An Introduction
to Health Psychology

An Introduction to Health Psychology

THIRD EDITION

Andrew Baum
University of Pittsburgh

Robert J. Gatchel
University of Texas Southwestern Medical Center at Dallas

David S. Krantz
Uniformed Services University of the Health Sciences

Boston, Massachusetts   Burr Ridge, Illinois   Dubuque, Iowa
Madison, Wisconsin   New York, New York   San Francisco, California   St. Louis, Missouri

McGraw-Hill

A Division of The McGraw-Hill Companies

This book was set in Palatino by Ruttle, Shaw & Wetherill, Inc.
The editors were Brian L. McKean and Larry Goldberg;
the production supervisor was Louise Karam.
The photo editor was Debra Hershkowitz.
The cover was designed by Joan Greenfield.
Project supervision was done
by Ruttle, Shaw & Wetherill, Inc.
Quebecor Printing/Fairfield was printer and binder.

AN INTRODUCTION TO HEALTH PSYCHOLOGY

This book is printed on acid-free paper.

2 3 4 5 6 7 8 9 0 FGR FGR 9 0 9 8 7

ISBN 0-07-022961-9

Library of Congress Cataloging-in-Publication Data

Baum, Andrew
    An introduction to health psychology / Andrew Baum, Robert J.
Gatchel, David S. Krantz.—3rd ed.
       p.   cm.
    Rev. ed. of: An introduction to health psychology / Robert J.
Gatchel, Andrew Baum, David S. Krantz. 2nd ed. 1989.
    Includes bibliographical references and index.
    ISBN 0-07-022961-9
    1. Medicine and psychology.   I. Gatchel, Robert J. An
introduction to health psychology.   II. Gatchel, Robert J.
III. Krantz, David S.   IV. Title.
R726.5.G38   1997
616'.001'9—dc20   96-35210

http://www.mhcollege.com

About the Authors

ANDREW BAUM received his B.S. in psychology from the University of Pittsburgh in 1970 and his Ph.D. from the State University of New York at Stony Brook in 1974. He is currently the Director of Behavioral Medicine and Oncology in the University of Pittsburgh Cancer Institute and Professor of Psychiatry and Psychology at the University of Pittsburgh. He has studied chronic stress and long-term consequences of traumatic or persistent stressors since 1972 and has focused more specifically on mental health and psychological and physical symptoms of victims of disasters and motor vehicle accidents. Dr. Baum also studies the effects of stress on immune system activity and psychosocial and biobehavioral aspects of cancer. He has edited, co-edited, or co-authored more than 30 books and authored or co-authored more than 125 scientific and professional publications.

Dr. Baum received a Centennial Award from the American Psychological Association (APA) for activities on behalf of psychological science (in 1992) and the Award for Outstanding Contributions to Health Psychology from the Division of Health Psychology of the APA (in 1985). He is a fellow of several professional societies including the Academy of Behavioral Medicine Research, Society of Behavioral Medicine, American Psychological Association, and the American Psychological Society; was president of the Division of Health Psychology in 1989; and is currently treasurer of the Academy of Behavioral Medicine Research and secretary-treasurer of the Council of Directors of Health Psychology Training. He is editor of the *Journal of Applied Social Psychology* and co-editor of *Psychology & Health* and the APA/Health Psychology book series *Application and Practice in Health Psychology.* He was the chair of the National Institute of Mental Health's Health Behavior and Prevention Initial Review Committee.

ROBERT J. GATCHEL received his B.A. in psychology from the State University of New York at Stony Brook in 1969 and his Ph.D. in clinical psychology from the University of Wisconsin in 1973. He is currently professor in the Departments of Psychiatry and Rehabilitation Science at the University of Texas Southwestern Medical Center at Dallas, where he is the Director of Graduate Research, Division of Clinical Psychology. He has conducted extensive clinical research, much of it supported by grants from the National Institutes of Health (NIH), on the psychophysiology of stress and emotion, the comorbidity of psychological and physical health disorders, and the etiology, assessment, and treatment of chronic stress and pain behavior. He has published over 150 scientific articles and book chapters and has authored or edited 12 other books, including *Psychophysiological Disorders: Research and Clinical Applications* (with E. Blanchard), *Psychological Approaches to Pain Management: A Practitioner's Handbook* (with D. Turk), and *Fundamentals of Abnormal Psychology* (with F. Mears).

Dr. Gatchel is a Diplomate of the American Board of Professional Psychology and is on the Board of Directors of the American Board of Health Psychology. He is also the recipient of a Research Scientist Development Award from NIH. He is on the editorial boards of numerous journals and is a member or fellow of several professional organizations, including the American Psychological Association, the Academy of Behavioral Medicine Research, and the Society for Psychophysiological Research.

DAVID S. KRANTZ received his B.S. in psychology from the City College of New York in 1971 and his Ph.D. from the University of Texas at Austin in 1975. He is currently Professor and Director of Graduate Studies in the Department of Medical and Clinical Psychology at the Uniformed Services University of the Health Sciences and Professor of Psychiatry and Medicine at Georgetown University Medical Center. He has conducted extensive research on stress and health. The focus of Dr. Krantz's research has been on biobehavioral factors in coronary heart disease, with emphasis on behavioral triggers of acute cardiovascular events such as myocardial ischemia and sudden death. Dr. Krantz has authored or co-authored over 120 scientific and professional publications, including *Behavior, Health and Environmental Stress*, and co-edited *Behavioral Assessment and Management of Cardiovascular Disorders* and *Handbook of Psychology and Health: Cardiovascular Disorders and Behavior*.

Dr. Krantz was the recipient of the Early Career Scientific Award (in 1982) from the American Psychological Association (APA) and the Annual Award from the APA Division of Health Psychology (in 1981). He is a fellow of several professional organizations, including the American Psychological Association, American Psychological Society, Academy of Behavioral Medicine Research, and the Society of Behavioral Medicine. He currently serves as editor-in-chief of the journal *Health Psychology* and is a past president of the Academy of Behavioral Medicine Research.

To Jesse Slater Sachs, in loving memory.
She endures in many incarnations.

—AB

To my deceased father, John P. Gatchel, who served as an
important role model during my formative years and who
provided me with intelligent guidance through the years.

—RJG

To my wife Marsha and children Michael and Della.

—DSK

Contents

Foreword

When the first edition of *An Introduction to Health Psychology* was being written almost fifteen years ago, the area of *health psychology* was small, relatively new, and not particularly well defined. The authors of the first edition, Robert J. Gatchel and Andrew Baum, not only met the challenge of relating psychological processes to health and illness in a coherent, comprehensible, and scholarly manner, but they were also instrumental in structuring a major new subdiscipline within psychology. Today health psychology is recognized as an important subdiscipline of psychology throughout most of the computer-literate world. Within the United States, the journal *Health Psychology,* with approximately 9,000 subscribers, is the third most subscribed primary journal of the American Psychological Association. Its editor, David S. Krantz, is recognized as an eminent scientist and scholar of considerable breadth. Not surprisingly, as an author of both the second and third editions of this text, he has made major conceptual contributions.

The true context of health psychology, as depicted by the three authors of the present text, has to be understood not only as a subdiscipline of psychology but also as an integral component of *behavioral medicine.* Behavioral medicine is the interdisciplinary field concerned with the development and integration of biomedical, behavioral, psychosocial, and sociocultural knowledge and techniques relevant to understanding health and illness. It is also concerned with the application of this knowledge and these techniques to disease prevention, diagnosis, treatment, and health promotion. Thus, the domains of behavioral medicine include not only academic disciplines such as anthropology, biochemistry, genetics, immunology, molecular biology, neuroscience, psychology, and sociology but also such healing professions as medicine, dentistry, and nursing. Within the field of behavioral medicine, health psychologists have played a large and important role, because of the analytic tools they possess and the vigor with which they have successfully interacted with other academics and professionals to address important aspects of health and illness. The three authors of the present volume have been preeminent in both health psychology and behavioral medicine and are thus well qualified to describe the full richness of the tapestry that comprises contemporary health psychology.

A particular strength of the first two editions was the emphasis placed on an implicit biopsychosocial model of health and illness. As in the present edition the earlier versions provided scholarly coverage of such topics as stress, coping, psychosocial risk, and cognitive-behavioral treatment of physical disorders as well as biopsychosocial approaches to the pathogenesis and management of AIDS, cancer, coronary heart disease, pain, and other afflictions. In this edition these topics still receive extensive coverage, but are augmented by important discussions of dispositions that appear to affect health and health behaviors, assessment of quality of life in medical patients, assessment of pain behaviors, psychoneuroimmunology, psychosocial aspects of organ transplantation, and the development of health promotion programs. The discussions are concise, insightful, and cogent.

In conclusion, the present text provides a scholarly, comprehensive, readable introduction to health psychology. The authors have done an outstanding job of organizing, codifying, synthesizing, and explicating the key concepts relating relevant behavioral, biomedical, psychosocial, and sociocultural processes to health and illness. It is apparent that the authors are not only academic scholars who are able to translate complex concepts into readily comprehensible formulations, but also distinguished working scientists with sufficient perspective to grasp the full implications of these formulations for research, practice, and the further development of health psychology.

Neil Schneiderman
James L. Knight Professor of Health Psychology
University of Miami

Preface

Twenty years ago, health psychology was a new, promising field of inquiry. Today, it has grown dramatically, fulfilling some of its early promise and opening creative new lines of investigation that will fuel its further growth. In this short time, we have learned a great deal. We have learned that behavior is a basic and influential component of health and that it can make disease more or less likely. Diet and drug use, exercise, stress, and other behaviors have demonstrable effects on a range of physiological systems and health outcomes. Disease processes, such as those involved in cardiovascular disorders and hypertension, are clearly tied to behavior and to emotional experiences. How people behave when they are ill or whether they seek medical attention for symptoms also determines the eventual costs of a disease or the severity of its impact. From basic research and intervention to contributions to public policy, health psychology has become an important discipline within and outside the field of psychology.

Health psychology is an exciting area of study, in part because it considers so many levels of influence and because the *relationships* it studies are inherently interesting and important. It shares the excitement of basic discoveries with more basic social, cognitive, and physiological fields of psychology. Effective applications of research to problems of health and well-being, including successful intervention with patients, are also thrilling and rewarding aspects of this field. Health psychology is exciting because it deals with very important outcomes, literally with life and death, and because it has uniquely important contributions to make to our understanding of behavior, of health, and of disease. It has become one of the most active areas within psychology and has clearly defined roles for psychologists in the health care arena. At a time when opportunities seem to be shrinking all around us, the opportunities in health psychology continue to grow. The vibrancy of our field, its breadth, rigor, and importance, are among the reasons for its dramatic growth and continued success.

Psychologists have always been concerned with issues of illness and health. Historically, they generally limited themselves to mental health settings and issues such as psychotherapy, mental retardation, and schizophrenia. This focus has changed during the past twenty years, with an increased involvement in all areas of health and illness, not just mental health. Integrating research and theory from clinical psychology, social psychology, biopsychology, experimental psychology, and the like, health psychology has expanded and broadened its scope. This text provides a comprehensive review of this work and of the many medically related topics and areas that are being changed by the health psychology specialty.

We each have taught courses in behavioral medicine and health psychology over a period of many years to a varied audience—psychology undergraduate and graduate students, medical and dental students, nurses, and other health care professionals and trainees. These experiences have provided the opportunity to explore the best methods for presenting the field to a diverse audience. This book is intended to provide a broad introduction to health psychology and to the interface of psychology and the medical world. We have provided a balanced presentation of both the broad issues in the field as well as of specific content topics that are especially relevant today for better understanding health and illness. We have been able to draw on feedback from instructors who have used the previous two editions of the text to better crystallize the information and to more specifically tailor it to the needs of students, instructors, and health professionals in the field.

The reader will be exposed to important psychological theories, concepts, and assessment/treatment methods of psychology as they apply to the area of health and illness. In presenting this material, we were aware that we would be addressing readers who differ in backgrounds and expertise in psychology as well as in terms of basic psychobiological principles and professional service delivery experience. As a consequence, we have been careful to clearly describe important concepts and terms in a manner that does not require a strong background in these areas. We also provide basic material where it is needed. We have tried to use clear, understandable language without introducing complicated jargon or, conversely, oversimplifying basic concepts and issues. It is our firm belief that our field must integrate physiological, psychological, and social aspects of behavior with state-of-the-art knowledge of biology and medicine. Consequently, we have written this book to consciously integrate medicine and these many levels of analysis in an accessible and understandable manner.

We have been impressed with the rapid advancement of this field since the completion of the second edition of this book. Accordingly, this new edition features updated discussions of material that was reviewed in the first editions, as well as expanded or new coverage of the central issues in health psychology. In particular, coverage of cancer-related issues including prevention and assessment and of health-related behaviors such as exercise, diet, and alcohol use has been expanded. Rapidly growing subspecialities, such as psychoneuroimmunology, are covered in detail. In addition, we describe differences between traditional and more innovative approaches to treatment and discuss the opportunities for health psychology associated with our rapidly changing health care system.

The organization of the text is similar to that of the second edition. The reader is first introduced to the important concepts and issues in the field of health psychology. After an introduction and historical overview of the field in Chapter 1, we provide a summary of physiological bases of behavior and health in Chapter 2. A "short course" in basic human physiological factors and mechanisms serves as a foundation for concepts and phenomena discussed in later chapters. We then discuss basic concepts and behaviors that span the entire field of health psychology: stress (Chapter 3) and control and learned helplessness (Chapter 4).

Starting in Chapter 5, which deals with cardiovascular disorders, we turn to more specific areas within the field of health psychology. Chapter 6 considers psychological aspects of immunoregulation, cancer, and AIDS. The prevalence and significance of psychophysiological disorders are discussed in Chapter 7, followed by coverage of the impact of hospitalization and patient behavior on health and illness in Chapter 8. A review of psychological assessment techniques in medical settings is presented in Chapter 9. This review is provided not only for those with clinical interests but also as an introduction for nonclinicians to procedures they are likely to encounter in their research and training activities. Chapter 10 reviews the various cognitive-behavioral treatment procedures that have been used effectively with problem behaviors often seen in medical settings. Pain and its treatment, which account for over 80 percent of all physician visits, are discussed in Chapter 11. In Chapter 12, we discuss three common appetitive problem behaviors that have significant health consequences—obesity, problem drinking/alcoholism, and smoking. We have selected these topics as vivid examples of how comprehensive psychological approaches can be applied to help us better understand the biological and psychosocial factors involved in these problem behaviors and, consequently, help to treat the behaviors more effectively. The text concludes with discussion of health psychology contributions to the promotion of health and prevention of disease.

We have diverse clinical and research interests and experiences in the field of health psychology, and we were trained in different subspecialities of psychology. None of us was originally trained as a health psychologist. No courses in health psychology even existed when we were in school! However, our backgrounds in social, clinical, and environmental psychology as well as in psychophysiology gave us a broad foundation for health psychology. This diversity greatly helped us provide a broad spectrum of expertise in the major topic areas covered. We all embrace a biopsychosocial orientation, a common thread throughout the fabric of this text. A concerted effort was made to provide an equitable balance among review summaries, major theories, hallmark research studies, and important clinical applications for each content area presented. Our intent was to foster a strong foundation and better appreciation of how psychology successfully interacts with medical illness and health issues.

No text of this type is possible without the aid of many dedicated people. We are especially grateful to a number of colleagues who read drafts of the earlier editions and provided helpful critiques and suggestions about chapters in the new edition. Extensive revisions were made as a result of their expert comments. We would particularly like to thank Tonya Y. Schooler for her helpful comments on several chapters. We thank the reviewers of this edition for their thoughtful comments and suggestions: Christian S. Crandall, University of

Florida; Lynn A. Durel, University of Miami; Dennis E. Elsenrath, University of Wisconsin, Stevens Point; George B. Walz, Indiana University of Pennsylvania; Carol S. Weisse, Union College; and Kathleen D. Zylan, Lynchburg College. We would also like to thank and acknowledge the help and support we received from the staff at McGraw-Hill, particularly from Brian McKean and Susan Elia. Their persistence and expertise were greatly appreciated. Finally, special thanks are due to Michele Hayward and Susan Hagan for their tireless help in preparing the book and to Tina Racan, Laurie Hall, Shiela McFeeley, Carol Gentry, and Nicole Lundgren for their valuable assistance in its preparation.

Andrew Baum
Robert J. Gatchel
David S. Krantz

CHAPTER 1

Overview of Health Psychology

One of the major medical revolutions of the recent past has been organ transplantation. Although once the topic of dreamers and science fiction novels, organ transplantation is now a reality. Heart, lung, kidney, liver, and other vital organs have been successfully transplanted for several years, and the number of centers that perform them has increased dramatically. As we can see in Figure 1.1, liver transplants nearly doubled between 1985 and 1994, whereas heart transplants increased by 40 percent and lung transplants increased more than 20-fold (*Scientific Registry*, 1995). There were many medical and technological developments that made all this possible: Organs can be removed and maintained for sufficient periods of time, patients can be kept alive and functional while their old organs are removed and new ones are "connected," and drugs that can suppress the body's immune responses that lead to organ rejection are now available. However, not all the advances that enable us to transplant organs are biomedical. Research and theory about behavior and stress have also played an important role.

How important is health psychology for organ transplantation? Consider some questions that a surgeon might ask: Are there any ways to indicate how well a prospective transplant patient will adjust to postsurgery demands? Can you improve the extent to which patients will comply with their medication schedule? Can you tell me anything about patients that will help to gauge their likelihood of survival? The complexity of transplant procedures and the heavy demands of postsurgery recovery (such as immunosuppressive medication that must be taken) led some transplant teams to require that a transplant patient should have a caregiver in the postsurgery period. Therefore, concerns about adjustment and quality of life have emerged, and approaches to improving the degree to which patients comply with medication and lifestyle change indicate that prescriptions are of great importance. All of this assumes that the organs are available to conduct transplants. Relatively few people sign organ donor cards or agree to donate organs after death, and thus there are not enough organs to go around. As a result, people must wait months or years for

1

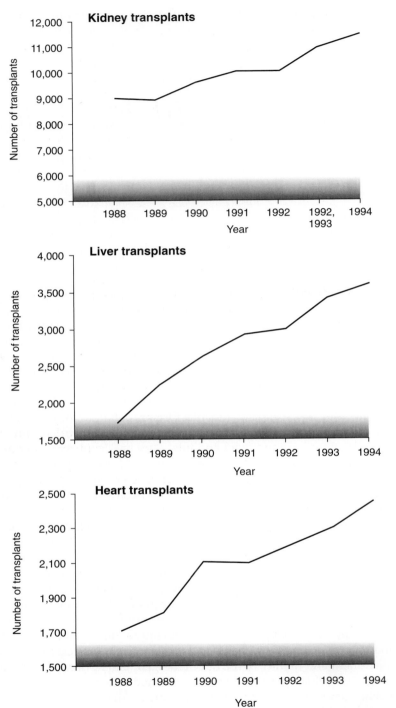

FIGURE 1.1. Once thought to be impossible, organ transplantation is a rapidly growing medical procedure that has dramatically affected health care. Transplantation of hearts, livers, and kidneys has increased considerably since the mid-1980s.
Source: Adapted from data received from the *Scientific Registry,* Number of U.S. Transplants. Richmond, VA: United Network for Organ Sharing, July 31, 1995.

a suitable organ, often while they are very sick. Some die before an organ can be found. Increasing organ donation and changing attitudes about donating organs is an important job for health psychologists. If you think this will be easy, just think about how difficult it can be to get someone to give blood!

There is a growing literature in health psychology that addresses these issues, and we have learned a great deal about the psychological aspects of organ donation, compliance, and adjustment and survival after organ transplantation (see Canning, Dew and Davidson, in press; Dew et al., 1994; Kormos et al., 1994). We will not review this literature here, other than to say that psychological factors appear to be directly and indirectly related to both organ donation and posttransplant survival. More importantly, we have considered an example that is just one of many reasons for the rapid growth of health psychology. Health and illness are related to what we think and feel and what we do, and there are exciting and significant areas of investigation that need to be pursued. A new age of holistic medicine and unprecedented collaboration between psychologists and the health care system is dawning and you are in its vanguard.

As we have suggested, there was a time when psychology and medicine had little to do with each other. Despite shared origins, psychology and medicine embraced the dualism of mind and body, viewing the two as separable and autonomous systems. The "health" in psychology was mental health rather than a holistic mental and physical well-being. With the growing realization that health includes both mental and physical well-being and psychological variables are important in illness, a new association between psychology and medicine has developed. Psychologists have begun to participate more actively in the diagnosis, treatment, and prevention of medical problems and have become active members of medical teams. Moreover, psychologists have brought their special research skills and technology to bear on major problem areas, including the causes of illness, the nature of threats to health, and the care and management of patients and health care. Psychologists are applying hybrid theories and techniques to improve mood and quality of life and medical outcomes of disease. Before more specifically defining and discussing this growing area, which is most commonly referred to as health psychology or behavioral medicine, we will briefly review how medicine and psychology have been linked historically.

THE MIND-BODY RELATIONSHIP: A HISTORICAL OVERVIEW

The relationship between the mind and the body has long been a controversial topic among philosophers, physiologists, and psychologists. Are experiences purely mental, purely physical, or an interaction of the physical and the mental? Recent history has been a dualistic one, as predominant religious, philosophical, and scientific developments assumed that mind and body were separate. However, this way of thinking has not always been dominant. Ancient religious teachings and Chinese medicine took the position that good health was a matter of maintaining a good balance with the world around us, a spiritual product of mind and body together in harmony with nature (Stone, 1987).

Consistent with this concept, ancient civilizations from Greece to Rome and developing societies through the Middle Ages believed in a unity or strong relationship of mind and body. Gentry and Matarazzo (1981) point out that the belief that mind and body are closely related and work together, as evidenced by the dry mouth and racing heart associated with fear, anger or the headache triggered by emotional stress, are prominent in ancient literary documents from Babylonia and Greece. The ancient Greek physician Hippocrates, a founder of modern medicine in many ways, also considered mind and body as one, proposing one of the earliest theories of personality based on psychological properties of four bodily fluids or humors (see Figure 1.2). He argued that these biological factors were associated with specific personality attributes or temperaments. An excess of *yellow bile* was linked to a *choleric* temperament. It was assumed that this yellow bile prompted an individual to become chronically angry and irritable, hence the word choleric (angry), which literally means bile. An excess of *black bile* was considered to cause a person to be chronically sad or *melancholic,* hence the term melancholy, which literally means black bile. The sanguine or **optimistic** temperament was the result of excess blood in the system. Finally, the **phlegmatic** temperament, characterized by calm, listless personality attributes, was seen as being caused by an excess of the bodily humor *phlegm.*

Of course, this humoral theory of personality was abandoned long ago, along with a number of other prescientific notions. On a historical level, it points out how physical or biological factors have been seen through the ages

FIGURE 1.2. Hippocrates, for whom the physician's oath of conduct is named, was among the first to agree that mind and body were one.
Source: Corbis-Bettmann

as significantly interacting with and affecting the personality or psychological characteristics of an individual. Mind, a product of the brain and nervous system, was inextricably part of the body, and health and illness were products of the entire organism. It is difficult for some of us today to fully understand or appreciate the meaning of a unitary view of mind and body, so strong have been dualistic beliefs for the past few hundred years. But our longer history is one in which the dominant view has been more holistic.

This classical depiction of the interrelationship of mind and body lost favor in the seventeenth century. With the advent of physical medicine during the Renaissance, the belief that the mind influences the body came to be regarded as unscientific. The understanding of the mind and soul was relegated to the areas of religion and philosophy, whereas the science of understanding the body was considered a separate realm of physical medicine. This perpetuated the dualistic viewpoint that the mind and the body function separately and independently. Civilization's physicians, serving the multiple roles of philosopher-teacher, priest, and healer, had approached the understanding of mind-body interactions in a more holistic manner. They were now expected to focus exclusively on biological causes of disease.

The individual who is usually credited with the development of this dualistic viewpoint and the resulting move away from a more holistic approach was the French philosopher René Descartes. Descartes argued that the mind or soul was a separate entity that is parallel to and incapable of affecting physical matter or somatic processes in any direct way. This Cartesian dualism of mind and body became the preeminent philosophical basis of medicine. Although Descartes did indicate that the two entities could interact (he proposed that the pineal gland located in the midbrain was the vital connection between the mind and body), his basic tenet of dualism moved the newly independent field of medicine away from the holistic approach that emphasized psyche-soma interactions toward the mechanistic pathophysiology approach that has dominated medicine until relatively recently.

Ironically, the very discoveries of biological causes of disease and development of treatments and vaccines that led to control and prevention of many diseases were taken as evidence of the wisdom of treating the body separately from the mind. Until this time we knew little about the causes of disease or why some treatments seemed more effective than others. The plagues that devastated Europe during the Middle Ages were not well understood at the time (see Figure 1.3). We now know that they were caused by pathogens, but explanations for the disease were more spiritual or animistic at the time! Germs, infection, antiseptic treatment conditions, and the like are all relatively new concepts. The nineteenth-century discovery that microorganisms caused certain diseases revolutionized medicine but also produced further evidence of mind-body dualism. The development of drugs and vaccines against the most dangerous diseases also suggested that biological solutions were the best courses to pursue. During this scientific era of medicine mechanical laws or physiological principles became the primary permissible explanations of disease and psychological factors were discounted as mind or spirit. Such an orientation left a great many disorders unclassifiable and required some other explanation and categorization. As McMahon and Hastrup (1980) noted:

FIGURE 1.3. Several plagues struck Europe and other continents in the first two-thirds of the millennium. Rampant disease, borne by rats and other carriers, devastated towns and cities, causing great fear, sorrow, and disorganization.
Source: Corbis-Bettmann

There gradually emerged . . . an ambiguously defined diagnostic category designed to accommodate what we know today as "Psychosomatic" disorders. This category was called "nervous." . . . The apparent influence of "emotions of the mind" in such conditions made their etiology an enigma. It was agreed that if a physician had evidence that a patient was "only nervous," he should "stop further inquiry." He is then without the pale of rational medicine. . . . According to the received view, that which was caused by a psychological variable could itself be nothing but psychological. Thus the "nervous" condition became dissociated from physiological processes, and a somatic complaint of nervous origin was understood as having no physical basis (p. 206).

As a result of these changes and in spite of the problems suggested earlier, the *biomedical model* of illness and disease has dominated our view of health and health care. This model is based on the assumption that disease is caused by a **pathogen**—a virus, bacteria, or some other "germ" that enters the body and causes disruption and discomfort. The spirits or lack of harmony of ancient times were replaced by microorganisms. Efforts to defeat diseases were now directed toward killing or preventing infection. The result was the enormous change and growth of health care that eradicated many of the major diseases of history. While few can disagree that these have been significant advances in medicine and science, the dualism of the scientific revolution went too far. As important as biomedical causes of disease may be, psychosocial factors are very important as well. Fortunately, strict dualistic perspectives were tempered by scientists in medicine who saw things differently. For example, the work of

Bernard, one of the first prominent physicians to emphasize the contributions of psychological factors to physical ailments, was an important counterweight to the dualistic thinking of his time. Subsequently, Sigmund Freud and his disciples were influential in bringing the interaction of psychological and physical factors back to the forefront in accounts of various disorders. Although emphasis was still on the body, microorganisms, and biological determinants of illness, we were again becoming aware of other sources of influence.

THE DEVELOPMENT OF HEALTH PSYCHOLOGY

The sweeping changes caused by World War II changed the nature of psychology as well. Its science had become more applied as a result of the war, and its successes in aiding the war effort brought psychology more prominence and opportunity. Renewed emphasis on the physiological bases of behavior, successful application in areas ranging from architecture to law, and the transcendence of the "schools" of psychology have all helped to bring about a richer and more open discipline. The expectation that psychology can contribute to the solution of social problems and to progress in many other fields is now firmly entrenched, and psychological input into matters of health and illness has increased greatly.

At the same time, developing research in psychosomatic medicine was influential in the development of health psychology. Wolff (1950), for instance, made early contributions to the study of health and behavior with his extensive studies of the role of stress and adaptation in the development of disease states. He viewed illness as being caused by a number of factors, one of which was failure to adapt to the changes and stresses that are a normal part of life. Failure to adapt led to emotional and biological responses that could cause the onset of disease. Further, the particular ways in which people responded psychologically were linked to specific organs in the body and to specific kinds of ailments. Psychophysiological research provided basic evidence of the relationships between emotion and physiological responses (see Ax, 1953) and suggested that emotional and cognitive factors are extremely important in eliciting specific patterns of bodily response to threat (see Mason, 1975).

During the past two decades psychological contributions to medically relevant topics have become an important part of medical science, with growing interest in treating patients as "whole" human beings and the realization that psychological factors are significant in the course of almost any disease. Research in social psychology, clinical psychology, biopsychology, developmental psychology, and several other areas of psychology and behavioral medicine formed the early theoretical bases for this effort, and investigators from these fields came together as health psychology emerged. This developing science and practice of health psychology (see Table 1.1) is based on the belief that to understand health and disease comprehensively, one must view people as "individual mind-body complexes ceaselessly interacting with the social and physical environment in which they are embodied" (see Lipowski, 1977, p. 234).

Developments in psychology and medicine that led to the rapid development of health psychology and behavioral medicine in these forces shaped our

TABLE 1.1. Preventable Medical Conditions[a]

Condition	Number per Year	Deaths per Year	Cost per Patient ($)
Heart disease	7 million affected	500,000	30,000.00[b]
Cancer	1 million new cases	510,000	29,000.00[c]
Stroke	600,000 strokes	150,000	22,000.00
Injuries	2.3 million hospitalized[d]	142,500	570,000.00[e]
HIV	1–1.5 million infected[f]	Not reported	75,000.00[g]
Alcoholism	18.5 million persons	105,000	250,000.00[h]
Drug abuse[i]		Not reported	63,000.00[j]
Cocaine	1.3 million persons		
Intravenous drugs	900,000 persons		
Heroin	500,000 persons		
Drug-exposed babies	375,000 babies		
Low birthweight babies	260,000 babies born	23,000	10,000.00[k]

[a]The table reflects preventable medical conditions, including the number of those affected or cases reported, deaths per year for each, and the cost of treatment.

Notes: [b]284,000 bypass procedures are performed each year.

    [c]Lung cancer treatment.

    [d]177,000 are spinal cord injuries.

    [e]Lifetime, quadriplegia.

    [f]147,525 AIDS cases (January 1990).

    [g]Cost reflects lifetime treatment.

    [h]Cost of liver transplant.

    [i]Regular users.

    [j]5 years.

    [k]Intensive care.

Source: Health Insurance Association of America (HIAA). Source Book of Health Insurance Data, 1993. Washington, DC: Health Insurance Association of America, 1994, p. 8. Used with permission of HIAA.

view of health and behavior. Within more traditional fields such as social psychology and clinical psychology, researchers such as David Glass, Judith Rodin, Jerome E. Singer, Joseph Matarazzo, and Stephen Weiss had begun to study basic behavior-health interactions and new ways to explain and treat illness or health-impairing behaviors. At the same time, important insights into brain-behavior relationships and the discovery that basic biological activity can be controlled consciously by investigators such as Neal Miller and Neil Schneiderman set the stage for the explosion in research and theory that was to come. Everything was in place in the late 1970s and the development of graduate training programs focused on research programs, and other aspects of a formal discipline appeared. Health psychology was alive and well and began a passionate campaign to alter traditional evolution in health care and research on the role of behavior in health.

The advent of a formal health psychology has also had benefits for psychology. Just as neuroscience, cognitive science, and psychopharmacology have done, health psychology introduced new ways of thinking about the science of behavior, and the cross-pollination of health psychology and "older" areas of psychology has resulted in a hybrid science. With new outcomes under study, scientists in many areas have turned to study aspects of their particular area in the health arena. Health psychology has shaped new ways to work with patients, new areas or problems needing behavior change, and new social problems.

Health psychology is now a strong and vibrant discipline, with substantial representation in the major psychological societies all over the world. Health psychology has several of its own journals, handbooks, and annual conferences, and has grown to challenge more traditional ways of viewing the relationship of health and well-being to behavior. We will address these developments later in this chapter. For now it is sufficient to note that health psychology has strongly promoted prevention and an emphasis on maintaining people's health over treating and merely reacting to disease once it is manifested, arguing that prevention is less costly and more effective (Taylor, 1990). It has influenced medicine to the extent that many psychologists now work in medical settings and medical students more routinely receive training in the relations of health and behavior (Pattishall,1989). And it has challenged traditional models of disease and health, addressing directly the challenges of the changes in health and illness that have occurred in the past century.

Health psychology did not suddenly appear one day fully developed and ready to go. Instead, it emerged slowly, evolving much as psychology did, from a part of a mythology or philosophy of consciousness to a sophisticated science of behavior. Throughout history, one can find references to mind and behavior as factors in health and well-being. However, it has taken a long time for these notions to take hold and changes in how we have viewed the mind and body typify the turbulent development of the field. Now, in the face of considerable evidence that how people feel, what they believe, and what they do can affect their health, preeminent universities, medical centers, and other parts of medical science and the health care establishment have begun to integrate health and behavior research and to practice with traditional biomedical perspectives. The initial results of this revolution are promising and the partnership between health psychology and medicine is growing.

THE CHANGING NATURE OF HEALTH AND ILLNESS

The importance of mind-body interactions and of research on the relationships between behavior and health is further suggested by the rapidly changing nature of health care and the current major threats to good health (see Table 1.2). At the end of the century life expectancy for both men and women in the United States has increased by 50 percent, a change made possible in part by breakthroughs in treating and preventing infectious illnesses such as polio, influenza, rubella, and smallpox (Matarazzo, 1985). With the elimination of these diseases through vaccination, treatment with antibiotics, and improved sanitation, "new" diseases have become more prominent and now take into account most of the deaths in this country. In Canada up to one-half of premature mortality has been attributed to lifestyle or behavior, and these findings are similar to those reported in the United States (see Ouellete et al., 1979; Lalonde, 1974). Cancer deaths, for example, have tripled since 1900, and heart disease, cancer,

TABLE 1.2. Leading Causes of Death, 1990[a]

Cause	1990 Number	Rank
All causes	2,148,463	—
Heart disease	720,058	1
Malignant neoplasms[b]	505,322	2
Cerebrovascular disease	144,088	3
Injuries (unintentional)	91,983	4
Chronic obstructive pulmonary disease	86,679	5
Pneumonia and influenza	79,513	6
Diabetes mellitus	47,664	7
Suicide	30,906	8
Chronic liver disease and cirrhosis	25,815	9
HIV infection	25,188	10
Homicide and legal intervention	24,932	11
Nephritis, nephrotic syndrome, and nephrosis	20,764	12
Septicemia	19,169	13
Atherosclerosis	18,047	14

[a]The table shows the number and rank for top causes of death in the United States in 1990. Data include all races and are based on the National Vital Statistics System.

Notes: [b]The code numbers for the cause of death are based on the International Classification of Diseases, 9th revision. Categories for the coding and classification of human immunodeficiency virus (HIV) infection were introduced in the United States beginning with mortality data for 1987. The number of HIV infection deaths based on the National Vital Statistics System differs from the number of deaths among acquired immunodeficiency syndrome (AIDS) cases reported to the Centers for Disease Control (CDC) AIDS Surveillance System. 1. Cancer.

Source: U.S. Department of Health and Human Services. Public Health Service. Centers for Disease Control and Prevention. National Center for Health Statistics. Health, United States, 1992. Hyattsville, MD: Public Health Service, 1993, pp. 49–51. Primary source: Center for Disease Control and Prevention. National Center for Health Statistics. Vital Statistics of the United States, Vol. II: Mortality, Part A. Washington, DC: U.S. Government Printing Office; data computed by the Division of Analysis from data compiled by the Division of Vital Statistics.

and acquired immune deficiency syndrome (AIDS) are now major killers. These diseases have no "magic bullet" cure or vaccine, but they are, in some respects, diseases caused by lifestyle and behavior. Diet, smoking, exercise, stress, and substance use are all behavioral factors that are associated with development of today's most feared illnesses. Califano (1979) noted that at the turn of the century 580 deaths out of every 100,000 U.S. citizens were due to a group of infectious diseases that include influenza, pneumonia, diphtheria, tuberculosis, and gastrointestinal infections. Today these diseases take into account only 30 deaths per 100,000 citizens. This rapid decline in deaths from infectious agents, he argued, has been accompanied by increased numbers of deaths from diseases caused or facilitated by preventable, behavioral factors such as smoking (see Figure 1.4).

One of the reasons for this revolution was the development of antibiotics. As Sterling (1995) recently concluded:

> Sir Alexander Fleming discovered penicillin in 1928, and the power of the sulfonamides was recognized by drug company researchers in 1935, but antibiotics first came into general medical use in the 1940's and 50's. The effects on the hidden world of bacteria were catastrophic. Bacteria which had spent

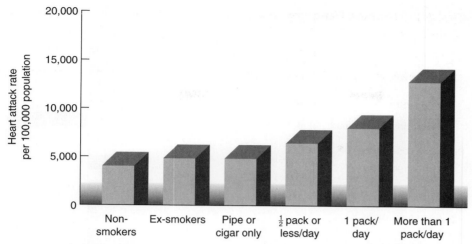

FIGURE 1.4. Age-adjusted rates of first heart attack for white males aged 30 to 59, United States, categorized by smoking status.
Source: Adapted from J. A. Califano, Jr. *Healthy People: The Surgeon General's Report on Health Promotion and Disease Prevention.* Washington, DC: U.S. Government Printing Office, 1979.

many contented millennia decimating the human race were suddenly and swiftly decimated in return. The entire structure of human mortality shifted radically, in a terrific attack on bacteria from the world of organized intelligence. At the beginning of this century, back in the pre-antibiotic year of 1900, four of the top ten leading causes of death in the United States were bacterial. The most prominent were tuberculosis ("the white plague," *Mycobacterium tuberculosis*) and pneumonia (*Streptococcus pneumoniae, Pneumococcus*). The death rate in 1900 from gastroenteritis (*Escherichia coli,* various *Campylobacter Species,* etc.) was higher than that for heart disease. The nation's number ten cause of death was diphtheria (*Corynebacterium diphtheriae*). Bringing up the bacterial van were gonorrhea, meningitis, septicemia, dysentery, typhoid fever, whooping cough, and many more.

At the end of the century, all of these festering bacterial afflictions (except pneumonia) had vanished from the top ten. They'd been replaced by heart disease, cancer, stroke and even relative luxuries of postindustrial mortality, such as accidents, homicide and suicide. All thanks to the miracle of antibiotics (p. 90).

Within the past decade observable changes in the lifestyles of Americans reflect directly on these behavioral factors associated with heart disease, cancer, and other modern illnesses. Data from the 1981 Surgeon General's report (Harris et al., 1981) suggested that many people have taken steps to exercise, to change their diets, to quit smoking, and so on. The thrust of the Surgeon Generals' reportings through the 1990s also suggests that behavioral factors are vital for guarding citizens' health. We can see this heightened concern everywhere; people are looking for healthier foods and ways to exercise, or otherwise looking for ways to safeguard their health. Although some of these trends

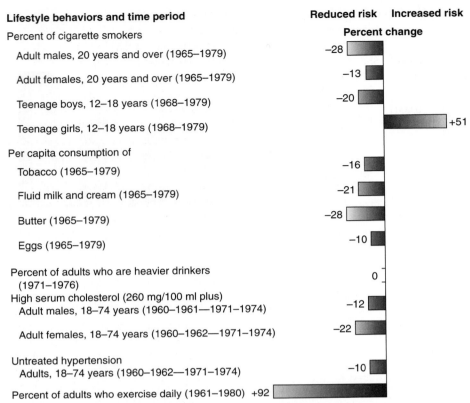

FIGURE 1.5. Recent changes in lifestyle behaviors that affect health.
Source: Adapted from P. R. Harris. *Health United States 1980.* U.S. Department of Health and Human Services Pub. No. (PHS) 81-1232. Washington, DC: U.S. Government Printing Office, 1981.

are not positive, as in recent increases in smoking among teenage girls, most trends reflect a growing awareness of lifestyle as a determinant of health (see Figure 1.5).

Changes in major health problems since 1900 also require different kinds of health care. Pneumonia or other infectious diseases are acute illnesses and can be treated with antibiotics or antiviral drugs. Further, people recover from these diseases quickly. However, heart disease, cancer, diabetes, and other chronic illnesses are difficult to treat, require expensive interventions (e.g., surgery, chemotherapy), and usually continue to cause difficulties for very long periods of time. As a result, years of expensive treatment and care are needed. In order to appreciate this, consider the fact that treatments for heart disease, for example, are designed to correct or reverse damage to the cardiovascular system that has accumulated over a lifetime! Cancer treatments often require surgery, radiation therapy, and highly aversive chemotherapy, and diseases such as hypertension and diabetes often require lifelong restrictions on activity and use of ameliorative drugs or insulin. Our health care system has and is changing to reflect greater concern for these chronic, hard-to-treat illnesses.

At the same time, this system has been affected by the fact that people with heart disease and cancer tend to be older than those patients with major diseases used to be. Improvements in public health and elimination of many fatal infectious illnesses have resulted in dramatic gains in life expectancy. In part this is due to the greater number of people who now survive childhood. However, older people develop diseases too, and their care and treatment often differ from younger patients. Increases in some diseases, such as cancer, may be due, in part, to the aging of our patient population. The importance of prevention, lifestyle change, and new ways to treat chronic diseases and the necessity that health care continue to change to meet these challenges seem evident.

Health care in our country *is* changing rapidly, providing new opportunities and a strong *raison d'être* for health psychology. Four major problems face our nation's health care system today: (1) health care costs are rising dramatically and exhausting too much of our resources; (2) the number of uninsured people in the system is too large; (3) health care outcomes are often mediocre or not cost-effective, and (4) there are substantial barriers to effective health care of vulnerable or underserved groups within our society (National Institute for Health Care Management, 1994). These problems have dictated new ways of conceptualizing health care, including President Clinton's ill-fated health care reform program, and changes in traditional medical insurance and the advent of "managed care." Behavioral research and intervention in health care settings offer several possible remedies for some of these problems.

First, and perhaps most importantly, health psychology interventions are cost-effective. "Blended care," or the integration of psychological and behavioral medicine approaches to treatment and prevention appears to be fairly inexpensive to introduce into health care settings and yields substantial savings in subsequent need for health care (see Table 1.3). To the extent that these interventions can reduce people's need for office visits and shorten postsurgical stays in the hospital, they will reduce costs and reliance on traditional health care. (See Chapter 8.)

At the same time, the application of psychological principles to screening programs and outreach offers some promise of incorporating more vulnerable and underserved segments of society in the health care system. Some groups,

TABLE 1.3.

Reduction in frequency of medical and surgical treatments as a result of various clinical behavioral medicine interventions:

Total ambulatory care visits	−17%
Visits for minor illnesses	−35%
Pediatric acute illness visits	−25%
Office visits for acute asthma	−49%
Office visits by arthritis patients	−40%
Average hospital length of stay for surgical patients	−1.5 days
Cesarean sections	−56%
Epidural anesthesia during labor and delivery	−85%

Source: From D. S. Sobel. Mind matters, money matters: The cost-effectiveness of clinical behavioral medicine. In S. J. Blumenthal, K. Matthews, and S. M. Weiss, *New Research Frontiers in Behavioral Medicine: Proceedings of the National Conference,* 1994, p. 25.

for example, have proven resistant to preventive and screening efforts. Epidemiological investigations, while effective in identifying resistant groups and factors associated with isolation from health care, have not suggested ways of modifying individual behaviors and attitudes that may interact with socioeconomic, racial, and location-based barriers to active participation in the health care system.

METHODOLOGICAL DEVELOPMENTS

Changes in our views about mind and body, weaknesses in traditional biomedical models, and the recognition that health and illness are results of interactions among genetic, biological, environmental, and behavioral factors (see Baum, 1993) have required a different way of describing health and illness. In response to this need and as a result of these changes, psychology has seen the development of research on environmental and social determinants of mood and behavior. At the same time, medicine has begun to apply some of this work to its practice. The result has been a shift in the implicit models that we use to explain health and illness. Consider the parallel change that occurred when American psychology was changed forever by the advent of behaviorism. Where models of behavior had been mentalistic and focused on the structure and content of consciousness, behaviorists insisted on studying observable behavior and came to regard operant conditioning as the source of behavior. In health psychology, the biomedical model has been supplanted by what has been called the *biopsychosocial model,* which considers psychological and social determinants of health and well-being along with more traditional biological factors (see Engel, 1977; Schwartz, 1982; Temoshok, 1985).

Biological factors, including *bodily processes that promote disease and genetic predispositions that may contribute to them,* interact with psychological factors and social variables, and these interactions have pervasive effects on health. Social factors in the model would include personal relationships, one's sense of community and social support, and one's socioeconomic status (see the box "Doing the Right Thing—The Human Capital Initiative"), whereas psychological factors range from mood to self-esteem or coping style. Together these factors determine one's health and well-being. The model also suggests that there is potentially an enormous number of factors that could be involved, and choosing those factors to study can be challenging. For example, if one considers health and illness by using the biopsychosocial model, one might end up with the possible sources of influence depicted in Figure 1.6. Clearly, behavior itself is important, but it can also interact with biological factors and social conditions, suggesting a bewildering array of potential factors. The strength of the biopsychosocial model, its inclusiveness, also makes it very complicated to study properly. However, the biopsychosocial model is also more powerful in predicting or explaining health outcomes.

How does one go about studying the relationships between the psyche and bodily tissue damage or resistance? The following example will demonstrate the complexity of the problem. Assume that you are interested in the relationships between personality and illness. You first devise a personality scale that distinguishes people along a personality dimension, dividing people into

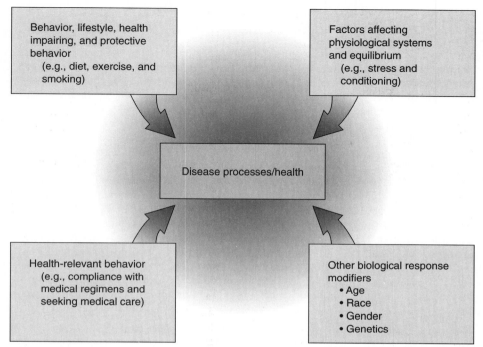

FIGURE 1.6. Factors contributing to disease processes and health.
Source: From A. Baum. Disease processes: Behavioral, biological, and environmental interactions in disease processes. In S. J. Blumenthal, K. Matthews, and S. M. Weiss (eds.), *New Research Frontiers in Behavioral Medicine: Proceedings of the National Conference,* 1994, p. 25.

"X" and "Not-X" categories. You develop the hypothesis that all people with the "X" trait are more likely to develop high blood pressure than those without this trait. To test your hypothesis, you assemble a pool of 2,000 potential subjects, carefully matched on a number of variables such as education and income, and administer your personality scale to each subject. You recruit 500 people in each category, then you take each subject's blood pressure and inquire as to his or her history of high blood pressure (or lack thereof). When you tabulate your data, the findings are remarkable: Not only do 70 percent of the "Xs" have a history of high blood pressure whereas only 10 percent of the "Not-Xs" have such a history, but the mean blood pressure of "Xs" is 20 mm of mercury higher than that of the "Not-Xs." Such results initially prompt you to believe that you have discovered the cause of high blood pressure.

The only problem with these results is that they have not demonstrated that your personality trait causes high blood pressure. Your evidence is correlational in nature: It shows that the personality trait "X" is related to high blood pressure, but it does not show that the factors are causally linked. It is possible, for example, that a third factor (perhaps "X" types eat more salt or fat or smoke more) is related to your personality type and actually causes high blood pressure. In such a case your conclusion about the personality causing high blood pressure would be incorrect. This is a common problem in psychol-

Doing the Right Thing—The Human Capital Initiative

As further evidence of psychology's increasing involvement in the science and practice of health care, the American Psychological Association in collaboration with the American Psychological Society and a dozen other professional societies, eight Institutes of the National Institutes of Health, and several private health policy institutes and organizations, produced a document outlining a research agenda in health and behavior. Part of the *Human Capital Initiative* (HCI), an effort by the behavioral science community to develop national behavioral science research agendas in particularly important areas, is the document that addresses "Doing the Right Thing: A Research Plan for Healthy Living." Each HCI document outlines a sustained research effort and describes areas in need of attention and support. Health was identified as one of the six original areas of broad concern.

Doing the Right Thing was published in 1995 and outlined four major areas of concern. The top priorities in implementing this research initiative were: (1) *chronic disease* and the basic behavioral processes in the prevention, development, and treatment of chronic illness; (2) acceleration of scientific investigation and enhancement of *health promotion*; (3) extension of research and health care to *traditionally understudied groups* such as women and minorities; and (4) reshaping of the health care system to bring more attention to bear on health promotion and disease prevention. To achieve these, strategies were outlined to understand better the interaction of behavior, biology, and environment in the development and course of diseases such as cancer, heart disease, AIDS, diabetes, and arthritis. At the same time, research should address early detection and screening programs, risk evaluations, interventions to support good quality of life, and ways to assist nonmedical caregivers (e.g., spouses caring for ill partners) in providing extended care to those who are ill.

Health promotion and disease prevention are the least costly approaches to health care. Preventing a disease is far more efficient and cost-effective than is treating it. Research in service of this objective must identify health-enhancing and health-impairing behaviors and their bases if we are to change them, and we should try to understand interactions between patients and health care providers to help frame prevention programs. Evaluation of socioeconomic influences on health are also important, and research and access to care should be extended to groups that have historically been understudied or underserved. This includes understanding different patterns of acquisition and maintenance of health-related behaviors and ways of enhancing preventive and self-care programs in all segments of society. Finally, the research plan calls for developing information systems and assessment tools, improving access to health care, and refocusing models of training in medicine and other health care professions (including psychology) to bring about more effective collaboration, and development of effective preventive activities.

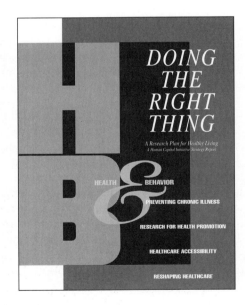

Source: From *Doing the Right Thing: A Research Plan for Healthy Living.* Washington, DC: American Psychological Association, 1995.

ogy, but it takes on a special significance in studies of health and illness. For example, based on your data, can one refute the possibility that high blood pressure causes personality trait "X" to develop? The answer, of course, is "No". Being an "X" may cause people to develop high blood pressure, however it is equally possible that finding out that they have high blood pressure causes people to develop trait "X."

There are a number of ways to improve upon the preceding basic research design. We have outlined a **retrospective study** in which people are asked to recall past events or in which present conditions are used to explain these past events. Studies of Type A behavior or social support, measured *after* an event such as a heart attack, are retrospective in that they use a measure of behavior or support to predict back to a prior event.

This kind of study is relatively easy to do if one has access to an appropriate population of patients. *Prospective studies* in which an attempt is made to predict future events are more costly and time-consuming. A prospective version of *your* study might entail, for example, administering your personality measure to your 2,000 subjects, recruiting 500 "Xs" and 500 "Not-Xs," and then studying all 1,000 regularly over 5 years to determine which subjects develop high blood pressure. Once a year blood pressure could be recorded from all subjects, and you could ask them about whether they were diagnosed with high blood pressure.

Suppose that only 10 of the subjects have high blood pressure when the scale is initially administered. After 5 years it is found that 150 subjects have high blood pressure and that of these 120 are "Xs." Are these data any more revealing than those obtained in the retrospective study? The answer is, "Yes." Although the data are still correlational, and therefore they still do not provide a solid basis for causal inferences, they allow you to eliminate one important alternative explanation. These findings do not support the conclusion that high blood pressure causes personality change to trait "X." You have predicted who would develop high blood pressure (or at least 80 percent of them) on the basis of a personality trait measured *before* subjects developed this problem. Since the trait assessment preceded subjects' learning that they had high blood pressure, it is not likely that the relationship between personality and blood pressure was caused by blood pressure.

As we will see, many retrospective and prospective studies have been conducted. In some cases retrospective studies yield the same results as prospective efforts, and in other cases they do not. However, the prospective study of illness is not guaranteed to work in all cases. It is important to consider a number of other problems. The choice of indicators is one potential problem. If you are interested in a specific illness, how do you define it? Typically, only extreme cases are studied, as many people with mild cases of an illness are undiagnosed. Thus, someone with very high blood pressure would be more likely to have a recorded history of high blood pressure than someone with moderately high blood pressure.

Or, if you are interested in factors affecting influenza in a given community, relying on diagnosed cases would reflect only those cases of flu that are seen by the health care system. We know that many people who get the flu treat it at home, and these cases would never be included in statistics from clinics or other sources. Another problem is the sheer complexity of the human body and the number of factors that can influence health. Blood pressure is regulated by many biological systems. The sympathetic nervous system can affect it, as can the pituitary gland, the kidneys, and several other systems. (We will discuss these physiological systems in the next chapter.) Identifying causal factors or spelling out their sequence is often impossible given our present state of knowledge. These complexities are a formidable obstacle to studying the causes and development of illness.

Another problem facing the psychologist in studying health and illness is the choice of variables and the operationalization of these variables. Operationalization refers to the translation of concepts into methodology. In learning psychology, for example, we may operationalize the conceptual variable motivation or hunger as food deprivation for 24 hours. The operational definition is believed to reflect the conceptual variable, but we cannot always be sure that this is accurate. If we are interested in studying causes of lower back pain or of headache, we normally must rely upon subjects' reports of discomfort. However, there is no assurance that these reports are comparable or that they reflect the same sensation in all patients. Using physiological measurements strikes most of us as being more objective, and the assumption is often made that such recordings are more reflective of a given condition than are self-reports. However, physiological activity can usually be interpreted in many ways as well. Thus, data that we believe are indicative of a particular condition may instead be related to another one. We should never assume that physiological response data are necessarily any more reliable than self-report data.

The selection of appropriate subject groups is another important problem that needs to be considered. Biases in selection can undermine our best research efforts. In a study of stress at Three Mile Island (TMI), for example, this problem was particularly evident (see Baum and Fleming, 1993; Baum et al., 1983). If we are interested in the health consequences of the stress caused by the TMI nuclear accident, who should be studied? The "experimental" group of people exposed to the accident who may be experiencing stress could be drawn randomly from people living near the crippled nuclear plant. However, with whom should they be compared? What is the appropriate comparison group? If we decide that it should be people living 50 to 100 miles or more away, we have not taken into account the fact that simply living near *any* power plant could be stressful. As a result, we find that the TMI group is more stressed than the comparison group, we will not be able to tell whether this stress is caused by living near TMI or by living near *any* power plant. In order to take this into account, we could add a second control group—this time of people living near a coal-fired power plant. Now, if the TMI group is more stressed than either control group, we can say that this stress is not caused by living near a power plant. However, another possibility still cannot be ruled out—the fact that living near any *nuclear* plant is stressful. In order to eliminate this possibility, we must add yet another control group drawn from people living near an undamaged nuclear plant. If the data still show that TMI residents are more stressed than the control groups (and that the control groups are all about the same), we can then conclude that these differences are unique to the TMI accident. However, without indications that the TMI residents were comparable to the control participants *before* the accident and that they changed after it, we still cannot be absolutely sure that the accident caused distress.

There is yet another problem, which is more relevant to convincing people of the veracity of your findings than to generating the findings. Many disease states, such as cancer, heart disease, and hypertension, have a long development period. They develop slowly and are often not detectable for many years. This reflects the gradual wear and tear on the body associated with stress and the slow accumulation of pathologic processes and damage in the body. It is very difficult to identify when this development began (if such a point exists), and as a result, it may be hard to convince people that a particularly salient (and therefore recognizable) event was the cause. Returning to our TMI example, even if we find in 10 years that in comparison to people living elsewhere four times as many Three Mile Islanders have hypertension, controlling for age and the like, how do we convince people that the presence of TMI was *the* cause?

In spite of the extensive and challenging problems in health psychology and the inherent challenges of "experimenting" outside the laboratory, research has produced interesting and important findings. Interdisciplinary methodologies have evolved to deal with many of these problems. Research in health psychology uses human and animal models and studies health and behavior in the laboratory and in the field. Conducting research with patients or in the health care system can be difficult, and communicating and collaborating with other disciplines can be frustrating. However, the future is an interdisciplinary one, in which psychology can make important contributions. The opportunity to offer input into an exciting and basic enterprise where the outcomes *life and death*—are often more dramatic than psychologists are used to makes grappling with these thorny issues worth our time and effort. Like the efforts to apply psychology to environmental problems and other issues that consistently defied attempts to exert experimental control and rigor (Singer and Glass, 1975), the drive to apply psychology to health ultimately will be successful.

Modifiable versus Nonmodifiable Risk

Before moving on, we need to make one other point. As you research health psychology in more detail or conduct your own studies, you may find that although you can find *statistically* significant results, they are often small and of questionable *clinical* significance. The distinctions between these two forms of significance are important and health psychologists often hear such criticism. Clearly, the burden of proof is on us; we must demonstrate that the kinds of changes we can accomplish or the variables that we study have a real impact on health and illness or the processes that lead to disease. However, once we have done so, we also need to recognize that even small increments in risk for disease or decreases in one's ability to resist infection are important because most behavioral or psychological determinants of health and illness are *modifiable*. They can be changed. If one is at risk for heart disease because of family history, that risk cannot be changed. But to the extent that risk is due to one's diet, smoking, and lack of exercise, *this risk can be reduced.* The fact that many behavioral or psychological risks for illness or determinants of poor health can be changed increases the importance of studying them.

BEHAVIORAL MEDICINE AND HEALTH PSYCHOLOGY

Behavioral medicine represents the broad integration of the behavioral sciences with the practice and science of medicine. In an enlightening historical overview of the emergence of health psychology Schofield (1969) emphasized that although the research and services of psychologists traditionally were primarily limited to three health areas—psychotherapy, schizophrenia, and mental retardation—there was a growing opportunity and need for psychological research in a number of other health areas (Matarazzo, 1980). Specifically, the 1964 report of the President's Commission on Cancer, Heart Disease, and Stroke indicated that these health areas were targets for well-funded research, treatment, and prevention programs. The research opportunities for psychology in the field of health stimulated the interest of the American Psychological Association (APA) and ultimately resulted in the development in 1978 of the Division of Health Psychology (Division 38 of the APA), which publishes its own journal, *Health Psychology.* At about the same time, an important meeting at Yale and the founding of the Academy of Behavioral Medicine Research and the Society of Behavioral Medicine marked the formal beginning of behavioral medicine. The *Journal of Behavioral Medicine* was also established early in this process. Currently a large number of courses and even subspecialty areas of study in behavioral medicine and health psychology are being developed in psychology, psychiatry, and other programs throughout the world. The International Federation of Behavioral Medicine Societies publishes its own journal, which includes research from around the world, and several other relevant journals have appeared.

Although behavioral medicine is now recognized as an important area, there is still some debate among professionals in the field concerning just what behavioral medicine is. A widely accepted definition was originally developed at the Yale Conference on Behavioral Medicine and later was articulated by Schwartz and Weiss (1977). Their definition viewed the area as an amalgam of elements from behavioral science disciplines, such as psychology, medical sociology, and health education, that have relevant knowledge that can assist in health care, treatment, and illness prevention. Thus they emphasized the interdisciplinary nature of behavioral medicine.

Matarazzo (1980) suggested that the field of behavioral medicine should actually be broken down into specific areas. He suggests that the term behavioral medicine should be used for the broad interdisciplinary field of scientific investigation, education, and practice that concerns itself with health, illness, and related physiological dysfunctions. This is similar to Schwartz and Weiss's (1977) definition. *Behavioral health,* he proposes, is a term to describe the new interdisciplinary subspecialty within behavioral medicine that is specifically concerned with the maintenance of health and the prevention of illness and medical dysfunctions in currently healthy individuals (see Figure 1.7). For ex-

"Basically, there's nothing wrong with you that what's right with you can't cure."

FIGURE 1.7. Gradually, doctors, nurses, and patients are coming to realize that people have considerable intrinsic resources to battle illnesses and to keep themselves healthy. What we do and who we are have an important effect on our health.
Source: Drawing by D. Reilly, © 1993; The New Yorker Magazine, Inc.

ample, educational effects directed at the maintenance of good health through proper diet and exercise fall into this subspecialty. Finally, **health psychology** is a more discipline-specific term encompassing psychology's primary role as a science and profession in both of these domains. Health psychology is the aggregate of the specific educational, scientific, and professional contributions of the discipline of psychology to the promotion and maintenance of health, the prevention and treatment of illness, and the identification of etiologic and diagnostic correlates of health, illness, and related dysfunction. (Matarazzo, 1980, p. 815)

We offer this as a general definition of health psychology. In the chapters that follow we will present important areas of health psychology that have contributed, or that have the *promise* to contribute significantly to our understanding of health and illness.

SUMMARY

This first chapter provides a brief historical overview of how medicine and psychology have been linked. Until recently the concept of a dualism between mind and body dominated the field of medicine. Currently there is a movement toward an integrated, holistic approach to health and illness and a renewed effort toward employing psychological approaches to medical diagnosis and treatment. Psychology has a great deal to offer the study of health and illness, especially in methodology.

Behavioral medicine should actually be broken down into specific areas; those areas were defined: the term *behavioral medicine* should be used for the broad interdisciplinary field of scientific investigation, education, and practice that concerns itself with health, illness, and related physiological dysfunctions; *behavioral health* describes the new interdisciplinary subspecialty within behavioral medicine that is specifically concerned with the maintenance of health and the prevention of illness in currently healthy individuals; and *health psychology* is a more discipline-specific term encompassing psychology's primary role as a science and profession in both of these former domains. Throughout this text advances in the area of health psychology will be highlighted.

If we return to the advent of the age of organ transplantation that we described in the beginning of this chapter, we can see how the problems and challenges associated with transplantation "beg" health psychology attention. While issues related to organ donation and attitudes toward transplantation are applied concerns of more traditional fields of psychology, ethical, clinical, and scientific questions of immediate relevance to health psychology become clear as well. How will increasingly common organ transplantation affect our prevailing views of life and people's intuitive theories of health and illness? How will the demands of transplant surgery and postsurgery compliance with medical treatments affect recurring disease? What are the effects of giving extended care to transplant patients? Are there consequences of chronic immunosuppression that are designed to prevent rejection of the organ? These and other important questions fall nicely within the new field of health psychology.

RECOMMENDED READINGS

Healthy People 2000. National Health Promotion and Disease Prevention Objectives. National Institutes of Health, 1991.

Matarazzo, J. D. Behavioral health and behavioral medicine: Frontiers for a new health psychology. *American Psychologist*, 1980, *35*, 807–817.

Matarazzo, J. D. Behavioral health's challenge to academic, scientific, and professional psychology. *American Psychologist*, 1982, *37*, 1–14.

Rodin, J., and Salovey, P. Health psychology. *Annual Review of Psychology*, 1989, *40*, 533–579.

Taylor, S. E. Health psychology: The science and the field. *American Psychologist*, 1990, *45*, 40–50.

CHAPTER 2

Physiological Bases of Behavior and Health

Imagine an underwater city far beneath the surface of the ocean. In order to survive, such a city would require a supply of air, water, and food, and the means to distribute these nutrients to all the people living there. A shell or wall to keep water out and to keep residents safe from outside threats would also be necessary. It would need police or some other protection against outside invaders and internal chaos, a way to put out fires and to cope with emergencies, and a way to transport its people to and from work and play. The underwater city would also need a way to purify, reuse, and/or eliminate "used" air and waste products from food and industry. And it would require a system of communication from person-to-person as well as emergency systems for rapid communication and mobilization. With all of these things, an underwater community might survive, although as one can easily see, such an existence would be fragile and require constant vigilance.

In many ways this undersea habitat is similar to the human body. Our respiratory system provides our bodies with oxygen and also removes "waste air" (carbon dioxide). Our digestive system provides food to the body, bringing complexes of nutrients into the mouth and stomach where it is broken down and into the intestines where it is absorbed. Waste is also removed by this system. These nutrients or fuels, once they are made usable (e.g., food made into glucose) are distributed to all parts of the body by the cardiovascular system and its extensive system of highways (arteries, veins, and capillaries). The shell of the city is like our skin, the largest organ of the immune system and our principal defense against outside invaders such as bacteria or viruses. Just as a crack in the undersea walls could spell disaster, a cut in the skin is a way in which pathogens often invade the body. Fortunately, we also have the equivalent of police and fire protection too: The immune system and aspects of inflammation processes act to contain, neutralize, and destroy invaders. The liver, kidneys, and the excretory system help to process food and waste and to take away waste. In addition, the brain and extensive nervous and endocrine systems that act as messengers are responsible for communication and rapid mobilization during periods of danger or emergency.

The human body is a temple; it is intricately designed to assure its survival and is capable of enormous accomplishment. But the human body is also very fragile and so complex that the breakdown of one system (or even part of a system) can cause chaos and dysfunction. We left several systems out of the preceding example, but if we add back the muscle systems, skeletal system, and reproductive system, for example, the interactions and interdependencies of these systems of the body become even more complicated. When everything is working correctly, all the systems function as they should, and all the body's needs are being satisfied, we are happy and productive. When one or more systems go awry or are disrupted by some external event, we get sick, are sad or upset, and/or do not function as well as we should.

Health psychology, whether it focuses on health maintenance or on prevention or treatment of illnesses, is concerned with basic interactions among behaviors, thoughts, feelings, and the functioning of the body. Although not all of health psychology is directly concerned with biological systems or measures, health and illness are biological states as much as they are psychological. Ultimately, behavior must affect or interact with biological functions to affect health or illness. A working knowledge of how the body functions is necessary because behavioral interactions with physiological systems are critical to studying health and behavior. How the nervous and endocrine systems manage the body, and how this management or activity is disrupted by stress are among the central concerns of health psychologists. In this chapter we will review some basic biological processes that affect health and illness as well as physiological aspects of behavior and health that relate to the material in the rest of this book. We will briefly cover many of the systems of the body and genetic influences on behavior and health. This material is basic to discussions of specific aspects of health and illness in coming chapters, and you may want to refer back to this chapter often.

One of the first things that we learn in health psychology is that the mind and body are thoroughly and inextricably intertwined. Beginning with the central nervous system, consisting of the brain and spinal cord, behavior and biological responses are integrated and made to work together to ensure the proper functioning of the organism. The physiological aspects of behavior and the ways in which physiological responses are changed during emotional response attest to this linkage. Without an understanding of both realms, and a genuine effort to integrate them as interlocking systems, our knowledge of each one suffers. For this reason, we cannot emphasize enough the importance of learning about the ways in which the body works and how it is part of our thoughts, feelings, and behaviors. This chapter will provide the reader with a brief introduction to the systems of the body.

SYSTEMS OF THE BODY

The human body consists of billions of cells that are organized into organs or other structures that make up many systems, including the cardiovascular, nervous, immune, digestive, and endocrine systems. Some organs and systems maintain conditions that are needed for life, by either producing or circulating necessary oxygen and nutrients to all areas of the body. Other systems are supposed to regulate these energy-producing or distributing systems, whereas others protect the body and its systems from infection or disease. Although at one time these systems were thought to be independent of each other, they do not function autonomously. We now know that *these systems are related to one another, participate in regulating each other, and work together to maintain optimal health and well-being.* Although each system is important, we cannot review every system here. (Interested readers can readily study these systems in a standard medical physiology text.) In this chapter we will restrict our attention to regulatory systems—nervous and endocrine, those systems that collect and distribute essentials of life throughout the body—cardiovascular, respiratory, digestive system, and the immune system that protects us from outside challenge by bacteria, viruses, and parasites.

The Nervous System

The primary regulatory system of the body is the **nervous system**, aided by activity by the **endocrine system**. Stress and other aspects of behavior and health are mediated primarily by these systems. These systems act to communicate, integrate, and regulate activity by the body as a whole, by stimulating most of the systems of the body or inhibiting activity as needed. Both systems are channeled through the **hypothalamus**, a section of the brain that regulates the internal functions of the body, including temperature, blood flow, and body weight. Extending down from the hypothalamus, the nervous system consists of billions of **neurons**—nerve cells—that communicate with one another and carry messages to and from all parts of the body. These nerve cells are specialized for rapid transfer of information. The **cell body** is the central area of the neuron, and extending from this part of the cell are **dendrites**, which are branched projections that receive information from other neurons. Once messages are received, they are transferred down the **axon** from the cell body to the **synaptic knobs** or vesicles, where information is passed to dendrites of interconnected neurons. Neurons are arranged, dendrite to axon, connected by tiny synapses or spaces between two neurons. In this way information is transferred across the synapse between cells and signals from one neuron are transmitted to another neuron, which, in turn, communicates with other cells in the same manner.

The ways in which information actually "leaps" across the synapse from knobs to dendrites had been a mystery until the discovery of **neurotransmitters** and **receptors**. Information is conveyed from the dendrites and cell body down the axon to the synapse as electrical impulses, but this energy does not transfer directly to other neurons. When electrical impulses reach the synapse, they stimulate the synaptic vesicles to release chemicals, called neurotransmitters, that bind to receptors on the next neuron's dendrites. In this way nervous system activity is transmitted directly from neuron to neuron, making very rapid communication possible through the release of neurotransmitters and the binding of those chemicals to receptors in the synapse. Receptors are places on cells that allow chemical messengers to bind to and communicate with the cell.

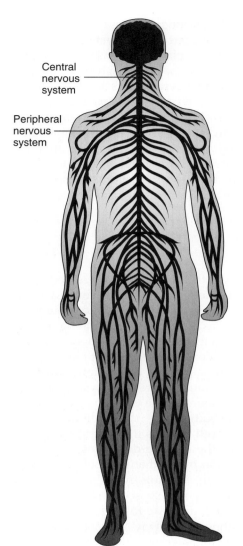

Central
nervous
system

Peripheral
nervous
system

FIGURE 2.1. The human central nervous system (CNS) and peripheral nervous system (PNS).
Source: Adapted from J. Pinel. *Biopsychology.* Copyright © 1993 by Allyn & Bacon. Reprinted by permission of the publisher.

Each neuron is capable of releasing and receiving several different neurotransmitters that affect different organs. They also differ in whether they signal increased or decreased activity. The endocrine system also interfaces with the nervous system at a number of places, using chemical messengers to stimulate, slow, or otherwise govern response by organ systems. The interaction of the endocrine and nervous systems is also accomplished through specialized receptors, where particular hormones can bind and do their work. For example, epinephrine and norepinephrine seek out adrenergic receptors to bind to target tissue so that they can influence an organ or system function. When epinephrine binds to beta-adrenergic receptors on the heart, it increases activity by the heart muscle. However, not all effects of epinephrine are stimulatory. For example, when it binds to beta receptors on immune cells, epinephrine appears to inhibit immune functions. Endocrine and nervous system activity also interact in other ways. Release of messengers from the hypothalamus can affect both nervous and endocrine systems' activities simultaneously. This joint regulation of bodily function is also evident in the pituitary gland, a key regulatory center of the brain, which is made up of separate neural and endocrine tissues.

Most descriptions of the nervous system refer to two levels of organization. The first is the **central nervous system (CNS)** and the second is the **peripheral nervous system** (see Figure 2.1). These classifications may be further subdivided. For example, the peripheral system is often described as having somatic and autonomic components.

The Central Nervous System

The CNS is the command post of the body. Under most circumstances it regulates and integrates all other bodily functions. It consists of only two parts—the brain and the spinal cord—but these two parts are enormously complex (see Figure 2.2).

The brain, the large mass of nervous tissue located beneath the skull, is organized in layers emanating out from the center. Toward the middle are the areas responsible for bodily processes and survival. The **brain stem**, located at the point where the spinal cord widens as it enters the skull, is regarded as the center for regulating life-support systems. Included in or near this core are several structures.

These areas of the brain have different functions, but each is essential for survival. The **hypothalamus** communicates with nearly all brain regions and initiates much of the activity in the periphery by way of its links with the pituitary and to the sympathetic nervous system. As we will see, hypothalamic regulation of the pituitary plays a major role in stress responses and in reproductive hormone activity. Similarly, its control of sympathetic and parasympathetic nervous systems arousal is basic to responses to change or threat. The **thalamus**, located nearby, is also involved in emotional responses and plays an important role in relaying information, sensation, and pain perception.

The **medulla oblongata** is a critical relay center for incoming sensory information and outgoing signals that "tell" us what to do. The basic and involuntary functions of survival, including breathing, heart function, and digestion are regulated by this center and associated autonomic nuclei. At the same time, the *reticular formation* facilitates communication between the brain and the body, extending upward from the brain stem to the hypothalamus and sorting incoming information to help the higher brain to process all this information. The reticular formation also governs arousal and sleep and is responsible for alerting the cortex that danger or demand is present. By prioritizing input, this system helps to alert the brain to the most pressing changes or demands on the organism and to activate the bodily systems that are most appropriate for responding. Finally, the **cerebellum** ("little brain"), shaped like the larger brain, governs muscle tone, balance, and the coordination of movements and activities.

Surrounding the central area of the brain is the **limbic system**, which includes the hippocampus, olfactory bulbs, septum, and amygdala. The limbic system is believed to play a role in emotions, particularly those related to

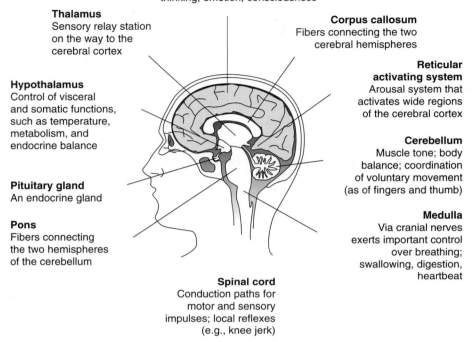

Cerebrum
(Surface: cerebral cortex)
sense perception; voluntary
movements; learning, remembering,
thinking; emotion; consciousness

Thalamus
Sensory relay station
on the way to the
cerebral cortex

Corpus callosum
Fibers connecting the two
cerebral hemispheres

**Reticular
activating system**
Arousal system that
activates wide regions
of the cerebral cortex

Hypothalamus
Control of visceral
and somatic functions,
such as temperature,
metabolism, and
endocrine balance

Cerebellum
Muscle tone; body
balance; coordination
of voluntary movement
(as of fingers and thumb)

Pituitary gland
An endocrine gland

Medulla
Via cranial nerves
exerts important control
over breathing;
swallowing, digestion,
heartbeat

Pons
Fibers connecting
the two hemispheres
of the cerebellum

Spinal cord
Conduction paths for
motor and sensory
impulses; local reflexes
(e.g., knee jerk)

FIGURE 2.2. Cross section of the brain—major structures of the brain and their functions.
Source: Adapted from Ernest R. Hilgard, Richard C. Atkinson, and Rita L. Atkinson. *Introduction to Psychology,* Sixth Edition. Copyright © 1975 by Harcourt Brace Jovanovich, Inc. Reprinted by permission of the publisher.

anger, sexual arousal, and pain. These structures are involved in the regulation of aggression, memory, and learning, and some associated centers regulate reward and reinforcement. The **hippocampus** also appears to play a role in the regulation of hypothalamic control of the pituitary (see the next section). The outer area of the brain farthest from the core is the **cerebral cortex**. Here reside such intellectual abilities as learning, memory, and consciousness.

The **spinal cord** is also a mass of nervous tissue, but it occupies the vertebral canal that runs through the center of the body. It is protected by bone and is organized in segments. Each segment is associated with specific muscles, organ systems, or functions. Within the spinal cord, cell bodies are responsible for receiving and transmitting sensory and motor information. Sensory information is received from nerves emanating from the periphery and is sent to the brain. Information from the brain is similarly transmitted to the peripheral nerves that reach the cord. In this way the spinal cord serves as the link between the brain and the rest of the body. *Afferent* stimulation provides information coming into the CNS from sensory nerves in the periphery, whereas *efferent* stimulation would be information sent from the brain to the many organs and organ systems. All of these transmissions of information are sent through the spinal cord.

The Peripheral Nervous System

All the nerves in the body that are outside the CNS constitute the peripheral nervous system. Of the many ways of viewing this massive system's components, the most common involves distinguishing between the somatic and autonomic nervous systems. Although both are composed entirely of peripheral nerves, they serve different functions. The *somatic system* connects with voluntary muscles and consists of nerves between the sensory and motor organs. Walking, running, or lifting an arm is governed by the somatic nervous system. This system also provides the central nervous system with its only access to external information through sensory organs and nerves.

The **autonomic nervous system**, on the other hand, connects with involuntary muscles in organs such as the lungs, stomach, and kidneys. The autonomic system controls the viscera, the organs that produce and/or distribute nourishment to the body and rid it of waste products. These are the functions of the body that are basic to continued survival. Although it operates below the level of awareness, we are often aware of its effects. It is sometimes called the **visceral system** since its primary function is control of the viscera or the internal organs. While we now know that we can exert volitional control over some autonomic functions such as breathing, this system normally operates on "automatic" to preserve optimal functioning of the body.

The autonomic nervous system can be subdivided into the sympathetic and parasympathetic nervous systems. Again, distinctions are not always clear but the classification is useful. The two systems generally affect the same organs but do so in very different ways (see Table 2.1). As we will see, these two systems often work against, or in opposition to each other.

The **sympathetic nervous system (SNS)** arouses many systems of the body to work harder and to increase blood flow and glucose production. It is a *catabolic* system, meaning that it generally works to break down stored energy into available and usable energy. The SNS is responsible for arousing or mobilizing the body for action, stimulating organs that must increase activity in order to ready an organism to act and inhibit organs that are not involved in such a mobilization. For example, SNS activity increases respiration so that we get more oxygen, increases heart rate and blood pressure (which reflect increasing distribution of oxygen and glucose), increases conversion of stored energy to usable energy, constricts blood vessels to organs that are not needed, and reduces blood flow to the digestive system and to the skin. Blood flow to the gut is reduced to quiet activity there, whereas dilation of vessels to the muscles generally allows increased blood flow to areas that will be needed to act. As we will see in the next chapter, this readying or preparation by the body, described by Cannon (1927) as the fight-or-flight response, is basic to stress. For the present it is sufficient to think of the sympathetic system as

TABLE 2.1. Comparison between the Sympathetic and the Parasympathetic Nervous System

	Sympathetic	Parasympathetic
General function	Catabolism	Anabolism
Activity	Long-lasting	Short-acting
Specific actions		
Pupil of eye	Dilates	Constricts
Salivary glands	Scanty, thick secretion	Profuse, watery secretion
Heart rate	Increase	Decrease
Contractility of heart (force of ventricular contraction)	Increase	—
Blood vessels	Generally constricts	Slight effect
Bronchial tubes of lungs	Dilates lumen	Constricts lumen
Sweat glands	Stimulates	—
Adrenal medulla	Secretes epinephrine and norepinephrine	—
Genitals	Ejaculation	Erection
Motility and tone of gastrointestinal tract	Inhibits	Stimulates
Sphincters	Stimulates	Inhibits (relax)

Source: Based on A. C. Guyton. *Textbook of Medical Physiology.* Philadelphia: Saunders, 1981, p. 715.

being responsible for arousing an organism and preparing various organs to meet an emergency quickly and with maximum strength.

Whereas the sympathetic nervous system is concerned with arousal, the **parasympathetic nervous system** is concerned with calming or reducing arousal of various organisms. As noted earlier, in a sense the two are opposites: The parasympathetic system counteracts arousal (the sympathetic system) when it is no longer needed. (See Figure 2.3.) It is an **anabolic system** in that it restores the body's reserves of stored energy. Although not always the case, the parasympathetic system has the opposite effect on an organ from the SNS. After the sympathetic system has increased heart rate, the parasympathetic system slows it down. Whereas SNS activity reduces digestive system activity, parasympathetic stimulation increases digestion. Since both systems affect the same organs, sometimes it is difficult to know which system is responsible for an effect, but, clearly, they operate at the same time and may work together to produce some bodily changes.

All the differences between the two systems are not based on function. The activity of the SNS is generally an all-or-nothing response. That is, the entire body is affected together—all organs are usually affected at once. Sympathetic arousal is also relatively long-lasting. Endocrine functions associated with sympathetic activity, as we will discuss in the next section, serve to extend the arousal generated by SNS activity. Increases in parasympathetic activity are more short-lived and much more specific, and individual organs can be affected in a more or less isolated manner.

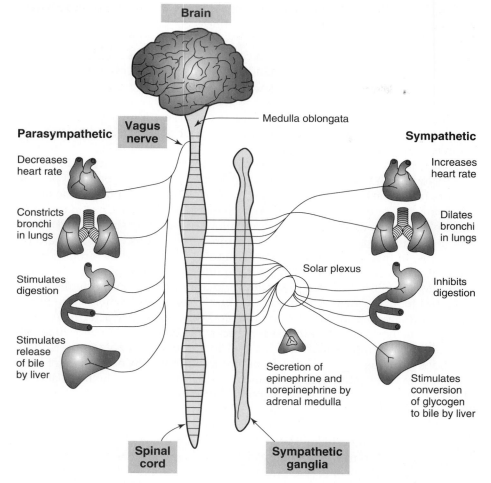

Brain

Medulla oblongata

Parasympathetic

Vagus nerve

Sympathetic

Decreases heart rate

Increases heart rate

Constricts bronchi in lungs

Dilates bronchi in lungs

Stimulates digestion

Solar plexus

Inhibits digestion

Stimulates release of bile by liver

Secretion of epinephrine and norepinephrine by adrenal medulla

Stimulates conversion of glycogen to bile by liver

Spinal cord

Sympathetic ganglia

FIGURE 2.3. The sympathetic and parasympathetic nervous systems. Although affecting the same organs, they have different effects.
Source: Adapted from Ernest R. Hilgard, Richard C. Atkinson, and Rita L. Atkinson. *Introduction to Psychology,* Sixth Edition. Copyright © 1975 by Harcourt Brace Jovanovich, Inc. Reprinted by permission of the publisher.

Related Endocrine Activity

The SNS, because of its association with arousal, was readily implicated in the stress response and has been implicated as a factor in several major diseases. However, sympathetic arousal is not just produced by nervous system activity, and endocrinological aspects of SNS arousal have consequently been of interest too. As early as the turn of the twentieth century, the role of endocrine activity in stress was of interest to researchers (see Cannon and de la Paz, 1911). This activity is accomplished mainly through one primary ganglia of the SNS, the adrenal medulla. The adrenal medulla is part of the adrenal glands, which sit atop the kidneys and play a major role in regulating body function. Stimulation of the SNS causes the adrenal medullae and sympathetic neurons to release large quantities of two hormones, **epinephrine** and **norepinephrine** (also known as adrenaline and noradrenaline). These two substances are members of the general hormone class **catecholamines**. Epinephrine is secreted primarily by the adrenal glands, whereas norepinephrine is primarily released by sympathetic neurons and also serves as a neurotransmitter in the nervous system.

Once released by the adrenal medullae or nerve endings, these hormones enter the bloodstream and are carried throughout the body, binding to adrenergic receptors on organs, and affecting blood vessels or other structures to regulate their activity. Adrenergic receptors are receptors for adrenal hormones and include alpha- and beta-adrenergic subtypes. Depending on the type of receptors (alpha or beta), it will "prefer" to bind with either epinephrine or norepinephrine. For example, norepinephrine in the bloodstream has many of the same effects as does sympathetic stimulation, constricting some blood vessels and increasing resistance or the force required to move blood through arteries and veins. In this regard it functions to support and extend the arousal generated by the nervous system because the effects of hormones in circulating blood last longer than those generated primarily by nervous system stimulation. Epinephrine has similar long-lasting effects, and when epinephrine reaches the heart, it increases heart rate and other coronary activity. At other places in the body catecholamines constrict some blood vessels and dilate others, inhibit gastrointestinal activity, and increase a number of other bodily functions. Although epinephrine is similar to norepinephrine in most of its effects, it is more effective than norepinephrine in stimulating the heart and less effective in constricting blood vessels. Epinephrine also appears to have stronger regulatory effects on immune cells and may be more closely linked to emotional experiences than is norepinephrine.

As we have suggested, adrenal medullary activity and release of epinephrine and norepinephrine exert many effects by augmenting SNS action. As a result, these hormones have very far-ranging effects on nearly every system in the body. The fact that they stimulate some organs and inhibit others may seem confusing but this actually makes sense. If we keep in mind what the functions of sympathetic activity are and then consider each system or area of the body separately, we can see that blood vessels to the muscles would be dilated in order to increase blood flow to them (we need our muscles when dealing with emergencies) and vessels to the digestion system would be constricted in order to minimize blood flow to the gut (which we do not need as acutely!). An effective augmenting hormone would have these selective effects, inhibiting some systems and energizing others. Catecholamines have such effects and are important regulatory hormones for the study of health and behavior.

A second endocrine system often implicated in stress and involved in regulating bodily activity is the hypothalamic-pituitary-adrenal (HPA) axis. While both systems involve the adrenal glands, they are governed by different parts of these glands. (The activities of these adrenal systems are depicted in Figure 2.4.) One adrenal gland is located above each kidney and each is made up of two parts: the medulla, which we have already considered, and the adrenal cortex. As we have suggested, adrenal medullary activity is caused by and

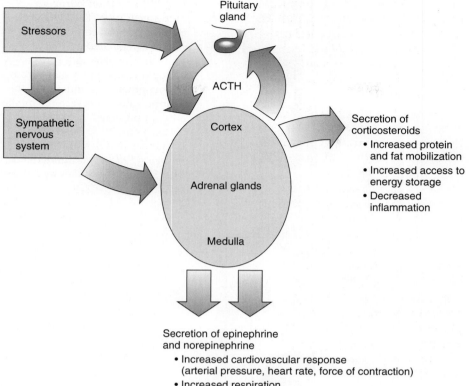

FIGURE 2.4. Diagram of stress-related activities of the adrenal glands.

similar to sympathetic stimulation. Activity by the adrenal cortex is stimulated by secretions of the **pituitary gland**. Activity of the HPA axis begins with the release of corticotropin releasing hormone (CRH), which stimulates the pituitary to release hormones that stimulate the adrenals to produce corticosteroids (see Figure 2.5).

The pituitary is a major center of regulatory activity in the body. Often called the *master gland* because it controls so many functions, the pituitary gland secretes a number of hormones. Metabolism, reproductive function, and to some extent immune and nervous system activity are affected by these hormones. One hormone is **adrenocorticotropic hormone (ACTH)**, which stimulates the adrenal cortex release of corticosteroids. These hormones are very different from the catecholamines, and have different functions. They play a major role in regulating metabolic activity throughout the body and are also involved in control of inflammation and immune system activity. There are two

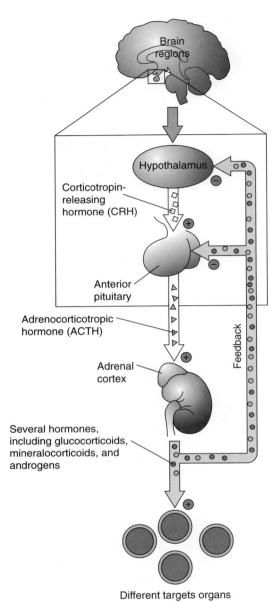

Brain regions

Hypothalamus

Corticotropin-releasing hormone (CRH)

Anterior pituitary

Adrenocorticotropic hormone (ACTH)

Feedback

Adrenal cortex

Several hormones, including glucocorticoids, mineralocorticoids, and androgens

Different targets organs

FIGURE 2.5. Adrenocorticoid hormone regulation. The level of circulating adrenal cortical hormones is regulated in several steps that involve both corticotropin-releasing hormone from the hypothalamus and adrenocorticotropic hormone secreted by the anterior pituitary.
Source: From M. R. Rosenzweig, A. L. Leiman, and S. M. Breedlove. *Biological Psychology.* Sunderland. MA: Sinauer Associates Inc., 1996, p. 232.

basic forms of corticosteroids: **glucocorticoids,** which help to regulate levels of glucose in the blood, and the mineralocorticoids, which affect the use of minerals and regulate electrolyte balance in the blood. In humans the primary glucocorticoid is called *cortisol,* whereas in other animals it is typically *corticosterone.*

Cortisol has a number of effects on carbohydrate metabolism. It also inhibits inflammation of damaged tissue. More important for our purposes, cortisol appears to accompany stress. Most situations that are considered stressful, including trauma, heat, cold, and even sympathetic stimulation, elicit large increases in cortisol secretion. The exact role played by cortisol in the stress response is not as clear as that played by the catecholamines. It is likely that cortisol helps to speed up the body's access to its energy stores of fats and carbohydrates, thereby supporting arousal. It is also not clear whether the increased secretion of cortisol is caused by parallel activation of the pituitary and the SNS or is stimulated first. However, it is clear that both systems are related to the stress response.

The negative feedback loop involved in HPA-axis activation has helped to reveal an important role of the hippocampus in HPA activity. Recall that the secretion of CRH by the hypothalamus and the resulting release of ACTH from the pituitary stimulate the adrenals to release cortisol. This response continues until the quantity of cortisol in circulation is sufficient. This is signaled when cortisol binds to glucocorticoid receptors on the pituitary and apparently in the hippocampus, which tells the system to stop the secretion of the messengers that call for further cortisol release. Damage to hippocampal tissue is associated with strong cortisol reactions and slower shutoff of the HPA axis (see Mendelson and McEwen, 1993). Aging, stress, and other conditions may cause loss of the hippocampal function and reduce the elasticity of the HPA axis.

The Endocrine System

The adrenal glands are part of the endocrine system (see Figure 2.6), which generally serves as a complementary system to the nervous system in regulating many bodily functions. Nervous system communication with bodily systems is by way of nerves and neuron transmission, whereas endocrine communication is by release of hormones. The endocrine network consists of many different glands that secrete hormones directly into the circulating bloodstream, and also includes the pituitary, thyroid, and the reproductive organs. Hormones secreted into the bloodstream travel to various organs that they affect and bind to appropriate receptors on these organs. For example, epinephrine binds to adrenergic receptors, including alpha- and beta-adrenergic receptors. When binding is achieved, the organ is stimulated or inhibited depending on the receptor type and location, and regulatory activities are accomplished. If binding to these receptors is blocked, for example, by a different substance that also binds to these receptors, the organ is not affected. Thus, beta-blocking drugs, or drugs that bind to and block beta receptors, are one class of commonly used medications for hypertension. By binding to beta-adrenergic receptors on the heart and preventing stimulation by epinephrine by blocking its binding to these receptors, these drugs help to reduce hypertension related to cardiac activity. (See Figure 2.7.) The epinephrine cannot attach itself to these receptors because they are already occupied by the beta-blocker.

The hypothalamus regulates the release of hormones by secreting messengers such as CRH, which signals the pituitary to secrete ACTH, which elicits cortisol release. There is some evidence that CRH is also involved in sympathetic activation. Other regulatory hormones released by the hypothalamus include the *thyrotropin releasing factor* and the *gonadotropin releasing hormone*, which trigger the pituitary to signal for the release of thyroid hormone and sex hormones. The combined release of stimulatory hormones, from the brain to

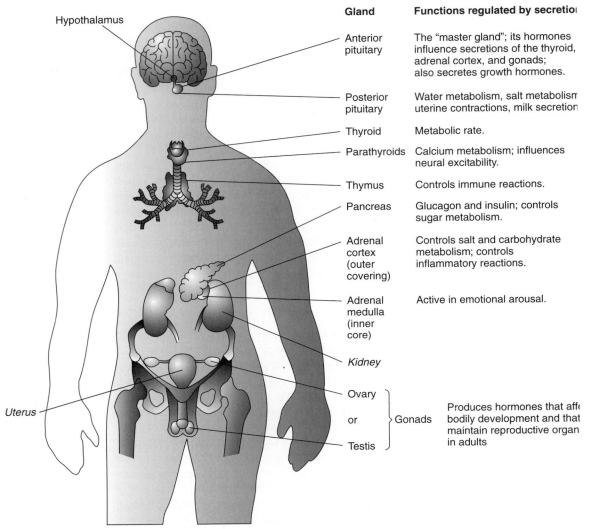

Gland	Functions regulated by secretion
Anterior pituitary	The "master gland"; its hormones influence secretions of the thyroid, adrenal cortex, and gonads; also secretes growth hormones.
Posterior pituitary	Water metabolism, salt metabolism, uterine contractions, milk secretion
Thyroid	Metabolic rate.
Parathyroids	Calcium metabolism; influences neural excitability.
Thymus	Controls immune reactions.
Pancreas	Glucagon and insulin; controls sugar metabolism.
Adrenal cortex (outer covering)	Controls salt and carbohydrate metabolism; controls inflammatory reactions.
Adrenal medulla (inner core)	Active in emotional arousal.
Kidney	
Ovary or Testis } Gonads	Produces hormones that affect bodily development and that maintain reproductive organs in adults

FIGURE 2.6. The endocrine system includes the adrenal glands, sitting on top of the kidneys, as well as many other glands and organs.
Source: With permission from A. M. Schneider and B. Tarshis. *Elements of Physiological Psychology.* New York: McGraw-Hill, Inc., 1995, p. 356.

regulatory glands and eventually to target organs, all have built-in negative feedback loops that shut down hormone release when levels are excessive or unnecessarily high. For example, the release of CRH by the hypothalamus stimulates pituitary release of ACTH and adrenal release of cortisol. High or rising levels of cortisol signal decreases in CRH and ACTH release, shutting the system off again. These regulatory relationships result in responsive and efficient systems.

36   We have already discussed the function of adrenal activity during sympa-

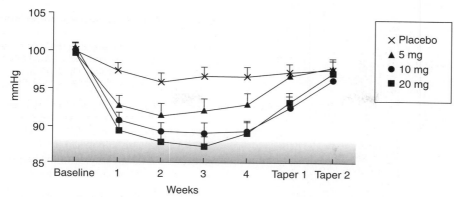

FIGURE 2.7. Resting diastolic blood pressure over time by treatment group using three doses of beta blockers.

✕ Placebo ▲ 5 mg ● 10 mg ■ 20 mg

Source: Copyrighted and reprinted with the permission of Clinical Cardiology Publishing Company, Inc., and/or the Foundation for Advances in Medicine and Science, Inc., Mahwah, NJ 07430-0832, USA.

thetic arousal. The endocrine system has a number of other purposes as well. These include influencing growth, regulating sexual development and functioning, and controlling or facilitating reproduction, renal (kidney) function, thyroid activity, and immune system surveillance. The thyroid affects metabolic rate, protein synthesis, and oxygen utilization. The reproductive glands, regulated by the pituitary, release several hormones that affect reproductive function and sexual differentiation and activity. During pregnancy hormonal changes signal necessary changes for sustaining a maturing fetus and for delivering a live infant. During aging hormonal agents affect cognitive function, immune function, and a range of other activities.

The Cardiovascular System

The heart, and hence the cardiovascular system, has been of interest to scientists, healers, and poets for a long time. This "seat of love and passion" is critical for survival. Without it we cannot (or could not) survive. Like a heating or plumbing system in a building, the cardiovascular system shunts nutrients to cells that need them, carries endocrine messengers to target organs, and transports oxygen throughout the body. It removes carbon dioxide (CO_2) from cells and conveys immune defenses to distal parts of the body as well. Like an unending conveyor belt, the extensive system of arteries, veins, and capillaries picks up and drops off its cargo where available or needed. As we will see, the blood that flows through these vessels also contains elements to protect the vessels from hemorrhage.

The cardiovascular system consists of the heart, the arteries that carry oxygenated blood to the various parts of the body, the small arteries or capillaries, and the veins that return oxygen-depleted (but CO_2 rich) blood to the heart. (See Figure 2.8). The heart, generally thought of as the most important muscle

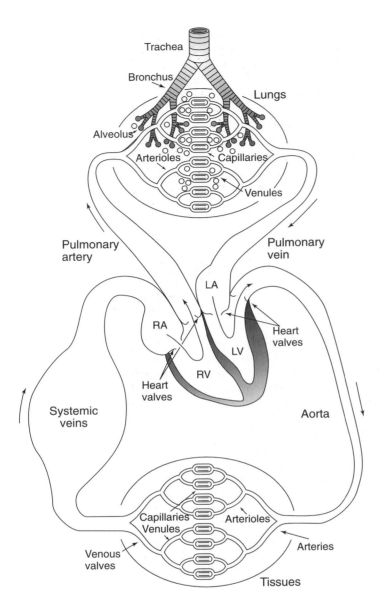

FIGURE 2.8. The cardiovascular system. The heart, blood vessels, and lungs provide for exchange of gases between the atmosphere and the tissues. The right and left side of the heart are two pumps arranged in series on the same circuit. The oxygenated blood (arterial blood) returning from the lungs by the pulmonary veins enters the left atrium (LA) and the left ventricle (LV). Contraction of the latter expels the blood into the aorta, which ramifies into numerous arteries for distribution of the blood to the tissues. The end branches of the arteries (arterioles) give rise to the exchange vessels (capillaries) where oxygen and foodstuffs pass to the tissues and carbon dioxide and waste products are taken up by the blood (venous blood). The capillaries reunite to form the venules and veins, which return the venous blood to the right atrium (RA) and right ventricle (RV). The contraction of the right ventricle propels the blood into the pulmonary artery and its branches. In the pulmonary capillaries the carbon dioxide diffuses to the small air sacs (alveoli), and oxygen is taken up from the latter by the blood. The presence of valves in the heart and the limb veins ensures forward movement of the blood.
Source: From J. T. Shepherd and P. M. Vanhoutte. *The Human Cardiovascular System: Facts and Concepts.* New York: Raven Press, 1979, p. 3.

in the body, is the pump that is responsible for the circulation of blood throughout the body.

The Heart

The heart is composed of four parts or chambers that work in sequence to bring blood into the heart and then to pump it out again. Blood, after passing through the body, enters the right atrium and then the right ventricle. This blood has little oxygen left and so is sent into the pulmonary artery and through the lungs, where it disposes of CO_2 and is replenished with oxygen.

Next it flows into the left atrium of the heart through the pulmonary vein and then into the left ventricle. The heart pumps the oxygenated blood from the left ventricle into the arterial system, through which blood carries nutrients to all parts of the body. The arteries and capillaries that branch off them eventually run into veins that return blood to the heart, forming a closed circulating system.

The motion of blood through the heart is governed by the opening and closing of valves that connect the various chambers and by the regular sequence of contraction and relaxation of the heart muscle. The phases of contraction and relaxation are referred to as the *cardiac cycle*, and consist of systole and diastole. During **systole**, or the contraction of the heart, blood is pumped out of the heart and blood pressure increases. As the muscle relaxes (**diastole**), blood pressure drops and blood is allowed into the heart. This rhythm is maintained in a number of ways. The primary mechanisms are the atrioventricular and sinoatrial nodes, areas that emit impulses and stimulation regulating heart rhythms. These nodes are innervated by the sympathetic and parasympathetic nervous systems. An **electrocardiogram (EKG)** measures the impulses of these nodes and can indicate whether the firing pattern (and hence the activity of the heart) is normal or unusual. **Arrhythmias** are unusual patterns of heart-muscle contraction and relaxation.

Since the heart is innervated by both the sympathetic and parasympathetic systems, it can be regulated through stimulation by these systems. The heart rate or the strength of heart contraction can be altered to provide more or less blood to the body. Both faster pumping and increased strength of contraction result in greater blood flow to the body, whereas slower pumping and weaker contractions have the opposite effect. Excessively rapid heart rates can result in an overall decrease in heart strength, which may decrease the amount of blood pumped. The heart is also sensitive to aspects of blood flow and regulates itself accordingly. Autoregulation of the heart rate is affected by the amount of blood flowing from the veins into the heart. Since tissues throughout the body regulate the blood circulation through them, the return of blood in the veins may vary. The heart must therefore adapt to changes in the amount of blood being returned for oxygenation and recirculation. The more venous blood returned, the more blood the heart will have to pump back out, so during periods of relatively high returns of venous blood, the heart rate increases to contend with the surplus.

Blood Composition and Circulation

Blood is mostly liquid, consisting of a variety of cells suspended in **plasma**, the liquid part of blood. Its red color comes from **red blood cells,** which are the most common cells in blood. These cells are formed in the bone marrow and are the primary carriers of oxygen. Hemoglobin in red blood cells picks up oxygen and transports it through the body by way of the circulatory system. In addition, **white blood cells** (leukocytes) and **platelets** are suspended in the plasma. As we will see, the white blood cells are part of our immune system. Platelets are flat cell fragments that stick together when necessary to form blood clots and to stop bleeding. Together, these cells, the plasma, and other elements such as lipids (fat) and glucose circulate through blood vessels to provide vital nutrients and protein to the body. Changes in the concentration of cells and liquid in blood can have disastrous consequences. For example, stress appears to increase the viscosity of blood and the stickiness of platelets, increasing the possibility of blood clots and potentially heart attacks (Patterson et al., 1994) (see Chapter 5).

Blood pressure is related to heart muscle activity but is also determined by the remaining parts of the cardiovascular system, the blood vessels. **Arteries** carry blood from the heart to other organs and tissue; with the exception of the pulmonary artery, they carry oxygenated blood. The **capillaries** are tiny vessels that carry blood to individual cells, and the **veins** return blood to the heart after its oxygen has been used up. These vessels are responsible for peripheral circulation and may dilate or contract at times. When arteries narrow, their resistance to blood flow increases. Other events will also affect arterial pressure, including the phase of the cardiac cycle (resistance is the greatest during expulsion of blood from the heart). Blood pressure is a measure of this resistance, actually measuring the force built up to overcome resistance in the arteries. As peripheral resistance increases, the force that is necessary also increases. During systole this force is at its highest point, and during diastole it falls to its lowest point. Thus, systolic blood pressure is higher than diastolic blood pressure.

There are a number of ways to increase or decrease arterial pressure, but we will not deal with them here. It is sufficient for our purposes to understand that blood pressure is related to the rate at which the heart is pumping, the resistance in the arteries, and various other bodily processes. It is regulated by several systems and reflects generally upon cardiovascular function.

Coronary Arteries

Blood pressure, how much fat is in the blood, and other factors affect several processes that may lead to heart disease. We will discuss these in Chapter 5. However, before leaving this critical organ system, we need to recognize that the heart, being living muscle tissue, must also receive nourishment. Although it is easy to forget about this with everything else that is going on, this is a vital process. If the heart does not receive enough oxygen, ischemia and tissue death are possible. The coronary arteries carry oxygen-rich blood to the heart and cardiac veins and return the used blood to the circulatory system. When these arteries narrow or become blocked, heart attacks or other dangerous conditions can result. In other words, atherosclerosis or other blockage of these coronary arteries are critical events in coronary heart disease. As we will see in Chapter 5, coronary artery disease is a leading cause of death in the United States.

The Respiratory System

Closely linked to the cardiovascular system, the **respiratory system** provides the blood with oxygen and rids it of carbon dioxide (CO_2) before it is pumped through the body. As we have already noted, blood returns to the heart full of CO_2 waste, and it must exchange this waste for oxygen before it can be recirculated. This process occurs in the lungs, the most important organ of the respiratory system. This is because they are air exchangers, pushing out bad air and pulling in good air. The lungs are large organs located in the chest. Air is brought to the lungs through bronchial tubes that branch into smaller and smaller tubes, called **bronchioles**. At the end of each bronchiole there are air sacs, called **alveoli**. These tiny structures have permeable membranes that permit the exchange of gases, allowing oxygen to be exchanged for CO_2. The respiratory system also includes the nose, mouth, pharynx, trachea, lungs, diaphragm, and a number of abdominal muscles. Without these other organs, the lungs would not function very well at all. Like the heart in the cardiovascular system, the lungs are important but cannot work by themselves.

When we breathe, air is brought in through the nose and mouth, then passed to the lungs through the pharynx and trachea. Once the air reaches the lungs, oxygen is exchanged for CO_2 in the capillaries in the lungs. Respiration is controlled by both voluntary and involuntary muscles. Unlike the heart, the lungs can be stopped voluntarily. We do this when we hold our breath. (It would certainly be difficult to swim underwater if we could not stop breathing temporarily.) We cannot do it very long, however, because there is a respiratory center in the medulla of the brain that monitors the CO_2 levels in the blood and initiates respiration involuntarily when necessary. Under normal circumstances this brain center regulates the rate of respiration to assure optimal levels of blood gases.

The lungs are readily damaged by inhaling cigarette smoke, by air pollution, or by toxic substances and pathogens. Lung cancer and emphysema, major chronic debilitating respiratory diseases, share strong environmental and behavioral etiologies and are major threats to many peoples' health and well-being. The respiratory system has a number of ways to protect itself, including small hairs in the lining of the nose that trap germs and other things that do not belong. When a particle of dust or other foreign matter irritates nasal passages, we sneeze, and this reflex is aimed at expelling the irritant. If irritation occurs in the lungs, coughing serves a similar function. Finally, the sticky mucus lining of the nasal passages and other parts of the respiratory system also trap foreign particles, holding them until they are expelled (see the discussion of the immune system).

The Digestive System

The digestive system, or **gastrointestinal (GI) system**, is responsible for processing the food that we eat and converting it to usable substances. Extending from the mouth, salivary glands, and esophagus, through the stomach, small and large intestines, and the anus, the digestive system is a long, complex, and poorly understood system (see Figure 2.9). As food passes through this large, circuitous system, it is broken down into various nutrients by chemicals and juices (e.g., saliva) that are secreted by organs along the way. These nutrients are absorbed into the bloodstream and carried to other areas of the body. Waste is disposed of at the end of the system.

Digestion occurs in stages, beginning with chewing and the action of salivary enzymes in the mouth that begin to break up food that we eat. As food slips down the **esophagus**, it is pushed toward the stomach by a process called **peristalsis**. These contractions continue as food reaches the stomach and is

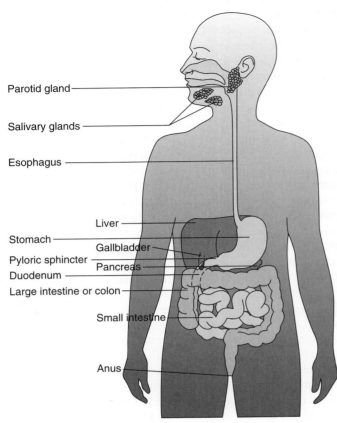

Parotid gland

Salivary glands

Esophagus

Liver

Stomach

Gallbladder

Pyloric sphincter

Pancreas

Duodenum

Large intestine or colon

Small intestine

Anus

1. Chewing breaks up food and mixes it with saliva.
2. Saliva lubricates food and begins its digestion.
3. Swallowing moves food and drink down the esophagus to the stomach.
4. The primary function of the stomach is to serve as a storage reservoir. The hydrochloric acid in the stomach breaks food down into small particles, and pepsin begins the process of breaking down protein molecules to amino acids.
5. The stomach gradually empties its contents through the pyloric sphincter into the duodenum, the upper portion of the intestine, where most of the absorption takes place.
6. Digestive enzymes in the duodenum, many of them from the gallbladder and pancreas, break down the protein molecules to amino acids and starch and complex sugar molecules to simple sugars. Simple sugars and amino acids readily pass through the duodenum wall into the bloodstream and are carried to the liver.
7. Fats are emulsified (broken into droplets) by bile, which is manufactured in the liver and stored in the gallbladder until it is released into the duodenum. Emulsified fat cannot pass through the duodenum wall and is carried by small ducts in the duodenum wall into the lymphatic system.
8. The large intestine absorbs most of the remaining water and electrolytes from the waste, and the remainder is ejected from the anus.

FIGURE 2.9. The digestive system enables us to use the food we eat. Starting with chewing, the digestive system breaks down food into constituent nutrients, helps us to absorb some of these, and excretes the waste that is left.
Source: From J. Pinel. *Biopsychology.* Copyright © 1993 by Allyn & Bacon. Reprinted by permission of the publisher.

mixed with gastric acids and enzymes. These acids and enzymes break down the food further as it sits in the stomach and is gradually emptied into the intestines. Passage through the **small and large intestines** occurs at variable speeds as food goes through the final breakdown and is absorbed through the intestinal lining into the bloodstream. This is aided by secretions from the pancreas, liver, and gallbladder, including bile and pancreatic enzymes that help to reduce fat to tiny particles that can be absorbed. Absorption, mostly of water, continues in the large intestine, and undigested material is converted into waste material that is stored in the rectum.

Stress, anxiety, smoking, and other behaviors can affect digestion at any one of these stages, from making us chew less thoroughly or drying our mouths and reducing the amount of saliva to slowing the rate at which the stomach empties into the intestines or food is absorbed in the intestines (see Breslin et al., 1994). Another problem can occur particularly when there are defects in the stomach's mucosal lining, which protects it against acids secreted in the stomach. Stress can increase the amount of acid in the stomach by increasing release and by slowing emptying, and too much acid may give rise to ulcers.

Digestion, like respiration, "collects" food, water, and oxygen and makes it usable by the body. The circulatory network and cardiovascular system distribute these nutrients, and the nervous and endocrine systems regulate these and other vital systems. A number of other systems contribute to these functions. There are systems to create and rid our body of waste (**renal system**), to regulate sexual activity and reproductive functioning (**reproductive system**), and to clean, detoxify, and regulate metabolism and related activities (**hepatic system**). These are certainly important systems, and diseases of these systems are serious and warrant behavioral research attention. However, we will not review them here. (Interested readers are directed to Recommended Readings at the end of this chapter to learn more about them.) We will turn our attention now to the immune system, a complicated but vital system that will take some explaining!

The Immune System

Unlike many of the systems that we have already discussed, the complex array of immune organs and cells are not primarily concerned with transporting nutrients or signaling the body to work in special ways. Instead, the immune system is responsible for providing defense against pathogens and "foreign" agents—particles and substances that do not "belong" in the body. Bacteria, viruses, abnormal cells, transplanted tissue, and allergens are all subject to attack by the immune system. The largest immune organ is the skin, and this exterior defense constitutes the primary defense of the body. It protects us against most of the pathogens we encounter. Sometimes pathogens get in through a cut in the skin, and in this case, local defenses against the entry of pathogens in the body (such as inflammation) (see Figure 2.10) also protect us against most organisms. This is also true for pathogens that we breathe in or swallow. For example, microorganisms that we breathe are trapped by cilia and mucus in the nose and trachea, and the *mucociliary escalator* removes these foreign particles from the lungs. Similarly, immune and gastric processes disable or destroy most antigens entering the digestive system. Some pathogens may penetrate these systems, however, and require more complex defenses.

The task of the immune system is enormous, and to meet this challenge, it has evolved into a very complex system. Among other things, it must learn to discriminate between what belongs in the body—what is *self*—and what does not belong, or is foreign—what is *not self*. The targets of immune system activity are **antigens,** defined as substances or organisms that are "not self," that are foreign, or that have been altered so as to no longer "belong." Thus, the pollen that we breathe, viruses that infiltrate our bodies, bacteria, cancer cells, and in-

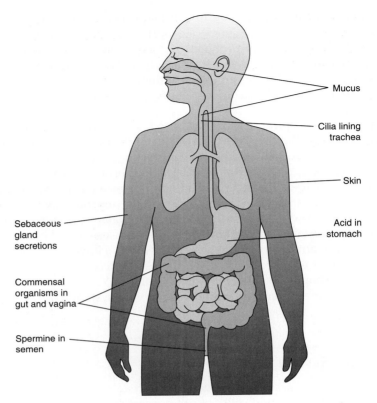

Mucus

Cilia lining
trachea

Skin

Sebaceous
gland
secretions

Acid in
stomach

Commensal
organisms in
gut and vagina

Spermine in
semen

FIGURE 2.10. Exterior defenses. Most of the infectious agents that
an individual encounters do not penetrate the body's surfaces but
are prevented from entering by a variety of biochemical and physical barriers.

fected cells (e.g., cells that normally would be considered "self" in which a virus is now living) are antigens, and they all set off immune reactions. The process by which the distinctions are made between antigens and particles that belong in the body are only partly understood.

Another important distinction when describing the immune system is its ability to respond to new viruses or other antigens and its memory for and *enhanced* reaction to antigens that it has already encountered. The former is called *innate* or *nonspecific immunity* and it is accomplished by cells that do not need to have "seen the antigen before" in order to attack it. In other words, nonspecific immunity involves defense against any foreign presence, new or old. Natural killer cells, monocytes and macrophages, and neutrophils are agents of nonspecific immunity and will attack antigens regardless of previous experience with them. This response is often enough to overcome the invaders but may not always be successful. Our backup, or heavy artillary, is an even stronger immune response, mediated by T and B lymphocytes, that occurs when an antigen has been encountered before. During an initial encounter with an antigen it is "presented" to T cells by other immune cells, and a *memory* for the antigen is created. After this initial encounter, the system retains T and B cells that possess memory for the antigen. In future encounters with the antigen these memory cells are able to unleash an even more ferocious defense of the body.

The ability to develop memory for antigens is the basis of acquired immunity to certain viruses or other pathogens, by either having had an illness or getting a vaccine for it. If you have had an illness, your response to the virus in a subsequent exposure will be stronger because there are memory cells for it and they will overcome the pathogen. This same principle is involved in vaccines, and childhood diseases like mumps, measles, and chickenpox can now be controlled by vaccinating children, injecting dead virus or a harmless modification of the virus that allows the body to create a memory for it. When people then come in contact with the virus, the body is able to overwhelm it with combined nonspecific and specific attacks by the immune system.

FIGURE 2.11. Immune cells originate in the bone marrow and develop along with blood constituents from common progenitor cells, called stem cells. From these cells come lymphocytes, polymorphonuclear leukocytes, platelets, erythrocytes, plasma cells, mast cells, and macrophages.
Source: From J. Janeway and C. A. Travers, *Basic Concepts in Immunology.* Copyright © 1994 by Garland Publications, Inc. Reprinted by permission of the publisher.

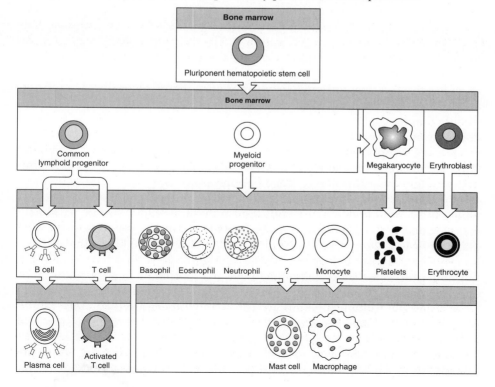

Leukocytes and Lymphocytes

The complexity of the immune system is quickly seen in the number of different organs and cells (**leukocytes**) that are involved in combating antigens. (see Figure 2.11). Several parts of the body are involved in the production and regulation of leukocytes (white blood cells) that are the primary mechanisms of the immune system function. These cells are produced in the **bone marrow**, soft tissue found in the center of many bones. Some cells migrate to the **thymus**, located in the center of the chest. Slowly shrinking in size as an individual grows older, the thymus helps to develop these lymphocytes and produces several substances involved in the immune system function. These cells, called T lymphocytes (T for thymus-derived), are agents of cell-mediated **immunity**; cells that mature in other immune system organs, known as B lymphocytes, are agents of **humoral** immunity. Humoral immunity operates primarily through the activity of antibodies that are produced by B cells. Cellular immunity is conveyed by cells that actively attack invaders and often works in conjunction with antibody release.

Lymphocytes are what many people call white blood cells. (There are many other kinds of white blood cells, however, including macrophages and neutrophils). As noted, there are two types of lymphocytes, B cells and T cells. The former produce **antibodies**; upon contact with an antigen, B lymphocytes produce a number of plasma cells, each of which produces antibodies and secretes them into the bloodstream. Plasma cells derived from the same B cell produce identical antibodies that are tailored to combat a particular antigen.

Antibodies are made up of one of five types of **immunoglobulin (Ig)**, each of which has a different function or mode of action. The most common is IgG, and its primary function is to cover antigens with a substance that facilitates destruction by other immune cells. IgM is effective primarily against bacteria. IgA is located primarily in fluids such as saliva, and helps to destroy antigens as they enter the body. IgE attaches itself to other immune cells and directs them to act when encountering an appropriate antigen, whereas IgD exerts effects on cell activity. In general, antibodies neutralize or coat antigen so as to disable it and to increase its "visibility" by other components of the immune defense (see Figure 2.12).

Some T lymphocytes act as controllers in the immune system. (See Figure 2.13.) **Helper cells** function to activate B cells and other components of the immune system, whereas others, called **suppressor cells**, reduce activity by these cells. This is a very simple description of these functions; the processes by which the T lymphocytes carry out their regulatory functions are extremely complex and not altogether clear. The identity of suppressor cells is not fully known nor is its activities well understood. However, we know that some T lymphocytes are more concerned with killing antigens than with regulating immune processes. These cells, called **cytotoxic cells**, form a third kind of T cell that binds with antigens and destroys them. If we divide these T lymphocytes according to their function, we can see that there are regulatory T lymphocytes and *effector* cells that kill antigens and reject foreign tissues and grafts.

Many lymphocytes as well as monocytes secrete **lymphokines**, which are different from the antibodies secreted by plasma cells. Lymphokines are chem-

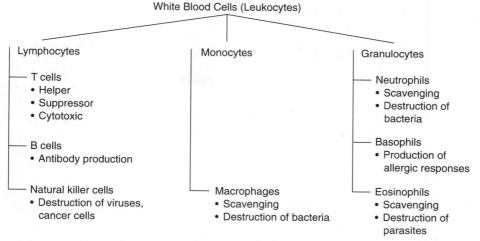

FIGURE 2.12. Major classes of leukocytes, or white blood cells, include lymphocytes, granulocytes, and monocytes (which mature into macrophages).

ical messengers much like hormones that are used by one immune cell to stimulate or inhibit activity by another immune cell. Among the lymphokines that have been identified there are interleukin–1, interleukin–2, and interferon, which help to direct cellular immune reactions. Interferon appears to initiate or regulate antiviral activity by cells, inhibit replication of viruses, and affect the function of a variety of immune cells. Interleukin–2 also affects an array of immune functions, and there is some evidence that these lymphokines are involved in communication with other systems in the body.

Another kind of lymphocyte, the natural killer (NK) cell, is similar to cytotoxic T cells except that they have granules in the cell body that are used to **lyse** (cut through the membrane of) target cells. These large granular lymphocytes do not require prior experience with an antigen to attack it, and are thought to play a major role in combating viruses and cancer.

NK cells make up a relatively small proportion of total lymphocyte populations, but their ability to target and destroy tumor cells or normal bodily tissue that has become infected appears to be very important. Many components of the immune defense are unable to detect and/or eliminate viruses after they have taken up residence in a host cell, and the immunosurveillance function against tumor growth shown by natural killers may represent a primary natural defense against tumor growth and metastasis.

These many cells are distributed throughout the body, and as we have noted, they travel through the blood to areas in which are needed. All cells are not in circulation all the time though, and many lymphocytes reside in the spleen or in one of many **lymph nodes**, located throughout the body. These areas are staging areas for cell activity and release cells when they are needed. Lymph nodes are extremely important, not only because they provide this staging area for lymphocytes, but because they also contain **macrophages** (see below)—another type of immune cell—and trap antigens that approach them.

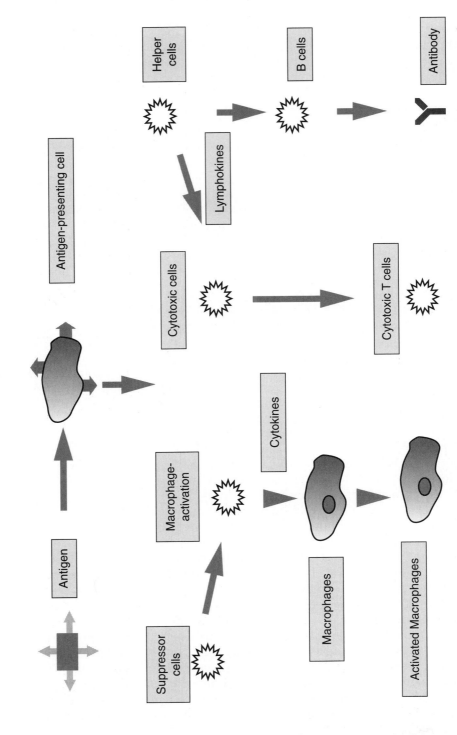

FIGURE 2.13. Cell-mediated immune responses follow presentation of antigen and activation of T cells, regulated by suppressor and helper cells. Some cells release cytokines which activate macrophages to enhance their functions. Cytotoxic T cells are activated by antigen and are helped by helper T cells. Helper cells also cooperate with B cells in the production of antibody.

They are all linked by a system of lymphatic vessels, similiar to blood vessels, carrying **lymph** into the bloodstream. Lymph is a fluid that is made up largely of lymphocytes, macrophages, and antigens that have entered the system and have been caught. By filtering through the lymph nodes, lymph not only carries away antigens that have been trapped there but also delivers the leukocytes into circulating blood, where they search out and destroy other antigens.

Neutrophils and Monocytes

Other types of leukocytes carry out different functions. Perhaps the most primitive form of the immune agent is the **neutrophil**. Neutrophils are developed and released from bone marrow and circulate for about a day before losing potency and leaving the body by way of several pathways. They play an important role in the destruction of bacteria and the prevention of infection. They are very numerous and travel to areas that have suffered injury by squeezing through blood vessels into damaged tissue. In many cases they function as killer cells, becoming sticky and adhering to tissue in the vicinity of a wound or inflammation. Once there, they can destroy bacteria in the area. The process by which this process unfolds appears to be directed by other immune cells and by a process called **chemotaxis**, by which chemical stimuli released by other cells attract neutrophils to the point of invasion by a pathogen. Neutrophils kill invading microorganisms by engulfing them with pseudopods (extensions of the cell body) and releasing chemicals that lyse the enemy cells.

White blood cells that engulf antigens are called **phagocytes**, a term referring to their ability to surround and ingest microorganisms or inert particles. **Monocytes** circulate in the bloodstream much like neutrophils, leaving circulation in less than a day. However, they do not die when they leave the bloodstream. Instead, they mature and *become* larger, more effective phagocytes, called macrophages. In this form they enter many different bodily tissues and organs and dispose of antigens that are already disabled by other immune processes or that have been coated by antibodies. Macrophages also ingest antigens that have been trapped in lymph nodes and secrete substances similar to lymphokines, called **monokines**. These substances affect activity by other cells and are, with lymphokines, called **cytokines**.

Summary

The cells of the immune system, depicted in Figure 2.12, have many different functions. Sometimes they may not function quickly, effectively, or in optimal numbers, and compromise the defense of the organism against pathogens. Depending on what functions are inhibited, different kinds of infections could be expected. Changes in neutrophil activity, for example, might increase the likelihood of bacterial infection, and changes in NK cells might affect tumor growth. In addition, the immune system can turn on the body and initiate responses to "self"—the immune system may attempt to kill or neutralize part of the body. This type of dysfunction is an autoimmune disease, and requires different kinds of treatment from other illnesses. We will discuss some of these issues in greater detail in Chapter 6.

GENETIC INFLUENCES ON HEALTH
AND BEHAVIOR

Genetics exert important effects on behavior and health. Darwin proposed that the great diversity among species was a result of variations that prove to be adaptive to the environment being transmitted to offspring. Favorable or adaptive variations in a plant or animal in a given environment would increase the probability that the plant or animal would survive to transmit those variations to offspring. Extinction of a species was the result of the failure of adaptive evolution; "survival of the fittest" was the result of successful adaptive evolution. Successive generations would thus be infused with qualities from past generations that fit well into a particular environment. This principle was called **natural selection**. Although most or all the mutations and variations responsible for differences among members of the same species are random, they are responsible, in large part, for determining which survive and which do not.

Darwin suggested that each part of an organism produced in its cells substances called **gemmules** that contained a type of blueprint for that cell and the organism. These gemmules, he believed, were collected in the semen and transmitted through sexual reproduction. Although neither Darwin nor anyone else at that time fully understood the rudimentary mechanisms of heredity and genetics, Darwin's theory of evolution rested on the centerpiece of heredity and genetic transmission.

One of the many scholars and intellectuals who admired and studied Darwin's work, Sir Francis Galton was also one of the first to study the influences of genetics on behavior and intelligence. Indeed, Galton is often considered the father of **eugenics** (a term he coined), which is the study of human genetics with the goal of "improving" human characteristics. In 1869 he published a text entitled *Hereditary Genius* in which he presented evidence suggesting that intelligence and talent were inherited characteristics. His general argument, laid out in this book and in several of his earlier articles, was that certain talents and abilities tended to run in families. He studied a number of famous (and highly intelligent) families and noted that they produced a larger than usual number of gifted individuals. Further, he noted that the closer the family relationship, the more likely the exceptional trait was to be expressed. Eminence in a given field was directly related to family membership, and a child's chances of being famous increased as closer relatives achieved this status. (Later in this chapter we will return to this issue of intelligence and heredity.)

Neither Darwin nor Galton understood the basic mechanisms of heredity and gene transmission. Mendel, however, carried out a detailed, lifetime study in an attempt to explain how inherited characteristics might be acquired. Using ordinary garden peas as his subject population, he worked for years in his monastery gardens, crossing certain shapes of peas with other shapes to produce **hybrids** (literally meaning a cross-mating between two subspecies). Generally, he found that given traits were passed on from one generation to the next in a rather systematic fashion that could be predicted mathematically.

Mendel actually uncovered the basic workings of hereditary transmission. Although neither he nor anyone else knew of the actual existence of genes at this time, he was nonetheless aware of their effects. He concluded that inherited characteristics are determined by combinations of hereditary units received from each parent's reproductive cells, cells that we know as **gametes**.

Mendel also correctly recognized that some gene factors are more potent than others for a given trait. For example, in the case of his plants the color of pods and the form of pods were traits. Since each parent contributes a given gene for a particular trait, each trait is determined by pairs of genes. The gene from each parent may be either **dominant** or **recessive**. Dominant genes always prevail when present. A dominant gene from one parent and a recessive from the other would lead to the expression of the dominant trait. Recessive genes are not able to be expressed unless both are recessive; two recessive genes are the only situation that allows the expression of recessive traits. Parents having both dominant genes for a given trait would breed true, or produce offspring with the obvious expression of that trait. If one parent had the recessive gene, the parents would produce mixed offspring (see Figure 2.14). In recessive inheritance, also noted by Mendel, neither parent may express the trait but both may have recessive genes for it; therefore, it could be expressed in an offspring. Thus, Mendel observed that what you see is not always what you get. Even though an organism may not appear to have a particular trait (the trait is not expressed), the organism may possess recessive genes for that trait. The characteristics observed in the organism are called **phenotypes**; what the organism contains, both expressed and nonexpressed, is called **genotype**. A short plant has shortness as a phenotype (you can actually see the shortness), but this plant may contain recessive genes for tallness (the genotype). Mendel determined the phenotype through mere observation, but the genotype was determined by looking at the inbreeding history of the organism.

Mendel's work showed that a single trait seen in the offspring is a result of paired genes that were acquired from the parents, one coming from the germ cell of the female, the other coming from the germ cell of the male. An acquired trait is the result of two discrete bits of genetic information coming from each parent. The variation within and between species, a phenomenon that fascinated Darwin, was now partly explainable by Mendel's laws: It was a result of the passing on of genetic material from both parents.

BEHAVIORAL GENETICS

As we noted earlier, Mendel, Darwin, and other early researchers in the field of genetics were chiefly interested in how physical or anatomical features were transmitted from parents to offspring. In more recent years another focus has emerged from the observation of *behaviors* that could be transmitted from parent to offspring. This field is called **behavioral genetics**. Behavior, or rather a number of diverse phenomena such as intelligence, aggression, emotionality, mental illness, and criminality, appears to show some of the same hereditary patterns as do physical characteristics like eye color. The three major methods

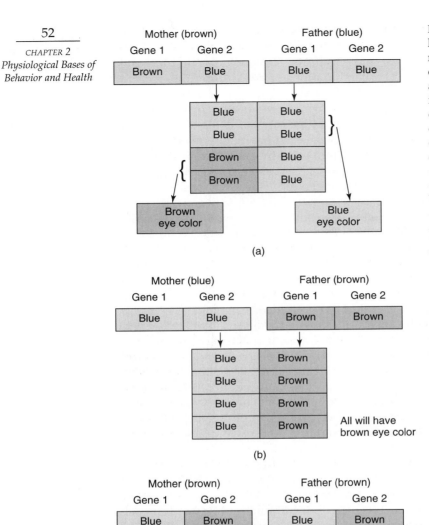

FIGURE 2.14. An example of how recessive and dominant genes combine. Blue eye color is a recessive trait and will only be expressed in a child if both parents contribute a blue eye color chromosome. This can occur in (*a*) where one parent has two blue eye genes (and has blue eyes) and the other has one of each (and brown eyes). In this case offspring will have blue eyes 50 percent of the time. In (*b*) the father has two brown eye color genes and always donates one brown chromosome. Offspring will always be brown-eyed because brown eye color is dominant. In (*c*) both parents have brown eyes. Can they have a blue-eyed child?

of genetic investigation of humans are family studies, twin studies, and studies of adopted children.

Family Studies

Family studies assess each member of a family in order to determine whether the prevalence of a certain characteristic exceeds that found in the general population. Of critical importance in such studies is the requirement that the considered characteristic be precisely defined. If this requirement is not met, then meaningful comparisons with a norm cannot be made. However, when unique patterns or mutations can be documented in many members of a family, it can suggest genetic linkages and heritability. For example, research has identified specific genetic mutations that appear to be related to breast and ovarian cancer and that occur among affected members of families that share this genetic defect.

Family studies are generally the weakest kind of evidence to support the presence of genetic predisposition to a certain personality characteristic. Since family members not only have the same genes but also have the same environment, it is impossible to determine whether the relationships found are due to genetic or environmental factors.

Twin Studies

Twin studies can provide a somewhat stronger test of the possible presence of genetic factors because they compare persons raised in a highly similar environment who are either genetically identical (**monozygotic twins**) or similar but not identical (**dizygotic twins**). Twin studies are the most popular method of evaluating human inheritance. Monozygotic twins develop from the same fertilized egg ovum, and thus share the same set of inherited genes. As a result, they are often called **identical twins**. Because they are genetically identical, any observed differences between the twins can be attributed to environmental factors. Dizygotic twins develop from two separate fertilized eggs, and therefore are not any more genetically alike than other brothers and sisters (i.e., they share 50 percent of their genes). Any observed differences found between these **fraternal twins** can be ascribed to a combination of genetic and environmental factors. Any differences found between monozygotic and dizygotic twins raised in the same environment would be evidence for possible genetic involvement.

Twin studies, although strongly suggestive of the presence or absence of genetic factors, must be interpreted with some caution. We can argue that monozygotic twins not only are alike genetically, but also share a more nearly identical environment than dizygotic twins. They are of the same sex and commonly tend to be dressed alike, treated alike, and usually confused with each other by other people. One way of overcoming this argument is to examine monozygotic twins who were separated from each other very early in life and then reared apart. But because of the time and expense involved in conducting such studies, only a small number of cases have been studied, primarily in the area of psychopathology. For example, in the investigation of schizophrenia, twin studies have suggested that there is a genetic predisposition for this disorder. However, the small number of cases in these studies prevents any definitive conclusion (Rosenthal, 1970).

Another point concerning twin studies is worthy of comment. Identical twins, in comparison with fraternal twins or normal siblings, have a greater risk of retardation and pregnancy and birth complications (Hanson and Gottesman, 1976). Such an observation raises some questions about identical twin studies and the possibility of genetic involvement because of the likelihood that trauma to the central nervous system (e.g., birth complications), and not genetic factors, predisposes twins to develop certain forms of psychopathology and personality characteristics. Similarly, although twins may be reared apart, they share the same environment for 9 months and this environmental sameness may be responsible for some similarities that appear to have a genetic basis.

Adoption Studies

Finally, another type of study—the adopted child study—attempts to eliminate the possible developmental effect of being raised in a similar environment. Such studies examine children who were adopted away from their original biological family at birth and raised by another family. These people have the genetic endowment of one family and the environmental learning experiences of another family. A number of meaningful comparisons can be made by using this method. For example, we can determine whether the adopted child resembled his or her biological parents with regard to the psychological characteristic in question. Other comparisons are also helpful in determining the impact of genetic endowment in a different environment.

Convergence

The strongest support for the heritability of a particular personality characteristic or trait comes from the convergence of evidence from family studies, twin studies, and studies of adopted children. If it is found that there is familial similarity in a trait, if monozygotic twins are significantly more similar than dizygotic twins on that trait, and if adopted children resemble their natural parents more than their adoptive parents, then some involvement of heredity for that trait is beyond dispute. In the field of psychology, the only trait for which all three methods of investigation have clearly converged is the intelligence quotient (IQ), suggesting that there is a significant inherited component in intelligence (Buss and Plomin, 1975). However, the problems inherent in studying or interpreting data on intelligence makes this conclusion controversial and the topic has been debated often. The extent to which inherited intelligence contributes to overall intelligence is not clear.

This is a very complex issue with a great deal of political and social significance, and the scientific and sociopolitical debate will probably continue in one form or another for some time. Recent discussion of heritability and IQ include the publication of the book, *The Bell Curve: Intelligence and Class Structure in American Life* (Herrnstein and Murray, 1994) and criticisms of this approach to studying heritability and IQ (see Waldman et al., 1995).

Abnormal Behavior and Genetics

There is also considerable evidence to suggest the importance of genetic factors in various forms of abnormal behavior such as schizophrenia (see Mears and Gatchel, 1979). This evidence comes from the three major types of studies that we have discussed: family studies, twin studies, and studies of adopted children. At the outset we should point out that a major problem in such research is confusion concerning just what schizophrenia is and how it can be reliably diagnosed and measured. On the top of the problems of studying heritability there is the fact that schizophrenia consists of a complex array of symptoms that may differ from person to person and that may change in a given person over time. The reader is referred to a thorough review of this problem provided by Mears and Gatchel (1979).

A number of family studies have demonstrated that the more closely a person is related to a schizophrenic, the higher the probability is that the person will develop schizophrenia. Although findings varied considerably among these studies with reported risk factors ranging from 0.2 to 12.0 percent, 12 of the 14 studies showed a risk factor for related individuals of above 1 percent, which is roughly the expected occurrence of this disorder in the general population (Rosenthal, 1970). Similarly, studies of twins suggest a greater concordance rate of schizophrenia in identical twins than in fraternal twins (Ban, 1973; Kallman, 1946). The concordance rate for identical twins was approximately five times larger than the concordance rate for fraternal twins. As we can see in Table 2.2, there is a great deal of disparity in the concordance rates reported in the various studies, but concordance is usually much greater for identical than for fraternal twins.

Adopted Child Studies

If it could be determined that children who are born to schizophrenic mothers but *not exposed to the potentially traumatic experiences of being raised in a schizophrenic family* still develop schizophrenia at the same rate as children who

TABLE 2.2. Concordance Rates Between Monozygotic and Dizygotic Twins in the Major Twin Studies of Schizophrenia

Study	Monozygotic (Identical) Twins		Dizygotic (Fraternal) Twins	
	Number of Pairs	Percent Concordant	Number of Pairs	Percent Concordant
Luxemburger, 1928a, 1934 (Germany)	17–27	33–76.5	48	2.1
Rosanoff et al., 1934–1935 (United States and Canada)	41	61.0	101	10.0
Essen-Möller, 1941 (Sweden)	7–11	14–71	24	8.3–17
Kallmann, 1946 (New York)	174	69–86.2	517	10–14.5
Slater, 1953 (England)	37	65–74.7	115	11.3–14.4
Inouye, 1961 (Japan)	55	36–60	17	6–12
Tienari, 1963, 1968 (Finland)	16	0–6	21	4.8
Gottesman and Shields, 1966 (England)	24	41.7	33	9.1
Kringlen, 1967 (Norway)	55	25–38	172	10
Fischer, 1968 (Denmark)	16	19–56	34	6–15

Source: From D. Rosenthal, *Genetic Theory and Abnormal Behavior.* New York: McGraw-Hill, 1970. Copyright © 1970, McGraw-Hill Book Company. Used with the permission of McGraw-Hill Book Company. See original source for full references.

are born to schizophrenic mothers and raised by them, then this would be convincingly strong support for the presence of a genetic predisposition. Heston (1966) conducted a study in which 58 adoptees born to hospitalized schizophrenic mothers were examined. Adopted individuals who did not have schizophrenic mothers (the control group) were simultaneously examined. Participants in the two groups were matched for age, sex, and duration of time in child-care institutions. Independent diagnoses made by several psychiatrists and based on a wide variety of information showed that schizophrenia was found only in those children who had schizophrenic mothers. Approximately one-half the children of schizophrenic mothers demonstrated major forms of psychopathology such as neuroses, psychopathy, and mental retardation. Much larger-scale adoptee studies also have shown that children of schizophrenic parents who were adopted by other families had significantly greater schizophrenic characteristics than a matched control group of adopted children whose biological parents had no history of psychiatric hospitalization for schizophrenia (see Kety et al., 1971).

Conclusions

Taking into account all the results found in family studies, twin studies, and adoptee studies, one is likely to conclude that genetic factors play an important role in the etiology of schizophrenia. However, the fact that the concordance rates are far from 100 percent suggests the involvement of other factors. Currently a widely held position proposes a diathesis-stress formulation of schizophrenia (see Chapter 3). It is assumed that some people inherit a diathesis (or predisposition) toward the development of schizophrenia, but schizophrenia will actually develop only in those predisposed individuals who are exposed to particular experiences as stressors (Meehl, 1962; Zubin and Spring, 1977).

Genetic Bases of Disease

Genetic factors also play a prominent role in the development of many physical diseases. We will briefly discuss their role in four prevalent diseases: diabetes, essential hypertension, breast cancer, and colon cancer. Before doing so, however, it should be pointed out that research on these genetic factors has stimulated the growth of new areas in medicine. The first has to do with the development of genetic testing techniques for detecting the susceptibility gene in various illnesses. The development of these genetic risk-factor testing methods will concomitantly be an important area for health psychology. It will prompt the need to establish a better understanding of how individuals deal psychologically with the information that they possess a gene risk factor that might ultimately lead to the development of a potentially fatal disease. Moreover, many people may be offered the options of increased surveillance or prophylactic surgery in order to prevent fatality from the disease. What will be the best method of offering such options? A second important area of medical development is genetic engineering. It may be possible to alter genes that are responsible for a predisposition to a certain disease. Evaluating the success rate of such methods, as well as the best decision-making process for a person to use who may have moral or religious concerns, will be important areas of research in health psychology.

Hypertension

Genetic factors clearly play an important role in the development of hypertension (see Smith et al., 1987). Although we will discuss some of these factors in more detail in Chapter 5, we will consider here some of the evidence suggesting a genetic factor in hypertension. Research has concluded that if one parent has high blood pressure, his or her offspring will have almost a 50–50 chance of developing it; if two parents have high blood pressure, the probability increases to approximately 95 percent (Taylor, 1995). The operative factor in this pattern appears to be a possible genetic predisposition to greater changes in blood pressure and heart rate that occur throughout the day and night. For example, a recent study by Somes et al., (1995) showed these kinds of influences in monozygotic and dizygotic twins.

Diabetes

There are two major types of diabetes, both characterized by abnormally high levels of blood glucose. As reviewed by Polonsky (1993), *Type I diabetes*, also known as insulin-dependent diabetes mellitus (IDDM), usually appears during childhood or adolescence. This appears to be due to genetic and autoimmune processes that have negative effects on pancreatic beta cells, which are the primary sources of **insulin**. Insulin helps to store glucose in cells by helping to move it from the bloodstream into cells for storage. The resulting insufficient level of insulin effects an inability of glucose to be normally absorbed into the tissues, resulting in hyperglycemia and other metabolic problems. *Type II diabetes*, also known as non-insulin-dependent diabetes mellitus (NIDDM), usually appears after the age of 40. It is thought that this chronic hyperglycemia is the result of significant resistance to insulin as well as the dysfunction of beta cells. It has been estimated that Type II diabetes is 7 to 10 times more prevalent than Type I diabetes (Polonsky, 1993). Overall, about 5.5 million Americans have been diagnosed with diabetes (Herman, Teutsch, and Geiss, 1987).

There has been a great deal of research with humans and animals evaluating the possible genetic bases of susceptibility to diabetes. This research suggests that the risk for both Type I and Type II diabetes is at least partly genetic (Braunwald, 1994).

Breast Cancer

In Chapter 6 we will discuss cancer. While genetic aspects of cancer vary greatly with different types of cancer, some appear to be associated with genetic defects or mutations. Two types of cancer that have received increasing attention in recent years by genetic researchers are breast cancer and colon cancer. As pointed out by Weber (1996), the clustering of breast cancer in certain families was first noted by physicians in ancient Greece. Evidence of similar clusters of disease within families has led to the general conclusion that genetic factors are responsible for 5 to 10 percent of all breast cancer. The first major susceptibility gene for breast cancer was identified as BRCA1. A great deal of research is now being conducted to detect reliably and to understand the process of BRCA1 mutations. [Interested readers are referred to a review of this specific susceptibility gene (Shattuck-Eldens et al., 1995).] As noted by Dhingra, Hittelman, and Hortobagyi (1995), the knowledge and interpretation of such specific genetic changes as well as their biological consequences, will eventually lead to methods to prevent and treat them effectively. We will consider these issues again in Chapter 6.

Colon Cancer

Finally, there is good evidence of a heritable component of colon cancer risk (see Lynch et al., 1992), and genetic risk identification is possible in some cases (see Burt, DiSario, and Cannon-Albright, 1995). Since the prevalence of colon cancer is significant, further development of refined screening strategies for both rare and common cases of colon cancer is receiving a great deal of scientific attention. Again, continued genetic research will lead to more precise and accurate screening methods and improved diagnostic and therapeutic options for these diseases.

SUMMARY

In this chapter we have discussed the physiological systems involved with behavior and health. It is important to know both psychological and somatic aspects of the body and behavior in order to understand better the topics of health psychology.

Most aspects of body function are mediated by the nervous and the endocrine systems. The brain [part of the *central nervous system (CNS)*] is the command post for the body. The *peripheral nervous system* extends out to the muscles and organs of the body from the spinal cord. At various points along the way connections with the *endocrine system* coordinate the chemical support that it gives to the nervous system function. One of the most important links is between the endocrine system and the *sympathetic nervous system (SNS)*, a subdivision of the peripheral nervous system that controls arousal and stimulation of bodily functions. The *parasympathetic nervous system* works to counter the effects of the sympathetic system. Endocrine activity supports the *SNS* through the use of long-lasting hormones that extend the arousal generated by the nervous system. Norepinephrine and epinephrine, hormones also called *catecholamines,* are produced in the *adrenal medulla.* The *adrenal cortex,* controlled by the *pituitary gland,* secretes a number of hormones that regulate glucose levels in the blood and spur other metabolic functions.

The *cardiovascular system* is responsible for the circulation of blood through the body. The *arteries* carry oxygenated blood away from the *heart* to the *capillaries,* where it is used by the cells and where carbon dioxide (CO_2) is returned. The capillaries then carry the blood to the veins, which lead back to the heart. The heart is composed of four chambers that work in sequence to bring the blood into the heart and to pump it out again. The motion of the blood through the heart is governed by the valves that connect the four chambers. The sympathetic and parasympathetic nervous systems regulate the heart, and the heart is sensitive to blood-flow changes itself. Blood pressure is related to the activity of the heart and the contraction of the blood vessels.

The respiratory system provides the blood with oxygen and rids it of CO_2. Respiration is controlled voluntarily and involuntarily—there is an area in the medulla that overrides voluntary control when necessary.

The *digestive system,* or *gastrointestinal (GI) tract*, is responsible for processing the food that we eat. It includes the mouth, esophagus, stomach, large and small intestines, and anus. As food passes through the GI tract, various nutrients are absorbed into the bloodstream and carried to other areas of the body. The GI tract seems sensitive to emotion, and it appears to involve sympathetic and parasympathetic system activities simultaneously.

The *immune system* is responsible for the protection of the body from germs, bacteria, and other pathogens that attempt to invade the body. Several lines of defense exist, beginning with cells and tissue designed to trap viruses or other "Not-self" particles as they enter the body. Other components of the immune system neutralize, ingest, or kill these antigens once they have entered the body. The function of the immune system appears to be regulated by *T cells* and the *lymphokines* that they secrete, but this direction is dependent on the function by other lymphokines, macrophages, and granulocytes.

Genetics has an impact on behavior and health. Galton is considered the father of *eugenics*, the study of human genetics with the intent to improve the human species. However, there is no evidence that eminence is transmitted in a simple way. *Behavioral genetics* is the study of behavior transfer from the parent to the offspring. *Family studies, twin studies, and adopted child studies* are the three most common methods of behavioral genetic study. Some interesting research in behavior and genetics shows that schizophrenia may have a genetic component.

RECOMMENDED READINGS

Hassett, J. *A primer of psychophysiology*. San Francisco: Freeman, 1978.

Isaacson, R., Douglas, R., Lubar, J., and Schmaltz, L. *A primer of physiological psychology*. New York: Harper & Row, 1971.

Obrist, P. *Cardiovascular physiology*. New York: Plenum Press, 1981.

Plomin, R., DeFries, J., and McClearn, G. *Behavioral genetics*. San Francisco: Freeman, 1980.

Roitt, I., Brostoff, J., and Male, D. *Immunology*. St. Louis: C. V. Mosby, 1985.

CHAPTER 3

Stress

When you are busy, you may start to feel pressure to do things more quickly and to ignore demands that do not seem to be related to getting your work done. This time urgency is interrupted by worries that you will not get it all done in time and have the alertness and energy to help you get it done. Your mind is racing, your heart is beating fast, and you are able to work harder and faster than you normally can. At the same time, you find yourself more irritable and angry when you are interrupted. You lose your appetite, drink more and more coffee, and have a few beers or drinks when you are done for the day so that you can unwind. You realize that you have not jogged for days, and when you eat, it is usually some fast food or junk food that is readily available and quickly consumed. As you approach your deadline or shortly after completing your work, you notice that you are not feeling well and have some problems getting other things done.

This unpleasant state that we have just described is not unusual and many or most of us have experienced or do experience these kinds of situations. What we feel, how our body responds, and what happens to us after we complete our work are part of the **stress** that we experience in these situations. Stress is as common as any emotional state and is experienced in different intensities and durations. It helps us to perform better when we need to and helps us to be more alert when vigilance is necessary. However, it can have some unfortunate effects as well, and stress is of interest because it appears to be central to health psychology research and practice.

Stress is a central concept in the study of health and behavior for a number of reasons. Stress is so common and widespread that we can safely say that everyone experiences it, and the term itself has become enormously popular as a lay explanation for any number of aches, pains, and maladies. We often speak of stress as if it were pressure, or some negative force that can explain unusual behaviors and sensations. But stress is not only "popular" among lay people: Scientists have investigated stress more thoroughly than most other concepts. For nearly one hundred years, investigators have tried to learn about the events that cause stress and the ways in which stress alters normal bodily functioning. It is extremely important as both a process that helps us to adapt to environmental changes and one that has a central role in the pathophysiology of a number of chronic illnesses. Stress is thought to be a psychological or physiological precursor of illness and has been used as an explanation for spontaneous outbreaks of inexplicable illnesses. It is also used as a catchall for emotional reactions, such as anxiety, discomfort, or depression. From a cursory reading of psychological and medical texts we can derive a fairly broad definition of stress. Yet stress actually refers to a process that is not only specific but also central to the relationship between people and their surroundings.

As we will see, as stress unfolds the entire body is altered. Biochemical, physiological, behavioral, and psychological changes, many of which are directly related to health, occur as part of this reaction. We will begin our study of stress by reviewing major theories of stress, discussing evidence supporting each concept, and reviewing the various concepts used to explain how stress works. We will use a combination of these theories to provide a framework for discussing some of the specific causes and effects of stress.

THE MODERN CONCEPT OF STRESS

Stress can be defined as the *process by which environmental events threaten or challenge an organism's well-being and by which that organism responds to this threat.* This general definition assumes that organisms live in a world that contains various threats (e.g., from predators) and challenges (e.g., finding food) and that the world poses constantly changing demands that require organisms to adjust continually. There are specific responses that are helpful in these situations. It is useful to run from predators and to search for and gather food when hungry. Stress, when aroused, helps us to run faster, to be more vigilant for food, or otherwise to act more quickly or with greater efficacy. In other words, stress acts to amplify specific coping responses or attempts to overcome or adapt to a stressor. It does not make the responses, it makes them better. Environmental events that pose threats or challenge are called **stressors**. Under certain conditions these events give rise to a stress reaction, characterized by such symptoms as fear, anxiety, and anger. This is by no means the only way to define stress, nor is it the most precise definition that one can use. We will return to the definition of stress later. For now, it is useful to think about stress in its environmental and evolutionary context.

As we suggested earlier, some people have argued that stress is adaptive and helpful, a "hard-wired" pattern of physiological and psychological changes that help us to adjust to changes and threats in our world (see Chapter 2). When it is activated, stress increases our strength, alertness, and speed so that we can better cope with threats or adjust to changes. It readies us to act and can make our responses more effective. This pattern, some believe, is important for survival and was naturally selected throughout evolutionary processes because of these prosurvival characteristics. Cave people or others of our early ancestors dealt primarily with basic survival needs—shelter, food, safety—and a mechanism that increased their strength, speed, and vigilance should have helped them to fight off predators, to hunt and successfully procure food, and to flee when the odds against them were overwhelming. One can easily see how a response that supports and enhances our reactions to danger would be selected and transmitted to offspring. As a result, most of us respond similarly to stressors. As human society has changed and much of our protection from predators or other threats has been institutionalized, the usefulness of this action pattern is no longer as clear. Most of us no longer hunt and gather our food, or must seek out shelter and protection each day. Whether the stress response that helps us to fight or flee successfully still serves us well is an interesting question and an important part of the study of stress.

There are many questions through the ages that have been asked about stress, questions that cannot really be answered. For example, was life more stressful in prehistoric times or are there equally challenging and threatening stresses today? If you think about it, there are still many sources of harm and threat in our daily lives, and although we no longer must worry about saber-toothed tigers lurking behind the next rock, we do worry about crime, finding and keeping a job, having friends, and staying healthy. If you think about the kinds of problems we deal with in the same way that we discussed our ancestral past in the last paragraph, you will quickly see that the same adaptation sequence characterizes our daily lives. In order to survive and prosper, we engage in more or less continuous adjustment to changes in our surroundings. Sometimes changes are minor and we adjust to them without even being aware of it. However, at other times these changes are more severe and a conscious effort is needed to adapt to them. Snowstorms and cold spells require substantial adjustments as we must get around in snow and keep warm. The closing of a plant where one works also requires adjustment, and we must manage our loss of self-esteem as well as money, support, and the basis for planning for the future. Announcements of exams, loss of a grandparent or close friend, or other major life events also require adjustment.

Most of you will recognize that events such as moving away from home for the first time or studying for final examinations are sufficiently challenging and threatening to require considerable effort to succeed. As a result, they are associated with some negative sensations and unusual behavior. On a different level, extreme events such as loss of a loved one, living through a natural disaster, loss of a job, or family problems often cause changes in mental and physical health. It is not always clear that arousal of stress is useful in all of these situations and when stress is unusually prolonged or intense, these responses may actually harm us. Stress can be viewed as the primary process by which stressors cause health-related change. When stressors occur, a complex physiological and psychological response is evoked, and it is this response that in many cases is used to explain negative outcomes.

We are suggesting that stress is a general activation pattern in which the body "turns itself on," becomes more alert and vigilant, and gathers strength to permit strong, quick reactions and/or sustained resistance to a stressor. Mind and body are one in this process as central nervous system (CNS)-mediated reactions affect and are influenced by our thoughts, fears, and memories. Although there is still a great deal that we do not know about stress, research has revealed some important facts and relationships that help to explain its source (stressors), its characteristics, and its effects.

63

What Is Stress?

WHAT IS STRESS?

Lay definitions of stress are primarily concerned with two factors: the *pressure* or tension that people feel and the implication that this pressure is *aversive*. When people say they are stressed, they often are referring to the negative emotions and anxiety that they feel when they have too much to do or must cope with something that is unpleasant. Stress can also be defined by people as the presence of events that require a great deal of effort or that cause them to experience tension and negative emotions. In this case stress is the object or event causing discomfort. Consequently, stress is usually thought of as negative, as a state in which people are very busy or have too much to do, or are in a position to lose something they value. Most of us cannot define stress in much greater detail. Stress is pressure; stress is the tension created by pressure; stress is unpleasant.

One consequence of such general notions of stress is that when people talk about stress, they are often referring to only one part of it. If they focus on the pressure placed on us by environmental events, they are looking outward at the environmental events and forces that affect people. If they focus on the effects of that pressure, the tension or mental state of the recipient of pressure, they are looking inward at biological and psychological events. In fact, stress is both. *Stress is the process by which environmental events (stressors) challenge or threaten us, how these threats are interpreted, and how they make us feel.*

Another factor contributing to the superficiality or circularity of definitions of the general understanding of stress is that it cannot really be described as a thing in the way that most of us would like to describe it. As we have noted, it is a process, unfolding in a sequence of events and feelings and involving a number of factors that by themselves can be very complex. It involves environmental and psychological events, interpretations of them, and behavioral and physiological responses. Stress is, as Lazarus and Launier (1978) suggest, a transaction between people and the environment. Because it is the basis of give-and-take adjustments that characterize people's relationships with the environment, stress is a critical transaction indeed! Stress is the process by which environmental events challenge or threaten us, how they are interpreted, how they make us feel, *and how we respond and adjust to them.*

This definition includes five interacting elements (see Figure 3.1). *Stressors,* sources of challenge or danger to the organism, are usually external to the organism and can be thought of as environmental causes of harm or loss. Disasters, examinations, illnesses, major accidents, and other events that demand a great deal of effort in order for us to regain a sense of well-being are all examples of stressors. Stressors are not always environmental, and instead may be symbols of threat, reminders of past harm, or other psychological representations of danger. In this way dreams or unwanted thoughts about a stressor may cause stress themselves. Regardless of their origin or the kinds of dangers

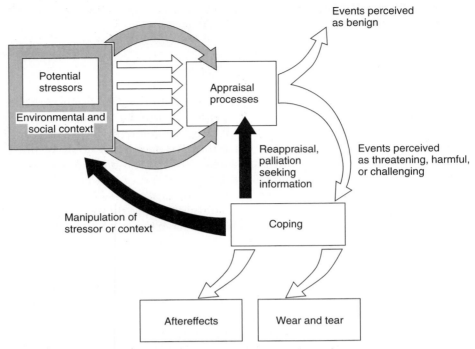

FIGURE 3.1. Stress as a psychophysiological process.

that these events pose, they all evoke some kind of response from the organism. *There are no events that are stressful for everyone*, as exceptions can always be found in even the most extreme stressors. However, some stressors that pose strong threats to life or limb, that involve considerable loss of life or property, or that require extensive effort and energy for successful adaptation are almost always stressful. In general, the weaker the threat demand or loss is, the greater is the variation in whether people view the event as stressful. In the case of a very strong threat most people will experience stress. With a weaker threat, people will differ more in how they respond.

Response during and after exposure to stressors may be physiological, behavioral, cognitive, emotional, or a combination of all of these. Typically, physiological and emotional responses are tied to arousal-heightened brain activity and increased physiological responding. Stress increases the body's readiness and general state of activity, and this arousal is linked with cognitive variables to our experience of emotions. Various interpretations of arousal may lead to different outcomes (see Schachter and Singer, 1962), and there is reason to assume that **appraisals** of stressors and evaluations of their effects and how best to deal with them also occur. Cognitive and behavioral variables may also be linked to **coping**—our responses to the stressor that constitute our attempts to remove the stressor or to insulate ourselves from its effects. If *coping* is successful, the organism returns to normal physiological and psychological arousal as the threat is eliminated or minimized. When this occurs, the organism has adapted either cognitively—by making itself unaware of the stressor or by re-assessing the degree of threat—or behaviorally—by removing or reducing the threat. Finally, in cases in which adaptation is not achieved, consequences of stress are likely, ranging from illnesses to changes in mood and behavior. As we will see, there are costs associated with stress even when coping is success-ful and adaptation is achieved.

Stress begins with our anticipation of or encounter with a stressor and un-folds as we become aware of its danger, mobilize to cope with it, and either succeed or fail in adapting to it. The stressor's danger is evaluated, coping strategies are selected, the body mobilizes itself to combat the stressor, and coping is put into action. If adaptation is successful, the effects of the stressor diminish. If it is unsuccessful, stress persists, arousal is not reduced, and pathological end-states such as mental or physical illness become more likely.

There are several aspects of this depiction of stress that are not universally accepted. Although most agree that a stressor and awareness of it are neces-sary to evoke a stress response, theories about the mechanisms by which awareness is made vary greatly. Some believe that appraisals and interpreta-tion are necessary, whereas others suggest that such structures are unnecessar-ily mentalistic. The evidence seems to suggest appraisal does occur; there are too many instances in which interpretation or evaluation of stressful situations is necessary to explain different responses. We may not know right away if something is dangerous, especially if we have never seen it before. We learn properties of events that cause us harm, and we distinguish between those that we feel are threatening and those that we feel are not. It is very difficult to ex-plain the variety of stress responses by different people to the same stressors without looking to some interpretation evaluation mechanism such as ap-praisal. These ways of viewing stress have evolved over thousands of years, and we turn next to the formal development of this concept with an emphasis on modern scientific theory.

Early Conceptions of Stress

As we have suggested, stress appears to have had evolutionary significance and may be as old or older than our species. Although much of what we know about stress has come to light in the past one hundred years, stress has been a focus of theory in medicine for centuries. Hippocrates separated suffering caused by disease (*pathos*) from the toil involved in resisting and fighting it (*ponos*). In doing so, he suggested a stresslike aspect of illness reflecting the en-ergy and wear and tear associated with attempts to combat disease. When you have a cold, some of your symptoms are unique to colds as your body fights off the cold virus. In addition, you feel a kind of general fatigue and malaise that you recognize as similar to past experiences with many illnesses (such as the flu). This ponos is a product of the body gearing up and preparing itself to fight the disease, just as stress is a reflection of general arousal/stress re-sponses in the face of a threat or challenge. In both cases, costs of coping are likely. Since Hippocrates' time many similar notions have appeared (see Selye, 1956), but it was not until the beginning of the twentieth century that the no-tion of stress was formalized.

Cannon (1914, 1928, 1929) was among the first to use the term *stress* and clearly suggested that it had physiological and psychological components. In studying emotions, he referred to "great emotional stress" to describe a powerful psychophysiological process that appeared to influence emotion. He viewed stress as a potential cause of medical problems and felt strongly that emotional stress could cause disturbances of a physiological nature. As was discussed in Chapter 2, he provided a simple description of the readying function of the sympathetic nervous system that we have already described. When threatened, organisms prepare to respond, to "fight or flee," by producing a heightened arousal state. This is accomplished partly by the secretion of epinephrine and other chemicals produced by the body that increase the speed and intensity of response. When you are suddenly confronted with danger (e.g., you are driving your car at high speed and it goes off the road), you experience sensations (such as rapid heart rate, dry mouth, and rapid breathing) as your body rapidly readies itself to respond. In this case the arousal occurs in an instant and increases the speed with which you can respond and get the car back on the road. In some instances, where resistance is feasible, arousal should increase the ability to overcome danger or threat, whereas in other situations it will enhance our ability to flee.

Psychobiologic Stress Models

Hans Selye's research on stress, spanning a 40-year period, was a watershed for stress research. He did much to popularize the notion of stress and to bring it to the attention of scientists in many disciplines. In doing so, he stimulated an extensive empirical literature, much of which was from his laboratory (see Selye, 1976).

Selye's work on stress began accidentally. In studying sex hormones, he found that injections of extracts of ovary tissue into animals caused an unexplainable triad of responses: enlargement of the adrenal glands, shrinkage of the thymus gland, and bleeding ulcers in the digestive system. Following up on this discovery, Selye found that extracts of other organs caused the same triad of responses, and that substances not derived from bodily tissue also caused these responses. Eventually, he found the same responses to be characteristic of many different events, such as injection of insulin, application of heat or cold, exposure to x-rays, exercise, and so on. Each time he applied something painful or harmful, changes in the adrenal and thymus glands and in the acid sensitive gastrointestinal lining were observed. He referred to these changes as a *universal triad* of stress effects, and argued that the responses that caused these changes were nonspecific because they appeared to be caused by *any* noxious or aversive event.

Selye's notion of nonspecific response has come under more fire than any other aspect of his theory. Because nearly everything he did to the organisms was associated with the same pattern, Selye believed that stress was a specific syndrome—it followed certain specific patterns and affected specific organs—but that it was *nonspecifically induced* (Selye, 1956). The specific syndrome of stress was always the same despite being caused by many different agents. Thus, the opening round of a stress response would be the same regardless of what specific event had signaled it.

Selye (1956) illustrated this notion by comparing stress response to a burglary:

> Suppose that all possible accesses to a bank building are connected with a police station by an elaborate burglar-alarm system. When a burglar enters the bank, no matter what his personal characteristics are—whether he is small or tall, lean or stout and no matter which door or window he opens to enter—he will set off the same alarm. The primary change is therefore nonspecifically induced from anywhere by anyone. The pattern of the resulting secondary change, on the other hand, is highly specific. It is always in a certain police station that the burglar alarm will ring and policemen will then rush to the bank along a specified route according to a predetermined plan to prevent robbery (p. 58).

Criticisms of Selye's theories (see Mason, 1975) have focused on the fact that this notion of nonspecificity seems to rule out psychological mechanisms in determining response to a stressor. As we will see, many of these criticisms are appropriate. Yet it is possible to allow for appraisal in this process if we assume that the nonspecific nature of stress is limited to our initial responses to a stressor. If only the initial phase of responding to stress is nonspecific, late reactions may be mediated by a variety of factors, including appraisal. Selye devised the **general adaptation syndrome (GAS)** to describe three stages of response (see Figure 3.2). First, as the organism becomes aware of a stressor or the presence of noxious stimulation, the *alarm reaction* is experienced. Here the organism prepares to resist the stressor. Adrenal activity and cardiovascular and respiratory functions increase, large amounts of glucocorticoids are released, and the body is made ready to respond. When reserves are ready and circulating levels of corticosteroids have reached peak levels, the organism enters a **stage of resistance**, applying various coping mechanisms and typically achieving suitable adaptation. During this stage there is a relatively constant resistance to the stressor, but there is a decrease in resistance to other stimuli. When these reactions are repeated many times or when they are prolonged because of a recurring problem, the organism may be placed at risk for irreversible physiological damage. Selye believed that this is the result of a third stage of the GAS, **exhaustion.** Adaptive reserves are depleted by long-term or repeated conflict with stressors, and resistance is then no longer possible. The

FIGURE 3.2. Diagram of Selye's three-stage general adaptation syndrome.

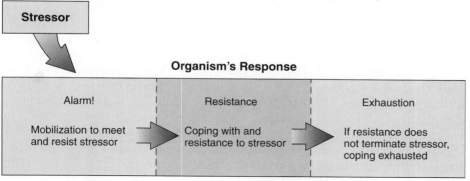

result of exhaustion is likely to be the onset of *diseases of adaptation*, illnesses such as kidney disease, arthritis, and cardiovascular disease.

The picture that Selye draws for us of a rise and fall in response to threat is a useful one. But Selye also believed that our adaptive abilities are limited. Under most conditions we can cope with a stressor, resist and overcome it, and our physiological state returns to normal. However, if we do not overcome the stressor during resistance, we cycle back to alarm, experience a new release of steroids, and continue to resist. We can cycle back and forth between alarm and resistance many times, but repeated, prolonged, or sufficiently strong stressors may deplete our ability to resist further. Resistance results in wear and tear on the body that can use up its ability to resist.

The importance of the GAS is in its depiction of how stress can lead to resistance and physiological damage. Research has indicated that stressors cause many kinds of changes that Selye outlined. For example, Levi (1965) has linked aggression-provoking stimuli to increased adrenal activity, and others have shown that major changes in people's lives are related to increased cortisol levels (see Mason, 1975; Schaeffer and Baum, 1984). Situations of overload, involvement, or lack of control are likely to result in increased physiological response as well (see Frankenhaeuser, 1976). The specific mechanisms by which the body can mobilize and resist, however, are still under investigation.

As we mentioned earlier, Selye's nonspecific response was based on the fact that the triad of responses occurred in the presence of any noxious event. Nonspecific aversive events caused this response. Since then researchers have found evidence of specific responding or patterning of adrenal corticosteroids for different stressors. For example, Mason (1975) reported different patterns of epinephrine, norepinephrine, and corticosteroid secretion associated with stressors varying in uncertainty or anger and fear elicitation. We will not deal with this issue in great detail here. It is enough to recognize that Mason and other researchers were concerned with the role of aversive events in evoking the secretion of hormones and transmitters by the adrenal glands. More importantly, Mason clarified the role of psychosocial stimuli in stress.

Mason argued that psychological distress precedes adrenal response and may be necessary for a physiological reaction to occur. There may be circumstances in which the nonspecific stress response occurs without psychological input, but the best evidence suggests that awareness of a noxious condition and attempts to deal with it are crucial. This awareness does not need to be conscious in the common use of the term because of the body's ability to attack foreign substances unbeknownst to the individual. Mason's own work has shown that physical stressors, such as the application of heat, do not elicit adrenal activity when psychological factors involved in the perception and sensation of the stressor were eliminated (see Mason, 1975). One study compared two groups of dying patients, one composed of people who remained in a coma until they died and the other made up of patients who remained conscious until they passed away. Autopsies indicated that the conscious group showed symptoms of stress, such as enlarged adrenal glands, whereas those who were not conscious showed no such symptoms (Symington et al., 1955). Similar findings from a massive nightclub fire in which many people died also suggest that stress requires conscious processing of threat or harm (Adler, 1943). Survivors of the fire were more likely to be free of posttraumatic stress symptoms if they had lost consciousness during the disaster. Similarly, Mason (1968) studied starving animals that were fed non-nutritive pellets so that they thought they were eating. Compared with animals that did not receive anything to eat, those who ate non-nutritive pellets exhibited fewer symptoms of stress.

Marianne Frankenhaeuser (1975) also conducted a number of studies during this questioning of basic aspects of stress and showed that stress has a strong psychological component. Frankenhaeuser focused on epinephrine and norepinephrine responses rather than on corticosteroids, extending the readying function described by Cannon. For example, these hormones can affect emotional and cognitive functioning and are secreted in response to purely psychological events (Frankenhaeuser, 1972). In one study increases in levels of epinephrine and norepinephrine were associated with decreasing amounts of control over electric shock (Frankenhaeuser and Rissler, 1970), and in another both understimulation (not having enough to do) and overstimulation (having too much to do) were associated with rises in epinephrine and norepinephrine levels (Frankenhaeuser et al., 1971). An interesting study by Patkai (1971) showed that increased output of the "stress hormones" epinephrine and norepinephrine is associated not only with noxious or aversive events, but also with pleasant but uncontrollable events. Each subject participated in four sessions. During one session the subjects played a game of chance, a modified bingo game that was generally regarded as being pleasant. In another session they viewed gruesome surgery films, and in a third session, unpleasant and tedious tasks were performed. Subjects also spent one session in "neutral inactivity" in order to provide a control for their other experiences. Epinephrine secretion among subjects was the highest in the pleasant but uncontrollable setting (playing the game), the next highest in the less pleasant conditions (e.g., tedious task session, film session), and the lowest in the inactivity session. Both pleasant and unpleasant events evoked biochemical symptoms of stress (see Figure 3.3).

Up to now we have seen social and psychological variables progressively integrated with biological aspects of stress to create a more complete view. The biological bases of stress are important because they are responsible for much of what we feel or do under stress. However, the psychological side, in terms of both causes and effects, is of great significance as well in initiating, managing, and resolving episodes of stress. If psychological factors alter bodily functioning in ways that facilitate illness or injury, an important link between psychology and health will be revealed.

Psychological Stress

Against the backdrop of research and theory on the physiological response to threat, Lazarus (1966) and others have added and expanded important psychological dimensions to the stress concept. The notion of psychological appraisal and the belief that the stress process can be initiated or influenced by psychological events is consistent with the models already described. However, research and theory in biological and psychological traditions developed independently of each other, and only recently have researchers tried to integrate the two into unified theories of stress. Lazarus's theories were almost as exclusively psychological as Selye's were physiological.

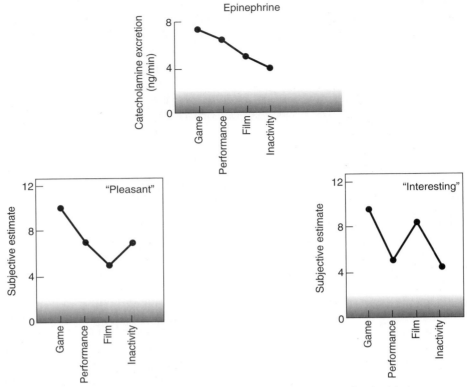

FIGURE 3.3. Mean epinephrine levels and ratings of pleasantness for the bingo game (pleasant condition), task and film (less pleasant conditions), and inactivity sessions. Higher levels of epinephrine were associated with pleasant and unpleasant events. *Source:* Reprinted from P. Patkai. Catecholamine excretion in pleasant and unpleasant situations. *Acta Psychologica,* 1971, *35,* 352–363, with kind permission from Elsevier Science-NL, Sara Burgerhartstraat 25, 1055KV Amsterdam, The Netherlands.

Lazarus (1966) made the study of stress more complex and challenging. Like other aspects of behavior, psychological stressors cannot be measured directly. Instead, they must be inferred from responses or defined in terms of the situations in which they arise. Stress can be measured in many ways, including asking people how they feel, observing performance on tasks, or measuring levels of epinephrine and norepinephrine (Baum, Grunberg, and Singer, 1982). Since stress causes negative mood states, performance deficits on some tasks, and increased secretion of catecholamines by the adrenal glands, stress may be measured by observing these effects. Similarly, stressors may be grouped or labeled in terms of where they occur, what they involve, or their characteristics. As a result, we can discuss occupational stress, urban stress, and examination stress, or we can focus on the duration of the stressor (acute/chronic) or other characteristics. The problem is that the impact of the death of a parent, losing a job, or being exposed to crowding is greater than the sum of its effects. What does it mean to experience such stress?

Lazarus (1966) emphasized the role of perception and cognitive appraisal in the stress response. He suggested, for example, that unless we perceive a situation as threatening, we will not experience stress. Thus the animals in Selye's experiments may have had to perceive danger before an alarm reaction and subsequent phases of the GAS could occur. In support of this hypothesis we can return to the study by Symington et al. (1955) that found that patients who were dying from injury or disease showed no stress response, as measured by adrenal activity, as long as they were unconscious. It is possible that blocking a person's ability to appraise a situation as stressful can prevent the onset of the stress response.

Appraisal

Over the course of more than 30 years Lazarus developed a model of stress that is based on the significance of psychological factors such as appraisal and coping (see Figure 3.1). Lazarus argued that in order for an event to be a stressor, it must be appraised as threatening, harmful, or posing excessive demand. We evaluate the pressures we encounter, and only those appraised to be threatening evoke a stress response. If you fail an examination, a number of factors will enter into your appraisal of the event. You may consider how much the failure will affect your final grade, whether you feel that the failure was your fault or the fault of a bad test, how failure will affect your self-esteem, or the extent to which you care about grades or tests. If the failure will not count toward your grade, if it does not threaten your self-esteem, or if you do not care how you did on the exam, you probably will not experience stress. If, on the other hand, the failure is perceived as threatening, stress is more likely.

A series of studies conducted by Lazarus and his associates during the 1960s provided support for this perspective. In one study Lazarus et al. (1965) had subjects view a gruesome and stressful film depicting woodshop accidents such as a worker cutting off a finger and another worker being killed by a wooden plank driven through his body. Subjects were told that either the events had been staged and no one was really being hurt or the events were real but the film would help to improve safety in such settings. A third group of subjects were given no explanation. Both sets of instructions were effective in reducing arousal during the film, presumably because they allowed appraisal of the film in a less threatening manner. It can be argued, for example, that subjects who were told that the film had been staged would not find the film as gruesome as those who believed that the carnage was real.

The role of appraisal processes in the stress process has been widely demonstrated and generally accepted. More recent work has focused on long-term coping and on the kinds of appraisals that can be made. Lazarus and Launier (1978) identified a number of possible appraisals, including the evaluation of an event as *irrelevant* (the event in question will not affect me), *benign* appraisals (the event is positive), and harmful or threatening interpretations that may lead to stress. Stressful appraisal may involve evaluation of harm or potential loss; threat of danger, harm, or loss; and challenge.

Coping

When exposed to a potentially stressful situation, we appraise the setting and make judgments about how threatening it is to us. This primary appraisal can lead to other appraisals. After a situation is judged to be threatening and stressful, secondary appraisals are made. No longer concerned with assessment of danger, we turn our attention to the dangers or benefits of different modes of coping with perceived threats. The perception of danger motivates a search for coping responses that will reduce this threat.

Consider an example of this sequence in a familiar and relatively low-threat event. Imagine that your peers at college exclude you from their activities. When impromptu parties come up, you are the last to find out. People go to the movies without inviting you to come along or go to dinner without waiting for you. You feel isolated from your fellow students. When you talk to them, they are polite but say little. If you are the kind of person who derives self-esteem or gratification from being part of the "gang," you are more likely to appraise this as threatening and aversive than if you prefer the role of "loner." Let us say that you are of the former persuasion. You are upset by the situation and wish to respond. During a second appraisal aimed at what you should do you may consider several approaches. You can do nothing or even withdraw further—the benefits of which are that you do not have to expend energy or risk the rejection that might result from a blatant attempt to join the group. The costs of this coping option are continued isolation and loss of self-esteem. On the other hand, you can make a strong effort to join the group, risking embarrassment and rejection for the possible benefit of being accepted into the group. A third alternative might be to increase your participation slowly in the group or to change your behavior if you conclude you are doing something the others do not like. The risks and benefits are similar to those of the second alternative except that the risk of embarrassment is reduced but the period of time before you feel that you "belong" is greater. You may try to find out why you are being treated as you are in order to understand it better. Finally, you may reinterpret the situation, deciding that you do not want to join the group and/or find another group that is more accepting. In reinterpreting rejection by the group in a positive light, you may reduce loss of self-esteem, but you are still not a member of the group.

In this example your response to the situation will depend on two kinds of appraisals. First, you must interpret the situation and consider its potential for threats, harm, or challenge. Second, you must consider your response choices. Obviously, evaluation of your choices is based on your interpretation of the situation and the nature of the threat you see. One of the first things you may try to do to is to find out why the members of the group are acting as they are. Seeking information about them and the situation will help in making subsequent coping decisions. In addition, you may consider previous experiences like this or how you or others have coped with previous stressors. Once a decision is made, you can "test" the usefulness of whatever you choose to do by reevaluating the situation from time to time to see if your strategy is working. By weighing the costs and benefits of these choices, you select a coping strategy and continually evaluate its efficacy.

Coping behavior is an important part of the stress response. Lazarus and Folkman (1984) proposed that stress responses can take manipulative or accommodative forms. They may be *direct action* responses, where the individual tries directly to manipulate or alter his or her relationship to the stressful situation. Changing the stressor by direct action would include solving a problem that was causing distress or leaving the scene if a bully threatens us. We can address the problem or abandon the situation. In these ways we can change the setting, flee, or otherwise remove the physical presence of the stressor. Alternatively, people may *seek information* about the situation so that they can understand it and predict related events. They may also do nothing: *Inhibition of action* may be the best course of action in some situations. Finally, *intrapsychic* or *palliative coping* may be necessary. Here the individual accommodates the stressful situation by reappraising the situation or by altering his or her "internal environment." One can think of this as actively learning to live with the stressor, reinterpreting or denying it, or just "hunkering down" and taking it until it is over. Distraction and reappraisal, taking drugs, using alcohol, learning to relax, creating or using psychological defense mechanisms, and engaging in meditation are all examples of this kind of coping (Lazarus and Folkman, 1984).

There are now several ways to categorize coping, and some researchers have gone so far as to suggest that some people have coping styles or habitual ways of responding to stress. For example, people may use problem-focused coping, or do wishful thinking about a stressful situation, or they may seek and use social support, avoid stressors or thoughts about them, or use self-blame coping to different degrees (Vitaliano et al., 1990). Although use of problem-focused coping is generally thought to be good (it is productive to try to act directly to eliminate the stressor), such coping is not usually effective when stressors are not controllable or readily manipulated (see Baum et al., 1983). In such cases reappraisal or avoidance may be more useful (Cohen and Lazarus, 1973; Collins et al., 1983). Alternatively, flexible coping styles, in which one's approaches to coping with stressful situations are tailored to the situation and changeable across settings appear to be effective (Lester et al., 1994). Optimism, control, and coping are related to one another and to outcomes of stressful encounters (Scheier and Carver, 1987). We will return to this in Chapter 4.

Theories of psychological stress have continued to evolve, and stress has increasingly been portrayed as an emotional state (see Lazarus, 1991, 1993). The experience of threat, harm, or excessive demand is unpleasant, motivating us to remove or reduce it or to minimize our discomfort. Not all stressors are negative events (getting married and having a baby are on balance positive events but are also stressful). However, it is usually the negative aspects of these events that are stressful (see Baum, 1990). In other words, getting married is stressful, not because one is in love or is about to live and share one's life with another person but, rather, because of the hassles associated with weddings and the uncertainties of entering into new relationships. Marriage and the birth of a baby are good events, but the disruption, sleep deprivation, and loss of freedom may be stressful. Selye (1984) proposed that *distress*—stress associated with negative events—is different from *eustress*—stress associated with positive events—but most stress researchers have not embraced this distinction. Negative events are more likely both to be seen as stressful and to be related to symptoms of ill health (see Brown and McGill, 1989; Thoits, 1986), but positive events can pose threats as well. Even Selye (1984) argued that regardless of whether the stressor is positive or negative, the effects on the body are always the same. It appears that responses to positive events may be similar to negative ones because stress is typically induced by negative aspects of these events. In subsequent sections of this chapter we will consider factors that affect the experience of stress. Differences in stressors, appraisal, and response will be discussed in their relationships to one another. It should be remembered that although presented as discrete factors, they cannot be isolated in practice. Aspects of one factor necessarily affect the others.

STRESSORS

Although some events are threatening to almost no one, most of them carry a range of potential problems. Some or all of these problems may be appraised as stressful under certain conditions. The properties of the stressor can affect its appraisal but usually cannot determine reactions directly. Lazarus and Cohen (1977) have described three general categories of stressors drawn along a number of dimensions: how long the stressor persists, the magnitude of the response required by the stressor, and the number of people affected by the stressor.

Cataclysmic events are stressors that have sudden and powerful impact and are more or less universal in eliciting a response. These events usually require a great deal of effort for effective coping. War, torture, imprisonment, natural disaster, and nuclear accidents are unpredictable and powerful threats that generally affect all of those touched by them. The floods in the American Midwest and the more common tornadoes, hurricanes, and other natural disasters (Baum, 1987; Rubonis and Bickman, 1992; Ironson et al., in press) are in this category of stressors. One study suggested that concentration camp survivors who had developed cancer showed poorer coping than cancer patients who had not been in camps and that concentration camp survivors may be more vulnerable to stress associated with the disease (Baider and Sarell, 1984).

The powerful onset of a cataclysmic event may initially evoke a freezing or dazed response by victims. Coping is difficult and may bring no immediate relief. When a severe storm hits an area or when an earthquake occurs in a region, it can be extremely frightening and dangerous, it can cause severe disruption of people's lives, and it can cause damage or loss whose impact will not fade for years (see Figure 3.4). However, because the actual event is brief, the severely threatening aspects of such a stressor dissipate rapidly. Some cataclysmic events cause less physical damage but do not fade quickly. At Love Canal in upstate New York, for example, the discovery of toxic wastes and associated dangers to area residents was a slow process with little physical destruction. When recovery is allowed to proceed without the return of the stressor, rebuilding progresses and full recovery is generally achieved. In the case of Love Canal, where rebuilding is not what is needed (nothing was actually destroyed), the damage already done is less important than the damage that may as yet come. In such cases, recovery may be more difficult (Baum, 1987).

The fact that cataclysmic stressors usually affect large numbers of people at one time is also important in the rate of recovery. Individuals have no specific immunity when many homes are damaged, many people are injured, and so on. Because people helping each other seems to be a logical way of speeding recovery and rebuilding, disasters often lead to an increase in social cohesion

FIGURE 3.4. Earthquakes and mudslides can cause great damage, destruction, and disruption. Surprisingly, most people cope effectively and recover from disasters fairly quickly.
Source: Reuters/Corbis-Bettmann

in affected communities (see Quarantelli and Dynes, 1972). People draw together after a disaster, providing each other with comfort as well as support and assistance in recovery. Centers for homeless victims may be set up, and those housed in them may form attachments with one another. People may help one another to search through debris for personal belongings, may help the police to maintain order, or may render assistance in many other ways. Sometimes whole communities will band together to meet threats or to repair damage already incurred. Of course, not all major disasters dissipate quickly, and residents cannot band together to fight a stressor indefinitely. When a disaster persists in an apparently unresolvable manner, it can lead to problems of a different kind.

Similar to cataclysmic events, personal stressors are strong and may be unexpected. *Personal stressors* include those events that are powerful enough to challenge adaptive abilities in the same way as do cataclysmic events but that affect fewer people at any one time. This distinction is important; affiliative and socially comparative behaviors have been identified as styles of coping with a focused, specific threat (see McGrath, 1970; Schachter, 1959), and social support has been shown to moderate the effect of stress (see Cobb, 1976). In other words, having people around to provide support, help, comparison for emotional and behavioral responses, and other assistance can reduce the negative impact of a stressor. With cataclysmic events, people are able to share distress with others undergoing the same difficulties. The second class of stressors, however, affects fewer people at a time, resulting in fewer people in the same situation with whom they can share. The death of a parent, for example, is generally an intensely painful loss and is often borne primarily by a small group or only a few people. Losing your job, unless there are general layoffs, can be very stressful and lonely.

Background stressors are persistent, repetitive, and almost routine stressors that are part of our everyday lives. Lazarus and Cohen (1977) have labeled this third group of stressors daily hassles—stable, repetitive, low-intensity problems encountered daily as part of one's routine. Daily hassles are different from other stressors in many ways (see Table 3.1). First, they are by themselves considerably less powerful than the stressors noted previously. Cumulatively, over time, they may pose threats that are equally serious, but individually the stressors do not generally pose severe threats. Second, they are chronic. Their impact persists over relatively long periods of time, and the effects of exposure

TABLE 3.1. Sample Items from the Hassles Scale

Directions: Hassles are irritants that can range from minor annoyances to fairly major pressures, problems, or difficulties. They can occur few or many times. Listed in the center of the table are a number of ways in which a person can feel hassled. First, circle the hassles that have happened to you *in the past month*. Then look at the numbers on the right of the items you circled. Indicate by circling a 1, 2, or 3 how *severe* each of the *circled* hassles has been for you in the past month. If a hassle did not occur in the last month, do *not* circle it.

Hassles	Severity
	1. Somewhat severe 2. Moderately severe 3. Extremely severe

Hassles	1	2	3
(1) Misplacing or losing things	1	2	3
(2) Troublesome neighbors	1	2	3
(3) Planning meals	1	2	3
(4) Inconsiderate smokers	1	2	3
(5) Don't like fellow workers	1	2	3
(6) Having to wait	1	2	3
(7) Health of a family member	1	2	3
(8) Not enough money for clothing	1	2	3
(9) Not enough money for housing	1	2	3
(10) Concerns about owing money	1	2	3

Source: From A. D. Kanner, J. C. Coyne, C. Schaefer, and R. S. Lazarus. Comparison of two modes of stress management: Daily hassles and uplifts versus major life events. *Journal of Behavioral Medicine*, 1981, 4, 1–39.

are gradual. Thus, living in a very noisy neighborhood may not pose severe threats all at once—one exposure to noise is easily coped with and not particularly threatening. However, noise is not usually a one time event. Rather, it is repeated often and may persist indefinitely. In this context the notion that things are getting better may not be common. The point at which the worst is over may never occur as things slowly become worse and worse. People can cope with individual episodes of noise even if it is uncontrollable (see Glass and Singer, 1972), but the cumulative effects of chronic exposures to noise over time appear to be more severe (Cohen, 1980).

Some chronic stressors, including job dissatisfaction (Frankenhaeuser and Gardell, 1976; Kahn and French, 1970), neighborhood problems (Harburg et al., 1973), and commuting (Singer, Lundberg, and Frankenhaeuser, 1978) may contribute to background stress. Finding out that one has a serious illness such as AIDS or cancer is also stressful, and the diagnosis, treatment, and survival of these diseases may be chronic and debilitating (see Antoni et al., 1992; Kaplan et al., 1995). Theorell et al. (1985) reported greater systolic blood pressure elevations among those in high-demand, low-control occupations (such as waiters, drivers, and cooks) than among those in more controllable or less demanding settings. Crowding encountered repetitively in one's neighborhood, on commuter trains, or in apartment buildings may form part of an individual's background (Baum and Paulus, 1987). In dormitory settings, for example, it is unlikely that a single episode of unwanted contact in which you encounter someone you do not like will present severe adaptive demands. Rather, the sum total of instances of unwanted contact may be responsible for the stress experienced if these encounters are repeated often or cannot be avoided (Baum and Valins, 1977). Chronically high levels of social interaction on the job may also cause problems; over a 2-year period, higher levels of social contact were associated with increased serum triglycerides and uric acid levels (Howard, Cunningham, and Rechnitzer, 1986).

Finally, the benefits of sharing with others in order to cope may not be as important here. Even if large numbers of people are affected, the duration and magnitude of individual exposure may be so brief as never to raise the need for affiliation. Crowded subway rides are episodic bouts with stress. However, the stress is not severe and can usually be coped with (although it may become increasingly difficult to do so over time). Such an aversive experience probably will not be of sufficient intensity to cause people to band together to provide each other with support and comfort. Consider the worker who must get up at 5 a.m. each morning, commute an hour each way to work on a crowded train, and work in a noisy and congested area of a big city. Each individual episode with the crowded train ride or each encounter with noise may not present much of a problem and the presence of familiar people, even if we do not know them, may be somewhat comforting. Noise and commuting combined may pose more of a problem, but they can be adapted to as well. Add other problems encountered regularly, and the cumulative adaptive difficulty becomes more demanding. Although adaptation may still be possible, the background level of stress becomes higher. As exposure becomes more chronic and these problems are encountered regularly, costs may continue to mount. At some point these daily hassles may exceed one's adaptive abilities, resulting in too much wear and tear on the body and placing one at risk for major psychological and physiological response to acute stressors. The worker with a high background stress level may overreact to unrelated stressors or become so responsive that he or she shows exaggerated responses to them. The comforting value of other people may be replaced by a desire to avoid further social interaction and patience and tolerance for frustration may disappear. As a result, he or she may overreact to a child's disobedience, a friend's carelessness, or some insignificant hassle with a neighbor.

Chronic Stress

Chronic stressors are not necessarily of small magnitude like hassles or many everyday events. Some may be substantive and result in long-term disruption and problems. For example, residents of the area around Three Mile Island (TMI) were faced with the chronic threats inherent in believing that they may have been exposed to radiation (Figure 3.5). The consequences of such expo-

FIGURE 3.5. The accident at Three Mile Island in 1979 raised fears of a nuclear explosion, reactor meltdown, or other catastrophes. Many people living nearby believed they were exposed to radiation and worry about whether they or their children will suffer ill health as a result.
Source: Conklin/Monkmeyer

sure are long term; they take years to become detectable, and people who think they were exposed may worry about the possibility that they or their children will develop cancer or show genetic abnormalities *sometime in the future.* This can produce a chronic uncertainty that may give rise to persistent stress. Research has shown that some of these people have exhibited chronic elevations in blood pressure, cortisol, catecholamines, and symptom reporting over a period of several years (Baum and Fleming, 1993; Davidson and Baum, 1986) (see Figure 3.6).

Part of the problem at TMI appears to be the involvement of toxic substances. Radiation is often considered a prime example of environmental hazards. Other studies suggest that the presence of toxins appears to intensify or prolong stress responding (Fleming, 1985). Another instance of this is provided by a study of mothers who took diethylstilbestrol (DES) while pregnant (Gutterman et al., 1985). During a 25-year period (1948–1971) DES, a synthetic estrogen, was used to improve prenatal child health and to reduce spontaneous abortion, but use was stopped after studies indicated a risk of cervical and vaginal cancer for female children (Gutterman et al, 1985; Herbst, Ulfelder and Poskanzer, 1971). However, by the time DES use was halted, millions of women had taken it and many of them had children who were apparently at risk for health threats. The results of questionnaire assessment of the psychological well-being of a sample of these mothers suggested few symptoms of chronic stress and, for the most part, good adjustment. When other chronic stressors were present, however, psychological health was affected by a history of DES use. Thus, for example, women who had used DES had poorer mental

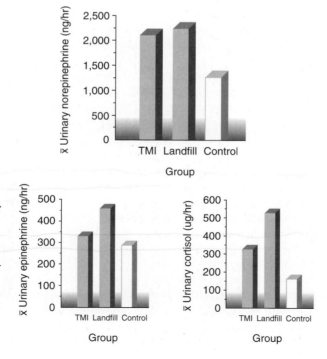

FIGURE 3.6. Mean urinary epinephrine, norepinephrine, and cortisol levels among people living near the Three Mile Island (TMI) nuclear power plant, near a hazardous landfill, and near no known hazards (control group).
Source: Adapted from A. Baum and I. Fleming. Implications of psychological research on stress and technological accidents. *American Psychologist*, 1993, 48(6), 665–672.

health when they were exposed to other threats or problems as well (Gutterman et al., 1985).

It should be clear that some stressors are very intrusive, physical, and universally threatening (such as natural disaster), whereas others are more culturally determined, less universal, and more psychological. Crowding and spatial invasion, for example, are culture-bound in that responses to varying densities and proximities are specific to cultural norms and meanings (see Aiello and Thompson, 1980; Hall, 1966). These kinds of stressors are based on psychological processes involved in appraisal and are far less universal than such things as earthquakes or floods.

APPRAISAL

Factors that affect the way we interpret stressors include environmental, social, and psychological variables. Individuals who possess great wealth, coping skills, or resources (e.g., friends, possessions) may not be as prone to appraise a given event as threatening. As a result, they tend to be less affected by the stressor. The upper middle-class resident of a large city, for example, may be less likely to experience difficulty from urban stressors than a poorer resident, as he or she may be better able to avoid aversive urban conditions. Attitudes toward the sources of stress will also mediate responses. If we believe that a stressor will not cause us any permanent harm, our response will probably be less extreme than if the danger carries the threat of lasting harm. If our attitudes are strongly in favor of something that may also cause us harm, we may reappraise threats and make them less alarming. Thus the dedicated urbanite might interpret crowding as exciting and "alive," jokingly proclaiming "We've got nature under control—we use asphalt." The array of environmental and psychological variables associated with each encounter with stress determines the response.

Harm/loss assessments typically involve analysis of *damage that has already been done* (Lazarus and Launier, 1978). The properties of a sudden event such as a tornado may predispose people toward this type of appraisal since damage is done very quickly and people will be more concerned with existing damage than with the possibility of more damage (see Figure 3.7). Of course, harm and threat appraisals can be coexistent if more tornadoes and damage are predicted. Bereavement is also likely to reflect a harm/loss evaluation, although when someone has been chronically ill, bereavement may also occur in anticipation of loss. Further, loss may imply threat, the second type of appraisal that can be made. In addition to loss of the loved one, we may also perceive demands that will occur after death.

Threat appraisals are concerned *with future dangers*. If warning is given of the approach of a tornado, it may initially be appraised as a threat. The stress of moving away to college, of learning to live with a roommate, and of similar events is largely anticipatory. Likewise, waiting to take an exam may be more stressful than taking it or even than failing it. The ability to foresee problems and to anticipate difficulties allows us to solve or prevent their occurrence. It also allows perception of threat and anticipatory stress.

FIGURE 3.7. The changing nature of stress is illustrated in these two pictures. The approach of a killer tornado will give rise to threat appraisals and people may take action to protect themselves or their loved ones. If one of these loved ones is killed by the storm, appraisals are more likely to be of harm or loss and coping must change to deal with new kinds of stress.

Source: David Petty/Photo Researchers (*left*); Freda Leinwand/Monkmeyer (*right*)

Challenge appraisals focus on the *possibility of overcoming the stressor,* not on the harm or potential harm of the event (Lazarus and Launier, 1978). Some stressors may affect us beyond our ability to cope, but all of us have a range of events within which we are confident of our ability to cope successfully. Stressors that are evaluated as challenges fall within this range. The event may be seen as potentially harmful, but we feel that we can prevent harm from occurring. The magnitude of the stressor, our estimates of our coping resources, our styles of coping with problems—all of these determine whether an event is seen as challenging or threatening.

Mediation of Appraisals

These appraisals, as well as secondary appraisals of coping, are a product of perceptions of the stressor, interpretation and prediction of its characteristics and consequences, and opinions about the severity and duration of these consequences. These judgments are, in turn, affected by a number of conditions, such as social support or gender, that alter our perceptions of stressors and our decisions about how to cope. If you are faced with a big exam, several factors may affect how you respond. Having a lot of support means you can get people to help you study, answer your questions, and generally support you throughout the ordeal. Women may use this social support more extensively than men, and the different ways that people choose to cope may make a difference as well. These and other factors also affect how we view and respond to potentially stressful events. Before considering the nature of stress responses and consequences, we briefly discuss several important mediating conditions that shape our experiences with stress.

Social Support

One of the most important and well-studied mediators of stress is social support, the feeling that a person is cared about and valued by other people and that he or she belongs to a social network (see Cobb, 1976). The notion that people need to be embedded in groups of people who provide love and a sense of belonging is not new. Many philosophers have spoken of the social needs of people, and psychologists have postulated needs for social caring and nurturance (see Fromm, 1955; Maslow, 1954; Murray, 1938). Many have long believed that interpersonal relationships can somehow protect us from many ills. However, the effects of having or not having social and emotional support have not always been clearly shown.

The fact that social support can be measured in a number of ways makes research difficult to interpret or integrate (Cohen and Wills, 1985). The number of people that an individual sees on a regular basis can be directly observed, or people can estimate this number (see Berkman and Syme, 1979; Killworth and Bernard, 1976; Ludwig and Collette, 1970). For a broader definition of social support, estimates of the number of people one considers to be friends; the types of nonfriend contacts, such as clergy or family; and the importance of each (see Caplan, Cobb, and French, 1975) can be collated. A number of other measures include evaluations of broad social networks at home and at work, the perceived importance of social ties in general, and the degree to which these relationships satisfy various needs (Pilisuk and Parks, 1980). Measures of perceived social support tap feelings of the adequacy and usefulness of social support as well as ratings of the availability of different kinds of support (Cohen and Wills, 1985).

Further complicating the study of social support is the fact that we derive many kinds of support from people (Wills, 1985). *Esteem support* refers to the effects of other people in increasing feelings of self-esteem: We may feel better about ourselves if a group of friends and acquaintances think well of us. We may also get necessary information from social interaction, which Wills calls *informational support*. *Social companionship* is defined as support derived from social activities, and *instrumental support* refers to the physical aid one can get from friends. If your car breaks down, your friends may bolster your self-esteem by assuring you that it was not your fault (esteem support), providing information about how to get it repaired (informational support), taking you with them to a party (companionship), or giving you a ride to the garage to get your car towed (instrumental support). Consistent with the notion that social support may be differentially effective in different situations or among different people, Kamarck, Annunziato, and Amateau (1995) found that stress-buffering effects of affiliation under stress were limited to stressors characterized by high social threat among women (see Figure 3.8) (Kamarck et al., 1995, p. 188). These effects tended to be stronger among hostile or socially avoidant participants.

Kamarck and his colleagues (1995) found that support was helpful, but only when threat was present. However, other studies have found effects of support that appear to be independent of stress. These issues have led to the formulation of two basic mechanisms by which social support affects stress. One posits that social support is beneficial regardless of whether we are

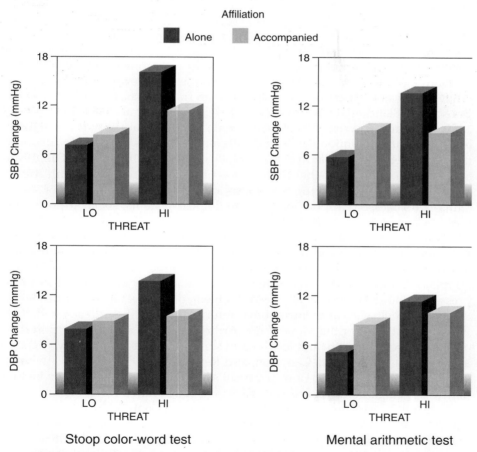

FIGURE 3.8. Effects of condition (Threat and Affiliation) on covariance-adjusted blood pressure responses to Stroop color-word test and mental arithmetic test.
Source: From T. W. Kamarck, B. Annunziato, and L. Meriwether Amateau, Affiliation moderates the effects of social threat on stress-related cardiovascular responses: Boundary conditions for a laboratory model of social support. *Psychosomatic Medicine,* 1995, 57, 189.

stressed and that not having social support is stressful by itself. This hypothesis is called the *direct* or *main effect hypothesis* and stands in opposition to the alternate, *stress-buffering hypothesis*, which views social support as beneficial because it buffers or helps us to cope with stress (Cohen and McKay, 1984; Cohen and Syme, 1985). Evidence actually supports both views; sometimes social support appears to be helpful to people even when stress is low, and it is plausible that having very little support generates stress on its own (see House et al., 1988). Differences in findings may be attributable to the outcome variables used (e.g., psychological, physiological), to the nature of the situation studied, to the characteristics of the people involved, and to other variables (Fleming et al., 1982; Wills, 1985; Winemiller et al., 1993). Both the direct and stress-buffering models of social support describe the relationship between one's social reality and stress (Cohen and Syme, 1985).

The extent of the effects of social support are evident in the many studies that have found relationships between social support and various aspects of physiological activity (Uchino, Cacioppo, and Kiecolt-Glaser, in press). In general, having more social support is associated with lower heart rate, blood pressure, and catecholamine levels, and stronger immune function. This appears to occur in several very different cultures; studies have reported that more support is linked to lower blood pressure among Samoan men and women, African-American men and women, and other groups (including white Americans, Hispanics, men and women from Jamaica, and people from Brazil) (see Bland et al., 1991; Dressler, 1991; Dressler et al., 1986, 1992; Janes, 1990; Janes and Pawson, 1986; Spitzer et al., 1992). Social support has similar effects on catecholamine levels and different measures of immune function (see Arnetz et al., 1985; Baron et al., 1990; Fleming et al., 1982; Levy et al., 1990; Seeman et al., 1994). Whether these effects are due to interactions with stress, as suggested by the buffering hypothesis, or are due to direct results of social support (or lack of support) on these biological systems, social support appears to be a critical variable in health and disease.

However, there are also instances in which social support may be harmful for chronically ill men and women. A study of recently diagnosed rheumatoid arthritis patients found that patients reported "problematic support" or attempts by family and friends to be helpful that actually contributed to a depressed mood (Revenson et al., 1991). Problematic support included instances of advice or help such as giving patients information that they already had, that was incorrect, and/or that upset them. Arthritis patients are able to report discrete instances of helpful and less helpful supportive acts from family, friends, and medical staff (Lanza, Cameron, and Revenson, 1995). Similarly, there is support that is not contingent on a patient's behavior but, rather, is seen by the patient as being offered *because he or she is ill* (Coates and Wortman, 1980).

Among the explanations that have been offered, Cobb (1976) notes the possibility that social support helps people to be flexible and to alter roles and identities as stressors demand. Others have considered the role of affiliation in the reduction of distress (see Schachter, 1959) and the possibility that support reduces cardiovascular or endocrine systems reactivity (Gerin et al., 1992; Lepore et al., 1992; Manuck, 1994). In addition, it is reasonable to assume that opportunities and calming influences of social comparison and affiliation are related to social support. Membership in a social network may assure beneficial role and comparison levels, and may affect the degree to which we view an event as stressful or help us to choose the "best" way of coping with a stressor (Posluszny, Hyman, and Baum, in press).

85

Appraisal

Exercise

A number of ways of reducing stress have been devised, and we will consider several of these in greater detail in Chapter 10. For now it is important to note that there are some conditions or activities that appear to be associated with less stress in everyday life. Among these is exercise, which seems to be an effective means of keeping stress levels down (Blumenthal and McCubbin, 1987; Cox, Evans, and Jamieson, 1979; Holmes, 1993; Keller, 1980; Sinyor et al., 1983). In one study regular exercisers and those who did not exercise frequently were exposed to a laboratory stressor; those who exercised showed stronger, more rapidly recovering hormonal responses to the stressor (Sinyor et al., 1983). Brown and Lawton (1986) conducted a study of 220 adolescent women in order to determine relationships among stressful life circumstances, measures of physical and psychological well-being, and exercise. The primary assumption regarding exercise was that regular physical exertion would result in less susceptibility to the negative effects of stress. Findings first showed that life events were related to reported illness and that illness reports were related to depression. Exercise was negatively associated with depression and positively associated with age. More important, those women reporting high stress exhibited more stress-related illness if they did not exercise regularly.

Other research on exercise has also been reported, much of it dealing directly with cardiovascular risk factors. Subjective reports of mood are more positive among exercisers, and the reduction of anxiety or depression can be achieved by initiating physical training programs (see Berger, 1984; Folkins and Sime, 1981; Markoff, Ryan, and Young, 1982). Exercise is associated with lower levels of cardiovascular reactivity (changes in blood pressure and heart rate when a stressor is introduced) and less risk for hypertension (see Dimsdale et al., 1986). Lower resting blood pressure and heart rate are also linked to exercise (Jennings et al., 1986).

Dispositional Variables

Research has suggested that there may be gender differences in the way in which our bodies respond during stress. A meta-analysis of studies of acute stress responding, for example, suggests that men may respond more strenuously to stressors than do women, particularly if one considers systolic blood pressure response (Stoney, Davis, and Matthews, 1987). Stress hormones, such as catecholamines, have also been studied and evidence indicates that men exhibit greater epinephrine response during stress but show more comparable levels of norepinephrine and cortisol (Frankenhaeuser, 1983). We will consider gender differences in stress response in more detail in a later section of this chapter and other dispositional variables in Chapter 4. Here we consider a few examples of personality or coping style differences in stress appraisal and response.

The existence of "high-stress" or "high-risk" personalities, or of other personal variables that affect appraisal of stressors, has been considered in many studies (see Friedman and Booth-Kewley, 1987). Grinker and Spiegel (1945) noted that only a relatively small number of air combat crews serving during World War II ever developed serious stress-related disorders. Some of the airmen studied had previously established neuroses that made them more susceptible to the stress of battle.

More recent research suggests there are personality styles or predispositions to cope in certain ways that are related to stress and stress consequences (see Kobasa et al., 1985; Wiebe and McCallum, 1986). Coping styles or behavior patterns have also been identified, and these styles appear to affect the ways in which events are appraised as well as which types of coping are involved. Work on a number of these dimensions, including repression sensitization (or monitor/blunter), arousal seeking, screening, and denial have indicated that people differing on these dimensions may not interpret situations in the same way (see Byrne, 1964; Janis, 1958; Mehrabian, 1977; Zuckerman, 1971). Differences in vigilance and avoidance coping where some people cope by maintaining vigilance whereas others avoid thinking or encountering stressors, also predict some stress effects (see Kiyak, Vitaliano, and Crinean, 1988; Wong and Kaloupek, 1986). Avoidance coping can backfire and make eventual coping more difficult (Mullen and Suls, 1982; Suls and Fletcher, 1985) whereas hypervigilance can also have negative effects (see Miller and Mangan, 1983). A study by Baum et al. (1981), for example, suggests that individuals who handle overload by screening and prioritizing demands are less susceptible to the effects of crowding than are people who do not cope in this way. Optimism, pessimism, and one's prevailing world view are also important determinants of stress impact (see Janoff-Bulman, 1985; Scheier and Bridges, 1995). We will consider some of these factors in Chapter 4.

Gender

Research has identified consistent gender differences in stress outcomes, whether they are physiological reactions to threat or harm or different appraisals or emotional reactions to stressful conditions. In general, men exhibit stronger blood pressure and hormonal responses during or after stress, with two notable exceptions. Although several studies have found larger blood pressure responses among men exposed to stressors, there is also evidence that women exhibit larger increases in heart rate than do men (Baum and Grunberg, 1991). Similarly, there is evidence of larger increases in epinephrine and norepinephrine among men but stronger cortisol responses among women (see Baum and Grunberg, 1991; Gallucci et al., 1993). Stoney et al. (1988) found that women show smaller increases in low-density lipoprotein cholesterol and blood pressure during three different stressful tasks. Low-density lipoprotein cholesterol increases during stress, and high levels of this cholesterol fraction have been associated with atherosclerosis and coronary heart disease, indicating one possible reason for differential vulnerability to cardiovascular disease among men and women (Kannel, Castelli, and Gordon, 1979; Stoney et al., 1987). Menstrual cycle factors do not appear to be related to stress-related changes in immune function (Caggiula et al., 1993), and research has not found differences in how women's and men's immune systems respond to stress (see Bachen et al., 1994).

Women usually report greater distress and more symptoms of stress than do men, possibly because women are more willing to report negative emotions or because they experience greater threat or demand when faced with a stressor. Some researchers have suggested that women are more sensitive to symptoms or bodily changes than are men, suggesting that differences in self-report reflect greater accuracy of self-perception by women. We do not as yet know why these differences exist, and research on gender as a determinant of stress responses has continued to examine reasons for these differences.

One plausible reason for some gender effects is the possibility that, in general, women experience more stress as part of their daily lives. This seems particularly true in families in which women work. We know that women often assume more roles in the family than do men, and in a dual-career family women often have primary responsibility for cooking, cleaning, child-care, and other household chores, *as well as fullfilling the demands of their job*. Although good marriages appear to reduce stress for many women, the inequalities inherent in many relationships seem to affect men and women differently (see McLaughlin, Cormier, and Cormier, 1988). This is complicated by the finding suggesting that single women also experience more distress than do single men and that married women without children report less stress than do comparable men (Fisk, 1993). In addition, as society gradually changes and expectations become more egalitarian, gender differences in experienced stress and inequalities in the home and workplace are slowly disappearing (Barnett, 1993).

PHYSIOLOGICAL ASPECTS OF THE STRESS RESPONSE

Despite the sometimes overwhelming nature of stressors or the likelihood that they will be appraised as threatening, stress cannot be defined without reference to the response made by the organism. These physiological, cognitive, and behavioral reactions or effects are important aspects of the stressor-stress process and help arouse us and make us ready to respond, increasing vigilance and motivation to do something to adjust.

Because stress affects nearly every system in the body and all aspects of consciousness, one needs to measure its effects at several different levels (see Baum et al., 1982). Physiological and biochemical measurements of stress allow inferences about emotional states and provide markers of those bodily responses that are most affected by stress. As noted earlier, catecholamines and corticosteroids, secreted by the adrenal medullae and cortex, respectively, are centrally involved in stress responding (see Cannon, 1929; Frankenhaeuser, 1973; Glass et al., 1980; Mason, 1975). Catecholamine secretion also reflects sympathetic arousal; the adrenal medullae are innervated by the sympathetic nervous system, and secretion of epinephrine and norepinephrine appears to be part of the sympathetic arousal. Thus, secretion of catecholamines is also associated with systemic reactions in the body (Ax, 1953). Increases in blood pressure, heart rate, or other measures of cardiovascular response, referred to as **cardiovascular reactivity** (i.e., faster heart rate, higher blood pressure), have been measured, and stress appears to increase the release of opioids, such as beta-endorphins (see Meyerhoff, Oleshansky, and Mougey, 1988). Stress also produces changes in muscle potential, and measures of skin conductance have also been used to show the effects of stress. Generally speaking, many stressors appear to cause the same kind of general physiological response. However, stress responses go far beyond activation of the sympathetic and HPA (hypothalamic-pituitary-adrenal) systems and the organ systems that they affect. In stress the whole body reacts, with changes often driven by these endocrine and neural changes. Nearly all hormones are affected, as are most muscle groups, the digestive and immune systems, and systems and structures ranging from the liver to immune cells and blood platelets.

Reactivity

The construct of **reactivity** has been a useful way to think about some of these bodily changes during stress, not just because reactivity seems to be associated with susceptibility to disease but also because causes of differential reactivity may reflect very basic genetic-environmental interactions. *Reactivity* may be defined as the extent to which one or more indices of physiological functions change when an acute stressor is introduced. In studies in the laboratory participants typically sit quietly for a period of 20 to 30 minutes while baseline recordings of blood pressure and heart rate are recorded, and are then exposed to a challenging task or stressful situation such as working on a difficult puzzle or giving a speech. Many different responses can be measured, and reactivity in measures of cardiac activity, vascular resistance, immune function, and endocrine changes have been reported (see Kamarck et al., 1993; Kasprowicz et al., 1990; Manuck et al., 1991; Zakowski et al., 1992). Reactivity is indexed, regardless of what is being studied, as a result of the stressor and is frequently expressed as a change from the baseline, at either peak or average stressor levels.

Of some interest is the fact that differences in reactivity seem to be independent of the perceived stressfulness of the challenge used. That is, higher and lower reactors (those who show greater or smaller changes from the baseline to the stressor) report experiencing comparable levels of stress in most studies. It is not simply a matter of more stress means more response. High reactors show larger responses in instances of comparable stress as well. This reinforces the belief that reactivity reflects some constitutional variability, either by itself or in combination with environmental experiences. Research has treated reactivity as a dispositional variable, associated with behavior patterns such as Type A, and as consequences of chronic stress (Fleming et al., 1987; Krantz and Manuck, 1984; Uchino et al., 1995; Wilson et al., 1995).

Another interesting characteristic of reactivity is that different stressors appear to elicit changes in different systems or measures and that people vary in how they respond to these variable stressors. Some stressors and/or people seem to be sensitive to changes in cardiac output or activity by the heart, whereas others are associated with changes in resistance in the blood vessels (see Kasprowicz et al., 1990). The former changes, related to increased force and the rate of heartbeats, appear to be mediated through beta-adrenergic receptors activation (see Chapter 2) (Girdler, Hinderliter, & Light, 1993; Light and Sherwood, 1989). Evaluation of the meaning of these differences, as well as the importance of physiological reactivity in the general stress-disease relationship, will be considered further in Chapter 5.

Effects of Physiological Changes

Bodily changes and somatic consequences of stress are important for a number of reasons. First, as we have seen, increased catecholamine and corticosteroid secretion is associated with a wide range of other physiological responses, such as changes in heart rate, blood pressure, breathing, muscle potential, reduced inflammation, and changes in other bodily functions. Prolonged or sudden elevation of circulating catecholamines may damage tissue, as is suggested for the pathogenesis of atherosclerosis (see Schneiderman, 1983). Research on similarities of stress and infusion of epinephrine on plasma lipid concentrations has indicated that both independently cause increases in free fatty acid, total low-density lipoprotein, very low-density lipoprotein, and high-density lipoprotein cholesterol (McCann et al., 1995). Catecholamines also appear to affect cognitive and emotional functioning, and elevated levels of epinephrine or norepinephrine in the blood may affect mood and behavior, immune system function, and activity in other systems.

In order to view this link more fully, we must review Cannon's (1914) work suggesting that epinephrine has a salutary effect on adaptation. By arousing the organism, epinephrine provides a biological advantage to the organism, enabling it to respond more rapidly to danger. When we are extremely frightened or enraged, we experience an arousal that may be uncomfortable but that readies us to act against the thing that frightens or angers us. Stress-related increases in catecholamines may facilitate adaptive behavior. In fact, studies have shown superior performance on some tasks among subjects who were injected with epinephrine (Frankenhaeuser, Jarpe, and Mattell, 1961) and also among people who produce larger amounts of catecholamines in the face of challenge (see Frankenhaeuser, 1971). However, arousal has also been associated with impaired performance on complex tasks (see Evans, 1978).

There may be cognitive benefits of stress, but it is also evident that the "fight-or-flight" model, derivable from Cannon's work, is inadequate for predicting response to danger in our complex society. Aside from the wear and tear on our bodies generated by repeated or prolonged stress, a number of less desirable outcomes are likely when stress does not abate readily. Most of the research that finds support for facilitating aspects of stress has considered acute situations in which adjustment leads to a decrease in stress. The consequences of unabated stress or repeated exposure to stress, as in the case of background stressors, have only recently come under study. Among these consequences are decrements in the ability to cope with subsequent stress, aftereffects, and, in some cases, physiological dysfunction, tissue damage, or death.

Many biological changes occur as a direct or indirect consequence of stress. The extent to which they are part of the adaptive response itself or products of these responses is sometimes unclear. Immune system changes do not appear to be adaptive. Although suppression of immune system activity could reflect a conservation of energy, it may, instead, be a product of neural and hormonal changes that are part of the stress response. We will discuss these issues in greater detail in Chapter 6.

EMOTIONAL AND PSYCHOLOGICAL ASPECTS OF THE STRESS RESPONSE

Emotions occur as part of stress or can occur independently. They are usually thought of as powerful responses to positive or negative events. *Emotional response* is not unlike the stress response: Heightened sympathetic arousal, sensations in the viscera, unhappiness, and excitement can all be characteristic of emotion. Also, like stress, emotions typically motivate people to try to dispel, avoid, overcome, or prolong the source of emotional arousal. This seems like an awfully complicated way of defining such a common state. We are all familiar with emotions—we are sometimes sad, sometimes happy, and sometimes angry. Yet the true nature of emotions is still a matter of debate. As with many things, the common is more mysterious than the unusual.

Anxiety disorders are emotional problems that are characterized, as the term suggests, primarily by the presence of anxiety. *Anxiety* is defined as a generalized state of fear or apprehension. The afflicted individual experiences anxiety and distress in everyday situations that do not normally elicit such behavior from other persons. These disorders are distinguished by diffuse and often severe "free-floating" anxiety that may not be related to any one immediate situation or object threat. In such cases the individual may not be able to identify the source of fear or apprehension. Physiological symptoms, reflective of heightened autonomic nervous system arousal, include an elevated heart rate and blood pressure level, sweating, intestinal distress, and muscular tension and weakness. Anxious people also report problems with insomnia, worry, forgetfulness, difficulty in concentrating, irritability, and frequently mild depression. Besides their clinically high level of anxiety, people with anxiety disorders often experience acute episodes of panic.

Depressive disorders are marked by disturbances of mood that can cause a great deal of debilitating distress for the afflicted person. *Depression* is characterized by a dejected mood, loss of the desire to do things, general tiredness, and the inability to concentrate. It can be a significant problem that seriously interferes with an individual's everyday functioning. With the intensification of a dejected mood, the individual often loses interest in the world and lacks the motivation and desire to get involved in tasks. The future looks bleak, and the person believes that nothing can be done to change this condition. Moreover, the depressed individual may experience crying spells; loss of appetite, weight, sleep, and sexual desire; and may want to avoid people.

Generally, negative psychological consequences of stress are not all as severe or debilitating as these "clinical" consequences. However, decreases in problem-solving abilities, increases in general negativity, impatience, irritability, feelings of worthlessness, and emotionality may all be part of a stress response.

As we have already noted, stress can cause cognitive deficits as well as improved performance. Cognitive deficits may, in turn, be caused by behavioral strategies that are used for coping: We may "tune out" loud noise or narrow our field of attention (see Cohen, 1978; Deutsch, 1964). We may also be unable to concentrate or unwilling to put effort into a task (see Glass and Singer, 1972). At this level response may become more specific to the stressor that is being experienced. Behavioral aspects of the stress response may reflect the specific causes of discomfort as the organism copes with the stressor.

Aftereffects, on the other hand, do not appear to be specific to certain stressors; they appear to reflect more general effects. Defined as consequences that are experienced after exposure to a stressor has terminated, these effects fit into Selye's (1976) notion of limited adaptive energy. As exposure to stress increases, the adaptive reserves are depleted, causing aftereffects and reductions of subsequent coping ability. Evidence for the existence of poststressor effects comes from a number of sources, including research on the effects of noise (see Cohen et al., 1986; Glass and Singer, 1972; Evans et al., in press; Rotton et al., 1978; Sherrod and Downs, 1974; Sherrod et al., 1977), crowding (Evans, 1979; Sherrod, 1974), and electric shock (Glass et al., 1973). However, explanations for these effects are not as clear.

Aftereffects of exposure to stressors include decreases in cognitive ability, reduced tolerance for frustration, aggressiveness, helplessness, decreased sensitivity to others, and withdrawal (Cohen, 1980). These postexposure consequences seem to be affected by the perception of control during exposure to the stressor, with fewer aftereffects following experiences in which participants felt that they had control (Cohen, 1980). One explanation for this is that aftereffects are related to the amount of effort expended in coping with a stressor. Since perceived control appears to ease the difficulties posed by a stressor, it should reduce the effort needed to adapt, and therefore reduce aftereffects. Thus, costs of adaptation may be reflected by aftereffects, and we should expect to find them when people have successfully coped (Cohen et al., 1986).

Psychological effects that linger or persist may also reflect consequences of adaptation. Calhoun (1967, 1970) has referred to refractory periods, in which an organism recovers from a bout with a stressor, as crucial to the effects of population density in animal populations. If recovery is interrupted by another encounter, increased stress-relevant problems are likely. Further, depletion of catecholamines in the brain as a result of severe or prolonged stress has been associated with death in studies using animals (see Weick, Ritter, and Ritter, 1980). One particularly severe psychological syndrome that may develop out of stress responding is posttraumatic stress disorder.

Posttraumatic Stress

Posttraumatic stress disorder (PTSD) is a diagnostic category in the DSM–IV (*Diagnostic and Statistical Manual of the American Psychiatric Association,* 4th ed.) that includes several characteristics. The complex of disorders included in this category has evolved since its inclusion in DSM, and some symptoms or criteria for diagnosis have changed. Initially, PTSD was reserved for people who had experienced a threat or event that was so severe and overwhelming as to be considered *outside the range of normal human experience.* These events are similar to Lazarus and Cohen's (1977) cataclysmic events and include war, torture, and disasters. Other events, such as rape, are comparable to Lazarus and Cohen's second category of powerful but more personal stressors and may also give rise to PTSD. More recent descriptions of PTSD have softened this criterion somewhat, and the range of events that may cause PTSD has been expanded to include anything that is highly threatening to life and limb. Although stressors do not need to be rare or unusual, they still must be severe and capable of causing powerful stress responding. These stressors can be called *traumatic stressors*, events that are so powerful that they *threaten life or well-being, severely tax or overwhelm coping capabilities, and challenge the assumptions that people make about the world and the way it works.*

There is no test that one can apply to determine whether events qualify as traumatic stressors. However, although some stressors may "fall on the line" between traumatic stressors and nontraumatic events, most stressors do not. Some researchers have provided a framework for evaluating traumatic stressors (see Table 3.2). Disasters, rape, assault, serious house fires or motor vehicle accidents, war, diagnosis of life-threatening illness, loss of a loved one, and exposure to mass casualties (such as in the case of recovery efforts following an airplane disaster) are traumatic stressors. They are all powerful events, involve intense threats with very important consequences, require intense coping, and make us reevaluate our opinions about the world. The intensity of each kind of event may vary, and one would expect that the severity of the stressor is correlated with the strength of the stress responses. All of these can cause profound consequences of stress, including PTSD.

Other characteristics of PTSD include *social withdrawal* and *emotional numbing* (so that one no longer "feels" very intensely or experiences most emotions strongly). *Hyperarousal,* or states characterized by unusual hormonal patterns, exaggerated startle responses, and difficulty in sleeping, is also common among PTSD patients. In addition, the often unwanted *reexperiencing* of memories or feelings associated with the original event is a key PTSD symptom. Together these characteristics define most cases of PTSD and reflect a very severe consequence of traumatic stressors.

Historical Developments

As you might expect, interest in and awareness of severe consequences of stress is not new. In character, PTSD actually is a new name for an "old" ailment. Syndromes such as *shell shock,* which is similar to PTSD, have been noted for centuries. Railroad accidents during and after the industrial revolution

TABLE 3.2. Common Dimensions of Traumatic Stressors[a]

1. Threat to life	5. Violent or sudden loss of a loved one
2. Severe physical harm or injury	6. Witnessing or learning of violence to a loved one
3. Receipt of intentional injury/harm/loss	7. Learning of serious illness or exposure to toxic agents
4. Exposure to the grotesque	8. Causing death or severe harm to someone else

[a]These characteristics of stressors appear to be associated with traumatic stress.
Source: Adapted from B. L. Green, Identifying survivors at risk: Trauma and stressors across events. In J. P. Wilson and B. Raphael (Eds.), *International Handbook of Traumatic Stress Syndromes.*

were among the first events associated with causing symptoms that defied traditional medical explanation. Initially the disorder was called *railway spine* because many physicians thought that the symptoms were caused by compression or microlesions of the spine that were suffered in the accidents. This syndrome included inexplicable pain and weakness, psychological malaise, and general disability (see Trimble, 1981). Industrial accidents were also associated with these symptoms, and some argued that the problems that victims experienced were psychological rather than physical.

Organic theories of railway spine involved physical causes such as small, undetectable damage to the spine. One of the major champions of the organic theory of these ailments was John Erichsen (1882), who argued that the symptoms observed in trauma victims were caused by molecular changes in the spinal cord that were caused by concussion or sudden twisting.

In 1883 Herbert Page, a London surgeon, disputed Erichsen's views about railway spine. Page argued that there was little evidence to support organic bases of the diseases that Erichsen suggested and that nervous shock was not a function of molecular disruptions of the spinal cord. Instead, Page (1885) began to investigate and describe psychological dimensions in his treatment of disorders following accidents. Fear and alarm were hypothesized to explain sequelae of these traumas. The horror of experiencing a railway accident was part or all of the syndrome (Trimble, 1981), and Page argued that, "the medical literati abounds with cases where the gravest disturbances of function, and even death . . . have been produced by fright and by fright alone" (Trimble, 1981, p. 26). Over the next 40 years the debate continued with new advocates of both positions. Twentieth-century warfare, however, was more influential in the debate than were the debaters' well-constructed positions, as war exposed people to new and unspeakable horrors. Nervous shock or disruption of normal functioning was due to fear and emotional distress and not to physical damage to the nervous system. Erichsen and other physicians only grudgingly recognized that Page's theory was useful.

However, the tendency to attribute unusual behavior and symptoms to organic causes persisted. During World War I, for example, cases of PTSD-like syndromes were referred to as shell shock because it was widely believed that the concussion of huge artillery shells used in that conflict caused central nervous system damage that caused the observed symptoms. Mott (1919) suggested that these symptoms, which are the same as those noted in railroad and industrial accidents, were brought about by physical damage to the brain due to carbon monoxide or changes in air pressure. However, this did not explain cases of shock or distress among those people who were not exposed to the exploding shells, and Southward (1919), in reviewing 589 cases from World War I, concluded that most cases were psychological in origin and not due to organic changes. Several researchers reported the same conclusions based on studies of World War II victims: They viewed the symptoms as part of a neuropsychological disorder (see Kardiner and Spiegel, 1941; Ross, 1941). Our experience in the two world wars as well as in the Korean war convinced psychiatrists, psychologists, and others that traumatic stress, regardless of what it was called, could inflict serious, long-term mental health consequences.

Recognition of the psychological effects of extreme stress and trauma has led to different views of the lingering or chronic consequences of these events.

Vietnam veterans, for example, have been studied and treated for PTSD and seem to have experienced a higher incidence of PTSD than have veterans of other wars. The extent and severity of distress among Vietnam veterans contributed to the evolution of PTSD as an independent diagnostic category. It is difficult to determine whether the Vietnamese War generated more cases of posttraumatic stress than did previous wars, in part because researchers and clinicians were more aware of it in the 1960s and 1970s than they had been before, and therefore were more likely to find it. This vigilance and readiness to treat PTSD has also been characteristic of more recent conflicts in the Middle East and Persian Gulf.

The importance of these historical developments is not in whether the Vietnamese War was worse than other wars or created an unusually large number of psychological casualties. Studying the characteristics of that conflict and others will tell us a lot about causes of the disorder as well as about conditions that make people more or less vulnerable to its effects. For example, patterns of response to traumatic stressors suggest that only a minority of people undergoing a traumatic event experience severe distress and PTSD. Estimates vary somewhat, but in general about 15 percent of those serving in Vietnam developed PTSD (see Kulka et al., 1988). An additional 11 percent were judged to have partial PTSD, indicated by the presence of symptoms but not a diagnosable disorder (see Kulka et al., 1988). Similarly, the incidence of PTSD among victims of other traumatic stressors suggest that most people recover well and do not develop PTSD (see Table 3.3). The search for factors that affect how likely an individual is to develop PTSD after experiencing a traumatic event is important in treating and preventing this syndrome and in understanding how stress causes such profound disturbances.

The search for factors influencing response to traumatic stressors has focused on characteristics of the event and of the victim. Certain kinds of events or exposure variables (e.g., how close one is to a tornado) seem to increase the likelihood of PTSD. A closer inspection of the data in Table 3.4 suggests that stressors of human origin, that is man- or woman-made stressors, appear more

TABLE 3.3. Summary of Rates of PTSD for Different (Selected) Kinds of Traumatic Stressors

Stressor	PTSD(%)	Citation
Tornado	2	North et al., 1989
Cyclone	8	Fairley, 1984
Volcano	2	Shore, Tatum and Vollner, 1986
Tornado	4–21	Steinglass and Gerrity, 1989
Earthquake	32	Conyer et al., 1987
Airplane crash landing	54	Sloan, 1988
Dam break and flood	44	Green et al., 1989
Plane crash into hotel	29	Smith et al., 1989
Motor vehicle accidents	18	Delahanty et al., 1996

likely to cause PTSD than are natural disasters. This is consistent with several accounts of the differences in traumatic stressors (e.g., Baum, et al., 1983; Green, 1993). The scope of an event, how many people it affects, how long it lasts, and how suddenly it occurs also contribute to the extent of postdisaster impact (Barton, 1969; Berren, Beigel, and Ghertner, 1980). How deliberate or intentional human-caused stressors are judged to be also seem important. Natural events are unintentional by definition, but human-caused events vary in how deliberate they seem (see Green, 1993). Those that are thought to be errors or unintended mishaps should be less stressful and disruptive than events that appear to have been intentional (Green, 1993).

Although all of these characteristics may increase the likelihood that one experiences PTSD, the personal impact of these events is ultimately the key factor in one's vulnerability to traumatic stress. The extent of the personal impact of an event, the perceived control over a future impact, how one is prepared to deal with a stressor, and one's beliefs and expectations about traumatic stressors all affect how we experience traumatic events (see Berren et al., 1980; Delahanty et al., 1996; Dougall et al., 1996). Social support, previous mental health problems, coping, and a variety of other factors also affect how severe the impact of a stressor may be or how likely a victim is to develop PTSD (see Baum, Fleming, and Singer, 1983; Green, Wilson, and Lindy, 1985; Hartman and Burgess, 1993; Raphael, 1986). While research must further specify the conditions associated with vulnerability or resistance to PTSD and other severe stress reactions, we have learned a great deal already.

Physiology of PTSD

One of the aspects of PTSD that has attracted attention is the physiological basis of PTSD or extreme stress. Studies of Vietnam veterans many years after their experiences have revealed persistent physiological response patterns much like those associated with stress. One consistent finding is that PTSD patients exhibit substantially higher levels of epinephrine and norepinephrine in their urine than do other psychiatric inpatients (Mason et al., 1986; Yehuda et al., 1992). Severity of PTSD symptoms was significantly correlated with norepinephrine levels. Symptoms of PTSD were also correlated with catecholamine levels in urine (Davidson and Baum, 1986). However, another study found evidence of lower levels of cortisol in PTSD patients than in patients with major depressive disorders or other inpatients (Yehuda et al., 1993).

This is not an isolated finding. In another study urinary cortisol in Holocaust survivors with PTSD were lower than in Holocaust survivors who did not have PTSD (Yehuda et al., 1995). Cortisol was inversely related to the severity of PTSD, indicating that those suffering the most severe distress were those with the lowest levels of cortisol. But not all studies of traumatic stress find decreases in cortisol or show that lower cortisol correlates negatively with distress. In a study of subway drivers involved in "person under train" accidents, illness outcomes were associated with high cortisol levels (Theorell et al., 1992). And the effects of traumatic stress on cortisol are not always the same. Research on women with PTSD who had been abused as children found no evidence of decreased cortisol or larger catecholamine/cortisol ratios (Lemieux and Coe, 1995). However, lower cortisol among men with PTSD has been a consistent finding in research on Vietnam veterans. For example, Yehuda and colleagues (1995) found that combat veterans with PTSD showed enhanced suppression of cortisol when dexamethasone, a synthetic glucocorticoid, was administered. This may have been due to the possibility that PTSD patients have more glucocorticoid receptors compared to "normal" men. Regardless of the cause, PTSD seems to be associated with a specific pattern of stress hormones that are characterized by elevated catecholamine and often with suppressed cortisol responses (Mason et al., 1990; Yehuda, Giller, and Mason, 1993). Fear conditioning, sensitization, and memory processes appear to be causes of those abnormalities (Southwick et al., 1994).

Adrenergic hormones are not the only ones to show changes in PTSD. Research indicates that exposure to endogenous opioids has a suppressive effect on natural killer cell function among PTSD patients, whereas it increases this measure of immune system status among drug-free, healthy volunteers (Mosnaim et al., 1993). Stress among PTSD patients appeared to affect the way in which opioids influenced the immune function. Similarly, an investigation of twenty-six 51-year-old men with PTSD and 20 healthy controls of about the same age found significantly lower levels of beta-endorphins (an endogenous opioid) in PTSD patients and lower morning cortisol levels in control subjects (Hoffman et al., 1989). Other studies have found that among veterans with PTSD sympathetic reactivity to events reminiscent of combat is greater than that among control subjects (Blanchard et al., 1982; Brende, 1982; Malloy et al., 1983). Presentation of stimuli that reminded people about a traumatic stressor also elicited larger catecholamine increases in PTSD patients than in controls (McFall et al., 1990). Studies of disaster victims also reveal lasting stress symptoms associated with the posttraumatic stress syndrome, including correlate reports of intrusive thoughts and dreams and levels of sympathetic arousal (Davidson and Baum, 1986). Psychological distress, including anxiety and depression, is also found in chronic stress situations, suggesting that PTSD may represent an extreme consequence of lasting stress caused by unusually severe stressors.

STRESS AND ILLNESS

One of the major areas of investigation in health psychology is the impact of stress on health and illness. Chapters 5 through 7 are devoted to exploring the link between stress and various illnesses, demonstrating the relationships among stress, behavioral and physiological changes, and such illnesses as coronary heart disease and cancer and the links to psychophysiological disorders such as hypertension and hives. Research clearly indicates that behavioral factors and stress are involved in the development of many illnesses. (See the box, "Stress and Herpes Simplex.") Before turning to these points, we will consider basic issues in stress and illness.

Mechanisms of Behavioral Influence

Krantz et al. (1981) argued that general behavioral links to illness can be reduced to three basic mechanisms—namely, direct psychophysiological effects,

Stress and Herpes Simplex

Herpes simplex refers to two distinct but highly related common viruses, one of which causes cold sores and another of which causes genital herpes infection. Nearly all of us have been exposed to the first kind, called herpes simplex virus (HSV-1), and some of us have recurrent episodes of cold sores that result from HSV-1. However, we do not have cold sores all the time and some of us rarely or never have them. This is because herpes viruses can become latent infections; once they invade bodily tissue they become dormant and remain in this latent, inactive state until they are temporarily reactivated. These periodic reactivations are responsible for the clinical signs that we see, such as cold sores, and scientists are trying to learn what processes govern the latency and reactivation of these viruses.

When we initially come in contact with the HSV, it replicates at the site of infection (e.g., the skin) and then migrates up a neuronal axon that is near the site of initial infection and takes up residence in the neuron cell body. For HSV-1, for example, this is usually in the trigeminal ganglion in the head. Once in the cell body, the virus begins to replicate but is stopped early in this process and becomes latent. When reactivated, the virus is transported back down the axon and creates clinical signs of oral (HSV-1) or genital herpes (HSV-2), including a cold sore, itching, or soreness. Once infected, we are always infected; as far as we know, the body never completely eliminates the virus. However, it is ordinarily held in check—latency—most of the time by immune and nervous system processes.

The search for causes of reactivation has considered illness, challenges to the immune system, stress, and fatigue (Jenkins and Baum, 1995). A complex of immune factors, including interleukins, antibodies, and endocrine and neuropeptide activity may be the key factors in the regulation of genetic expression that signals latency and reactivation. This is consistent with the predominant theories about HSV latency, which hold that some breakdown in cellular or humoral immune processes cause temporary reactivation, which is reversed when the immune function returns to normal (see Glaser et al., 1985). Another theory, the ganglion trigger theory, suggests that the latency of HSV is broken by a ganglion "trigger" such as the surgical section of neurons or infection with pneumococcal pneumonia virus (Dalkvist et al., 1995; Stevens, Cook, and Jordan, 1975; Walz, Price, and Notkins, 1974).

Although stress could effect these kinds of interruptions of latency and is often mentioned as a cause of cold sores or genital herpes symptoms, evidence linking stress to reactivation of HSV is not compelling (Dalkvist et al., 1995; Jenkins and Baum, 1995). Recent research examined the effects of catching a cold, the amount of sleep, exposure to sunshine, and emotional distress on recurrence of HSV-1 and -2 over a 3-month period by using daily reports of these predictors. Results indicated that recurring HSV-2 infections were reliably preceded by "reduced and decreasing" emotional health beginning about 10 days before clinical symptoms were apparent (Dalkvist et al., 1995). Women exhibited a stronger relationship between mood and recurrence than did men. Poor sleep 3 to 8 days before recurrence was observed among men. Colds did not affect the reactivation of HSV-2 but was the strongest predictor of the reactivation of HSV-1 (hence, the term "cold sores"). The strong effects of colds appeared to mask effects of mood, making it difficult to determine the extent of the impact of emotional distress on HSV-1 reactivation (Dalkvist et al., 1995). Clearly, more research is needed, both to understand how best to prevent and treat the reactivation of HSV and to understand better the basic bodily response to latent and active viruses.

health-impairing and protective behaviors, and reactions to illness. These same mechanisms can be applied to stress and its actions (see Baum, 1993; Krantz et al., 1985) (see Figure 3.9). For example, we have already seen that stress has several effects on bodily functioning and homeostasis. These direct alterations

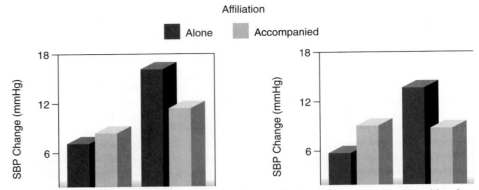

FIGURE 3.9. Stress affects health by altering how we behave when ill or well and by direct effects on our bodies.
Source: From A. Baum. Behavioral, biological, and environmental interactions in disease process. In S. Blumenthal, K. Matthews, and S. Weiss (Eds.), *New Research Frontiers in Behavioral Medicine: Proceedings of the National Conference.* Washington, DC: American Psychological Association, 1994, p. 62.

of bodily processes and tissues occur as part of the readying activity associated with stress. Stress can cause neural and endocrine change that alters the normal functioning of the organism (e.g., changing cardiovascular reactivity or immune system functioning). These physiological changes, in turn, may cause or facilitate the development of illnesses ranging from coronary heart disease to gastrointestinal disorders and cancer. This is somewhat inconsistent with the notion that stress is adaptive and actually helps us to cope with the world. However, it also appears that when stress responses are abnormally intense or prolonged, they can damage organ systems and contribute to disease processes. We have seen abundant evidence that stress can cause a number of physiological and biochemical changes. Now we will see that some of these changes can be linked directly to illness.

A second general mechanism is behavioral changes due to stress that, in turn, have effects on physiological processes that contribute to disease. The evidence for this mechanism, the effects of habits or lifestyles, is also formidable. Cigarette smoking, diet, lack of exercise, coping styles, and other aspects of one's lifestyle have been linked to both physiological changes and the onset of illness. To the extent that stress increases or alters these behaviors, it may contribute to illness.

The third mechanism is concerned primarily with behaviors that affect the treatment of illness. Once people are ill, their behavior is critically important; they must report their symptoms and seek help for them, adhere to the recommendations made by physicians or other health care professionals, and otherwise do what will best help them to recover. Reactions to illness, such as one's willingness to report symptoms or to seek medical attention, obviously affect the course of an illness. If we fail to report noticeable changes in bodily functions or delay reporting these changes, we run the risk of allowing an illness to progress to a point where it is more difficult to treat. In addition, response following the diagnosis of disease is important. Failure to follow treatment regimens or to change lifestyles will usually retard recovery or a cure.

In practice, these three mechanisms are difficult to separate completely and should not be thought of as exclusive or independent processes. Stress and the psychological and physiological effects that accompany it may be exacerbated or moderated by one's characteristic coping style or reaction to being ill. However, the distinctions among these mechanisms are important in explaining the ways in which behavioral factors can affect health and illness. They are also complicated by the fact that stress can affect disease processes at several different points in the development of an illness (Baum, 1994). Most diseases have an initiating point or a series of events that mark the beginning of the disease. In heart disease this initial event may be the original insult to a coronary artery wall or the beginning of atherosclerosis. In cancer the initial event is a mutation of cells and the formation of small, usually undetectable neoplasms. In HIV disease and AIDS the initial event is infection with the HIV. We know that stress and sudden increases in catecholamine release can damage blood vessel walls, and may be responsible for the initial development of plaque formation in the vessel (Schneiderman, 1983; see Chapter 5). We also believe that stress can affect mutation or cellular processes involved in initial cancer events. There is evidence, for example, that stress slows the ability of cell nuclei to repair themselves after being damaged (Glaser et al., 1985) (see Chapter 6). There are also reasons to believe that stress affects physiological processes that could resist the HIV when it is contracted through sexual activity, drug use, or other means. Also, several stress-related behaviors such as alcohol and drug use, affect the likelihood of coming in contact with the virus at all! (see Chapter 6).

Stress not only affects the likelihood or the beginning of disease processes or infection, it also affects the *progression* of disease. Heart disease, cancer, HIV disease, arthritis, and other illnesses do not suddenly appear. They develop, often slowly, over a period of years, and are often not detected until they have developed to be large enough or to cause symptoms that are apparent to the afflicted individual. Heart disease develops over decades of life; as blood vessels slowly narrow, heart activity is altered, and/or other changes predispose people to life-threatening events like heart attacks. Similarly, cancer starts as a tiny mass of neoplastic cells, slowly developing into palpable tumors that spread (metastasize) and cause organ system dysfunction. HIV disease also develops at variable speeds, as the virus destroys more and more T cells and slowly disables the body's immune defenses. Stress appears to affect the rate of progression of these and other diseases, to varying extents, and does so by affecting physiological systems directly or indirectly (by altering behaviors) or by affecting reactions to diagnosis and treatment of the disease (Baum, 1994).

Finally, stress can affect the onset of disease events or life-threatening manifestations of disease as well as the extent of the disability caused. Heart disease often leads to heart attacks, and stress contributes to these events by increasing demand on the heart, constricting key blood vessels, and increasing the stickiness of platelets in the blood, thereby increasing the possibility of a clot forming and occluding coronary artery blood flow. Cancers are not characterized by such dramatic changes in condition and usually are not marked by a sudden life threat. However, the likelihood of recurrence, survival time, and the severity of pain and disability associated with advanced cancers are affected by stress. Finally, the progression from HIV disease to AIDS and the onset of life-threatening opportunistic infections may be affected by stress (Antoni et al., 1992).

In general, chronic stress has a greater chance of affecting our health, although acute events may trigger illness episodes or sudden death. The normal course of resistance and adaptation to stress is not always successful, and when it is not, persistently elevated hormonal, cardiovascular, behavioral, and emotional aspects of stress may begin to have effects on disease processes such as atherosclerosis (House and Smith, 1989). In addition, chronic stress may alter typical acute reactions to stress (see Fleming et al., 1987; Pardine and Napoli, 1983). (We will deal with these and other diseases in greater detail in Chapters 5 through 7).

An example of the complicated relationships between stress and disease processes will be informative here. We know, for example, that alcohol use can be bad for our health. Although moderate use of alcohol may not cause problems or may actually protect us from some diseases, heavier use is associated with cancer, some infectious illnesses, and HIV disease (see Breslin and Baum, in press). We also know that stress affects alcohol use although the mechanisms underlying this relationship are not known. Some have argued that stress and negative emotional states are relieved by alcohol; if we feel bad or uptight, drinking helps us to relax and feel better (see Conger, 1956; Sher, 1987). A second mechanism may be that stress changes our bodies enough actually to alter the way that alcohol affects us. Thus, stress may reduce the psychopharmacological impact of drinking alcohol (see Grunberg and Baum, 1985). Stress inhibits activity in the digestive system, and because alcohol is absorbed through this system, absorption could be slowed by stress (Minnick, Miller, and Wehner, 1995). At the same time, stress affects activity in the liver and some have argued that catecholamine and glucocorticoid release can stimulate alcohol metabolism there. Both of these stress-related changes could reduce the mood-altering impact of an alcoholic drink, first by making it take longer for alcohol to be absorbed into the bloodstream, and second by speeding detoxification and removal of alcohol from the system.

A recent study examined these possibilities, looking at the effects of an acute stressor on blood alcohol concentrations in the laboratory (Breslin, Hayward, and Baum, 1994). A total of 63 volunteers were studied; all participants consumed an alcoholic beverage (one part vodka to three parts cranberry juice) after some predrink measures were taken. Immediately after the drink, they were exposed to one of two stressors (watching a gruesome film or putting their hands in very cold water) or to a nonstressful control condition. Assessments of the degree of participants' intoxication, blood alcohol, and metabolism of alcohol were then collected over several hours following the stressor. Results suggested that the stressor decreased the time from completing the drink to peak blood alcohol levels (see Figure 3.10; Breslin et al., 1994, Figure 3) and increased rate of elimination of alcohol (see Figure 3.11; Breslin et al., 1994, Figure 4). Apparently, stress alters the body in ways that affect how alcohol is processed, and from these findings it looks as though stress reduces the subjective impact of drinking alcohol. Because people under stress would have to consume more alcohol to get to the same blood alcohol level than if not under stress, this may be one mechanism by which stress increases alcohol use!

Life Events, Stress, and Disease

As discussed many times in this book, traditional accounts of illness view it as a biomedical phenomenon. Sickness is caused by germs or by some internal malfunction. Many health professionals have tended to assume that illness is simply a matter of biology and not affected or caused by what we do or how we respond to the demands of our environment. However, there are many illnesses that do not fit this biomedical model. Diseases can be caused, at least partly, by our behavior patterns and our psychological response to our surroundings. Hypertension and heart disease are not contagious; they do not seem to be caused by germs or pathogens. Rather, they develop over the course of a person's life and are apparently caused by a number of factors, including diet, working habits, smoking, and response to stress. As Eliot and Buell (1981) have noted, "These disease states [coronary and hypertensive heart disease] appear to be the major epidemic afflictions of industrialized

FIGURE 3.10. Mean latency (minutes postdrink) to peak blood alcohol content for subjects in the cold pressor (CP), film stressor (FS), and warm pressor (WP) conditions. HR = heart rate; SBP = systolic blood pressure; DBP = diastolic blood pressure.
Source: From F. C. Breslin, M. Hayward, and A. Baum. Effect of stress on perceived intoxication and the blood alcohol curve in men and women. *Health Psychology,* 1994, *13*(6), 483.

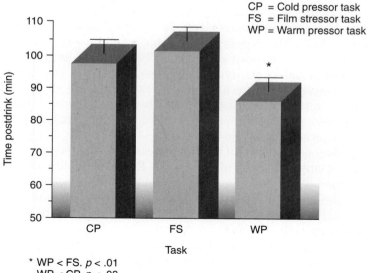

* WP < FS. $p < .01$
  WP < CP. $p < .08$

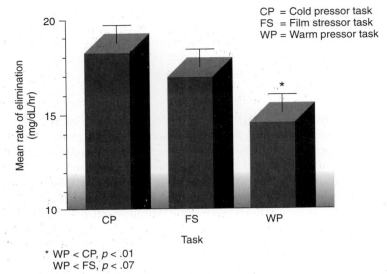

FIGURE 3.11. Mean rate of alcohol elimination (adjusting for daily expenditure of energy) on the initial portion of the descending limb for the CP, FS, and WP stress conditions.
Source: From F. C. Breslin, M. Hayward, and A. Baum. Effect of stress on perceived intoxication and the blood alcohol curve in men and women. *Health Psychology,* 1994, *13*(6), 484.

communities in the 20th century. Indeed, the prevalence of coronary heart disease and hypertension parallels the increasing complexity of social systems and social order whether we are speaking of animals or mankind" (p. 25).

The study of links between psychological factors and disease states is relatively new. However, research has already identified a number of relationships. In an attempt to include some psychosocial contributions to disease in the etiology of illness, researchers have devised the **diathesis-stress model of illness** (Levi, 1974). All elements are *continually* interacting with one another. *Physiological predispositions* toward a certain illness (such as genetic weakness or biochemical imbalance), *psychosocial stimuli* or events that trigger bodily changes or disease (e.g., stress and how we respond to it), and previously experienced *environmental conditions* will jointly determine many disease states. Biological factors are still viewed as important, but other factors, including psychological variables, are also critical.

A great deal of evidence of a stress-illness link has been provided by the study of life change or stressful life events. Research on life events is essentially concerned with correlating the frequency of change caused by different events and the onset of illness. In other words, life change or stressful life events research assumes that the greater the amount of change one experiences, the greater is the likelihood that one will become ill. The idea that such change could predispose illness is not new, but the study of life events is a fairly recent phenomenon, beginning in earnest with Holmes and Rahe's (1967) Schedule of Recent Experiences and Social Readjustment Rating Scale.

This scale provided an extensive listing of events and changes that occur from time to time (see Table 3.5). (See Chapter 9 for further information on these instruments.) Initially, respondents simply checked those events that had occurred in their lives in a given time period, and the number of events experienced was used as an index of life change for that period. Someone who had committed a misdemeanor, who had taken a vacation, and whose spouse had recently begun work was given a score of 3, whereas someone who had gotten divorced and been fired from work received a score of 2.

The problems with such a gross scoring method are obvious. Such a method indicates greater life change for the first person in the preceding example, whereas common sense suggests that change was greater for the second person. Despite the fact that gross summation measures did show relationships to illness, numerous changes have been made. In some studies weights— or relative degrees of life change caused by each event—were generated by panel ratings; other studies asked subjects to assign their own weights (see Holmes and Rahe, 1967; Rahe, 1975; Rahe et al., 1980).

Initial research using these scales was generally retrospective in nature. Subjects reviewed their experiences over a prior time period, and these recollections were translated into life change scores. These studies reported a consistent increase or clustering of life events causing change and requiring adjustment during the year preceding the diagnosis of illnesses such as infectious disease, metabolic disturbance, and heart disease (see Garrity and Marx, 1979; Jacobs et al., 1970; Rahe, 1975). In a prospective study Rahe, Mahan, and Arthur (1970) reported a linear relationship between life change and illness rates among enlisted men during 6-month cruises aboard U.S. navy ships. Studies of Native Americans suggest that life events are significant predictors of illness and hospitalization, whereas studies in India indicate that major life events are related to more psychosomatic symptoms and stress (Lepore, Evans, and Palsane, 1991; Williams, Zyzanski, and Wright, 1992). Other studies indicate that life change is associated with a wide range of behavioral and health outcomes, including accidents, academic performance, cardiovascular risk, drug use, and illness (see Bruns and Geist, 1984; Garrity and Ries, 1985; Rahe, 1987).

To the extent that these measures reflect stress, stressful life event measures can predict illness. However, a number of major criticisms have led to attempts to devise alternative ways of assessing life events (see Dohrenwend and Dohrenwend, 1974; Monroe and Simons, 1991; Rabkin and Struening, 1976).

Some researchers have argued that individual ratings of events are important and that the many different aspects of life events should be considered. For example, Pilkonis, Imler, and Rubinsky (1985) reported a study that used both life events checklists and interviews to identify the characteristics of life events that are most important. They found three general factors: desirability of an event, control, and required readjustment. How positive an event was, how much control subjects felt that they had over an event, and how much effort was required to cope with the event were also significant factors. Problems associated with recall ability, memory biases, reliability of measurement, and the frequent causal relationships among stressful life events must be considered (Hudgens, 1974; Rose, Jenkins, and Hurst, 1978).

The interaction of specific life events is a particularly important factor that

TABLE 3.4. The Schedule of Recent Experiences

Life Event	Value
Death of spouse	100
Divorce	73
Marital separation	65
Jail term	63
Death of close family member	63
Personal injury or illness	53
Marriage	50
Fired at work	47
Marital reconciliation	45
Retirement	45
Change in health of family member	44
Pregnancy	40
Sex difficulties	39
Gain of new family member	39
Business readjustment	39
Change in financial state	38
Death of close friend	37
Change to different line of work	36
Change in number of arguments with spouse	35
Mortgage or loan for major purchase	31
Foreclosure of mortgage or loan	30
Change in responsibilities at work	29
Son or daughter leaving home	29
Trouble with in-laws	29
Outstanding personal achievement	28
Wife begins or stops work	26
Begin or end school	26
Change in living conditions	25
Revision of personal habits	24
Trouble with boss	23
Change in work hours or conditions	20
Change in residence	20
Change in schools	20
Change in recreation	19
Change in church activities	19
Change in social activities	18
Mortgage or loan for lesser purchase (car, TV, etc.)	17
Change in sleeping habits	16
Change in number of family get-togethers	15
Change in eating habits	15
Vacation	13
Christmas	12
Minor violations of the law	11

Source: Reprinted by permission of the publisher from T. H. Holmes and R. H. Rahe. The social readjustment rating scale. *Journal of Psychosomatic Research,* vol. 11. Copyright @ 1967 by Elsevier Science. See the original text for complete wording of the items.

is rarely considered. According to the values in Table 3.5, a divorce is rated 73 life change units and remarriage counts an additional 50 units. As a result, we could assume that an individual who is divorced and remarried within a year or so would have experienced substantial life change. However, for many people a quick remarriage may reduce the change or disruption caused by the divorce, canceling out some stress and making life less stressful. For others the 123 life change unit sum might be more meaningful. Without assessment of individual perceptions and qualitative ratings of these kinds of events, problems like this will persist.

Another problem is the possibility that life events also reflect mood and symptom experience (see Schroeder and Costa, 1984). In other words, several of the events listed in these checklists are either "contaminated by mood" or symptoms of health consequences that these scales are made to predict. In Table 3.4, many of the listed life changes have associated mood changes that are strongly related to the events themselves, and some—life "changes in sleeping habits" or "changes in eating habits"—may actually be symptoms of illness. Brett and her associates (1990) have argued that pessimism or a negative mood can affect reporting of life changes and illness, and that observed correlations between life change and illness may reflect this confound rather than a real relationship (Brett et al., 1990).

Regardless of these issues, studies using a variety of measures have reinforced the belief that life events and health are linked. A study of naval submarine students examined the relationships between life events and both self-report and medically documented indices of health. Using a cross-lagged panel design, researchers correlated life events for two different periods of time with measures of health. Negative life events were associated with measures of health as self-report and medical record measures showed significant correlations with the occurrence of events (Antoni, 1985).

SUMMARY

Stress has been a topic of concern for centuries and was formalized in the early twentieth century by Cannon (1914, 1928, 1929). The scientific study of stress was given further impetus by the work of Selye (1956, 1976). Additional theoretical refinements were provided by researchers such as Mason (1975) and Frankenhaeuser (1972), who emphasized psychological factors as important determinants of the experience of and response to stress.

The physiological stress response is rather well documented. Two different systems appear to be operative. In the first system stimulation of the sympathetic nervous system causes the adrenal medullae to secrete large quantities of catecholamines—neurotransmitter hormones that increase the heart rate and other coronary activity—to constrict blood vessels, to inhibit gastrointestinal activity, and to increase a number of other bodily functions. In the second system the pituitary gland secretes a hormone (ACTH) that stimulates the adrenal cortex to produce corticosteroids, particularly cortisol. Cortisol affects carbohydrate metabolism and is an anti-inflammatory agent.

Sources of stress, or stressors, have been studied by many disciplines—particularly psychologists, epidemiologists, and sociologists. Lazarus and Cohen (1978) have considered three general classes of stressors: (1) cataclysmic phenomena; (2) powerful events that challenge adaptive abilities in the same way as cataclysmic events but affect fewer people; and (3) "daily hassles." On another level, the appraisal or interpretation of stressors has been considered, primarily by psychologists. The key issue at this level is whether or not the stressor will be perceived as threatening. Responses to stressors are determined by the extent to which the stressors are perceived as harmful, rather than by the objective danger (Lazarus, 1966). Lazarus and Launier (1978) have specified the following types of interpretations:

1. Harm or loss assessments involving analysis of the damage that has already occurred.
2. Threat appraisals concerned with future dangers.
3. Challenge appraisals focused on the possibility of overcoming the stressor.

The final determination of the degree of harm or threat presented by a stressor will be affected by several mediating variables, such as attitudes toward the availability and extent of social support systems, and certain dispositional variables such as perceived control and coping styles.

The physiological response to stress is accompanied by behavioral responses as well. As noted by Lazarus (1966), individuals may respond to stress with action directed toward the source of stress, or they may respond by palliative coping methods. Behavioral and psychological responses will be affected by factors such as the accuracy of expectations and individual susceptibility to stress (i.e., the "stress-prone personality") and can be accompanied by consequences such as anxiety, depression, increased symptom reporting, decreases in problem-solving abilities, and heightened aggressiveness.

Several points can be emphasized in relation to the organization of stress into source, transmission, and recipient levels. First, the three components are interactive. So, for example, recipients may engage in direct action to modify a stressful situation that they perceived as threatening, or they may reappraise the nature of the situation so that it does not seem to be dangerous. Second, some stressors may be intense enough to override the recipients' coping mechanisms and to produce a debilitating response despite resistance. Third, the influence of variables such as appraisal and coping is not limited solely to the time during which the stressor is actually present. For example, evaluation processes may begin well in advance, may be affected by the recipient's prior experience, and may influence evaluation of future stressors. Many effects of stress, particularly physiological ones, are similar whether the source of stress is psychological or physical. Although there are subtle differences in endocrine response among stressors, response to stress is, for the most part, nonspecific. Finally, it is not always possible to identify accurately the source of stress. In fact, some types of psychological anxiety may be viewed as psychological stress where the source cannot be clearly identified.

Stress and behavioral response to it can affect health and facilitate, if not cause, some illnesses. Stress has direct physiological effects on the body, and the cumulative wear and tear on the system caused by recurring stress can eventually cause damage to the system. Lifestyle and coping style are also important, partly because they help to determine the impact of stress and partly because they lead people to adopt habits that may predispose them to illness. Finally, the way that people react to being ill is important.

RECOMMENDED READINGS

Baum, A., and Singer, J. E. (Eds.) *Handbook of psychology and health*, vol. 5, *Stress*. Hillsdale, NJ: Erlbaum, 1987.

Cohen, S., Kessler, R., and Gordon, L. (Eds.), *Measuring stress*. New York: Oxford University Press, 1995.

Cohen, S., and Syme, L. (Eds.), *Social support and health*. New York: Academic Press, 1985.

Glass, D. C. and Singer, J. E. *Urban stress*. New York: Academic Press, 1972.

Sapolsky, R. M. *Why Zebras Don't Get Ulcers*. New York: Freeman, 1994.

Selye, H. *The stress of life*. New York: McGraw-Hill, 1976.

CHAPTER 4

Control and Learned Helplessness

You wake up in the middle of the night with a strange pain in your side. You have never felt it before, and you cannot think of anything unusual that you did to cause it. Your response to this situation will ultimately depend on how worthwhile you think seeking care might be and how likely it is that you can treat the problem. If you believe that you are responsible for what happens to you, that what you do will make a difference, you are apt to try to reduce the pain until morning and then to see a doctor right away. If it was really uncomfortable, you might seek care sooner. *But you would do something!* If you believe that you cannot affect your health or that nothing you do will cure or make your condition worse, you may not do anything at all! Perceived control and one's sense of responsibility and efficacy are potentially very powerful determinants of health-related behavior.

Infants and very young children do not appear to understand simple chains of cause and effect. They do something, something else happens, but it seems to take some time before the child understands that he or she caused it to happen. Early on in life children may learn that a parent (or better yet a bottle or breast) follows quickly when they cry, but whether or not they understand that their crying caused food and/or comfort to appear is not clear. The recognition of the *causal connection* between what one does and what happens is called *control* and perceptions of control appear to be central aspects of human development and healthy behavior.

Consider the socioeconomic gradient in health that we discussed in Chapter 2. One explanation for the greater incidence and severity of several diseases and health problems in lower socioeconomic groups is that poorer or more poorly educated people may not have a strong sense of control and may not see many connections between their efforts and rewards. Any number of factors could be responsible. For example, discrimination against a minority can inhibit perceived control among members of that minority group. Conversely, education may help us to cope with or to avoid stress. When people learn that their behaviors are not related to particular outcomes, they may exhibit *learned helplessness*.

Control is also an important mediator of stress. In Chapter 3 we briefly considered this factor, but its importance as a determinant of behavior and a factor in health and illness are larger than this. Research on both human and animal populations has clearly shown that being able to control a noxious event, believing that one can control the event, or perceiving that one can control other aspects of the environment can reduce the impact of a stressor. In this chapter we will consider control primarily as it relates to health and stress. We will also discuss the consequences of losing or not having control and some styles of explaining or coping with the world that seem to be related to perceptions of control.

CONTROL

On a general level, control means being able to determine what we do or what others do to us. It is the belief that we make our own decisions and determine what we do (Rodin, 1986). Most of us will agree that having control and keeping it are important. But why is control such an important motivator and influential determinant of our mood and behavior?

Control is one of the most basic processes in our daily interaction with our environment and other people. Kelley (1967) suggested that people may spend a great deal of time and energy trying to explain how and why things happen as they do. This is done, according to Kelley, to achieve a sense of control over one's surroundings. Like ancient mythology, which was created to provide explanations for natural events that made them more predictable, we create or maintain a sense of control over our surroundings to help us cope with them. White (1959) wrote about control as an intrinsically reinforcing goal that directs much of our behavior related to being able to predict and manipulate our surroundings. Having control is rewarding regardless of whether it will make any real difference in what happens. White (1959) referred to the desire for control as *effectance motivation* and thought of it as an innate need. As such, control is something that we all want to have, and not having it is unpleasant and motivates our attempts to gain it.

Other views of control emphasize its role in one's developing sense of mastery over an environment. As children, we gradually developed a sense of control and predictability over our surroundings, one that we defined or seek to improve as adults. Achievement of *efficacy* or a sense of control over the environment was seen as a pleasant state and therefore reinforcing. Bandura (1977a) also implied inherent gratification accompanying a sense of control. He describes self-efficacy as the belief that one can do what is necessary to get desired outcomes. Rodin, Rennert, and Solomon (1980) have suggested that control may be an inherent motivator, but not in all situations. Control is useful or important only in those instances where it *will actually make a difference*. If control will not really have much of an effect on what happens in a given situation, it will not be terribly important.

Regardless of whether control is inherently reinforcing, whether it is a primary or secondary drive, or whether it is valued solely for its instrumental value (i.e., its value in helping to achieve goals), control appears to be important to people. The desire to believe that we have control over things that happen, to know how we will be affected by them, and to interpret events as being under our control, is pervasive in our culture. Such an outlook is charicatured in comedian George Carlin's portrayal of cats—animals we often believe are always "in control." Cats, says Carlin, can have the most frightening and disastrous accidents, but they always calmly recover, proclaiming "I meant that!"

Illusion of Control

To some extent these tendencies may cause us to assume incorrectly responsibility for events over which we do not have any control. Most of us have at one time or another believed that our luck in a game of Monopoly was actually due to our skill at rolling the dice, or that something we did or did not do caused our favorite football team to lose. Mistakenly believing that an outcome was directly determined by us rather than by chance or other factors has been called the **illusion of control** (Langer, 1975). This illusion provides us with a sense of control (perceived control) even when actual, objective control does not exist. This optimistic outlook appears to affect health behaviors as well as other activities and feelings (see Taylor, 1983).

The illusion of control was studied in research by Wortman (1975) and Langer (1975). In the former subjects were awarded prizes as a result of drawing marbles (different prizes were associated with different marbles) and what each got was determined by the marble selected. Some subjects were allowed to draw the marbles themselves, whereas others were not (the experimenter picked them). Despite the fact that the drawing was determined by chance in both cases, when subjects could link their behavior (drawing the marbles) to the prize they received, they reported more perceived control over the situation.

Research on illusions of control suggests that people tend to overestimate how much control they really have (see Taylor and Brown, 1988). There are a number of reasons for this. Most real-world events are complex, and outcomes are usually determined jointly by chance or external factors and ability (Langer, 1975). As a result, it is often difficult for us to determine the real causes of an event. Reasons for thinking that something happened by chance or because of something we did may determine attributions as much as the actual event does. For example, you may blame yourself for bad things that happen to you or blame other people or chance for them. Doing the latter would seem to protect self-esteem more effectively. If we can shift blame for something bad or accept responsibility for a desirable event and thereby bolster our self-esteem, we are likely to do so.

The value of illusions of control when coping with serious or chronic disease is not clear, and there is some debate about whether they are harmful or protective in such situations (Alloy and Clements, 1992). Taylor (1983) argued that illusions of control provide an advantage when dealing with illness because they help us to adjust to changing situations. Self-generated feelings of control among patients with chronic or progressive disease appear to reduce anxiety and depression and to improve adjustment (Taylor et al., 1991) (see Table 4.1). Similarly, those cancer patients with more perceived control over the disease exhibit better adjustment to having cancer (Hilton, 1989; Taylor, Lichtman, and Wood, 1984; Thompson et al., 1993). Perceived control also appears to minimize depression among cancer patients, protecting them from the emotional distress associated with this dysphoria (Marks et al., 1986). Positive illusions seem to be most protective when people get bad news about something (Taylor and Brown, 1988). However, other studies suggest that perceived control and illusions of control can be harmful when people finally recognize the limits of their control (see Affleck et al., 1987).

Self-Blame

Illusions of control are related to the possibility that people *create* or unrealistically assume control over uncontrollable situations by blaming themselves for them. In other words, people sometimes blame themselves for things for which they could not have been responsible. However, the findings of research on this topic have been mixed. Some studies have found that assuming responsibility for misfortune or victimization is beneficial (see Baum et al., 1983; Bulman and Wortman, 1977; Dirksen, 1995; Jacobs et al., 1994; Janoff-Bulman, 1979). Other studies suggest that self-blame is negative and associated with distress (see Fairbank, Hansen, and Fitterling, 1991; Morrow, Thoreson, and Penney, 1995; Troop et al., 1994; Williams, Robinson, and Geisser, 1994). In part, the reasons for this inconsistency are due to differences across situations, in definitions and operationalizations of self-blame or assumption of responsibility, and the use of separate concepts of behavioral and characterological self-blame (see Anderson et al., 1994; Janoff-Bulman, 1979). Behavioral and characterological self-blame differ in how stable or how easy they are to change: Attributing

TABLE 4.1. Correlations between Control Ratings and Global Adjustment of AIDS Patients by Subjective Health Status

Variable	Total Sample (N = 24)	Subjective Health	
		Low (N = 12)	High (N = 12)
Personal control			
Day-to-day symptoms	0.56[b]	0.67[a]	0.36
Maintaining health	0.59[b]	0.68[a]	0.25
Medical care and treatment	0.55[b]	0.71[a]	0.28
Total personal	0.69[c]	0.68[c]	0.36
Vicarious control			
Day-to-day symptoms	−0.09	−0.31	−0.10
Maintaining health	−0.46[a]	−0.73[a]	−0.10
Medical care and treatment	−0.47[a]	−0.68[a]	−0.22
Total vicarious	−0.53[b]	−0.82[b]	−0.22

Note: A positive number means that high perceptions of control were correlated with good health.
[a]$p < .05$.
[b]$p < .01$.
[c]$p < .001$.
Source: From S. E. Taylor, V. S. Helgeson, G. M. Reed, and L. A. Skokan. Self-generated feelings of control and adjustment of physical illness. *Journal of Social Issues*, 1991, 47(4), 101.

responsibility to one's character, a difficult thing to change, appears to be associated with less positive outcomes. Behavioral self-blame refers to blaming a behavior or action that can more readily be changed in the future.

An example may help. Let us say that you are injured by a car that runs a red light and hits you while you are crossing the street. Clearly, the accident was not your fault. The driver broke a law, ignoring the signal to stop. However, you may come to decide that there were things that you could have done to avoid the accident and you assume some responsibility for the event—you could have been more careful; you should have crossed at a different corner; or you were supposed to have been visiting a sick relative and should not have been there in the first place! Such attributions to behavioral causes are often useful in bolstering our sense of control ("If I do these things correctly next time, I can avoid another accident") and seem to help us adjust. However, attributing the accident to some aspect of our character ("I'm the type of person who gets into an accident") will not increase perceived control or help us to deal with our injuries.

In addition to differences in types of self-blame, there is also evidence that the effects of using self-blame to increase perceived control may be time-dependent. Reidy and Caplan (1994) studied men with spinal cord injuries during hospitalization and 18 and 24 months after discharge. These patients were asked to assign blame for their injury to themselves, the environment, luck, or other people's actions. Nearly all of them changed their ratings of self-blame over time, and those who used increasing amounts of self-blame over time were the most depressed 2 years after the injury occurred (Reidy and Caplan, 1994). The extent to which control is enhanced by taking responsibility for misfortune may change over time and differences in behavioral or characterological self-blame may also be affected by the passage of time.

Alternatively, the meaning of taking blame for something negative may change or represent different kinds of control. For example, in a study of serious automobile accidents victims who believed that they caused the accident actually showed less distress and better adjustment in the year following the crash than did victims who thought the other driver caused the accident (Delahanty et al., 1996). However, of those victims who thought that they caused the accident, those who reported self-blame in a coping inventory exhibited *more* distress than the others. When people in another study attributed causes of their failure to quit smoking to themselves, their sense of self-efficacy determined the meaning and implications of assuming responsibility for failure (Grove, 1993).

Determinants of Control

People do not always overestimate how much control they have, and a number of factors appear to affect perceptions of control. When people have had experience with an uncontrollable event, they may judge their ability to control events in the future more realistically. This seems to be true even if there is something to be gained from believing that one could control future outcomes. Parker, Brewer, and Spencer (1980) reported a study of residents in a California area that had been devastated by a brush fire. A year later victims who had decided to rebuild rather than relocate reported that they would have less control over the outcome of another fire than did a group of people who had not been affected by the fire.

Corah and Boffa (1970) examined *choice,* another aspect of control. Subjects were exposed to loud bursts of noise. Members of one group were told how they could, if they desired, escape the noise. The others were also given either escape or no-escape instructions, but they were not told that they could choose between escaping and not escaping. Several measures were used to assess the stress response in the subjects. Overall, subjects who were given a choice showed somewhat less stress—less discomfort and lower skin conductance readings—than did no-choice subjects. Corah and Boffa (1970) suggest that the perception of control provided by having been given a choice influenced appraisal of threat and reduced arousal associated with stress.

Learning about one's abilities to control things around them is another important determinant of perceived control. Throughout daily comings and goings we have many opportunities to observe whether our behaviors actually affect what happens. A lifetime of experience characterized by successful control of what happens teaches us that we can control the things and events around us, contributing to perceptions of *self-efficacy* (see Bandura, 1986). In other words, our experiences indicate that we can exert control and that we can gain the things that we want (e.g., fame, fortune, status). People with a strong sense of self-efficacy believe that they can master most situations and play a major role in determining what they get. Similarly, people with a strong belief in their ability to control things around them are more likely to try to exert control.

Another way to think of this is in terms of *locus of control,* one's beliefs and expectations about the factors that determine what happens to them (Rotter, 1966). Some people, often with a strong sense of self-efficacy, believe that *they* cause the events around them and are said to have *internal* locus of control. Others feel that these events are caused by *external* factors, such as luck or the actions of other people. Those of us who have internal locus of control believe that we control most of what happens to us, whereas those of us who are more externally oriented believe that these events are caused by factors beyond our control. Because they represent differences in basic motivation and are likely to be applied in a given situation, notions of self-efficacy and locus of control have been important parts of a number of theories and interventions in health psychology.

Control, then, refers to our *real* or *perceived* ability to determine outcomes of an event. When our behavior is perceived as being causally linked to outcomes, perceptions of control are likely. When outcomes cannot be tied to behavior, it is more difficult to believe that we are in control. Much of the recent interest in control has dealt with two issues: (1) the effects of believing that one has control and that outcomes depend on one's behavior and (2) the effects of believing that outcomes are not contingent on behavior and therefore are not controllable. The first issue has been concerned most directly with the mediating effects of perceived control on response to aversive stimulation and stress.

The second issue has been concerned with learned helplessness and the debilitating effects of believing that one cannot control what happens.

Control and Stress: the Executive Monkey

Control appears to be an effective mediator of exposure to aversive stimulation. Whether it is perceived or real, useful or not, it seems to make a difference in the ways that people respond to stress. A number of studies of both human and animal subjects have demonstrated this pattern. One of the first major studies considering the impact of control on health-relevant outcomes found evidence contrary to the view that control reduces the impact of stress. Brady and his associates (see Brady, 1958; Brady et al., 1958; Porter et al., 1958) found that shock delivered over a fairly long period of time was associated with an increased incidence of gastric ulcers in monkeys. The pattern of their data suggested that most of the ulcers in the gastrointestinal tract occurred during rest, when shocks were not being delivered. This suggested a parallel with human executives who are responsible for serious decisions and who have control and responsibility. These executives might also show increased incidence of ulcers. In order to test this notion, Brady et al. (1958) designed a study that placed monkeys in situations analogous to those experienced by executives—hence the popular reference to the study as the "executive monkey" study (see Figure 4.1).

As part of an avoidance task, pairs of monkeys were exposed to shock. One monkey in each pair, designated as the "executive," was taught a response to avoid the shock for both animals in the pair. The other monkey was yoked to the executive and could do nothing to affect the shock. Both received shock in the same intensities and frequencies; the only difference between them was that one had the ability to avoid (control) the shock.

The executives were quite good at learning to avoid the shock, and the number of shocks received by the animals was thus kept low. However, within 2 months of the study, all of the executives had either died or become so incapacitated that they had to be euthanized. Equally surprising was the finding that these executives had developed extensive gastric ulcerations. Autopsies of sacrificed monkeys who had no control but who had received the same amount of shock showed little if any lesioning. Apparently, the control and responsibility associated with the executive role *increased* rather than decreased stress-related illness. One interpretation of this result was that the need to be constantly vigilant increased stress for the executives.

Subsequent work by Weiss (1968; Weiss and Miller, 1971) suggested that the results of the executive study were artifactual and were caused by sampling error rather than by processes related to control or hypervigilance. The executive in each pair of monkeys in the study was initially selected on a speed-of-learning basis. The monkey that learned the avoidance response first was made executive, and its slower colleague was placed in the uncontrollable condition. Unfortunately, research suggests that more emotional monkeys learn this response fastest, and as a result of the selection criteria, monkeys in the executive group were also more emotional (see Weiss, 1968; Weiss and Miller, 1971). Since heightened emotional reactivity can be linked to increased

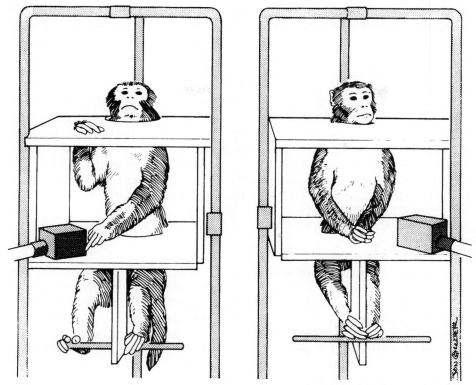

FIGURE 4.1. Each pair of participants in the executive monkey study received shocks, but only one could control when they occurred. Illustration by Jon Coulter, 1996.

susceptibility to stress, and therefore the development of ulcers, control may not have been responsible for the executives' demise.

Research by Weiss (1968) conducted to "correct" this problem has provided evidence that control reduces the impact of stress. In a situation similar to the one used with the monkeys rats were considered in groups of three. One rat in each group was the executive and was taught to avoid shock; a second was yoked to the executive position and received equivalent shock with no ability to avoid it; and a third was not exposed to shock at all. The sampling error in the executive monkey studies was eliminated and results were directly opposite those obtained with the monkeys. Rats who received shock when they had no control over it suffered more severe somatic consequences of stress than did the executives. However, both groups showed more deterioration than did the no-shock controls. The ability to avoid the shocks did not completely neutralize stress in this setting.

These results indicated that the opportunity to control an aversive event is an important determinant of the response to a stressful situation. Predictability, a form of control conveyed by knowing when or for how long a stressor will last, has been shown to have similar effects on stress in animals. Again using a three-group design, Weiss (1968) exposed rats to unpredictable, predictable, or no-shock conditions and found that unpredictable shock was associated with increased corticosteroid production and gastric ulceration as compared with predictable or no-shock treatments. A number of studies have examined the effects of perceived control over the delivery of electric shock or negative outcomes. Early studies with both human and animal subjects suggested that self-administration of shock was associated with fewer symptoms of arousal or disruption than was shock administered by others (see Haggard, 1946; Mowrer and Viek, 1948). Pervin (1963) also found evidence of this by measuring subject preferences for self-delivered versus experimenter-delivered shocks. Not surprisingly, self administered shock was preferred even though the intensity and duration of shocks to be delivered were the same. Similar evidence of preference for, or reduced arousal under, self-administration of shock has been provided by other studies (see Le Panto, Moroney, and Zenhausem, 1965; Staub, Tursky, and Schwartz, 1971).

Control, Stress, and Health

As an important mediator of stress and critical determinant of behavior, control should affect our health or bodily states that may affect health indirectly. In general, this is the case. For example, optimists, who have strong expectations for being able to control things, have better health behaviors and fewer illnesses, and are more likely to treat their illnesses than are pessimists, who have less control (see Lin and Peterson, 1990). (We will discuss optimism in more detail later in this chapter.) Internal locus of control is associated with better adjustment to chronic illness (Marks et al., 1986), and the use of cognitive control was related to adjustment to cancer in another study (Taylor, Lichtman, and Wood, 1984). Self-efficacy is also important, as a prominent factor in theories of attitude-behavior relationships (see Rogers and Rippetoe, 1987) and as a factor in recovering from chronic illness (see Kaplan, Atkins, and Timms, 1984).

The effects of control have been shown clearly in stressful occupational settings. A model of disease risk that considered the demand and control characteristics of stressful occupations suggests that low control and high demand jobs are not harmful (Karasek et al., 1982). Other studies conducted by Frankenhaeuser and her colleagues at the University of Stockholm (see Frankenhaeuser and Gardell 1976; Frankenhaeuser and Johansson, 1982) also indicate this pattern. Those workers whose jobs were self-paced—that is, those who could determine how fast and/or when they did their assigned tasks—showed fewer symptoms of stress than did workers whose jobs were machine-paced or otherwise determined for them (see Figure 4.2). The degree to which the job was under the workers' control was related to excretion of catecholamines and self-reported distress.

The controllability of a stressor appears to affect the magnitude of corticosteroid release during stress. Studies have suggested that corticosteroid elevations during stress are greater when the stressor is uncontrollable or inescapable than when it can be avoided or terminated, but these differences do not appear to be very large (see, Maier, Laudenslager, and Ryan, 1985). It has also been reported that corticosteroid levels decline more slowly after inescapable or uncontrollable shock than after shock that is controllable (Swenson and Vogel, 1983).

FIGURE 4.2. Workers on assembly lines or in other jobs where the workload is high but individuals' control over the pace of work is low appear to experience more stress than other workers.
Source: Michael Hayman/Photo Researchers

Another endocrine response during stress that appears to be influenced by control is the release of endogenous opioid peptides such as beta-endorphins. These substances are similar to morphine and other opiates that exist outside the body and are used as analgesics (pain reducers). However, they are produced inside the body. Among other things, they reduce pain, affect eating behavior, and are part of stress responses and involved in immune system regulation. Research suggests that these opioids are also released when one perceives that he or she does not have control (Maier et al., 1985). Inescapable shock produced an opiate-based analgesia, whereas escapable shock did not (Jackson, Maier, and Coon, 1979). Further, although both controllable and uncontrollable stressors appear to produce brief poststressor analgesia, only that produced by inescapable stressors can be eliminated by administering opiate antagonists such as naloxone (see Hyson et al., 1982). Thus, there seem to be two different types of analgesia after stress experience; only one is based on endogenous opiate activity, and that type is more likely to be produced by uncontrollable stressors (Maier et al., 1983). In humans increasing self-efficacy and perceived control also affected opioid and endocrine reactions during stressful encounters (see Bandura et al., 1987). In another study the development of a strong sense of mastery or self-efficacy over things by which people were frightened has positive effects on the immune system, heart rate, and endocrine activity (Wiedenfeld et al., 1990).

Control also appears to be important in the effects of stress on immunity. One study found that rats exposed to escapable shock exhibited a stronger immune response than did rats exposed to inescapable shock (Laudenslager et al., 1983). In another study by Maier, Laudenslager, and Ryan (1985) natural killer (NK) cell activity was evaluated in light of the controllability of stress. Rats were exposed to escapable or inescapable shock, and the ability of NK cells to kill cancerous target cells was measured. Both stressor conditions reduced the cytotoxicity of NK cells, but inescapable stress resulted in greater suppression than did escapable stress. These and other studies suggest that control does affect a number of physiological systems and measures. However, it does so in conjunction with stress. There are few studies of control under low stress conditions. The physiological effects of control during stress are consistent with what one would expect if control were acting on response by reducing stress rather than through any effects of its own. Consequently, it is likely that these results reflect the impact of control on stress and, in turn, on the effects of stress rather than on the independent effects of control.

A number of investigators have studied the effects of perceived control on mood and the consequences of stress (see Glass and Levy, 1982). Among the first programmatic investigations of this subject was the research conducted by Glass and Singer during the late 1960s and early 1970s. Initially interested in noise as a stressor, Glass and Singer (1972) set out to document the physiological and behavioral consequences of exposure to bursts of loud, unwanted sounds. Two noise tapes were used in most of their experiments. One, with fixed intermittent bursts, presented noise to subjects at the same point in every minute. Thus, a subject listening to the fixed intermittent tape heard 9-second bursts of noise about 60 seconds apart. The occurrence of each burst was predictable. The second basic tape used varying intervals between bursts of noise and also varied the length of each burst. This random, intermittent delivery of noise was not easily predicted. Noise was heard at different times throughout each of the 20 to 25 minutes of the study, and the duration of each burst varied. The noise used was recorded at 108 decibels (dB), about what one would hear "if operating a riveting machine." No-noise conditions were measured at approximately 40 dB.

In one study Glass and Singer (1972) measured skin conductance during exposure to noise as well as the effects of the noise on task performance. Subjects reported to a laboratory and were exposed to either loud (108 dB), soft (50 dB), or no-noise (40 dB) conditions. In the noise conditions, one-half the subjects were exposed to the predictable tape and one-half to the unpredictable noise tape. Skin conductance readings showed that initially loud noise was associated with greater arousal than soft or no noise regardless of its predictability. However, as the experiment wore on, these differences disappeared. Apparently, subjects got used to the noise quickly. By the end of the experimental session there were no differences in skin conductance among the treatment conditions. These findings were replicated, extended to other measures (e.g., heart rate), and were found for different age groups (Glass and Singer, 1972). In most of these studies physiological response to the noise diminished as the session progressed.

Glass and Singer (1972) also considered the effects of noise on task performance. Three standardized tests were administered during exposure to the noise. Subjects worked on fairly simple tasks that required concentration. As with physiological measures, whatever performance effects of noise that were seen were small, appeared early in the session, and disappeared by the end of the session. Noise did not produce task performance deficits. Another study (Finkelman and Glass, 1970) indicated that when overloaded by a second task during noise exposure, subjects exposed to unpredictable noise showed poorer performance than did subjects exposed to predictable noise. By and large, however, initial investigations suggested that noise by itself did not appear to have major effects on physiological responding or task performance.

The pattern of results was very different when aftereffects were examined. As you will recall from Chapter 3, aftereffects refer to changes in behavior or performance that appear after the termination of a stressor. Glass and Singer (1972) found few effects of noise during its administration, but when performance on tasks *after the noise* was considered, more consistent effects appeared. Two types of postnoise tasks were administered. In one type subjects' tolerance for frustration and persistence was measured by asking the subjects to solve unsolvable puzzles. In the other type concentration abilities were tapped by having subjects work on a proofreading task, reading a passage to find errors that had been systematically inserted.

Subjects in the unpredictable noise conditions were less persistent and spent less time on unsolvable puzzles than were subjects in predictable noise conditions, and proofreading errors increased for those exposed to unpredictable noise. In a study reported by Glass, Singer, and Friedman (1969) subjects were exposed only to unpredictable noise. One-half the subjects were given the same treatments as before, whereas the others were led to believe that they could shut the noise off if they so desired. The subjects in this perceived control group were told about a switch on the arm of their chair that, if thrown, would stop the noise for the remainder of the session. Subjects were urged not to end the noise unless it was absolutely necessary but were told that they could terminate the noise if they wished. The perception of control over the noise was successful in reducing performance decrements following the noise. The belief that subjects could terminate the noise was associated with more persistence on the unsolvable puzzles and better proofreading scores than was exposure to the noise without perceived control (see Figure 4.3).

The perception that one has lost control that he or she once had also appears to *cause* stress. In a series of studies in college dormitories Baum and Valins (1977) found that some dormitory designs placed students in residential settings that made control over social contact difficult to maintain. In these environments small local groups did not form readily; interaction with neighbors was frequent, and often unwanted; and residents complained about a great deal of uncontrollable contact. Apparently, these students experienced difficulty in regulating when, where, and with whom they interacted. This loss

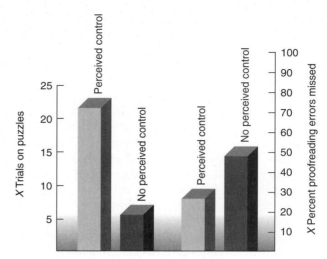

FIGURE 4.3. Perceived control over noise resulted in more persistence on the puzzles and in fewer proofreading errors than did the absence of control.
Source: Based on D. C. Glass and J. E. Singer. *Urban Stress.* New York: Academic Press, 1972. Copyright © 1972 by Academic Press, Inc., and adapted with permission.

of control over social experience was associated with withdrawal, negative affect, and a limited form of learned helplessness. The effects of prolonged exposure to uncontrollable events on students' motivation to assume control over situations outside their dormitories reflect more general consequences of loss of control.

The importance of control in mediating between environmental threats and demands on the one hand and our health on the other is also suggested by research linking controllability of stressors to diseases such as cancer. As we will see in Chapter 6, a number of behavioral factors seem to be related to cancer, and as Visintainer and Seligman (1983) note, there is substantial anecdotal evidence linking cancer with lack of control. In a study reported by Seligman and Visintainer (1985) rats were injected with live tumor cells and then put through procedures similar to Weiss's (1968) studies—one escapable stress group; one yoked, inescapable group; and one no-shock control group. Rats exposed to the inescapable condition were more likely to develop tumors and to die than were rats in the other two conditions. These differences were not small, as about 73 percent of those in the inescapable condition developed tumors whereas only one-half of the animals in the other conditions succumbed.

Another study, of long-term loss of control and the effects of early and adult experience with controllable and uncontrollable stress, exposed animals to escapable, inescapable, or no-shock conditions at an early age and/or later in life (Seligman and Visintainer, 1985). Within 1 month of birth, rats were exposed to one of the three conditions, using shock as a stressor. Each animal received four sessions of training, with escapable-condition animals yoked to inescapable-condition animals to assure comparable numbers of shocks. Then when the rats were 90 days old, all were injected with tumor cells and randomly assigned to "retraining" as adults: A third of each previous group—escapable, inescapable, no-shock as young rats—was given adult experience with escapable, inescapable, or no-shock. In this way the effects of helplessness training during childhood, as adults, or both together were evaluated.

Table 4.2 presents the percentage of animals that rejected tumors or inhibited their growth in each combination of conditions. Early helplessness training alone seemed to have little effect on adult tumor rejection, as about one-half of each group receiving no adult shock training did not develop tumors. Escapable shock during early experience appeared to enhance immune defense against tumors regardless of adult experience. Inescapable shock was associated with poorer results. When young rats were exposed to uncontrollable shock and then to either escapable or inescapable shock as adults, the rejection rate was much lower than for other animals. This was also true for animals that were given no shocks during early experience but were given inescapable shocks as adults.

Thus, early helplessness is important in determining tumor growth when uncontrollable events also occur during adulthood, and it seems to affect tumor growth when controllable events are experienced by adults as well. Only when no shocks were encountered as adults were the effects of early exposure to uncontrollable shock eliminated. Conversely, early experience with controllable shock seemed to protect the animals later: When these animals were exposed to either controllable or uncontrollable shock as adults, tumor rejection was higher than in any other conditions. Childhood experience that suggests that the world is controllable appears to "immunize" animals to the effects of adult stress but has no effects when adult experience is stress-free (Seligman and Visintainer, 1985).

LEARNED HELPLESSNESS

Control may be best thought of as a relationship between what we do and what happens to us. But what happens when control is not available—that is,

TABLE 4.2. Childhood and Adult Experience with Controllable and Uncontrollable Stress-Affected Tumor Rejection

		Early Experience		
		Escapable Shock (%)	Inescapable Shock (%)	No Shock (%)
Adult Experience	Escapable shock (%)	65	30	52
	Inescapable shock (%)	70	26	27
	No shock (%)	48	57	51

Source: Adapted from M. E. P. Seligman and M. A. Visintainer. Tumor rejection and early experience of uncontrollable shock in the rat. In F. R. Brush and J. B. Overmier (Eds.), *Affect Conditioning and Cognition: Essays on the Determinants of Behavior.* Hillsdale, NJ: Erlbaum, 1985.

when we cannot, under any conditions, gain some sense of control over what happens to us? Work by Seligman (1975) and others suggests that repeated exposure to noncontingent relationships, when our behavior and what happens appear to be independent, can cause us to become helpless. People exposed to uncontrollable conditions may learn that they cannot affect what happens and cease trying to do so. Repeated exposure to uncontrollable events "teaches" us to expect responses and outcomes to be noncontingent, and the reaction that this produces has been called **learned helplessness**.

Examples of noncontingent relationships are all around us. Try as we might, there does not seem to be anything we can do to make a certain kind of weather occur. Even washing the car does not always make it rain! But many situations do seem to be controllable, and losing control in these situations may make us feel worse than if we never had control at all!

We all know what helplessness is—the feeling that we cannot do anything, that everything we try to do ends up as failure. Psychologists have long been aware that when an individual repeatedly fails to accomplish a goal or to exert control effectively over something, he or she not only may stop trying in that setting, but also may become unresponsive in new environments where success might be more readily achieved. When a student finds that nothing he or she does seems to improve his or her grades, helplessness is likely and motivation and mood can suffer. Symptoms of this kind of experience can take many forms; among college students, for example, helplessness is associated with putting off doing their schoolwork, lower grades, and depression (McKean, 1994). More importantly, these symptoms may persist beyond the helplessness exhibited in the setting where failure occurred. Seligman (1975) argued that people can *learn to be helpless* in a number of settings, learning that their attempts to control or succeed will likely not be successful.

According to Seligman (1975), the primary cause of learned helplessness is the recognition that response and outcome are independent—that the probability of achieving a given outcome is the same whether or not responses are made. Once repeated exposure to uncontrollable events has caused the organism to learn that the outcomes cannot be affected, responding ceases. As an example, consider a common procedure used for experimentally inducing learned helplessness. You are in a situation in which aversive stimulation (e.g., noise, electric shock) is being administered. The stimulation is completely unavoidable; although there are a number of buttons and levers for you to push, nothing you do prevents the noise or shock from being delivered. After several trials you learn that there is nothing that you can do to change the outcomes of each trial, and thus you stop trying. For the remainder of the session you passively accept the noxious stimulation.

It is not surprising that you would stop trying to control the noise or shock in such a situation. What is surprising, and of potentially greater harm, is the fact that this passivity can generalize to other settings. Experiences with uncontrollable events seem to affect motivation and cognitive ability in other settings as well as in the situation in which it was first learned.

Seligman (1975) conducted a great deal of research on the learned helplessness phenomenon. Early work with animals showed that lack or loss of control can have serious behavioral consequences. **Noncontingent** relationships between response and outcomes were associated with passivity in dogs (see

Overmier and Seligman, 1967; Seligman, Maier, and Geer, 1967). Typical of these studies was a situation in which a dog was given unavoidable electric shocks while confined in a harness. This uncontrollable trauma was followed by a test phase in which the dog was placed in a two-chambered cell and electric shocks were again administered. In this second phase, however, the dog could control the trauma since it could escape the shock by jumping into the other chamber. Usually, dogs exposed to uncontrollable shock first did not learn this escape behavior, remaining passive and continuing to endure the shock.

This kind of helplessness conditioning, where learning that one cannot affect outcomes, has also been explored with human subjects. These studies have largely been conducted in the laboratory, and as a result, may not be indicative of true helplessness conditioning. However, research has demonstrated that real-world helplessness conditioning does occur (Barlow, 1988; Baum, Aiello, and Calesnick, 1978; Mineka and Kelly, 1989). These studies have found evidence of motivational loss, emotional disturbance, and cognitive impairment as a function of repeated exposure to an uncontrollable situation. Hiroto and Seligman (1975) and Krantz, Glass, and Snyder (1974) conducted studies in which human subjects were placed in settings analogous to the training situations used to study dogs, namely, exposure to controllable or uncontrollable noise. In subsequent test phases, where all subjects could control the noise, those who had been exposed to controllable noise in the first part of the study quickly learned to control it in the second part. Subjects exposed to uncontrollable noise initially were unable to solve the situation and to learn to control the noise; most of them sat passively while the noise continued. Glass and Singer (1972) also reported evidence of helplessness as a result of exposure to uncontrollable noise. As you will recall, uncontrollable noise caused aftereffects. Subjects were less persistent on unsolvable puzzles when they had been exposed to uncontrollable or unpredictable noise.

Consequences of Learned Helplessness

More research needs to be conducted to determine whether helplessness can have serious effects on people in real settings. However, it appears that helplessness is a real problem among the elderly and among people with chronic illnesses (see Daltroy and Liang, 1991; Kane, 1991). There are case studies that suggest that helplessness can have serious consequences (see boxes "Hopelessness and Death," Case Example 1 and Case Example 2), and data collected by Baum, Aiello, and Davis (1979) indicate that helplessness may interfere with seeking help from doctors and heighten sensitivity to symptoms. Other studies show that learned helplessness can interfere with recovery from brain and spinal cord injuries, can reduce quality of life following injury, and can slow one's recovery from surgery (see Chovaz et al., 1994; Moore and Stambrook, 1995). Research at the Los Angeles International Airport has also suggested that uncontrollable aircraft noise is associated with helplessness and poorer health among children (see Cohen et al., 1986).

One consistent finding is that elderly people living in nursing homes or long-term care facilities are vulnerable to learned helplessness (Barder, Slimmer, and Le Sage, 1994) (see Figure 4.4). Short-term care is not as likely to cause

FIGURE 4.4. Nursing homes and other institutions for the elderly or infirm often reduce residents' sense of control and responsibility to low levels. This loss of control can cause helplessness. Adjusting to changes in these environments can be stressful as well.
Source: Ursula Markus/Photo Researchers

symptoms of helplessness, but residing in these settings for 7 weeks or more was (Barder et al., 1994). Research on relocation of the elderly has also shown effects of control and helplessness. When older people were moved from familiar surroundings to unfamiliar ones, especially in institutions, negative consequences were common (see Schulz and Brenner, 1977). The more similar the old and new environments were, the less severe were the consequences (Schulz and Aderman, 1973; Schulz and Brenner, 1977; Shrut, 1965). If steps are taken to provide a greater sense of control over a new environment, such as making people responsible for some aspect of the environment or providing them with information about it, helplessness appears to be minimized and health is improved (see Krantz and Schulz, 1980; Langer and Rodin, 1976; Rodin and Langer, 1977).

Seligman (1975) has argued that learned helplessness may also be associated with depression. There are a number of parallels between helplessness and depression, and since the kinds of events that produce depression are similar to those that cause helplessness, Seligman believed that the two may be linked. Both are characterized by *passive behavior, negative expectations* ("I won't be able to do this"), and *hopelessness*. Seligman believed that helplessness may, in fact, be one *cause* of depression. Generally, depressed people have failed on a number of occasions: They may have lost a job, experienced rejection, or lost control over their lives. This kind of learning history could result in a conditioned helplessness as well as a depressed mood. Thus, helplessness training may contribute to the development of depression.

Although links between helplessness and depression do appear to exist, the relationship is far more complex than research initially suggested. A great deal of work by Seligman (1975) and others (Beck, 1976; Cohen and Tennen, 1985; Peterson, Rosenbaum, and Conn, 1985; Rizley, 1978) has indicated that depression and helplessness are related, and a number of reformulations of the helplessness theory have appeared to allow incorporation of some of the known cognitive determinants of depression. Klein and Seligman (1976) compared depressed subjects with nondepressed subjects. Subjects were pretreated with escapable, inescapable, or no-noise conditions. Following experience with noise, they were presented with solvable problems. Performance on the second task was poorer for nondepressed subjects when noise was inescapable. Depressed subjects given no helplessness training performed equally poorly. Both depressed subjects and nondepressed subjects given helplessness training showed poorer performance than did participants who were exposed to escapable or no-noise conditions.

Weaker evidence of similarities between helplessness and depression was reported by Gatchel, McKinney, and Koebernick (1977). While depressed, subjects exhibited poorer performance on the test task regardless of pretraining with controllable or uncontrollable outcomes. Untreated, depressed subjects performed much like nondepressed subjects after helplessness training. However, reductions in skin conductance were observed among helpless subjects, whereas increases in skin conductance appeared among depressed subjects. Despite behavioral similarities between helplessness and depression, the investigators concluded that there may be different underlying processes and deficits for each subject.

Research on depressed patients indicates other similarities to depression. Some features of helplessness appear to be related to neuroendocrine symptoms of depression (Samson et al., 1992), but studies of noncollege populations have provided mixed results. Some suggest that depression and helplesslike behavior are not related, whereas others provide evidence of such a link (see Greer and Calhoun, 1983; O'Leary et al., 1978). The best evidence of a link between helplessness and depression is provided by studies of attributions and explanatory styles (see the next section).

Some studies have since found evidence of helplessness conditioning following exposure to uncontrollable *positive* events, consistent with the idea that contingency is the crucial determinant of learned helplessness (see Tennen and Eller, 1977). One study found that noncontingent feedback while playing a video game generated symptoms of learned helplessness among college students (Fox and Oakes, 1984). However, research on helplessness has not always conformed closely with Seligman's (1975) initial formulations. For example, Roth and Bootzin (1974) observed performance on a test task after subjects had been pretreated with contingent, noncontingent (random), or no reinforcement of their responses. Unexpectedly, those receiving noncontingent reinforcement exhibited better performance on the second task and reported greater feelings of control than did the other subjects. Roth and Bootzin (1974) concluded that they had violated the subjects' expectations of being able to

Hopelessness and Death
Case Example 1

When in early 1973 medical army officer Major F. Harold Kushner returned from 5½ years as a prisoner of war in South Vietnam, he told me a stark and chilling tale. His story represents one of the few cases on record in which a trained medical observer witnessed from start to finish what I can only call death from helplessness.

Major Kushner was shot down in a helicopter in North Vietnam in November 1967. He was captured, seriously wounded, by the Viet Cong. He spent the next 3 years in a hell called First Camp. Through the camp passed 27 Americans: 5 were released by the Viet Cong, 10 died in the camp, and 12 survived to be released from Hanoi in 1973. The camp's conditions beggar description. At any time there were about 11 men who lived in a bamboo hut, sleeping on one crowded bamboo bed about 16 feet across. The basic diet was three small cups of red, rotten, vermin-infested rice a day. Within the first year the average prisoner lost 40 to 50 percent of his body weight and acquired running sores and atrophied muscles. There were two prominent killers: malnutrition and helplessness. When Kushner was first captured, he was asked to make antiwar statements. He said that he would rather die, and his captor responded with words Kushner remembered every day of his captivity: "Dying is easy; it's living that's hard." The will to live, and the catastrophic consequences of the loss of hope, are the theme of Kushner's story. . . .

When Major Kushner arrived at First Camp in January 1968, Robert had already been a captive for 2 years. He was a rugged and intelligent corporal from a crack marine unit, austere, stoic, and oblivious to pain and suffering. He was 24 years old and had been trained as a parachutist and a scuba diver. Like the rest of the men, he was down to a weight of 90 pounds and was forced to make long, shoeless treks daily with 90 pounds of manioc root on his back. He never griped. "Grit your teeth and tighten your belt," he used to repeat. Despite malnutrition and a terrible skin disease, he remained in very good phyical and mental health. The cause of his relatively fine shape was clear to Kushner. Robert was convinced that he would soon be released. The Viet Cong had made it a practice to release, as examples, a few men who had cooperated with them and adopted the correct attitudes. Robert had done so, and the camp

commander had indicated that he was next in line for release, to come in 6 months.

As expected, 6 months later, the event occurred that had preceded these token releases in the past. A very high-ranking Viet Cong cadre appeared to give the prisoners a political course; it was understood that the outstanding pupil would be released. Robert was chosen as leader of the thought-reform group. He made the statements required and was told to expect release within the month.

The month came and went, and he began to sense a change in the guards' attitude toward him. Finally, it dawned on him that he had been deceived—that is, he had already served his captor's purpose, and he was not going to be released. He stopped working and showed signs of severe depression: He refused food and lay on his bed in a fetal position, sucking his thumb. His fellow prisoners tried to bring him around. They hugged him, babied him, and, when this didn't work, they tried to bring him out of his stupor with their fists. He defecated and urinated in the bed. After a few weeks it was apparent to Kushner that Robert was moribund: although otherwise his gross physical shape was still better than most of the others, he was dusky and cyanotic.

In the early hours of a November morning he lay dying in Kushner's arms. For the first time in days his eyes focused and he spoke: "Doc, Post Office Box 161, Texarkana, Texas. Mom, Dad, I love you very much. Barbara, I forgive you." Within seconds, he was dead.

Robert's was typical of a number of such deaths that Major Kushner saw. What killed him? Kushner could not perform an autopsy, since the Viet Cong allowed him no surgical tools. To Kushner's eyes the immediate cause was "gross electrolytic imbalance." But given Robert's relatively good physical state, psychological precursors rather than physiological state seem to be a more specifiable cause of death. Hope of release sustained Robert. When he gave up hope, when he believed that all his efforts had failed and would continue to fail, he died.

A 76-year-old former horse trader, gambler, and adventurer had been admitted to the hospital in 1957 in a state of severe emaciation and with signs of taboparesis. His physical condition improved with treatment, but he remained confined to a chair or to a walker. He also had a chronic urinary infection, which proved resistant to treatment. His peevish, complaining attitude, constant demands, competition with and provocation of other patients, and cunning attempts to test the personnel made him a management problem. At the same time, several members of the team had a certain liking for this unusual patient. He showed strong, though ambivalent, attachment to the nurse, the charge aide, and the physician. It was possible to handle him only by a well-coordinated, rigid system of privileges and controls.

After the fire, this patient was transferred to the neurological ward where his former special privileges (such as providing him with cartons of milk at certain hours each day) and controls could not be maintained. The patient appeared dejected and sad. He did not express his bitter anger as usual and usually answered when addressed. Two weeks after the fire, he was found dead and the diagnosis was probably myocardial infarction. Autopsy was not performed.

Although the patient had been undernourished and feeble, there was nothing to indicate a critical condition and his death came as a complete surprise. Death was classified as "unexpected."

control the situation by providing random feedback and may have aroused reactance (Brehm, 1966) rather than conditioned helplessness. Since reactance is a purposive, control-seeking response to threats to one's freedom and sense of control, such an interpretation has persisted and has been incorporated into a number of investigations.

Wortman and Brehm (1975) formalized this notion when they proposed that helplessness is mediated by *expectations* for control. Initial exposure to uncontrollable outcomes will arouse reactance as long as an individual expects to be able to control the outcomes. Reactance is often a highly aroused state, where control or regaining freedom is an overriding concern and affect is likely to be angry and hostile. Thus, as long as we expect to control things in the situation, we will be reactant. However, with repeated exposure to uncontrollable outcomes, we may come to believe that we will not be able to control things in the situation and our expectations for control decrease. At this point helplessness is more likely. As reactance fades with waning expectations for control, purposeful behavior fades into more helpless behavior.

According to this model, people first resist loss of control and become helpless only when they have exhausted their ability to regain control. Our use of "resist" and "exhaust" here is not coincidental since Wortman and Brehm's (1975) description of helplessness is similar to Selye's description of stress. The similarity between these processes suggests that loss of control may serve as a stressor under some conditions and that helplessness may be an outcome of stress.

Research has been generally supportive of this model of developing helplessness. Pittman and Pittman (1979) found that expectations for control were related to whether subjects were reactant or helpless, and Baum et al. (1978) found that helplessness in college dormitories developed in ways that closely approximate Wortman and Brehm's (1975) description. Initial experience with uncontrollable events in the dormitories was associated with an angry, reactancelike response. This persisted for several weeks. However, after 7 weeks of residence, cumulative experience with uncontrollable social outcomes led to diminishing expectations for control and more helplesslike responding.

Attribution and Learned Helplessness

Application of the helplessness theory to humans required change and elaboration of the original theory to take into account greater complexity and range of human cognitive and coping advantages. For example, Abramson, Seligman, and Teasdale (1978) suggested that helplessness conditioning was affected by cognitive and attributional factors. They argued that when helplessness is being conditioned, people think about and attribute their lack of control or their inability to solve a problem to one or more of a number of possible causes. The degree to which helplessness is perceived to be personal—caused by one's own failings or lack of skill—or universal—caused by external factors such as the environment or the task itself—was one important dimension. Attributing lack of control to one's own failings and assuming personal responsibility for failure may cause more damage to self-esteem than will placing blame on other people or on the environment. None of us can control everything. There are many things, such as wanting immortality, that do not condition a generalized helplessness among most people because they are generally regarded to be beyond everyone's control. Thus, although specific behaviors may cease with either personal or universal helplessness, personal helplessness may be more costly.

An example can illustrate this distinction. Consider your reaction to a particularly difficult class. The subject is interesting and the classes seem to go well, but you have been unable to get a passing grade on any exams, quizzes, or papers. How should you respond? There are a number of cues in the setting that help. For example, if everyone you know in the class is having the same problem, the loss of control is more *universal* and less likely to be due to your personal failings. However, if everyone else is doing well in the class and you are the only one who is failing, the loss of control is more *personally caused*. Your reactions to these two situations may seem to be the same, though you might try harder in the situation characterized by your personal failure. Even if you gave up and stopped working hard under both circumstances, though, the reasons are probably different. If no one can get the material and pass the course, you may decide it is not worth the effort because the tests are too difficult or the course requirements are not within anyone else's reach either. However, if everyone else is having success, your failure may harm your self-esteem and suggest that you are not able to keep up. This could also undermine your confidence and performance in other courses.

Abramson and her colleagues (1978) also suggested that people distinguish between global and specific causes of helplessness—that is, whether uncontrollable events persist in a number of situations or are limited to only one or two. Global helplessness may be more debilitating, as its effects will generalize and characterize a number of settings. Judgments of *stability* are also made. The degree to which failure or lack of control is due to lack of ability—a stable characteristic that is difficult to change—or to lack of effort—an unstable, more easily changed characteristic—will affect helplessness. Stable character or environmental attributions will lead to more persistent helplessness since loss of control is expected to occur in more different places.

Evidence indicates that cognitive factors are important in the conditioning of helplessness at least some of the time. The notion that people have different tendencies or styles of making attributions is appealing because it helps to explain response to ambiguous situations in which control is not available (Seligman et al., 1979). When faced with a situation in which there are no clear causes, some people may tend to attribute events to internal causes, whereas others may be predisposed toward external attributions. Similarly, people may exhibit tendencies to attribute causes to global or specific events. Studies have shown that this individual difference variable affects the generalization of helplessness to new situations (Alloy et al., 1984; Mikulincer, 1986). Other studies offer varying degrees of support for the notion that varying the likely causes of failure to control a situation can have different effects on subsequent efforts to exert control (see Pillow et al., 1991; Wortman and Dintzer, 1978). In addition, attributional style is associated with symptoms of depression and school achievement among children (Donovan and Leavitt, 1985; Nolen-Hoeksema, Girgus, and Seligman, 1986).

Increased exposure to lack of control may sensitize people to the fact that some situations are not controllable and lead to reduced expectations and shortened "reactance" periods during future encounters with challenging or uncontrollable situations (see Baum and Gatchel, 1981). This is consistent with the finding that helplessness conditioning does not necessarily result in lower perceived control but, instead, may lead to higher and in some cases more accurate judgments of control during the helplessness training (Ford and Neale, 1985). It is also consistent with the cognitive exhaustion model of helplessness that predicts that people will not expend effort on tasks after exposure to uncontrollable situations (Sedek, Kofta, and Tsyzka, 1993). Research has further suggested that personally attributed loss of control or failure has facilitating effects rather than helpless effects.

Explanatory Style, Control, and Helplessness

The tendency for people to attribute negative or uncontrollable events to particular causes is called *explanatory style*. For example, depressive explanatory styles are characterized by consistent attributions for failure to stable, personal factors such as one's intelligence or personality. People with this explanatory style expect failure in most situations, in part because they attribute failure to conditions that are always present. Students with this kind of attributional tendency are more likely to become depressed than are students who do not exhibit these tendencies (Alloy et al., 1984; Metalsky et al., 1987), but these relationships do not always hold up. This attributional style is also associated with anxiety disorders (Heimberg et al., 1989) and in some cases the nature of negative events is more important in determining whether people become depressed than their attributions for these events (Hammen et al., 1989). Other studies suggest that stable, personal attributions for failure may be a result of rather than a cause of depression (Lewinsohn, Hoberman, and Rosenbaum, 1988). It is also possible that these negative explanatory styles are initially produced by depression but come to characterize one's outlook and cause depression in the future (Nolen-Hoeksema et al., 1992).

Explanatory styles are probably related to a number of other personal variables that affect health and illness. Anger, hostility, emotional suppression, fatalism, and pessimism are all thought to affect disease processes and health-related behaviors (see Scheier and Bridges, 1995). Together they can alter or bias the ways in which people view stressors, interpret what happens in their lives, and react to illness. In addition, they appear to affect the kinds of coping strategies that people use when exposed to stress. Anger and hostile styles may predispose people to view things as threats or as challenges to their sense of control, or to interpret unintended events as being intentional. (These styles are discussed in Chapter 5 and will not be described here.) These perceptions then help to determine emotional and behavioral responses and, ultimately, the outcome of each encounter with a stressor. These styles or tendencies are thought of as habitual reactions to changes in one's environment that affect appraisal of and response to stressful encounters. One of the more promising areas of research in health psychology is research on optimism and pessimism, appraisal and coping styles that appear to have strong effects on health-related behaviors and on disease.

OPTIMISM AND PESSIMISM

Research on the effects of being optimistic or pessimistic has grown rapidly and has taken several approaches. One early analysis focused on *unrealistic optimism,* or favorable outlooks that have no basis in reality (Weinstein, 1982, 1987). In one study undergraduates were asked to rate their risk of several health problems, including alcoholism, diabetes, skin cancer, and heart disease. Students rated their risk for about 75 percent of these problems as being lower than for other students, reporting that they were at greater risk only for developing ulcers (Weinstein, 1982). Older participants in a similar study showed the same optimistic bias in rating their risk of developing these diseases (Weinstein, 1987) and others have reported similar optimistic biases (see Peterson and DeAvila, 1995). Clearly, all people are not at lower risk for all health problems, so these findings suggested a bias or tendency to diminish one's own risk of illness.

One can argue that optimism is good, and as we will see, research indicates that it has benefits for people who are exposed to illness. However, if one maintains such optimistic views of health threats when the information he or she has is not consistent with this, problems can occur. People may rate their risk of heart disease or breast cancer as being low, but if this outlook persists in the face of chest pains or a lump in one's breast, proper interpretation of these symptoms may be suppressed and disease may go undetected. Clearly, unrealistic optimism may be harmful. Fortunately, many people do not remain optimistic about disease threats when they are ill or have been exposed to illness (Kulik and Mahler, 1987).

This raises questions about how important these optimistic biases really are and about differences in how strong people's beliefs about their risk of disease tend to be. If people change so readily when confronted with evidence of illness or exposure to its causes, how strong is this style anyway? Of course, most of the things that we do that turn out to affect our health are done while we are feeling healthy. Consistent with this, unrealistic optimism can reduce routine preventive and healthy behaviors that might otherwise be preferred.

Another view of optimism is less concerned with evaluation of one's risk for disease, focusing instead on broader expectations and ways of appraising what happens to people. In this view optimism reflects a fundamental bias to view the world as benign, controllable, and likely to yield positive outcomes. In this case optimism goes well beyond how people view their chance of becoming ill, referring to a tendency to see the world as a benevolent place and to look at the good side of things rather than to dwell on the negative.

This more global view of **optimism**, as well as its opposite, **pessimism**, has received a lot of research attention as a factor in coping and illness (see Horowitz et al., 1988; Mraczek et al., 1993). Most of this work has used a simple scale, the Life Orientation Test (LOT), to measure these styles. The LOT was developed by Scheier and Carver (1985) and consists of eight items, all designed to distinguish optimistic biases from more pessimistic ones. A quick look at some of these items is instructive and illustrates what their idea of optimism is. Statements like "In uncertain times, I usually expect the best," "I always look on the bright side of things," and "I'm always optimistic about my future" clearly reflect a positive world view, whereas items like "If something can go wrong for me, it will" and "Things never work out the way I want them to" depict a less confident, more pessimistic orientation (Scheier and Carver, 1985).

Implicit in this distinction are differences in perceived control or self-efficacy. To some extent positive outcomes are more likely for the optimist because he or she is able to make them come out that way. In contrast, pessimism is associated with less perceived control or correspondence between the way things work out and the way they "should have." For whatever reason, it seems reasonable to assume that optimists have stronger expectations that they can control their experiences than do pessimists.

Another important difference between optimists and pessimists is in how they cope with stress. Studies of college students have suggested that optimists are more likely to try to change the situation or to take direct problem-focused action against a stressor than are pessimists (Scheier, Weintraub, and Carver, 1986). Similar effects on coping have been observed in studies of traumatic stress, life-threatening illnesses or surgery, and other stressful situations (see Dougall et al., 1996; Scheier and Bridges, 1995; Scheier et al., 1989).

Research generally suggests that it is good to be optimistic. In one study optimism was associated with shorter hospital stays and better outcomes of coronary artery bypass surgery than was a more pessimistic outlook (Scheier et al., 1989). A study of rheumatoid arthritis patients and their caregivers also showed that optimism was associated with greater self-efficacy and patients' beliefs in their ability to control arthritis symptoms (Beckham et al., 1995). Pessimism has also been related to rumination, a cognitive style marked by continuous or repetitive thoughts about stressors or negative events (Nolen-Hoeksema, Parker, and Larson, 1994). In this study rumination was, in turn, related to lower levels of social support, greater stress burden, and high levels of depression. Pessimists are also more frequent users of health care services, view their risk of being exposed to life-threatening illnesses as very high, and adjust more poorly to diagnosis and treatment of breast cancer (Carver et al., 1994; Colligan et al., 1994; Fontaine, 1994).

The reasons for these effects are not yet clear although several hypotheses are being evaluated. As we have suggested, optimistic styles are related to perceived control and self-efficacy, which are also associated with more positive health outcomes. Similarly, these styles are related to particular kinds of coping responses in stressful situations, and these specific forms of coping are often more effective in helping people to deal with stress (see Carver et al., 1993; Scheier and Bridges, 1995). Pessimistic styles are also associated with depression and sadness, and the experience of sadness appears to make us view events as being beyond our control (Keltner, Ellsworth, and Edwards, 1993). Other evidence indicates that worriers tend to be more pessimistic and this, together with evidence linking pessimism with rumination, suggests the possibility that cognitive styles might contribute to differences between optimism and pessimism (see MaCleod, Williams, and Bekevian, 1991). The results of future research showing how optimism and pessimism exert their effects will underscore the important implications of integrative concepts that predict many aspects of health behavior and disease outcomes.

HARDINESS

A very different coping style or way of viewing the world is *hardiness*. Sometimes thought of as a personality style, hardiness refers to the belief that people have control over what happens to them, a strong sense of purpose or commitment to achieving particular goals, and an enduring "zest" for challenge (see Kobasa et al., 1982). Hardy people tend to be healthier than less hardy people in part because they can deal more effectively with stressors and stress (Kobasa, 1979). When confronted with a stressful situation, hardy people more effectively solve problems and are better at reappraising negative conditions as positive ones (see Contrada, 1989; Gentry and Kobasa, 1984; Williams, Wiebe, and Smith, 1992). In addition, hardiness appears to be correlated with social support, suggesting that hardiness may be a product of having good support and a strong sense of self-efficacy (Blaney and Ganellen, 1990). However, studies in which hardiness, social support, and health-protecting behaviors (e.g., exercise) were measured simultaneously indicate that hardiness is an independent factor in illness outcomes (see Kobasa et al., 1982, 1985). In one study hardiness seemed to protect against illness better than exercise or social support, but the three combined offered the most protection (see Kobasa et al., 1985) (see Table 4.3).

Hardiness appears to be important in protection from disease and is associated with more rapid and successful adjustment to a number of stressful situations. It is similar to observations of special qualities of some children, termed *resilience*. Resilience reflects the fact that some kids show an enhanced ability to deal with a stressor, quickly "shake it off," and return to "normal" while waiting for the next challenge (see Garmezy, 1983). This quality appears to affect

TABLE 4.3. Illness as a Function of the Number of Resistance Resources among Subjects High in Stressful Life Events

Resistance Resources, 1980	*n*		*Mean Illness*		*Illness Probability*	
	1980	1981	1980[b]	1981[c]	1980[d]	1981[a]
All three high	13	13	357.04	601.46	7.69	23.11
Two high	26	22	2049.27	1702.13	57.69	50.00
One high	32	24	3336.18	2715.58	71.87	62.50
None high	14	11	6474.35	5635.91	92.85	81.80

[a]The entries indicate the percentage of subjects in the various resistance resource categories falling above the illness median for all 71 subjects.
[b]For entries in this column, $F = 8.38$ ($p < 0.0001$).
[c]For entries in this column, $F = 4.94$ ($p < 0.003$).
[d]For entries in this column, Kandall's $Tau_C = 0.52$ ($p < 0.0001$).
[e]For entries in this column, Kandall's $Tau_C = 0.39$ ($p < 0.001$).
Source: Adapted with permission from Kobasa et al. Effectiveness of hardiness, exercise and social support as resources against illness. *Psychosomatic Research*, 1985, *29*(5), 529.

the quality of children's adjustment to serious stressors or previously experienced adverse conditions (see Werner, 1987). It is also similar to *stamina*, a term used to describe resiliency in old age. People with more stamina, characterized by a "triumphant, positive outlook" appear to cope with setbacks and stressors more effectively than do people who lack stamina (Colerick, 1985). Finally, hardiness is similar to self-efficacy because the commitment and sense of challenge that are part of the style or personality are products of one's sense of self-efficacy. Support for achieving a sense of autonomy is related to health behavior among adolescents (Turner et al., 1993) and may affect other behaviors as well. How all of these control-related elements fit together to predict how well people do when confronted by adversity remains to be studied. However, it is clear now that these control-related coping or explanatory styles are important and may offer some clues for ways to reverse helplessness.

SUMMARY

The role of perceived control as a determinant of stress is important in considering the effects of stress on health and well-being. The consistent finding that perceived control is associated with fewer or less severe consequences of exposure to stressors suggests that uncontrollable stressors are more likely to affect health adversely. The related findings that loss or lack of control can be a cause of stress further highlights the importance of considering control. Some studies have begun to identify instances in which control influences health outcomes. Coping and attribution of blame or responsibility appear to be related to perceptions of control and to illusions of control.

Research on learned helplessness suggests a number of links to health and illness. Prolonged or repeated exposure to settings or situations in which people have little or no control appears to be associated with reduced motivation, emotional disturbance, and cognitive impairment. Although the reasons for this are not clear and the ways in which helplessness is conditioned have not been clearly established, there is some evidence that helplessness occurs in natural settings as well as in the laboratory. When helplessness is minimized by enhancing an individual's sense of control, health outcomes appear to improve. One outcome of research on helplessness was the idea that the way that people explain things (explanatory style) affects their reactions to stressors and loss of control. Pessimism, optimism, and hardiness are explanatory styles or dispositions that appear to affect health and health behaviors.

RECOMMENDED READINGS

Abramson, L. Y., Seligman, M. E. P., and Teasdale, J. Learned helplessness in humans: Critique and reformulation. *Journal of Abnormal Psychology,* 1978, *87,* 49–74.

Mikulincer, M. Human learned helplessness: A coping perspective. Plenum Press: New York, 1994.

Peterson, C., Maier, S. F., Seligman, M. E. P. Learned helplessness: A theory for the age of personal control. New York: Oxford University Press. 1993.

Steptoe, A., and Appels, A. Stress, personal control and health. John Wiley and Sons: Chichester, England. 1989.

Wortman, C. B., and Brehm, J. W. Responses to uncontrollable outcomes: An integration of reactance theory and the learned helplessness model. In L. Berkowitz (Ed.), *Advances in experimental social psychology,* vol. 8. New York: Academic Press, 1975.

Cardiovascular Disorders and Behavior

Cardiovascular disorders, including coronary heart disease, high blood pressure, and stroke, are a major public health problem and are the leading cause of death in the United States and other Western societies (Higgins and Luepker, 1988; NHLBI, 1994) (see Table 1.2). In 1990, 720,058 U.S. deaths were caused by heart disease, compared with 505,322 deaths due to cancer. We have mentioned them often as examples of changing health threats and of diseases that are influenced by stress and behavior. Many physiological, environmental, and behavioral variables interact in the development of these diseases. For example, coronary heart disease (CHD) is a disorder that is a result of the individual's lifestyle; many of the causal agents can be modified, are related to habits of living, and are under the control of the individual. It is, therefore, not surprising that these cardiovascular disorders are widely studied topics in health psychology (Krantz, Grunberg, and Baum, 1985).

In the past 25 years there has been encouraging news that death rates from heart disease have been decreasing (NHLBI, 1994). These changes are due in part to dramatic medical developments such as drugs and improvements in medical technology. Heart transplant technology, bypass surgery, angioplasty, and drug therapies reflect recent advances in the biomedical treatment of the disease. At the same time, there is a new awareness of behaviors that are risk factors and attempts by individuals to modify risk factors for heart disease. Goldman and Cook (1988), for example, used the epidemiologic literature to estimate that about 40 percent of the reduction in cardiovascular mortality was due to improvements in medical care, such as drug treatments for high blood pressure and improvements in cardiac care. However, more than one-half the decline in death rates from CHD (54 percent) could be attributed to lifestyle changes, such as changes in fat consumption and cholesterol levels (30 percent), and reductions in cigarette smoking (24 percent). These data reinforce the important link between individual lifestyle and the risk of coronary disease.

136

CHAPTER 5
Cardiovascular
Disorders and
Behavior

CORONARY HEART DISEASE

As noted in Chapter 2, the heart muscle, like other organs, needs a supply of blood. Blood to the heart is delivered through the coronary arteries, which can become narrowed by fatty deposits, a condition called **atherosclerosis,** which is popularly known as "hardening of the arteries." **Coronary heart disease** refers to a set of conditions that are thought to result from coronary atherosclerosis. As the buildup (or *plaque*) on the inner coronary artery walls becomes hard and thick, it is more difficult for the blood to move through the narrowed vessels (see Figure 5.1). If the plaque becomes unstable and a complete blockage occurs, the result may be a heart attack or **myocardial infarction** (MI), which occurs when part of the heart does not get enough oxygen and other nutrients and begins to die. Sometimes the narrowing of the artery is not complete and some oxygen, but not enough, is supplied to the heart. This state reflects **myocardial ischemia**, which is at times accompanied by chest pain—a condition called **angina pectoris**. Myocardial ischemic episodes may become frequent and lead to MI.

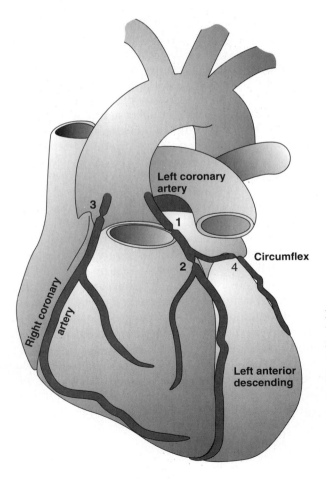

FIGURE 5.1. The coronary arteries: four points of narrowing due to atherosclerosis.
Source: Adapted from M. Franklin, M. Krauthamer, A. R. Tai, and A. Pinchot. *The Heart Doctors' Heart Book.* New York: Grosset and Dunlap, 1974. Reprinted with permission.

A coronary risk factor is a characteristic of the population or of the environment that increases an individual's likelihood of developing cardiovascular disease. Numerous studies by epidemiologists over the past 40 years have established a set of physical risk factors for CHD (see Table 5.1).

The more risk factors that individuals have, the greater is their likelihood of developing heart disease, and those who are likely to develop CHD can be identified with a moderate degree of accuracy.

Nonmodifiable Factors

Several of the coronary risk factors cannot be controlled. These include chronological age, sex, race, and family history. Unfortunately, the longer someone lives, the greater is his or her likelihood of developing heart disease because there is more time for plaque to accumulate in arteries. Nearly one-half of all coronary victims are over the age of 65. Throughout most of their lives, and especially at younger ages, men are at greater CHD risk than women, apparently because of protective effects of estrogen and other female sex hormones (Lerner and Kannel, 1986). In the United States African-Americans are more likely to develop CHD than whites, and this may be related to the fact that they are more susceptible to high blood pressure than are white Americans: High blood pressure is a major CHD risk factor. Last, but not least, among nonmodifiable risk factors is family history. Susceptibility to CHD can be transmitted genetically, and certain families appear to be at higher risk than others.

Modifiable factors

It is important to see, however, that even if individuals fall into the higher risk groups because they possess these noncontrollable traits, they can still minimize their risk by modifying certain habits. For example, cigarette smoking is a preventable behavior. The death rate from heart attack is higher among people who smoke than among people who do not smoke (see Ockene and Ockene, 1992). However, for those who give up the habit the death rate

TABLE 5.1. Risk Factors for Coronary Heart Disease

Nonmodifiable	Modifiable
► Age	► Hypertension
► Sex (being male)	► High low-density lipoproteins and low high-density lipoprotein levels
► Family history	► Cigarette smoking
	► Diabetes
	► Obesity
	► Sedentary lifestyle
	► Hostility and related personality traits
	► Psychosocial stress

begins to decrease almost to the level of those who have never smoked (Higgins and Luepker, 1988). Apparently, the pathophysiologic effects of smoking can be reversed.

High salt intake and obesity are other kinds of behaviorally related factors that can contribute to high blood pressure in some individuals, and thereby contribute to heart disease (Ockene and Ockene, 1992). Physicians have incorporated this information into their treatment of hypertensive patients by recommending that people with mild blood pressure elevations begin a program of dietary salt restriction or weight reduction before undergoing treatment with blood pressure-reducing drugs. High blood cholesterol is another major CHD risk factor that is partly related to dietary behavior. The body manufactures cholesterol, but also gets it from what the person eats. Therefore, a diet that is low in cholesterol and saturated fats will help to lower the level of blood cholesterol and to reduce this modifiable risk factor.

In the Seven Countries Study (Keys, 1980) a significant relationship between diet and heart disease was found. Greater intake of saturated fat and cholesterol were related to the risk of death from heart disease. Other international studies in several populations have shown similar associations (see Ockene and Ockene, 1992). Despite extensive research on the epidemiology of heart disease, there is still controversy as to the importance of such factors as diet and exercise in the development of coronary disease. For example, some studies have not found that dietary patterns within the population are predictive of later development of heart disease (Mann, 1977). Generally, the least controversial and most widely accepted risk factors are considered to be smoking, levels of cholesterol in the blood, and high blood pressure (Kannel et al., 1979).

Psychosocial Risk Factors

Behavioral scientists became interested in CHD for at least two reasons. First, as noted earlier, many standard risk factors involve behaviors that can be altered. Smoking is a potentially modifiable behavior, and high blood pressure, obesity, and serum cholesterol levels can be influenced by changes in diet and eating behaviors. Second, despite extensive research into the standard physiological risk factors, the best combinations of these factors still do not take into account the occurrence of heart disease in many individuals. The search has been broadened to examine interactions of potential new risk factors, social and psychological characteristics, and characteristics of the environment (Jenkins, 1983; Krantz, Baum, and Singer, 1983). Of these, we will discuss three active areas of research on behavior and cardiovascular disorders: (1) **chronic and acute stress** and factors such as **social support** that can moderate the effects of stress on cardiovascular pathology; (2) personality traits, such as hostility, anger, and Type A behavior, that may be risk factors for CHD, and depression, which can lead to poor prognosis in cardiac patients; and (3) individual differences in physiologic **reactivity** (responsiveness) to behavioral stressors.

Stress and Coronary Heart Disease

Stress appears to contribute to CHD in a number of ways, from triggering MIs or other cardiac events to the gradual buildup of plaque in blood vessels and changes in clotting properties of the blood. The most dramatic ways are acute stressors that set off cardiac episodes in susceptible individuals.

Acute Stress as a Cardiac Disease Trigger

Several studies have explored the relationship of stressful life events to the occurrence of MI and/or sudden cardiac death (see Krantz et al., 1996 for review). For example, Myers and Dewar (1975) observed that stressful life events were reported to have occurred among 40 of 100 sudden death victims in the 24 hours preceding death. Similarly, Cottington et al. (1980) found that loss events (e.g., death of a loved one, etc.) occurred to sudden death victims more frequently than to controls. However, these and related studies are subject to the criticism of biased recall of stressful events by relatives or friends of sudden death victims who served as informants in these studies. They share many limitations of retrospective studies that we discussed in the first chapter. Somewhat more convincing are studies that have prospectively explored whether emotional trauma or upset triggers MI or sudden death. The studies examine people who have undergone severe life crises. Parkes et al. (1969) followed up a large cohort of middle-aged widowers and observed a 40 percent increase in mortality in the first 6 months following bereavement: More than one-half of this increased mortality was attributed to cardiovascular causes. However, it is possible to explain the increased mortality among widowers in terms of other factors, such as changes in lifestyle during the grieving process or to unfavorable environments shared by the widower and the deceased.

An increase in deaths due to heart disease and rates of myocardial infarction following several general disasters and personal traumas has also been documented. One recent series of studies explored the effect of Iraqi missile attacks on Israel during the initial days of the 1991 Gulf War on fatal and nonfatal cardiac events among a population living close to Tel Aviv (Meisel et al., 1991). Cases of acute MI treated in the intensive care unit of a Tel Aviv medical center were elevated during the week following the missile attacks (January 17–25, 1991), compared with the week before the attacks and to an index period consisting of the same week a year earlier (see Figure 5.2). In addition, data showed an increase in the sudden death rate during January 1991 compared with the same period a year earlier.

A subsequent assessment of mortality statistics among the entire Israeli population during this period showed that on the day of the first missile strike, excess mortality was greater among women than among men (Kark et al., 1995). Moreover, this mortality excess occurred largely in the Tel Aviv area where the missile attacks occurred and was attributable to cardiovascular disease.

Another approach to studying psychological and behavioral antecedents of acute MI is to assess the occurrence of possible triggers before the events. Several studies of patients hospitalized for acute heart attack (or MI) have identified stressful events as possible external triggers occurring prior to onset. Tofler et al. (1990) reported that among 849 patients with acute MI, 48 percent reported one or more possible triggers, the most common of which was emotional upset. A more sophisticated approach has been employed by Mittleman et al. (1993, 1995), who used a novel epidemiologic methodology that com-

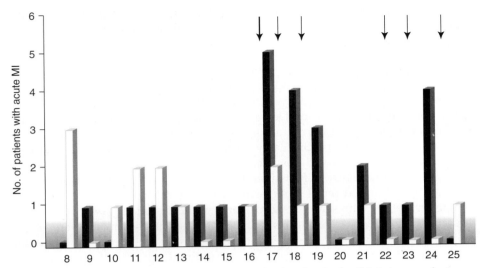

FIGURE 5.2. Daily incidence of acute myocardial infarction in the Tel Aviv area during January 8–25, 1991 (black bars), compared with same period in 1990 (white bars). Thick arrow = beginning of Gulf war; thin arrows = missile attacks on Israel.
Source: S. R. Meisel, I. Kutz, K. I. Dayan, H. Pauzner, I. Chetboun, Y. Arbel, & D. David. The Lancet, 1991; 338–661.

pared each patient's pre-MI activities with his or her usual levels of activities, to assess the immediate physical and mental triggers of the onset of heart attack. In a study of patients who were interviewed a median of 4 days post-MI, 2.4 percent reported episodes of anger within 2 hours prior to the MI onset. The risk of MI following episodes of anger was more than twice as high.

Researchers have also examined the relationship of several stress-related environmental characteristics to the development and worsening of cardiovascular disease (Ostfeld and Eaker, 1985). Some of this research deals with the influence of acute or short-term stressful life events, utilizing the "life change unit methodology" described in Chapter 3. These studies collect information about stressful life events or changes in peoples' lives and relate them to measures of heart disease. Unfortunately, these studies have not shown a very consistent ability to predict heart disease (Wells, 1985). One or a few stressful events may not contribute measurably to CHD since it is a chronic disease that progresses over time. Therefore, it has proven more productive to study the effects of chronic life situations, such as psychological and social conditions at work and in other life domains (e.g., home and family).

Chronic Stress and Coronary Heart Disease

In humans and animals, researchers have studied chronic stress arising from work and social situations. This research reveals that the effects of most stressful situations on physiology and behavior depend on psychological factors. As described in Chapter 3, if situations are not viewed or interpreted as harmful, threatening, or challenging, they can produce smaller and even opposite physiologic responses (Lazarus and Folkman, 1984). Therefore, the relationship of various psychological and social stresses (e.g., occupational conditions) to CHD seems to depend on the meaning of the situation to the individual and the way in which individuals perceive their life situations (cf. Cohen et al., 1986).

Occupational stress appears to be a coronary risk factor. Much of the research in the area of occupational stress and health has tried to determine which occupations are more stressful or which characteristics of particular occupations are causes of elevated risk of coronary disease (cf. Karasek and Theorell, 1990). This research is very promising because it suggests psychological dimensions of settings or individuals that can be modified in order to reduce stress.

Several broad types of working conditions have been associated with CHD risk. These include the psychological demands of the job, autonomy on the job—how much input they have in making decisions—and satisfaction on the job. Job demands refer to job conditions that tax or interfere with the worker's performance abilities, such as workload and work responsibilities. The level of job autonomy refers to the ability of the worker to control the speed, nature, and conditions of work. Job satisfactions include gratifications of the worker's needs and aspirations derived from employment (Wells, 1985).

Low levels of control over one's job and excessive workload seem to be a particularly important combination in heightening job-related stress. For example, studies by Marianne Frankenhaeuser (1979) in Sweden showing greater stress with machine-paced versus self-paced work were discussed in Chapters 3 and 4. The idea that personal control can lessen the negative effects of stress (see Chapter 4) has been applied to workplace effects on CHD by Karasek and his colleagues (Karasek and Theorell, 1990). They proposed that conditions of high work demands, combined with few opportunities to control the job situation (low decisional latitude), are associated with increased coronary disease risk.

Conditions of high demand and low control are called *high strain* situations. The Karasek "job-demand/control" hypothesis has been tested in several populations by applying a "job characteristics scoring system" based on responses to several national surveys of workers. These job characteristic scores can distinguish between occupations along the dimensions comprising job strain, as illustrated in Figure 5.3. This model has shown the ability to predict cardiovascular disease and mortality in studies of male Swedish workers and in studies of men and women in the United States (Karasek and Theorell, 1990; Karasek et al., 1988; Schnall et al., 1990). However, in a recent longitudinal study of patients who underwent diagnostic testing for coronary disease occupational stress was not related to the extent of disease or to subsequent cardiac morbidity or mortality (Hlatky et al., 1995). These negative findings may be attributable to the fact that the study group consisted of a selected group of largely symptomatic patients, and the effects of job strain may have been obscured or overwhelmed by the extent of disease in such a population. (See the box "Gender Differences in 'Total Workload': Do They Affect Health?")

An interesting study of occupational stress and CHD among women also illustrates how job conditions may contribute to coronary disease. Work and family demands and one's control over these situations are important buffers

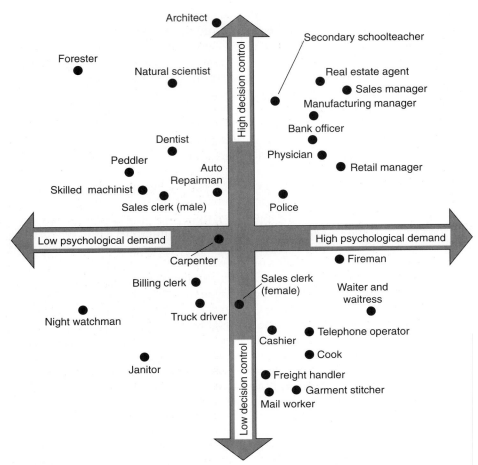

FIGURE 5.3. The dimensions of job strain with corresponding job categories. High demand and low control jobs led to the most CHD.
Source: Modified with permission from B. Nelson. Bosses face less risk than the bossed. *New York Times*, April 3, 1983. Copyright © 1983 by The New York Times Company.

of stress. Haynes and Feinleib (1980) analyzed data from the Framingham Heart Study, a major epidemiologic study of heart disease conducted by the National Institutes of Health. They wondered whether the increasing employment of women outside the home might adversely affect their cardiovascular health. In the mid-1960s, middle-aged women were examined for the development of CHD for the ensuing 8 years. Working women, that is, women who had been employed outside the home for more than one-half their adult years, were compared with housewives and with men. Results indicated that working women in general were *not* at a significantly higher risk of subsequent coronary disease than housewives. However, clerical workers, who perhaps have low job control; working women with children, who have high family demands; and women whose bosses were nonsupportive all were more likely to develop CHD. Interestingly, the likelihood of CHD increased linearly with the

Gender Differences in "Total Workload": Do They Affect Health?

The different factors that contribute to stress in working men and women are illustrated by a study that compared male and female managers and clerical workers at the Volvo automobile manufacturing plant in Sweden. Marianne Frankenhaeuser, Ulf Lundberg, and their colleagues (1989) tested study subjects in three different settings: at work, at home, and in the laboratory. The most striking gender differences were evident in comparisons of the male and female managers. Women managers gave the highest estimates of how much work outside the paid job contributed to their total workload. A questionnaire on their total workload asked subjects to state how responsibility was divided for different duties at home.

This survey revealed that the responsibility followed a traditional sex role pattern; that is, women maintained greater responsibility for home and children whether or not they worked. When physiological measurements were compared at work and at home in the evening after a day of work, the men's norepinephrine levels and blood pressure either decreased or stayed the same at home, whereas women's levels of blood pressure and norepinephrine *increased* in the evening at home. Thus, home and family responsibilities among working managerial-level women contributed a greater extent to the total workload than they did for men, and these responsibilities prevented the women from physiologically "unwinding" in the evening at home. Women managers were subjected to a heavy load both inside and outside their paid work. The question of whether this difficulty in unwinding will affect long-term cardiovascular or other health issues has yet to be answered.

number of children for working women, but not for housewives (Lacroix and Haynes, 1987) (see Figure 5.4).

Some aspects of the social environment, particularly social isolation, low social support, and lack of social and economic resources, can also increase an individual's risk of cardiovascular disease (Shumaker and Czakowski, 1994). Social support refers to the instrumental, emotional, and informational aid obtained from an individual's social ties and community resources (Cohen and Wills, 1985). It has been hypothesized that social support may serve as a buffer or mediator between life stressors and cardiovascular disease outcomes. On the other hand, the absence of tangible aid from a supportive social network may have direct adverse effects on health as well, for example, by impeding access to needed help or interfering with medical compliance. In studies in the United States and other countries people with strong social networks are at relatively lower CHD risk (Shumaker and Czakowski, 1994).

In industrialized societies rates of cardiac morbidity and mortality are inversely related to socioeconomic status, with disease rates higher among poorer individuals. The inverse association of CHD mortality with the socioeconomic level cannot be explained by the different use of medical care services by lower-class individuals (Marmot, 1983). Although it is known that the prevalence of standard CHD risk factors (e.g., high blood pressure, smoking) decreases with increasing socioeconomic status (SES), this is not sufficient by itself to explain all the increase in coronary mortality attributable to low SES.

Low social support and lack of economic resources appear to increase interactively the risk of adverse prognosis in CHD patients. Ruberman et al.

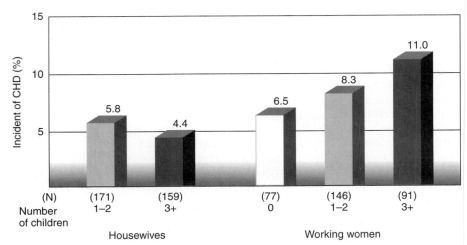

FIGURE 5.4. Eight-year incidence of coronary heart disease by the number of children among women aged 45 to 64 years. CHD increases with number of children among working women.
Source: Reprinted with permission from S. G. Haynes, M. Feinlieb, and W. B. Kannel. Women, work, and coronary heart disease. *American Journal of Public Health,* 1980, *70,* 133–141.

(1984) (see Figure 5.5) demonstrated that the level of education and social support resources—elements associated with socioeconomic level—are significant factors affecting survival for men after a first MI. In this study men with lower educational levels were likely to experience more isolation and life stress than men with higher levels of education, and they had mortality rates twice as high as men with more education and social support. More recently, two studies demonstrated that living alone led to a near doubling of the risk of recurrent heart attack or death in post-MI patients and suggested that unmarried male and female coronary artery disease patients without a friend or confidant (and patients with low household incomes) were at increased risk of cardiovascular death over a 5-year period (Case et al., 1992; Williams et al., 1992). Social factors presumably influence prognosis by influencing patients' psychological reactions to MI. For example, the poorly educated may be at increased risk of job loss following an infarction, and for those who live alone, the future may be even more bleak.

Type A Behavior Pattern, Hostility, and Coronary Heart Disease

The concept of a coronary-prone personality suggests that there is a set of emotions, behaviors, and personality attributes that characterize people who are likely to develop CHD. This idea has a history dating back to the last century when the noted physician Sir William Osler (1892) described the typical coronary patient as "not the delicate, neurotic person . . . but the robust, the vigorous in mind and body, the keen and ambitious man, the indicator of whose engine is always at full speed ahead." (cf. Dembroski et al., 1983, p. 59). In the twentieth century the Menningers (1936) suggested that the trait of *ag-*

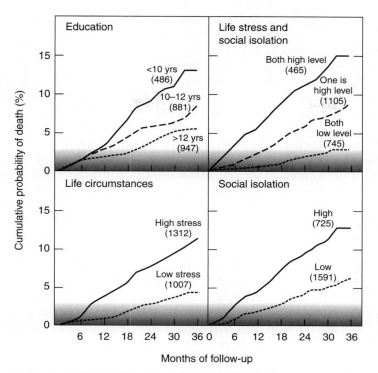

FIGURE 5.5. Cumulative mortality curves for male survivors of myocardial infarction according to (1) level of education, (2) life stress (life circumstances), and (3) social isolation.
Source: Reprinted with permission from W. Ruberman, E. Weinblatt, J. D. Goldberg, and B. S. Chaudhary. Psychosocial influences on mortality after myocardial infarction. *The New England Journal of Medicine,* August 30, 1984, *311*(9), 555, Massachusetts Medical Society.

gressiveness was common among those who developed CHD and could be a cause of disease.

Over the past 30 years opinions about what aspects of this personality or behavior pattern contributed to increased heart disease risk have changed dramatically. During the 1950s two cardiologists, Friedman and Rosenman (1959) described the Type A behavior pattern (TABP) as characterized by excessive competitive drive, impatience, hostility, and vigorous speech characteristics. A contrasting behavior pattern, called Type B, consisted of the relative lack of these characteristics and a more easygoing style of coping. Rosenman and Friedman developed a structured interview to measure Type A behavior based on the presence of observable behaviors such as speech characteristics and the *manner* in which subjects respond to questions, rather than rely on whether subjects describe themselves as impatient and competitive (Friedman and Rosenman, 1974). Several questionnaire measures were also developed to assess Type A behavior, the Jenkins Activity Survey (JAS) (Jenkins, Zyzanski, and Rosenman, 1971). These measures relied solely on subjects' self-reports of their own behavior (Matthews and Haynes, 1986) and have shown a weaker relationship to CHD than have interview based Type A measures.

Early studies showed that Type A traits were related to certain coronary risk factors, and also to the development of coronary disease. In one interesting study (Friedman, Rosenman, and Caroll, 1958) accountants were tested for their levels of serum cholesterol every 2 weeks over a 6-month time period. They found that cholesterol levels rose as the April 15 tax preparation period approached. The changes in cholesterol in this study could not be explained by dietary factors, suggesting that the intense feelings of time pressure produced by occupational deadlines could raise cholesterol levels.

Most studies conducted in the 1960s and 1970s to examine the relationship of Type A behavior to heart disease revealed a positive correlation between TABP and the risk of CHD in men and women, comparable with and independent of the effects of risk factors such as smoking and hypertension. Much of the evidence suggesting that Type A behavior is a risk factor for heart disease came from studies in the two major heart disease projects that included initially healthy individuals. The Western Collaborative Group Study (WCGS) began in 1960 and examined over 3,000 men for $8\frac{1}{2}$ years. At the end of the study those men assessed as Type A by interview and questionnaire were more likely to have developed heart disease than Type B men (Jenkins et al., 1974; Rosenman et al., 1975). In the Framingham Heart Study Type A behavior was a predictor of CHD among men in white-collar occupations and women working outside the home (Haynes et al., 1980).

However, since the 1980s most studies have failed to find a relationship between Type A and coronary disease (see Matthews and Haynes, 1986). In the multiple risk factor intervention trial or MRFIT project, a study was conducted to determine whether interventions to modify coronary risk factors such as smoking, high cholesterol levels, and high blood pressure in high-risk men would lessen the likelihood of coronary disease. Measures of Type A were obtained for over 3,000 MRFIT subjects, who were followed for 7 years. Type A behavior, as measured by the structured interview and by the JAS, was not related to incidence of a first heart attack (Shekelle et al., 1985). In addition, research reports appeared indicating that after a heart attack, Type B patients— and not Type A's—were more likely to die (Ragland and Brand, 1988).

The reasons for these inconsistent findings for Type A are not entirely clear, and some researchers have suggested that Type A behavior might not be a risk factor for some high-risk groups (as were tested in the MRFIT study) (see Matthews and Haynes, 1986). Others have argued that Type A behavior is more likely to be a risk factor in younger, as opposed to older, subgroups (Williams et al., 1988). Nevertheless, it appears that certain components of Type A—particularly anger, hostility, and vigorous speech characteristics— have remained correlated with coronary disease even in studies where overall or "global" Type A has not been related to CHD (Lipkus et al., 1994).

Anger, Hostility, and Coronary Heart Disease Risk

As noted earlier, Type A behavior consists of several behaviors, including competitiveness, time urgency, and hostility. It is possible that all of these behaviors do not contribute equally to coronary risk. Some behaviors have consistently emerged as correlates of CHD in these studies, characteristics relating to *hostility, anger,* and certain *speech characteristics* derived from the structured interview, and the characteristic of *not expressing anger or irritation* ("anger-in"). For example, a reanalysis of data from the WCGS study showed that "potential for hostility," vigorous speech, and reports of frequent anger and irritation were the strongest predictors of CHD (Matthews et al., 1977), and even in the MRFIT study, which was not able to find relationships between Type A and CHD, hostility characteristics were associated with an increased CHD risk (Dembroski et al., 1989).

The Cook and Medley Hostility Inventory (Cook and Medley, 1954), a scale derived from the Minnesota Multiphasic Personality Inventory or MMPI (see Chapter 9), has been shown to predict the occurrence of coronary disease. This scale (see Chapter 9) appears to measure attitudes such as cynicism and mistrust of others (Lipkus et al., 1994). In one study involving a 25-year follow-up of physicians who completed the MMPI while in medical school, high Cook-Medley scores measured when they were college students predicted incidence of CHD as well as mortality from all causes. This relationship was independent of the individual effects of smoking, age, and presence of high blood pressure (Barefoot et al., 1983) (see Figure 5.6). There is also evidence that low hostility scores were associated with lower death rates during a 20-year follow-up of nearly 1,900 participants in the Western Electric Study (Shekelle et al., 1983). In other studies hostility (e.g., assessed through analyses of behaviors and attitudes indicative of hostility derived from the Type A structured interview) were related to the development of CHD in initially healthy men and in high-risk participants in the MRFIT study (see Helmers et al., 1994 for review). Hostility scores on the Cook-Medley (1954) scale are

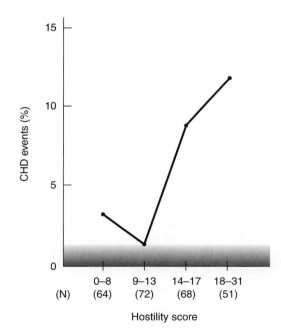

FIGURE 5.6. Relationship between scores on the Ho scale and CHD event incidence over a 25-year follow-up period.
Source: Adapted with permission from J. C. Barefoot, G. Dahlstrom, and R. B. Williams. Hostility, CHD incidence, and total mortality: A 25-year follow-up study of 255 physicians. *Psychosomatic Medicine,* 1983, 45(1), 60.

higher in low socioeconomic status groups, higher in men and nonwhites in the United States, and also positively related to the prevalence of smoking (Lipkus et al., 1994). Although this may indicate that some effects of hostility are due to gender or SES instead, one can also hypothesize that hostility may take into account some socioeconomic and gender differences in death rates from cardiovascular diseases (Stoney and Engbretson, 1994).

Psychological Depression in Coronary Patients

In addition to hostility, the presence of other psychological traits can effectuate an increased risk of poor health outcomes among CHD patients. As a result, they are important to consider as elements of effective cardiac patient treatment and rehabilitation. Signs and symptoms of clinical depression, including fatigue, exhaustion, and sadness, are prevalent among patients with CHD. Moreover, studies have reported that nearly one in five cardiac patients could be diagnosed as having the signs and symptoms of clinical depression (Carney et al., 1987; Frasure-Smith et al., 1993). However, despite this high prevalence, depression among post-MI patients is often untreated.

The presence of a major depressive episode in CHD patients is associated with poor psychosocial rehabilitation and increased medical morbidity (Carney et al., 1995). At least four studies have compared the clinical course of depressed versus nondepressed patients. Diagnosis of major depressive disorder at the time of coronary angiography was the best predictor of a significant cardiac event (death, reinfarction, bypass, angioplasty) during a 1-year follow-up period (Carney et al., 1987). Schleifer et al. (1989) reported a trend toward more frequent rehospitalization and second heart attacks in depressed patients. Kennedy et al. (1987) found a significant correlation between depression and cardiac arrhythmias, and mortality. More recently Frasure-Smith et al. (1993) prospectively followed 222 post-MI patients and observed that the diagnosis of major depression was strongly related to mortality in the 6 months following hospital discharge.

The increased risk of cardiac events associated with depression and low social support may be related to: (1) the indirect effects of these psychological and social factors on health behaviors (e.g., compliance with medical regimens or modification of risk factors) or (2) pathophysiologic changes associated directly with these psychosocial characteristics (Carney et al., 1995; Cohen et al., 1994). Studies have shown that compliance with medical therapeutic and exercise regimens is poorer in depressed cardiac patients (Carney et al., 1995), and a supportive social network is thought to be necessary to facilitate adequate compliance with medical regimens and the reduction of cardiac risk factors (Amick and Ockene, 1994). It has also been suggested that increased susceptibility to cardiac arrhythmias links major depression to sudden cardiac death in coronary patients (Carney et al., 1995). Recent studies have indicated that the presence of clinical depression can be associated with changes in neural and neuroendocrine function that can cause sudden death (Frasure-Smith et al., 1993). There is also preliminary evidence that depressed cardiac patients may be at increased risk of experiencing stress-induced ischemia (Jiang et al., 1994). Research on mechanisms linking depression, social support, and/or lack of economic resources to increased cardiac morbidity and mortality is in its early stages, and this area promises to be a fruitful area for exploration.

Social Conflict and Dominance in Animal Models

Research studies with animals have the benefit of being able to exert the kind of experimental control and to manipulate causal variables relating stress to cardiovascular pathology that would not be ethical with humans. Experimental studies of several animal species have shown that when animals are exposed to conditions that are stressful or that disrupt the social environment, increased coronary artery disease can result (Manuck, Kaplan, and Matthews, 1986). In recent years a particularly important series of studies in this area have been conducted at the Bowman-Gray School of Medicine (Kaplan et al., 1982). These studies are of *cynomolgous monkeys,* which is a particularly good species for studying the influence of behavior on atherosclerosis for two reasons. First, coronary disease pathology in these animals closely resembles that of humans. In addition, many major aspects of these animals' behavior, such as forming a social hierarchy and maintaining friendships and isolation, competition, and aggression are also important aspects of human behavior. Consequently, these animals exhibit behaviors that are analogous to those that have been implicated as potential contributors to coronary disease in humans. In their natural habitat these monkeys organize themselves through the establishment of stable hierarchies of social dominance. Dominant and submissive animals can be identified within a given group based on each animal's overt behavior.

Observations of these animals' social behavior have shown that the introduction of unfamiliar monkeys into an established social group is a powerful social stressor, leading to increased aggressive behavior as group members attempt to reestablish a social dominance hierarchy (Manuck et al., 1986). In recent studies these stressful conditions were created by periodically reorganizing social groups (called the *unstable* condition). Each group composed of five monkeys was, at intervals, newly exposed to three to four different monkeys. Unstressed animals in *stable* social conditions were assigned to similarly sized groups having fixed memberships over the duration of the study (Kaplan et al., 1982). Based on the patterns of their behaviors in the groups, monkeys were categorized as either dominant or subordinate.

In one study of male monkeys the dominant animals in the unstable social condition developed more extensive coronary atherosclerosis than their subordinate counterparts. However, differences were also evident between dominants and subordinates in the stable social condition. Under stable social conditions dominants were slightly *less* affected than subordinates, whereas dominant animals in the unstable condition showed the most aggression toward other animals and a disruption of positive social interactions. The psychosocial influences on development of atherosclerosis in this study were apparently independent of physical risk factors (e.g., cholesterol, blood pressure, etc.). This is similar to what is found in studies of Type A or "coronary-prone behavior" in humans. However, all animals had relatively high cholesterol levels because they were maintained on a diet high in saturated fat and cholesterol.

A second study examined whether social stress would show similar effects if monkeys were maintained on a low cholesterol, low fat diet (The American Heart Association "prudent" diet). With the same conditions created, dominant animals in the unstable condition again developed the most severe disease. However, comparing the extent of atherosclerosis across the two studies, results indicated that social influences on coronary disease development were greatly magnified in the presence of high cholesterol levels induced by diet (Manuck et al., 1986).

In a third study conducted with female monkeys subordinate animals developed *greater* coronary artery disease than did dominants (Kaplan et al., 1984), and as in the other studies with male animals, these effects could not be attributed to the physical risk factors. Reproductive function in many subordinate animals was also disrupted, and these behaviorally induced reproductive problems may have lessened these animals' "protection" against coronary disease.

These experiments demonstrate the effects of psychosocial stress in the development of coronary artery disease. Interestingly, the specific effects of stress depend on individual characteristics (e.g., level of dominance) that determine how objective conditions will affect each animal's behavior. Thus, we might conclude that these studies are similar to the occupational stress findings, indicating that the effects of stress depend on psychological processes such as the perception and/or the interpretation of demands on the individual. The aggressive behaviors observed in male monkeys that developed the most coronary disease also resemble some characteristics of Type A behavior and hostility observed to predict CHD in humans.

Physiologic Mechanisms Linking Stress to Coronary Disease

Many adverse effects of stress on cardiac pathology have been attributed to neural, endocrine, and cardiovascular effects of stress (Krantz et al., in press). It has long been known that wide individual differences exist in physiologic reactions to stress, and these reactions have been of interest to psychosomatic practitioners and researchers. A body of research now suggests that physiological responses (reactivity) to emotional stress may be involved in the development of CHD and/or high blood pressure (Krantz and Manuck, 1984; Manuck, 1994). As we saw in Chapter 3, we can measure "reactivity" by looking at cardiovascular and/or hormonal *changes* in response to stressors. For example, one commonly used task for determining reactivity is a competitive video game such as "Pong" or "Pac-Man." Subjects are hooked up to a blood pressure and heart rate monitor and are challenged to perform as well as possible on the game. Resting levels of heart rate and blood pressure are taken before the instructions are given, and these measurements are repeated throughout the time that the subjects perform the task. It turns out that there are wide individual differences in the magnitude of physiological responses shown during such a task, with some people (so-called "hot reactors") showing sizable increases to the challenging task, and others showing little or no increases. An underlying assumption in measuring reactivity in such a manner is that changes over resting levels in response to real-life or laboratory stresses give an index of how the body is responding during the challenges of everyday life and/or during exposure to environmental stress.

One school of thought is that psychological factors such as stress and hostility contribute to the development of CHD because they are related to the activity of the sympathetic nervous system (SNS) and to the activity of the adrenal glands (Krantz and Manuck, 1984; Schneiderman, 1983). Certain types of cardiovascular and endocrine reactions are thought to promote the development of coronary atherosclerosis and/or heart attack. Particular attention has been directed to the role of catecholamines, epinephrine and norepinephrine in leading to cardiovascular pathology. Apparently, high levels of catecholamines and repeated rapid increases in cardiovascular responses facilitate injury or damage to arteries, increasing the likelihood of plaque accumulation (see Ross and Glomset, 1976). Catecholamine elevation may also contribute to blood clot formation, thereby leading to heart attack (Muller et al., 1994).

It has been suggested that behaviors evidenced by hostile Type A persons are accompanied by the same kinds of cardiovascular and neuroendocrine responses thought to link psychosocial stress to CHD. Studies demonstrate that Type A's, compared to Type B's, display larger increases in blood pressure, heart rate, and stress hormones when confronted by challenging or stressful tasks (Matthews, 1982). Type A's do not seem to differ much physiologically from Type B's when they are at rest and not psychologically challenged.

It is also worth noting that, at least in coronary patients, some evidence indicates that there may be a psychobiological basis for Type A behavior that is inherited or acquired. In two studies of patients under general anesthesia for coronary bypass surgery—a situation where patients' consciousness is certainly minimized—Type A patients showed increased systolic blood pressure responses during the surgical procedure (Krantz and Durel, 1983). These results suggest that, at least among coronary patients, there may be an underlying constitutional basis for Type A behavior and that certain overt behaviors exhibited by Type A patients could *reflect* an underlying SNS hyperreactivity (Krantz and Durel, 1983).

Research has also examined the possibility that excessive reactivity to stress itself may be a risk factor for coronary disease. In one study of initially healthy men followed for 23 years (Keys et al., 1971) the magnitude of their diastolic blood pressure reactions to a cold pressor test (which involves immersing the hand in cold water) predicted later heart disease. In fact, this physiologic response was a stronger predictor than many of the standard risk factors assessed in the study.

Additional evidence of a relationship between cardiovascular reactions to stress and coronary disease was obtained in the Bowman-Gray monkeys described earlier. In studies of male and female cynomolgous monkeys fed on a cholesterol-rich diet, animals were exposed to a standard laboratory stressor—threat of capture—that produced large heart rate elevations (Manuck, Kaplan, and Clarkson, 1983; Manuck et al., 1986). There were large individual differences in heart rate reactions to stress, and animals were categorized as either high or low heart rate reactors. At the end of the study high heart rate reactors had nearly twice the amount of coronary atherosclerosis than did low heart rate reactors (see Figure 5.7). Interestingly, the heart rate responses correlated with the animals' behavioral characteristics, with high heart rate reactivity associated with aggressiveness in male monkeys and submissiveness in female monkeys.

There is also great interest in behavioral methods for reducing reactivity. Among the behavioral techniques used for this purpose are cognitive techniques, relaxation training, biofeedback, and aerobic exercise (Jacob and Chesney, 1986; Matthews et al., 1986) (see Chapter 8).

Research has also focused on myocardial ischemia—the inadequate supply of blood to the heart that can occur in the presence of atherosclerosis. This cardiac event has been studied as an intermediate measure for understanding mechanisms by which mental stress may trigger clinical events (Krantz et al., 1996). Recent technological developments have made it possible to monitor the electrocardiogram (EKG) in CHD patients when they are out of the hospital and going about their usual daily activities (see Cohn, 1986). This research has demonstrated that ischemia occurs frequently in the absence of chest pain (so-called **silent ischemia**). Cardiac patients' perceived level of physical and mental activity appears to coincide with EKG evidence of ischemia during daily life (Barry et al., 1988; Gabbay et al., 1996). The majority of episodes of silent is-

FIGURE 5.7. Amount of coronary atherosclerosis in high heart rate and low heart rate reactor monkeys.
Source: Adapted with permission from S. B. Manuck, J. R. Kaplan, and T. B. Clarkson. Behaviorally induced heart rate reactivity and atherosclerosis in cynomolgous monkeys. *Psychosomatic Medicine,* 1983, *45,* 95–108.

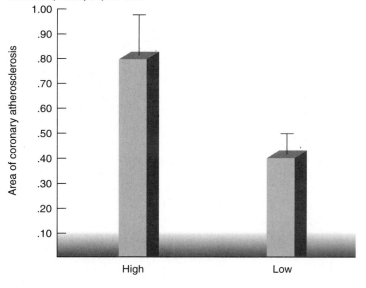

chemia occur during daily activities involving low or moderate levels of physical activity. Examples of such activities are talking on the phone, doing clerical work, and conversing with a friend. These findings have also suggested that as the intensity of both mental and physical activities increases, they are increasingly likely to produce transient ischemia (Krantz et al., 1996).

153

*Treatment and
Preventive
Implications of
Behavioral Risk
Factors*

Because high levels of exercise are relatively infrequent, and mental activities are more frequent during daily life, mental activities may be a more common trigger of transient ischemia (Barry et al., 1988; Gabbay et al., 1996). More recently the experience of intense anger was identified as a potent trigger of daily life ischemia. Researchers have also used a variety of ways to evaluate the effects of mental stress on the heart in coronary patients; this suggests that in the laboratory mental stressors such as mental arithmetic or giving a speech in front of an audience can provoke ischemia in many coronary patients. This ischemia is usually silent and appears to exhibit a somewhat different physiological profile (e.g., occurring at lower heart rates and most frequently not associated with anginal pain) from ischemia triggered by exercise. Ironson et al. (1992) reported that an anger-inducing stressor, compared to other stressors, was a particularly potent psychological stressor in its ability to trigger cardiac dysfunction.

Treatment and Preventive Implications of Behavioral Risk Factors

Since there is evidence that traits of hostility, anger, and Type A behavior and unhealthy habits such as smoking and a high fat diet are associated with heart disease, is there anything we can do to modify or prevent these behaviors? Hostility, Type A behavior, and other lifestyle factors are the result of long learning histories, and changes in these factors are difficult for most people to achieve (see Chapter 13).

Modifying Hostility and Type A Behavior

A variety of clinical interventions have been used to decrease Type A behavior in either persons with elevated levels of other CHD risk factors or samples of coronary patients. Most of these studies have shown that elements of Type A behavior can be decreased to some extent in subjects who are motivated to change (Suinn, 1982). Unfortunately, changes in Type A in these studies were primarily measured by self-reports, and it is unknown whether changes in self-perception correspond to actual changes in behavior. Accompanying changes in Type A, some studies also measured changes in traditional CHD risk factors such as cholesterol or blood pressure. The findings from these studies are inconsistent (Suinn, 1982). These results are not surprising considering that the therapeutic regimens are not typically directed at decreasing risk factor levels other than Type A.

Thorough studies comparing the effects of different interventions to reduce Type A behavior have been conducted in healthy individuals (see Roskies et al., 1986). However, the most important and ambitious Type A intervention study to date is the Recurrent Coronary Prevention Project (Friedman et al.,

1986). The major purpose of this project was to determine whether the constellation of Type A behaviors—focusing on anger, impatience, aggressiveness, and irritability—could be modified in a large group of heart attack patients and whether such behavior changes would lower the recurrence of heart attacks and deaths from CHD. Beginning in 1979 over 1,000 patients were recruited for the 5-year intervention study.

Patients were assigned to one of three groups: a cardiology counseling treatment group, a combined cardiology counseling and Type A modification group, or a no-treatment control group. The cardiology counseling included encouragement to comply with dietary, exercise, and drug regimens prescribed by the participants' personal physicians as well as education about CHD and its treatment and counseling about psychological problems, other than Type A, associated with the postcoronary experience. The Type A counseling included drills to change specific Type A behaviors (see Table 5.2), focused discussions on beliefs and values underlying Type A behavior, rearrangement of home and work demands, and relaxation training to decrease physiological arousal.

The results of the study showed that 4½ years later the rate of heart attack recurrence for the Type A behavioral counseling group was significantly lower than for the cardiology counseling and control groups (Friedman et al., 1986). These results are unique in demonstrating, in a controlled experimental design, that altering Type A behavior reduces coronary disease recurrence in postheart attack patients.

TABLE 5.2. Example from the Recurrent Coronary Prevention Project's *Drill Book* Used in the Type A Behavioral Group Treatment

Day of Week	October
Monday	Set aside 30 minutes for yourself
Tuesday	Practice smiling
Wednesday	Practice removing your grimaces
Thursday	Eat more slowly
Friday	Recall memories for 10 minutes
Saturday	Verbalize affection to spouse/children
Sunday	Linger at table

1.[a] "The only future we can conceive is built upon the forward shadow of our past"—Proust.
2. "If you make the organization your life, you are defenseless against the inevitable disappointments"—Peter Drucker.
3. "The moment numeration ceases to be your servant, it becomes your tyrant"—Anonymous.
4. "Habit is the hardiest of all the plants in human growth"—Anonymous.

[a]Reflect on the first quote daily for the first week, the second daily for the second week, and so on.
Source: From C.E. Thoresen et al. Altering the Type A behavior pattern in post-infarction patients. In D.S. Krantz and J.A. Blumenthal (Eds.), *Behavioral Assessment and Management of Cardiovascular Disorders.* Sarasota, FL: Professional Resource Exchange, 1987, pp. 97–116.

Social Support and Counseling to Reduce Life Stress

155

*Treatment and
Preventive
Implications of
Behavioral Risk
Factors*

Another perhaps more cost-effective approach to preventing stress-related morbidity and mortality in patients with heart disease was described in the Ischemic Heart Disease Life Stress Monitoring Program (Frasure-Smith and Prince, 1987, 1989), conducted in Montreal. This study made use of evidence that periods of increased life stress may precede recurrent heart attack. Patients who had experienced a heart attack were assigned to either a *treatment group* (N = 229) or to a *control group* (N = 224). Patients assigned to the *control group* did not receive life-stress monitoring and an intervention but, instead, received routine medical follow-up care. In the *treatment group* patients were contacted by phone on a monthly basis and asked about 20 symptoms of distress such as insomnia, feelings of depression, inability to concentrate, and so on. When stress levels exceeded a critical level (more than 4 out of 20 possible symptoms), a project nurse made a home visit to assess the causes of increased distress, attempting to help the patient with whatever life problems seemed to be producing the distress. Over the year of the program, about one-half the patients in the treatment group had high enough stress levels for intervention. On average, study nurses provided each high stress patient with 5 to 6 hours of home nursing contact, including teaching patients about coronary disease, counseling, providing social and emotional support, and referring patients to cardiologists or other health professionals as needed.

The study hypothesized that by reducing stress, the program would result in a reduction in cardiac mortality and in cardiac recurrences. Results showed that for the year of the project, cardiac deaths were reduced by 50 percent, and that the reduced death rate persisted for 6 months beyond the end of the program. In addition, although there were similar rates of MI recurrences, during the 7 years following the program there were fewer MI recurrences among patients in the treatment group (see Figure 5.8).

The most obvious explanation for the outcomes obtained in the Ischemic Heart Disease Life Stress Monitoring Program is that the program provided patients with a sense of social and emotional support that helped to reduce depression and feelings of helplessness and distress. This helped to reduce physiological arousal and its adverse effects on the cardiovascular system. The special clinical features of the program, including selection for treatment based on stress scores and individualized tailoring of interventions to patients' needs, may have also been responsible for the program's success.

The Lifestyle Heart Trial

One of the most important intervention studies conducted to date is the one designed by Dean Ornish and colleagues (1990). These researchers conducted a controlled study of 28 patients with significant coronary artery disease documented by coronary angiography—a procedure to assess the severity of blockages in coronary arteries. Patients were randomly assigned to either an **experimental group** or to a usual care **control group**. Experimental group patients were given a lifestyle modification program consisting of a very low fat vegetarian diet, stress management training, support consisting of biweekly

156

CHAPTER 5
*Cardiovascular
Disorders and
Behavior*

Long-Term Outcomes of IHD Stress Program

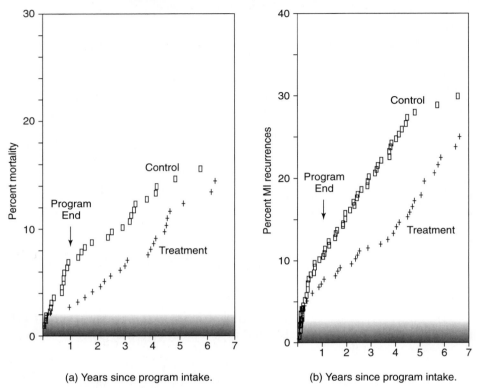

(a) Years since program intake. (b) Years since program intake.

FIGURE 5.8. (*a*) Cumulative out-of-hospital mortality (sudden deaths) in the treatment and control groups. (*b*) Cumulative MI recurrences in the treatment and control groups. *Source:* Adapted with permission from N. Frasure-Smith and R. Prince. Long-term follow-up of the ischemic heart disease life stress monitoring program. *Psychosomatic Medicine,* 1989, *51,* 495.

yoga and meditation conducted in group sessions, 1 hour daily individual practice, smoking cessation, and moderate levels of aerobic exercise. Patients assigned to the control group were not asked to make lifestyle changes other than those recommended by traditional cardiology care. The intervention lasted for 1 year, and the extent of progression of coronary disease was assessed in all patients by comparing coronary angiography at the study onset and after 1 year of "healthier living."

The study results demonstrated that there was, on average, a slight reduction (regression) in the extent of stenosis (or blockage) in coronary arteries in the experimental group, whereas the controls showed continued progression in the severity of vessel damage. Overall, 82 percent of the patients in the experimental group had an average change toward regression of disease. Interestingly, the degree of measured regression of disease was related to the overall extent of adherence to the intervention among the study subjects. The most compliant subjects showed the most improvement in disease status, and the least compliant patients showed the least change (see Figure 5.9).

BEHAVIORAL FACTORS IN HYPERTENSION

Essential hypertension refers to a condition in which the blood pressure is chronically elevated and for which no single cause can be identified. The frequency of this condition in the United States is estimated at about 15 percent of the population, or more than 35 million people. The prevalence of this disorder increases with age, is more common among African-Americans than among other groups in our population, and below the age of 50 is less frequent among women than men (Higgins and Luepker, 1988). Hypertension is considered to be asymptomatic—no particular symptoms are associated with it. People with hypertension are not usually aware of changes in their temperament or in bodily sensations. However, it is a serious and potentially deadly disease. Untreated hypertension increases the risk of stroke, heart attack, and kidney and vascular disease. Fortunately, because of recent strides in the medical treatment of hypertension, it usually can be controlled. However, because the disease has no observable symptoms and the drugs used to treat it may have unpleasant side effects, patients do not always comply with drug treatment regimens and the problem of maintaining adherence to treatments is considerable (see Chapter 8).

A number of factors have been associated with risk for hypertension, including age, family history of hypertension, "borderline" high blood pressure, dietary intake of salt, and obesity. Like CHD, there are numerous social, environmental, and cultural factors that interact with genetic background in predisposing individuals to hypertension. Considerable attention has been paid to studying the role of stress and personality factors in the development of this disorder. Many findings of research examining risk factors for hypertension are controversial because of the complex interactions among behavioral, physiological, and genetic factors. In addition, essential hypertension is probably not a single homogeneous disease. Instead, changes in blood pressure are thought to progress over a period of years from moderately elevated or borderline levels to more appreciably elevated levels, called "established" hypertension.

Several different pathogenic changes or conditions can lead to blood pressure elevations, and different physiological and/or behavioral mechanisms are implicated at different stages of the disorder. For example, individuals with borderline hypertension are commonly observed to have an elevated output of blood from the heart but little evidence of increased resistance to the flow of blood in the body's vasculature (Julius and Esler, 1975). This physiological pattern is consistent with an increased activation of the SNS (see Chapter 2), which is the body's initial reaction to psychological stress. Indeed, high levels of blood and tissue catecholamines—such as those produced by stress—have been found in some hypertensive humans and animals (Julius and Esler, 1975). However, in older individuals with more established hypertension the heart's output of blood is normal or even decreased and resistance to flow of blood is elevated.

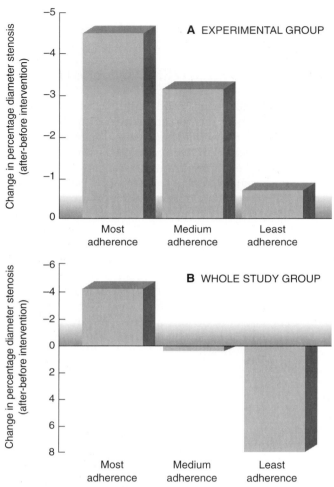

FIGURE 5.9. Correlation of overall adherence score and
changes in percentage diameter stenosis in experimental
group only (A) and in whole study group (B) from the
Lifestyle Heart Study.
Source: D. Ornish, S. E. Brown, L. W. Scherwitz, J. H. Billings,
W. T. Armstrong, T. A. Ports, S. M. McLanahan, R. L. Kir-
keeide, R. J. Brand, & K. L. Gould. The Lancet, 1990; 336:132.

Evidence from animal research and from studies of human twins indicates
that genetic factors are important in the development of hypertension (Pickering, 1977). In humans, however, it is likely that sustained hypertension is produced by an interaction of environmental and genetic factors. Population studies reveal a difference in the prevalence of hypertension among various social
and cultural groups, a difference that cannot be taken into account by genetic
factors alone (Henry and Cassel, 1969). For example, even though African-
Americans in the United States experience more hypertension than do whites,
prevalence of this disease is more common among the poor than in middle-

class black Americans (Harburg et al., 1973). Animal research also has provided examples in which environmental factors, such as dietary salt intake or stress, can lead to sustained blood pressure elevations—but only in certain genetic strains (Dahl et al., 1962). Sociocultural and psychological studies of humans, in conjunction with research on animals, have identified some factors related to behavior that might play a role in the development of hypertension. These factors include dietary intake of salt, obesity, and psychological stress.

Salt Intake

Much has been written about the role of salt in essential hypertension, largely because excessive intake of sodium acts on the kidneys to increase the volume of blood. However, studies indicate that high salt intake may be related to high blood pressure levels only in some cultures and population groups. For example, among people who live in tribal societies, sodium intake is often low, as is the prevalence of hypertension (Page et al., 1970). As individuals move or become acculturated to newer societies, the prevalence of hypertension increases. This phenomenon has been discussed in terms of increasing stress due to acculturation, but it has also been argued that acculturation is associated with increased salt intake, which plays an equally important role in the development of hypertension (Page et al., 1970). Clearly, both the salt and stress explanations for the increased prevalence of hypertension in modern societies have some merit, and research suggests that salt consumption and exposure to stress may interact to produce blood pressure elevations (Friedman and Iwai, 1976; Haythornethwaite et al., 1992).

There is also evidence that decreasing sodium intake in the diet of hypertensives will lower blood pressure, and in healthy people progressively greater salt intakes will result in proportional blood pressure increases (Luft et al., 1978; Parjis et al., 1973). The reduction of salt intake has become an important part of the nonpharmacological treatment of hypertension. In accordance with our prior discussion of genetic–environmental interactions, we should note that high salt intake is correlated with increased prevalence of hypertension only in certain populations or groups.

Obesity

Obesity is another social and cultural phenomenon that plays an important role in hypertension. There is an increased prevalence of hypertension in obese persons although the precise reasons for this remain to be determined (Shapiro, 1983). Some researchers have thought that obese patients merely consume more sodium, but recent studies have demonstrated that weight loss without salt restriction can result in significant decreases in blood pressure (Reisen et al., 1978). For this reason, weight loss is an important behavioral method for managing high blood pressure.

Stress, Sociocultural Factors, and Essential Hypertension

As noted earlier, there is an increased risk for hypertension among African-Americans compared with whites in the United States and among persons of lower socioeconomic status compared with those of higher socioeconomic status. Although these relationships have been observed for a long time, we still do not have a widely accepted explanation for these race or social class differences. Possible explanations include differences in dietary patterns, exercise habits, or the social and physical charactersitics of the environments in which these individuals live and work (Krantz et al., 1987). Some studies have suggested that differential exposure to stress or certain environments (e.g., urban high crime settings) that require sustained vigilance as well as recurrent mobilization of coping resources to ward off harm may raise blood pressure (Anderson and Armstead, 1995; Benson and Guttman, 1971; Henry and Cassel, 1969). It is well documented that poorer people and minority groups in this country are overrepresented in such environments.

There are related anthropological studies that show that more traditional or less developed rural populations living in small, cohesive societies (e.g., nomadic tribes in Africa, Australian Aboriginies, etc.) have low blood pressures that do not increase with age. However, when members of these societies migrated to areas where they were suddenly exposed to western culture, they rapidly developed high blood pressure levels that did increase as they got older (Henry and Cassel, 1969). This result suggested that the new living conditions had some stressful effects that became evident over the course of the life span. Another study supporting the role of stress in hypertension is a study of residents of Detroit (Harburg et al., 1973). Four areas were categorized as "high stress" or "low stress" based on socioeconomic status, crime rate, population density, residential mobility, and marital breakup rates. Blood pressure levels were highest among black high stress males, whereas white and black low stress areas did not differ in blood pressure levels.

Research has also shown that people engaged in highly stressful occupations, such as air traffic controllers, have more than four times the prevalence of hypertension when stress is high than individuals of similar age in other professions (see Figure 5.10) (Cobb and Rose, 1973). Current studies of urban bus drivers in several places in the world suggest that they also have higher rates of hypertension than demographically comparable groups of people. The high rates of hypertension observed in these occupational groups is consistent with the job demand/control hypothesis advanced to explain the relationship between occupational stress and CHD (Karasek et al., 1982). Specifically, hypertension may occur more frequently in jobs that are demanding but in which there is little opportunity or flexibility to deal with these demands (see Figure 5.3).

Experimental studies with animals further suggest that stress can produce hypertension in predisposed individuals. Classic studies by Henry and his associates (see Henry and Stephens, 1977) have shown that psychosocial stimuli can cause hypertension in mice. In an early study mice that had been kept in isolation were housed in a specially designed cage where they were forced to interact with a number of other animals who in a common space when they went to obtain food or water. Those animals that were previously isolated showed chronic elevation of blood pressure in response to frequent contact with others. Other studies indicate that hypertension can be induced in animals that are exposed to stressors such as fear, shock, or experimentally produced conflict (Campbell and Henry, 1983). However, unlike humans, animals'

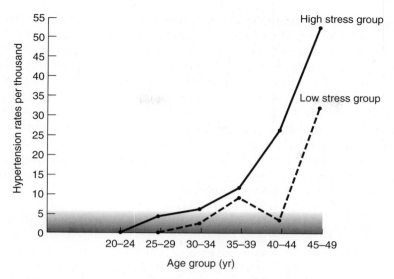

FIGURE 5.10. Incidence of hypertension as a function of stress. High stress air traffic controllers (men working at high traffic towers) show greater prevalence of diagnosed hypertension than do low stress controllers (men working at low traffic towers).
Source: Adapted from S. Cobb and R. M. Rose. Hypertension, peptic ulcer, and diabetes in air traffic controllers. *Journal of the American Medical Association,* 1973, 244(4), 489–492. Copyright © 1973 by the American Medical Association and adapted with permission.

blood pressure tends to normalize when the stressor is removed unless the animals are genetically predisposed to hypertension. Consistent with the notion that genetic–environment interactions are important in the development of hypertension, research has revealed that strains of animals that are susceptible to hypertension are also most likely to show stress-induced blood pressure elevations (Friedman and Iwai, 1976).

There is also evidence in humans to suggest that excessive stress and salt consumption can interact to produce blood pressure elevations. Haythorne-thwaite et al. (1992) studied medical students during periods of high exam stress and during vacation periods when stress was lower. One-half the students were randomly assigned to consume salt tablets and the other half to consume placebo tablets during a 2-week period of high or low stress. Results of the study indicated that high sodium intake during the high stress period was associated with greater elevations in resting systolic and mean arterial pressure than "normal" salt intake in the placebo condition. High salt intake during the low stress period was also not associated with blood pressure elevations. These results suggest that some forms of hypertension or blood pressure elevations may result from the interaction of psychosocial stress with periods of high salt intake.

The idea that emotional and behavioral stimuli affect the development and/or maintenance of high blood pressure is also consistent with results of human studies, indicating that techniques such as biofeedback and relaxation training can be used to modify the stress-induced components of high blood pressure, and thereby reduce blood pressure in hypertensive patients (Shapiro, 1983). There have been a number of studies showing small but significant decreases in blood pressure (e.g., 15 mmHg systolic and 10 mmHg diastolic blood pressure) after a series of training sessions with biofeedback or relaxation methods such as meditation, progressive relaxation, or yoga (Shapiro et al., 1977) (see Figure 5.11). Comparative studies of these various behavioral techniques indicate that none of them is clearly superior to the others, each producing modest declines. Interestingly, these reductions in blood pressure are achieved without any side effects or medical contraindications, thus heightening the attractiveness of stress-reducing techniques as nonpharmacologic adjuncts for the treatment of hypertension.

Race Differences in Stress Reactivity

A higher resting blood pressure and greater prevalance of hypertension among African-American, compared with white adults in the United States is a consistent epidemiologic finding. In order to explain these findings, researchers in the 1980s began to examine racial differences in reactivity to stress as one potential contributor to the higher hypertension morbidity in blacks. Several studies observed that blacks, compared with whites, showed higher blood pressure levels or greater increases in cardiovascular activity due to laboratory stressors (see Anderson, McNeilly, and Meyers, 1992 for review). There is also evidence that the mechanisms of blood pressure increases due to stress may be

FIGURE 5.11. Comparison of nondrug techniques in reducing blood pressure levels, with means derived from a review of the literature (Psychor. = psychotherapy; Sugg. = suggestion). The white bars indicate the lowest and highest falls in systolic (S) and the dark bars indicate the lowest and highest falls in diastolic (D).
Source: Adapted with permission from A. P. Shapiro. The non-pharmacologic treatment of hypertension. In D. S. Krantz, A. Baum, and J. E. Singer (Eds.), *Handbook of Psychology and Health* (vol. 3), *Cardiovascular Disorders and Behavior.* Hillsdale, NJ: Erlbaum, 1983.

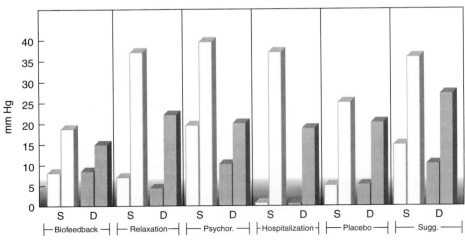

somewhat different in blacks who are more likely to show increases in total peripheral resistance and constriction of the vasculature, whereas whites tend to show greater increases in cardiac output in response to stress. In order to explain these differences, Anderson et al. (1992) have proposed that the greater exposure to social and environmental stressors among blacks, rather than the effects of genetic differences, results in greater sodium retention by the kidneys among blacks and a correspondingly greater tendency for vascular constriction. Further research is clearly needed to assess the role of stress reactivity in the genesis of hypertension and the relevance of an environmental and/or genetic model of stress reactivity to hypertension in blacks.

Compliance with Antihypertensive Treatment Regimens

Any discussion of behavioral factors and hypertension is incomplete without considering the issue of patient compliance with treatment regimens. Hypertension is a progressive, asymptomatic, and irreversible disease if not treated. Thus, patients must be persuaded to undertake treatment that may last for a lifetime and may have side effects and considerable inconvenience. When patients comply and adhere to treatment, blood pressure can be reduced and there is good evidence that the negative health effects of hypertension can be avoided. However, the asymptomatic nature of the disease and the side effects that often result from drug treatments frequently result in poor compliance with medication taking. As described in Chapter 8, good communication between the doctor and the patient is important, and the patient must be effectively educated as to the benefits of treatment. In addition, by making other lifestyle changes such as modifying diet, losing weight, and exercising, the dose of the drug required can be reduced. In some patients with mild blood pressure elevations the necessity of taking drugs can even be avoided.

SUMMARY

Many environmental, behavioral, and physiological variables interact in the development of cardiovascular disorders. The risk factors for coronary heart disease (CHD) include nonmodifiable factors such as aging, male sex, and a family history, as well as controllable factors such as serum cholesterol, smoking, and hypertension.

Psychosocial risk factors for CHD have also been identified. These include occupational and social stress, the hostility and anger components of Type A behavior, and physiologic reactivity to stress. In cardiac patients the presence of acute stress, low social support, lack of economic resources, and psychological depression also appear to be important psychosocial risk factors.

With regard to occupational stress, low levels of control over the job combined with high job demands seem to heighten job stress and to increase the risk of CHD. An interesting primate animal model has demonstrated that dominant animals placed in an unstable social environment develop more extensive atherosclerosis than dominant animals in stable environments or than socially subordinate animals. Studies of this animal model have also demonstrated a relationship between cardiovascular responses to stress (reactivity) and the development of coronary artery disease.

These identifications of psychosocial risk factors for coronary disease have led to several promising behavioral and psychosocial interventions to aid in the treatment and prevention of coronary disease in high-risk individuals. Three such behavioral and psychosocial interventions with coronary patients were described: a cognitive-behavioral intervention directed at lessening hostility and Type A behavior (The Recurrent Coronary Prevention Project); a tailored social support and counseling intervention delivered by a nurse directed at reducing life stress (The Ischemic Heart Disease Life Stress Monitoring Program conducted in Montreal, Canada); a lifestyle modification program consisting of a very low fat vegetarian diet, a stress management training and group supporting individual practice, stopping smoking, and performing moderate levels of aerobic exercise (Dean Ornish's Lifestyle Heart Trial).

In this chapter we have also discussed biobehavioral influences on essential hypertension, a condition in which the blood pressure is chronically elevated. These include excessive salt intake, obesity, and stress. Evidence indicates that genetic and environmental factors interact in development of hypertension. With regard to the role of stress, there is evidence that societies characterized by rapid cultural change, as well as individuals in certain high stress occupations, are more prone to hypertension. Studies in animals also indicate that stress can result in hypertension although, unlike the human condition, blood pressure tends to normalize when the stress is removed. The effectiveness of behavioral stress-reducing techniques such as relaxation training, biofeedback, and meditation in lowering blood pressure is also consistent with the role of stress in the development of this disorder.

RECOMMENDED READINGS

Carney, R. M., Freedland K. E., Rich, M. W., and Jaffe, A. S. Depression as a risk factor for cardiac events in established coronary heart disease: A review of possible mechanisms. *Annals of Behavioral Medicine*, 1995, *17*, 142–149.

Krantz, D. S., Kop, W. J., Santiago, H. T., and Gottdiener, J. S. Mental stress as a trigger of myocardial ischemia and infarction. *Cardiology Clinics of North America*, 1996, *14*, 271–287.

Ockene, I. S., and Ockene, J. K. *Prevention of coronary heart disease*. Boston: Little, Brown and Company, 1992.

Shumaker, S. A., and Czakowski, S. M. *Social support and cardiovascular disease*. New York: Plenum Press, 1994.

Siegman, A., and Smith, T. W. *Anger, hostility, and the heart*. Hillsdale, NJ: Erlbaum, 1994.

CHAPTER 6

Psychoneuroimmunology, Cancer, and AIDS

For most of us when we think about the immune system, we think about infectious illnesses caused by viruses or by bacteria. Influenza, pneumonia, tuberculosis, polio, and the common cold are such illnesses. We get them *if* we are exposed to the virus or bacteria that causes the illness and *if* the virus or bacteria is not overcome by the immune system. When something happens to our immune system, we are more likely to catch a cold or other infectious illness that we may be exposed to in passing. However, the immune system also appears to play a major role in cancer, serving as one defense against malignancy and metastasis—becoming cancerous and spreading to distant sites in the body. Also, the immune system seems to be a primary target of the virus that causes AIDS. In fact, the most lethal aspect of AIDS, including the development of *opportunistic infections*, occurs as a consequence of impairment of the immune system.

These diseases directly involving immune system activity are major health threats throughout the world. Cancer is the second leading cause of death in the United States, and HIV disease and AIDS have become major health problems. Importantly, there appear to be a number of behavioral factors that affect people with cancer and AIDS or that contribute to illness development and progression. Some of these involve influences on the immune system, and a new field, **psychoneuroimmunology,** has been developed to study genetic, hormonal, neural, and psychological interactions with immune system activity and surveillance. Other factors are related to health-impairing behaviors, such as smoking, and to health-protecting behaviors, such as exercise. Finally, reactions to being ill, undergoing treatment, and otherwise dealing with disease may affect the course of disease or how sick we get.

This chapter considers this new field of psychoneuroimmunology and then focuses on biobehavioral factors in infectious diseases, cancer, and HIV disease/AIDS. (Each of these topics warrants more attention and interested readers are referred to Recommended Readings at the end of this chapter for more detailed accounts of these areas.)

Knowledge about the immune system and how it works has expanded rapidly in the past decade, partly because of the introduction of new technologies that can be used to examine and assess immune system status and function. As discussed in Chapter 2, we now know that there are many different cells that participate in immune responses and that these cells undergo transformations and evolutions throughout their lifetime. We also know that they are not autonomous cells operating independently of other bodily systems. Both nervous system influence and endocrine involvement in immune system activity have been noted, and there is reason to believe that the influence works both ways—that is, the immune system may also affect the nervous and endocrine systems. A field of study has recently grown around these ideas, called neuroimmodulation or *psychoneuroimmunology*. This field is important not only because of what it tells us about how behavior and systems of the body interact, but also because the immune system constitutes our major defense against infectious diseases and cancer.

PSYCHONEUROIMMUNOLOGY

The name of this field indicates a lot about this area of study. It includes three areas of bodily functioning formerly thought to be relatively independent. Psychological influences and the function of the nervous system have long been seen as interrelated, but the association of both with the immune system is a new and important development. Research on the effects of psychological and central nervous system (CNS) influences on the immune system and mutual influences of the immune, nervous, and endocrine systems has grown rapidly and clearly indicates that these systems are interrelated. The notion of an independent immune system has been discredited, and we have begun to clarify the ways in which the immune system interacts with other bodily systems. In this chapter we will examine some of this research, considering conditioning of the immune system as well as evidence that stress can influence the responsiveness of this system. We will then turn our attention to two diseases that are closely related to the immune system function—cancer and AIDS.

The Immune System

As you will recall, the immune system consists of a number of organs, cells, and factors that work together to prevent or combat infectious illnesses. Most potential pathogens never enter human hosts; the skin serves as a formidable barrier, and strong defenses in the digestive and respiratory systems are able to neutralize antigens that enter the body through the nose or mouth. However, when foreign particles are able to elude this defense and enter the body, a complex and highly interdependent chain of immune events result and is usually sufficient to neutralize or destroy them. These immune responses are "orchestrated" by lymphocytes—white blood cells that are precommitted to react only to specific antigens and to circulate as memory cells that are ready to clone themselves and to proliferate when the presence of these antigens is detected. When the antigen is actually encountered, B lymphocytes and T lymphocytes act through interdependent arms to neutralize and destroy the invader. These cells tell each other what they are doing as well as what target cells should be doing through the release of cytokines. They are also affected by endocrine and peptide changes, such as those that occur during stress.

Measuring Immunity

There are several ways of examining immune status that have been used in psychoneuroimmunology. Some are indirect; one can infer the immune function by measuring the rate of immune-sensitive tumor growth or of viral activity or antibodies to a virus. If the immune system protects against tumor growth or viral replication, rapid growth or replication would suggest poorer defensive function. Similarly, latent viruses such as herpes simplex (HSV) and the Epstein-Barr virus (EBV) are maintained by the immune system in a *latent state*. This latency is protective and prevents the virus from multiplying, destroying host cells, and infecting new cells. When the immune control of this inactive latency is reduced by stress, immunosuppressive drugs, or other agents, the virus reactivates and begins to replicate, causing antibodies to the virus to be produced. Measures of antibody titers—the amount of antibody present in a sample—can thus serve as a marker for whether the virus is active, and if it is—increased antibody titers—the indication is that the immune regulation of viruses is impaired (Jenkins and Baum, 1995).

Other common measures of immune status are more direct. One alternative is to measure the numbers of different immune cells in circulation by counting cells and lymphocyte subpopulations in a sample of blood. This tells us which and how many cells are in the bloodstream and reflects on the overall immune defense. To some extent these measures are limited in human studies by the fact that many immune cells live in lymph nodes or the spleen and that we cannot measure these cells in studies of people. The meaning of changes in the number of cells is clouded by this fact: The extent to which changes in the number of cells reflect the release of cells from storage in the spleen or lymph tissue or the migration of cells from circulation to interstitial sites where they are needed is not yet known. However, because the proper immune function probably depends on the adequate number of circulating white blood cells and on the balance of types of lymphocytes and other immune cells, these quantitative measures are useful and often necessary.

Another limitation of measures based on the number of cells is that it does not indicate anything about how well cells are working. If, for example, increasing cell numbers are due primarily to the premature release of underdeveloped cells, having more will not necessarily strengthen immunity. Measures of the capacity of individual cells to do their jobs, called *functional measures*, capture these aspects of cell activity. Together with cell numbers, they provide a good estimate of immune defenses. In many cases these measures are based on the natural reactions of immune cells. Recall, for example, that immune cells are capable of rapid and extensive replication when stimulated. Called *proliferation* or *blastogenesis*, this process allows conservation of energy by making it possible to maintain relatively low numbers of circulating cells. When an antigen is encountered, many replicates of the appropriately marked lymphocytes will be made to deal with the invader. In general, the stronger this proliferative response is, the better the system is thought to be operating. Assays of cell proliferation are conducted by culturing immune cells with mitogens or other stimuli that cause cell activation and replication and by measuring the number of replicates that are produced. Similarly, the ability of natural killer cells to attack and kill can be measured by culturing cells with tumor cells and by measuring the number or percentage of tumor cells that are killed.

Research in psychoneuroimmunology has already indicated that immune responses, greatly simplified in the previous summary, are governed by complicated sets of factors, including emotional and CNS-mediated variables. The "psycho-neuro" influences appear to operate at several levels, including (1) the distribution and migration of immune cells in circulation or interstitial fluid, (2) the strength of the replication/proliferation response by lymphocytes when stimulated, and (3) the efficacy or level of activity (such as the ability to kill foreign cells, and the production of cytokine). Evidence for psychological and neurally mediated influence in these stages of the immune system is uneven, and many mechanisms underlying immune changes are not known. It is fairly clear, for example, that stress suppresses some immune functions, depending on how long the stress lasts, gender, and other variables. Proliferation of lymphocytes appears to be poorer during or after stress than when no stress is experienced, and some studies indicate that stress reduces functions such as the ability to lyse (kill) target antigens. However, we know less about how these changes occur or whether they have clear health-related manifestations or consequences.

Endocrine Pathways

We know of at least one major pathway by which stress and emotional factors may affect the immune system. The endocrine system has been likened to a "second nervous system" in that it operates together with the nervous system in communicating with the various regions and systems of the body. Hormones are like signaling agents that work to increase or decrease release of other peptides and molecules. Each hormone may have several functions and may communicate with an impressive range of organs and glands. The adrenal hormones are a good example of this, having demonstrable effects on the immune system as well as on the cardiovascular system and other endocrine glands. Respiration, sweating, and a number of other functions are also affected. Adrenal medullary hormones are agents of the sympathetic nervous system (SNS) and act to strengthen and prolong the arousal of organ systems achieved by neural SNS activity. Epinephrine, released primarily by the adrenals, and norepinephrine, released distally in many regions of the body, also appear to affect the immune system. Together with other hormones they are an important pathway by which immune status can be altered (Ballieux, 1994).

These adrenal hormones interact with lymphocytes by way of adrenergic receptors on lymphocytes. Research suggests that beta-adrenergic receptors, which bind epinephrine, have a suppressive effect on cell productive activity when stimulated (Bachen et al., 1995). In other words, when circulating epinephrine encounters and attaches itself to beta receptors on lymphocytes, the result is a decrease in the cell's function. When catecholamine levels are manipulated (e.g., they are increased by infusing epinephrine), lymphocyte proliferation is suppressed by high levels of epinephrine and is enhanced at lower levels (Crary et al., 1983).

Another adrenal hormone, cortisol, is also an important immunomodulator. Produced by activation of the hypothalamic-pituitary-adrenal axis (HPA) (see Chapter 2), cortisol is a primary glucocorticoid responsible for anti-inflammatory and glucose utilization. Glucocorticoids, together with ACTH, which elicits glucocorticoid release from the adrenal cortex, have a wide range of immune system effects. Damage to thymus and lymph tissues, reduced antibody production by B cells, decreased cytokine production, poorer lymphocyte proliferation, and decreases in the number of cells in circulation are associated with elevated glucocorticoid levels (Munck and Puyre, 1991). Much of the research on which this conclusion is based is animal research, and cortisol has not shown equally strong effects on the human immune function.

Conditioning and Immunity

One way to demonstrate that the immune system is not autonomous is to show that it can be conditioned—for example, it can be made to respond to neutral stimuli paired with agents that affect it directly. We know from research on biofeedback (see Chapter 10) and from other studies that a number of bodily systems can be altered by operant and classical conditioning techniques. Miller (1969) and others have shown that physiological responses previously thought to be involuntary, such as heart rate, can be conditioned or shaped by instrumental procedures. People can learn to increase or decrease their heart rate, fingertip temperature, and even their brain waves (cf. Gatchel and Price, 1979). Drug effects have also been found to be conditionable; the effects of opiates may be elicited by neutral stimuli (such as the setting in which one takes drugs) in much the same way as by the drugs themselves (see Siegel, 1977).

The first systematic investigations in psychoneuroimmunology were Ader and Cohen's (1975) studies of conditioning and immunity. This research was based on a particularly powerful form of conditioning—learned taste aversion. It had been discovered that for animals, when illness and novel, neutral taste stimuli are paired, they develop an aversion to the previously neutral taste (see Garcia et al., 1974). Thus, if an animal is given a sweet-tasting fluid and then made ill (by injection or exposing it to radiation), it will avoid drinking the sweet-tasting liquid after this encounter. The strength of this paradigm is underscored by the fact that this learning seems to require only one pairing of the neutral and unconditioned stimuli. Once the pairing has been accomplished, the animal will avoid the conditioned stimulus. Anecdotes about people's experiences with illness also give support to the single-trial nature of conditioned taste aversion. Many people report that there are times when they are ill that they eat something, vomit later, and develop an aversion to the food that they had eaten before becoming ill. However, experience also tells us that this conditioning is not universal and depends on many factors.

Ader and Cohen (1975, 1981) found that immune system changes could also be conditioned to neutral taste stimuli. They had been using cyclophosphamide (CY)—a drug with immunosuppressive properties—to cause nausea and vomiting. In the course of their taste aversion studies they discovered that their animals were sick, and subsequent investigation produced evidence of conditioned immunosuppressive effects as well (Ader, 1981). In a series of elegant studies designed to follow up on this possibility these researchers found that a single pairing of a taste stimulus and CY produced an association between the taste and the immune status. Following a single pairing of saccharin-flavored water with CY, subsequent exposure to the saccharin water alone produced effects of CY, including immunosuppression.

In most of these studies conditioned animals were provided saccharin-flavored water to drink while unconditioned animals received plain water or saccharin that was not paired with the unconditioned stimulus. After allowing 15 minutes for drinking the animals were injected with CY. Three days later all the animals were injected with an antigen, intended to "set off" an immune response, and subgroups of each conditioning group were again given saccharin or plain water. Thus, animals who had received CY after drinking the saccharin solution the first time were now exposed to saccharine or plain water. Subsequent injections of CY or saline further divided these groups. (See Table 6.1.)

The results were as predicted: Animals exposed to the pairing of saccharin and CY exhibited immunosuppressive effects when reexposed to the saccharine alone. As can be seen in Figure 6.1, the placebo group, never exposed to CY, showed the strongest antibody response to the antigen, followed by the nonconditioned animals that had received CY after drinking plain water and had subsequently been given saccharin water. The conditioned groups showed weaker antibody responses, particularly when saccharin was presented immediately after the introduction of the antigen. The pairing of the two stimuli and the subsequent presentation of saccharin produced a weaker antibody response. Animals receiving CY alone showed almost no response to the antigen (Ader and Cohen, 1975).

Various combinations of conditions were used to rule out alternative explanations and/or to identify mechanisms by which this conditioned immunosuppression was accomplished. Replications of the basic studies produced comparable findings, again showing evidence of conditioned immunosuppression of antibody response to antigens (Ghanta et al., 1994; Maier, Watkins, and Fleschner, 1994; Rogers et al., 1979; Spector et al., 1994; Wayner et al., 1978). Generally, evidence is fairly strong that at least some immune system responses can be conditioned to neutral stimuli. More recent work has sought to identify the mediators of conditioned immunosuppression and its relationship to morphine or other drug conditioning (Coussons-Read et al., 1994).

Although most of these studies were done on animals, some evidence of conditioning of immune responses in humans has been reported as well. One study paired sherbet and white noise with injections of epinephrine (which causes brief increases in natural killer (NK) cell activity) and measured NK cell responses after subsequent exposure to the neutral stimuli. Elevated NK cell numbers and activity were enhanced by re-presentation of these stimuli in the absence of the epinephrine injection (Buske-Kirschbaum et al., 1992, 1994).

The importance of this finding may be seen in several ways. It not only serves as confirmation of earlier conditioning studies, it provides new information about how conditioning of autonomic responses may occur. These studies have been critical for the development of interest and research in psychoneuroimmunology, and the applicability of these studies is potentially im-

TABLE 6.1. Design of Conditioning Studies Showing Conditioned Immunosuppression

Column groups: **DAYS AFTER CONDITIONING** (0, 3, 6, 9) and, nested, **DAYS AFTER ANTIGEN** (0, 1–2, 3, 4–5, 6). The "Sample" column corresponds to 9 days after conditioning / 6 days after antigen.

Group	Adaptation (3)	Cond. Day (0)	Subgroup	0 (Antigen)	1–2	3	4–5	Sample (9 / 6)
Conditioned	H₂O	SAC + CY	US	H₂O + CY	H₂O	H₂O	H₂O	Sample
				H₂O	H₂O	H₂O + CY	H₂O	Sample
			CS₀	H₂O + Sal	H₂O	H₂O	H₂O	Sample
				H₂O	H₂O	H₂O + Sal	H₂O	Sample
			CS₁	SAC + Sal	H₂O	H₂O	H₂O	Sample
				H₂O	H₂O	SAC + Sal	H₂O	Sample
			CS₂	SAC + Sal	H₂O	SAC	H₂O	Sample
Nonconditioned	H₂O	H₂O + CY	NC	SAC + Sal	H₂O	H₂O	H₂O	Sample
				H₂O	H₂O	SAC + Sal	H₂O	Sample
Placebo	H₂O	H₂O + P	P	H₂O	H₂O	H₂O	H₂O	Sample

From R. Ader, *Psychoneuroimmunology.* San Diego: Academic Press, 1981, p. 286.

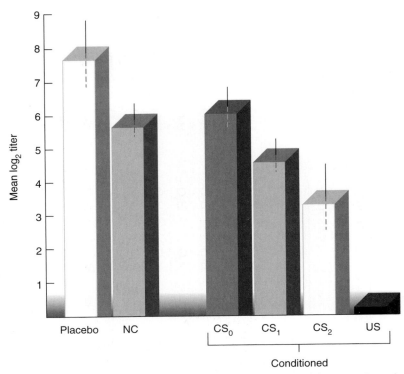

FIGURE 6.1. Antibody titers (mean ± SE) obtained 6 days after injection of antigen. NC, nonconditioned animals provided with saccharin on day 0 (day of antigen) or day 3; CS_0, conditioned animals that did not receive saccharin following antigen treatment; CS_1, conditioned animals reexposed to saccharin on day 0 or day 3; CS_2, conditioned animals reexposed to saccharin on days 0 *and* 3; US, conditioned animals injected with cyclophosphamide following antigenic stimulation.
Source: Reprinted, by permission the publisher, from R. Ader and N. Cohen. Behaviorally conditional immunosuppression. *Psychosomatic Medicine,* 1975, *37,* 334–340.

portant as well. It has been shown that conditioned immunosuppression reduces the graft versus host rejection response (see Bovbjerg et al., 1982), suggesting that the rejection of transplanted tissue may be reduced through careful application of a conditioning paradigm. The use of conditioning in bone marrow transplants to help suppress the immune system rejection of the graft has been described (Storb, 1994). This would have important implications for transplant surgery and required suppression of rejection by the immune system. It is also possible that conditioning could be used to reduce the medication doses required in cancer chemotherapy.

Recent findings indicate that antitumor functions of some lymphocytes can also be conditioned: Animals were exposed to the pairing of camphor odor with the injection of an immunomodulator and responded to the odor alone by showing increases in cytotoxic T and NK cell activity (Ghanta et al., 1994). The presentation of a novel stimulus during initial chemotherapy and the subsequent presentation of the now-conditioned stimulus with a smaller dose of whatever drug is being used might produce needed effects and reduce the aversive nature of the procedures. Studies of conditioned nausea in cancer treatment, however, suggest that some of these aversive effects may also become associated with the conditioned stimulus. Conditioned nausea appears to be accompanied by changes in immune measures, particularly among anxious patients (Fredrikson et al., 1993). In general, this supports the notion that conditioning might be used to modulate the dose of chemotherapy that is required.

Stress and Immunity

A number of studies have suggested that stress is associated with suppression of the immune system and that it may result in decreased immunocompetence. **Immunocompetence** refers to the ability to recognize and reject that which does not belong in the body. Thus, *immunocompetence* may be defined as the degree to which an antigen is identified, destroyed, and disposed of by a host of cells and processes. The occurrence of an infection or the development of a tumor may reflect a deficiency in immunocompetence, which may be temporary or long term. These simple definitions belie the complexity of the immune system but provide scientists with a working notion of what they are seeking to measure. If we want to learn whether stress affects immunocompetence and increases the likelihood of infectious illness, we would study immune system response as a means by which this occurs. The notion of immunocompetence provides us with some hint of what we will measure. Many measures of immunocompetence can be used, varying from the observation of tumor growth to counts of numbers of lymphocytes and estimates of how active lymphocytes are or how well they do their jobs.

Tumor Growth

Some studies consider tumor growth as an index of immunocompetence. It has been suggested that the immune system serves an **immunosurveillance** function, wherein immune cells scout for signs of tumors and help to destroy them while they are small. In other words, immune cells are on guard against the development of tumors and by acting against these tumors as soon as they are detected, immune cells protect against systemic disease. If stress or some other event interferes with this function, tumors may be allowed to grow to a size that the immune system can no longer deal with easily. At the same time, suppression of various immune system functions leading to a generalized reduction of immunocompetence may also allow more rapid growth of tumors. Of course, studies that show greater tumor growth after exposure to stress do not necessarily show that immune system changes cause these effects. Other processes and systems are also affected by stress and could be involved.

Studies that look at tumor growth as a function of stress have generally found evidence of stress-related changes. Sakakibara (1966) exposed one group of animals to bright, flashing light for 8 hours each day, a second group to continuous light, a third to continuous darkness, and a control group to normal lighting conditions. Chemically induced tumor growth was measured over a

20-week period, and results showed that the first group, exposed to flashing light, developed tumors more rapidly and nearly 80 percent of the animals in the group developed tumors. In the second group tumor growth took longer and was less common (64 percent); in the third group tumor growth took still longer and was less likely (24 percent). The control mice showed the same latency in tumor development as the mice that were kept in darkness and exhibited a similar incidence of tumors (36 percent developed tumors).

Stressors do not need to be unusual or severe to affect tumors. This was suggested by a study of prolonged handling of mice. Simply taking mice from their cages and holding them is stressful for them, and research suggests that handling them for 2 weeks results in decreases in antibody production, spleen cell production of cytokine, and proliferation of cells to antigen challenge (Street and Mosmann, 1991). This broad immune system suppression is accompanied by reduced ability to fight off tumors. Animals were handled every day for 2 weeks. At the end of the 2 weeks, a tumor cell line was injected into the animals. Tumor growth and lung metastases were measured 1 to 3 weeks later. Tumor development and metastases were substantially greater in handled mice than in nonhandled controls (Brenner et al., 1990).

Other studies of tumor growth are not as clear or consistent with the notion that stress decreases immunocompetence and increases tumor growth. Newberry et al. (1976) found no effects of electric shock on tumor growth in rats, whereas Henry and his colleagues (1975) found that isolation was associated with more rapid development of tumors in mice. Other studies report evidence of reduced tumor growth due to stress (see Marsh and Rasmussen, 1959; Nieburgs et al., 1979). In an extensive series of studies, Riley and his colleagues (1981) found evidence of stress effects on tumor development and some conditions that affect host resistance to the tumors. Using a number of stressors, these researchers found associations between increases in corticosteroid secretion and decreases in the time required for development of tumors (Riley, Fitzmaurice, and Spackman, 1981). Stress was associated with dramatic differences in mortality following implantation of tumors in female mice; 20 days after tumor implant more than 40 percent of mice that had been stressed prior to receiving the tumor had died, compared with only 20 percent of animals exposed to low stress conditions. By day 25 after implants more than 80 percent of stressed animals and only 40 percent of low stress animals had died.

Other studies suggest possible mechanisms by which these effects are generated. Riley and colleagues (1981) found rapid decreases in the number of circulating white blood cells following stress and damage to thymus tissue associated with elevations in corticosterone after stress (Riley et al., 1981; Spackman and Riley, 1975). Administration of corticosterone independent of stress was also found to be associated with enhanced tumor growth. Although other changes are also important and have been noted, the role of corticosteroids in stress effects on tumor growth appear to be important.

Lymphocyte Responsiveness

Another way to measure immunity is to study the ability of its parts to do their jobs. This index of immune function measures how reactive a cell is when it is called into action. If lymphocytes are very responsive, they will do their work well; if they are slow, weak, or inactive, they will not. As a result, many studies have used measures that tap important components of the overall immune defense such as how large a response is made by T and B cells to challenges or stimulation by antigen. Blood is drawn, prepared, and challenged in vitro by any of a number of stimulating **mitogens**, including concanavalin A (ConA), phytohemagglutinin (PHA), and pokeweed. Many studies have used these mitogens (which are powerful substances that cause lymphocytes to multiply) to stimulate cells and to mark cell activity. The resulting value from this test yields an estimate of how strong a response is being made by lymphocytes. Proliferation of lymphocytes in the presence of mitogens, called **blastogenesis**, is thus studied. If exposure to a mitogen results in large increases in cells, the immune system is considered strong.

Several studies have considered stress due to bereavement as a factor in immune function. Bartrop et al. (1977), for example, studied both T and B cells following the death of a spouse and found that lymphocyte response to PHA and ConA was reduced during the 2 months after the death compared with response by a control group (See Figure 6.2.) The number of T and B cells was comparable across time and group. Stein and colleagues (1985) have reported several studies of immune changes associated with depression and bereavement (see Schleifer et al., 1980, 1983, 1984). They studied a small group of men whose wives were dying, assessing immune function before the spouse's death as well as 5 to 7 weeks after. Again, the number of cells did not appear to change, but responsiveness of cells to mitogens was significantly different from pre- to post-bereavement samplings. Control group subjects showed no changes over time.

A study relating the occurrence of life events to changes in immune status also showed effects of stress on immunity (Locke et al., 1978). When life changes were frequent and reported distress was high as well, measures of NK cell activity were the lowest. This finding is similar to that reported by Greene, Betts, and Ochitull (1978), indicating that high stress and poor coping were related to a poorer immune function. Other studies have reported a poorer lymphocyte response to mitogens among people subjected to sleep deprivation and among astronauts following the return to earth (see Fisher et al., 1972; Palmblad et al., 1976, 1979).

Other distressed states also appear to be related to immunocompetence. Among spinal cord injury and stroke patients, NK and T cell function were suppressed for several months after the injury but recovered somewhat with rehabilitation (Cruse et al., 1993). Stein, Keller, and Schleifer (1985) reported that inpatients who were classified as depressed exhibited a poorer response to mitogen challenge. Depression has been linked to substantially weaker NK cell activity in other studies when compared with nondepressed people (Irwin et al., 1990), and other studies have suggested that psychiatric patients have poorer immune system control of viruses and fewer T-helper lymphocytes (see Krueger et al., 1984). Despite some controversy, there appear to be effects of depression related to the immune function (Herbert and Cohen, 1993; Stein, 1989).

Stressors do not need to be exotic or extremely powerful to affect immune system status. Several studies conducted among students have shown changes

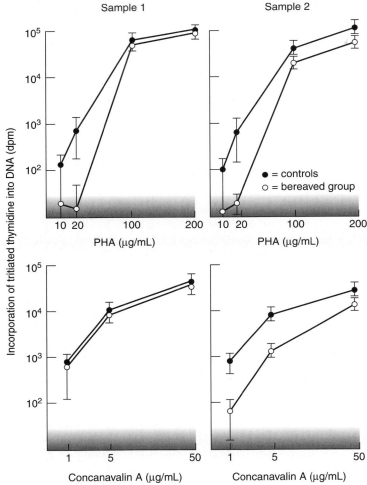

FIGURE 6.2. The effect of bereavement on lymphocyte proliferation after challenge with phytohemagglutinin (PHA) and concanavalin A in vitro. Sample 1 was obtained shortly after and sample 2 about 8 weeks after bereavement.
Source: Reprinted, by permission of the publisher, from R. W. Bartrop et al. Depressed lymphocyte function after bereavement. *Lancet* 1977, *I*, 834–836.

in different indices of immune function as a function of examinations. Kiecolt-Glaser and her colleagues (1986), for example, reported decreased NK cell activity due to exams in medical school, compared with levels exhibited 1 month earlier (Kiecolt-Glaser et al., 1984) (see Figure 6.3). Loneliness was also associated with lower NK cell activity, and subsequent studies found that examinations were also associated with a decreased number of NK cells (Glaser et al., 1986). Percentages of T cells that may be classified as helper cells were also found to be lower among medical students during exams than they had been earlier, and production of interferon, an important lymphokine, was sup-

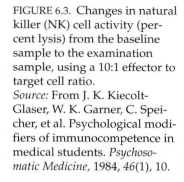

FIGURE 6.3. Changes in natural killer (NK) cell activity (percent lysis) from the baseline sample to the examination sample, using a 10:1 effector to target cell ratio.
Source: From J. K. Kiecolt-Glaser, W. K. Garner, C. Speicher, et al. Psychological modifiers of immunocompetence in medical students. *Psychosomatic Medicine,* 1984, 46(1), 10.

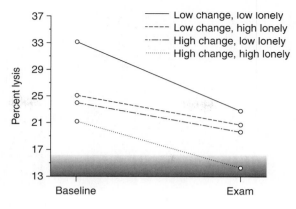

pressed among students during exams relative to preexam levels (Kiecolt-Glaser et al., 1986). Further, examinations were associated with decreased proliferative responses to mitogen challenge (Glaser et al., 1985).

A somewhat different approach to documenting immune system status is to examine antibody titers to latent viruses. This is an indirect approach because it uses the outcome (antibody titers) to measure how well the immune system maintains the virus in a latent state. Some viruses, such as herpes simplex or Epstein-Barr, remain dormant in the body following initial infection. In other words, after the first infection with such a virus, the immune system may control the virus but cannot destroy or eliminate it. The virus remains in a latent state, sufficiently suppressed by immune system activity to keep it in check. When the virus is active, B cells secrete an antibody to destroy it; when the virus is latent, antibody secretion is much lower as the virus is not freely circulating through the body. If something happens to weaken the immune system control of latent viruses and they become active, antibody titers to the virus will *increase.* Thus, more antibodies for latent viruses suggest poorer immune function, particularly in the absence of changes in antibodies to nonlatent viruses. Treatment of patients with immunosuppressive drugs, such as in chemotherapy, has been shown to increase antibodies to latent viruses (Kiecolt-Glaser and Glaser, 1987). Results of studies measuring antibody titers to latent viruses have also provided evidence of stress-related changes in immune function. Loneliness and examination stress were found to be associated with elevated antibody titers to the Epstein-Barr virus among medical students (see Glaser et al., 1985) (see Figure 6.4).

Studies of lymphocyte function have yielded a number of important findings, including the general one that stress reduces some aspects of immunity. They also suggest that other studies have capitalized on inoculations to examine the ability of the immune system to develop antibodies for a "new" antigen. For example, one can study responses to vaccination and how quickly the immune system starts making antibodies for the antigen that was injected. Glaser and his colleagues (1992) studied the extent to which stress and anxiety affected how quickly students produced antibodies to hepatitis B during the three-shot vaccination process for this disease. Those who did not show evidence of antibody production were more responsive to stress associated with examinations (Glaser et al., 1992). Subsequent investigation by others has also

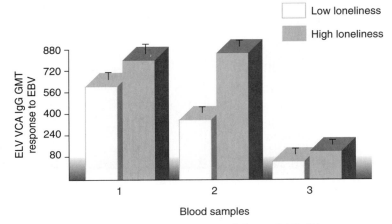

FIGURE 6.4. Changes in the GMT (±SE) of EBV VCA IgG immune response to Epstein-Barr virus (EBV) in high and low loneliness medical students across the three sample points.
Source: Adapted from R. Glaser, J. K. Kiecolt-Glaser, C. E. Speicher, and J. E. Holiday. Stress, loneliness and changes in herpes virus latency. *Journal of Behavioral Medicine,* 1985, *8*(3), 255.

produced evidence of stress effects in response to vaccination to hepatitis B and the search for mechanisms by which the sensitizing effects of inoculation are inhibited is underway. It is possible to reverse this pattern, prevent stress-related decreases in immune function, and/or increase function among stressed individuals to "normal" levels. In a study of residents of old-age homes subjects were given one of three treatments (Kiecolt-Glaser et al., 1985). In one treatment they were trained to relax; in another they were provided with enhanced social contact; and in the third no intervention was applied. Subjects in the first treatment group were the only ones to show changes, but these changes were important. Relative to baseline and other groups, subjects given relaxation training exhibited heightened NK cell activity and lower antibody titers to latent viruses and reported fewer stress-related symptoms. Similar findings have been noted with medical students, among whom the most frequent relaxation practice was associated with higher levels of lymphocytes, and among undergraduates who were taught different ways to relax (see Kiecolt-Glaser et al., 1986).

Acute Stress and Immunity

A relatively new area of investigation has been the study of acute stress and immune function. As we have seen, studies of stressors such as bereavement have shown some relationship between chronic stress and immunity, but the nature of these studies precluded the investigation of mechanisms. If studies of stress could be moved to the laboratory where experimental control could help to rule out alternative explanations, a better picture of how stress affects the immune system could be gained. However, it was not known whether relatively mild stressors such as those that one could use in a laboratory study would reliably affect immune function. After all, a "stressful task" is not nearly as strong a stressor as bereavement, losing one's job, or even examinations. It was also not at all clear that changes in immune function would occur rapidly enough to be seen in a typical laboratory study lasting 2 or 3 hours.

The first studies of acute stress and immune function answered both of these questions (Manuck et al, 1991; Weisse et al., 1990; Zakowski et al., 1992). Manuck and his colleagues studied a variety of immune indicators in subjects who worked on stressful tasks—the Stroop test and mental arithmetic. These stressors, involving difficult performance under time pressure, have been shown to be effective in eliciting cardiovascular reactivity (see Chapter 5). These investigators found that the challenging, stressful tasks increased blood pressure and decreased lymphocyte proliferation to mitogen stimulation. A similar study using a different stressor (a gory surgery film) also produced evidence of suppressed proliferation to mitogen challenge (Zakowski et al., 1992). These studies were partly consistent with another, earlier study using yet a different stressor (Weisse et al., 1990). Together they suggested that brief laboratory stressors could produce reliable changes in immune function in an hour or less. Further, they indicated that these changes were correlated with measures of cardiovascular or endocrine reactivity, suggesting sympathetic arousal as one mechanism of this change (Manuck et al., 1991; Zakowski et al., 1992).

Since these initial studies, acute, rapid changes in immune function have been linked to other brief laboratory stressors as well as to parachute jumping (see Figure 6.5) (Cacioppo et al., 1995; Schedlowski et al., 1993). Changes in immune system activity have been detected within 2 to 5 minutes of the start of a stressor (Bachen et al., in press; Delahanty et al., 1996), have been associated with differences in types of stressors (Bachen et al., 1992; Zakowski et al., 1994), and are reduced when beta-blockers—medicine that blocks beta receptors and prevents epinephrine from stimulating cells or organs—are applied prior to the stressor (see Bachen, 1994). There is also evidence that NK cell numbers and activity increase immediately after an acute stressor (see Figure 6.6) (Delahanty et al., 1996; Naliboff et al., 1991; Schedlowski et al., 1993) but decrease below baseline levels an hour or more after the stressor (see Cohen et al., 1993; Schedlowski et al., 1993; Sieber et al., 1992).

Chronic Stress and Immunity

Although these and other studies provide reasonably clear evidence that acute stress is associated with transient immunological changes, the nature of these changes is a little less clear when chronic stress and longer-term effects are considered. Monjan (1981) suggested that chronic stress may have the opposite effects that acute stress has; that is, chronic stress may *enhance* some aspects of immune system function. Earlier studies of rats exposed to crowding for 1 or 5 weeks prior to immunization produced fewer circulating antibodies in crowded animals than in uncrowded animals, but after 5 weeks crowded animals showed an enhanced effect to immunization (Joasoo and McKenzie, 1976; Solomon, 1969). Similarly, Monjan and Collector (1977) varied the duration of noise stress in a study of mice and found differences in immune system effects depending on the length of noise exposure. All mice were exposed to 15 minutes noise per day, spread out evenly over a 3-hour period. Duration was varied comparing mice exposed to the noise for different numbers of days, and

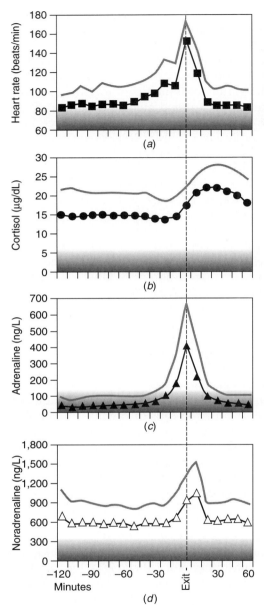

FIGURE 6.5. Heart rate frequencies (*a*) and plasma levels of cortisol (*b*), adrenaline (*c*), and noradrenaline (*d*) before, during, and after the long jump at 10-min intervals from 120 min before to 60 min after the jump. Data are expressed as mean ± standard deviation: (SD).
Source: Adapted from M. Schedlowski, R. Jacobs, G. Stratmann, et al. Changes of natural killer cells during acute psychological stress. *Journal of Clinical Immunology,* 1993, *13*(2), 121.

the results of the study showed that acute noise exposure (fewer days) was associated with suppression of immune responsiveness while longer-term stress was associated with enhancement of immune function. (See Figure 6.7.) Consistent with this, results of a study by Sklar and Anisman (1979) showed that a single day of noise stress reduced resistance to tumor growth, whereas 10 days of noise stress resulted in enhancement of resistance and slower tumor growth.

A likely explanation for these suppressing and enhancing effects of stress is that adaptation or habituation of stress responding is responsible for differ-

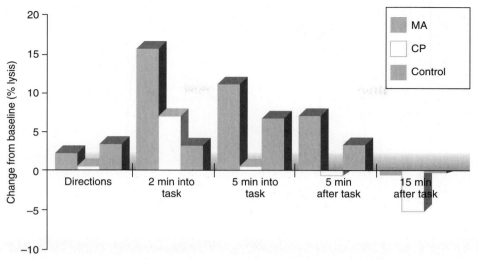

FIGURE 6.6. Change in mean NK cell activity (% lysis) averaged across effector: target ratio from baseline to blood draws 2-6. MA = mental arithmetic group; CP = cold pressor group.
Source: Adapted from D. L. Delahanty, A. L. Dougall, L. Hawken, et al. Time course of natural killer cell activity and lymphocyte proliferation in response to two acute stressors in healthy men. *Health Psychology,* 1996, *15*(1), 52.

ent effects. Recall from Chapter 3 that organisms adapt to stressful experiences; after repetitive exposure to the same stressor, response to it decreases and may disappear entirely. This appears to occur as a result of psychological adaptation and successful coping rather than as a result of changes in physiological systems. In other words, as people or animals deal with a stressor or "get used to it," biological responses slowly diminish and return to normal. In the studies of stress and immune system function just discussed it is possible that the animals adapted to the stressor when it was chronic, and therefore were exhibiting fewer stress responses after 10 days than they were after 1 or 2 days. If so, one could expect that the immune system function would return to normal or might even exceed baseline levels over a short period of time (many physiological systems show a rebound effect when a suppressing force is removed, actually exceeding basal levels briefly). This has been used to explain other observations of initial suppression and subsequent recovery or enhancement of immune function during chronic stress in animals (see Riley et al., 1981). However, another study found a delayed but persistent suppression of NK cell function among mice following exposure to a stressor (Kandil and Borysenko, 1987) suggesting that adaptation did not occur in this case or that other processes are also involved in temporal dynamics of stress-related immune function changes.

Studies of chronic stress and immune response in humans have provided more support for the notion that adaptation is an important factor in the course of immune system activity. Kiecolt-Glaser and colleagues (1994) have argued that findings showing adaptation and/or enhancement of immune system function during chronic stress may have been due to the nature of the

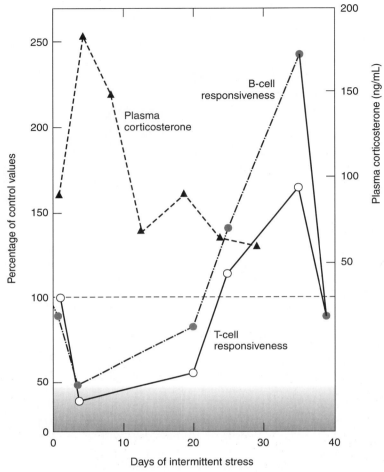

FIGURE 6.7. Immunosuppression is followed by immunoenhancement during a chronic stress experiment. Plasma corticosterone levels were elevated during the period of immunosuppression but dropped as the animals apparently became adapted to the chronic stress.
Source: Adapted by V. Riley, M. Fitzmaurice, and D. Spackman. Psychoneuroimmunologic factors in neoplasia: Studies in animals. In R. Ader (Ed.), *Psychoneuroimmunology.* New York: Academic Press, 1981, p. 82.

stressor. Physical stressors, such as noise, that were used in some studies just discussed may be more easily adapted to than are the complex chronic stressors that people encounter naturalistically. They reported a study of family caregivers for patients with Alzheimer's disease—a progressively debilitating disease that places great demands on those responsible for patient care. Arguing that people should adapt less readily to such a stressor, they studied a group of 34 caregivers and compared them with a control group of matched, noncaregiving participants. The length of care provided ranged from new diagnoses to 11 years, with a mean of more than 33 months. The results of a battery of immunological assessments suggested that caregivers had suppressed immune systems; cellular immune system control of latent viruses was poorer, percentages of T lymphocytes and T-helper lymphocytes were lower, and the helper/suppressor ratio was smaller among caregivers than among controls (see Esterling et al., 1994, in press; Kiecolt-Glaser et al., in press). These data suggest that stress can give rise to persistent changes in immunity and that these changes can occur in several components of immunosurveillance (Bodnar and Kiecolt-Glaser, 1994).

Similar findings have been reported in newlyweds and couples undergoing marital conflict (see Malarkey et al., 1994; Kiecolt-Glaser et al., in press). Another study of humans exposed to chronic stress, comparing people living near the Three Mile Island (TMI) nuclear power plant with a control sample, also suggests that long-term stress can result in immune system change in an apparently negative direction. The nuclear accident at TMI was threatening and stressful for many area residents and symptoms of distress persisted for years afterward (see Baum et al., 1983). A very small sample of people living near the power plant who continued to exhibit symptoms of stress were studied more than 6 years after the accident there while comparable measures were collected among similar control subjects. Results showed a higher number of circulating neutrophils and a lower number of B cells, NK cells, and cytotoxic T lymphocytes among the TMI area residents (McKinnon et al., 1989). Data also indicated poorer cellular control over latent viruses among TMI subjects than among controls.

Stress appears to have direct psychophysiological effects on immunity: Stress is associated with bodily changes such as increased levels of cortisol, which can destroy immune tissue and alter the system's ability to function. However, there is another way in which stress can affect immunity, and that is a more indirect pathway through behavioral change. Stress does not only affect immune function directly through changes in physiological systems: It can result in increases in drug use, smoking, drinking, and so on, which could contribute to chronic effects on immunity. Do these behaviors have any implications for the immune system?

Smoking and the Immune System Function

Although on one level it seems obvious that smoking affects the immune system, specifying its effects and consequences has been tricky. One way that cigarette smoking affects immunity is straightforward enough: Tobacco and its products (e.g., smoke and tar) are antigens, interacting with the immune system to result in the production of specific antibodies. Some studies have shown that animals can be shown to experience allergic reactions to tobacco products and have argued that this allergy may be relevant to understanding coronary heart disease (CHD) and hypertension (see Fontana et al., 1959). Among humans, allergic reactions to tobacco extracts have also been found (Kreis et al., 1970; Panayotopoulos et al., 1974). Independent of its role as an antigen, cigarette smoking appears to affect immune status as well. Chronic smoking damages the respiratory tract mucus, thus reducing the number and function of cilia that normally trap invading microorganisms, dust, and other particles (see Ballenger, 1960; Regland et al., 1976). Impairment of this resistance increases the work that must be done by other agents of immunity. However, studies have also shown wide variation in the effects of smoking on mucosa, with some smokers showing evidence of damage and others showing little change or even enhanced resistance (Cameron et al., 1970; Yeates et al., 1975).

The consequences of smoking extend beyond mucociliary damage and include effects on macrophages and lymphocytes. Smoking appears to increase the number of macrophages in the lungs (see Holt and Keast, 1977). It has also been reported that the composition of macrophages is different in smokers from that in nonsmokers (Pratt et al., 1969) and that macrophages are capable of adapting to the effects of cigarette smoke (Holt and Keast, 1977). However, the macrophage function apparently is harmed by smoking; the ability of macrophages to engulf and destroy foreign material is reduced by cigarette smoke (Green and Carolin, 1967; Maxwell et al., 1967). Some studies have found no differences in the macrophage function among smokers and nonsmokers, and this effect may be more common among animals than among humans.

The numbers and function of T lymphocytes are also affected by smoking. In animals initial exposure to cigarette smoke appears to enhance proliferation of lymphocytes to mitogen stimulation, whereas prolonged exposure decreases proliferation (Carlens, 1976; Thomas et al., 1973). In humans the picture is more complex. An increased number of T cells has been found in young smokers, mirroring the findings with initial exposure of mice (Silverman et al., 1975). However, for older smokers or for those with a history of heavy, chronic smoking, there were no differences in the number of T cells between smokers and nonsmokers. Several other studies in humans have found few differences in T-cell numbers or function among smokers and nonsmokers, and the importance of smoking for cellular-based immunity has not been clearly established.

These findings, many based on animal studies, do not provide much information about whether smoking actually affects the immune system's illness-fighting activity. Other studies do suggest that smoking increases the incidence of infectious illnesses such as influenza. In one study those smoking more than 10 cigarettes a day showed increased risk for the flu, and in another study incidence of clinical and subclinical influenza among smokers was higher than among nonsmokers (Finklea et al., 1969; Waldman et al., 1969). Another study, of 39 healthy white men who smoked, looked at a range of hormonal and immune measures before and after 28 of them quit smoking for 1 month (Meliska et al., 1995). Some measures showed little change, but NK cell activity increased after smoking cessation and cortisol decreased. These changes were not correlated with each other, but these studies suggest that smoking has effects that may be associated with enhanced susceptibility to illness.

Generally, smoking affects bodily resistance to infection in several ways. In humans nicotine affects the lymphocyte function, and tobacco smoke has stimulatory effects at low levels and inhibitory effects in higher doses, with the overall effect suggesting immunosuppression (Holt and Keast, 1977). It appears that smoking affects lymphocytes and macrophages, and it may well be associated with mucociliary damage and destruction of tissue that helps to protect us from bacteria and viruses. Much work is still needed to determine more clearly how and when cigarette smoking affects immunity and resistance to disease.

185

*Psychoneuro-
immunology*

Alcohol and the Immune Function

There are a number of reasons to suspect that alcohol affects immune status. First, alcoholics tend to have poorer health and studies have long suggested that they are more susceptible to infectious diseases. Alcohol use has also been linked to some cancers, and anecdotal evidence also links heavy alcohol use with a range of ailments and health-related behavioral and biological risks (see Mufti, 1992). Studies of effects of experimentally manipulated alcohol levels have also shown some links, although this "circumstantial evidence" is correlational and the reasons for observed immune changes are not all known. Conclusions about alcohol and immunity can only be made with caution. For example, we know that a number of factors that could be responsible for the relationship between alcohol and infectious illness are not necessarily immunologic factors (see Adams, 1994). Alcoholics, for example, may also have poor nutrition, be exposed to more pathogens, or lack proper shelter and clothing (particularly if they are homeless). Any of these variables could be related to health in addition to *or instead of* alcohol consumption and these other factors could be the reason for alcohol-illness associations (see Waltz and Watson, 1992).

However, there are a number of indirect or correlational and experimental studies of alcohol and immunity at which we can look. For example, excessive alcohol consumption, over long periods of time, can cause liver damage and cirrhosis. In turn, alcohol-induced cirrhosis has effects on immune function, activating and elevating immune function whether or not activation is needed (Diez-Ruiz et al., 1995). Immune-mediated skin disorders are exacerbated by alcohol use (Higgins and duVirier, 1994) and bacterial infections appear to be more severe and frequent among people who consume substantial amounts of alcohol (Antony et al., 1993). However, research on these disease outcomes— that is, studies looking at relationships between alcohol and illness—rarely measure the presumed immune mediators and cannot draw conclusions about the causes of alcohol-related illness.

Alcohol also appears to have a number of direct effects on immunity although most studies have used animal models of alcohol administration. Conclusions about the effects of alcohol on lymphocytes and other immune cells can be drawn from this literature but should be applied cautiously. For example, the ability of macrophages in rabbits to move toward infections was reduced by the consumption of alcohol in quantities that approximated a 0.1 percent blood level in humans (Louria, 1963). Recall from Chapter 2 that one mechanism by which macrophages find sites where they are needed is by responding and moving toward chemical signals released by the body. Weakened chemotaxis by macrophages was also observed by Nungester and Klesper (1939) following the administration of as little as 100 mg/dL of ethanol, and other studies show that larger doses also retard the ability of human granulocytes to approach infected areas (Spagnuolo and MacGregor, 1975). In Spagnuolo and MacGregor's (1975) study continuous oral administration of alcohol (320 mL of 100 percent ethanol daily) for a week reduced chemotaxis by granulocytes, but similar administration of much smaller quantities (less than 100 mL of 100 percent ethanol) did not cause any impairment.

Alcohol also appears to be associated with weaker lymphocyte proliferative responses (Grossman et al., 1993a; Worlfe, Miner, and Michalek, 1993) and poorer macrophage antiantigen activity (Antony et al., 1993). Of more clinical significance is the fact that after infusion of alcohol immune activity against *E. coli* and *H. influenza* Type B was reduced, but it returned to normal levels 5 hours after administration (Johnson et al., 1969). There is also some evidence that alcohol may increase the replication of HIV, the virus that causes AIDS although there is considerable controversy about the role of alcohol in this disease (Bagasra et al., 1993). The killing ability of lymphocytes also appears to be affected by alcohol, with significant reductions of T-cell cytotoxicity observed following the administration of relatively high levels of alcohol (Kemp and Berke, 1973; Stacey, 1984). At lower levels of alcohol lymphocyte toxicity may be increased or unaffected (Kendall and Targan, 1980).

Recent discoveries about fetal alcohol syndrome and the consequences of fetal exposure to alcohol have led to interest in alcohol and child development. Several studies have tried to determine whether a child's lymphocytes can be affected by alcohol use by the mother during pregnancy. Monjan and Mandell (1980) studied children of alcoholics and found that their T cells exhibited poor DNA synthesis and inhibited proliferation. An investigation of nonhuman primates who had been exposed to alcohol *in utero* found that risk for serious infectious illness was greater among alcohol-exposed children as were some indices of immune function (Grossman et al., 1993a). Several other studies also suggest that alcohol retards the ability of lymphocytes to multiply when they are needed to deal with foreign material (see Atkinson et al., 1977; Johnson et al., 1981; Taylor et al., 1993). Further, lymphocyte activity appears to be suppressed among alcoholics and children with fetal alcohol syndrome (Johnson et al., 1981; Young et al., 1979).

Gender differences in alcohol-immune relationships have been studied, again mostly in animal populations. Grossman et al. (1993b) fed male and female Sprague-Dauley rats a liquid diet for 2 months. The diet contained ethanol in concentrations approximating 30 to 45 percent of their daily calories. Control animals also consumed a liquid diet, but no alcohol. Rats who drank ethanol showed weaker proliferative responses to mitogen challenge although this effect was stronger among female animals (Grossman et al., 1993b). Differences between males and females in alcohol-immune system relationships could have been due to different hormonal or immunological response patterns or to other factors and further research on this issue is necessary.

Fortunately, the effects of excessive alcohol use may be long-lasting but do not appear to be permanent. Alcoholics and moderate drinkers who were undergoing a program to quit drinking had delayed hypersensitivity reactions measured before, during, and after they became sober (Tonnesen et al., 1992). Results suggested that immune response became stronger the longer participants remained alcohol-free and that after 2 months delayed hypersensitivity responses were normal (i.e., comparable to the control group; Tonnesen et al., 1992). In another study interferon production was suppressed among alcoholics but recovered 30 days after participants stopped drinking (Windle et al.,

1993). Similar studies in animal populations also suggest that the immunological effects of alcohol use may persist for a while after alcohol consumption stops, but that responses eventually return to normal (Norman et al., 1991). Lasting effects on immunity appear to be most closely tied to heavy drinking, but there are reasons to believe that even social drinking may affect immune function and host defense (see Bounds et al., 1994; Breslin and Baum, in press).

To summarize, research provides some evidence of alcohol-related consequences for immune system function. Macrophages appear to be inhibited, moving more slowly to sites where they are needed and, perhaps, being produced in smaller numbers. Some lymphocytes also show effects, as T cell proliferation in the face of challenge and their cytotoxicity seems to be inhibited. However, several aspects of the immune system appear to be unaffected; no inhibition of antibody production has been observed and the overall number of lymphocytes is not reduced by alcohol (Caizza and Orary, 1976; Conge and Gouche, 1985; Lundy, 1975). The dose and chronicity of alcohol consumption also appear to be important. In most cases when alcohol is consumed in small or moderate amounts and drinking is irregular, effects are small and/or transient. Among alcoholics, however, effects are substantial and related to more widespread damage to bodily tissues, including the thymus.

Caffeine and Immunity

People tend to drink more coffee and other caffeine-containing beverages when they are under stress, and research suggests that this may hinder immune function. Studies have shown that high doses of caffeine suppress a range of functions, including increased mortality to *E. coli* bacteria (see Saxena et al., 1984). At low doses some evidence of enhanced immune function was observed. The addition of caffeine directly to cultures of spleen cells after antigen stimulation resulted in a reduction of antibody production (Laux and Klesiuns, 1973), but evidence suggests that whatever effects are found may likely be due to caffeine stimulation of cyclic adenosine monophosphate (AMP), which, in turn, can reduce the overall activity of lymphocytes (Borysenko and Borysenko, 1982). In this regard the immuno-enhancing or suppressing effects of caffeine should be similar to effects of catecholamines released during stress. Drinking coffee while under stress could produce particularly clear effects.

Summary

The importance of research showing direct psychophysiological effects on immune status or function and of behavioral influences on immune system activity lies in several areas. On the one hand, the notion that the immune, nervous, and endocrine systems are interrelated and integrated by the central nervous system (CNS) opens new possibilities for the study of regulation of internal bodily function and homeostasis. Conditioning studies show that the same processes by which heart rate or other peripheral responses may be regulated by an individual may apply to the immune system as well. Finally, the finding that stress can affect the immune system demands study of how stress may contribute to illness associated with immune system deficiency. Impaired immune system function clearly contributes to the incidence of infectious illness, although available research evidence has not clearly established stress-related immunosuppression as a cause of these illnesses. In another category, however, there are more devastating diseases directly related to immune system function—cancer and acquired immune deficiency syndrome (AIDS).

Stress, Immunity, and Infectious Illness

We have learned a great deal about our immune system and its relationships to endocrine and nervous system activity and biobehavioral processes such as stress or the use of drugs. As a result, the quality and scope of basic research on CNS mediation of bodily function and immunity have benefited greatly. However, studying psychological and neuroendocrine influences on the immune system is also important because they may affect our vulnerability to disease. Cancer, which appears to be dependent to some extent on immune system surveillance, and HIV disease and AIDS, diseases of the immune system, will be considered in the following sections. Before turning to them, we should consider what we know about stress and susceptibility to less dramatic or life-threatening diseases such as influenza or the common colds.

Although we have learned about many aspects of our immune system, we do not fully understand the scope of these activities, and how they all come together to combat pathogens that invade our bodies still offers unsolved mysteries. We know, for example, that stress is correlated with illnesses such as colds and flu, and this holds up across several ways of measuring stress (see Cohen and Williamson, 1991). Studies of life events that could be considered stressful and of daily hassles have shown that "high stress" people had more episodes of upper respiratory infections (URIs) and more symptoms of illness than did "lower stress" participants (see Graham et al., 1986; Meyer and Haggarty, 1962). Naturalistic studies of influenza susceptibility have also suggested that stress was related to greater vulnerability to flu (Clover et al., 1989). Some researchers have suggested that this may be due to greater exposure to germs among stressed groups, but there is no good evidence that this is the case (see Cohen and Herbert, in press). Further, because these studies are correlational, we have no way of knowing whether stress-related events are involved or whether independent factors take into account observed effects. These findings, together with research suggesting that stress is associated with increased viral activity (see Jenkins and Baum, 1995; Kiecolt-Glaser and Glaser, 1987; Luborsky et al., 1976) offer circumstantial evidence of a relationship between stress and infectious illness. What we should be able to say is that *stress increases susceptibility to colds and flu* in a well-controlled study of people who are systematically exposed to infectious agents such as cold viruses.

Fortunately, such research has been done. Recent studies of viral challenges, in which stress is measured at the start of the study and people are randomly assigned to exposure to either a cold virus or a benign agent (e.g., saline), offer strong evidence of a stress-illness relationship. Briefly, participants are brought to a clinical unit or hotel, stress and other variables are measured at the start of the study, and participants are housed in semi-isolated conditions for a week. Early in this week participants are given an inhaler containing a cold or flu virus or saline, and this exposure is the primary experimental manipulation of the study. As a result, all participants in one group are directly exposed to the virus, whereas none in the other group is exposed. Differences in illness rates, severity, and disease characteristics are the major dependent variables in these studies. The first of these studies, investigations, of nearly 400 people exposed to a virus or saline, showed that stressful life events, perceptions of stress, and negative mood were related to whether participants got sick (Cohen et al., 1991). Although immune function changes due to stress are hypothesized as a cause for this greater vulnerability, data reflecting on this were not available. Other studies also suggest enhanced susceptibility to infection and severity of illness as a result of mood and stress, but the mechanisms underlying this are still not clear (Stone et al., 1993; Cohen et al., 1995). Despite these promising advances, we still do not have definite evidence of stress-enhanced vulnerability to viral infection or of how this occurs.

Stress, Immune Function, and Healing

Another way in which stress or other behavioral influences on immunity may have implications for health and well-being is in wound healing. Cellular immune functions play a role in inflammation and healing processes when the skin is cut or abraded and cytokines such as interleukin-1 appear to play a role in healing too. Stress suppresses all of these functions under a number of conditions and can interfere with healing. The best way to test this idea would be to create wounds and to measure how rapidly they heal, comparing stressed and nonstressed (or less stressed) participants.

Such a study has been reported (Kiecolt-Glaser et al., 1995). Thirteen caregivers for Alzheimer's disease patients and a like number of lower stress control subjects (ages 47 to 81) were recruited and agreed to undergo a "punch biopsy," a procedure used to biopsy skin tissue. The biopsy created a small circular wound on subjects' nondominant arm (each wound was about 4 mm). Each wound was dressed in the same way and for the same amount of time. Observation and photographs of the wounds were made until healed and were used to measure the size of the wound at each point in time after injury. Blood samples were also taken and used to measure interleukin-1.

Caregiver participants showed slower wound healing than did controls; it took stressed caregivers nearly 49 days to heal completely, whereas control subjects healed in 30 days (Kiecolt-Glaser et al., 1995) (see Figure 6.8). In addition, caregivers had larger wounds than did controls throughout the study although these differences were the greatest 6 to 21 days after the injury (see Figure 6.9). Interleukin-1 measures also suggested that caregivers had a weaker response than did controls, resulting in lower amounts of cytokine. Finally, caregivers showed poorer healing than did controls when peroxide was applied to the wounds.

This study strongly suggests that wound healing is affected by stress and other immune system modulators. How well this applies to larger or more severe wounds, wounds that are sutured (as in surgery or to seal up a deep cut), or wounds associated with other medical procedures (such as the resection of the ureter in prostate surgery, and the healing of breast tissue after lumpectomy) remains to be seen. However, this study provides additional evidence of clinically significant results of stress-related immunosuppression.

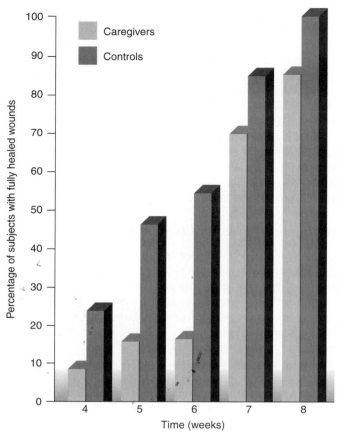

FIGURE 6.8. Percentage of caregivers and controls whose wounds had healed with time.
Source: Adapted from J. K. Kiecolt-Glaser, P. T. Marucha, W. B. Malarkey, et al. Slowing of wound healing by psychological stress. *The Lancet*, 1995, *346*, 1195.

CANCER

Cancer is the second leading cause of death in the United States. It is an "old" disease that we have known about for a long time, but it still defies ready description. We are learning about its causes but as yet we do not know all of them or how to prevent cancer, and treatments for cancer are still imperfect. We have been successful in learning how to prevent and cure some forms of cancer, but many others still cause thousands of deaths every year. Within the past decade, interest in biobehavioral aspects of cancer has increased. One reason for the increased interest in cancer is its continued growth in our population, in part due to the growing number of older people who are more likely than younger people to develop cancer (Krantz et al., 1980). Other reasons are

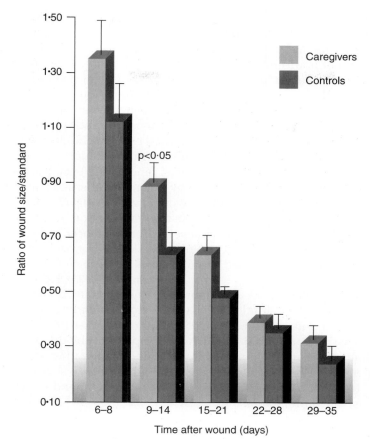

FIGURE 6.9. Average wound size during first 5 weeks of the study. All wound measurements for a subject during a given week were averaged to provide a single value for the interval for each subject who had not yet healed.
Source: Adapted from J. K. Kiecolt-Glaser, P. T. Marucha, W. B. Malarkey, et al. Slowing of wound healing by psychological stress. *The Lancet,* 1995, *346,* 1195.

related to risk factors for cancer, including smoking, diet, and increased levels of suspected carcinogens in our environment—food additives, asbestos, chemical wastes, defoliants, and radiation. All of these seem to have increased as well although many people are quitting smoking and we are also trying to reduce other exposure to "causes" of cancer. Further, detection and diagnoses of cancer are more likely now, and survival is becoming increasingly common.

Cancer is actually a set of related diseases in which altered cells of the body—cancer cells—multiply in unrestrained and rapid fashion, generating tumors or clusters of cells whose growth is also uncontrollable. All tumors are not cancerous; benign tumors do not grow uncontrollably and do not spread to other parts of the body. This spreading of cancerous cells, called **metastasis,** is characteristic of malignant tumors. Basic to the growth of malignant, cancerous neoplasms is damage to the DNA inside cells. The rapid increases in abnormal cells cause a diversion of nourishment from functional cells and eventual invasion of bodily tissue by the cancerous growth. This proliferation of cancer cells may cause damage or death of organ systems and the organism.

Genetic and environmental factors figure prominently when one reviews the possible causes of cancer (see Table 6.2). Some cancer risk is conveyed genetically. Daughters of women with breast cancer, for example, appear to be at greater risk themselves, and this risk is caused by a genetic characteristic called BRCA-1, that can be measured. Women with this mutation seem to have substantially greater risks of developing breast cancer. However, because up to 90 percent of all breast cancers are caused by other, noninherited factors, not having the mutation is no insurance that a woman will not develop the disease.

Environmental factors include exposures to radiation, toxic chemicals, or other agents (e.g., the sun) that may cause or promote cancer. Exposure to radiation is a risk factor for breast cancer, leukemia, skin cancer, and other neoplastic diseases, and toxic chemicals and viral infections also appear to enhance the risk for cancer (see Armitage, 1993; Dawes, 1992; Lambley, 1993). However, alone or together with genetic factors, environmental conditions still do not take into account all cancers. Behavioral and lifestyle factors, including stress, smoking, diet, alcohol use, and exercise, may all contribute to disease processes.

In discussing cancer and psychological aspects of the disease, we should keep in mind that cancer has a long growth period under most conditions, posing challenges to the study of its causes. In addition, we should distinguish "cause" from factors that facilitate or allow the growth and development of neoplasms, called promoters.

Behavioral Factors and Cancer

Despite the fact that there are a hundred or more different forms of cancer, some general theories of how cancer begins and develops have been formu-

TABLE 6.2. Risk Factors for Breast Cancer

1. Family history (genetic)	Increases risk
2. Obesity (exposure to estrogen variables)	Increases risk
3. Postmenopausal hormone replacement	Increases risk
4. Age at birth of first child	Increases risk
5. Age at menarche	Increases risk
6. Oral contraceptive use	Increases risk
7. Age at menopause	Increases risk
8. Benign breast disease	Increases risk
9. Radiation exposure	Increases risk
10. Alcohol use	Increases risk
11. Height	Increases risk

Source: Adapted from J. R. Harris, M. E. Lippman, U. Veronesi, and W. Willett. Breast cancer (first of three parts). *The New England Journal of Medicine,* 1992a, *327,* 319–328.

lated. Cancer develops from a mutation or other change in cell function and is promoted by a number of factors that "help" it to develop into large, hard-to-control measures or tumors. One belief is that cancer is related to genetic cell defects that are triggered by a number of environmental or physiological factors (see Cohen et al., 1979). Another belief suggests that the breakdown or temporary dysfunction of the immune system, which routinely attacks and kills mutagenic or alien cells or tumors, is responsible for cancer. Basically, this latter theory posits a "surveillance" function in the immune system similar to the immunosurveillance function discussed earlier. By recognizing and killing precancerous cells under conditions of normal functioning, the immune system protects the body from invasion by alien cells or uncontrolled tumor growth. However, when this surveillance role is suppressed by any of a number of physiological, social, or psychological events, the immune system may fail to detect and kill cancerous cells, allowing tumors to develop unhindered. There is evidence, for example, that NK cells are involved in cancer protection (see Herberman and Holden, 1978). If these cells are responsible for surveillance and early destruction of tumors, disruption of their activity (as appears to occur during or after stress) could have important implications for cancer. Recall that research evidence suggests that NK cells are very responsive to variations in stress and coping.

Studies addressing this surveillance notion have been criticized on methodological grounds, so evidence is yet inconclusive. Increased tumor growth and metastases in animals are associated with depressed NK cell activity, and there are several studies linking NK activity to stress (see Gorelick and Herberman, 1989; Herbert and Cohen, 1993). Research also suggests that psychological factors affect the course of the disease once established. Greer (1991) has shown that attitudes, beliefs, and behavioral style can influence the course of the disease. In a 15-year study of women with breast cancer "fighting spirit" was associated with better long-term outcomes than was coping that featured "stoic acceptance" (see Table 6.3). Supportive groups appear to increase survival of advanced cancer patients (see Fawzy and Fawzy, 1994; Spiegel et al., 1989) and other data, largely in the form of correlations, link personality variables or coping styles with the length of survival, recurrence, and the general course of illness (see Derogatis, Abeloff, and Melisaratos, 1979; Rogentine et al., 1979). These studies indicate that the rate at which the disease progresses—

TABLE 6.3. Psychological Responses and 15-Year Outcome

Psychological Responses	Still Alive	Died from Cancer	Died from Other Causes	Total
Fighting spirit	4	2	4	10
Denial	5	5	—	10
Stoic acceptance	6	24	3	33
Anxious	—	3	—	3
Helplessness	1	5	—	6

Source: From S. Greer, Psychological response to cancer and survival. *Psychological Medicine*, 1991, 21, 43–49.

rather than the factors that first caused it—is associated with psychological variables and stress.

Stress and Cancer

The search for behavioral factors that affect the onset of cancer appears largely concerned with three factors: mood, lifestyle variables such as smoking, and variables such as stress that are associated with the immune system. Studies have suggested that the loss of a close and important person is associated with reduced immune competence or the onset of cancer (see Bartop et al., 1977; Tache, Selye, and Day, 1979). Depression also appears to be linked to the likelihood of dying from cancer (Persky et al., 1987) and to the duration of survival or disease-free periods (Levy et al., 1985; Derogatis et al., 1979). Recall, for example, that in a study of men who had recently lost their wives, Schleifer et al. (1980) found that their immune systems showed marked depression during bereavement. Analysis of relationships between depression and immune function are also consistent with this (see Herbert and Cohen, 1993). Whether stress has a systematic impact on the initiation of cancer is not yet known.

Some studies examining mechanisms by which stress-induced immunosuppression might cause or facilitate cancer have yielded promising results. Sklar and Anisman (1981) had concluded that stress probably did not cause tumors to appear but, rather, affects the growth of neoplasms. Glaser et al. (1985) found evidence of stress effects in one of the basic bodily defenses against carcinogens: DNA repair within cells was disrupted due to stress-related reductions in the level of an enzyme that helps to repair cellular DNA and to minimize damage due to cancer-causing agents. The same link was identified in another study of psychiatric patients varying in reported distress. Those reporting more stress showed poorer DNA repair in lymphocytes than those reporting less stress or than nonpatient controls (Kiecolt-Glaser et al., 1985). These studies begin to show us the ways in which stress may affect immune function and disease states.

Smoking and diet have been established as risk factors for cancer, and the routes by which they exert this influence are varied. Smoking can affect the immune system and reduce immunosurveillance, possibly increasing the chances for a tumor to grow. Other immune system functions are also affected by smoking, and direct organ system damage is also possible. Dietary factors have been associated with cancer as well (Glanz, 1994; Levy, 1983). Recent research has also suggested a link between alcohol consumption and cancer (see Heirch et al., 1983). In combination with smoking, alcohol consumption has been found to contribute to risk for several types of cancer (see Flanders and Rothman, 1982; Herity et al., 1982). High fat intake appears to be related to risk for colon cancer and breast cancer (Henderson et al., 1990), and increase cancer risk (see Wynder et al., 1963). Dietary variables may be factors in findings relating cultural background with cancer. For example, it was found that Japanese-American women were more likely to develop breast cancer when they lived in the United States; the "Americanization" of these women was associated with increased susceptibility to breast cancer (Wynder, 1963). Because social and cultural differences are so complex and include so many possible causes, it is difficult to determine which variables are responsible for differences in cancer rates. However, the pronounced differences in diet across cultures is one likely agent.

Stress in general appears to be involved in the etiology and progression of cancer although there is no direct evidence of this in humans (see Goodkin et al., 1993). Measures of stress such as life events, emotional loss, and demand are related to having cancer and to poorer prognoses (see Cooper et al., 1989; Forsen, 1991). Studies of animals exposed to stress have noted damage to tissues involved in immunity, such as the thymus (which, as you will recall, is part of Selye's triad of responses), and lowered immune functioning (Solomon and Amkraut, 1979). Further studies have reported that crowding or noxious stimulation can increase the incidence of spontaneous cancers (Ader, 1981b). Similarly, stressed animals are more susceptible to a range of infectious diseases (see Solomon and Amkraut, 1979; Friedman, Glasgow, and Ader, 1969).

The reasons for this relationship are not known. Some researchers have proposed that sympathetic arousal associated with stress or the pituitary-adrenal-cortical responses described by Selye (1976) may be responsible. The latter notion is supported by findings showing reduced immune responses in humans following corticosteroid therapy (see Rinehart et al., 1975). These reductions in the ability of the body to combat infection were apparently caused by increased levels of corticosteroids in the body.

Adjustment and Coping with Cancer

Cancer can be a frightening, painful disease and the aversive treatments for it also make cancer tough to deal with. Adaptation to life with cancer can be difficult. Cancer is (1) often life threatening, (2) sometimes painful, and (3) unusually an unpleasant, fatigue-causing disease. Its treatments, including surgery, radiation, chemotherapy, and newer immunotherapies, are often difficult because of unpleasant side effects, and people with cancer may feel shunned or isolated from other people because of their disease (see Holland et al., 1979; Nerenz et al., 1982). Finally, cancer treatment and surveillance are long-term commitments and often cause disruption as well as worry as people adjust to being healthy again (see Cella and Tross, 1986). These events are stressful and cause emotional distress (Lerman et al., 1991). Adjustment to these demands appears to be important, not only for one's well-being and mood, but also to minimize stress and its potential to alter bodily defenses and to affect the course of the disease. Recurrence of the disease may be due to stress and is also clearly a cause of further distress; symptoms of stress disorders such as PTSD have been associated with recurrence and are exacerbated by the suddenness of the recurrence (Cella et al., 1990).

Coping or how people find meaning in what is happening to them is an important determinant of stress and quality of life among cancer patients and their families (Cooper and Faragher, 1993). Patients and family members report using a variety of coping strategies to deal with fear, anger, disruption, feeling ill, and other aspects of cancer (Ptacek, Ptacek, and Dodge, 1994) and how well stress is coped with is related to depression, anxiety, hostility, and lower self-esteem among patients (Katz, 1994). Previous or chronic experience with major stressors appear to decrease patients' ability to cope (Peretz, 1994). Several investigators have reported that more stoic, nonexpressive styles of coping are not well suited to cancer (see Cooper and Faragher, 1993; Eyesenck, 1994). When combined with avoiding social support, this nonexpressive coping style may constitute a risk factor for cancer and other health threats (Kotler, 1994).

Some investigators have suggested that men and women cope differently when faced with major stressors such as having cancer. One study found that there were no differences in how much distress was reported but that women were more adaptive in this situation and appeared to be most assisted by social support (Fife et al., 1994). Among parents of children with cancer, fathers and mothers seemed to adjust well to the situation and used similar means to deal with disruption and worry (Roberts et al., 1994).

Coping by family members is important because the health and well-being of the family affect the mood and well-being of the patient. In addition, stress and disruption associated with having a family member ill with cancer can have substantial costs for family members. Being a parent of a child with cancer is stressful, as is being the child of a parent with cancer (Compas et al., 1994; Hall and Baum, 1995; Wittrock et al., 1994). Substantial strain and stress are also likely when family members become caregivers for patients (see Blood et al., 1994). Siblings of children with cancer are also affected although cohesive families help brothers and sisters to cope with the illness of their sibling (Cohen et al., 1994). For example, family caregivers for patients undergoing chemotherapy for cancer report being depressed or experiencing stress, and coping styles and social support determine the extent to which a negative mood is experienced (Reardon and Agdin, 1993).

Social Support and Cancer

Social support appears to be an important resource for people dealing with the stress associated with cancer. By physically helping patients to meet the demands of treatment or by providing emotional support, this assistance seems to be invaluable. Recent research indicates that emotional support from friends and family is protective and associated with longer survival (Ell et al., 1992). Support from the family makes adjustment to having cancer easier, and loss of support can be devastating (Lichtman and Taylor, 1988). Studies suggest that a lack of close interpersonal ties is often associated with cancer (Thomas and Duszynski, 1974). Almost one thousand medical students were interviewed and then followed for 10 to 15 years. Those who had developed cancer after 15 years reported that they did not have very much family closeness. Other research suggests that social support has effects on the immune system that appear to be related to cancer progression and, possibly, to the initiation of the disease (see Levy et al., 1990). Survival and better prognoses have been associated with social support (see Funch and Marshall, 1983), although these effects do not extend to all patients. Social support is also related to perceived control and how well people are integrated into their social environment (Ell et al., 1992).

A primary source of support for cancer patients is the spouse or significant other in a relationship. When these partners are viewed as being supportive and patients are satisfied with their assistance, patient well-being is enhanced (Pistrang, 1995). This was the case even when other support might be available. If a patient had a troubled or problematic relationship with his or her partner, well-being suffered regardless of the availability of support from other people (Pistrang, 1995). Having positive support also appears to affect how people cope with the stressors associated with cancer, and with more positive emotional outcomes as well (see Ell et al., 1992). For example, support is related to depression among cancer patients. Although up to 50 percent or more of cancer patients suffer moderate to severe symptoms of depression, support and quality of life were strongly related to emotional symptoms that the patient reported (Godding et al., 1995).

An important development in the treatment of cancer has been the recent investigation of using groups to provide support and psychotherapy for cancer patients. Being isolated or having few friends and social contacts is associated with the elevated risk of mortality as well as with all-cause morbidity (see Berkman and Syme, 1979; House et al., 1988). A study of cancer patients indicated that women with little social support or contact with others were more likely to die from the cancer (Reynolds and Kaplan, 1990), and studies suggest that married cancer patients survive longer than do unmarried patients (Goodwin et al., 1987). The kind of support that might be derived from being in a group with others dealing with similar cancers appears to be associated with a better quality of life and long survival among cancer patients (see Ell et al., 1992; Waxler-Morrison et al., 1991). This has been recognized and group psychotherapy has been studied, but clear evidence to support this clinical procedure has only recently been reported. Some studies do not find evidence of social support affecting cancer outcomes (see Cassileth et al., 1985), but most report some associations (see Reynolds and Kaplan, 1990; Neale et al., 1986).

One series of studies of a 1-year group psychotherapy intervention for women with metastatic breast cancer have produced very encouraging results (see Spiegel et al., 1989). Following these women for several years after the intervention, Spiegel and his colleagues at Stanford found that women who received the group intervention lived an average of 18 months longer than women given standard care (Spiegel et al., 1989). In addition, the group intervention was associated with better mood, more effective coping, less pain, and better mental health (Spiegel and Bloom, 1983; Spiegel et al., 1981).

Another series of studies of a similar group intervention have also found a significant effect of group support and therapy on survival, this time of advanced melanoma patients (Fawzy et al., 1993). Six years after the 6-week intervention, patients randomly assigned to receive the intervention had a survival advantage and reported a better mood than did controls (Fawzy et al., 1993). In addition, quality of life was enhanced and immune function, measured as NK cell activity, was better among patients who got the intervention (Fawzy et al., 1990). Some studies have not reported dramatic benefits of group psychotherapy, but the support and opportunity for social comparison, expression of emotional distress, and enhanced coping skills that are part of these interventions appear to have clear benefits for cancer patients (Posluszny et al., in press).

The usefulness of these psychosocial interventions has been questioned, and a recent review and meta-analysis summarizes some of the overall findings of this literature (Meyer, 1995). The review found 45 studies of treatment/control group comparisons and the general conclusions that were drawn were that emotional adjustment is improved and treatment and disease-related symptoms are decreased among patients given these special psychosocial treatments (Meyer, 1995). The specific type of intervention—that is, whether patients received counseling, behavioral interventions including relaxation, education, or social support—did not make a difference in the nature of benefits for patients (Meyer, 1995). (See the box "How Much Does Behavior Affect Cancer?")

Personality Factors and Cancer

The immune system's role in cancer is still not fully known. Despite promising findings and some apparent relationships, much work remains to be done.

How Much Does Behavior Affect Cancer?

If we could answer this question now, on the basis of existing research, we would have accomplished a lot. We do not yet know all the answers to this question, but evidence is mounting that behavioral factors play a very large role in the development and consequences of cancer. An example of this is a recent article in the *Washington Post*, reporting the results of a state health study of cancer rates in Maryland. Under the headline "Most MD Cancer Behavioral," the article reports that 40 percent of cancers in Maryland were likely related to smoking and tobacco use and another 20 percent to diet, meaning that behavioral phenomena were involved in the majority of the 47,000 cancer

deaths in Maryland from 1987 to 1991. In the state survey nearly 30 percent of cancer deaths in Maryland (1987–1991) were from lung cancer alone, underscoring what we now know is a pervasive health threat associated with cigarette smoking (see Figure below), and when we add oral cancers (not depicted), colon and breast cancer (which have dietary components at least), and other forms of cancer associated with smoking or diet, we are taking into account a lot of the variance in cancer with just two behavioral factors!

Source: Adapted from the *Washington Post*, February 1995, A1–A8.

Cancer Deaths and Cases in Maryland

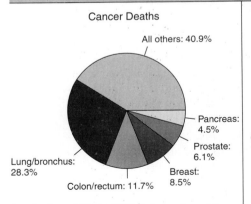

Cancer Deaths

All others: 40.9%
Pancreas: 4.5%
Prostate: 6.1%
Breast: 8.5%
Colon/rectum: 11.7%
Lung/bronchus: 28.3%

Deaths from 1987 to 1991 by type of cancer; the total number of deaths was 47,435.

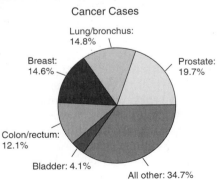

Cancer Cases

Lung/bronchus: 14.8%
Prostate: 19.7%
Breast: 14.6%
Colon/rectum: 12.1%
Bladder: 4.1%
All other: 34.7%

New cancer cases, by type, in 1992; the total number of new cases was 20,047.

However, other dimensions are also being explored. Wittkower and Dudek (1973) suggested that psychological factors are involved in the onset of cancer, and some research has suggested the possibility of a cancer-prone personality (see Le Shan, 1959). Several characteristics that seem to be associated with cancer have been identified. The first includes a tendency to keep in resentment and anger rather than express it and a "marked inability to forgive." In addition, research suggests that cancer victims are ineffective in forming and/or maintaining close, long-term relationships with other people. They are more likely to be loners without extensive social support systems. Third, they engage in more self-pity than what might be considered normal. Also, these people tend to have poor self-images. Thus, the cancer-prone individual "puts on a happy face and denies any sense of loss, anger, distress, disappointment, or despair" (Scarf, 1980, p. 37) while living an inner life of self-pity, insecurity, and a certain degree of loneliness. Other research has described the cancer-prone person as pleasant, compliant, and passive, or as an extreme expressor or suppressor of anger (Greer and Morris, 1975; Renneker, 1981).

This research has come together in the notion of the Type C cancer-prone personality (see Table 6.4). Characterized by repression of emotional expression, this pattern has been linked to the risk of cancer as well as to how well one does with the disease (see Cumming et al., 1993; Kune et al., 1991; Neuhaus et al., 1994). The appraisal, coping, and defense styles associated with the Type C personality are correlated with one another (Clement, 1994). Whether a cause of the risk or simply a correlate, the inhibited emotional style characterizing the Type C personality appears to be related to cancer and programs to alter these personality characteristics in "healthier" directions seem to reduce some health risks (see Grossarth-Maticek et al., 1991).

Another approach to studying Type C personalities is to study similar conditions. One such condition is alexithymia, a state defined by the inability to experience or express emotions. A study of alexithymics and healthy controls by using development of cervical intraepithelial neoplasia (CIN) as an index of the cancer course revealed that alexithymia and CIN were related (Todarello et al., 1994) and that alexithymics had lower levels of lymphocytes. These findings provide further evidence of a link between personality variables reflecting emotional inhibition and vulnerability to cancer (Todarello et al., 1994).

Optimism and pessimism also appear to be related to cancer, at least as far

TABLE 6.4. Type C Cancer-Prone Personality

- Denial and suppression of emotions
- Pathological niceness
- Avoidance of conflicts
- Exaggerated response to social desirability
- Overcompliance
- Overpatience
- Rigid control of emotional expressiveness

Source: From H. J. Baltrusch, W. Strangel, and I. Titze. Stress, cancer, and immunity: New developments in biopsychosocial and psychoneuroimmunologic research. Congress on Brain and Immunity (1991, Naples, Italy). *Acta Neurologica,* 1991, *13*(4), 315–327.

as adjustment to having cancer is concerned. Pessimists showed poorer adjustment 3, 6, and 12 months after breast surgery, were less satisfied with life, and generally experienced less well-being than did more optimistic patients (Carver et al., 1994). They also coped less effectively, using more denial and helplessness (Carver et al., 1992). Personality may also affect attending screenings or efforts to prevent or detect cancer. In one study repressiveness was correlated with the number of relatives with cancer among women who did not attend breast-screening tests (Chaitchik and Kreitler, 1991).

One of the problems in determining whether there is a personality style that predisposes someone to get cancer is causality. If you find that certain types of people develop cancer more often than others, is this sufficient to show a personality cause? The answer, clearly, is "No." Most studies of personality factors and cancer have compared cancer patients with healthy control subjects after the patients have become ill (Fox, 1976). The inference often made is that any differences observed between patient and nonpatient groups existed prior to the onset of illness and were responsible for it. This is difficult to prove, and as Fox (1976) *suggests*, cancer causes a number of perceptual and cognitive changes that could affect or produce differences between patients and nonpatients. Chemotherapy agents are toxic and may have effects on mood as well. Some studies have shown differences between cancer and noncancer patients that existed before the disease status was known, but the data do not clearly support the idea that personality factors contribute to cancer (Fox, 1976; Krasnoff, 1959; Perrin and Pierce, 1959; Stavraky, 1968). It is possible, though, that personality may be related to behaviors that are associated with cancer, such as smoking and poor diet (Fox, 1976).

Personality variables may not be as important in the cause of cancer as in its progression. Research has suggested that personality profiles in which behavior is overly polite and passive are associated with rapid progression of cancer and early death compared with the longer time course of illness exhibited by people who are more aggressive (see Derogatis et al., 1979). Levy et al. (1985) reported that apathy, depression, and fatiguelike behavior were associated with poorer biological status (lower NK cell activity) among women with primary breast cancer. However, this could be true of a number of degenerative or progressive diseases—the fact that combative people live longer (because they "fight" harder). In addition, women who were rated as being "well adjusted" or who reported low levels of social support also showed lower NK cell activity. Those who were seen as being better adjusted may have, in fact, been exhibiting symptoms of learned helplessness and as a result appeared more compliant and cooperative (see Chapter 8). The relationship between personality and disease progression requires further study.

Cancer Screening and Early Detection

Cancer screening is still seen as an important defense against the disease, as early treatment of small tumors has the greatest likelihood of success. However, getting people to go to screenings, to self-examine, or otherwise to try to monitor and detect early symptoms of cancer is often difficult. This has been particularly true for early detection of cancer by African-Americans (Tessaro et al., 1994). Social support and health beliefs are important and those with more social ties were most likely to undergo routine mammograms in a study of African-American women (Bundek et al., 1993). Compliance and adherence with preventive recommendations is affected by many variables. We will consider these in Chapter 8. However, even knowing the seven warning signs of cancer and monitoring for them can aid in early detections and effective cancer treatment (see Figure 6.10).

Research has sought to identify factors that increase the likelihood that people will do the things that are necessary for early detection of cancer. How effective early detection is in helping to treat disease, how your friends and associates feel about the screening procedures, and how emotional we become when thinking about screening programs appear to be related to whether people participate (see Montano and Taplin, 1991). For example, mammography and prostate examination are effective ways to keep vigilant for early stages of disease but are made less likely by their aversiveness or inconvenience. Perceived risk is also important, and, in general, people who believe that they are at greater risk are more likely to have screenings done (Blalock et al., 1990).

It is very difficult to study psychological or behavioral components of cancer, and this limits our ability to determine their roles. The relatively long period of time over which cancer develops—some forms require 20 years or more before they can be detected—is the basic problem. Studies must be retrospective, and recollections may be affected by the knowledge that one has cancer. Also, since we do not know when the disease began, it is difficult to attach significance to psychological events. How does one know, for example, that loss of a spouse affected the disease if one cannot determine whether the disease started around the time of the loss?

FIGURE 6.10. Monitoring of signs of cancer is very important in early detection of cancer. The American Cancer Society, the National Cancer Institute, and other groups issue information like this that can alert us as to when we should seek help for troubling symptoms. Often the early warning signs of disease can only be monitored by the individual. That means by you!

Seven Warning Signs of Cancer

See a doctor right away if you have:

- A sore that doesn't get better
- A nagging cough, or unusually hoarse voice
- Indigestion (very bad upset stomach more than once in a while) or problems with swallowing
- Changes in a wart or mole
- Unusual bleeding or discharge
- Thick spot or lump in breast or anywhere else
- Change in bowel or bladder habits

Doctors can answer many questions and give you any tests you need. If you are between the ages of 20 and 40, have yourself checked for cancer once every 3 years. If you are over 40, get checked every year.

HIV DISEASE AND AIDS

Since its "discovery" in the early 1980s AIDS has quickly become one of the most deadly and feared diseases in history (Glasner and Kaslow, 1990). Like cancer, it involves the immune system, but in different ways. It is caused by infection with **human immunodeficiency virus (HIV)** and has a number of immunologic effects, including decreases in T lymphocytes, some types of immunoglobins, T-helper lymphocytes, and reduced responsiveness of lymphocytes to antigens (see Coates et al., 1987; Lange and Dax, 1987). As its name suggests HIV causes immune systems to become weak and to permit the development of infections that we normally would be able to fend off. Because the virus attacks T-helper cells specifically, it disrupts cellular immunity and increases victims' susceptibility to opportunistic infections. Thus, many AIDS patients develop other illnesses, which are actually the cause of their death. Among the opportunistic infections identified in AIDS patients are pneumocystis carinii pneumonia and Kaposi's sarcoma (a rare cancer).

Because AIDS is a comparatively new disease, we are still learning about it. We have learned a lot. Exposure to HIV is not the same as having AIDS. We can think of the illness on a spectrum from one extreme—someone who has just been infected by the virus—to the other—someone who has developed AIDS. From the initial infection one can be said to have the HIV disease whether or not any symptoms are experienced. Once exposed, an individual may develop the disease or simply exhibit chronic symptoms and immunosuppression. Some individuals who are exposed do not immediately develop AIDS; of those who tested positive for the AIDS virus (seropositive, i.e., having antibodies for HIV), less than one-half had developed AIDS by 1985 (Goedert et al., 1986) and the rates of progression of HIV disease to AIDS is not well understood. Approximately 50 percent of those becoming infected with HIV develop AIDS within 10 years (Friedland, 1990).

How the disease progresses and identification of factors that increase or decrease its progression are topics of important research. Some researchers have suggested that the virus may remain dormant for varying periods before becoming active and causing AIDS. They believe that this is similar to the way in which latent viruses, such as herpes, emerge periodically to cause illness. Others have suggested that what appears to be a latent period is actually one in which the body's immune system is successfully fighting the infection and preventing its spread. The lack of symptoms in this phase, leading others to call it latency, may actually be due to a virtual draw between the virus and immune system. The body is still able to replace cells lost in the battle, but the virus is not eliminated or slowed. Most researchers believe that all or at least a majority of those who are HIV seropositive will eventually develop AIDS. Estimates of deaths from AIDS through 1991 approach 200,000 Americans. At the end of 1991, 350,000 AIDS cases had been reported (Thurn, 1992). The disease continues to spread with estimates of HIV-infected individuals exceeding 10 million (Thurn, 1992). It is not just an American phenomenon; it threatens most of the world's population. In some countries the epidemic has been more destructive than in the United States.

As we have already suggested, HIV disease represents a continuum of medical outcomes and illness experiences beginning when one is infected by the HIV and progressing through AIDS and subsequent death. Seen this way, AIDS is actually an endpoint—the final, lethal stage of a progressive chronic illness. The actual infection, accomplished through exposure to bodily fluids containing active HIV, may not have any symptoms and is ordinarily detected by a blood test for antibodies to HIV. If someone is infected by HIV (i.e., HIV has taken control of at least a few T cells), the body produces antibodies against HIV. If there is no infection, there are no antibodies and the individual is said to be *seronegative*. If there is active infection, there are antibodies against HIV and the individual is said to be *seropositive*. Some transient flu symptoms and enlarged lymph nodes may be experienced, but, generally, infection and early stages of the disease are asymptomatic.

Staging of the disease is still undergoing changes, and several ways of categorizing the severity of HIV disease have been devised. Most researchers use symptoms of immunosuppression as criteria. Early stages are asymptomatic and, as suggested earlier, without a blood test people may not even know that they have the disease! As the disease progresses, the number of T-helper cells decreases, thrush and bacterial or fungal infections may develop, and allergic-type responses may be compromised. These changes may be accompanied by night sweats, confusion, loss of appetite, skin rashes, diarrhea, dementia, and, eventually, with opportunistic infections, cancer, viral illnesses, and parasitic diseases. As noted previously, most deaths from AIDS are actually "complications" from AIDS; the diseases that usually kill AIDS patients are the result of AIDS and immunosuppression. (See the box "Education and Counseling for Individuals with a Positive HIV Test.")

Transmission of AIDS

HIV is spread by the exchange of bodily fluids during sex, the sharing of needles or other drug paraphernalia, and blood transfusion, and from mother to child prior to delivery (Coates et al., 1987). The disease was initially found in the United States among identifiable subgroups (e.g., homosexuals) and was apparently spread within these groups (e.g., by sexual contact in the gay community). Thus, male homosexuals are one of several high-risk groups; the others include intravenous drug users, prostitutes, bisexual men, and hemophiliacs (who require frequent blood transfusions). High-risk groups in this case are defined by *high-risk behaviors*, such as having unprotected sex, having sex with multiple partners, and injecting drugs of abuse. Because the virus was more common among gay men, those having unprotected sex in this population are considered to be at high risk. Estimates of the percentage of AIDS cases among gay or bisexual men have ranged up to three-quarters of AIDS cases, with intravenous drug users, hemophiliacs, and transfusion recipients behind them in reported incidence of the disease (Centers for Disease Control, 1986). Another "problem group" is pregnant women who test positive for the HIV antibody or young children with HIV infection. The virus does not appear to be communicable by casual contact but, rather, requires intimate contact

Education and Counseling for Individuals with a Positive HIV Test

When someone tests positive for the virus that causes AIDS, what can be done for him or her? It is not currently known what the likelihood of developing AIDS is once someone has been infected, and we do not know enough about the disease to predict how long it may take for the disease to develop. Studies indicate moderate rates of disease among seropositive people over 3- to 4-year periods, showing that about one in five people testing positive for the virus actually gets AIDS (Goedert et al., 1987; Kaplan et al., 1987). Further complicating this is the fact that we do not know what factors affect the development of the disease. There appear to be genetic factors involved (Eales et al., 1987), but stress and other psychosocial variables may be important as well. The need for programs for education and counseling for seropositive individuals is clear.

One such program has been described by Morokoff, Holmes-Johnson, and Weisse (1987). Patients were given a thorough medical screening and evaluation, including retesting for HIV antibodies, laboratory analysis of immune status, and rediagnosis. This is followed by psychosocial evaluation by a social worker, chaplain, and psychiatrists, and patients are assigned to a support group meeting at least once a week. Finally, an educational program is presented, including a discussion of the relationships between stress and the immune function, medical and legal aspects of HIV positive status, stress management, safer sex practices, and alcohol and drug abuse.

The support groups focus on management of grief, depression, feelings of helplessness, anger, fear of dying, and related issues. Educational programs are directed primarily at providing information relevant to problems considered in the support groups as well as coping and self-management skills that may help people to deal with their situation. One lecture deals specifically with the ways in which people react to the knowledge that they are seropositive for HIV. This provides a normative context within which individuals may evaluate and work through their fears and concerns. The stress management instruction is designed to help patients regain a sense of control over their lives and, perhaps, to reinforce immune system response. A lecture about safer sex practices deals with the very mundane but vitally important issue of how to avoid the further spread of the virus.

In attempting to address the information needs and emotional concerns of the individual who is positive for the AIDS virus, this program represents an important example of the kind of treatment program that will not only help those already infected but also contribute to the prevention of further transmission of the disease. The problems that go along with a positive test for the virus are great and difficult to cope with in the isolation that may follow disclosure of the diagnosis. Education about the nature of AIDS, its biological and psychological characteristics, and coping skills may improve the health and well-being of these people as well as help to prevent the spread of the disease.

and substantial exposure to infected blood or semen to be transmitted from one person to another.

Reported cases have increased dramatically since 1978 (see May and Anderson, 1987). As many as 40,000 new HIV infections are reported in the United States each year, suggesting that we are not doing enough to prevent its spread (Stryker et al., 1995). In one study of gay men done in San Francisco the percentage of tested individuals who were seropositive—who showed evidence of infection with HIV—increased from less than 10 percent in 1978 to more than 70 percent in 1985 (Centers for Disease Control, 1986). Similar results have been reported in studies of homosexuals in London and intravenous drug users in Italy (Angarano et al., 1985; Carne et al., 1985). The time needed for reported cases to double has decreased steadily since the discovery of the epidemic, and the number of cases of AIDS has risen rapidly (see Figure 6.4) (May and Anderson, 1987).

Again, it is important to understand that high-risk behavior, and not membership in a group, introduces risk. If IV drug users always use clean needles and never share their "works" with other people, their risk is not really affected by being IV drug users. Similarly, monogamous gay men are not at risk for HIV infection unless they contact it from another source. The most common mode of transmission is through sex, and unprotected anal sex is a highly risky behavior. For anyone, then, unprotected sex and numbers of partners are high-risk behaviors, and this risk is amplified if one or more of these partners is a member of a high-risk group. As far as we know, heterosexual transmission is possible (in other parts of the world, the disease is primarily spread through heterosexual contact) but the mechanisms by which transmission occurs are not yet known.

A number of treatments have been proposed and promising drugs have been developed. As of this writing, one drug, AZT, has been used widely. Early studies indicate that AZT may inhibit the spread of the virus, but whether it improves immune function is not clear (Selwyn, 1986). Despite the life-lengthening effects of AZT, its ultimate value remains to be seen as long-term survival and possible side effects are evaluated. Combinations of drugs have shown great promise as well. However, *there is currently no cure for AIDS or a vaccine to prevent infection by HIV.* Because of this, prevention is particularly important, as once an individual develops the disease, the prognosis is not good. Behavioral principles become very important as a result of this situation because the ways in which the disease is transmitted are largely controllable. In other words, the spread of AIDS can, it is believed, be stopped or greatly reduced by having people avoid high-risk behaviors and/or change their behavior so as to minimize risk. Use of condoms during sexual intercourse, for example, greatly reduces the chances of spreading the disease in this manner. Thus, getting people to adopt safer behaviors seems to be one of the only avenues by which we may be able to deal with AIDS, at least for the present.

It appears that anyone can get AIDS, and predictions suggest that the disease is spreading into the heterosexual community and over the next few years will begin to affect a significant number of heterosexuals. However, because the initial spread of the disease has occurred in two or three groups, most attempts to change behavior have taken shape within those groups. There is some evidence, for example, that health education programs have increased knowledge about the disease and how it is spread among gay men, and that sexual behavior that appears to have been associated with the spread of AIDS has decreased (see McKusick, Hortsmann, and Coates, 1985). Emphasis has been on **safer sex**, taking precautions such as **condom** use to reduce the spread of HIV during sex, and on reducing the number of sex partners and other aspects of sexual activity that increase the transmission of the illness. However, these interventions have not been wholly successful; in some reports gay men state that they have continued high-risk behavior. College students, regardless of sexual orientation or lifestyle, are at risk because of frequent sexual contact and because they may not engage in "safe" practices due to a sense of invulnerability or the belief that if any of their partners had AIDS, they would let others know (see Hirschom, 1987). Some allow the belief that only homosexuals and drug users get the disease to dissuade them from taking proper precautions.

Research on interventions and on the risk-taking behavior among drug users suggests that most drug users engage in behavior that can spread the disease. Data show that nearly 90 percent of drug users with AIDS shared needles and that a majority of drug users share needles regularly (Black et al., 1986; Friedland et al., 1985). Data also suggest that drug users are aware of the risks but that they engage in risky behaviors anyway (Coates et al., 1987). Complicating attempts to intervene is the addictive nature of the behavior; because drugs are addictive, stopping drug use is difficult, leaving modification of how one takes the drugs an "easier" target.

Psychosocial Consequences of AIDS

AIDS is a frightening illness with a number of consequences other than deterioration of the immune system. Those who have AIDS may find themselves isolated from social support networks as friends and family withdraw from them. The decision of how and when to disclose that one has AIDS may generate social consequences of its own and require disclosure of a lifestyle or habit that one had previously kept hidden from family and friends (Coates et al., 1987). Thus, the nature of the disease and conditions by which it is transmitted may cause people to provide less support for victims just when they need it the most.

Psychiatric impairment and emotional complications of AIDS and ARC are relatively common, with estimates that more than one-half of AIDS patients and three-quarters of ARC patients show diagnosable emotional disturbances and psychological disorders (Holland and Tross, 1985; Selwyn, 1986). The higher rate of distress among ARC patients may reflect the uncertainty of their prognosis, although seropositive but healthy individuals show a lower rate of distress (Selwyn, 1986). The effects of stress among patients with AIDS or ARC may be responsible for some of these disturbances as well as for variations in the progression of the disease due to factors such as immunosuppression, poor diet, smoking, and so on.

Stress and emotional problems are likely among those who test positive for HIV but who are not ill (see the box "With a Positive HIV Test"). The knowledge that one has tested positive can generate profound distress and has been associated with psychiatric problems. Several studies have shown that problems such as depression, anxiety, fear, and adjustment problems can occur as a result of testing, although other research has suggested that the testing procedures and knowledge of one's HIV status can have little or even positive effects (Selwyn, 1986). Social support is again useful to buffer some stress associated with the disease; both positive and negative interactions appear to be beneficial (Siegel et al., 1994).

Research and interventions aimed at reducing stress among people with HIV disease have focused on the notification that one has tested positive for

HIV and the acute stress period immediately following learning that one is HIV positive. Among the investigations examining adjustment to the news and learning to live with the disease, several researchers have found that the active coping style, social support, and interventions using relaxation exercises determine how well people adjust (Antoni et al., 1992; Lutgendorf et al., 1994). More comprehensive interventions using aerobic exercise and cognitive behavioral stress management have shown promising effects as well. In general, HIV positive men appeared more immunosuppressed shortly after notification than did those who were HIV negative (Esterling et al., 1992). The interventions buffered some of this effect, resulting in improved immune status and mood (Antoni et al., 1991; LaPerriere et al., 1991). Similar effects on mood were found in a study of an educational "stress prevention" intervention with men after learning that they were HIV positive (Perry et al., 1991). Education and counseling were also associated with less stress in another sample of HIV positive people, apparently by helping to shape effective coping (Fishman et al., 1990; VanDevanter et al., 1990).

Neuorological consequences of the disease are also serious and may further complicate psychosocial adjustment. AIDS dementia, which refers to a variety of CNS problems, appears to be common among AIDS patients (Selwyn, 1986). Symptoms of CNS impairment include memory problems, difficulty in concentrating and in coordination of motor skills, balance problems, and severe impairment of impulse control and decision making. These problems further affect attempts to stop the spread of the disease, and may interfere with its management and treatment. Impairment occurs not only among AIDS patients but also among those testing positive for the HIV antibody as well. In about 25 percent of cases dementia-related symptoms are detected before any signs of AIDS or ARC appear (Navia, Jordan, and Price, 1986), a fact that suggests parallel CNS and immune effects of the virus and the usefulness of neuropsychological testing in diagnosing and managing the illness.

Preventing HIV Disease

Because there are no effective cures for HIV disease and AIDS, and because of the likelihood that once infected by HIV, people are likely to develop AIDS, attention has focused on *preventing the initial exposure to HIV*. Some investigators have studied ways of reducing the likelihood that someone with HIV disease will spread the virus to other people, focusing on the behavior of prostitutes, on determining factors that lead people to take risks, and by studying the behavior of people already infected by the virus (see Hospers et al., 1994; Sheeran and Abraham, 1994; Vanwesenbeeck et al., 1994). For example, studying determinants of condom use, which presumably minimized the likelihood of spreading the virus during sex, can suggest ways of increasing the use of condoms among HIV positive people. Other efforts have focused on preventing behavior that puts seronegative people in a situation in which they could become infected, such as the use of IV drugs. These programs are generally directed at learning what causes people to put themselves at risk and how to prevent it.

Generally, we think of ourselves as rational decision makers, so initial efforts to prevent HIV exposure has to educate people. If we know how to avoid a deadly disease, we should be able to avoid it. Unfortunately, information and education appears to be necessary but insufficient to prevent risky behavior. Educational campaigns have increased awareness and knowledge in many high-risk and potentially high-risk groups (see Fisher and Fisher, 1992; Muller et al., 1995). Yet people have resisted the admonitions of public health campaigns and have not generally eliminated behavior placing them at risk. More targeted interventions that provide skills and knowledge have had better success. In addition, research suggests that optimism, stress, and coping affect high-risk behavior and quality of life among HIV positive people (see Reed, 1993; Taylor et al., 1991, 1992).

This discussion of AIDS is necessarily brief and does not approach the complex problems that the epidemic presents. A number of behaviorally based prevention and treatment programs have been developed, and some of these will be discussed in detail in Chapter 13. The role of psychological variables in the progression of disease is also important, and some studies have begun to address the effects of psychosocial variables. Research has, for example, suggested that stress may affect the immune system so as to increase immunosuppression and contribute to the progress of AIDS (see Coates et al., 1987; Solomon et al., 1987). Personality characteristics may also be associated with better or poorer coping and with different prognoses (see Temoshock, Sweet, and Zich, 1987). In cases of victimization, research indicates, for example, that self-blame can enhance coping by reaffirming one's sense of control (see Chapter 8). In the case of ARC this holds up, but among AIDS patients, self-blame contributes to negative emotional states, suggesting different perceptions and implications (Temoshok et al., 1987). Additional research is needed to clarify these issues, to understand better the role of psychological variables in the disease, and to develop further effective prevention and treatment.

SUMMARY

The importance of psychological and neural interactions with the immune system has become increasingly clear in the past decade and suggests a number of important facts. Immunocompetence appears to be conditionable, providing evidence of psychological mediation of immune responsiveness and suggesting a number of significant practical and research issues. Stress appears to affect immunocompetence as well, indicating the possibility that psychophysiological states do predispose one to a range of infectious illnesses. Tumor growth appears to be affected by stress, more rapidly when growing during stress than immediately after exposure to a stressor. Lymphocytes and other agents of immunity are also weakened by stress. Further research is necessary to determine whether these changes are associated with increased susceptibility to illness.

In this chapter we also discussed two diseases that involve the immune system—cancer and AIDS. Both are often fatal and frighten people immensely, but they involve very different processes and are affected by many psychosocial variables. The notion of immunosurveillance was considered and discussed as a possible contributor too, and the role of personality factors in cancer was also considered. Similarly, in the case of AIDS a number of psychological variables of possible importance to the development and/or progression of the disease were presented. The importance of behavioral factors in both diseases is clear, although lack of effective treatments for AIDS makes behavioral issues involved in treatment and prevention particularly prominent.

RECOMMENDED READINGS

Adler, R. (Ed.), *Psychoneuroimmunology*, New York: Academic Press, 1981.

Burish, T., Levy, S., and Meyerowitz, B. (Eds.), *Cancer, nutrition, and eating behavior.* Hillsdale, NJ: Erlbaum, 1984.

Fox, B. Premorbid psychological factors as related to cancer incidence. *Journal of Behavioral Medicine*, 1978, *1*, 45–134.

Glaser, R., and Kiecolt-Glaser, J. *Handbook of human stress and immunity.* San Diego, CA: Academic Press, 1994.

Jemmott, J. B., and Locke, S. E. Psychosocial factors, immunologic mediation, and human susceptibility to infectious diseases. *Psychological Bulletin*, 1984, *95*, 78–108.

Temoshok, L., and Baum, A. (Eds.), *Psychosocial aspects of AIDS.* Hillsdale, NJ: Erlbaum, 1988.

Psychophysiological Disorders: Psychological Factors Affecting Medical Conditions

"It's all in your head." "You imagined your symptoms or caused them on purpose." All of us have heard that kind of explanation for some illnesses and have seen the impatience that people show when one's illness has no detectable physical causes. Psychophysiological disorders have no physical causes—they are psychogenic or of psychological origin—but all of them are not "in people's heads." They are real illnesses with real symptoms and real consequences.

Ancient philosophy, medicine, and religion treated mind and body as one. In Chapter 1 we discussed Hippocrates' theory of personality that relied on predominant bodily fluids to explain why people behave as they do. Plato, an ancient Greek philosopher generally regarded as a major contributor to western philosophy and civilization, once observed:

> As you ought not to attempt to cure the eyes without the head, or the head without the body, then neither ought you to attempt to cure the body without the soul . . . for the part will never be well unless the whole is well.

As we suggested in Chapter 1, dualistic thinking in areas such as medicine and psychology is again being evaluated and replaced with more holistic theories. In part, this is due to undeniable evidence that physical illness can have psychological causes and consequences. Among the many kinds of evidence that mind and body are at least intimately connected, the fact that physical diseases can have psychological causes ranks among the most important cause. **Psychosomatic disorders**—now called psychophysiological disorders—are real illnesses. They are characterized by physical symptoms or a breakdown of various bodily organs/systems that are caused by or linked with psychosocial factors. Through the ages perspectives on how closely interrelated these physical and psychosocial dimensions of disease and illness were have greatly changed and have significantly altered the manner in which these disorders have been viewed and treated. Today it is widely accepted and believed that there are complex interactive relationships between psychological factors and physical illness.

The close interplay of psychological and physiological processes involved in psychophysiological disorders makes their diagnosis and treatment particularly difficult. The symptoms of psychophysiological disorders are usually similar to those in systemic disease. As a result, distinctions between these types of disorders are usually made on the basis of etiology. For example, in the case of hypertension, renal hypertension is a systemic disease caused by kidney malfunctioning. Essential hypertension (discussed in Chapter 5) is classified as a psychophysiological disorder because it has no known biological cause. In other words, it is **idiopathic**. However, even though psychological factors appear to cause or maintain chronic elevation of blood pressure in the disorder, the physical problem is nevertheless very real.

To some extent psychophysiological disorders parallel stress-induced illnesses and many of the same mechanisms may also apply here. However, we still do not know enough about the process by which psychological factors produce changes in health and illness. In the field of medicine as a whole the exact causes of many disorders are not totally understood. Since many other causes are possible, all of them are tested until one is indicated. The general rule of assessment for psychophysiological disorders has been that all physical causes must be ruled out before psychological causes are considered. A particular case of hypertension, headache, or any other problem is psychophysiological *only after a complete medical evaluation has ruled out organic factors* as the primary cause, and only where good evidence exists for emotional factors that are antecedent or coincident to the disorder.

Most medical explanations of disease have been *functional* in nature: That is, they do not explain the antecedents of symptoms of a disorder but, rather, only explain the functional disturbances that they cause. For example, they tell us about the relationship between high blood pressure and renal dysfunction, but they do not indicate why at a particular point in time the kidneys stopped functioning properly. The contribution of the field of psychosomatic research to medicine has been to provide a historical explanation of a disorder as well, in order to allow the prediction of who might be at risk for a particular disorder and under what conditions the predisposed person is most likely to develop it. Unfortunately, this field initially overemphasized the unitary role of psychological predisposition in disease processes. A great deal of psychological research was conducted without the recognition of physiological and genetic factors that interact in predisposing us to a particular disorder. Later in this chapter we will again consider the diathesis-stress model of illness (see Chapter 3), which was proposed to take into account these complex interactions.

CLASSIFICATION OF PSYCHOPHYSIOLOGICAL DISORDERS

The Diagnostic and Statistical Manual of Mental Disorders (DSM) was adopted by the American Psychiatric Association in 1952 as its official way of classifying mental disorders. In the original DSM version there was a category called psychosomatic disorders. Nine major categories of disorders were described and the major difference among them was the affected part or system of the body.

212

CHAPTER 7
Psychophysiological
Disorders:
Psychological Factors
Affecting Medical
Conditions

Disorders were classified as psychosomatic illnesses if a clear medical etiology could not be found. The use of this exclusion rule reflects the same biases that most of us carry around. For example, when your stomach hurts, you probably think first about physical causes—something you ate or some virus that you caught. Only when we cannot find a clear biological cause do most of us think about being unhappy, nervous, or under stress as causes. But can we really make ourselves sick by worrying or being upset? Evidence suggests that these emotional factors can cause or contribute to physical illness.

As the DSM was used, several problems were identified. The category for psychosomatic disorders was particularly troublesome; with the increasing recognition that psychological or emotional factors were important as causes of disease or in exacerbation of its symptoms, a change was needed in this classification system. Research had shown that psychological factors were involved in the etiology and development of a number of illnesses that are not typically thought of as psychosomatic, ranging from neurological diseases such as multiple sclerosis to infectious diseases and malignancies such as tuberculosis and cancer. The early DSM did not take this into account and made this diagnosis difficult to use.

In 1968 a modified version (the DSM-II) was developed in collaboration with the World Health Organization (WHO). The term *psychophysiological disorder* replaced psychosomatic disorder in an attempt to repudiate the older view that psychological and somatic indices could be differentiated. A newer and considerably revised version—the DSM-III—was published in 1980, followed by the DSM-III-R in 1987. In these versions the category Psychological Factors Affecting Physical Conditions replaced the psychophysiological disorders category in another attempt to emphasize the extent to which psychosocial factors affect almost all physical disorders (see Table 7.1).

This section or category included traditional psychophysiological disorders as well as any physical condition in which psychological factors are significant in causing, exacerbating, or prolonging the disorder. This newer system relieved clinicians from having to describe a given condition exclusively in psychological or organic terms. Returning to our earlier example, we now are able to describe your stomachache as caused by both physical (e.g., what you ate) and psychological (e.g., upset) factors.

The American Psychiatric Association's most recent revision of the DSM—the DSM-IV—was published in 1994. In this version there is a requirement to specify the type of factors affecting a medical condition. Moreover, the cate-

---

TABLE 7.1. DSM-III-R Diagnostic Criteria for "Psychological Factors Affecting Physical Conditions"

A. Psychologically meaningful environmental stimuli are temporally related to the initiation or exacerbation of a specific physical condition or disorder (recorded on Axis III).
B. The physical condition involves either demonstrable organic pathology (e.g., rheumatoid arthritis) or a known pathophysiologic process (e.g., migraine headache).
C. The condition does not meet the criteria for a somatoform disorder.

Source: Reprinted with permission from *Diagnostic and Statistical Manual of Mental Disorders* (rev. 3rd ed.). Copyright 1987 American Psychiatric Association.

gory has been broadened to include important public health concerns, in addition to the effects of psychiatric **comorbidity** (the co-occurrence of mental and physical illness) on medical outcome (Stoudemire and Hales, 1991). Table 7.2 summarizes these diagnostic criteria. They again reinforce the view that psychosocial factors are intimately linked with physical functioning and illness.

MAJOR FORMS OF PSYCHOPHYSIOLOGICAL DISORDERS

In Chapter 5 we considered one of the most common and potentially dangerous forms of psychophysiological disorders—essential hypertension. Here we will briefly review some of the other prevalent forms of psychophysiological disorders. In all of these disease states stress and emotional factors play a major role in their etiology, exacerbation, or maintenance (Gatchel and Blanchard, 1993).

TABLE 7.2. Diagnostic Criteria for the "Psychological Factors Affecting Medical Condition" Category

A. A general medical condition (coded on Axis III) is present.
B. Psychological factors adversely affect the general medical condition in one of the following ways:
    1. The factors have influenced the course of the general medical condition as shown by a close temporal association between the psychological factors and the development or exacerbation of, or delayed recovery from, the general medical condition.
    2. The factors interfere with the treatment of the general medical condition.
    3. The factors constitute additional health risks for the individual.
    4. Stress-related physiological responses precipitate or exacerbate symptoms of the general medical condition.

Choose name based on the nature of the psychological factors (if more than one factor is present, indicate the most prominent):

Mental disorder affecting . . . [*Indicate the general medical condition*] (e.g., an Axis I disorder such as a major depressive disorder delaying recovery from a myocardial infarction)
Psychological symptoms affecting . . . [*Indicate the general medical condition*] (e.g., depressive symptoms delaying recovery from surgery; anxiety exacerbating asthma)
Personality traits or coping style affecting . . . [*Indicate the general medical condition*] (e.g., pathological denial of the need for surgery in a patient with cancer; hostile, pressured behavior contributing to cardiovascular disease)
Maladaptive health behaviors affecting . . . [*Indicate the general medical condition*] (e.g., overeating; lack of exercise; unsafe sex)
Stress-related physiological response affecting . . . [*Indicate the general medical condition*] (e.g., stress-related exacerbations of ulcer, hypertension, arrhythmia, or tension headache)
Other or unspecified psychological factors affecting . . . [*Indicate the general medical condition*] (e.g., interpersonal, cultural, or religious factors).

Source: From A. Stoudemire and R.E. Hales. Psychological and behavioral factors affecting medical conditions and DSM-IV: An overview. *Psychosomatics*, 1991, *32*, 5–12.

214

CHAPTER 7
Psychophysiological
Disorders:
Psychological Factors
Affecting Medical
Conditions

Asthma

Since 1970 cases of asthma in the United States and other western countries have increased dramatically: As many as 10 to 15 million individuals in the United States suffer from asthma, and prevalence of the disorder has increased by 50 percent or more (see Asthma, 1992; Taylor and Newacheck, 1992). Although we have developed better treatments for this potentially reversible disorder, the number of asthma-related deaths has increased as well. Explaining and changing this trend and reducing costs associated with treating asthma (they exceeded $6 billion in 1990; Weiss, Gergen, and Hodgson, 1992) are greatly needed.

There is considerable debate over the exact definition of asthma and specific distinctions such as *asthma attack, asthma flare, and asthma episode,* but a comprehensive definition views asthma as a lung disease that affects our ability to breathe by obstructing airways, narrowing airways, having inflammation, and/or inducing airway hyperresponsiveness of air passages to a variety of stimuli (see Figure 7.1).

Asthma is most dangerous during asthma *attacks* or episodes of acute airway obstruction. The frequency and regularity of these attacks is variable: For

FIGURE 7.1. Model of asthma.
Source: Adapted from T. L. Creer and B. G. Bender. Asthma. In R. J. Gatchel and E. B. Blanchard (Eds.), *Psychophysiological Disorders: Research and Clinical Applications.* Copyright © 1993, Washington, DC: American Psychological Association.

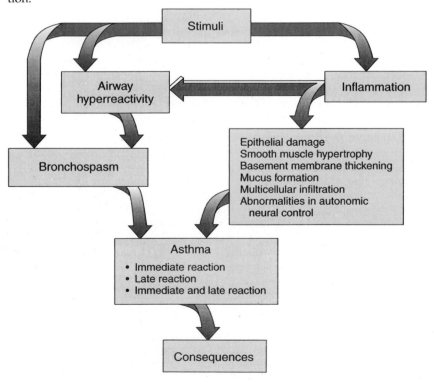

some people they are rare and for others they are more common; and for some people they are usually "set off" by specific conditions (e.g., allergic reactions), whereas for others they are unpredictable. Asthma attacks also vary in severity. Differences in the pattern of episodes and the severity of each attack have contributed to problems in studying, treating, and classifying asthma (see Creer and Bender, 1993; Sheffer, 1991).

A colleague once suggested that if you want to learn about how asthma feels, put a straw in your mouth and, breathing only through the straw, run or walk up several flights of stairs. The supply of air through the straw quickly becomes inadequate. This is similar to what happens during an asthma attack. As the airway closes up or is obstructed, one's air supply becomes inadequate. If we could learn the causes of these changes, we might be able to reduce or eliminate severe or disabling episodes of illness but the nature of these causes or "triggers" remains unclear. Another perplexing characteristic of asthma relates to its reversibility. Although a majority of patients show complete reversibility of airway obstruction with appropriate treatment, others do not obtain total reversibility of their asthma with intensive therapy. Asthma is a very complex disorder with a great deal of individual variation in intensity and frequency of symptoms.

Rees (1964) isolated three causal factors when examining the case histories of children with asthma. The *allergy factor* reflected situations in which some substance (e.g., an allergen such as pollen or dust) caused a biochemical reaction that constricted the bronchi in the lungs. The *infection factor* included bacterial or viral etiology, with the most common type of respiratory infection being acute bronchitis. Rees noted that 35 percent of the asthmatic children he studied had their first asthmatic attacks during a respiratory infection. Finally, *psychological factors* such as anxiety, depression, and other emotional reactions were considered to be potential causes of an asthmatic attack.

Some research has evaluated potential causes of asthma (see Creer and Bender, 1993; Williams et al., 1958), but more progress has been made in learning about important factors in asthma management (see Bauman et al., 1989; Quirk and Jones, 1990). One such investigation looked at knowledge after implementing an educational intervention that was intended to increase what children know about the disorder (Taggart et al., 1991). Attacking the psychological bases of the disorder and understanding the causes of attacks and other changes in asthma are necessary to treat it better. Improving asthma management by those with the disorder should reduce the number and severity of attacks and improve quality of life. Compliance with medical recommendations regarding both lifestyle and the use of medication is also an important determinant of the severity of asthma (see Creer and Bender, 1993). Continued development of behavioral and medical treatments for people with asthma should help to contain the impact of the disorder.

Dermatological Disorders

Diseases of the skin have long been thought of as having clear psychological causes (Gil et al., 1988). Dermatitis is a term for any inflammation of the skin, and the most common form, **atopic dermatitis**, is marked by redness, painful sores, scratching, and thickening of the skin (Friedman et al., 1993). Atopic der-

216

CHAPTER 7
*Psychophysiological
Disorders:
Psychological Factors
Affecting Medical
Conditions*

matitis is fairly common and takes into account about one-fifth of all patients treated in dermatology clinics (Faulstiche and Keane, 1987). Stress, emotional upset, separation from loved ones, and bereavement have been proposed as antecedents to this inflammatory disorder, and there is some evidence to support this view (see Faulstiche et al., 1985; Gil and Sampson, 1989).

Psoriasis is also relatively common; it is marked by red spots or patches of thick, scaly skin. Most of us are familiar with another kind of dermatitis, namely, acne. **Acne** appears to affect grades in school, unemployment, low self-image, anxiety, and anger in some cases, although many sufferers deal with it and emerge well adjusted (see Cunliffe et al., 1989; Motley and Finlay, 1989; Van der Meeren et al., 1985).

Emotional or psychological factors also appear to cause these skin disorders. The skin appears responsive to emotions, and persistent emotional upset can change blood circulation beneath the skin that can be damaging. These circulatory changes may play a role in some dermatological disorders, and they may be resistant to medical treatment if treated while stress is still present. Emotional or stress-reducing treatments can be successful in treating acne (Hughes et al., 1983).

These disorders may leave some residual scars if the skin was especially itchy and continually scratched. They may also leave "psychological scars" since most cases are clearly visible and often unsightly, contributing to self-consciousness, a poor self-concept, and disruption of social relationships. Skin disorders are not life-threatening psychophysiological disorders like hypertension, but they can disrupt one's life and level of self-esteem.

Headache

Headaches are among the most common modern medical complaints (Linet et al., 1989). They can result from a wide variety of organic causes, including tumors, systemic infections, and concussions or from a range of other biological causes as well as psychological factors such as tension. The vast majority of headaches are psychophysiological in nature and can be divided into two major categories: (1) **migraine headaches** and (2) **tension-type headaches**. Many headache sufferers have a combination of both vascular (migraines) and tension components. Headache is common in the general population. Chronic problems with migraine headaches occur in about 5 to 10 percent of the population, whereas approximately 30 to 40 percent experience chronic problems of tension headaches.

Migraine headache is a vascular (blood vessel) disorder caused by a loss of tone in the major extracranial blood vessels, leading to painful dilation and throbbing pain. A pain-threshold chemical (bradykinin or neurokinin) is thought to be released at the side of the dilated vessels, causing an inflammatory reaction. Edema develops (i.e., the walls of the blood vessels become filled with fluid), resulting in a sharp, painful, and throbbing sensation in the head. The pain is often only on one side of the head. Migraine headaches are often preceded by an **aura**—a subjective sensation or visual interference alerting the person that the headache is about to start. Such prodromal or early warning symptoms that precede migraine headaches can include blurred vision, nausea, vomiting, and dizziness.

Migraine headaches usually do not occur during stress; rather, they occur during the poststress period. These headaches are also associated with anxiety and depression, are more common among low-income or less well-educated people, and, interestingly, are *least* common in the northeastern United States (see Breslau et al., 1991; Cook et al., 1989; Nappi et al., 1991; Stewart et al., 1992). They are most common in western and mountain states (Stewart et al., 1992). They can last anywhere from a few hours to several days. Up to 20 percent of men and 30 percent of women experience migraine headaches at some time in their lives (Hatch, 1993), and they are most common between the ages of 35 and 45 (Stewart et al., 1992).

Tension headaches are very different from migraine headaches. They appear to be caused by sustained contraction of the head and neck muscles (Hatch, 1993) and often last for days or weeks. They frequently begin during a stressful period (Wallasch, 1992). Research has not found a relationship between tension headaches and hyperreactivity during stress (Flor and Turk, 1989; Hatch et al., 1992). There are no significant prodromal symptoms, and the headache itself consists of a nonthrobbing ache, with a sensation of tightness frequently described as a feeling of having a "tight band" around the head.

A number of emotionally stressful events appear to precede or accompany the emergence of symptoms in chronic headache sufferers. Headache triggers are events or changes that can cause headaches (see Table 7.3). For example, Wolff conducted a number of studies using an "emotional provocation technique" to precipitate headaches in patients (Dalessio, 1972). The psychological stress produced by this technique, in which patients were criticized for their behavior, actually triggered headache attacks. Heightened sensitivity to pressure-type pain may be an underlying cause of tension headaches (Lous and Olesen, 1982; Schoenen et al., 1991), but stress management techniques have been successfully applied to ease the discomfort associated with these headaches (see Blanchard, 1988).

Irritable Bowel Syndrome

Irritable bowel syndrome is a general term for a functional disorder of the lower gastrointestinal tract. Epidemiological research suggests that the lifetime prevalence of irritable bowel syndrome ranges up to 17 percent of the adult population of the United States (Drossman et al., 1982; Whitehead et al., 1982).

TABLE 7.3. Diathesis-Stress Model of Psychophysiological Disorders

IF	*Individual Response Stereotypy* (Constitutional predisposition to respond physiologically to a situation in a particular way)	AND	*Inadequate Homeostatic Restraints* (May be due to stress-induced breakdown, previous accident or infection, or genetic predisposition)	AND	*Exposure to Activating Situations* (Either exposure to actual external activating/stressful situations or misperception of an ordinary situation or event as stressful)
			THEN *Psychosomatic Episodes*		

Source: From R.A. Sternbach, *Principles of Psychophysiology*. New York: Academic Press, 1996. Copyright © 1996 by Academic Press. Reprinted with permission.

218

CHAPTER 7
Psychophysiological
Disorders:
Psychological Factors
Affecting Medical
Conditions

Thus, although irritable bowel syndrome is a relatively minor health problem (it is not terribly severe or life threatening), it is a major source (in terms of prevalence) of everyday distress. In addition, many patients with symptoms of irritable bowel syndrome exhibit distress (Blanchard, 1993).

The broad criteria for irritable bowel syndrome include at least 3 months of continuous or recurrent symptoms of abdominal pain or discomfort, which is relieved with defecation and/or associated with a change in the frequency of defecation or in the consistency of the stool. Recent criteria from an international conference in Rome, Italy, have established these symptoms as basic to irritable bowel syndrome and provide a working definition of what it entails (Thompson et al., 1992). Treatments include hypnosis, biofeedback, education, and stress management in place of or together with pharmacologic intervention (see Blanchard, 1993; Guthrie et al., 1991; Harvey et al., 1989).

Ulcers

An *ulcer* is a lesion or sore in the lining of the stomach or in the upper part of the small intestine or duodenum that lies immediately below the stomach. There are two general types of ulcer, based on where the lesion is located. **Gastric ulcers** are located in the stomach and **duodenal ulcers** are intestinal. Although these two forms have certain characteristics in common, there are also significant differences. For example, duodenal ulcers are usually associated with an increase in gastric secretion of hydrochloric acid and pepsin, whereas gastric ulcers can be characterized by normal, subnormal, or elevated gastric secretion levels. Another important difference is that emotional factors appear to play a more important role in duodenal ulcer than in gastric ulcer (Yeager and Weiner, 1970). Indeed, gastric and duodenal ulcers are viewed by clinicians as separate disorders that are associated with different causes (Kirsner, 1968). Thus, the general term *ulcer* can be misleading because it refers to at least two diseases that differ in their location, history, and response to treatment. Recently some ulcers have been found to be caused by bacteria that can readily be treated with antibiotics. However, other ulcers are not as easily explained.

Ulcers are not as common in the general population as are some other disorders, with a prevalence rate of about 2 percent. Of these, the majority are duodenal ulcers, which tend to occur at an earlier age than do ulcers in the stomach (Young et al., 1987). They are sometimes "quiet," in the sense that they cause no pain or discomfort and remain unnoticed and unreported. More often the individual feels discomfort, ranging from a "burning sensation" in the stomach, usually the first sign of an ulcer, to severe pain (as the lesion grows larger). These symptoms can be accompanied by nausea and vomiting. Many ulcers heal by themselves, although treatment can reduce the pain and speed up recovery (Welgan, Meshkinpour, and Hoehler, 1985). However, if the ulcer perforates blood vessels in the walls of the stomach, vomiting of blood will occur. Continued hemorrhaging and internal bleeding are life threatening.

Duodenal ulcers appear to be produced by excessively high levels of gastric secretion of hydrochloric acid. The stomach produces this acid to aid in the digestive process and it helps to break down food (see Chapter 2). The walls of the duodenum and the stomach have a protective mucous lining that is usually resistant to this mildly corrosive acid. When acid is produced but food is no longer present, or when the rate of stomach emptying is slowed down and acid stays in the stomach longer, the acid may begin to eat away the protective mucous lining. Among those individuals who cannot tolerate excessive secretion, this may occur quite rapidly. When the output of acid is excessive and a particular site is no longer resistant to the acid, an ulcer will develop.

The most popular explanation for ulcers suggests that psychological stress causes excessive secretion of acid in the absence of food (see Wolf and Wolff, 1947). This notion is based on both animal and human research demonstrating a relationship between stress and secretion activity. There have been numerous examples of patients exposed to emotionally stressful situations showing an increase in the volume and acidity of gastric secretion (see Wolf, 1965). In research with animals it has been demonstrated that the persistent exposure of rats to stress (unpredictable or uncontrollable electric shock) leads to a significant increase in ulceration rate (see Weiss, 1968, 1971b).

Rheumatoid Arthritis

Rheumatoid arthritis is now thought to be an autoimmune disease but was long considered to have important psychological properties. As a result, we discuss this disease here. It is a chronic inflammatory disease, accompanied by considerable pain and deterioration of joints throughout the body. Autoimmune processes that attack the joints and exaggerate inflammatory reactions are among the suspected causes. The progressive inflammatory nature of this disease leads to the formation of *pannus* (a granulation tissue) that can accelerate the destruction of cartilage, bone, and tendons. These destructive effects, together with swelling, change the afflicted joint physically as well as cause pain. About 10 in 100 people are affected by rheumatoid arthritis, with women almost three times as likely as men to be affected. Approximately 60 percent of patients with rheumatoid arthritis show progressive disability (Young, 1993). Currently, there are no cures for the disease.

The importance of psychological factors throughout the course of rheumatoid arthritis has been recognized (Zautra and Manne, 1992). Most clearly, it is associated with a number of stressors with which patients must cope, including a variety of physical symptoms and manifestations of the disease such as joint and generalized pain, swelling, and fatigue. Pain is greater among people who are anxious or depressed (Brown, 1990; Hawley and Wolfe, 1988; Lorig et al., 1989). There are also side effects of medication limitations on daily activities and a good deal of uncertainty about the course of the disease and the absence of a cure. Finally, feelings of hopelessness and despair may occur as pain becomes unbearable (Stein et al., 1988). These psychological factors can affect the time course of the disease if they are not appropriately dealt with.

Pain appears to be the principal source of stress among arthritis patients (Affleck, 1988) and is most often the cause of seeking medical care (McKenna and Wright, 1985). It has been linked to distress and negative mood and is determined to some extent on how well people cope with the disease (Brown et al., 1989). Active coping, such as when one tries to keep busy or otherwise to distract one's attention from the pain, appears to be effective, resulting in

220

CHAPTER 7
Psychophysiological
Disorders:
Psychological Factors
Affecting Medical
. Conditions

fewer or less severe bouts of pain (Brown and Nicassio, 1987; Flor and Turk, 1989). More passive or "giving in" coping strategies, such as wishful thinking, restricting one's activities, or becoming dependent on others, and more negative, pessimistic reactions are associated with more severe and disabling pain (Brown and Nicassio, 1987; Keefe et al., 1989; Revenson, 1993). These coping effects among arthritis patients appear to affect self-esteem, disability, and other aspects of the disease as well (Zautra and Manne, 1992). Psychological determinants of arthritis pain appear to be more strongly related to pain than are measures of disease severity. The number of swollen joints and the extent of sedimentation in the joints are positively correlated with pain, but anxiety, depression, and distress appear to be more closely related to arthritis pain (Affleck et al., 1991; Hagglund et al., 1989).

Several behavioral and cognitive-behavioral approaches to reducing pain and distress among arthritis patients have been described. As with similar programs, emphasis has been on stress management, problem solving, and coping enhancement. By providing education, support, and coping skills, these interventions have been successful in reducing pain, improving physical functioning, and helping patients' adjustment to chronic illness (Achterberg et al., 1981; O'Leary et al., 1988; Radojevik et al., 1992). Particularly important are problem-solving and skills instruction and implementation since rheumatoid arthritis can be chronic, progressive, and debilitating.

Temporomandibular Disorders

Temporomandibular disorders (TMD) are a collection of different disorders that involve pain in the oral cavity and grinding of teeth or other unusual activity. These disorders are usually classified into two diagnostic groups. The first includes disorders of the muscles in the face, head, neck, and shoulders. Other TMDs involve the jaw. Although not mutually exclusive (some patients with facial pain may also have disorders of the jaw), they ordinarily occur independently (Glaros and Glass, 1993). Symptoms can include headache, earache, dizziness, ringing in the ears, and neck and back pain. Estimates of prevalence of these disorders vary. Some studies suggest that one-half of us are afflicted, whereas other reports indicate that about one-third of the general population suffer TMD symptoms (Gale, 1992; Glaros and Glass, 1993). The lowest estimates are based on health care utilization for TMD, with fewer than 5 percent seeking medical attention (Dworkin et al., 1990; Shiffman et al., 1990).

Behavioral and psychological factors play an important role in the disorder. Anxiety and depression play a part in the initiation and development of TMD, and several other psychological and physiological causes have been identified (Glaros and Glass, 1993). Facial muscle reactivity and higher levels of facial muscle activity at rest appear to be related to TMD, and poorer muscle discrimination has been found in TMD patients (Flor, Schugens, and Birbaumer, 1992; Kapel et al., 1989). Emotional factors also appear to be important, particularly in maintaining chronic pain from TMD. Depression, sensitivity to pain, anxiety, and distress are more likely among TMD patients than among healthy controls (Magni et al., 1990; McCreary et al., 1991). Programs that teach patients about the disorder, how to relax, and how to reduce pain and distress have been used to treat TMD (Glaros and Glass, 1993), and biofeedback appears effective in decreasing both facial muscle activity and pain (Burdette and Gale, 1988; Dalen et al., 1986; Funch and Gale, 1984).

ETIOLOGY OF PSYCHOPHYSIOLOGICAL DISORDERS

Relatively broad theoretical models were originally used to conceptualize the causes and consequences of psychosomatic disorders. One model was equally useful for any or all disorders. Simply put, it was assumed that psychosomatic disorders occur because of a *bodily weakness*, either a *weak organ*, such as the stomach (ulcers), or a *weak physiological system*, such as the cardiovascular system (essential hypertension). Furthermore, it was assumed that this bodily weakness could be inherited or develop as a result of disease (e.g., if a respiratory infection predisposes someone to develop asthma).

An extension of this *weak organ/system theory* was the idea that people have specific physiological responses to particular situations. These patterns, including reactions to stressful events, are inherited. The term *specific-response pattern approach* was used to convey the assumption that individuals tend to respond physiologically to stressful situations in their own idiosyncratic ways. It has often been shown that individuals differ in responding physiologically to situations (see Lacey, 1967). One person may demonstrate an increase in heart rate and blood pressure level but little increase in muscle tension; another person in the same situation may display very little increase in heart rate and blood pressure but a large increase in muscle tension. This difference in response patterns is known as *individual response stereotypy* and reflects individual differences in the stereotypic way of responding to situations. As an early example of these individual differences in a clinical population, Malmo and Shagass (1949) demonstrated that under stress, patients with cardiovascular symptoms showed larger increases in cardiovascular response than in muscle tension. Patients with muscle tension headaches showed an opposite pattern.

The next part of the theory proposes that the organ or symptom that is most constantly activated—the weak organ or system—may be susceptible to breakdown and development of a psychophysiological disorder. That is, if you persistently respond to situations with a greatly elevated blood pressure level, this may stress the cardiovascular system and cause a disruption of its homeostatic mechanism. As a result, you may be more susceptible to hypertension. By the same reasoning, those of us with weak digestive systems would expect to develop ulcers or irritable bowel syndrome and those of us with weak joints or bones might develop arthritis.

A major shortcoming of this general model was its lack of predictive validity. Generally, it has not been able to take into account the fact that most people who respond in a specific way do not develop psychophysiological disorders. For example, not all of us with a significant degree of cardiovascular activation in novel or challenging situations eventually develop a cardiovascular disease such as hypertension.

It is generally accepted that genetic factors play an important role in predisposing individuals to various psychophysiological disorders (Weiner, 1977). For example, Mirsky (1958) showed that pepsinogen levels of ulcer patients were significantly higher than those of patients without ulcers. Pepsinogen is a good

222

CHAPTER 7
Psychophysiological
Disorders:
Psychological Factors
Affecting Medical
Conditions

measure of gastric secretion activity because many investigators view an excess of pepsinogen as a cause of ulcers. Together with hydrochloric acid, it is the primary active agent in gastric digestive juices. In an initial study, Mirsky found significant individual difference in pepsinogen levels in newborn infants. Infants with high pepsinogen levels were likely to be members of families in which overall pepsinogen levels were high. In addition, twin studies showed that pepsinogen levels for identical twins were very similar (Mirsky, Fritterman, and Kaplan, 1952; Pilot et al., 1957). This provided early evidence that some important contributing factors in the development of ulcers are inherited.

The first purely psychological formulation of psychosomatic disorders was Freud's classic elaboration of conversion hysteria. Although conversion hysteria was not considered a psychosomatic disorder because there is no actual organic dysfunction, the basic psychological mechanisms in both were similar. When socially unacceptable and forbidden thoughts or impulses occur but cannot be expressed, they will be repressed and alternative channels for getting rid of them will be sought. If appropriate ways of doing so are not available or cannot be found, reactions such as those that occur in hysterical conversion reactions are likely to occur. For example, an individual's wish to strike a significant other may be unacceptable because of the threat of severe punishment or social sanction; and if repression cannot adequately dispose of this impulse, then the individual might develop paralysis of the arm. This is a compromise coping method that allows the simultaneous discharge of energy in a defense against the action. Repressed instinctual impulses were thought to be expressed at a somatic level through the production of the somatic symptom that has a meaningful symbolic relationship to the psychic event.

The notion that specific illnesses were caused by internal conflicts was elaborated by Alexander (1950). The resulting theory of *psychogenesis* dominated the field of psychosomatic medicine for several years. Unlike Freud, Alexander emphasized the association of specific personality patterns, rather than a single conflict, to particular illnesses. He rejected the view that conversion could take into account the occurrence of any physical illness. For example, he suggested that each of the psychosomatic disorders has its own unique combination of personality and conflict factors or *nuclear conflicts* and personality characteristics. His formulation was based to a large extent on clinical observation of patients undergoing psychoanalysis. Repressed psychic energy could be discharged directly to the autonomic nervous system, leading to impairment of visceral functioning.

A more recent psychodynamic formulation of psychosomatic disorders centered around the concept of **alexithymia**. Sifneos (1967) and Nemiah (1973, 1975) argued that the psychosomatic process is often characterized by *alexithymia*, a cluster of cognitive traits dominated by an inability to describe one's feelings. According to Nemiah (1975), the alexithymic personality displays an inability to describe feelings verbally, very little fantasy, and an inability to make any significant internal psychological changes in the course of psychodynamically oriented psychotherapy (Gatchel and Blanchard, 1993). This deficit is assumed to be a major cause or factor in maintaining psychosomatic disorders.

Another theory, based loosely in the psychodynamic tradition, was the **specific attitudes theory** proposed by Graham and colleagues (Graham et al.,

1962; Graham, Stern and Winokur, 1958). These investigators conducted a series of studies of specific attitudes about a distressing life situation. These specific attitudes were thought to be related to susceptibility to particular psychophysiological disorders because they reflected what individuals felt was happening to them and what they wanted to do about it. Clinical interviews with patients suffering from various psychophysiological disorders identified several specific attitudes, and in a study of 128 patients with 12 different psychosomatic disorders or symptoms patients with the same disorder showed similarity in describing their attitudes toward events that occurred just before the appearance or worsening of their symptoms (Grace and Graham, 1952). The associations found included the attitudes for **hypertension**—*the person feels threatened with harm by an ever-present danger and, as a result, needs to be on guard, watchful, and prepared*—ulcers—*the person feels deprived of what is due him or her and wants to seek revenge and to get even*—and migraine headaches—*the person feels that something has to be achieved and then relaxes after the effort.*

A number of these theories, particularly the psychoanalytic approach, were viewed as unscientific because of weaknesses inherent in clinical data. The result was some formulations of psychosomatic disorders. Support for these theories has been inconsistent, in part because they ignored many sources of influence in disease outcomes. Harold G. Wolff's (1953) research on stress and disease was highlighted by careful description and measurement of both psychological and physiological factors under investigation. He focused on conscious rather than unconscious emotions. For example, Wolff studied a patient with a fistula into his stomach allowing observation of the GI tract. This well-known study of gastric functioning systematically evaluated changes in gastric secretion and motor activity under different emotional stress conditions (Wolf and Wolff, 1974). Aggressive states of anger and resentment were associated with increases in gastric secretion and motor activity. However, emotional states of fright and depression led to decreases in gastric activity. (See the box "A Case Study of Stress in an Ulcer-Gastrointestinal Reaction.")

Dissatisfied with early theories, many investigators who were interested in the role of psychological factors in psychophysiological disorders also began to shift their attention to the role of more easily and reliably quantified situational variables such as bereavement and separation as precipitating events (see Engel, 1967; Schmale, 1958). This research established the fact that behavioral and physiological responses to separation and other environmental stressors are correlated with coping mechanisms (Weiner, 1977). Indeed, as we have reviewed earlier in this text, in the growing area of stress research, the impact of any potentially stressful event can be significantly influenced by how a person appraises or copes with it. Coping may prove to be important to consider in any comprehensive model of psychophysiological disorders as well. Together these considerations suggest that a diathesis-stress model may be most appropriate to explain psychosomatic disorders.

The confluence of physiological, genetic, and psychological variables determines many psychophysiological states and must be considered if we are to understand these disorders. This kind of complex determination is reminiscent of the biopsychosocial model we discussed in Chapter 1 and the diathesis-stress model discussed in Chapter 3. This model was proposed to include some psychosocial contributions to disease in models of the etiology of illness (Levi,

224

CHAPTER 7
*Psychophysiological
Disorders:
Psychological Factors
Affecting Medical
Conditions*

1974). This model is a relatively simple statement of the ways in which psychosocial, environmental, genetic, and physiological elements should be considered in the description of disease (Sternbach, 1966). All elements continually interact with one another. Physiological predispositions toward a certain illness, such as genetic weakness or biochemical imbalance, psychosocial stimuli (e.g., stress and how we respond and cope with it), and previously experienced environmental conditions jointly determine many disease states.

Research has provided more support for the diathesis-stress model than to any of the others that we have described, and it now constitutes a basic assumption of research on stress and illness. For example, Ader (1963) bred rats for their susceptibility to gastric lesions under conditions of restraint stress (restraint and immobilization have been found to be significant stressors for rats). Individual differences in susceptibility to gastric lesions were due to individual variations in serum pepsinogen levels. However, Ader found that ulcer-susceptible rats exposed to restraint conditions were more likely to develop ulceration than were other rats, and this was true only when the rats were restrained at the peak of their circadian activity cycle (Ader, 1963).

Many variables—genetic, physiological, situational, behavioral/personality—clearly need to be taken into account in any comprehensive understanding of these disorders. As we have noted, significant progress is also being made in biomedical research on the pathogenesis of these disorders. Unfortunately, parallel progress has not as yet been made in research on psychological factors. More recent evaluations of specific behavioral characteristics and successes of cognitive behavioral interventions provide useful avenues for future investigation.

TREATMENT OF PSYCHOPHYSIOLOGICAL DISORDERS

The disturbing organic symptoms of some psychophysiological disorders, such as bleeding ulcers and cardiovascular disease, often demand immediate as well as long-range medical treatment. In such cases medication and dietary patterns must be prescribed to deal effectively with the physical symptoms of the disorders. Simultaneously, treatment directed at modifying the psychological/behavioral causes and stressors should be administered.

Traditionally, drug therapy has been the major form of treatment of these disorders. For example, minor tranquilizers are commonly prescribed to reduce anxiety and emotional tension associated with them. These tranquilizers can help to reduce intolerable levels of stress and can work in combination with cognitive-behavioral psychotherapy. However, the indiscriminate use of minor tranquilizers alone, without an attempt to deal with the situational or interpersonal factors that are involved, will not bring about much permanent improvement. In addition, side effects such as drowsiness may be associated with drug therapies and people may develop tolerance for a particular drug or dosage level. If this medication is terminated after prolonged and heavy usage, severe withdrawal symptoms such as insomnia, tremors, and hallucinations may occur.

A number of therapeutic techniques have been effective in treating anxiety and stress-related disorders. In Chapter 10 we will discuss various cognitive-

A Case Study of Stress in an Ulcer-Gastrointestinal Reaction

Edward Polowski was examined by a specialist in internal medicine and then referred to a clinical psychologist for further evaluation. The patient complained of a longstanding problem of severe cramps and diarrhea whenever he ate highly seasoned foods or encountered any type of stressful situation. This problem was diagnosed as an irritable colon when the patient was a child. Since that time, he had been treated by a series of physicians, all of whom confirmed this diagnosis. The patient reported the medications prescribed for him had varied in effectiveness, and he had recently been in severe discomfort.

Edward was 35 years old, married, and the father of a six-year-old boy and a two-year-old girl. He was a college graduate with a degree in library science and had been a librarian in the same city library since he graduated from college. Edward stated that he began having unusually severe gastrointestinal symptoms at the time that a new director was appointed to the library a number of months ago. . . .

Edward related that he had numerous occurrences of intestinal difficulties ever since childhood. These episodes were associated with circumstances such as his mother or teacher insisting that he do something he did not want to do. He also became ill when he had to make a public appearance such as participating in his first communion or in a play at school. His mother tended to be quite concerned about making him comfortable when he had intestinal symptoms, although she always told him that it was just a "nervous stomach." She said that she knew how he felt because she was also troubled with a "nervous stomach" when she was anxious or upset.

When Edward was nine years old, his mother took him to her physician because Edward was in severe discomfort. He was in the midst of an episode of cramps and diarrhea that lasted for about a week. The onset of the symptoms was associated with Edward's complaints that his new teacher was too strict and forced him to keep going over material he had already mastered. Edward stayed home from school during the latter part of that week, and the physician prescribed some medication which relieved a great deal of the discomfort. Mrs. Polowski pleaded with the doctor to call the school principal and explain the reason for Edward's symptoms. This was done and Edward reported that his teacher became somewhat more flexible in relation to his school activities. Edward had other occurrences of cramps during that school year, but none as severe as the earlier occasion.

Edward also had periodic intestinal problems while he was growing up, but these attacks usually lasted for just a few hours at a time. In high school, he experienced another prolonged occurrence of intestinal symptoms during a final examination period. Edward generally received good grades in school, but he was always quite anxious before a test because he was afraid that he would not do well. He was very anxious during these particular examinations because he had received lower grades than he had expected on some of his previous tests. He therefore studied a great deal and ignored his mother's assurances that he would do well on the exams.

Edward began having intestinal symptoms during the examination period, and the symptoms did not subside, even with medication, until ten days later when he went to a physician. He was given a complete medical examination, including a number of special tests of the gastrointestinal tract. These tests revealed no structural defects or damage, and the problem was again diagnosed as chronic irritable colon. Edward was given a new medication to take when he felt that the symptoms were about to recur.

Source: From Gloria Rakita Leon. *Case Histories of Deviant Behavior: An Interactional Perspective,* 2nd ed. Boston: Allyn and Bacon, 1977. Copyright © 1977 by Allyn and Bacon, Inc. Reprinted with permission.

226

CHAPTER 7
Psychophysiological
Disorders:
Psychological Factors
Affecting Medical
Conditions

behavioral approaches to treatment. Some cognitive-behavioral approaches have been shown to be effective in treating a wide range of psychophysiological disorders (Gatchel and Blanchard, 1993).

SUMMARY

Psychophysiological disorders, formerly called psychosomatic illnesses, are characterized by physical symptoms or dysfunctions in various organs of the body that are intimately linked with psychological factors. The relationship between the mind and the body has long been a controversial topic among philosophers, physiologists, and psychologists. Today it is assumed that psychological factors are important in all diseases. The current view of these disorders is that they are the result of many causes—physical, psychological, and sociocultural. It is the search for the unique interaction of these factors that interests investigators of psychophysiological disorders. Common forms of psychophysiological disorders—bronchial asthma, dysmenorrhea, headache, neurodermatitis, and peptic ulcer—demonstrate the role of physiological and genetic factors in these disorders. Major psychological formulations have been proposed to take them into account. A review of these various orientations emphasizes the importance of considering genetic, physiological, and psychological factors in a comprehensive diathesis-stress model of psychophysiological disorders.

RECOMMENDED READINGS

Gatchel, R. J., and Blanchard, E. B. (Eds.), *Psychophysiological disorders: Research and clinical applications*. Washington, DC: American Psychological Association, 1993.

Lipowski, Z. J. Psychosomatic medicine: Past and present, Part 1. Historical background. *Canadian Journal of Psychiatry*, 1986, *31*, 2–7.

Melamed, B. J. (Ed.). Special section: The interface of mental and physical health. *Health Psychology*, *14*(5), 1995.

Robinson, R. J., and Pennebaker, J. W. Emotion and health: Towards an integrative approach. In Strongman, K. T. (Ed.), *International review of studies on emotion volume 1*. Chichester, West Sussex, England: Wiley, 1991.

Weiner, H. *Psychobiology and human disease*. New York: Elsevier Science, 1977.

CHAPTER 8

Health Care and Patient Behavior

When people are sick, we can usually tell even if there are no visible symptoms such as runny noses, fatigue, or other signs of physical weakness. People act differently when they are sick. Some people adopt a dependent, helpless role and want others to take care of them. Others run to see a doctor or to the student health service for every little complaint, ever-vigilant for signs of illness or injury. Still others take a more self-sufficient approach, refusing to seek medical attention for all but the most serious bouts of illness, choosing by themselves treatments like over-the-counter drugs, and trying not to let being sick interfere with what they are doing.

Clearly, these behaviors have different implications for how people are treated by others when they are ill and for how their ailments might be treated. For example, those who enjoy the secondary gains from being dependent and cared for may actually take longer to get better, in part to maintain those "advantages." Hypervigilant or overly concerned people are often not taken very seriously because of the many false alarms generated by their reporting of every symptom or minor discomfort. Also, although a more stoic approach may have value and make people more credible when they are very ill, those who do not alter their routine because they are sick may spread the illness to other students, coworkers, or friends, and may make their own illnesses last longer.

These differences in how we react to being sick are important factors in health and well-being. In general, we should think of health care as an environment of sorts, and illness or "sick behavior" as an "entry point." Once we seek medical attention for a problem or illness, new and potent influences, such as hospital or clinic settings, medical tests, surgery, and the like, are introduced and these factors may have effects on important health outcomes. The extent to which we adapt to hospital settings, cope effectively with aversive medical procedures or surgery, cope with being ill, and comply with our health care providers' recommendations and prescriptions are potent determinants of recovery and well-being.

The study of patient behavior in health care settings and in relation to medical procedures has constituted a major area of study in health psychology. Although many principles governing this behavior resemble those already associated with behavior in other settings, there are special twists and concerns in dealing with medical settings. In this chapter we will deal with issues of the behavioral effects of hospitalization, coping with the stress of surgery, illness behavior, and compliance/adherence to medical regimens.

COPING WITH HEALTH CARE

As we have noted several times, medical care costs in the United States have increased at a very rapid rate (Enthoven and Kronick, 1989). In order to reduce the costs of health insurance and health care, our system is turning to health maintenance organizations (HMOs) and to other forms of *managed care*—health care that controls costs by providing treatment guidelines to hospitals and doctors. These kinds of health care systems rely on guidelines for appropriate treatments to determine a cost per patient per year, making it important for these systems to keep costly procedures or tests to a minimum. In addition, primary physicians manage patients' care by acting as gatekeepers for referrals within the system. These changes have affected and will affect health care in many ways. One result of increasing pressure on the health care system to reduce costs may be the reduction of doctors' and hospitals' ability to attend personally to patients' needs. For example, the duration of hospitalization for various procedures is being reduced (Shumaker and Pequegnat, 1989). Moreover, during the time that patients are in hospitals the reductions in the number of professional staff and in their level of training may intensify patients' fears and affect the quality of patients' personal interactions with the hospital staff.

Hospitalization

Hospitalization is often necessary when surgery is needed, intensive care procedures are required for treatment, expensive or scarce resources are necessary, or tests are required. In many cases the care that people receive in the hospital is superior to that which is available elsewhere. However, there are some negative aspects of hospitalization—emotional and behavioral effects that can interfere with proper treatment. Some people associate hospitals with fearful things such as pain or death; others dislike the disruptiveness of a hospital stay, the extreme dependency and loss of control that accompany hospitalization or the dehumanizing aspects of how people are treated in the hospital. Some people dislike or fear the image of the hospital as a complex, chaotic, and confusing environment where more harm than good occurs. Such fears are then compounded by the real problems with which hospitals must deal, including the tendency to treat people as if they were objects, or to withhold desired information, or otherwise to streamline necessary activities.

Although these kinds of experiences are not necessarily typical, one of the more dramatic and stubborn problems creating patient distress is the **depersonalization** of hospital patients by the staff. *Depersonalization* refers to treating a patient as if he or she were not a person. Too often patients are treated as an insurance number, a body to be operated on, a mouth to be fed or medicated, or an object to be watched, moved, or treated. Of course, some concern for the patient is demonstrated, but patients are often expected to remain passive, cooperative, and uninvolved in treatment (Goffman, 1963). Staff members tend to develop this one-dimensional view of patients because it facilitates staff operations and increases the number of people who can be treated. Most staff cannot provide the kind of friendly and personalized interaction that many patients want. The staff's time pressures and workload often require a more efficient, time-conscious style. All hospital patients do not experience this kind of treatment. Some hospitals have attempted to personalize their systems and some physicians provide more information, but many must rely on depersonalizing procedures in order to cope with the economic and logistical pressures of processing the many patients that arrive each day.

The result of this depersonalization is a set of expectations that may have unexpected results. In some cases the needs of the system (e.g., to see as many patients as possible) and the care provider (e.g., to spend more time with individual patients to learn more about them) are contradictory. In such cases different interpretations of patients' behavior are likely. An example of this is the depiction of good and bad patients by Taylor (1979). She describes the experience of hospitalization in terms of control and **learned helplessness** (discussed in Chapter 4). Patients are *supposed* to remain cooperative, unquestioning, and passive so that they are more easily managed by hospital staff. Most patients adopt this **good patient role**, suppressing their desires for more active involvement in their treatment. The good patient who is compliant, asks for little, and makes few complaints often facilitates staff functioning and is usually well liked by the staff. However, some patients do not suppress these needs, becoming angry or hostile and exhibiting **psychological reactance**. These patients assume a bad patient role, described as engaging in such behaviors as smoking against medical advice and making frequent requests and apparently unreasonable demands for more time and attention.

Taylor (1979) argued that these roles may involve more than superficial compliance. Although good patient behavior may be good for the staff, it may not be good for the patient. Conversely, bad patient behavior is disruptive to the staff, but it may have aspects that will help the patient's recovery. Are good patients trying to be cooperative, or is their behavior a result of having learned that they are helpless in hospital settings? It is not difficult to find sources of helplessness training, given the depersonalization and loss of control cues present in the hospital. The helpless patient will be less likely to try actively to improve his or her condition. New pains or sensations may not be reported and other information may be withheld since the helpless patient believes that he or she is unable to influence recovery. Second, helplessness may inhibit decision making. Patients asked to make decisions about their care may be unable or unwilling to do so. If the good patient role is like being helpless, "good patients" may experience some consequences of learned helplessness discussed in Chapter 4. In addition, good patients may withhold valuable information that might speed the treatment process or may have difficulty arriving at informed decisions.

Is the "bad" patient any better off? Taylor (1979) described this patient as reactant, refusing to become helpless and responding to hospitalization with anger and attempts to gain control. The staff, of course, may see these demands as annoying and as interfering with their routine. As we would expect, this kind of behavior can have negative consequences for patient health. If the patient begins to feel ignored or disliked (which may be an accurate perception since the staff may become irritated at the patient's behavior), arousal and suspicion of the quality of care may result. A negative emotional and physical state may also result. Also, the bad patient's important complaints may not be taken seriously by the staff, and thus health care may suffer. The bad patient, however, may have some advantages over his or her good counterpart. Since control has not as yet been yielded, decision making may be more effective. And because this patient maintains at least the illusion of control over hospital routine, readjustment to normal life after release from the hospital may be easier.

The processes involved in good and bad patient behavior are summarized in Table 8.1 (Taylor, 1979). At this point they remain descriptive of the kinds of roles adopted in hospital settings, and researchers are currently studying these issues. At least one study has reported evidence suggesting that "good" patients may indeed be a result of learned helplessness conditioned in the institutions (Raps et al., 1982). Attempts to provide control and responsibility in hospitals to counteract helplessness training have met with some success in countering helplessness-type effects that arise when individuals have to stay in institutional settings (see Langer and Rodin, 1976).

Stress and Surgery

One of the most common hospital experiences is surgery. Coping with surgery or aversive medical examinations is therefore an important aspect of health care. Most surgery is still performed in hospitals despite efforts to reduce escalating costs by performing many medical procedures in shorter hospital stays or on an outpatient basis (Burke, 1992). The apprehension and fear associated with the anticipation of surgery, as well as the alarm and distress commonly associated with recovery, may affect the ways in which a patient reacts to the situation and, consequently, the course of his or her recovery. Because there may be less opportunity to provide care to patients following surgical procedures, psychological interventions have become increasingly important as a means of preparing patients for the physical and psychological difficulties that they may face during the postoperative period (Contrada, Leventhal, and Anderson, 1994) (see Figure 8.1).

Janis (1958) was among the first to study systematically the response to surgery. In one investigation he interviewed patients before and after major surgery. On the basis of the presurgery interview patients were classified by how much fear they showed as the time for surgery approached. Some were extremely fearful, expressing constant concern, anxiety, and feelings of vulnerability. Others expressed more moderate fear, their worries were real but less prominent, and they sought out information about their surgery from physicians and staff. A third group of patients exhibited little if any fear while awaiting surgery. Their reports suggested that they were denying fear rather than dealing with it, and these patients were more angry than worried. Janis

TABLE 8.1. The Possible Consequences of Loss of Control, Good Patient Behavior, and Bad Patient Behavior in Hospital Patients

State	Behaviors	Cognitions	Affect	Physical State	Response from Staff
Loss of control (depersonalization)	Nondiscriminant information seeking and use; complaints to staff.	Inadequate expectations; confusion	Anxiety	Heightened physical reactions to symptoms and noxious medical procedures; possible increased need for medication, lengthened hospital stay.	Nonperson treatment
Good patient behavior (helplessness)	Compliance Passivity Learned helplessness Inability to take in information Failure to provide condition-relevant information	Feelings of helplessness, powerlessness, possible denial or fatalism.	Anxiety and depression	Possible norepinephrine depletion; helplessness also related to sudden death and gradual erosion of health.	Responsiveness to emergencies but routine failure to solicit information from patient.
Bad patient behavior (reactance)	Complaints to staff Demands for attention, mutinous behavior Possible self-sabotage	Commitment to a right to know; suspicion (or paranoia) regarding condition, treatment and staff behavior.	Anger	Heightened catecholamine secretion and hydrocortisone production; possible aggravation of blood pressure, hypertension, tachycardia, angina. Eventual depletion.	Condescension; ignoring patients' complaints; "medicate to placate"; psychiatric referrals; possible premature discharge.

Source: Reprinted, by permission of the publisher, from S. E. Taylor. Hospital patient behavior: Reactance, helplessness, or control? *Journal of Social Issues*, 1979, 35, 156–184.

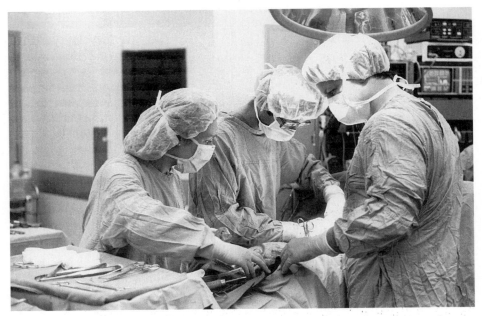

FIGURE 8.1. Psychological preparation for surgery has helped to reduce stress and to improve patients' mood and health. Patients receiving information about the surgery before the surgery do better later than those who are not given this information.
Source: Will and Deni McIntyre/Photo Researchers

found that the moderate fear group, those patients who were fearful but who did not exhibit extreme fear, showed less postoperative emotional problems (Janis, 1958).

Janis explained this finding by arguing that moderate levels of fear are optimal for developing defenses and coping strategies for surgery. Moderately fearful patients seemed to be realistic in approach, seeking information about what would happen to them and how to cope with these events. This information was rehearsed (learned) and provided a basis for confidence about the outcome of the surgery. Extremely fearful or nonfearful patients did not seek information or prepare for surgery and thus were less able to deal with surgery when it occurred. This explanation was supported by findings indicating that patients who had been given information about the unpleasant sensations that would follow surgery showed better recovery than did patients who had not received this information. Those who had been given information were less angry before surgery, showed greater confidence in their surgeon, and displayed less emotional distress after surgery. Information provided a basis for patients to engage in *the work of worrying* and to prepare for upcoming surgery (Janis, 1958).

Since these studies a lot of work has investigated the effects of providing information to patients before surgery as an intervention to reduce the stress of medical interventions (Gil, 1984; Rogers and Reich, 1986). Several studies suggest that providing accurate information about sensations of discomfort or pain that are likely after surgery reduces the aversiveness of these experiences when they occur (Contrada et al., 1994; Heater, Becker, and Olson, 1988; Janis and Leventhal, 1965). This research has also clarified the mechanisms by which psychological preparations for surgery can lessen stress and enhance recovery, and suggested effective interventions for both adults and children who are undergoing stressful medical procedures.

Three basic types of information may be given to patients awaiting surgery (or any frightening or aversive medical examination or procedure). The first concerns what people will feel (e.g., pains, discomforts). This kind of information is **sensory** in focus and corresponds fairly well with the kind of information Janis (1958) studied. The second does not deal with sensations but, rather, with objective characteristics of what will be done during the surgery or examination. This procedural information is focused externally rather than on the patient. A third type of information, coping information, deals with coping skills—that is, providing ways of dealing with pain and discomfort when it arises. Sensory information would likely include pains that would be felt, whereas procedural information might include the different steps in the surgery. Coping might include breathing exercises or other ways of reducing pain and distress. Research has indicated that these different kinds of information are not equally useful and that their effects vary across different situations (Contrada et al., 1994; Devine and Cook, 1983; Johnston and Vogele, 1993; Mavrias et al., 1990).

Imagine that you are in the hospital for surgery. You know that surgery can be dangerous and unpleasant and that recovery can be painful. Why would you want to know what you will feel after surgery? This information allows you to become acquainted with the problems you could encounter so that you are not surprised by them later. If you are told that, among other things, you might feel a sharp pain in your stomach, you will be less likely to experience surprise when such a pain materializes. If you do not have accurate expectations of what you might feel, such a pain might frighten you—you might think that something has gone wrong or that you are in danger. Armed with accurate expectations, however, you view pain as a normal result of the surgery and the recovery process rather than as a danger signal. As a result, the pain experience will be less threatening and hence less stressful. In this regard there is considerable evidence that having accurate sensory expectations reduces distress.

Procedural information, which does not address interpretation of sensations, appears to reduce distress by providing patients with a sense of control over what is happening to them. When surgery or examination is more predictable, this type of information gives patients some sense of control and confidence. Coping information (i.e., behavioral instructions), on the other hand, provides patients with real control since it teaches them ways of relieving pain and discomfort when they wish to do so (Lawlis et al., 1985; Manyande et al., 1995). Both sensory and procedural information appears to reduce surgical stress, and coping information is effective when paired with sensory information (knowing how to cope with a pain is only useful when the pain is accurately anticipated). This simple intervention can reduce distress, length of hospital stay, and other aspects of postsurgery adjustment (see Anderson, 1987;

Heater et al., 1988; Johnson, 1984; Ludwick-Rosenthal and Neufeld, 1988). Information of this kind is also associated with a better mood and outcomes of aversive medical procedures and exams as well (see Johnson and Leventhal, 1974) (see Figure 8.2).

Emotional Support and Patient Interventions

As we have seen in other chapters, social support is usually a good thing and giving patients more social support seems to enhance the recovery of severely ill patients. This suggests that a major component of psychosocial intervention for patients undergoing stressful medical procedures is providing emotional support, usually in combination with coping and procedural information (Felton et al., 1976; Wolfer and Visintainer, 1975). Emotional support includes efforts to reduce patients' concerns and/or to raise their spirits (Contrada et al., 1994; Devine and Cook, 1983). In most studies emotional support has also been evaluated in combination with information and coping skills interventions. For example, in an early study patients undergoing abdominal surgery received either special care involving a combined intervention consisting of encouragement, information about sensations, breathing exercises to reduce pain (Egbert et al., 1964) or routine treatment that involved no such interventions. After surgery patients in the special care group were able to leave the hospital sooner and were given fewer narcotics (see Figure 8.3). (See the box "Hospital Roommates, Stress, and Recovery from Surgery: Extending Laboratory Research into Health Field Settings.")

FIGURE 8.2. Heart rates before and after an aversive medical tube insertion. *Source:* Adapted with permission from J. E. Johnson and H. Leventhal. Effects of accurate expectations and behavioral instructions (coping information) on reactions during a noxious medical examination. *Journal of Personality and Social Psychology,* 1974, 29(5), 716. Copyright © 1974 by the American Psychological Association.

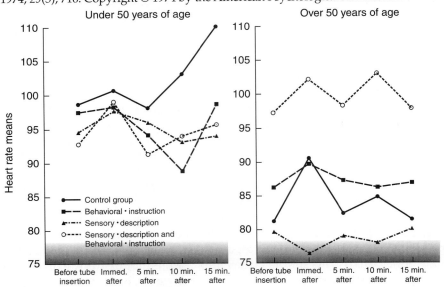

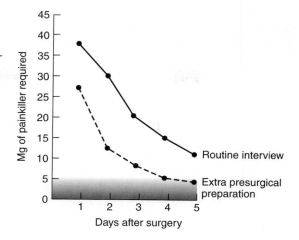

FIGURE 8.3. Graph depicting the different medication requirements of surgery patients given standard or special interviews before surgery. Those given extra information received less pain killer (morphine) after surgery. *Source:* Reprinted by permission from L. D. Egbert, G. E. Battit, C. E. Welch, and M. K. Bartlett. Reduction of postoperative pain by encouragement and instruction of patients. *New England Journal of Medicine,* 1964, 270, 825–827.

Other Interventions for Surgical Distress

Other cognitive and behavioral interventions designed to reduce distress have also been developed and assessed. These have included the use of procedures such as relaxation training to reduce distress and to facilitate recovery (see Contrada et al., 1994). One popular behavioral approach has been to expose patients to films or videotapes of patient models who are successfully coping with the aversive procedure. Modeling treatments were developed originally from the social learning theory (Bandura, 1977b; see Chapter 10) and have been used to treat psychological disorders such as phobias. Modeling procedures usually involve viewing an individual who is successfully coping with the procedure in question. Therefore, depending on the particular disorder, they convey information about procedures and may provide coping information as well. Anderson (1987) prepared patients for cardiac surgery by having one group of patients (information preparation group) view a videotape of interviews with former cardiac surgical patients that provided procedural and sensations information. A second group (information plus coping group) saw the first informational videotape and also watched a sound and slide show that taught them relaxation exercises for reducing postoperative distress. A control group was given the routine hospital preparation procedure consisting of presenting pamphlets describing the procedure and a neutral interview. Results indicated that both experimental groups reported less emotional distress and were judged by nurses as making better physical and psychological recoveries. They also had nearly one-third fewer episodes of hypertension following surgery (see Figure 8.5).

Another recent study tested the efficacy of a guided imagery procedure to reduce distress and physiological arousal in abdominal surgery patients (Manyande et al., 1995). One group of patients was instructed to imagine specific preoperative and postoperative discomforts such as hunger, pain, and nausea. During this imagery procedure these patients were told to imagine that they felt able to cope with these sources of distress. A comparison group of surgical patients received only background information about the hospital. Results

Hospital Roommates, Stress, and Recovery from Surgery: Extending Laboratory Research into Health Field Settings

People waiting for surgery, unless they have a private room, typically spend their time in the presence of other patients who are roommates. A set of interesting studies by Kulik and Mahler (1987, 1990) examined the effects of assigning patients who were about to undergo surgery to various types of hospital roommates. They based their study hypotheses on the theory of social comparison proposed by social psychologists more than 35 years earlier (Festiginer, 1954). Schachter (1959) adapted this theory to propose that people in novel, threatening situations turn to others for a variety of reasons, including the desire to reduce anxiety and to assess the appropriateness of their feelings. The theory further suggested that anxious people would seek to affiliate with similarly anxious others.

Kulik and Mahler (1990) first surveyed patients about to undergo coronary bypass surgery and found that, contrary to the theory's predic-tions, patients preferred to room with postoperative patients because these patients had already had surgery and could provide them with important information about how to cope with the surgery they were about to undergo. Next they assigned patients about to undergo coronary bypass surgery to a roommate who was either similar or dissimilar in surgical status (i.e., either preoperative or postoperative) and either similar or dissimilar in the type of operation (i.e., either cardiac or noncardiac). Their results indicated that patients who had a postoperative roommate before surgery and were less anxious were more ambulatory postoperatively and released from the hospital more quickly than were patients who roomed with another preoperative roommate. A subsequent study replicated these findings with patients who were undergoing a variety of types of surgeries (Kulik, Moore, and Mahler, 1993).

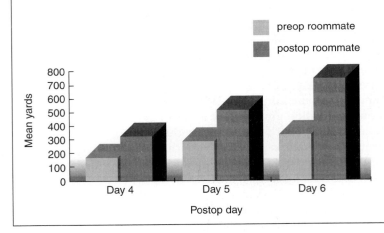

FIGURE 8.4. Postoperative ambulation (self-report) as a function of postoperative day and roommate similarity (similar = preop). *Source:* Adapted from J. A. Kulik and H. I. M. Mahler. Effects of preoperative roommate assignment on preoperative anxiety and recovery from coronary bypass surgery. *Health Psychology*, 1987, *6*, 534.

indicated that imagery patients felt that they had coped better with the procedure and had lower blood levels of cortisol both before and after the surgery.

Interventions with Children

Psychological interventions have also been designed for and used with children to reduce the distress associated with aversive medical and surgical procedures (Saile et al., 1988). Several studies have found that information can reduce the distress that children experience following an operation (see Peter-

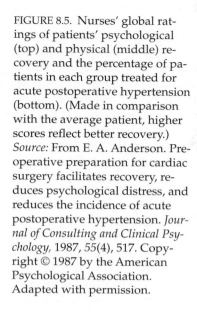

FIGURE 8.5. Nurses' global ratings of patients' psychological (top) and physical (middle) recovery and the percentage of patients in each group treated for acute postoperative hypertension (bottom). (Made in comparison with the average patient, higher scores reflect better recovery.) *Source:* From E. A. Anderson. Preoperative preparation for cardiac surgery facilitates recovery, reduces psychological distress, and reduces the incidence of acute postoperative hypertension. *Journal of Consulting and Clinical Psychology,* 1987, *55*(4), 517. Copyright © 1987 by the American Psychological Association. Adapted with permission.

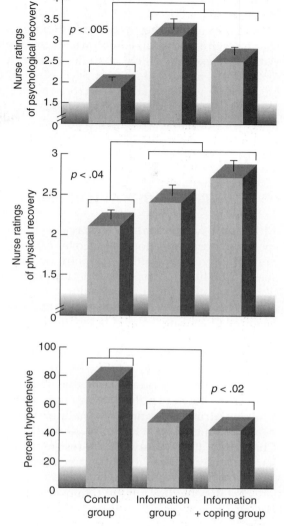

son and Shigetomi, 1982; Varni, 1983). One popular approach that has been validated by research involves the use of various modeling and cognitive-behavioral interventions to reduce distress in children who are undergoing surgery or other stressful procedures (see Faust, 1991; Jay et al., 1991). In one of the original studies to use these procedures with children Melamed and Siegel (1975) studied a group of hospitalized children who were scheduled to undergo various surgical procedures. The investigators used a modeling film entitled "Ethan Has an Operation" and compared its effects with a control film of a child on a nature trip. The modeling film was narrated by a 7-year-old pediatric patient model and demonstrated procedures and events that children encounter during hospitalization, including blood tests, going into surgery, and the use of anesthesia. Results of their study indicated better preoperative and postoperative adjustment among those children who saw the modeling film.

Subsequent studies used other coping skill interventions and relaxation training with hospitalized children (Campbell, 1995; Zastowny et al., 1986). With some exceptions, these studies demonstrate the effectiveness of these interventions, and some form of psychological preparation for hospitalization has become widespread in pediatric medical practice (Peterson and Ridley-Johnson, 1980). In addition, research has examined the situations in which the presence of a parent reduces a child's distress (Lumley et al., 1990) and when distracting a child during an aversive procedure is beneficial (Manne et al., 1992).

HEALTH BEHAVIOR AND ILLNESS BEHAVIOR

Although psychosocial and behavioral factors are important in affecting response to hospitalization and recovery from surgery, the majority of behaviors of interest from a health standpoint occurs outside the hospital. Most of us spend little time in hospitals and may go to great lengths to avoid hospitalization. Many of us self-diagnose our symptoms and treat them with over-the-counter remedies from the drug store and never even see a doctor much less a hospital! Our health-related behaviors in our everyday environments are very important.

As you will recall from Chapter 3, there are three basic mechanisms linking behavior to illness or poor health. Two of these are of relevance here—lifestyle and reactions to the sick role. Personal habits and patterns of behavior have been shown to influence the onset of a number of illnesses. Taking drugs, smoking, drinking, eating, and failing to exercise can all impair health. These behaviors are often referred to as **health behaviors**. As we will discuss in Chapter 12, these behaviors are resistant to attempts to change them and are hard to study because their negative effects are gradual and often not immediately noticeable.

Health behaviors refer to actions we take that may affect health *while we are healthy*. Once we decide that something is wrong, we can think of them differently. Responses to the fact that one is perceiving symptoms or could be ill are **illness behaviors** (McHugh and Vallis, 1986; Mechanic, 1986) and are more easily identified and have received a great deal of attention. These responses include attitudes toward seeking medical attention, methods of interpreting symptoms, and preferred styles of health care. Compliance, perhaps the most thoroughly researched aspect of health and illness behaviors, will be treated separately in a later section.

Beginning with early writings of medical sociologists (Goffman, 1961b; Parsons, 1951), a number of researchers have focused their work on aspects of behavior associated with the **sick role**, including cognitions and behavior that occur when people define themselves as being ill or having been diagnosed with a disease (Kasl and Cobb, 1966). To some extent this research was generated by the repeated observation that certain types of behaviors or events were associated with illness (McHugh and Vallis, 1986). Examples of such behaviors include both the "privileges" of being sick such as being excused from normal responsibilities and obligations as well as the negative aspects of illness such as being stigmatized with all the attendant social awkwardness and decreased attractiveness that being sick entails. The process of recognizing that one is ill usually takes place in several steps. According to Mechanic (1986; see also McHugh and Vallis, 1986), people must pay attention to the symptoms that they are experiencing, make an evaluation that these symptoms are illness-related, and then act on this evaluation by defining themselves as ill and either seeking medical care or treating themselves in some way.

Determinants of Help-Seeking

Seeking medical attention or otherwise interacting with the health care system is a critical first step in dealing with illness or the threat of illness. From looking for a diagnosis and treatment to getting preventive vaccines, we deal with this system at several levels. When ill or uncomfortable, people seek information and help, but the conditions under which they do so depends on a number of factors, including perception and interpretation of symptoms, cultural or learned patterns of response to symptoms, and previous experiences in medical settings.

These factors are very complicated. As an example, consider how people perceive and interpret symptoms. The ways in which sensations are interpreted as being medically relevant or as benign have been of considerable interest to health psychologists. Symptoms are generally considered to be discrete sensations that are experienced at certain times. Nausea, headaches, cramps, and the like are episodic—they occur and recur for specific periods of time. Yet evidence suggests that many sensations that we call symptoms occur more or less continuously—most people experience these somatic sensations much of the time (see Krantz et al., 1980; Mechanic, 1986; Zola, 1966). Minor pains or discomfort may vary in intensity or in whether they interfere with ongoing activities, but they are often not noticed. The degree to which people are *aware* of symptoms or are willing to report them and to seek information about them seems to vary.

Many factors appear to affect our awareness and the reporting of symptoms. Situational constraints or excesses may increase or decrease awareness. Research has indicated that people become more aware of bodily sensations when they are bored and less aware of sensations when they are fully occupied with a task (Fillingham and Fine, 1986; Pennebaker and Brittingham, 1982). This suggests that when we do not have anything to do, we pay more attention to symptoms and try to figure out what they signify. Withdrawal appears to be associated with heightened awareness of symptoms (Pennebaker, 1979). How one views the world or how optimistic one is also affects symptom reporting (Scheier et al., 1995). The ways in which sensations are also labeled and reported are determined by situational, cultural, and psychological influences (see McHugh and Vallis, 1986; Mechanic, 1986; Zola, 1966).

Although symptoms are hard to pin down and may or may not mean that something is wrong, our interpretations of symptoms and subsequent action are affected by the actual sensations experienced. Discomfort in different intensities and/or locations is interpreted differently. However, a number of social psychological factors are also important. For example, women are more likely to report symptoms and to seek medical attention than are men (Baum and Grunberg, 1991). Partly due to this, women more accurately report symptoms when they are present but also mention them more often when they are not present (Gonder-Frederick et al., 1989). Lower social status is also associated with greater symptom reporting (Kaplan, 1993; Koos, 1954). Help-seeking is frequently but not necessarily related to stress or to the extent of reported symptoms. Intervening factors such as social support and prior medical or psychological history appear to be reasonable predictors of help-seeking (see Bieliauskas, 1980; McHugh and Vallis, 1986).

Stress affects whether people interpret symptoms as danger signs and/or seek medical attention, but it is not the only variable that affects the use of health services. Mechanic (1978) conducted a study in which the patterns of health care by a large sample of college students were monitored. Distress was important, but so were the student's sex and relationship to social networks. Higher status, less religious students were most likely to seek psychiatric help, younger students were most likely to seek counseling assistance, and women were most likely to use health services in general.

Another factor in how one reacts to symptoms is one's mental health. Health psychologists as well as mental health specialists have become increasingly concerned about the interrelationship between psychological and physical disorders (Melamed, 1995). It has become evident that in many cases patients with diagnosable psychological problems, such as clinical depression or anxiety, interpret symptoms as physical illness and seek help from primary care physicians such as internists or family practitioners, and not from psychologists, psychiatrists, or other mental health practioners (Katon and Sullivan, 1990; Miranda and Munoz, 1994). Estimates range from 15 to 33 percent of hospitalized medical patients who suffer from psychological disorders, such as anxiety or depression, compared with 2 to 4 percent in the general population (Katon and Sullivan, 1990). In addition, it appears that there is a substantial **co-morbidity** of psychological and physical disorders (Cohen and Rodriguez, 1995). That is, psychological and physical disorders seem to coexist in the same individuals. What are the mechanisms that link psychological disorders to physical illnesses? Cohen and Rodriguez (1995) have suggested a number of biological, behavioral, cognitive, and social pathways by which emotional disorders, such as depression or anxiety, could influence physical disorders (see Figure 8.6). Biological pathways include endocrine or central nervous system effects of emotional disorders, including changes in cortisol or neuronal activity in the brain. The most relevant are the proposed effects of emotional disorders on health practices (e.g., adherence to regimens), cognitive pathways that affect the interpretation of symptoms (e.g., bodily preoccupation that can accompany depression), or social pathways (e.g., disturbances in relationships that may lead to seeking health care). Cohen and Rodriguez (1995) also suggest pathways in the opposite direction and try to explain how physical disorders can promote psychological disturbances as well. These would include the effects of sick role behaviors on mood, effects of physical illness on feelings of perceived stress and loss of control, and ways that social disruptions can alter mood and anxiety.

An important clinical application of recognizing the influences of emotional disorders on the use of health care services has been the development of

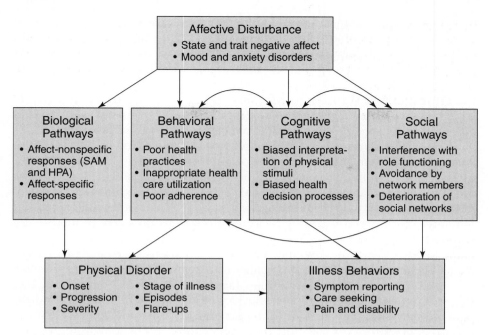

FIGURE 8.6. Pathways linking disturbances to physical disorders. The paths identified in the model move in only one direction from affective disturbance to physical disorder. The absence of alternative paths is not intended to imply that they do not exist. SAM = sympathetic-adrenal medullary system; HPA = hypothalamic-pituitary-adrenocortical axis.
Source: From S. Cohen and M. S. Rodriguez, Pathways linking affective disturbances and physical disorders. *Health Psychology,* 1955, *14*(5), 376. Copyright © 1995 by the American Psychological Association. Adapted with permission.

interventions designed to reduce the use of health care services (Cummings et al., 1992; Pallak et al., 1995). These studies have shown that targeting psychological or mental health treatment for medical patients can reduce their use of primary care services, lowering medical costs considerably (see Friedman et al., 1995, for a review of the ways that health psychology interventions might lead to reduced costs incurred in medical care).

Preferences for Types of Care

Different people have different preferences for the type of care they receive. Some like to get a lot of information—what the physician is doing and finding and what it means—whereas others do not. Some want to take care of themselves; others want professionals to do it. Some want friendly physicians; others want businesslike interactions. Recent research has looked at whether these kinds of preferences represent any systematic bias in patterns of using health care facilities. For example, how much should a doctor tell his or her patients? One approach to answering this and other questions is to measure patients' preferences for health care (Krantz, Baum, and Wideman, 1980). Research on providing information to surgery patients has indicated that choice or control enhances recovery from surgery. But other studies suggest that there are not always direct benefits of increased patient control. By the same token, some individuals may benefit more than others from an active and informed role in their health care. An example of this research has been modification of the locus of control concept and development of a health-specific index of the locus of control (Wallston and Wallston, 1984). This scale, which discerns the degree to which an individual feels able to control his or her health, has been used in order to identify people who benefit from differently focused programs.

Krantz and his associates (1980) developed a scale called the Health Opinion Survey (HOS) in order to measure patients' preferences for more or less active participation in health care and for a more or less informed role in this process. The items in this scale (see Table 8.2) assess the degree of involvement that patients want when making decisions about their health. Preferences for self-care—as opposed to letting health professionals take care of them—and preferences about what they are told about their health are measured.

In stressful and time-pressed health care situations there is evidence that the HOS can be useful in matching patients to treatment interventions in a way that minimizes stress and maximizes favorable health care outcomes. One study of patients undergoing oral surgery (Auerbach et al., 1983) varied the type of information given prior to the procedures. When patients were given specific preparatory information about procedures, patients with high information preferences showed better adjustment during surgery. However, when given only general information, patients with low information preferences fared better (see Figure 8.7). In a second study (Martelli et al., 1987) patients were given preparatory interventions that were either emotion-focused—designed to reduce negative emotion and distress—problem-focused—offering objective information about surgical procedures and sensations—or mixed—involving interventions that combine both features. Again, results indicated that adjustment and satisfaction were better when high HOS information preference subjects were given problem-focused information and low HOS information preference subjects were given emotion-focused information.

Patient preferences have also been studied in recovery from coronary bypass surgery (Mahler and Kulik, 1991). People with greater preferences for behavioral involvement experienced greater pain behavior but were more ambulatory and had shorter hospital stays after surgery. More recently, in patients undergoing hemodialysis for kidney disease, it was demonstrated that high levels of preferences for behavioral involvement were associated with better dietary adherence for patients receiving dialysis at home (where self-care is greater) but poorer dietary adherence when receiving treatment in a dialysis center (Christensen et al., 1990).

Coping with Chronic Illness

One of the most challenging areas in the field of health and behavior involves patient responses to chronic diseases. Most of us have been ill for more than a day or two, but few of us have been ill for weeks, months, or years. Many diseases, such as diabetes, hypertension, heart disease, and cancer, are not illnesses that one gets over and forgets. In general, they are not cured by treatment. Diabetes, arthritis, and hypertension, for example, are essentially

TABLE 8.2. Health Opinion Survey

The following questions ask for your opinions about different kinds of health care. For each statement below, decide whether you *agree* or *disagree* and circle the answer that *best* fits your opinion. Each person is different, so there are no "right" or "wrong" answers. Please try to circle an answer for each question, and don't leave any blank. Even if you find that you don't completely agree or disagree with a statement, choose the *one* answer that comes *closest* to what you believe.

For each question, circle only one answer that comes the *closest* to what you believe:

1. I usually don't ask the doctor or nurse many questions about what they're doing during a medical exam.	AGREE DISAGREE
2. Except for serious illness, it's generally better to take care of your *own* health than to seek professional help.	AGREE DISAGREE
3. I'd rather have doctors and nurses make the decisions about what's best than for them to give me a whole lot of choices.	AGREE DISAGREE
4. Instead of waiting for them to tell me, I usually ask the doctor or nurse immediately after an exam about my health.	AGREE DISAGREE
5. It is better to rely on the judgments of doctors (who are experts) than to rely on "common sense" in taking care of your own body.	AGREE DISAGREE
6. Clinics and hospitals are good places to go for help since *it's best for medical experts to take responsibility* for health care.	AGREE DISAGREE
7. Learning how to cure some of your illness without contacting a physician is a good idea.	AGREE DISAGREE
8. I usually ask the doctor or nurse lots of questions about the procedures during a medical exam.	AGREE DISAGREE
9. It's almost always better to seek professional help than try to treat yourself.	AGREE DISAGREE
10. It is better to trust the doctor or nurse in charge of a medical procedure than to question what they are doing.	AGREE DISAGREE
11. Learning how to cure some of your illness without contacting a physician may create more harm than good.	AGREE DISAGREE
12. Recovery is usually quicker under the care of a doctor or nurse than when patients take care of *themselves*.	AGREE DISAGREE
13. If it costs the same, I'd rather have a doctor or nurse give me treatments than do the same treatments myself.	AGREE DISAGREE
14. It is better to rely less on physicians and more on your own common sense when it comes to caring for your body.	AGREE DISAGREE
15. I usually wait for the doctor or nurse to tell me about the results of a medical exam rather than asking them immediately.	AGREE DISAGREE
16. I'd rather be given many choices about what's best for my health than to have the doctor make the decisions for me.	AGREE DISAGREE

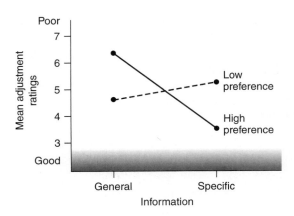

FIGURE 8.7 Mean adjustment ratings for subjects differing in preference for information and specificity of information received. *Source:* From S. M. Auerbach, M. F. Martelli, and L. G. Mercuri. Anxiety, information, interpersonal impacts, and adjustment to a stressful health care situation. *Journal of Personality and Social Psychology,* 1983, *44*(6), 1291. Copyright © 1983 by the American Psychological Association. Adapted with permission.

lifetime diseases that are controlled rather than cured. The use of dietary restrictions, insulin, analgesics, diuretics, beta-blocking drugs, and vasodilating drugs may allow people with these diseases to live normal lives, but the underlying conditions remain. These diseases require special coping skills and health care. Patients must deal with physical problems related to the illness as well as the nature of treatment. They must cope with pain, other symptoms that produce discomfort, physical impairment, and/or changes in cognitive abilities associated with their disease and with their treatment. Some forms of treatment, such as chemotherapy for cancer or various antihypertension medications, have aversive side effects that may be more uncomfortable and disruptive than are actual symptoms of the disease.

Coping with chronic illness means coping with all of these things. One's daily life changes as old ways of doing things are disrupted or abandoned. At the same time, new fears are present and plans for the future may need to be changed. Chronic illness and treatment of these disorders can create formidable difficulties for patients and care providers. Many important coping issues are common to a broad range of diseases, and several psychological concepts, such as denial, control, and social support, are important in coping with a variety of chronic diseases, including coronary heart disease, cancers, arthritis, and AIDS.

For example, many important resources that people need and use in coping with chronic illnesses come from family and friends. The social strains that are likely to follow the diagnosis and/or the treatment of a chronic illness may vary by disease and are affected by a number of variables. However, social support is often crucial to patients. Friends and family may draw away from victims of diseases such as AIDS and cancer, even though their support may be extremely important to the patient at that time. On the other hand, there is also some evidence of families drawing together in the face of such a crisis (Masters, Cerreto, and Mendlowitz, 1983). Nevertheless, evidence is accumulating that social support from family and friends predicts outcomes (including mortality) from diseases such as coronary heart disease (Shumaker and Czakowski, 1994) and cancer (Ell et al., 1992). One study (Christensen et al., 1994) showed that perceived family support was a predictor of the length of survival in patients with severe kidney disease. It has also been reported that lower levels of social support are related to immune system deterioration in male patients with the HIV virus (Theorell et al., 1995).

Also related to the difficulties in coping with chronic illness is the tendency of care providers to withhold or oversimplify information about the illness or its implications. Some physicians, for example, do not always tell patients that they have cancer or other fatal diseases when prognosis is not good. Among the reasons for this was the fear that patients would become depressed or suicidal. One study found that physicians were reluctant to disclose information fully to patients (Mount et al., 1974). However, the tendency of physicians to withhold information has diminished somewhat since the 1960s and 1970s. Most physicians now tell some or all patients about their cancer diagnoses (Greenwald and Nevitt, 1982). However, some information is still frequently withheld, which can pose problems for many patients (Bedell and Delbanco, 1984).

Research has examined coping with specific diseases ranging from cancer and arthritis to diabetes, kidney disease, and chronic lung disease (see Cox and Gonder-Frederick, 1992; Hegel et al., 1992; Kaplan et al., 1984; Zautra and Manne, 1992). Research has also addressed coping in relation to physical disability in the elderly (Wilcox et al., 1994) and among caregivers of Alzheimer's disease patients (Kiecolt-Glaser et al., 1994). In this chapter, rather than consider each of a broad range of chronic illnesses and how coping affects patients' responses to each disorder, we will, instead, consider the older and more established literature on rehabilitation and coping in patients who have experienced a heart attack as an example of the issues underlying management of chronic illness. Clearly, the problems of active participation, as in the case of insulin self-administration in diabetes or the severe side effects of treatment and fears associated with cancer or terminal illnesses, make them different from heart disease (see Davis et al., 1987; Van Komen and Redd, 1985). For our purposes here, however, the discussion of postheart attack demands will be illustrative of many major variables and processes in chronic diseases.

Recovering from Heart Attack

As is the case with most chronic diseases, many nonmedical problems resulting from the onset of coronary disease are almost as severe as the primary illness itself. Complex and demanding social, vocational, and psychological adjustments are required of patients and their families. Recovery from heart attack (also referred to as myocardial infarction or MI) requires the interaction of medical and psychological processes at many levels, and important recovery outcomes may depend on the patient's interpretation of illness and the success and failure of psychological coping mechanisms. Programs that aim to reduce distress and to facilitate adjustment after an attack are associated with reduced mortality as well as improved quality of life (Lewin et al., 1992).

The process of recovery from heart disease is usually divided into an acute (in hospital) phase and a convalescent (posthospital) phase. Three of the major concerns of the recovering heart patient after release from the hospital are *survival* (fears of death and recurrence of disease), the effects of illness on the *ability to resume work activities*, and the effects of illness on *sexual functioning*

(Croog, 1983; Dillard, 1982). It appears that most post-MI patients are reemployed after 1 year, with delays or failures to resume work occurring more often among blue-collar workers, relatively less educated people, and patients with long-lasting depression or emotional distress (Doehrman, 1977; Krantz and Deckel, 1983).

The family can play an important role in influencing the course of the patient's recovery and rehabilitation. (See the discussion in Chapter 4 on social support interventions in post-MI patients.) As most coronary patients are middle-aged males, particular emphasis has been placed on how the wife can affect the way that the husband copes with his disease (Croog, 1975, 1983). Conflicts between husband and wife or overprotectiveness on the part of the spouse can interfere with the recovery process (Garrity, 1975; Wishnie, Hackett, and Cassem, 1971).

Depression is considered to be one of the major problems in cardiac convalescence and rehabilitation (Carney et al., 1995) (see Chapter 4). During recovery patients must confront the realities of disability and deal with changes in lifestyle that are forced upon them. Moreover, after the period of hospitalization some patients are reluctant to resume their normal activities or to return to work—often to an extent that is not justified by their medical disability. One common reaction of this group of patients, termed **cardiac invalidism**, is characterized by excessive dependency, helplessness, and restriction of activity.

The onset of acute MI is a stressful and potentially uncontrollable crisis for most cardiac patients (Krantz, 1980; Krantz and Deckel, 1983). In addition to physical pain and fear of death, patients are confronted with uncertainties about employment and family activities. Restrictions of lifestyle and some fear and uncertainty may persist for months or even years beyond the acute phase of illness. The control-and-predictability model of heart attack recovery (Krantz, 1980) suggests that adverse consequences occurring after acute MI are mediated in part by feelings of helplessness induced by illness and by potentially threatening hospital procedures. Thus, individuals who feel relatively more competent, less depressed, and less threatened (all reflections of perceived helplessness) during the acute phase of illness will fare better emotionally, behaviorally, and physiologically at later points in the recovery process. Further, procedures that enhance the patient's behavioral control—providing choices, encouraging participation—or cognitive control—providing information, increasing environmental predictability—should facilitate recovery from acute MI.

Positive events can even be mistakenly interpreted as sources of stress. When patients are ready to transfer from a coronary intensive care unit to the general medical ward, adverse reactions are frequently observed as the nurse-patient and physician-patient relationships in the coronary care unit (CCU) may be suddenly disrupted. In one study most patients showed adverse emotional reactions to the transfer (Klein et al., 1968). Despite the fact that transfer was a sign of recovery, patients showing adverse reactions interpreted being moved as a sign of rejection by the staff. In addition, the patients felt considerable uncertainty about who their physician would be and about other aspects of their treatment because changes in treatment programs between the two locations were often abrupt as well. Preparation for the transfer, having the same physician-nurse team follow each patient, and daily visits by the same nurse who provided information and helped with adjustment reduced new cardiovascular complications. The potential importance of interventions in post-MI patients also received support from a study conducted by Cromwell et al. (1977).

Several other factors and behaviors also affect recovery (Hackett et al., 1988). For example, Figure 8.8 summarizes findings from a study of the likelihood of death among a group of men who had survived an initial heart attack. Plotted over a 3-year period, these findings show that less education, more stress, and more social isolation were related to a greater likelihood of dying (Ruberman et al., 1984). Recovery from a heart attack and other major disease events is affected by the resources one has to resist stress and isolation, how much stress is experienced, and how one copes with these stressors.

Quality of Life

It should be evident from the areas that we have reviewed in this chapter that medical treatments not only affect physical health status and survival, but they also have a significant effect on the quality of patients' lives and their ability to function in their day-to-day activities (Kaplan, 1994). It has been suggested (Kaplan, 1994; Kaplan and Bush, 1982) that the purpose of health care is twofold: to make people live for a long period of time and to improve the quality of their lives before death. Consider the following examples. As we noted earlier, some patients do not return to work and normal activities after a heart attack, becoming so-called cardiac invalids. Clearly, for these individuals their treatment might have been successful from a purely medical or survival standpoint, but the quality of their lives is diminished. Similarly, treatments such as chemotherapy may be available to patients with advanced forms of cancers, but the severe side effects of treatments become an important consideration for them in deciding whether extending their lives for several months is worth the diminished quality of life offered by the treatments.

For this reason, measurement of **quality of life**—rather than just medical status or mortality alone—has become an important outcome in health care. Quality of life has been operationalized in different ways, including assessment of the individual's expectations and whether they are met (Kaplan, 1985) and the impact of treatment on all aspects of the patient's life, not only on objective physical health and mortality (Bergner, 1989; Testa et al., 1993). How well people can do things such as dress themselves or care for their home reflects functional aspects of quality of life, whereas mood, satisfaction, and fulfillment reflect its more spiritual aspects. Studies have shown that the construct of quality of life incorporates a number of dimensions (see Bergner, 1989; Kaplan and Bush, 1982). These dimensions include (1) *physical symptoms* that the patient experiences; (2) *functional status*—their ability to take care of themselves and to conduct activities of daily life; (3) *role activities*—the ability to work at one's job and at home; (4) *social functioning*—including personal interactions and intimacy; (5) *emotional status*—anxiety, stress, depression; (6) *cognitive and intellectual functioning*—memory and analytical ability; (7) *general energy level and vitality*; (8) *perceptions of one's own health*—the sense of positive well-being; and (9) general *satisfaction* with life.

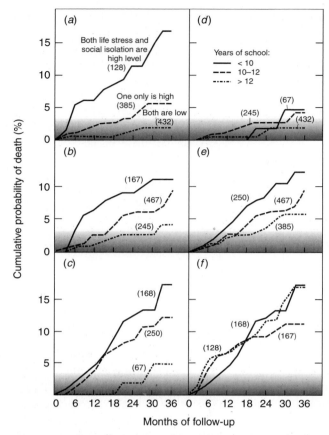

FIGURE 8.8. Cumulative mortality curves according to education and specified psychosocial variables for male survivors of myocardial infarction. (*a*) More than 12 years of school; (*b*) 10 to 12 years of school; (*c*) less than 10 years of school; (*d*) both life stress and social isolation are low level; (*e*) either life stress or social isolation is high level and the other is low level; (*f*) both life stress and social isolation are high level.
Source: From W. Ruberman, E. Weinblatt, J. D. Goldberg, and B. S. Chaudhary. Psychosocial influences on mortality after myocardial infarction. *New England Journal of Medicine,* August 30, 1984, *311*(9), 552–559.

An interesting and useful approach to assessing incorporating quality of life assessments into the evaluation of health care outcomes has been taken by Kaplan and colleagues (see Kaplan, 1994; Kaplan and Anderson, 1988). This approach combines weighted measures of symptoms and functioning to derive a numerical assessing of patients' well-being for a particular point in time, the quality-adjusted life year (or QALY). This index often can produce different results from approaches that only evaluate biological outcomes. Consider an example drawn from the treatment of prostate cancer in elderly men. There are three main treatment options available for this disorder: surgical removal of the prostate, radiation therapy, and "watchful waiting," or close evaluation and supervision by a physician (see Kaplan, 1994). The first two treatments, which emphasize tumor eradication and aggressive treatment, in contrast to the more passive watchful waiting, carry risks of complications that may reduce life satisfaction (e.g., impotence and incontinence). By using QALY as an index, researchers were able to balance the risk of the cancer metastasizing against the potential quality of life effects of the three possible treatments (Fleming et al., 1993). When the QALY approach was applied, results indicated that the three treatments were essentially identical in their expected results and should be a matter of the patient's preference. Thus, waiting, rather than aggressive treatment of prostate tumors, is shown to be a legitimate option for elderly men.

ADHERENCE TO MEDICAL REGIMENS

One of the most important and thoroughly researched aspects of health behavior is patient adherence (or compliance) in following a physician's advice or prescribed medical regimen. **Compliance with medical regimens** generally refers to following the advice or instructions of a health care professional. The term **adherence** is often used since it implies more voluntary action on the part of the patient. We will use the terms *compliance* and *adherence* interchangeably here. Taking medication when one is supposed to and not discontinuing it until told to do so, going on a prescribed diet, quitting smoking—these are all instances of complying with a physician's advice. **Noncompliance** (or nonadherence) refers to failure to follow advice—the degree to which a patient does not adhere to what he or she was told (Becker, 1991; Sackett and Haynes, 1976).

The problem of poor adherence is widespread in many areas of health care and is a serious and prevalent health care problem that may cause a serious breakdown in the treatment process. By not following doctors' orders, people risk more serious illness or prolongation of current problems, and failure to take prescribed preventive measures (such as getting a vaccine) can also have serious consequences. For example, estimates indicate that patients' errors in administering medications could account for up to 15 percent of hospitalizations among the elderly (Gryfe and Gryfe, 1984), and errors with medications are one of the primary reasons for hospitalization among diabetic children (Drash, 1987). Despite the importance of compliance in health care and the prevalence of noncompliance, progress in implementing ways to improve adherence to various health care regimens has been slow (Dunbar-Jacob, 1993). This suggests that the reasons for not following these orders are deeply ingrained and resistant to modification.

Extent of Noncompliance

How much of a problem is noncompliance? Unfortunately, this question is not easily answered. There are many different kinds of compliance—adhering to preventive regimens, taking medication, and making lifestyle alterations—and our ability to measure them is often very limited. Studies of treatment of a wide variety of illnesses, including hypertension, glaucoma, coronary heart disease, and diabetes, have indicated that only 40 to 70 percent of patients comply with physicians' prescriptions or advice (Becker, 1991; Haynes, Taylor, and Sackett, 1979). This also appears to be true for people who take drugs for mental health problems. Among patients given drugs for depression, nearly one-third stopped taking the antidepressive medication in the first month of treatment and 44 percent stopped in the first 3 months of treatment (Lin et al., 1995). Other estimates are even more dismal, ranging as low as 30 percent or less for several diseases (Podell, 1975), and rates of compliance with preventive procedures advised by health care providers are even lower (Gordis, Markowitz, and Lillienfield, 1969). Compliance with some forms of treatment appears to be better. Compliance with chemotherapy for cancer patients, for example, appears to be very high among adults, with estimates of better than 90 percent of patients complying with treatment (Taylor, Lichtman, and Wood, 1984).

Noncompliance is manifest at many points in the health care process. Some patients do not show up for appointments, whereas others do not follow advice. It has been found that many patients fail to fill prescriptions for medication, discontinue medication early, fail to make recommended changes in daily routine, and/or miss follow-up appointments (Sackett and Haynes, 1976).

Measuring Compliance

Unfortunately, the inability to measure noncompliance precisely has hindered attempts to solve this problem. The various ways in which compliance and noncompliance are assessed are not always accurate, and each one provides a separate set of problems. Should patients simply be asked what they have done? Can patient reports be assumed to be reliable? There is some evidence suggesting that these reports are sometimes accurate (see Francis, Korsch, and Morris, 1969), but most studies indicate that this is not a good way to measure noncompliance (see Epstein, 1992; Rudd, 1993). Since most patients wish to be thought of positively, they cannot be expected willingly to portray themselves negatively by admitting to adherence failures.

Research also indicates that asking physicians for estimates of their patients' rates of compliance is also not very reliable (Finney et al., 1993; Kasl, 1975). More objective measurements appear to be somewhat better, but they remain problematic as well. Counting pills remaining in a patient's prescription is one possibility, as are pharmacy checks to determine when prescriptions are refilled. This quantitative approach tells us if the proper amount of medication was removed from its container in a given interval. It really does not tell us much more. Patients can and do dispose of remaining medication to make doctors think that they took all of it, and these counts do not allow any inferences about whether the medication was taken properly or all at once.

Using clinical outcomes—whether or not the patient improves—as an index of compliance also has obvious limitations. Such an approach assumes that proper adherence to regimen will always effect a cure and that cures will not be achieved if a patient does not comply. There are many factors governing a patient's progress, of which compliance is only one. If a patient does not improve, it may have little to do with adherence. If the patient was misdiagnosed, it is likely that the medication prescribed would not work at all.

A. Direct
  1. Blood levels
     a. Medication
     b. Metabolite
     c. Marker
  2. Urinary excretion of
     a. Medication
     b. Metabolite
     c. Marker (tracer)
B. Indirect
  1. Therapeutic or preventive outcome
  2. "Impression" of physician (predictability)
  3. Patient interview
  4. Filling of prescription
  5. Pill count
  6. Metabolic consequences

Source: From D. L. Sackett, R. B. Haynes. *Compliance with Therapeutic Regimens.* Baltimore: Johns Hopkins University Press, 1976. Copyright © 1976. Reprinted by permission of the Johns Hopkins University Press.

Another way to measure compliance is to measure traces of a prescribed medication in blood or urine (see Table 8.3). Examination of urine can yield concentrations of a prescribed drug, and studies using this kind of measure have yielded somewhat more reliable estimates of compliance than have other methods (Epstein, 1992; Gordis, 1976). However, there are a number of problems with this approach as well (Basco and Rush, 1995). Unless repeated measurements are taken, these tests provide estimates of drug usage at a given point in time only. It cannot be determined, for example, whether a patient with the appropriate drug concentration has been taking the medication regularly or did so just before his or her appointment. Similarly, differences in metabolism or biochemical response to drugs across individuals can cloud the meaning of these assays (Epstein, 1992).

These problems with assessment of compliance can be illustrated by a recent study of medication adherence among diabetic and psychiatric patients (Babiker, 1994). Several methods were used to measure compliance with the oral medication, including pill counts, with a questionnaire asking for patients' reports about their compliance and by assays for traces of the drug in urine. The pill counts and other measures gave different impressions of compliance, and surprise (unannounced) visits to count pills resulted in different levels of compliance than did scheduled visit assessments (Babiker, 1994).

In recent years a new technology has been developed to assess medication compliance that will permit greater accuracy and allow the measurement of detailed, pill-by-pill medication intake. A pill-container device has been developed called the medication event monitoring system (or MEMS) (Aprex Corporation, Fremont, California; see Cramer et al., 1989). This container, which looks like a regular pill container with a slightly larger cap, records in memory each time it is opened or closed. Research with this device has shown promise in better documenting the relationship between medication intake and disease outcomes (Epstein, 1992; Rudd, 1993).

Nevertheless, measurements of compliance and noncompliance have remained imperfect estimates of patient behavior. Obviously, a patient who reports that he or she has failed to comply with a regimen, who does not show improvement, and who does not show traces of medication in blood samples may be confidently labeled as a noncomplier. When multiple measures are not used, or when these measures do not correspond (e.g., the patient says he or she did not comply but urine assay suggests he or she did), interpretations are more difficult.

Determinants of Compliance

A large number of studies have been addressed to understanding causes of noncompliance and identifying factors that affect compliance (Dunbar, 1993; Shumaker, Schrom and Ockene, 1990). Many approaches have been taken, including searches for personality variables or demographic characteristics that could be related to compliance, examination of the role of the interaction between doctor and patient, and consideration of health beliefs as a factor. Before turning to each of these approaches, we should consider general factors that may affect compliance.

Aspects of the Regimen

Aspects of the prescription regimen itself are likely to affect compliance (see Figure 8.9): If there are unpleasant side effects of the prescription or if it is too complex ("take two blue pills every 3 hours, a white pill after meals and at bedtime, and two green pills 2 hours after each white pill"), compliance will probably be low. Anything that makes it easier to follow a regimen, such as providing special food in weight loss programs, appears to increase adherence and success (Jeffrey, 1995). Compliance decreases as the length of treatment increases. If medication is prescribed over a long time, for example, it is more likely to be discontinued early (Dunbar, 1990). Further, if the financial cost of complying is great, compliance will be less likely. The greater the effort required for compliance or the greater the lifestyle change necessitated, the lower compliance is likely to be. In other words, a number of social or environmental factors will probably exert fairly general influences on adherence to regimens (see Becker, 1991).

Personality and Background of the Patient and the Physician

Some researchers have focused on personal attributes of the patient that may affect compliance. For example, having social support from family and friends appears to be associated with better compliance (Doherty et al., 1983; Sherwood, 1983). Ley (1977) noted that some patients are complainers and that others accept advice more readily. Those who complain regardless of what is done or said will be less satisfied with the physician and, as a result, will be less compliant. Some patients are generally predisposed not to follow advice.

FIGURE 8.9. Such things as the size, shape, and "swallowability" of pills may affect whether people take medication as prescribed.
Source: Blair Seitz/Photo Researchers

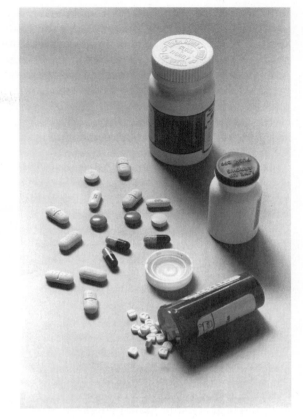

Evidence for such personality effects, however, has not been found consistently (Lutz et al., 1983).

Another approach emphasizing personal attributes has been to examine the relationships between various background demographic variables such as education and adherence to prescribed regimens. Some evidence suggests that factors relating to cultural, social, or educational status or income level are correlated with compliance (Strain, 1978). If a person cannot read, cannot afford to fill a prescription, or has social or cultural objections to certain prescriptions, compliance may be affected. Few studies have shown any relationships between such variables and compliance. However, mood appears to be related to compliance and well-being, and positive or optimistic expectations increase adherence (Baekeland and Lundwall, 1975, Leedham, 1995). Depressed mood appears to reduce adherence (Carney et al., 1995).

Researchers have recently begun to look at characteristics of physician behavior—particularly characteristics that affect the physicians' ability to communicate effectively with patients—that are related to their patients' adherence to regimens. DiMatteo and colleagues (1993) conducted a longitudinal study of 186 physicians and patients whom they were treating for diabetes, hypertension, and heart disease. General patient adherence to medication, exercise, and diet recommendations were examined over a 2-year period. Analyses in the study controlled for baseline levels of patient adherence and for patient characteristics that were predictive of adherence in previous analyses. Results of the study revealed that physicians' level of job satisfaction, the number of patients seen per week, and physicians' tendency to answer questions were among the factors that predicted compliance. These results indicate that physician characteristics that affect communication style have an impact on adherence.

Doctor-Patient Interaction and Compliance

Although patient characteristics do not appear to be primary determinants of compliance, evidence suggests that factors relating to the quality of doctor-patient interaction and their communication are related to compliance. One such communication-related factor is patient satisfaction with the physician. If patients are satisfied, they will be more compliant; if they are dissatisfied, they will be less compliant. People seem to be more resistant to persuasive appeals made by physicians with whom they are dissatisfied. A number of variables inherent in the doctor-patient relationship will determine satisfaction. For example, formal and businesslike interactions between the doctor and the patient were associated with patients' dissatisfaction, as were passive interactions (Korsch and Negrete, 1972). The ways in which physicians obtained and provided information were also important. Antagonistic or authoritarian styles were not satisfying, but physicians' ability to reduce tension in the consultation was associated with satisfaction (Davis, 1968).

Korsch and her colleagues (Korsch, Freeman, and Negrete, 1971; Korsch, Gozzi, and Francis, 1968; Korsch and Negrete, 1972) examined the satisfaction with medical consultation of children. Mothers' satisfaction with consultation and treatment of their children was assessed, and communicator variables were again implicated as determinants of satisfaction. If doctors were seen as businesslike, satisfaction was lower than if doctors were thought to be warm and caring. Further, more than 80 percent of those who thought that the physician had been understanding were satisfied, as compared with only one-third of those who did not feel that the doctor tried to understand their concern. Mothers who rated their children's doctors as good communicators were more satisfied than were mothers who saw the doctors as poor communicators (Korsch, Gozzi, and Francis, 1968). Finally, mothers whose expectations were not met, including information that they expected to receive that was not provided, were less satisfied than were mothers who were provided with what they had expected to receive. If they expected a diagnosis, a discussion of causes of an illness, or some other piece of information and this was not provided by the physician, then satisfaction with the physician was reduced. These thwarted expectations represent unmet needs and sources of disappointment for patients and may reflect the fact that physicians often do not address patients' concerns (Thompson et al., 1995).

The relationship between satisfaction and compliance with medical advice was directly investigated by Francis, Korsch, and Morris (1969). If dissatisfied with the communicator (doctor) or the content of the consultation, mothers were less likely to comply with the advice. Table 8.4 (Francis et al., 1969) illustrates this relationship. Further supporting this fact are recent findings indicat-

TABLE 8.4. Patient Compliance and Satisfaction with Medical Advice

Patients' Report	Percent Highly Compliant
Doctor businesslike	31
Doctor friendly and not businesslike	46
High satisfaction with consultation	53
Moderate satisfaction with consultation	43
Moderate dissatisfaction with consultation	32
High dissatisfaction with consultation	17

Source: Reprinted by permission from V. Francis, B. M. Korsch, and M. J. Morris. Gaps in doctor-patient communication. *New England Journal of Medicine,* 1969, *280,* 535–540.

ing that physicians' nonverbal skills are associated with patient satisfaction and compliance (DiMatteo, Hays, and Prince, 1986).

Comprehension and Compliance

Ley and Spelman (1967) have argued that cognitive and informational factors are largely responsible for failures to comply with prescribed regimens. The failure of many people to follow doctors' orders is not due to dissatisfaction, personality, or the like but, rather, to genuine problems in understanding and remembering what they are told. In one study more than one-half the patients studied misunderstood doctors' instructions; in another study, almost one-half of what was told to patients was quickly forgotten (see Boyd et al., 1974; Ley and Spelman, 1967). Patients generally know what the doctor is trying to tell them, and noncompliance for reasons such as "I don't like the doctor" should be less common than noncompliance because "I don't understand what I am supposed to do." In support of this Ley and Spelman (1967) list three determinants of failure in the doctor-patient interaction:

1. Often the material presented by the doctor is too difficult for patients to understand.
2. Sometimes patients do not understand basic physiology or anatomy and do not possess elementary medical knowledge.
3. Sometimes patients are under misconceptions that are so incorrect that they interfere with proper comprehension.

There is evidence indicating that people often lack basic information about physiology or medicine. Boyle (1970) found that one-half of those people studied did not know where the kidneys, stomach, lungs, or heart were located, and that one-quarter of these people did not know where the intestine was. Riley (1966) asked people about their understanding of doctors' orders and found that erroneous information even about common aspects of diet and medication was frequent. For example, almost three-fourths of those tested did not know that Alka-Seltzer contained aspirin.

Models for Explaining Compliance: The Health Belief Model

We already know that behaviors of the physician that increase satisfaction or trustworthiness affect compliance and that discrepancy of prescribed and preferred behaviors is also influential. What other factors will affect the acceptance of doctors' orders? Several attempts have been made to understand compliance behavior within the context of larger theoretical models of health behavior. In Chapter 3 we discuss several theoretical approaches to preventive health behavior, including the theory of reasoned action (Ajzen and Fishbein, 1980) and the health belief model. Each of these models has been applied to explain compliance with regimens as one form of health behavior. In this section we describe applications of the *health belief model* (Becker, 1991; Rosenstock, 1974) to the area of compliance.

The health belief model considers three sets of factors in predicting people's behavior. First, one must take into account the patient's readiness to act, or perceived necessity of action. This is determined by the perceived severity of the disease state that exists or that could occur and the perceived susceptibility to the illness or its consequences—how likely the patient feels disease onset really is. If a patient does not believe that an illness is severe or that he or she has a good chance of becoming ill, readiness to act will be low—there will be no reason for such readiness. If, on the other hand, the illness is seen as severe and the patient believes that there is a good chance of coming down with it, readiness to act will be higher. We are far more likely, for example, to get flu shots if the kind of flu expected is believed to be severe, unusual, and highly contagious than if it is thought to be mild and relatively rare. Risk perceptions are important determinants of health behavior and tend to be more optimistic than is warranted (Kulik and Mahler, 1987; Weinstein, 1989).

The second set of considerations in this model involves the estimation of costs and benefits of compliance. In order to comply, the patient must believe that the advocated regimen will be effective and that the benefits of following it will outweigh the costs. Side effects, disruptiveness, unpleasantness, and other negative aspects of a regimen must be countered by the benefits of treatment—the reduction of severity or susceptibility to an illness—if patients are to be expected to comply.

The third factor that the health belief model also posits is the need for a cue to action, something that makes the subject aware of potential consequences. Internal signals that something is wrong (e.g., pain, discomfort) or external stimuli such as health campaigns or screening programs are necessary to initiate health behaviors and to motivate the analysis of readiness, costs, benefits, and so on.

This model has been useful in predicting compliance. Although the doctor's perceptions of the severity of the patient's condition do not affect compliance, perceptions of severity and susceptibility *by the patient* are related to compliance (Becker, 1991; Richardson et al., 1995). Particularly when preventive health behaviors are considered, patients who believe they are likely to become ill and that this would have severe consequences are more likely to take some action. This has been shown in many areas, including treatments prescribed during preventive dental instruction, cancer screening, and heart disease testing (Fink, Shapiro, and Roester, 1972; Haefner and Kirscht, 1970). This also appears to be the case in adherence to lifestyle changes such as dieting, where perceptions of risk, benefits of lifestyle change, and self-efficacy seem to be important (Brownell, 1995).

Research has also considered perceptions of efficacy of treatment and cost-benefit analyses in decisions on whether or not to comply with prescribed regimens. When medication is involved, simple beliefs regarding the likelihood that it will improve the patient's condition are very potent determinants of compliance (Becker, 1991). Any questions of the safety of treatment, side effects, or distress associated with treatment become very powerful barriers or reasons not to do as advised, and thus reduce the likelihood that patients will do as they were told (Becker, 1991).

These kinds of findings are neither surprising nor difficult to explain. What the health belief model attempts to do is to consider patients' subjective states regarding their health rather than objective characteristics of it. *Actual severity* of an illness is not related to compliance, but *patient perception* of severity is. Revisions in the model have expanded its range to include intentions as well as beliefs (Becker, 1991). In addition, the model has been expanded and updated into a health decision model (Becker, 1991; Eraker, Kirscht, and Becker, 1984) to better incorporate and quantify factors relating to patients' decisions about the risks, benefits, and quality of life.

Naive Health Theories

Another consideration of determinants of compliance, related to the health belief model in its social psychological approach, has been proposed by Leventhal, Nerenz, and Leventhal (1982). Like the health belief model, this approach considers patient beliefs in determining compliance, but it does so with greater emphasis on the processes involved. Also called commonsense models of illness (Meyer, Leventhal, and Gutmann, 1985), these notions about health, symptoms, and illness can lead patients to drop out of treatment. Thus, one major determinant of compliance is the naive theory that a patient constructs in order to explain or predict an illness, as in the case of a patient with high blood pressure who complies periodically with taking medication. The patient believes that whenever her blood pressure is high, she gets headaches. This naive causal connection is reinforced by the fact that whenever she gets a headache, she takes her blood pressure and finds that it is elevated. Thus, she takes her medicine only when she gets a headache. If she were to take her blood pressure at times when she did not have a headache, she would see that it was elevated then as well and the basic fallacy of her theory would be exposed. Yet this selective monitoring effectively reinforces her belief and makes it a central aspect of self-treatment. In addition, once these naive theories are developed, they affect the way in which new information is interpreted and remembered (Bishop and Converse, 1986).

This description is particularly powerful because it can explain noncompliance by someone who intends to comply, believes that severity and vulnerability are sufficient to warrant action, and so on. The headaches serve as a cue to action, and this account is therefore consistent with the health belief model. Despite the fact that research indicates that people cannot reliably predict changes in blood pressure by focusing on symptoms such as headaches (Bauman and Leventhal, 1985), people connect events together in naive theories that can interfere with and reduce compliance. These theories also provide readily testable interventions aimed at exposing the fallacious aspects of patients' commonsense theories about their health.

Increasing Compliance

All these theories or explanations of compliance and noncompliance have been used in attempts to improve patients' adherence to advice or prescription (Glasgow, 1995; Lemanek, 1995). Correcting erroneous beliefs about either health or illness and bodily function in general has been attempted in a number of educational campaigns. Some educational interventions have affected short-term adherence to drug regimens, but many others have not been particularly successful (Haynes, 1976; Lin et al., 1995) although psychoeducational programs that also provide support appear to increase compliance more effectively (Devine and Reifschneider, 1995). Information about drugs has been provided by pharmacists and in patient package inserts (see Figure 8.10), and physicians and their assistants have attempted to provide patients with information about their treatment (see Dunbar-Jacob, 1993). These attempts have been somewhat successful but do not provide an adequate solution to the problem.

Other attempts have considered personalization of treatment to reduce the costs of compliance. Here the treatment regimen is designed to fit with a given individual's lifestyle. Disruptiveness—the degree of change required to comply—can thereby be minimized, and health behaviors can be attached to well-learned aspects of an individual's daily routine. On an individual level such

FIGURE 8.10. Pharmacists and other health care professionals seek to provide people with information about the drugs that are prescribed for them. Pharmacists are excellent sources of information about side effects, the effects of different drugs when taken at the same time, and other aspects of medication prescriptions.
Source: Ulrike Welsch/Photo Researchers

tailored regimens are easier to comply with, and some attempts on a larger scale have reported encouraging results (Haynes, Taylor, and Sackett, 1979; Schneider and Cable, 1978). A novel intervention that required participants to make verbal and written commitments to comply with a medication regimen also increased compliance (Putnam, 1994). Again, there is reason to believe that such approaches help, but these solutions do not address the whole range of noncompliers.

Some approaches attempt to modify doctors' behaviors so as to make physicians more informative, better communicators, or just warm and sensitive (DiMatteo, 1994). If doctors' behaviors can be made more satisfying for patients, compliance should increase. Many programs to accomplish this and to improve patient skills as well have been proposed but few have been comprehensively tested (see DiMatteo, 1994; Korsch et al., 1971). In any case, these programs are consistent with research findings and make good sense. Focusing doctors' attention on patients' worries and concerns; providing clear, jargon-free information; and adopting a friendly, caring attitude should improve adherence with most prescriptions (Korsch et al., 1971).

Other programs have been directed toward making communication between the doctor and the patient more effective and comprehensible. Thus, increasing the number of questions that patients ask increases their involvement in health care, possibly gives them more information, and appears to increase satisfaction with the physician visit (Roter, 1984). Ley et al. (1976) found that many patients were unclear about some of the information they had been told when medication was prescribed. They did not know, for example, what they should do if they forget to take a pill, or whether or not the effects of the medication would be immediately apparent. These aspects of the regimen about which little was known were associated with decreasing compliance. In order to reverse this problem, leaflets were prepared that provided information about medications. These leaflets were of three kinds: Some were easy to understand, some were moderately difficult, and others were difficult. Some patients received no leaflet, and others received a leaflet of one of the three levels of difficulty. Results indicated that the leaflets improved the accuracy of pill-taking, but only when the leaflets were easy or of moderate difficulty. Very difficult leaflets did not significantly improve compliance.

Supervision has also been considered an effective way to increase compliance because the act of reporting regularly to someone that you are following your regimen and your health is improving is a reinforcing situation. Consider the elementary school student who works hard so that she can get good grades. When she takes these grades home and shows her parents, she is made to feel good about herself—she is proud, is reinforced by parents, and comes to associate good feelings with good grades. On the other hand, presenting one's parents with poor grades is aversive and humiliating. One can apply this to the hypertensive patient. The patient who complies with prescribed medication and diet and who achieves some degree of blood pressure control is made to feel good when visiting the doctor. On the other hand, the noncompliant patient may be scolded and generally made to feel uncomfortable whenever visiting the doctor. Thus, increased supervision or more frequent visits to the doctor should improve compliance, as the patient seeks to avoid the aversive consequences of having failed to do what was supposed to be done. Research has confirmed that supervision is effective, increasing adherence up to 60 percent in some studies (McKenney et al., 1973; Taylor et al., 1978; Wilber and Barrow, 1969). When supervision is subsequently reduced to normal levels, however, compliance returns to its initial levels. Because supervision is expensive and the effects of increasing supervision do not generalize beyond treatment, this is not a preferred solution to compliance problems and has not received much attention in the past few years.

Related to this strategy is the use of self-monitoring or self-supervision to increase compliance. Haynes (1976), for example, asked noncompliant hypertensive patients to keep a record of their blood pressure and found that there was increased compliance during self-monitoring. However, this program was successful only when the records were reviewed by medical personnel. When patients were left on their own, compliance decreased. Without the threat of confrontation with a disapproving authority, self-monitoring did not have a lasting effect on compliance.

Enhancing family and social support can also increase compliance (Becker, 1991; Dunbar-Jacob, 1993). For example, enhancing support strategies for the patient through provider home visits and assigning family members a role in carrying out the health care regimen has been studied in hypertensive patients with some success (Dickinson et al., 1981). Similarly, adherence to surveillance activities such as breast self-examinations or testicular self-examination to detect cancer early in a more treatable stage may be influenced by social support (Finney et al., 1995).

The influences of medical environments, personal preferences and beliefs, information, and the like are undeniable. The patient is a behaving organism, processing information and responding to different settings in ways that can influence health. The study of health behavior and response to medical settings is one of the most important aspects of health that psychologists can study. Since the psychological perspectives are focused more on these issues than on other biomedical fields, unique and lasting contributions can be made.

SUMMARY

In this chapter we reviewed the effects that various medical settings have on patient behavior. Although hospitalization is sometimes necessary, the hospital stay is often considered a negative experience. The patient can be depersonalized, forced to yield control of his or her body to people who are strangers, and the patient must submerge identity and adjust to loss of privacy. Patients who assume a cooperative role have been termed *good patients*, whereas those who are less cooperative are considered *bad patients*. Although good patient behavior may help the staff, there is evidence that the noncompliant patient may retain more control and have an easier time readjusting to life outside the hospital.

Much interesting health behavior occurs outside the hospital. Response to illness has received a lot of attention and the sick role has been the subject of much study. Cultural background can influence the way that people react to symptoms of illness. Determinants of whether patients seek medical care include their perception and interpretation of symptoms, cultural or learned patterns of response to symptoms, and their previous experience in health care settings. Interpretations of and response to symptoms are affected by the actual sensations experienced, but also are based on a set of social and psychological factors. The complexities of the situational and personality processes involved in the psychology of physical symptoms has become an important area of study.

There is also an increasing awareness of the influence of psychological disorders on the use of the health care system. A significant minority of patients suffer from symptoms of anxiety or depression, and often people seek care for physical symptoms that can be better treated as aspects of psychological disorders. Studies have shown that the use of health services can be reduced by providing mental health treatment to patients who need it. People seem to prefer different styles of health care. The Health Opinion Survey (HOS) measures patients' preferences for more or less active participation and more or less information in health care. Attitudes toward treatment approaches can be measured reliably, and these attitudes influence a variety of illness behaviors and responses to aversive medical procedures.

It is also evident that medical treatments not only affect physical health status and survival, but also have a significant effect on the quality of patients' lives and their ability to function in their day-to-day activities (Kaplan, 1994). For this reason, measurement of *quality of life*—rather than just medical status or mortality alone—has become an important outcome in health care. One approach to assessing the impacts of various medical treatments has been the measurement of quality-adjusted life years (QALY), which combines weighted measures of symptoms and functioning to derive a numerical assessing of patients' well-being for a particular point in time.

Compliance (or adherence) to regimens is one of the most researched areas of health behavior. Compliance is a measure of adherence or cooperation with the doctor's advice. Factors that influence compliance include aspects of the regimen (e.g., its complexity), the information supplied about treatment, and the information supplied about drugs. Perhaps the most important influence on compliance is the effectiveness of the doctor-patient communication and the nature of doctor-patient interaction, including the patient's satisfaction. Among several models to predict adherence to regimens, the *health belief model* considers the patient's readiness to act, the costs and benefits of action, and a cue to action—factors that make the patient aware of the need to act. In addition, some patients construct naive health theories, connecting an unrelated symptom with a disorder and complying only when the symptom arises. This often explains noncompliance in those that intend to comply. Attempts at increasing compliance have included making physicians better communicators, increasing patients' satisfaction by other means, and increasing contact with medical personnel. These interventions have met with varying degrees of success.

RECOMMENDED READINGS

Contrada, R. J., Leventhal, E. A., and Anderson, J. A. Psychological preparation for surgery: Marshalling individual and social resources to optimize self-regulation. In

S. Maes, H. Leventhal, M. Johnston (Eds.). *International review of health psychology*, vol. 3. Chichester: J. Wiley, 1994.

Davis, C. *Patient practitioner interaction: An experiential manual for developing the art of health care*. Thorofare, NJ: Slack, 1989.

Friedman, H.S., and Dimatteo, M. R. *Interpersonal issues in health care*. New York: Academic Press, 1982.

McHugh, S., and Vallis, T. M. (Eds.). *Illness behavior: A multidisciplinary model*. New York: Plenum Press, 1986.

Shumaker, S. A., Schrom, E. B., and Ockene, J. (Eds.). *The handbook of health behavior change*. New York: Springer, 1990.

CHAPTER 9

Psychological Assessment in Medical Settings

Measuring things is one of the most basic aspects of science. Weight, size, and height of objects; temperature, acidity, and mineral content of water; and atomic weight and other characteristics of the basic elements are all expressions of qualities of things and are specified by different measures. For example, if someone asks you how old you are on your twentieth birthday, you have several measures of age available. The most common unit of measuring age is years and you could reply, "I'm 20." This means that you have lived for 20 years. Alternatively, you could express your age in different units (240 months, 1,040 weeks, 7,300 days, 175,200 hours, or 10,512,000 minutes old). Or you could use a different reference point, such as "I'm a junior" (signifying that you are old enough to be in your third year of college), or "I'm old enough to vote" (indicating that you are older than 18). Most things can be measured in many different ways. When you measure them, you want the measures that you use to be *reliable,* or reproducible over time, and *valid*—actually measuring what you want to measure.

Reliability is an issue, particularly when something is supposed to be stable over time. If you want to measure someone's attitudes about AIDS or HIV disease, you would want a measure that will be stable over time so that you will know that the measure you took last week will be the same next week. If you have a reliable measure, you do not have to keep measuring it. This is very clear in considering personality variables or traits that people are supposed to have. Good measures of optimism, Type A behavior, or coping style should be consistent over time. If you told people a different age every time they asked how old you are, their measures of your age would be inaccurate and someone who did not know the correct answer would have difficulty choosing which answer to use. These conceptions of reliability apply primarily to characteristics that are supposed to stay the same.

Equally important is validity. You must know that your measure actually measures what you think it measures if you are to draw any conclusions from it. If you study a situation in which you are manipulating the salience of a prevention message advocating regular blood pressure screening, your study will depend on people actually responding to the differences you have created. If participants in your study do not notice the message, cannot hear it, or otherwise do not actually process it, your results will not be based on the messages or differences between them. Likewise, if your measure of intention to have your blood pressure checked is not a good measure of this intention, your results will be suspect.

In health psychology measurement takes many forms. Outcome measures range from indexes of disease characteristics or severity to intermediate biological outcomes such as blood pressure or hormones, to behaviors, coping, and a variety of indicators of stress. These latter measures are diverse and can be confusing. There are many more methods of measuring assessment of personality variables, coping style, social support, distress, psychological disorders, and a number of other aspects of health and behavior than we can consider in this chapter. We will, however, describe some of the major measures used in health psychology and discuss some of the advantages and disadvantages of each.

ASSESSMENT IN PSYCHIATRIC SETTINGS

Until recently the major form of psychological assessment in medical settings used evaluation methods developed for psychiatric populations. A significant problem with this has been the fact that patients in a medical population are not always similar to patients in a psychiatric population. In research on prevention and health promotion, potential participants would usually be healthy and active people, whereas in research on patient populations, psychopathology is less likely than people who were mentally healthy before becoming ill who are now faced with extraordinary threats. Of course, standard psychological tests may provide some general information about the overall level of emotional health and the presence of potentially debilitating symptoms such as anxiety and depression. Fortunately, a number of diagnostic tests have been developed with medical populations in mind. Before discussing these tests, we briefly review traditional psychiatric classification and assessment methods that are still commonly used in many medical settings.

Classification of Psychological Disorders

Classification involves the arrangement of various forms of abnormal behavior into specific categories. The descriptive categories help to organize our thinking concerning the causes, symptoms, and treatment of abnormal behavior. They also aid in communicating the various types of psychological problems that individuals may experience.

The German psychiatrist Emil Kraepelin is credited with developing the first systematic and widely accepted classification system of mental disorders. He noted that certain symptom patterns occurred with sufficient regularity to allow one to identify and classify mental disorders on the basis of these symptoms. The classification schema that he developed is the basis of our present-day diagnostic system. A guiding philosophy behind *his* work was the belief that once various forms of mental illness were successfully distinguished and classified, one would be able to predict the outcome of a specific type of disorder.

The *Diagnostic and Statistical Manual of Mental Disorders (DSM)* was adopted by the American Psychiatric Association in 1952 as its official classification schema of mental disorders. We have already described its birth in 1952 and its gradual evolution into the American Psychiatric Association's current DSM-IV (1994). The larger goal of this classification system is to allow mental health professionals throughout the world to compare types of disorders, incidence of occurrence, and other relevant data concerning mental disorders by categorizing the wide variety of psychological disorders seen in hospital and clinical settings.

The DSM-IV includes a comprehensive list of categories. Moreover, the manual illustrates each disorder along several different dimensions. The first dimension spells out the essential features of each disorder or syndrome, giving an overview of the salient behaviors of the disorder. These would include symptoms such as fatigue or chronic worry. In addition, associated factors, or accompanying symptoms, are listed along with the age of onset, progression or course, and social impairment characteristic of the disorder. The sixth dimension deals with the **complications** of each disorder, including disorders or events (such as suicide) that may result from the initial problem. Depression, for example, may have complications such as drug abuse.

The seventh dimension for each disorder lists **predisposing factors**. Several conditions appear to make it more likely that someone will develop a disorder. Prevalence, the proportion of adults who may develop this problem, is described, as is the sex ratio, or relative frequency of diagnosis for women and men. Finally, familial pattern—whether a disorder is more common among family members—and differential diagnoses are also listed. This last dimension includes disorders with features similar to those of the problem in question. For example, opioid withdrawal has symptoms that are remarkably similar to influenza. Thus, influenza would be considered a differential diagnosis—a problem that would need to be distinguished from opioid withdrawal.

Multiaxial Classification

One of the hallmarks of the DSM-IV is called *multiaxial classification*. The earlier DSM-II was basically a single category system. This means that if you were being evaluated, you would normally receive only one diagnostic label and be placed into one category. This approach assumes, for example, that schizophrenics do not ordinarily have sexual deviations or any other major problem. In a sense, the single category approach is based on the assumption that each subject is classified as a member of either *one* psychiatric category or *no* psychiatric category. Thus, a neurotic might be coded as a hysterical, conversion type but could not receive any other superimposed diagnosis. The DSM-III-R viewed this as highly unrealistic and impractical. The DSM-IV has also continued the multiaxial approach. The newer classification system avoids the possibility that people with several disorders could be falsely placed into a

TABLE 9.1. Multiple Axes of the DSM-IV

Axis I: *Clinical disorders*
Other conditions that may be a focus of clinical attention
This axis includes the major clinical disorders except for the personality disorders and mental retardation. Other conditions that may be a focus of clinical attention include conditions such as physical and sexual abuse, medication-induced disorders, noncompliance with treatment.

Axis II: *Personality disorders*
Mental retardation
This axis is for reporting personality disorders and mental retardation, both of which might otherwise be overlooked when attention is directed to the typically more fluid Axis I disorders. It is also used for noting prominent maladaptive personality features and defense mechanisms.

Axis III: *General medical conditions*
This axis is for reporting current general medical conditions that are potentially important and relevant to the understanding or management of the individual's mental disorder. The DSM-IV considers knowledge of the general physical health of the person to be a major part of the total diagnostic picture.

Axis IV: *Psychosocial and environmental problems*
This axis is for reporting psychosocial and environmental problems that may affect the diagnosis, treatment, or prognosis of mental disorders (Axes I and II). These may involve a negative life event such as the death or loss of a loved one, inadequacy of social support or personal resources, occupational problems, and so on.

Axis V: *Global assessment of functioning*
This axis is for reporting the clinician's judgment of the individual's overall level of functioning on a scale (the global assessment of functioning or GAF scale). The GAF scale is used for the current period (i.e., the level of functioning at the time of the evaluation), and may also be rated for other time periods.

Source: From American Psychiatric Association. *Diagnostic and Statistical Manual of Mental Disorders (DSM-IV).* Washington, DC: American Psychiatric Association, 1994. Copyright © 1994 by the American Psychological Association. Reprinted by permission.

single category, and each individual is scored according to broad categories or axes (see Table 9.1).

PSYCHOLOGICAL ASSESSMENT PROCEDURES

Attempts to develop an effective classification system stimulated efforts to construct effective and reliable techniques for the assessment of psychological disorders. The techniques developed have been quite diverse. In general, the different assessment tests can be classified as projective and nonprojective techniques. Projective techniques were developed by psychoanalytically oriented theorists who were interested in the hidden or covert aspect of an individual's personality. These methods, which are also referred to as unstructured tests, present the individual with a stimulus for which there is little or no well-defined cultural pattern of responding so that the individual must "project" his or her feelings, attitudes, motives, and manner of viewing life upon that ambiguous situation. These factors, which are assumed to be largely at the level of the unconscious, make up the person's "core" personality structure and determine the way in which an individual will behave. The two most frequently used projective tests in psychiatric settings have been the *Thematic Apperception Test (TAT)* and the *Rorschach Inkblot Test.*

The TAT was developed in 1938 by the Harvard psychologist Henry Murray. It consists of a series of 30 pictures with personal connotations and one blank card. The cards are presented one at a time, and the respondent is requested to make up a story (as complete and detailed as possible) suggested by each picture shown. Murray's main goal was to have respondents interpret the cards according to their tendencies to perceive in a certain way (i.e., **apperception**). Recurrent themes presented by the respondent are then interpreted in terms of needs or internal motivators, such as achievement or aggression, and presses or environmental determinants, such as rejection by others or danger. Unfortunately, there is no generally accepted system of scoring the TAT. This seriously limits the reliability and validity of the test, and as a result, it is not widely used in psychiatric or medical settings. However, there have been some special scoring procedures developed to measure specific themes on the TAT, such as the need for achievement (McClelland et al., 1953) and the need for power (McClelland et al., 1972).

The Rorschach test is administered by an examiner who presents a series of 10 bilaterally symmetrical inkblots. The person being examined is asked to describe what he or she sees or what the inkblot suggests. After responding to all 10 inkblots, the respondent is shown the inkblots again, and the examiner asks what characteristics of the inkblot determined the responses and interpretations.

Unlike the TAT, there have been a number of major scoring systems developed for the Rorschach test (see Beck, 1961; Exner, 1986; Klopfer et al., 1954). Exner is especially noteworthy for his efforts toward standardizing and developing objective criteria and norms for both children and adults. However, the Rorschach test was not developed with a medical population in mind; although it may provide some general information about the overall level of emotional health, it is probably not useful in a general medical population.

Many clinicians and researchers became dissatisfied with projective tests because of problems of reliability and validity. As a result, more psychometrically sound tests were developed that could be objectively scored and quantified. Out of this tradition, a variety of structured tests were devised to measure personality characteristics. Statistical norms for these tests are usually developed by administering the test to large groups of individuals at different times so that the way one individual responds to test items can be compared with the way certain kinds of other people tend to respond. Of these tests, the MMPI is perhaps the best known.

MMPI

One of the most popular and widely used personality tests is the Minnesota Multiphasic Personality Inventory (MMPI), which was originally developed by Hathaway and McKinley (1943). It was developed in order to provide mental health professionals with a comprehensive method to use in the description and diagnosis of abnormal behavior. The test originally consisted of 550 items covering a wide range of subjects, including statements concerning current and past behaviors, beliefs, attitudes, symptoms, and traits. American culture has changed a lot over the five decades since the original MMPI items were written, and concerns were raised about outmoded language and references to old and unfamiliar material and activities. As a result, a comprehensive re-standardization of the test was undertaken which resulted in the development and publication of the MMPI-2 in 1989.

The MMPI is scored for 10 psychiatric-personality scales as well as for 3 "validity" scales used to check for the subject's faking, misunderstanding, or sloppiness in taking the test. The 10 "clinical" or psychiatric-personality scales are the hypochondriasis scale (HS), the depression scale (D), the hysteria scale (Hy), the psychopathic deviance scale (Pd), the masculinity-femininity scale (Mf), the paranoia scale (Pa), the psychasthenia scale (anxiety) (Pt), the schizophrenia scale (Sc), the hypomania scale (Ma), and the social introversion scale (Si).

In addition, there are 3 "validity" scales: a lie scale (L), which measures frankness or deception in answering questions; an infrequency scale (F), which measures the degree of carelessness, confusion, or effort to deceive by subjects in answering the question; and a defensiveness scale (K), which is designed to detect defensiveness or subtle faking.

As the use of the MMPI grew, it became apparent that the scoring of the test limited its usefulness. People obtaining high scores on a particular scale often did not fit precisely into that diagnostic category, and many apparently normal people scored high on some of the clinical scales. As a result, new ways of classifying people by assessing combinations or patterns of scale scores on the MMPI were developed. This is the manner in which the MMPI is currently used. For example, high scores on both the Pd and Ma scales (not just the Pd scale) are associated with psychopathy and other antisocial forms of behavior. Empirically based manuals containing profile patterns along with case descriptions of patients with these profile patterns have been developed for clinical and personality assessment (see Dahlstrom, Welsh, and Dahlstrom, 1972). These manuals are "cookbook" interpretations of the MMPI that provide standards for comparison for their cases. These cookbook manuals have added to the popularity and widespread use of this personality inventory. There are now computer services that score MMPI profiles and provide a detailed printout of the cookbook interpretation.

The MMPI generally produces characteristic patterns for an individual who is suffering from a psychophysiological disorder that can be used to differentiate the person's behavior from symptoms of other clinical disorders and from nonpsychiatric patterns of behavior. The MMPI pattern shown in Figure 9.1 is typical for an individual who is suffering from a psychophysiological disorder. This 1-2-3 profile pattern (elevations in hysteria, depression, and hypochondriasis scales) is associated with symptoms that occur in various psychophysiological disorders.

The MMPI was revised in 1989, and the new MMPI-2 was published. The MMPI-2 is considered to be similar to and an improvement over the original MMPI in its reliability and validity (Greene, 1991). Studies using the MMPI-2

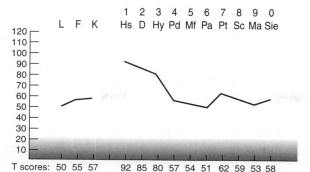

FIGURE 9.1. A 1-2-3 MMPI profile pattern (elevations in hysteria, depression, and hypochondriasis scales) that is typical for an individual suffering from a psychophysiological disorder.
Source: From H. Gilberstadt and J. Duker. *A Handbook for Clinical and Actuarial MMPI Interpretation.* Philadelphia: Saunders, 1965. Copyright © 1965 by W. B. Saunders Company. Reprinted by permission.

are beginning to appear in the scientific and clinical research literature, and it seems to be equally useful in predicting pain and/or illness. For example, differences in MMPI-2 profile types have been studied to see if they were related to surgical outcome in low back pain patients (Riley et al., 1995). In this study 71 patients who were to undergo spinal fusion surgery were given the MMPI-2. At least 6 months after surgery, patients were given a structured telephone interview during which information was gathered about their surgery. Results clearly showed that patients with some MMPI-2 profile types reported significantly more satisfaction and postsurgical improvement. The clinical implications of this research are significant since MMPI-2 personality profile data might now be used to predict a successful outcome from spinal fusion surgery. Traditionally, spinal fusion surgery has produced less than favorable outcomes for many patients (see Franklin et al., 1994), and the MMPI-2 may provide a way to screen out poor surgical candidates. For those patients with "inappropriate" MMPI-2 profile patterns alternative nonsurgical methods might have to be considered (cf., Mayer, Mooney, and Gatchel, 1991).

A word of caution is necessary about interpreting scores on the MMPI or any other single psychological assessment test. The fact that a person shows a profile pattern similar to that of a psychosomatic patient group does not necessarily mean that he or she is actually suffering from a psychophysiological disorder. It indicates only that the person is answering a series of questions on the inventory in a way that is similar to how diagnosed psychophysiological patients answer. Other factors can also cause this type of responding. Results of the test are only suggestive and should not be used as the sole basis for making a diagnosis. Before one can expect to make an accurate assessment, data generally must be gathered from multiple sources, such as self-report, observation by others, and physiological testing.

The Clinical Interview

The clinical interview, a basic and widely used method of assessment, is effective for exploring and delineating specific concerns, feelings, and problems that an individual may be experiencing. The type of information collected in the interview tends to differ depending on the interviewer's theoretical orientation. For instance, a behaviorally oriented assessor might be concerned with determining the specific stimulus/environmental conditions associated with abnormal behavior. In contrast, a psychodynamically oriented assessor would be interested in reconstructing the person's early developmental history as a means of determining underlying psychological characteristics that may be causing behaviors that are of clinical concern.

The degree to which an interview is structured may vary greatly. The vast majority of interviews are conducted in a very loose, unstructured format in which the interviewer determines the types of questions asked and the manner in which they are asked. This unstructured format can present a problem if you are interested in comparing material gathered by different interviewers. The differing experiences and clinical skills of the interviewers will make comparisons across interview data difficult, if not impossible.

An alternative is to impose more structure on the interview situation. One early structured interview system was the current and past psychopathology scales (Spitzer and Endicott, 1969). This system consisted of an interview protocol that was designed to gather specific information, with a guide focusing the clinician's attention on a uniform set of typical patient characteristics. Responses to a set of specific questions were scored on 6-point scales that measured the degree to which certain behaviors and feelings were present. Questions were always phrased in an identical manner so that the responses elicited could be secured and compared across patients. Assessment of the Type A behavior pattern with the *structured interview* procedure is another example of a structured interview method. We will discuss it later in this chapter.

More recently Spitzer and colleagues developed the Structured Clinical Interview for DSM-III-R or SCID (Spitzer et al., 1988). This is a standardized structured interview procedure in which subjects are asked specific questions to either rule in or rule out DSM-III-R diagnoses of psychopathology. Research has shown that it has good reliability (Skre et al., 1991; Williams et al., 1992). (See the box "DSM-IV: Psychological Factors Affecting Medical Condition.") A revised version has been developed for the newer DSM-IV. Methods such as these permit the collection of objective and quantifiable interview data, which can be compared over time and across different patient groups, and which produce a diagnostic statement about an individual.

Problems of Response Bias

One potentially significant and well-demonstrated difficulty associated with structured tests is the presence of response sets or biases. A **response set** or **bias** is a particular test-taking attitude that causes a person not to answer items on a test in terms of their manifest content. That is, he or she has a characteristic and consistent way of responding to items on the test regardless of what the

DSM-IV: Psychological Factors Affecting Medical Condition

The essential feature of Psychological Factors Affecting Medical Condition is the presence of one or more specific psychological or behavioral factors that adversely affect a general medical condition. (See Chapter 7.) There are several different ways in which these factors can adversely affect the general medical condition. The factors can influence the course of the general medical condition (which can be inferred by a close temporal association between the factors and the development or exacerbation of, or delayed recovery from, the medical condition). The factors may interfere with the treatment of the general medical condition. The factors may constitute an additional health risk for the individual (e.g., continued overeating in an individual with weight-related diabetes). They may precipitate or exacerbate symptoms of a general medical condition by eliciting stress-related physiological responses (e.g., causing chest pain in individuals with coronary artery disease or bronchospasm in individuals with asthma).

The psychological or behavioral factors that influence general medical conditions include Axis I disorders, Axis II disorders, psychological symptoms or personality traits that do not meet the full criteria for a specific mental disorder, maladaptive health behaviors, or physiological responses to environmental or social stressors.

Psychological or behavioral factors play a potential role in the presentation or treatment of almost every general medical condition. This category should be reserved for those situations in which the psychological factors have a clinically significant effect on the course or outcome of the general medical condition or place the individual at a significantly higher risk for an adverse outcome. There must be reasonable evidence to suggest an association between the psychological factors and the medical condition, although often it may not be possible to demonstrate direct causality or the mechanisms underlying the relationship. Psychological and behavioral factors may affect the course of almost every major category of disease, including cardiovascular conditions, dermatological conditions, endocrinological conditions, gastrointestinal conditions, neoplastic conditions, neurological conditions, pulmonary conditions, renal conditions, and rheumatological conditions.

The psychological factors affecting medical condition diagnosis is coded on Axis I, and the accompanying general medical condition is coded on Axis III.

[SPECIFIED PSYCHOLOGICAL FACTOR] AFFECTING . . . [INDICATE THE GENERAL MEDICAL CONDITION]

A. A general medical condition (coded on Axis III) is present.
B. Psychological factors adversely affect the general medical condition in one of the following ways:
   1. The factors have influenced the course of the general medical condition as shown by a close temporal association between the psychological factors and the development or exacerbation of, or delayed recovery from, the general medical condition.
   2. The factors interfere with the treatment of the general medical condition.
   3. The factors constitute additional health risks for the individual.
   4. Stress-related physiological responses precipitate or exacerbate symptoms of the general medical condition.

Reprinted with permission from the *Diagnostic and Statistical Manual of Mental Disorders,* Fourth Edition. Copyright © 1994 American Psychiatric Association.

items actually say. Three major forms of response sets have been shown to affect structured psychological tests: response deviation or dissimulation, response acquiescence, and social desirability.

Response dissimulation or **deviation** is the tendency to answer items in an uncommon direction in order to present an overly favorable or unfavorable picture of oneself. The MMPI validity scales were developed in an attempt to control for this factor to some degree. **Response acquiescence** refers to the tendency to agree with test items no matter what their content. On a personality test such as the MMPI the questions are worded so that agreement increases the scale score. That is, the total score on a scale is a direct function of how often the respondent agrees or responds "yes" to the items. The more often a person answers "yes" to an item that is part of the MMPI depression scale, for example, the higher his or her depression score will be. If a nondepressed person has an acquiescence response set and so answers "yes" to these items regardless of their content, then he or she will have a scale score that suggests the presence of depression.

Social desirability is the tendency to answer items in the most socially desirable manner regardless of what the truth is. In order to control for social desirability, certain inventories use a forced-choice question format. In this format, pairs of self-reference statements are presented simultaneously to the respondent, who is to choose the statement that is the most self-descriptive. The alternatives in each pair of statements are made equivalent in terms of social desirability. One can also measure the extent to which people respond in socially desirable ways by using inventories like the Marlowe-Crowne (Crowne and Marlow, 1964) or self-monitoring assessments (Snyder, 1974).

Obviously, a clinician or researcher has to be sensitive to the possibility of individuals who are falsifying their responses on a test. Many tests have validity scales to help isolate those cases in which falsification of responses occurs. Moreover, in most medical settings it can be assumed that a patient seeking professional help would not want to falsify his or her responses.

HEALTH ASSESSMENTS

We now turn our attention to assessment procedures specifically developed with a medical population in mind. In recent years the number of such procedures has been growing. We will review the most widely known and used of these methods. The first two to be discussed—symptom inventories that measure distress, the SCL–90 and the Millon Behavioral Health Inventory, are similar to the MMPI in their focus on the assessment of psychopathology. They are different, however, in that they were developed for use with medical populations rather than with a psychiatric population. We will also review methods developed to assess psychological characteristics associated with physical illness. The first of these—the Life Experiences Survey—was constructed to evaluate life change events, the stress of which has been shown to be associated with physical illness (see Chapter 3). Procedures developed for the assessment of Type A-B behavior characteristics will then be described along with several newer instruments measuring optimism, social support, quality of life, and other important health psychology variables. Finally, we will discuss one of the oldest forms of psychological assessment in medical settings—neuropsychological assessment.

The SCL-90 Rating Scale

The SCL-90 and SCL-90-R (Derogatis, 1977) are 90-item self-report symptom inventories that were developed to measure psychopathology in both psychiatric and medical outpatients (Derogatis, Lipman, and Covi, 1979). It was one of the first such scales developed with a medical population in mind. Each item is rated on a 5-point scale of distress (0 to 4) from "not at all" to "extremely." The inventory is scored on nine primary symptom dimensions plus three global indices of pathology. The nine primary dimensions are summarized in Table 9.2.

The SCL-90 is a useful clinical inventory that can provide an alternative to much more time-consuming inventories such as the MMPI. Moreover, as it was developed for use with outpatients, not just psychiatric patients, it may be helpful in a variety of research situations as well as diagnostic ones. However, a word of caution is needed concerning potential limitations of this test. In a recent study using this test with chronic low back pain patients Kinney, Gatchel, and Mayer (1991) found high interscale correlations of the SCL-90-R, indicating that it may be a single-factor instrument that assesses general psychological distress and not a multidimensional measure of different forms of psychopathology. Other investigators have also noted that the SCL-90-R may measure a single factor of general psychological distress and have questioned the validity of the various separate clinical scales when used with chronic pain patients (Dukro, Margoles, and Tait, 1985). There is no controversy, however, concerning its use as an effective screening device for general psychological distress in a medical population.

TABLE 9.2. The SCL-90-R is a 90-item self-report symptom inventory designed to reflect the psychological symptom patterns of respondents. Each item is rated on a 5-point scale of distress (0–4), ranging from "not at all" to "extremely." The nine subscales include somatization, obsessive-compulsive, interpersonal sensitivity, depression, anxiety, hostility, phobic anxiety, paranoid ideation, and psychoticism.

Instructions: Below is a list of problems that people sometimes have. Please read each one carefully, and choose the one that best describes *how much that problem has distressed or bothered you during the past 7 days including today.* Choose only one number for each problem and do not skip any items. If you change your mind, erase your first mark carefully.

> 0 = not at all
> 1 = a little bit
> 2 = moderately
> 3 = quite a bit
> 4 = extremely

1.	0 1 2 3 4				Headaches
2.	0 1 2 3 4				Nervousness or shakiness inside
3.	0 1 2 3 4				Repeated unpleasant thoughts that won't leave your mind

Source: Adapted with permission from National Computer Systems, Inc. Copyright © 1975 Leonard R. Derogatis, Ph.D.

The Millon Behavioral Health Inventory

The Millon Behavioral Health Inventory (MBHI) was developed with individuals undergoing evaluation or treatment in medical settings for physical disorders. Its major intent is to provide information relevant to behavioral assessments and treatment decisions about individuals with physical problems. Information is provided concerning factors such as the patient's style of relating to health care personnel and major psychosocial stressors as well as probable response to illness and treatment interventions. As we noted at the beginning of this chapter, traditional assessment methods designed for psychiatric populations (such as the MMPI) may not be totally valid for a medical population because the statistical norms and clinical signs may differ significantly. The MBHI was developed and standardized on a medical population.

The MBHI is a 150-item self-report inventory. It provides 20 clinical scales that measure dimensions relevant to psychosocial assessment and decision making with medical populations. These 20 scales are organized into four broad areas, including personality and coping styles, psychogenic attitudes related to stress, psychosomatic correlates such as allergic tendencies, and prognostic indices that predict complications or difficulties associated with illness.

Research has demonstrated the usefulness of the MBHI with certain medical problems. For example, Gatchel and colleagues (1985) evaluated the use of the MBHI in predicting the response of chronic headache sufferers to a behavioral treatment program. Results demonstrated that a number of scales significantly predicted response to treatment, as measured by the daily number of headaches, duration, intensity, and medication use. The emotional vulnerability scale was found to be the most general predictor of treatment outcome. High scorers for this scale (those who are generally poor responders to treatment programs) demonstrated the least amount of improvement in the headache measures. In another study Gatchel et al. (1986) evaluated the use of the MBHI in predicting improvement in the physical functioning of chronic low back pain patients who were undergoing a comprehensive multidisciplinary treatment program. Results revealed that various MBHI scales, especially the emotional vulnerability scale, were predictive of improvement in the overall physical functioning of these patients.

The Sickness Impact Profile

The Sickness Impact Profile (SIP), developed by Bergner and colleagues (1981), was designed to document the disability and behavioral impact of illness on medical patients. It can be used across a wide range of medical groups and illnesses of varying types and severities. The SIP is a standardized questionnaire with 136 items grouped into 12 scales ranging from physical, psychosocial, and independent (i.e., home management) categories. Each item in the questionnaire describes a specific dysfunctional behavior, and patients simply indicate whether or not each item applies to them.

Some impressive reliability and validity data for several patient populations have been reported (Bergner, 1984; Bergner et al., 1981). Research has also demonstrated its usefulness for assessing the degree of disability in patients such as those with chronic low back pain (see Follick, Smith, and Ahern, 1985). The SIP appears to be a useful assessment tool for measuring the degree of disability caused by a particular illness, across a number of different dimensions, in medical patients.

Stress and Life Change Assessment

In Chapter 3 we discussed research showing a relationship between life stress (defined in terms of self-reported life changes) and physical illness. The instrument most widely used in the initial life stress research was the Schedule of Recent Experiences (SRE), developed by Holmes and Rahe (1967). The updated form (Recent Life Changes) is a self-administered questionnaire containing a list of 55 events to which subjects respond by checking those events that they have experienced during the recent past (previous 6 months or 1 year) (See Table 9.3). We also discussed some major problems associated with this instrument. The SRE was based on the assumption that life changes per se are stressful regardless of the desirability of the events experienced. However, research has suggested that undesirable events (e.g., the death of a close family member) may have a significantly different, and perhaps a more detrimental, impact on individuals from desirable and positive events (e.g., outstanding personal achievement) (see Sarason, Johnson, and Siegel, 1978). A related problem with the SRE involves the quantification of life changes. Individuals differ greatly in how they are affected by events. The values derived from group ratings, which are used with SRE, may not necessarily reflect the impact that events have on particular individuals.

In response to these problems Sarason et al. (1978) developed a new measure of life stress called the Life Experiences Survey (LES). It is a 57-item self-report measure that allows the respondent to indicate events that he or she experienced during the past year. There are two portions of the scale. Section 1, designed for all respondents, contains a list of 47 specific events plus three blank spaces in which respondents can indicate other events that they have experienced. The events listed in this section correspond to life changes that are common to people in a wide range of situations. Section 2 consists of 10 events that are designed primarily for use with students, but they can be adapted for other populations. The events deal specifically with changes experienced in the academic environment. This and other, newer versions of the life change or life stress assessment may resolve many of the problems associated with earlier assessment of this variable.

One solution to this problem is to focus on perceived stress rather than measuring stressors. The Perceived Stress Scale (PSS) is a widely used 14-item questionnaire that measures the extent to which you appraise your life or events in it as stressful (Cohen, Kamarck, and Mermelstein, 1983). The 14 items include 7 positive and 7 negative questions about how often, in the past month, you found your life unpredictable, uncontrollable, or too busy (see Table 9.4). The questions are answered on 5-point scales from 0 = never to 4 = very often. The PSS is highly correlated with depressive and physical symptoms (Cohen, Kamarck, and Mermelstein, 1983). A brief 4-item version that is useful for phone interviews is also available.

Hewitt, Flett, and Mosher (1992) recently found two basic factors in the

TABLE 9.3. Items from the Recent Life Changes Questionnaire

Instructions for marking your recent life changes:

To answer the questions below, mark an "X" in one or more of the columns to the right of each question. If the event in question has happened to you within the past 2 years, indicate when it happened by marking the appropriate column: 0–6 months ago, 7–12 months ago, and so on. It may be the case with some of the events below that you experienced them over more than one of the time periods listed for the past 2 years. If so, mark all the appropriate columns. If the event has not happened to you during the last 2 years, leave all the columns empty.

After you have read all the events and indicated which events you experienced, go through the questionnaire again giving an adjustment score to those events you experienced. The adjustment score should be a score between 1 and 100 which reflects what you saw to be the amount of life adjustment necessary to cope with or handle the event.

	19–24 Months Ago	13–18 Months Ago	7–12 Months Ago	0–6 Months Ago	Your Adjustment Score
A. Health Within the time periods listed have you experienced:					
1. An illness or injury that: a. Kept you in bed a week or more, or took you to the hospital? b. Was less serious than described above?					
2. A major change in eating habits?					
3. A major change in sleeping habits?					
4. A change in your usual type and/or amount of recreation?					
5. Major dental work?					
B. Work Within the time periods listed, have you:					
6. Changed to a new type of work?					
7. Changed you work hours or conditions?					

Source: Adapted from R. H. Rahe. Epidemiological Studies of Life Changes and Illness. *International Journal of Psychiatry in Medicine*, 1975, 6, 131–146.

PSS. The first is a general distress factor, and the second concerns perceived coping ability. Both factors were related to symptoms of depression in women, but only the first was related to depression in men. Martin, Kazarian, and Breiter (1995) also found that the same two factors were discovered in other research (see Martin et al., 1995) but the extent to which one or both of these factors is related to distress in men and women is not clear. Gender differences

TABLE 9.4. Sample Items from the Perceived Stress Scale

The questions on this scale ask you about your feelings and thoughts during the *last* month. In each case you will be asked to indicate how often you felt or thought in a certain way. Although some of the questions are similar, there are differences between them and you should treat each one as a separate question. The best approach is to answer each question fairly quickly. That is, don't try to count the number of times you felt a particular way but, rather, indicate the alternative that seems like a reasonable estimate.

Question	0 Never	1 Almost Never	2 Sometimes	3 Fairly Often	4 Very Often
1. In the last month, how often have you been upset because of something that happened unexpectedly?					
2. In the last month, how often have you thought that you were unable to control the important things in your life?					
3. In the last month, how often have you felt nervous and "stressed"?					
4. In the last month, how often have you dealt successfully with irritating life hassles?					
5. In the last month, how often have you felt that you were effectively coping with important changes that were occurring in your life?					

Source: From S. Cohen, T. Kamarck, and R. Mermelstein. A global measure of perceived stress. *Journal of Health and Social Behavior,* 1983, 24, 385–396.

were also found in a study of male and female police officers (Norvell, Hills, and Murrin, 1993). Higher perceived stress was associated with more dissatisfaction with coworkers among female police officers but not among male officers. Men, on the other hand, who scored higher on the PSS, reported more physical symptoms and overall job dissatisfaction.

Another way to measure stress is to find out how much people think about what happened to them. After stressful events most people experience **intrusive thoughts** about the event. These thoughts are not controllable and seem to just "pop into your head." They appear to cause people to get upset and may be an important part of chronic stress (Baum et al., 1993). When these thoughts are upsetting enough, people avoid them or any reminders of the event.

The Impact of Event Scale (IES) was designed as a measure of subjective stress (Horowitz, Wilner, and Alvarez, 1979). The IES is a 15-item questionnaire that measures the frequency of intrusive thoughts and of avoidance behaviors associated with a specific event. You would be asked how often you thought of an event when you did not want to, and the intrusive thought subscale includes examples of unwanted thoughts, images, or feelings about an event. The avoidance behavior subscale includes behaviors associated with avoiding thoughts or reminders of an event (e.g., "I tried not to talk about it"). Subjects rate these items over the past 7 days using four response choices: "Not at all," "Rarely," "Sometimes," and "Often" (see Table 9.5).

Intrusive thoughts are currently thought to be a cause of chronic stress (see Baum, Cohen, and Hall, 1993). In the wake of stressful events people with high IES scores (more frequent intrusive thoughts and greater avoidance) are more stressed and report more symptoms and have a higher heart rate and blood pressure (see Davidson and Baum, 1986). Moreover, individuals with high IES

TABLE 9.5. Sample Items from the Impact of Event Scale

Below is a list of comments made by people after stressful life events. Please check each item, indicating how frequently these comments were true for you *during the past 7 days*. If they did not occur during that time, please mark the "Not at All" column.

You experienced the accident.

	Not at All	Rarely	Sometimes	Often
1. I thought about it when I didn't mean to.				
2. I avoided letting myself get upset when I thought about it or was reminded of it.				
3. I tried to remove it from my memory.				
4. I had trouble falling asleep or staying asleep.				
5. I had waves of strong feelings about it.				

Frequency

Source: Adapted from M. J. Horowitz, N. Wilner, and W. Alvarez. Impact of event scale: A measure of subjective stress. *Psychosomatic Medicine,* 1979, *41*, 209–218.

scores were more reactive (e.g., higher stress, increases in negative mood) to reminders of their stressful experience (Hall and Baum, 1995).

Measuring Type A Behavior and Hostility

As we saw in Chapter 5, the Type A behavior pattern was recognized early on as an independent risk factor for coronary heart disease. Much of the original work conducted in this area used the structured interview (SI) procedure developed by Friedman and Rosenman (1974). The SI was conceived and developed to elicit characteristics of the Type A syndrome. (See the box "Behavior Pattern Interview.")

The effective administration and assessment of the SI requires a period of supervised training. This is because assessment involves not only the evaluation of the specific content of answers, but also the general stylistics and mannerisms of the individual as he or she answers the questions. The way that something is said in the interview may be more important than what is actually said. Obviously, there is subjective evaluation involved in the SI; because it is not totally objective, the SI cannot yield a truly numerical quantification. In spite of this subjectivity problem, it has produced a high degree of interrater agreement in categorizing people as Type A or Type B (from 75 to 90 percent in various studies reviewed by Rosenman, 1978a).

Using the SI, one can classify people as Type A-1 or A-2, Type B or Type X (Rosenman, 1978a). Type A-1 characteristics include general expressions of vigor, energy, alertness, and confidence, and loud, rapid, tense, or clipped speech. This category also is indicated by the acceleration of speech at the end of long sentences, frequent interruptions, explosive speech, hostility, impatience, and the use of abrupt one-word responses such as "Never!" or "Absolutely!" Type A-2 people are not as extreme as A-1s. Thus, a Type A-2 might be in a hurry but not extremely impatient, occasionally use explosive speech, interrupt, or accelerate his or her speech, or otherwise show less hostile or aggressive characteristics of Type A-1. Type B subjects show little or no evidence of any of these characteristics: They are relaxed, do not interrupt, give long responses, speak in quieter voices, and do not exhibit hostile responding.

A Type X person is one who exhibits in almost equal proportions those characteristics attributed to Type A and Type B patterns. The Type X pattern occurs in only about 10 percent of the population.

As we learned in Chapter 5, one of the most important aspects of coronary-prone behavior is hostility (Helmers, Posluszny, and Krantz, 1994; Siegman and Smith, 1994). Depending on how it is measured, hostility appears to be a risk factor for coronary heart disease and for mortality in general (Matthews, 1988; Smith, 1992). Behavioral ratings from the structured interview have been used and are related to heart disease (Barefoot and Lipkus, 1994; Houston et al., 1992; Smith, 1992). The most widely used self-administered questionnaire assessing hostility is the Cook-Medley Hostility Inventory (Cook and Medley, 1954). The 50-item true/false questionnaire was derived from the MMPI (see Table 9.6). Blumenthal et al. (1987) suggest that the scale measures four behavior dimensions: anger and hostility, ineffective coping

Behavior Pattern Interview

Introduction: "I would appreciate it if you would answer the following questions to the best of your ability. Your answers will be kept in the strictest confidence. Most of the questions are concerned with your superficial habits, and none of them will embarrass you."

1. May I ask your age *please*?
2. What is your occupation or job?
   a. How long have you been in this type of work?
3. Are you *satisfied* with your job level? (Why not?)
4. Does your job carry *heavy* responsibility?
   a. Is there any time when you feel particularly *rushed* or under *pressure*?
   b. When you are under *pressure,* does it bother you?
5. Would you describe youself as a *hard-driving, ambitious* type of *man (woman)* in accomplishing the things you want, getting things done as *quickly* as possible, or would you describe yourself as a relatively *relaxed* and *easygoing* person?
   a. Are you married?
   b. How would your wife (husband) describe you—as *hard-driving* and *ambitious* or as relaxed and easygoing?
   c. Has she (he) ever asked you to slow down in your work? *Never?* How would she (he) put it—in *her (his)* own words?
6. When you get *angry* or *upset,* do people around you know about it? How do you show it?
7. Do you think you drive *harder* to *accomplish* things than most of your associates?
8. Do you take work home with you? How often?
9. Do you have any children? When they were around the ages of 6 and 8, did you *ever* play competitive games with them, like cards, checkers, Monopoly?
   a. Did you *always* allow them to *win* on purpose?
   b. *Why* (or *why not*)?
10. When you play games with people your own age, do you play for the fun of it, or are you really in there to *win*?
11. Is there any *competition* in your job? Do you enjoy this?
    a. Are you competitive off the job, sports, for example?
12. When you are in your automobile, and there is a car in your lane going *far too slowly* for you, what do you do about it? Would you *mutter* and *complain* to yourself? Would anyone riding with you know that you were *annoyed*?
13. Most people who work have to get up fairly early in the morning—in your particular case, uh-what-time-uh-do-you-uh-have-uh-to-uh-uh-get up?
14. If you make a *date* with someone for, oh, two o'clock in the afternoon, for example, would you *be there* on *time*?
    a. If you are kept waiting, do you *resent* it?
    b. Would you *say* anything about it?
15. If you see someone doing a job rather *slowly* and you *know* that you could do it faster and better yourself, does it make you *restless* to watch him?
    a. Would you be tempted to *step in and do it* yourself?
16. What *irritates* you most about your work or the people with whom you work?
17. Do you *eat rapidly*? Do you *walk* rapidly? After you've *finished* eating, do you like to sit around the table and chat, or do you like to *get up and get going*?
18. When you go out in the evening to a restaurant and you find eight or ten people *waiting ahead of you* for a table, will you wait? What will you do while you are waiting?
19. How do you feel about waiting in lines: *Bank* lines, or *supermarket* lines? *Post office* lines?
20. Do you *always* feel anxious to *get going* and *finish* whatever you have to do?
21. Do you have the feeling that *time* is passing too *rapidly* for you to *accomplish* all the things you would like to *get done* in one day?
    a. Do you *often* feel a sense of *time urgency*? *Time pressure*?
22. Do you *hurry* in doing most things?
    All right that completes the interview. Thank you very much.

Source: From R. H. Rosenman. The interview method of assessment of the coronary-prone behavior pattern. In T. M. Dembroski et al. (Eds.), *Coronary-Prone Behavior.* New York: Springer, 1978a, pp. 68–69.

TABLE 9.6. Sample Items from the Cook-Medley Hostility Scale

Read each statement and decide whether each is *true as applied to you or false as applied to you*. If a statement is *true or mostly true,* as applied to you, put an X in the column headed T. If a statement is *false or not usually true,* as applied to you, put an X in the column headed F. If a statement does not apply to you or if it is something you do not know about, make no mark.

Remember to give your own opinion of yourself. *Do not leave any spaces blank if you can avoid it.*

Statement	T	F
1. When someone does me wrong, I feel that I should pay him or her back if I can, just for the principle of the thing.		
2. I prefer to pass by school friends, or people I know but have not seen for a long time, unless they speak to me first.		
3. I have often had to take orders from someone who did not know as much as I did.		
4. I think that a great many people exaggerate their misfortune in order to gain the sympathy and help of others.		
5. It takes a lot of argument to convince most people of the truth.		

Source: Adapted from J. C. Barefoot, K. A. Dodge, B. L. Peterson, et al. The Cook-Medley Hostility scale: Item content and ability to predict survival. *Psychosomatic Medicine,* 1989, *51,* 46–57.

styles, neuroticism, and social maladjustment. Recent factor analysis of the items revealed several subscales, including cynicism, hostile attribution, aggressive responding, hostile affect, and social avoidance (Barefoot et al., 1989).

Optimism

Optimism is a dispositional variable that taps one's expectations and beliefs about how much control one has and about how likely one is to succeed or fail. As we discussed in Chapter 4, optimism is the general expectation that things will work out or that good things will happen, whereas pessimism is the general expectation that things will not work out. The Life Orientation Test (LOT) (Scheier and Carver, 1985) was developed to measure these expectations. If you were filling the test out, you would be asked to read through each of 12 items (see Table 9.7) and rate the extent to which you agree or disagree. Five-point scales are used to rate your agreement (0 = strongly disagree, 1 = disagree, 2 = neutral, 3 = agree, 4 = strongly agree). The score is based on 8 of the

TABLE 9.7. Sample Items from the Life Orientation Test

The next statements concern your way of looking at life in general. For each statement, indicate your opinion about it—whether you agree with it, or disagree, and how much. Try not to let your answer to one item influence your answers to other items. There are no correct or incorrect answers. Just express your own personal feelings. Here are the response choices:

> 0 = strongly disagree
> 1 = disagree
> 2 = neutral
> 3 = agree
> 4 = strongly agree

____ 1. In uncertain times, I usually expect the best.

____ 2. It's easy for me to relax.

____ 3. If something can go wrong for me, it will.

____ 4. I'm always optimistic about my future.

____ 5. I enjoy my friends a lot.

____ 6. It's important for me to keep busy.

____ 7. I hardly ever expect things to go my way.

____ 8. I don't get upset too easily.

____ 9. I rarely count on good things happening to me.

____ 10. Overall, I expect more good things to happen to me than bad.

Source: Adapted from M. F. Scheier and C. S. Carver. Optimism, coping, and health: Assessment and implications of generalized outcome expectancies. *Health Psychology*, 1985, *4*, 219–247. (The filler items are numbers 2, 6, 7 and 10)

12 items, as 4 are fillers and do not measure optimism. Can you tell which items are not part of the optimism score?

Among college students, a high score on the LOT (higher scores indicate optimistic orientations whereas low scores indicate pessimistic ones) is associated with distress: Optimists are less upset and uptight dealing with the daily demands of school or more demanding major life events such as serious illness (Carver et al., 1993; Scheier and Carver, 1992). This may be due to differences in coping, perceived control, or other advantages associated with optimism. New research will tell us more about this dispositional variable and its effects on stress and health.

Related to optimism and explanatory styles (see Chapter 4) are world assumptions, or the basic orientations or views that people have of the world and people around them. Some people have a positive view of the world and themselves, whereas others have more negative outlooks (Janoff-Bulman, 1989). Under normal conditions these assumptions are fairly stable and are believed to affect the appraisal of and the coping with traumatic events. Janoff-Bullman (1989) noted from her work with survivors of trauma that assumptive worlds are frequently changed by the experience of trauma. Victims feel less safe and more vulnerable as they realize that negative events are more common than they thought or that they occur randomly and without meaning.

The World Assumptions scale is a 32-item scale composed of three core categories and eight 4-item subscales. People indicate whether they agree or disagree with each of the statements on 6-point scales. The *Benevolence of the World* scale represents expectations about good and bad outcomes. The *Meaningfulness of the World* scale includes the assumption that events are not random but follow predictable laws and that people can exert control over them. The *Self-Worth* scale measures the assumption that the self is worthy and that precautionary behaviors prevent negative events.

Studies using this scale have found that assumptive worlds differ between victims of trauma and nonvictims. In general, victims see the world as more negative although the particular assumptions that change depend on the type of victimization. Janoff-Bulman (1989) assessed world assumptions in 338 undergraduate college students who were divided into victim or nonvictim groups. Victim status was based on having a history of incest or rape, experiencing a fire that destroyed their home, or being in an accident that resulted in their own serious disability. Victims and nonvictims differed on all three scales, with victims reporting less self-worth and that they saw the impersonal world as more malevolent. Minority group membership and experiences with injustice or victimization also appear to affect world view (Calhoun and Cann, 1995). Janoff-Bulman (1992) has also found these differences between victims and nonvictims in older subjects (ages 50 to 65) and in subjects that experienced other types of traumatic experiences such as bereavement (Schwartzberg and Janoff-Bulman, 1991).

Mood

The *Profile of Mood States (POMS)* is a 65-item scale measuring mood on 5-point adjective rating scales. It is easy to administer and requires approximately 5 minutes to complete (McNair, Lorr, and Droppelman, 1981). Its six scales are designed to measure tension-anxiety (T), depression-dejection (D), anger-hostility (A), vigor-activity (V), fatigue-inertia (F), and confusion-bewilderment (C). A total mood disturbance score can be calculated as a global measure of the affective state by summing the six scale scores (after reversing V).

The POMS is often used to measure mood in healthy individuals and has been used in various medical populations as well. For example, the POMS has been used to measure mood in multiple sclerosis and Parkinson's disease patients, to identify early effective symptoms that often predate cognitive changes in Huntington's disease patients, and to assess emotional symptoms secondary to toxic encephalopathy (such as fatigue, confusion, anger, and depression) (White, 1992). The POMS has also been used widely in HIV and cancer research and has norms for adult cancer patients who are entering treatment protocols for several kinds of cancer (Cella et al., 1989).

Social Support

As we have seen, having someone you can talk to about personal problems may decrease stress. Social support includes the extent to which you perceive individuals around yourself who would provide tangible support (like taking you to a doctor), self-esteem support, a sense of belonging (like inviting you to lunch), and appraisal support or help with opinions or reactions to events. Social support creates a feeling of well-being and security that may be especially important during times of stress. Social support is thought to operate during both the appraisal and the coping phases of the stress process. For example, friends may help to evaluate whether or not to interpret a professor's behavior as personally threatening and may help to provide strategies to cope with his or her interpersonal style.

Not surprisingly, there are many measures of social support. Some people count the number of friends they have, how often they interact, or measure other aspects of their social networks. Others measure perceived social support and may tap only global emotional support (see Fleming et al., 1982) (see Table 9.8), or more specific types of support (see Cohen and Hoberman, 1983). One of the most frequently used measures of perceived social support is the recently revised 4-Alternative Interpersonal Support Evaluation List (ISEL). The 40 items in the scale measure the four types of support listed earlier (tangible, self-esteem, belonging, and appraisal support). For each item one has four alternatives to choose from, ranging from definitely true to definitely false. The ISEL was developed by using college students, and an "adult" version of the scale was developed because of concerns with changing needs and strategies for social support over the lifetime.

Perceived Control

There are a number of ways to measure perceived control, ranging from ad hoc questions about specific and general control and feelings of helplessness to more systematic measures of locus of control and other aspects of perceived control (see Davidson et al., 1982; Wallston et al., 1994). One of the most widely known measures is the locus of control instrument that assesses expectations for control (see Chapter 4).

The Multidimensional Health Locus of Control (MHLC) scale was developed by Wallston and Wallston (1978) as a version of an earlier Health Locus of Control (HLC) scale (Wallston et al., 1976). The scales were designed to measure patients' beliefs about their health. Some of us believe that our health is determined by our own behavior (Wallston and Wallston, 1978), whereas others believe that it is more likely influenced by luck or other people. People who score high on the HLC are termed *"health externals,"* meaning they believe that their health is determined by external factors. *"Health internals,"* those who score low on the HLC, believe that their health is determined by their own actions.

Questions are answered on 6-point scales. There are a total of 18 items, measuring internal, external, and powerful others' locus of control. Two equivalent forms of the individual subscales were developed (Form A and Form B) so that subject familiarity with the wording of questions will not affect re-

TABLE 9.8. A Measure of Emotional Support from Other People—One Kind of Social Support

The following statements refer to thoughts that people have about themselves. Please rate the degree to which you agree or disagree with these statements. If you agree strongly, you might pick "1"; if you agree, but not strongly, you might pick "2" or "3." If you disagree, you would pick "5," "6," or "7," depending on how strongly you disagree. If you don't really agree or disagree, you would pick "4."

	Agree Strongly						Disagree Strongly
1. I often feel lonely, like I don't have anyone to reach out to.	1	2	3	4	5	6	7
2. When I am unhappy or under stress, there are people I can turn to for support.	1	2	3	4	5	6	7
3. I don't know anyone to confide in.	1	2	3	4	5	6	7
4. I used to have close friends to talk to about things, but I don't anymore.	1	2	3	4	5	6	7
5. When I am troubled, I keep things to myself.	1	2	3	4	5	6	7
6. I am not a member of any social groups (such as church groups, clubs, teams, etc.).	1	2	3	4	5	6	7

Source: From R. Fleming, A. Baum, M. M. Gisriel, and R. J. Gatchel. Mediating influences of social support on stress at Three Mile Island. *Journal of Human Stress, 8*(3), 14–22, 1982. Reprinted with permission of the Helen Dwight Reid Educational Foundation. Published by Heldref Publications, 1319 18th St. N.W., Washington, D.C. 20036-1802.

sponses if repeated measures are collected. More recently a third form (Form C) was developed. This form measures condition-specific health beliefs as opposed to general beliefs. Form C was developed for patients with cancer, rheumatoid arthritis, chronic pain, or diabetes, and can be adapted for use with any medical condition (Wallston, Stein, and Smith, 1994).

Coping

As we have seen, many researchers are interested in how people cope with the stressors they face in their lives. Whether the stressor is an exam, a family conflict, or diagnosis with a life-threatening disease, researchers are interested in the ways in which people deal with these events. Several measures of coping have appeared, and the most commonly used are the Ways of Coping (Folkman and Lazarus, 1980) and the COPE (Carver, Scheier, and Weintraub, 1989). The COPE is a 52-item measure divided into 14 scales. Five of the scales measure problem-focused coping and include active coping, planning, suppression of competing activities, restraint coping, and the seeking of social support. Five other scales, the seeking of emotional social support, positive reinterpretation, acceptance, denial, and turning to religion, can be described as emotion-focused coping. The remaining four scales assess the venting of emotions, behavioral disengagement, mental disengagement, and the use of alcohol.

The COPE is used to measure how a person usually deals with stressful situations, but it can also be used to measure how a person approaches a specific event. When dispositional coping is measured, people are asked to rate each of the items to reflect what they generally do and feel when faced with stressful events. When the situation-specific version of the COPE is used, people are asked to recall and think about a specific stressful event that has been or is being experienced. The four response options are: "I don't (didn't) do this at all," "I do (did) this a little bit," "I do (did) this a medium amount," "I do (did) this a lot." Research using the COPE, for example, has been used to describe coping methods used by early stage breast cancer patients (e.g., acceptance, positive reframing, and use of religion) (Carver et al., 1993). Some gender differences have been found for the kinds of coping responses reported by men and women (Scheier, Carver, and Weintraub, 1989).

The Ways of Coping Checklist (WCCL) (Folkman and Lazarus, 1980) was also designed to assess reactions to stressful events. In its original form the 68 items on the WCCL provided a variety of strategies that could be categorized as either problem-focused or emotion-focused coping methods. Vitaliano and his colleagues (1985) reported a factor analysis on the specific components of the WCCL, following a revision of the measure that added greater specificity to the emotion-focused subscale (Aldwin et al., 1980). Subscales measuring wishful thinking, self-blame, avoidance, and the seeking of social support were added to the coping profile obtainable with the WCCL. Each strategy is rated on a 4-point scale.

The WCCL has been used to examine coping strategies in a variety of stressful situations and has proven to be a valuable measure in studies of emotional and behavioral reactions to health-related events. It has also been useful in predicting the use of health behaviors as a specific coping mechanism. Baum, Fleming, and Singer (1983) administered the WCCL among a battery of self-report measures that were chosen to examine emotional, behavioral, and physiological response following exposure to the Three Mile Island (TMI) nuclear accident. More emotion-focused coping was related to lower levels of distress, whereas problem-focused coping was related to more distress. This seemed to be true because the sources of stress with which they were dealing were not readily controlled by residents of the area.

The WCCL has also been useful in studies of adaptation following a major life event such as the loss of one's spouse (Gass and Chang, 1989). High threat appraisal was related to both emotion- and problem-focused coping. Use of more problem-focused coping was related to better psychosocial health, whereas emotion-focused coping was linked to poorer psychosocial health. However, coping styles may be situation-specific, and the type of response that is appropriate or optimal for bereavement may not be generalizable to other stressful events (Grummon et al., 1994).

A different kind of coping scale is the Monitor-Blunter Style Scale (MBSS), designed to measure differences in the amount of information that you prefer to have about situations that you find threatening. Some people prefer to seek out information regarding the threat (monitors), and others use distraction to avoid thinking about the threat (blunters). The MBSS divides people into two separate subscales: high versus low monitoring and high versus low blunting.

People respond to a series of four descriptions of stressful scenes, each followed by eight questions—four dealing with monitoring and four with blunting behaviors.

Research using the MBSS has not shown that one style is always more adaptive than the other. The usefulness of either monitoring or blunting depends on the situation in which it is used. For example, Miller (1987) found that those who used a monitoring coping style during an acute threat of physical harm were more distressed and aroused than those who used a blunting style to cope (see Figure 9.2). However, Solomon, Mikulincer, and Arad (1991) found that soldiers involved in a war for at least 2 years who used monitoring strategies suffered less trauma-related psychopathology than those who used blunting strategies. Evidence suggests that when the threat and the resulting distress are short-lasting, denial or blunting are associated with less distress and arousal. However, when the threat is chronic or unresolved, monitoring results in less distress.

Pain

We will discuss pain in Chapter 11. Because it is the most common medical symptom and one of the hardest to measure, accurate measurement of pain is important. Subjective intensity, as assessed by one or two questions, is probably the most commonly used method for assessing pain (Jensen, Karoly, and Braver, 1986). However, current concepts of pain suggest multidimensional assessment of the pain experience (Turk, Meichenbaum, and Genest, 1983). The McGill pain questionnaire (MPQ) was the first comprehensive scale designed to assess the three major dimensions that patients use to specify subjective pain experience—sensory, affective, and evaluative (Melzack, 1975). It is one of the most widely used means of measuring pain (Dudgeon, 1993).

The original form consisted of 78 verbal descriptors of pain (Melzack, 1975). It also consisted of items designed to assess the intensity, pattern, and location of pain. It requires about 10 minutes to administer. The original validation of this questionnaire was done with a sample of 297 patients with 12 major diagnostic pain categories (e.g., arthritis, cancer, gastrointestinal, low back, menstrual, postsurgical). A short form of the MPQ was also developed (Melzack, 1987), measuring only the sensory and affective aspects of pain. The short form correlates with the standard inventory and consists of 15 descriptors (11 sensory, 4 affective) as well as measures of present pain intensity.

Both forms of the MPQ have been used extensively in clinical work and in treatment outcome research. It is applicable for many types of pain, including acute, chronic, and disease-related pain (see Appelbaum, 1988; Graham et al., 1980; Rybstein-Blinchik, 1979).

Sleep Quality

The quality and quantity of sleep that people get is an important variable in health and is now receiving attention as a possible health-related consequence of stress. Habitual sleep quality may be measured with the Pittsburgh Sleep Quality Index (PSQI) (Buysse et al., 1989). This 19-item, self-report question-

Vividly imagine that you are on an airplane, thirty minutes from your destination, when the plane unexpectedly goes into a deep dive and then suddenly levels off. After a short time, the pilot announces that nothing is wrong, although the rest of the ride may be rough. You, however, are not convinced that all is well. Check *all* of the statements that might apply to you.

_____ I would carefully read the information provided about safety features in the plane and make sure I knew where the emergency exits were.

_____ I would make small talk with the passenger beside me.

_____ I would watch the end of the movie, even if I had seen it before.

_____ I would call for the stewardess and ask her exactly what the problem was.

_____ I would order a drink or tranquilizer from the stewardess.

_____ I would listen carefully to the engines for unusual noises and would watch the crew to see if their behavior was out of the ordinary.

_____ I would talk to the passenger beside me about what might be wrong.

_____ I would settle down and read a book or magazine or write a letter.

FIGURE 9.2. Items from the Monitor-Blunter Style Scale.
Source: Adapted from S. M. Miller. Monitoring and blunting: Validation of a questionnaire to assess style information seeking under threat. *Journal of Personality and Social Psychology*, 1987, 52, 345–353.

naire was designed to capture a number of factors related to sleep quality, including both frequency and severity of sleep-related complaints. The PSQI identifies seven components of sleep quality that are summed into a global sleep quality index. The seven components are sleep latency (minutes to fall asleep), sleep duration (hours spent in bed), sleep efficiency (percentage of time in bed spent asleep), sleep disturbance (e.g., "cough or snore loudly"), sleep medications (frequency of use), daytime dysfunction (e.g., "trouble staying awake"), and sleep quality (general rating). Lower scores reflect better sleep (e.g., infrequent or mild complaint), whereas higher scores reflect worse sleep (e.g., frequent or more severe complaint).

A recent study showed that people who developed symptoms of PTSD (posttraumatic stress disorder) in the year following Hurricane Andrew in southern Florida had poorer sleep quality before the hurricane and continued to have poorer sleep quality 6 to 12 months after the hurricane (Mellman et al., 1995). A note of caution about these findings is needed, however. Pre-hurricane sleep quality was measured retrospectively, after symptoms of PTSD had emerged, and this could have affected memory or the reporting of predisaster sleep quality. However, similar findings have been reported from a study of rescue workers involved in rescue and cleanup operations following a plane crash in which all passengers and crew aboard were killed (Hall et al., under review). In this study sleep quality was a significant predictor of long-term psychological distress and perceived health. Poor sleep, measured prospectively, was associated with poorer health and more distress.

Quality of Life

The past decade has seen increased interest in health-related quality of life. When a patient is choosing a treatment option, he or she not only wants to know how effective the treatment is for "curing" the disease, but also wants to know how bad he or she will feel or if the side effects will permanently interfere with daily functioning. This is particularly relevant for treatments that can have severe side effects (Fleming et al., 1993).

There are now a number of measures of patient quality of life. These tools measure quality of life in patients with general medical illnesses. There are also specific measures for diseases such as cancer, and measures for assessing the quality of life for disease subgroups (i.e., prostate cancer versus breast cancer). The Memorial Sloan-Kettering Cancer Center has recently published a handbook of quality of life measures that includes the general quality of life questionnaires as well as cancer-specific instruments (Kornblith and Holland, 1994).

The MOS 36-Item Short Form Health Survey (SF–36) is a quality of life measure for patients with general medical illnesses (McHorney, Ware, and Raczek, 1993), and can be used in healthy populations as well. This questionnaire originated in the Medical Outcomes Study (MOS), a 2-year longitudinal study of patient outcomes in medical practice and clinical research (Tarlov et al., 1989). The questionnaire was developed to assess both physical and mental health aspects of life quality. The SF–36 was validated in a subgroup of 1,014 patients from the original MOS sample that had completed both the questionnaire portion of the study as well as a health examination within a 1-month period. Patients with minor medical conditions, serious medical conditions, psychiatric conditions, and both psychiatric and serious medical conditions answered questions about pain, general health perceptions, social functioning, and mental health.

Other measures of quality of life are more specific to the disease group or subgroup. One good example is the Functional Assessment of Cancer Therapy scale (FACT), a 28-item quality of life inventory designed for cancer patients (Cella et al., 1993). The general version (FACT-G) can be used for all types of cancer and includes subscales measuring physical, functional, social, and emotional well-being, as well as satisfaction with one's relationship with his or her doctor. The format for each item is a 5-point rating scale. The FACT is sensitive to changes in clinical status over time, as would be expected for a valid quality of life measure. FACT-measured quality of life also decreases with the onset of chemotherapy or immunotherapy in cancer patients (Bender, 1995). In addition, the FACT offers several versions tailored to specific problems associated with particular cancers, including breast, bladder, colorectal, head and neck, lung, ovarian, and prostate. There is also a measure for patients undergoing bone marrow transplants.

As we mentioned at the beginning of this text, behavioral medicine or medical psychology is a relatively young discipline. However, the collaboration between psychology and one medical specialty—neurology—has a much longer history. Beginning as a part of clinical psychology and then taking on an identity of its own, neuropsychology extends at least as far back as World War I. It represents the first major category of psychological practice addressed to nonpsychiatric medical patients. It can be viewed as the principal forerunner of modern behavioral medicine/medical psychology.

Neuropsychological assessment involves the search for behavioral manifestations or patterns of performance aberrations that are associated with specific brain disorders. It is an important assessment method because many of the currently used medical-neurological tests—the angiogram x-ray technique to detect a brain tumor, the measurement of the electrical activity of the brain, the examination of the retina to detect blood vessel damage, and the evaluation of perception and motor coordination—can assess gross brain damage but usually cannot detect more subtle dysfunctions. Neuropsychological test results may provide clues about the nature of such subtle disturbances (Lezak, 1976).

Neuropsychological evaluation can serve several purposes. First, it can help physicians to diagnose the presence/absence of organic brain dysfunction. It can also help to confirm or support a tentative diagnostic decision based on other assessment methods and can provide more definitive evidence of the behavioral/cognitive effects associated with a brain dysfunction condition. In addition, neuropsychological testing can provide a baseline measure of a patient's abilities, against which to compare later performance changes produced by surgery, medication, rehabilitation efforts, or time. Finally, this kind of evaluation can provide valuable information about the prognosis for improvement in many patients.

Halstead (1947) developed the first comprehensive neuropsychological test battery for the assessment of brain damage. It was subsequently revised by Reitan (1955) and further modified by Matthews and Klove at the University of Wisconsin. Reitan (1964) has empirically demonstrated that the neuropsychological test battery can reliably identify the etiology and location of certain brain lesions with a high degree of accuracy. The norms used in such identification were developed by comparing test performance patterns of patients with known organic disorders in specific parts of the brain to those of normal individuals with no known brain disorder.

The Halstead-Reitan Battery (HRB) consists of eight tests. For each of these an empirically derived cutoff is used to give a dichotomous classification of impaired-neurologic or unimpaired-normal. The impairment index derived is simply the number of scores in the impaired range. Several tests make up the HRB. The *Category Test*, which measures abstracting ability, is a nonverbal concept attainment test that requires the subject to abstract a general principle from a series of geometric stimuli. For example, figures varying in size, shape, color, and location, grouped by abstract principles, are projected on a screen. The subject's task is to figure out the principle involved. The principle might be that green is correct, or that upside-down is the correct answer.

The Tactile Performance Test measures tactile perception. The Trail Making Test measures visual attention and visual-motor tracking coordination. In this test the subject connects circles in correct numeric or alphanumeric sequence. There are also a Finger Tapping Test, which measures manual dexterity involving rapid finger movement in a counter, and a Speech Perception Test, which measures auditory perception. In the latter the subject listens to a series of tape-recorded nonsense words such as "theeks" or "theez." On an answer sheet he or she must select the correct word from among several alternatives.

The Rhythm Test measures auditory perception. This test, taken from the Seashore Scales of Musical Talents, requires the subject to make same-different judgments of rhythmic patterns. An Aphasia Screening Test, which tests for aphasia (the loss of the ability to read, write, or understand), assesses relatively gross sorts of aphasic symptoms and requires the subject to draw geometric figures. It is scored as normal, impaired in language, impaired in drawing, or impaired in both language and drawing. Finally, the Sensory Examination, which tests for touch, visual, and auditory functions, is derived from the classical neurologic examination.

In addition to these tests, a lateral dominance examination is administered that determines which hand is preferred on various manual-type tasks. Moreover, the Wechsler Adult Intelligence Scale-Revised (WAIS-R), which measures a variety of cognitive-verbal and motor-performance tasks, the Wide Range Achievement Test-Revised (WRAT-R), which evaluates basic academic skills, and the MMPI are frequently administered in order to provide an even more comprehensive understanding of the cognitive-psychological functioning of the individual. A clinical interview is also part of the full battery.

It should be noted that various normative guides for the clinical interpretation of neuropsychological test data have been developed (Heaton, Grant, and Matthews, 1991; Reitan and Wilson, 1985). They provide clinicians with standards against which to match their cases and to make the interpretation of test-battery results much more objective.

SUMMARY

In this chapter we have discussed the traditional forms of psychiatric classification and assessment methods and the more recent diagnostic tests developed with a medical population in mind. Early attempts to develop an effective psychiatric classification system stimulated simultaneous efforts to construct effective and reliable techniques for the assessment of psychological disorders. Although the techniques developed have been quite diverse, they can be classified into two major categories: projective techniques, such as the Thematic Apperception Test (TAT) and Rorschach Inkblot Test, and nonprojective techniques, such as MMPI. None of these tests, however, was developed with a medical population in mind. In recent years a number of assessment procedures have been developed specifically for a medical population. We reviewed the most widely known and utilized of these methods—the SCL-90, the Millon Behavioral Health Inventory (MBHI), the Schedule of Recent Experiences (SRE), the Life Experiences Survey (LES), and the Structured Interview

(SI). Finally, we also discussed the oldest form of psychological assessment in medical settings—neuropsychological assessment.

RECOMMENDED READINGS

Allen, J. P. The interrelationship of alchoholism assessment and treatment. *Alcohol Health and Research World*, 1991, *15*(3), 178–85.

Messick, S. Validity of psychological assessment: Validation of inferences from persons' responses and performances as scientific inquiry into score meaning. Conference on Contemporary Psychological Assessment (1994, Stockholm, Sweden). *American Psychologist*, 1995, *50*(9), 741–49.

Nezu, A. M., Nezu, C. M. Identifying and selecting target problems for clinical interventions: A problem-solving model. Special Section: Treatment implications of psychological assessment. *Psychological Assessment*, 1993, *5*(3), 254–63.

CHAPTER 10

Cognitive-Behavioral Treatment Techniques in Medical Settings

A friend has just learned that she has cancer. She is a little dazed, frightened, and agitated. You decide she is experiencing stress, and you know that stress will increase and continue to be a problem through the surgery and treatments to come. You learned in a class at school that stress can affect the immune system, how happy people are, and how long they live after developing cancer. It seems important to reduce the stress that your friend is experiencing and you set out to do this. But other than being supportive and helpful, what can you do? What are the best ways to go about reducing distress among the seriously ill or those at risk for disease?

The application of approaches from clinical psychology and psychiatry, modified to take into account use in medical settings and to provide new ways of reducing distress and enhancing psychological adjustment, has been a hallmark of health psychology. Although these cognitive-behavioral treatments are not all the interventions that health psychologists implement, they are a majority of them. More importantly, these interventions are empirically based and tested, and emphasize the patient's ability to help him- or herself rather than the therapist "taking care" of the patient. Skill development, coping, education, and support are primary components of these interventions. As a result, they are used, with some modification, in situations ranging from terminal illness and adjustment to aversive medical treatments to dietary or exercise interventions in the workplace or safer sex exhortations! In disease management alone, cognitive-behavioral interventions have proven useful in reducing pain, controlling hypertension, reducing depression or other emotional disturbances, managing symptoms and procedure-related distress, reducing conditioned nausea and vomiting, and increasing adherence and quality of life.

In this chapter we will discuss a variety of cognitive-behavioral treatment procedures that have been effectively employed with problem behaviors often seen in medical settings. The various cognitive-behavioral therapy techniques we will review have been found to treat effectively a wide range of maladaptive behaviors that have been resistant to other types of traditional treatment. Such findings highlight the clinical potency of these methods, as well as the learning principles on which they are based.

At the outset it should be noted that cognitive-behavioral (or behavioral-cognitive) treatment represents a broad class of therapies (Dobson and Block, 1988). Indeed, Lewinsohn et al. (1984) have pointed out that even though contemporary therapeutic approaches have been divided into those that primarily emphasize "behavior" and those that emphasize "cognitions," they are quite similar. Moreover, there is empirical support for the treatment efficacy of both approaches. The real problem confronting the practitioner at this point in time is selecting from among the wide range of these very promising and effective cognitive and behavioral approaches.

Ivan Pavlov (1849–1936), the eminent Russian physiologist, first described the process of classical conditioning with his work on the conditioned reflex. Reflexes are specific, automatic, unlearned reactions elicited by a specific stimulus. If you have ever touched a surface that you did not know was hot, such as a hot stove, you demonstrated a reflexive behavior—immediate withdrawal of your hand from the stove. Similarly, if a piece of dust suddenly enters your eye, your eye will automatically blink and begin to secrete tears. These **unconditioned reflexes** are automatic and have a great deal of survival value for the organism. Pavlov demonstrated that such unconditioned reflexes could be **conditioned**, or learned. While studying dogs in order to understand more fully the digestive process, he began to notice that many of the dogs secreted saliva even before food was delivered to them. He observed that this phenomenon occurred whenever the dogs either heard the approaching footsteps of the laboratory assistant who fed them or had a preliminary glimpse of the food. In order to investigate this phenomenon more systematically, Pavlov developed a procedure for producing a conditioned reflex. This procedure came to be called **classical conditioning**. It is one of the most basic forms of learning.

Pavlov conducted a series of well-known studies on the process of classical conditioning using dogs as experimental subjects. In these studies Pavlov studied situations in which a neutral stimulus or event (such as a bell) was presented to a dog just prior to the presentation of food (an unconditioned stimulus that normally elicits an automatic unconditioned reflex of salivation). After a number of such presentations the bell (now a conditioned stimulus) would elicit a conditioned or learned salivation response when presented by itself in the absence of food. The conditioned reflex of salivation occurred to the bell alone. This represents the process of classical conditioning and is based on the learned association or connection between two stimuli, such that the bell is associated with food, that have occurred together at approximately the same point in time. An association is learned between a weak stimulus (such as the bell) and a strong stimulus (such as the sight of food) so that the weak stimulus comes to elicit the response originally controlled only by the stronger one (i.e., salivation).

Operant or instrumental conditioning is a different form of learning that was originally formulated by Edward Thorndike and then more comprehensively developed by B. F. Skinner. Unlike classical conditioning, **operant conditioning** develops new behaviors that bring about positive consequences or remove negative events. In classical conditioning a new stimulus (such as a bell) is conditioned to elicit the same responses that had previously occurred to the unconditioned stimulus, whereas in operant conditioning a new response is learned. Behavior that produces food, social approval, or other positive consequences, or that reduces damaging or aversive events, illustrates operant behavior. The behavior "operates" on the environment to bring about changes in it.

Animal training, such as that involved in the learned performance of circus animals, involves basic principles of operant conditioning. Although operant training has existed for centuries, the behaviorist revolution in psychology provided the first carefully delineated methods and procedures of operant conditioning so that such training could be accomplished most efficiently. The key stimulus is **reinforcement**. *Reinforcement* refers to any consequence that increases the likelihood that a particular behavior will be repeated or that strengthens that behavior. **Extinction** involves the gradual decrease in the strength or tendency to perform a response due to the elimination of reinforcement.

An important procedure used in operant conditioning is **shaping**. In work on operant conditioning, the bar-pressing response of rats has been one of the most frequently studied processes. It is an easy response for rats to perform, it is a well-defined act, and it is easy to record automatically. However, when they are put into new situations, rats will not spontaneously find the correct sequence of behavior (e.g., approach the bar, rise up on hind legs, place front paws on the bar and press down toward the floor). Instead of waiting for the rat to stumble accidentally on the correct sequence, we use shaping, which is based on the process of successive approximations. Each time the animal comes closer to the bar or to pressing it, a reinforcement is provided until it learns the correct response.

Once a response is learned, one can introduce different **reinforcement schedules** in order to produce different patterns of responding. Reinforcement can now require variable numbers of bar presses or can be available every so often. Also, a *discriminative stimulus* can be introduced, so that the rat receives reinforcement for pressing the bar only when a certain light is on in the cage. The animal will soon learn not to respond when the light is off. In this manner the rat's bar-pressing behavior comes under **stimulus** (e.g., light) **control**.

This same shaping procedure is used in training circus and other animals to perform complicated acts. Dolphins can be shaped to leap out of the water, and lions can be taught to jump through flaming hoops. These techniques are used in virtually every zoo and marine animal show. These procedures are so powerful that Skinner and two of his early associates—Fred Keller and Marian Breland—worked on a project during World War II called "Project Pigeon," with the goal of training pigeons to guide a bomb toward a predetermined target. They were well on their way to completing the training of these "pigeon soldiers" when the war ended, removing the urgent need for this research.

Many behavioral treatment programs using operant conditioning principles have been developed. A number of these, including biofeedback, contingency management, and stimulus control procedures, will be discussed later in this chapter. Before we turn to these interventions, we should briefly consider another form of learning, called **observational learning**.

There has been a great deal of research indicating that learning can occur through simple observation without the presence of any form of tangible direct reinforcement. Such learning, besides being called *observational learning,* is sometimes called imitation learning, cognitive learning, vicarious learning, or modeling. *Observational learning* is defined simply as that learning which occurs without any apparent direct reinforcement (Bandura, 1969). Many behaviors can be acquired if an individual sees the particular behavior performed or modeled by another person.

One of the earliest laboratory studies of observational learning (Bandura et al., 1963) involved nursery school children. One group of children observed an adult model perform a series of aggressive acts, both verbal and physical, toward a large toy Bobo doll. Another group watched a nonaggressive adult, who simply sat quietly and paid no attention to the doll. A third group of children were not exposed to a model. Later, after being mildly frustrated, all children were placed in a room alone with the Bobo doll and their behavior was observed. It was found that the behavior of the two model groups tended to be similar to that of their adult model. That is, children who had viewed the aggressive adult performed more aggressive acts toward the doll in the free-play situation than the other groups and also made more responses that were exact imitations of the model's aggressive behavior. Those children who had observed a nonaggressive adult model performed significantly fewer aggressive responses than the aggressive model group.

SYSTEMATIC DESENSITIZATION

Systematic desensitization is a technique developed by Joseph Wolpe (1958) as a means of alleviating anxiety. He based his procedure on the principle of **counterconditioning**, in which an attempt is made to substitute relaxation (an adaptive behavior) for anxiety (the deviant or maladaptive behavior) in response to a particular object or situation. The procedure typically involves the pairing of deep muscle relaxation, which is taught by a progressive muscle relaxation technique developed by Jacobson in 1938, with imagined scenes depicting situations or objects associated with anxiety. Wolpe had his patients imagine the anxiety-related objects or situations because many of the fears treated were abstract in nature (e.g., fear of rejection by a loved one) and therefore could not easily be presented *in vivo* (in real life).

In this treatment procedure a graded hierarchy of scenes is constructed, consisting of items ranging from low-anxiety- to high-anxiety-provoking situations. The individual gradually "works up" this hierarchy, learning to tolerate more and more difficult scenes as he or she relaxes. The relaxation response tends to inhibit anxiety from occurring with the imagined scenes. This ability to tolerate anxiety-related imagery of objects or situations produces a significant decrease in anxiety in the related real-life situations. The therapeutic value of this procedure has been demonstrated with many anxiety-related disorders such as phobias (including fear of medical and dental procedures), insomnia, and stress-related psychophysiological disorders such as ulcers, asthma, and hypertension (see Rimm and Masters, 1974).

As an example of the effective use of systematic desensitization, consider a study of the efficacy of group-administered systematic desensitization in the treatment of individuals with an extreme degree of fear of dental procedures (Gatchel, 1980). Dental-phobic individuals were given six therapy sessions using the anxiety hierarchy depicted in Table 10.1. Phobic patients given systematic desensitization showed a significant reduction in dental anxiety compared with individuals who received no treatment. They also showed nearly 100 percent improvement in seeing the dentist. All these people were originally very fearful of seeing a dentist, indicating how effective desensitization procedures can be. This procedure has also been effective in the treatment of several medical phobias such as injection phobia and hemodialysis phobia. Moreover, it has been found to be effective in reducing anticipatory nausea, anticipating vomiting, posttreatment vomiting, and posttreatment nausea in cancer patients who were undergoing chemotherapy (Morrow et al., 1992).

Progressive Muscle Relaxation

Progressive muscle relaxation, which is an important component of the systematic desensitization treatment process, can often serve as a powerful therapeutic technique in its own right. Clinicians use it by itself to treat a wide variety of disorders, including generalized anxiety, insomnia, headaches, neck tension, and mild forms of agitated depression. Progressive muscle relaxation has also been effectively used in reducing the side effects of cancer chemotherapy (Burish and Jenkins, 1992). Its use is based on the premise that muscle tension is closely related to anxiety and that an individual will feel a significant reduction in experienced anxiety if tense muscles can be made to relax. Other techniques, such as autogenic training (Schultz and Luthe, 1959), biofeedback (which we will discuss later in this chapter), transcendental meditation, and yoga, are also commonly used to reduce physiological activation. This arousal is, in turn, assumed to be closely tied to anxiety.

TABLE 10.1. Graduated anxiety-provoking thoughts (least to most) for dental phobics (from Gatchel, 1980).

1. Thinking about going to the dentist.
2. Calling for an appointment with the dentist.
3. Getting in the car to go to the dentist's office.
4. Sitting in the waiting room of the dentist's office.
5. Having the nurse tell you it's your turn.
6. Getting in the dentist's chair.
7. Seeing the dentist lay out the instruments, one of which is a probe.
8. Seeing the dentist lay out the instruments, one of which is pliers used to pull teeth.
9. Having a probe held in front of you while you look at it.
10. Having a probe placed on the side of a tooth.
11. Having a probe placed in a cavity.
12. Getting an injection in your gums on one side.
13. Having your teeth drilled and worrying if the anesthetic will wear off.
14. Getting two injections, one on each side.
15. Hearing the crunching sounds as your tooth is being pulled.

The teaching of progressive muscle relaxation skills generally follows a fairly standardized procedure, in which individuals practice muscle relaxation directly by first discriminating tension and stress in various muscle groups and then relaxing these groups. For example, an individual would be requested to wrinkle his or her forehead and to notice the pattern and feeling of strain in these muscles. After maintaining the tension for about 10 seconds, the subject would be told to let the forehead muscles completely relax and to notice the difference in sensation at those places where tension and strain were previously felt. After a few minutes of relaxation the sequence is repeated again. The main goal of the training program is to teach individuals what relaxation of each muscle group feels like and to provide practice in achieving more relaxation. Once the individual is able to discriminate the patterns of tension in a particular muscle group, he or she is no longer told to tense before relaxing. Instead, he or she must relax the muscles from their present level of tension.

The relaxation procedure originally developed by Jacobson (1938) required training over many months, with hundreds of muscle sites trained. In normal clinical practice, however, a much more abbreviated form of training is usually applied. Several muscle groups are routinely included, ranging from right hand and left hand or forearm and wrist of both hands to mouth, cheeks, and jaw and chest, back, stomach, thighs, and feet. There have been a number of manuals published that detail different relaxation procedures (see Davis, Eshelman, and McKay, 1988).

Specific relaxation techniques and use of muscle relaxation therapy in general have proven useful in several instances (Smith, 1990). For example, in cancer patients it can often be used to effectively decrease pain, nausea, and anxiety associated with chemotherapy (Carey and Burish, 1988). Relaxation is also useful in controlling hypertension (Rosen et al., 1994) and Arena and Blanchard (1996) reviewed the efficacy of relaxation therapy for chronic pain disorders, noting that these interventions are sometimes as effective as pharmacological treatment. Potential side effects of pharmacological interventions gives a distinct advantage to muscle relaxation treatment programs that have no such side effects. (See the box "Abbrieviated Progressive Muscle Relaxation Training.")

Modeling

Bandura and his colleagues have shown that fear can also be reduced by having fearful individuals repeatedly observe models who effectively engage in the feared activities (see Bandura, 1971). This is based on the principle that the repeated observation that the feared performance does not lead to unfavorable or negative consequences will lead to the extinction or elimination of both anxiety responses and fear-arousing thoughts. This modeling procedure is often called *vicarious extinction.*

Even when one is using models, it is usually beneficial to employ a graduated hierarchy: Models perform a sequence of activities beginning with those that are the least feared and progressing to those that are the most feared. For example, in one modeling study conducted by Bandura, Grusec, and Menlove (1967), fear of dogs was treated by having fearful children observe another child interact with a dog in a graduated sequence. The fear-producing quality of the interactions was gradually increased by controlling the physical re-straints on the dog as well as the duration and degree of physical contact of the interactions. Subsequent studies have found that this modeling procedure is effective even when filmed models, and not live models, are used (Bandura, 1971).

Modeling procedures have been effectively used to reduce hospital- and surgery-related anxieties in children. Melamed and Siegel (1975) showed one of two films to children (aged 4 to 12) about to undergo surgery for hernias, tonsillectomies, or urinary-genital tract problems. One group of children were shown a film entitled *Ethan Has an Operation*. The film depicted a 7-year-old child who was hospitalized for a hernia operation.

The control group of children were shown a film of similar interest level but that was totally unrelated to the hospital situation. Children in both groups also received the standard hospital preoperative counseling procedures expla-nation by a nurse of what would happen on the day of surgery, with pictures and demonstrations, and visits by the surgeon and anesthesiologist.

Prior to surgery and again 3 to 4 weeks after the surgery, self-report, obser-vational, and physiological measures of the children's situational anxiety were obtained. Children who had viewed the hospital-related film showed less anxi-ety than the control group on all measures at both preoperative and postopera-tive assessment periods. This peer-modeling film had a significant effect on re-ducing anxiety in children above and beyond that produced by standard hospital preoperative procedures. Such peer modeling is probably especially important for young children because it is often easier for a child to under-stand another child than it is for the child to understand an adult.

In a similar study with children Robinson and Kobayashi (1991) evaluated the efficacy of three presurgical preparation programs with 28 children be-tween the ages of 4 and 13 who were scheduled for elective surgery. The basic component of all three programs was a peer-modeling film that followed a child going through a hospital admission for an elective surgery procedure. Self-reported fear ratings and observer ratings of anxiety were significantly lower among children in the preparatory program. All three films also had a positive effect on posthospital adjustment. Again, a presurgical intervention that provides information and a stronger sense of control can be therapeuti-cally beneficial for children who are undergoing surgical procedures (Robin-son and Kobayashi, 1991).

The same type of videotaped peer-modeling approach can also be used as a primary prevention program. For example, McFarland and Stanton (1991) as-sessed the effectiveness of a modeling program designed to prepare kinder-garten children for possible emergency room visits. Results clearly demon-strated that this preparation increased medical knowledge and reduced medical fears relative to children who were not receiving this preparation.

One of the important factors underlying the effectiveness of these model-ing procedures is the information given to subjects. As we discussed in Chap-ter 8, there is a growing body of research demonstrating the effectiveness of presurgery information in reducing the distress associated with surgery. For example, Robertson, Gatchel, and Fowler (1991) have demonstrated the effec-tive use of a videotaped behavioral preparation procedure for reducing anxiety in emergency oral surgery patients.

Abbreviated Progressive Muscle Relaxation Training

The following are general guidelines for an abbreviated muscle relaxation training procedure:

1. Instruct the subject to "make a fist with your dominant hand [usually right]. Make a fist and tense the muscles of your [right] hand and forearm; tense until it trembles. Feel the muscles pull across your fingers and the lower part of your forearm." Have the subject hold this position for 5 to 7 seconds; then say "relax," instructing him/her to just let her/his hand go: "Pay attention to the muscles of your [right] hand and forearm as they relax. Note how those muscles feel as relaxation flows through them" (10 to 20 seconds).

   "Again, tense the muscles of your [right] hand and forearm. Pay attention to the muscles involved" (5 to 7 seconds). "Okay, relax; attend only to those muscles, and note how they feel as the relaxation takes place, becoming more and more relaxed, more relaxed than ever before. Each time we do this you'll relax even more until your arm and hand are completely relaxed with no tension at all, warm and relaxed."

   Continue until subject reports his/her (right) hand and forearm are completely relaxed with no tension (usually two to four times is sufficient).

2. Instruct the subject to tense his/her (right) biceps, leaving his/her hand and forearm on the chair. Proceed in the same manner as above, in a "hypnotic monotone," using the (right) hand as a reference point (i.e., move on when the subject reports that his/her biceps feel as completely relaxed as his/her hand and forearm).

   Proceed to other gross-muscle groups (listed below) in the same manner, with the same verbalization. For example: "Note how these muscles feel as they relax; feel the relaxation and warmth flow through these muscles; pay attention to these muscles so that later you can relax them again." Always use the preceding group as a reference for moving on.

3. Nondominant (left) hand and forearm—feel muscles over knuckles and on lower part of arm.

4. Nondominant (left) biceps.
5. *Frown hard, tensing muscles of forehead and top of head* (these muscles often "tingle" as they relax).
6. Wrinkle nose, feeling muscles across top of cheeks and upper lip.
7. Draw corners of mouth back, feeling jaw muscles and cheeks.
8. Tighten chin and throat muscles, feeling two muscles in front of throat.
9. Tighten chest muscles and muscles across back—feel muscles pull below shoulder blades.
10. Tighten abdominal muscles—make abdomen hard.
11. Tighten muscles of right upper leg—feel one muscle on top and two on the bottom of the upper leg.
12. Tighten right calf—feel muscles on bottom of right calf.
13. Push down with toes and arch right foot—feel pressure as if something were pushing up under the arch.
14. Tighten left upper leg.
15. Tighten left calf.
16. Tighten left foot.

For most muscle groups two presentations will suffice. Ask the subject if he/she feels any tension anywhere in his/her body. If he/she does, go back and repeat the tension-release cycle for that muscle group. It is often helpful to instruct the subject to take a deep breath and hold it while tensing muscles, and to let it go while releasing. Should any muscle group not respond after four trials, move on and return to it later.

Caution: Some subjects may develop muscle cramps or spasms from prolonged tension of muscles. If this occurs, shorten the tension interval a few seconds, and instruct the subject not to tense muscles quite so hard.

Although the word hypnosis is not to be used, progressive relaxation, properly executed, does seem to create a state resembling a light hypnotic-trance state, with the subject more susceptible to suggestion. Relaxation may be further deepened by repetition of suggestions of warmth, relaxation, and so on. Some subjects may actually report sensations of disassociation from their bodies. This is complete relaxation and is to be expected. Subjects should be instructed to speak as little as possible while under relaxation.

In bringing subjects back to "normal," use the numerical method of trance termination: "I'm going to count from one to four. On the count of one, start moving your legs; two, your fingers and hands; three, your head; and four, open your eyes and sit up. One—move your legs; two—now your fingers and hands; three—move your head around; four—open your eyes and sit up." Always check to see that the subject feels well, alert, and so on, before leaving.

The subject should be instructed to practice relaxation twice a day between sessions. He/she should not work at it more than 15 minutes at a time, and should not practice twice within any 3-hour period. He/she should practice alone. Relaxation may be used for getting to sleep if practiced while the subject is horizontal; if the subject does not wish to sleep, he/she should practice sitting up. Properly timed, relaxation can be used for a "second wind" during study.

By the third session, if the subject has been practicing well, relaxation may be induced merely by focusing attention on the muscle groups and instructing the subject to "concentrate on muscles becoming relaxed, warm," and so on. However, if the subject has difficulty following straight suggestions, return to the use of tension release.

Behavioral Rehearsal

Allowing individuals to "act out" or "role play" their interpersonal problems and usual manner of behaving is used in many different forms of psychotherapy. In behavior therapy, role playing or behavioral rehearsal methods attempt to simulate real-life situations and to train individuals how to perform new behavior patterns. The therapist often "models" or "coaches" the appropriate behavior that a client may be lacking. A client lacking appropriate dating behavior, for instance, would be taught appropriate skills through behavioral rehearsal. Likewise, a patient undergoing an aversive medical procedure or surgery can learn ways to cope with it by rehearsing optimal response. Such procedures are being used more and more in teaching social skills for a variety of interpersonal situations.

Related to these procedures are **assertiveness training** techniques, used with individuals who experience distress and anxiety because of problems in asserting themselves. Because people sometimes lack the confidence or the skills to assert themselves and to make their wishes known, they fail repeatedly to represent their needs effectively and experience distress due to their inability to do so. This can create interpersonal anxiety. Salter (1949) developed a method to teach socially inhibited people how to express their feelings to others more strongly and effectively. Subsequently, McFall and colleagues (McFall and Lillesand, 1971; McFall and Marston, 1970; McFall and Twentyman, 1973) reported the therapeutic effectiveness of assertiveness training in reducing anxiety in various interpersonal situations.

Contingency Management

Contingency management refers to the process of changing the frequency of a behavior by controlling the consequences of that behavior. In the process of shaping a rat to press a bar, food reinforcement is developed only after the rat has made a correct response. The experimenter controls or manages the contingency between reinforcement (delivery of food) and a certain behavior (bar-pressing responses) in order to increase the frequency of that behavior. Any attempt to change the frequency of a behavior by systematically controlling consequences such as reinforcement is called **contingency management**.

We all use contingency management procedures in everyday life, although sometimes inconsistently. The parent rewards or punishes the child for some behavior, or the employer gives a bonus to an employee for some outstanding work performance. These are attempts to encourage or discourage particular behaviors by associating with them some consequence that is either desirable or undesirable. Behavior therapists have developed some systematic contingency management programs to alter a wide range of behaviors.

One particularly effective type of contingency management technique is the **token economy** program. Token economy programs have been shown to be effective in modifying and controlling deviant behaviors, even the bizarre behavior patterns and problems of schizophrenics in hospitalized settings (Ayllon and Azrin, 1968; Krasner, 1968). This approach has been among the most successful rehabilitation programs for hospitalized patients as well as in classrooms. In these programs undesirable behaviors are identified, and more desirable behaviors that are incompatible with the problem responses are defined. Individuals are systematically reinforced with tokens whenever they engage in the socially desirable behavior. Tokens are exchanged for something desirable such as candy or special privileges. Modifications of this, such as rewarding oneself for each day of abstinence after quitting smoking or having a new outfit for every so many pounds of weight that are lost, are common.

Stimulus Control

An important element in operant conditioning is the concept of a discriminative stimulus or cue. When we are driving a car, we routinely stop at a traffic light when it turns red. We are aware of the necessity of performing such a behavior in order to avoid getting a ticket or, even worse, being involved in a traffic accident. The traffic light serves as a discriminative cue or stimulus for the behavior (stopping the car) to occur. It informs us that a particular response is likely to be rewarded. As another example, a school-crossing sign is a discriminative stimulus for slowing down the speed of your car. Thus, a discriminative stimulus tells us when and where it is appropriate to emit a certain behavior in order to receive reinforcement or to avoid aversive consequences (e.g., receiving a traffic ticket for exceeding the speed limit).

Strictly defined, a *discriminative stimulus* is an environmental cue that informs us when it is likely that a response or behavior will be reinforced. Discriminative stimuli provide an occasion for the occurrence of an operant response. Behavior that is prompted by a discriminative cue or stimulus is termed to be under *stimulus control.* A wide variety of problem behaviors are under stimulus control, and many behaviors occur more frequently in some situations than in others.

In a classic study by Stuart (1967) the principle of stimulus control was used effectively in an obesity treatment program, giving rise to widespread use of behavioral programs for weight control. Stuart's original treatment program consisted of gradually restricting and eliminating stimuli that had come to elicit maladaptive eating behavior. For example, the program involved guidelines such as restricting eating to specific times and places; not eating while engaged in other enjoyable activities like watching television, listening to the radio, and so on; getting rid of fattening foods; and avoiding restaurants or grocery shopping when hungry. Stimulus control was dealt with by restricting eating to appropriate times and places and by eliminating eating cues from the environment.

Using this stimulus control approach, Stuart's program produced remarkable success. At a 1-year follow-up clients in the program had lost from 26 to 46 pounds. Although weight losses of this magnitude have not been consistently found in studies conducted since, the behavioral treatment of obesity has been effective (Stunkard, 1979). Later in this chapter we will review another effective behavioral weight reduction program developed by Mahoney, Moura, and Wade (1973). We will also discuss these issues in Chapter 12. These behavioral treatment programs continue to show success in significantly modifying some maladaptive overeating. Stimulus control procedures have also been found to be effective with a variety of other problem behaviors such as insomnia (Bootzin, 1973) and poor study habits (Goldiamond, 1965). Importantly, they are also useful in the comprehensive management of many medical disorders. One way of controlling asthmatic attacks, for example, is to learn the stimuli that may trigger an asthmatic attack and to avoid them. We can readily learn to become sensitive to stimuli such as a smoke-filled room, strong odors, or a setting requiring heavy physical exertion (Creer and Bender, 1994). In reducing pain the use of stimulus control is also indicated (Sanders 1996). It is not uncommon for patients to show more overt pain behaviors when in the presence of some people (such as a doctor), or when pain becomes a topic of conversation.

COGNITIVE-BEHAVIORAL THERAPY TECHNIQUES

In recent years there has been increased attention to modifying maladaptive cognitions as well as behavior. Albert Ellis (1962) originally developed **rational-emotive therapy (RET)** on the assumption that cognitions can produce emotions. He assumed that psychological disorders such as neuroses are caused by faulty or irrational patterns of thinking. Accordingly, he indicated that the focus of therapy should be directed at changing the internal or covert sentences that people say to themselves and that produce negative emotional responses. Summarizing the results of 172 case histories of clients whom he treated with either RET or traditional psychoanalytic therapy, Ellis (1962) found RET to be the more effective treatment. Although this was far from a controlled outcome evaluation study, it did suggest the potential effectiveness of his therapy technique. More important, it prompted more behavior therapists to begin to use his basic technique as a "cognitive-restructuring" method with a variety of behavioral disorders (Goldfried and Davison, 1976).

At the same time, Beck and colleagues (1979) began to develop a cognitive-behavioral therapy approach for the treatment of depression (Beck, 1967).

Their method focused on the cognitive distortions prevalent in the thinking, evaluation, and attitudes of depressed people. Therapy was directed at correcting these cognitive distractions that are assumed to underlie the depression. Their cognitive approach has also been effective (Beck et al., 1979).

Cognitive Restructuring

Meichenbaum (1972) has also successfully used a cognitive approach—termed **cognitive restructuring**—to modify anxiety. In this procedure the therapist determines the specific thoughts or self-verbalizations that are presumed to give rise to the anxiety. The therapist then assists the client in modifying these negative self-verbalizations and in replacing them with positive self-statements.

Like systematic desensitization, cognitive restructuring has been shown to be highly effective in reducing anxiety. In terms of the differential effectiveness of those two therapy techniques Rimm and Masters (1974) have suggested that systematic desensitization may be more effective with clients who show a relatively small number of phobias or fears, whereas those who experience multiple fears in a great many interpersonal situations might profit more from cognitive restructuring techniques. Additional research is needed to test experimentally the validity of their suggestion.

Another cognitive restructuring method that has been developed is **thought-stopping**. It is used with clients who experience distress because of repeated or obsessive thoughts that they have difficulty controlling. There are reasons to believe that suppression of disturbing thoughts may have negative effects on mood and health as well as result in more frequent distressing thoughts (Pennebaker, 1995; Schwartz and Kline, 1995; Wegner and Zanakos, 1994). However, if a patient can learn to start and stop thinking intentionally about a stressor, some control may be gained, and evidence shows that thought-stopping procedures are effective in dealing with obsessional thinking (Rimm and Masters, 1974).

These cognitive restructuring procedures are not only effective in treating anxiety experienced by neurotic individuals, but are also useful in reducing anxiety and stress. They may be effective in allowing patients to cope more successfully with stressors that are intimately linked with the precipitation or exacerbation of physical symptoms. Also, as we noted in Chapter 8, these procedures can be effective in reducing distress associated with surgery.

Self-Control Techniques

There has been a great deal of interest in developing self-control or self-management strategies for modifying problem behaviors. How can we best train an individual to control and alter his or her own behavior? There have been a number of self-control strategies developed, with the main goal of training people to use self-management methods for dealing with problem behaviors. For example, the obese person is taught to use self-control methods to lose weight, the heavy smoker to decrease smoking, the exceedingly tense person to manage stress.

An example of an early study of different self-control methods for treating obesity was the five-group study reported by Mahoney, Moura, and Wade

(1973). The design included a *control group*, which merely received information about the program with no specific treatment; *self-monitoring group*, which was asked simply to monitor its daily weight during the program; *self-reward group*, which used money as a reward (in such a procedure a therapist may instruct the client to set aside a specified amount of money toward the purchase of a desired item each time a certain amount of weight loss occurs); *self-punishment group*, in which a fine of a specified amount was levied if weight was not lost; and a *combined self-reward/self-punishment group*, in which the procedures of groups 3 and 4 were combined.

In the self-control groups (3, 4, and 5) subjects were given suggestions on the contingencies to be used (e.g., reward yourself for *x* amount of pounds lost), but they were free to self-reward or self-punish as they saw fit. Thus, the goal was to have them personally use a self-control strategy (contingent reinforcement) to help modify their weight.

Results of this study are summarized in Figure 10.1. Subjects in the two self-reward groups (groups 3 and 5) lost significantly more weight than the subjects in the self-punishment-only group (group 4). The fact that this latter group did not lose any more weight than the control and self-monitoring groups suggests that self-punishment is not a very effective procedure. Self-reward strategies appear to be the more powerful and promising techniques for self-regulated change of behavior. In such procedures:

FIGURE 10.1. Weight loss with different self-management procedures. *Source:* M. J. Mahoney, N. G. M. Moura, and T. C. Wade. The relative efficacy of self-reward, self-punishment, and self-monitoring techniques for weight loss. *Journal of Consulting and Clinical Psychology,* 1973, *40,* 404–407. Copyright © 1973 by the American Psychological Association. Reprinted by permission of the author.

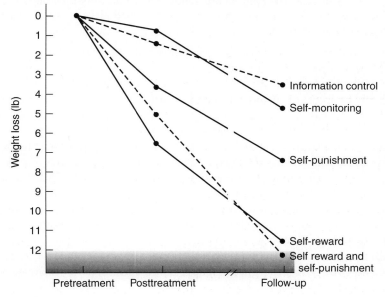

Individuals can reinforce themselves in a number of ways. Tangible rewards—such as money and gift certificates—have been shown to be effective in many applications. More recently, persons have been trained to self-reward privately (i.e., via a thought) as a means of strengthening or maintaining behavior. Likewise, they may enlist social support for their actions such that their self-reward strategies are supplemented by the compliments and encouragement of family and friends. (Mahoney and Arnkoff, 1979, p. 91)

Self-control procedures are effective in dealing with a wide range of problem behaviors. A comprehensive review of the various strategies can be found in Mahoney and Arnkoff (1979). These procedures are being widely used for a variety of medical conditions, such as the self-management of diabetes mellitus (Goodall and Halford, 1991). In these situations the basic approach is to encourage patients to pay attention to specific adaptive behaviors that they can control (Gatchel and Blanchard, 1994). The use of coping self-statements and self-reinforcement when adaptive behaviors are controlled is an important aspect of most cognitive-behavioral interventions (Turner and Romano, 1990).

Biofeedback

Before Harry Houdini performed one of his famous escapes, a skeptical committee would search his clothes and body. When the members of the committee were satisfied that the Great Houdini was concealing no keys, they would put chains, padlocks and handcuffs on him. . . . Of course, not even Houdini could open a padlock without a key, and when he was safely behind the curtain he would cough one up. He could hold a key suspended in his throat and regurgitate it when he was unobserved. . . . The trick behind many of Houdini's escapes was in some ways just as amazing as the escape itself. Ordinarily when an object is stuck in a person's throat he will start to gag. He can't help it—it's an unlearned, automatic reflex. But Houdini had learned to control his gag reflex by practicing for hours with a small piece of potato tied to a string. (Lang, 1970, p. 23)

Through the years other unusual instances of voluntary control over physiological functions have been noted in the scientific literature. Lindsley and Sassamon (1938) reported the case of a middle-aged male who had the ability to control the erection of hairs over the entire surface of his body. McClure (1959) noted the case of an individual who could voluntarily produce complete cardiac arrest for periods of several seconds at a time. Numerous instances of voluntary acceleration of heart rate were reported by Ogden and Shock (1939). Russian psychologist Luria (1958) described a mnemonist who had attained remarkable control of his heart rate and skin temperature. This individual could abruptly alter his heart rate by 40 beats per minute. He could also raise the skin temperature of one hand while simultaneously lowering the temperature of the other hand. It has also been documented that many yogis can control various physiological responses at will.

Such acts of bodily control have traditionally been viewed as rare feats that only certain extraordinarily gifted people could accomplish. However, in more recent years behavioral scientists have demonstrated that the average person can learn a degree of control over physiological responses. The principle training method developed and utilized in this learning process has been labeled **biofeedback**.

The biofeedback technique is based on the fundamental learning principle that we learn to perform a particular response when we receive feedback or information about the consequence of the response we have just made and then make appropriate adjustments. This is how we learn to perform the wide variety of skills and behaviors that we use in everyday activities. For example, we learn how to drive a car by receiving continuous feedback about how much we need to turn the steering wheel in order to turn the car a certain distance, or how much pressure we must apply to the accelerator in order to make the car move at a certain speed. If we were denied this feedback—as, for instance, by being blindfolded—we would never receive useful information about the consequences of our driving responses. We would therefore never be able to learn the appropriate adjustments needed to perform a successful maneuver with the car. Information feedback is thus very important. Indeed, Annent (1969) has reviewed numerous experimental studies demonstrating the importance of feedback in the learning and performance of a wide variety of motor skills.

The availability of feedback is also important in learning how to control internal physiological responses. Since we do not receive feedback of these internal events in day-to-day life, we cannot control them. However, if a person is provided biofeedback of, say, blood pressure via a visual display monitor, he or she can become aware of the consequences of blood pressure changes and how adjustments can be made to modify and eventually control it. Receiving feedback removes one's "blindfold," thus enabling one to learn how to control a response voluntarily. The recent development of sensitive physiological recording devices and digital logic circuitry has made it possible to detect small changes in visceral events and to provide subjects with immediate biofeedback of these events.

Since the initial pioneering experiments with animal subjects conducted in the late 1950s and early 1960s by Neal Miller (1969), there have been demonstrations of human subjects' learned control of a variety of what were once assumed to be "involuntary responses"—blood pressure, heart rate, sweat gland activity, skin temperature, neuromuscular activity, various brain wave rhythms, and even penile tumescence. Unfortunately, research evaluating the therapeutic effectiveness of biofeedback procedures has been plagued by a number of problems. There is still a lack of systematic, well-controlled studies that demonstrate conclusively the clinical effectiveness of these techniques. For the most part, claims of effectiveness have been based on uncontrolled group or single case studies. A great deal of research is still needed to determine whether biofeedback techniques are active therapeutic procedures or merely powerful placebo conditions. Reports have suggested that placebo factors play a significant role in clinical application of biofeedback (Gatchel, 1979; Katkin and Goldband, 1979). (See the box "The Placebo Effect.") Also, an important question that needs to be addressed in biofeedback evaluation research is whether biofeedback procedures are significantly superior to less expensive

The Placebo Effect

The *placebo effect* was originally shown to be an important factor in medical research when it was found that many times inert chemical drugs, which had no direct effect on physical events underlying various medical disorders, produced symptom reduction. Extensive literature on the placebo effect undeniably demonstrates that the *belief* by the patient that a prescribed medication is active, even if it is in fact chemically inert, often leads to significant symptom reduction (Shapiro, 1971). In a review of the placebo effect, Shapiro (1971) gives this definition:

A placebo is defined as any therapy, or that component of any therapy, that is deliberately used for its nonspecific, psychologic, or psychophysiologic effect, or that is used for its presumed specific effect on a patient, symptom, or illness, but which, unknown to patient and therapist, is without specific activity for the condition being treated. . . . A placebo, when used as a control in experimental studies, is defined as a substance or procedure that is without specific activity for the condition being evaluated. . . . The placebo effect is defined as the nonspecific, psychologic or psychophysiologic effect produced by placebos (p. 440).

In the area of drug therapy Shapiro (1971) notes that for centuries the use of medication has been largely a placebo-effect process, with chemically inert or inactive drugs producing therapeutic improvement in people who believed that these drugs or "magic potions" would help them. Frank (1961) has presented evidence that improvement in various physical and psychological problems can occur after a patient ingests a pill that a physician has suggested will help to alleviate the problem. Frank also notes that placebo effects are similar to many faith-healing procedures in which the individual believes he or she will be helped.

The placebo effect has also been found to be an active ingredient in psychotherapy/behavior therapy, especially when anxiety is being treated (Shapiro, 1971). As Shapiro (1971) indicates, the effect appears to be a "multidetermined phenomenon" that is not yet completely understood. It has also been shown to be an important factor in biofeedback treatment (Gatchel, 1979). One important psychological factor contributing to the placebo effect that has been shown to affect the outcome of psychotherapy is generalized expectancy of improvement (Wilkins, 1973). Research is continuing in this important field. In Chapter 11 we will review some research suggesting the importance of endorphins (endogenous opiatelike substances emanating from the brain) in mediating the placebo effect. Regardless of the exact psychophysiological mechanism ultimately found to be involved in this effect, therapists and physicians need to be aware of the potentially powerful and positive impact that the placebo effect can have in the treatment of a wide range of medical and psychological disorders.

and more easily administered methods such as muscle relaxation training and other behavioral techniques. Nevertheless, biofeedback has become a very important and widely used behavioral treatment technique.

Research has shown some degree of success in reducing the symptoms of essential hypertension with biofeedback. Blood pressure can be effectively reduced by using biofeedback (Glasgow and Engel, 1987). However, biofeedback is still an experimental form of treatment for hypertension, with little known about the exact physiological mechanisms involved in the process. Thus, it cannot be considered an alternative to pharmacologic treatment at this time. It should be noted, though, that a study reported by Luborsky et al. (1980) compared the relative efficacy of medication, relaxation training, and biofeedback during a 6-week treatment program with moderately hypertensive individuals. It was found that although patients given medication derived the most benefit even at moderate levels of medication, some patients experienced comparable benefits from the two behavioral treatments. These investigators suggest that hypertensive individuals who are strongly motivated to adhere to a behavioral treatment program should be encouraged to undergo such treatment first to assess whether it is beneficial before being put on medication. This is an interesting suggestion that certainly merits additional investigation.

Biofeedback is often used as one component in a more comprehensive behavioral intervention. For example, Fahrian et al. (1986) used a multimodal behavioral treatment that included biofeedback. They found that of the 54 medicated patients, 54 percent were able to eliminate their hypertensive medication while at the same time reducing blood pressure by 18/10 mmHg. There are other studies such as this. As Glasgow and Engel (1987) note, though, the variety of behavioral interventions reported to be effective for some patients is still quite great. More research is needed to develop a standard method of selecting the best behavioral treatment program to offer to specific patients.

The few cases available indicate that heart rate biofeedback seems to be effective in the treatment of cardiac arrhythmias such as sinus tachycardia, atrial fibrillation, and premature ventricular contractions (see Hatch, Gatchel, and Harrington, 1982). However, judgment must be withheld with regard to therapeutic value of biofeedback for such disorders generally until more research is conducted. Similarly, biofeedback appears to be useful in treating Raynaud's disease, a condition characterized by recurrent attacks of paroxysmal vasospasm in the hands or feet, commonly triggered by exposure to cold or emotional stress. Since specific vasomotor responding has repeatedly been shown to occur with skin temperature biofeedback in normal subjects (Taub, 1977), this would seem to be an appropriate technique for reducing vasospastic attacks of Raynaud's disease, and have shown that behavioral treatment, with biofeedback as a basic component, can be very effective and equal the best clinical effects of many medical and surgical interventions (Surwit and Jordan, 1987).

There have been many published reports of the clinical efficacy of biofeedback in treating **migraine headache**. A careful and critical review of this literature suggests that some caution should be maintained. Many early studies in the area are flawed by inadequate control groups, inappropriate statistical analysis, small sample size, brief pretreatment baseline and posttreatment follow-up periods, and the use of "treatment package" techniques that confound the effects of biofeedback with those of other components of therapy. However, in a review of the literature Blanchard and Andrasik (1987) concluded that temperature biofeedback combined with autogenic training is more effective than no treatment and possibly superior to placebo treatments.

Similarly, a number of controlled group outcome studies have shown that treatments involving biofeedback are more effective than inactive control procedures for tension headaches. A number of these studies have included follow-up evaluations conducted several months following the end of treatment, and the results indicate that clinical gains are often maintained. Moreover, the effects of biofeedback exceed those for medication placebo, biofeedback placebo, and psychotherapy placebo procedures (Andrasik and Blanchard,

1987). Research also suggests that biofeedback is useful in treating gastrointestinal disorders, epileptic seizures, nervous system disease, muscle pain, sexual dysfunction, and other disorders (see Gatchel and Price, 1979; Whitehead, 1992).

It has been amply demonstrated that some degree of self-control is possible over behaviors long assumed to be completely involuntary. It has also been shown that, with biofeedback, it is possible to extend voluntary control to pathophysiological responding in order to modify this maladaptive behavior in the direction of health. These are highly significant achievements. However, many important questions still remain as to how medically effective biofeedback will be. It would be extremely helpful also to compare biofeedback techniques with more traditional medical treatments, some of which have fairly well-established success rates. Combinations of medical and behavioral techniques should also be explored and evaluated. These studies will be most informative if they are designed so that the unique contribution of each individual technique, as well as the combined effect, can be isolated and reliably measured.

BROAD-SPECTRUM COGNITIVE BEHAVIORAL THERAPY

Lazarus (1971) has coined the term broad-spectrum behavior therapy to emphasize the fact that most behavior therapists employ several different treatment procedures for a specific disorder in an attempt to deal effectively with all the important controlling or causal variables. Just as traditional psychoanalytic therapy attempts to determine the underlying unconscious or "root" cause of a behavior disorder, cognitive-behavioral therapy seeks to assess the major causes of such behavior. However, the search is not for underlying unconscious causes, which are difficult to assess reliably but for the learned and environmental determinants or causes. As Bandura (1969) notes, if by "searching for the cause of a disorder" one means the search for the strongest and most significant causal and controlling variables, then the goal and task of all therapists, traditional psychotherapists as well as behavior therapists, is the same. The chief difference is that behavior therapists assume that the search for environmental determinants and the direct modification of behavior is heuristically the most feasible and effective approach, whereas traditional psychotherapists assume that it is more important to uncover and attempt to treat unconscious motivations of behavior.

Most behavior therapists therefore use several different treatment procedures for a specific disorder in order to deal effectively with all the important controlling or causal variables. Fortunately, behavior therapists have a number of very effective procedures in their treatment arsenal—systematic desensitization and its variants, progressive relaxation training, behavioral rehearsal and assertiveness training, self-control techniques, cognitive-restructuring and thought-stopping procedures, and biofeedback, to name a few that we have discussed in this chapter. For a more comprehensive review of these as well as other cognitive-behavioral techniques there are a number of excellent books available (see Bootzin, 1975; Dobson, 1988; Mahoney, 1974; Meichenbaum, 1977; Rimm and Masters, 1974).

The availability of a variety of different treatment methods gives broad-spectrum behavior therapy a major advantage over traditional forms of psychotherapy, in which the same general form of therapy is applied to all disorders. The traditional "general" psychotherapy approach has not been very successful in dealing with the various forms of abnormal and maladaptive behavior (Mears and Gatchel, 1979). Cognitive-behavioral therapy has taken the approach of developing specific treatment techniques to deal with particular disorders. In recent years there has also been more effort to individualize treatment so that the type of treatment employed is tailored to the specific disorder and characteristics of the patient. Goldstein and Stein (1976) published a text entitled *Prescriptive Psychotherapies*, which initially introduced the concept of attempting to outline the type of treatment that is most effective in dealing with specific disorders. Such an approach helps to ensure the appropriate matching of patient-therapist-treatment variables to produce the most successful therapeutic outcomes.

As an example of the broad-spectrum or multimodal approach to treatment, take the case of treating hypertension. In training an individual with hypertension to relax and voluntarily to lower his or her blood pressure level, the therapist might initially use progressive muscle relaxation and then blood pressure biofeedback. The therapist might also teach the patient new methods for more effectively coping with stressful situations, as blood pressure can be temporarily elevated as the result of inability to cope with perceived aggression or frustration (see Hokanson and Burgess, 1962). The individual might need to learn interpersonal social skills, such as assertiveness training, or cognitive restructuring techniques in order to cope more successfully with such stressors.

Other examples abound in the literature. For example, a cognitive-behavioral therapy package was developed for children who were undergoing painful medical procedures such as bone marrow aspirations and lumbar punctures (see Jay et al., 1991). The package consisted of filmed modeling, breathing exercises, imagery distraction, positive incentive, and behavioral rehearsal. These investigators have found that such a multimodal cognitive-behavioral treatment package significantly reduced children's procedure-related distress across self-report, observable behavior, and physiological indices of anxiety and distress. A recent text by Gatchel and Blanchard (1993) reviews a wide range of psychophysiological disorders for which multimodal cognitive-behavioral approaches have been effectively employed.

There have also been many effective **stress management methods** developed that combine a variety of cognitive-behavioral procedures for personal and work-related stress (Charlesworth and Nathan, 1982; Davis, Eshelman and McKay, 1988; Meichenbaum and Jaremko, 1983). Such methods use modalities such as cognitive restructuring, imagery and distraction, muscle relaxation, and biofeedback. There has been evidence for the treatment efficacy of such stress management treatment packages (Meichenbaum and Jaremko, 1983).

SUMMARY

In this chapter we have discussed a variety of cognitive-behavioral treatment procedures that have been successfully employed with problem behaviors often seen in medical settings. These techniques were developed on the basis of some major learning principles demonstrated to modify behavior—classical conditioning, operant conditioning, and observational learning-modeling. Systematic desensitization, developed by Wolpe, has been found to be effective in the treatment of a variety of medical phobias. Progressive muscle relaxation, which is an important component of the systematic desensitization treatment process, can often serve as a powerful therapeutic technique in its own right for the treatment of stress-related disorders. Modeling procedures, originally developed by Bandura, have been found to reduce fear and anxiety. Behavioral rehearsal procedures, such as assertiveness training, are used in teaching social skills for a variety of interpersonal situations. Contingency management procedures can be used effectively in a wide variety of settings (e.g., schools, homes, hospitals) to change behavior. They are also being used more and more to increase compliance to medical regimens. Stimulus control procedures have been found to be effective with a variety of problem behaviors such as obesity and insomnia. We also reviewed a number of cognitive-behavioral therapy techniques, such as cognitive restructuring and self-control methods. In addition, we reviewed the use of biofeedback for medically related disorders and pointed out its clinical utility. Finally, we noted the current trend of multimodal or broad-spectrum behavior therapy. This approach emphasized the use of several different treatment procedures for a specific disorder in an attempt to deal effectively with all the important controlling or causal variables involved.

RECOMMENDED READINGS

Andrasik, F., and Blanchard, E. B. The biofeedback treatment of tension headache. In J. P. Hatch, J. G. Fisher, and J. D. Rugh (Eds.), *Biofeedback: Studies in clinical efficacy.* New York: Plenum, 1987, pp. 281–322.

Beck A. T., Rush, A. J., Shaw, B. J., and Emery, G. *Cognitive therapy of depression: A treatment manual.* New York: Guilford Press, 1979.

Burish, T. G., and Jenkins, R. A. Effectiveness of biofeedback and relaxation training in reducing the side effects of cancer chemotherapy. *Health Psychology,* 1992, *11,* 17–23.

Glasgow, M. S., and Engel, B. T. Clinical issues in biofeedback and relaxation therapy for hypertension: Review and recommendations. In J. P. Hatch, J. G. Fisher, and J. D. Rugh (Eds.), *Biofeedback: Studies in clinical efficacy.* New York: Plenum Press, 1987, pp. 81–122.

Goodall, T. A., and Halford, W. K. Self-management of diabetes mellitus: A critical review. *Health Psychology,* 1991, *10,* 1–8.

Meichenbaum, D., and Jaremko, M. E. (Eds.), *Stress reduction and prevention.* New York: Plenum Press, 1987.

Surwit, R. S., and Jordan, J. S. Behavioral treatment of Raynaud's Syndrome. In J. P. Hatch, J. G. Fisher, and J. D. Rugh (Eds.), *Biofeedback: Studies in clinical efficacy.* New York: Plenum Press, 1987, pp. 255–280.

CHAPTER 11

Pain and Pain Management

Few topics in health psychology or medicine are like pain. It is clearly a physical sensation—when we touch something hot, we feel a sharp pain that tells us to withdraw our hand. When we cut ourselves, fall and scrape a knee, or otherwise injure ourselves, we feel pain, and it is real! Yet we also talk about pain that is not physical—the pain of breaking up with a girlfriend or boyfriend, or leaving home for the first time, or of saying goodbye to friends we will not see again for a year or more. Pain can have different sensory qualities—it can be shooting, burning, or throbbing pain, or it can be a dull ache that is just annoying enough to distract us from what we want to do. There is pain that is physical but pleasant, as in the pain associated with exercise and the pain associated with being hungry and having eaten too much. How can something be both physical and ethereal, both pleasant and unpleasant? As one of the most common complaints people bring to their doctors, nurses, and dentists, or as one of the best ways to diagnose what is wrong with a patient, or as the target of multimillion dollar drug development and marketing, pain is a complex component of health and well-being that has been and will continue to be the focus of a good deal of research. As hard as we have tried, however, we still are not exactly sure that we know what pain really is or how to detect it.

The scientific study of pain and the development of approaches to reducing pain have been extensive enterprises because pain is such a common complaint in medical settings. Hundreds of thousands actively seek relief from unbearable pain and most of us experience intrusive pain from time to time. At least one-third of us experience pain at some time that requires medical attention, and pain is responsible for almost 80 percent of medical complaints (Salovey et al., 1992). It has also been a significant problem because we have not been effective in treating pain. The success rates for traditional medical approaches to certain chronic pain problems (e.g., low back pain) rarely exceed 60 percent. Long-term success rates are often below 30 percent improvement (Loesser, 1974). Traditionally, one of the contributing factors to this poor success has been the way that medicine has dichotomized pain complaints as either "organic" or "psychogenic" in nature. This is, as you might expect, an overly simplistic conceptualization of pain. It has seriously hampered the physician's ability to understand fully the patient and her or his pain. As we will see in this chapter, pain is a complex phenomenon that involves physiological sensations and mechanisms but also significant behavioral/psychological components. A model of pain that integrates both physiological and psychological components has the best chance of allowing a comprehensive understanding of the pain process, and has important implications and practical applications for the assessment and treatment of individuals with pain.

THE PHYSIOLOGICAL BASES OF PAIN

The Physiology of Pain

Traditionally, pain has been conceptualized as some specific type of activity in the sensory nervous system. As Melzack (1973) noted:

> The best classical description of the theory was provided by Descartes in 1644, who conceived of the pain system as a straight-through channel from the skin to the brain. He suggested that the system is like the bell-ringing mechanism in a church: a man pulls the rope at the bottom of the tower, and the bell rings in the belfry. So too, he proposed, a flame sets particles in the foot into activity and the motion is transmitted up the leg and back into the head, where, presumably, something like an alarm system is set off. The person feels pain and responds to it (p. 126).

A more formal model of pain was proposed by Von Frey in 1894 (Melzack and Wall, 1965). This *specificity theory of pain* assumed that there were specific sensory receptors responsible for the transmission of sensations such as touch, warmth, and pain. Various sensory receptors were thought to have different structures, and these differences made them sensitive to different kinds of stimulation. Pain was viewed as having specific central and peripheral mechanisms similar to those of other bodily senses.

At approximately the same time that Von Frey was proposing his specificity theory of pain, Goldschneider presented an alternative conceptualization that was called the *pattern theory of pain* (Melzack and Wall, 1965). Goldschneider argued that pain sensations were the result of the transmission of nerve impulse *patterns* originating from, and coded at, the peripheral stimulation site. Differences in the patterning and quantity of peripheral nerve-fiber discharges were viewed as the cause of differences in the quality of sensation. A minimal tactile stimulus to an area might cause a feeling of touch, whereas stronger tactile stimuli would cause pain. If the same nerve fibers were stimulated and discharged, it was argued, then the difference in sensation had to be due to an increased discharge. The pattern of stimulation produced by a specific stimulus then had to be coded by the central nervous system. Therefore, the experience of pain was the result of central nervous system coding of nerve impulse patterns, and not simply the result of a specific connection between pain receptors and pain sites.

Research has shown that these theories are not sufficient to explain pain, but some support for each has been reported. In support of the specificity theory, for example, Bonica (1953) reported that there is a unique and specific experience of pain originating in the skin when appropriate stimulation is administered. Moreover, he also identified two sets of sensory fibers that had stimulus-specific conducting properties that were clearly involved in the transmission of pain. In partial support of the pattern theory Melzack and Wall (1965) found that skin receptors have some specialized properties by which they can transmit particular types and ranges of stimulation in the form of patterns of impulses.

However, a number of reported findings cannot be taken into account by either of them. For example, research (to be discussed in the next section) has indicated that psychological factors such as anxiety can significantly affect the pain experienced from a noxious stimulus. This intervening psychological mechanism is not taken into account by the specificity theory, which proposes a specific and direct stimulus-response chain. Another inadequacy of the specificity theory is its failure to explain why surgical intervention techniques that break the specific connection between peripheral body sites and central pain mechanisms (e.g., nerve severing) have not produced widespread therapeutic effects in alleviating chronic pain.

The pattern theory of pain, on the other hand, does not take into account the physiological evidence of nerve-fiber specialization that Bonica (1953) originally reported. Thus, although both the specificity and pattern theories take into account physiological mechanisms of pain perception, neither of them can comprehensively deal with the complex mechanism of pain perception. Moreover, the ever-evolving field of neurotransmitter mechanisms and the endogenous opioids have introduced additional complexities that these models cannot effectively incorporate. Pain is no longer viewed as the result of a straight-through transmission of impulse from the skin to the brain.

Recent research has demonstrated a number of structures within the nervous system that appear to be involved in pain. The term **nociceptor** has replaced the older term *pain receptor* in order to highlight the fact that these sensory units contribute to the pain experience rather than create it. Nociceptors are nerve endings that transmit pain. They are specialized transducer-like units that terminate in the skin, muscle, deep tissues, and the viscera (see Figure 11.1). There are two major groups of peripheral nerve fibers that are involved in nociception. **A-delta** fibers are small myelinated fibers that appear to mediate immediate or sharp pain (myelination of neurons increases the speed of transmission by the nerve). **C fibers** are even smaller nerve fibers that are unmyelinated. These slower-transmitting nerves appear to give rise to diffuse and dull or aching pain. Approximately one-half of C fibers are nociceptors.

There are two basic classes of these *A-delta* and *C fibers*. One class of these fibers include *mechanical nociceptors* that respond maximally to intense mechanical stimulation. The other class of fibers are called *polymodal nociceptors* because they respond maximally to mechanical *and* temperature stimulation. They may also be activated in tissue damage by chemicals released in the body such as serotonin, histamine, and prostaglandin.

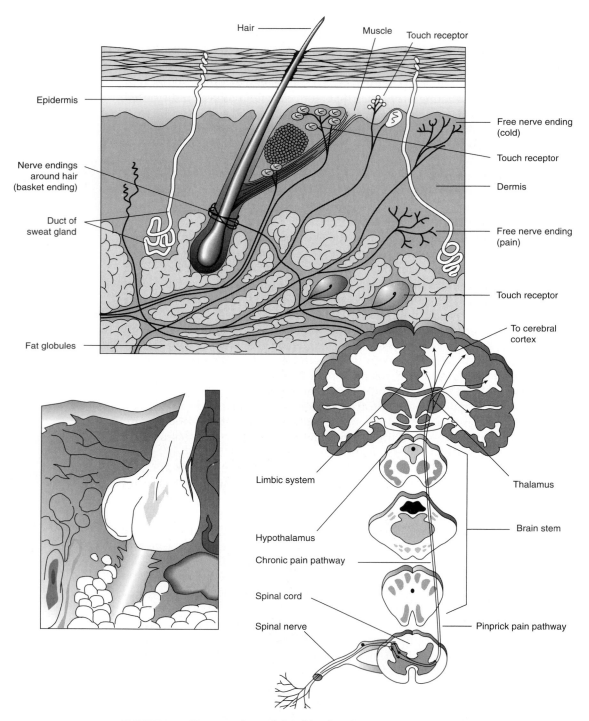

FIGURE 11.1. Cross section of the skin showing sensory receptors for pain, pressure, and temperature. Each serves a different function and provides distinctive sensory information.

These peripheral nerve fibers enter the spinal cord through the dorsal horn (see Figure 11.2) where they undergo considerable modulation from within the dorsal horn as well as descending impulses from higher brain centers. Neurotransmitters also affect the transmission of pain by these nociceptors. Substance P appears to be necessary for pain to be experienced, as do other chemical agents in the body (see Whipple, 1987). The incoming pathway from the dorsal horn crosses to the opposite segment of the spinal cord and then rises in the spinothalamic tract to the brain. It also reaches the cortex by alternative pathways to the reticular activating system with widespread subsequent radiation to lower and higher brain centers.

Thus, nociceptive stimuli travel from the periphery to the cerebral cortex via specific afferent pathways to specific brain sites. However, this pathway is subject to modulation along the way at several sites in the dorsal horn, the spinothalamic tract, and in lower and higher brain centers. This helps to explain why an incoming pain signal can be affected by other factors. As we will see next, the role of other sources of modulation has required changing conceptualizations of pain.

The Gate Control Theory of Pain

In 1965 Melzack and Wall introduced the **gate control theory** to take into account the many diverse factors involved in pain perception. The theory is not perfect and has its limitations, but it successfully introduced the scientific community to the importance of central and psychological factors in the pain perception process. It also gave form to the potentially significant role that psychological factors play (Melzack, 1993).

This theory assumes that there are a number of structures within the central nervous system that contribute to pain. The interplay among structures is critical in determining if, and to what extent, a specific stimulus leads to pain. Pain is not the result of a "straight-through" transmission of impulses from the

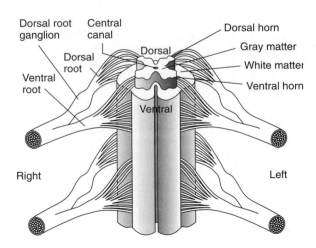

FIGURE 11.2. The peripheral nerves that are associated with two sections of the spinal cord.
Source: Adapted with permission from *Biopsychology* (3d ed.) © 1997 Allyn & Bacon; courtesy of John P. J. Pinel, Department of Psychology, University of British Columbia.

skin surface to the brain. Rather, the pathway is more complex, involving considerable opportunities for the alteration of incoming pain signals by other sensations and even by descending inhibiting impulses from higher brain centers.

In very basic terms, this gate control theory proposes the presence of a structure in the dorsal horn of the spinal cord that serves a gatelike function, increasing or decreasing the flow and transmission of nerve impulses from peripheral fibers to the central nervous system. Thus, sensory input is "reviewed and modified" by the gate before it evokes pain. It is further proposed that the degree to which this gate increases or decreases sensory transmission is determined by activity in large-diameter fibers (A-beta fibers) and small-diameter fibers (A-delta and C fibers), as well as by descending influences from the brain. Figure 11.3 presents a schematic of this gate control theory.

The gate control system in the theory is the substantia gelatinosa that modulates the amount of input transmitted from the peripheral fibers to the dorsal horn transmission (T) cells. This gate control mechanism is influenced by the relative degree of activity in the large-diameter A-beta fibers and the small-diameter A-delta and C fibers. Activity in the large fibers closes the gate, tending to inhibit transmission, whereas small-fiber activity opens the gate, tending to increase transmission. This spinal-gating is further influenced by efferent nerve impulses that descend from the brain. As a result, psychological processes such as anxiety, depression, attention, and past experience can exert influence directly on the pain perception process by altering gating at the dorsal horn. Melzack and Wall (1965) refer to this as the *central control mechanism*. This mechanism plays a major role in identifying sensory impulses from the periphery, assessing these signals in terms of past experience, and ultimately modulating properties of the gate control system.

FIGURE 11.3. The gate control theory of pain: (L) larger-diameter fibers; (S) small-diameter fibers; (SG) spinal gating mechanism; (T) spinal cord transmission cells.
Source: Reprinted with permission from R. Melzack and P. D. Wall. Pain mechanisms: A new theory. *Science*, 1965, *150*, 971–979. Copyright © 1965 by the American Association for the Advancement of Science.

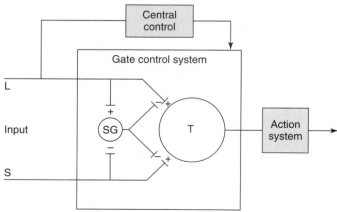

The output of the spinal cord T cells, determined by the interaction of the spinal-gating mechanism, can become very large. When this output exceeds a critical threshold level, it activates neuromechanisms that are the action system responsible for both pain perception and behavior. In other words, pain is experienced and responses to it are initiated.

This theory represented a significant advance in our conceptualization of pain. It was comprehensive enough to take into account the evidence suggesting specific types of pain receptors as well as allowing for the possibility that pain stimulation and transmission might occur in patterns of sensations. In addition, it allows for the significant role that downward central nervous system (CNS) mediation can play in pain perception. It also partially takes into account different types of pain as well as the different effects of time on the pain process (Fordyce and Steger, 1979). Finally, it views pain as a complex set of phenomena rather than a simple specific or discrete entity. Of course, as new understanding of pain neurophysiology, neurotransmission, and endogenous opioids increases, a more refined model will evolve.

One important outcome of this theory was the development of a procedure for artificially stimulating the nervous system in order to relieve pain. Electrical stimulators can be used on or beneath the surface of the skin, or implanted near the spinal cord. Electrical pulses are then administered in the vicinity of areas where pain is reported or in the region of the major nerves serving these areas. This procedure is based on the assumption that electrical stimulation activates the large-diameter fibers and thereby "closes the gate." Stimulation of activity in these large fibers is believed to activate cells of the substantia gelatinosa that inhibit the activity of transmission cells and, in turn, affect the action system responsible for pain perception and response. This electrical stimulation procedure often produces relief from pain during stimulation and for a period of time after stimulation. It should be noted, however, that not all individuals benefit from this type of treatment; moreover, the relief from pain is usually only temporary (Long, 1976; Melzack, 1975).

Neurochemical Bases of Pain

During the past 30 years there has been an explosion of interest and research in an endogenous opiatelike substance that constitutes a neurochemically based internal pain-regulation system. These chemicals are similar to morphine and other opiates, but they are produced inside the body in many parts of the brain and glands and are thought to play a significant role in pain reduction. They actually have a number of functions and appear to be important in eating as well as pain perception. The first major endogenous opioid to be clearly isolated was **enkephalin**. Since then, several other, similar substances have been identified, and we now believe that there are three basic families of opioids (Akil et al., 1984). **Beta-endorphins** are peptides that appear to project primarily to the limbic system and brain stem; **proenkephalins** are peptides that are widely distributed in the neuronal, endocrine, and central nervous systems; and **prodynorphins** are opioids found in the brain, gut, and the pituitary. The overall system of opioids is complex, with each family having a variety of forms, potencies, and active reception sites.

Investigators still do not know all the functions of the endogenous opioids and which factors are important in triggering their arousal. We have learned about **stress-induced analgesia**, paradoxical pain-reducing effects of stress related to the fact that stress causes opioid release. Another particularly interesting aspect of these opioids is their role in the placebo effect involved in the reduction of pain (see Chapter 10). In a number of painful conditions, up to one-third of those experiencing pain can get significant relief following the administration of a placebo (a nonactive drug or treatment). In other words, some people given sugar pills instead of a pain killer will get relief if they believe that they have taken a pain killer. The mechanisms involved in this placebo analgesia effect are not well understood, but the analgesic placebo effect and the analgesia produced by active narcotics appear to have very similar properties. For example, with repeated use over long periods of time, placebo analgesia becomes less effective (i.e., tolerance develops), and people get the urge to continue taking the placebo. They also have a tendency to increase the dosage of the placebo over time. An abstinence-withdrawal syndrome can appear when the use of placebos is suddenly discontinued, and giving a placebo may partially decrease or reverse withdrawal symptoms in narcotic addicts. People who react to placebos also experience significantly greater relief from postoperative pain after receiving narcotic analgesia (cf., Levine, Gordon, and Fields, 1978).

The study by Levine and colleagues (1978) provided initial insights into how opioids may be involved in this phenomenon. The effects of a placebo medication and a drug called **naloxone** on postoperative dental pain (produced by a major tooth extraction) were evaluated. Naloxone is an opiate antagonist; it blocks the effects of opiates, thereby increasing pain sensation. If placebo-induced analgesia is mediated by endogenous opioids, then naloxone, an opiate antagonist, should block these effects. Three hours after surgery, one-half of the patients received the placebo medication; the other half of the patients received naloxone. Four hours after surgery patients received the other medication. Patients were asked to report on the degree of pain they were experiencing after receiving their medications.

Some findings were simply replication. Patients given naloxone experienced, as expected, significantly more pain than when the placebo was administered. Since naloxone is an opiate antagonist, it should not reduce pain but, rather, it should block pain-reducing effects of naturally occurring opioids. Some patients' pain was reduced or unchanged (39 percent of the patients were found to be placebo responders), whereas placebo nonresponders' pain increased (61 percent of the patients were placebo nonresponders). This ratio of responders to nonresponders is similar to the one-third/two-thirds responder-nonresponder distribution usually found in the research literature. When naloxone was given as the second drug, there was no change in pain level in the nonresponders. However, there was an increase in pain levels among placebo responders. Naloxone blocked the opioids producing the pain reduction in the placebo responders. The results of this study showed that endogenous opioid release is involved in placebo analgesia. When opioid activity was blocked by naloxone, pain reduction was no longer apparent (Levine et al., 1978).

Future research will provide a clearer description of the variables actually involved in affecting endogenous opioid activity. Research on these opioid substances also suggest additional mechanisms for the downward efferent pain-inhibiting mechanisms that are not taken into account by the gate control theory (Snyder, 1977). This again indicates the importance of psychological processes in the pain perception process. In the next section we will discuss at greater length the influence of psychological processes on pain perception.

PSYCHOLOGICAL INFLUENCES ON PAIN PERCEPTION

The gate control theory of pain allowed for the significant role of downward CNS mediation in the pain perception process. A number of studies suggest that psychological factors have considerable effects on pain perception (Salovey et al., 1992; Turk, 1996). Among the first to emphasize the importance of the psychological status of an individual in determining his or her response to pain was researched by Beecher (1956). This belief was the result of his observation of wounded soldiers returning from battle during World War II. In a classic investigation Beecher (1956) studied requests for pain-killing medication made by soldiers taken to combat hospitals following wounds received in combat at Anzio. These soldiers' requests were compared with those made by civilians with comparable surgical wounds. Only 25 percent of the combat-wounded soldiers requested medication, and most of the soldiers either denied having pain from their extensive wounds or said they had so little that they did not think medication was necessary. In marked contrast, the civilians with similar wounds due to surgery experienced much more pain, with more than 80 percent requesting pain medication. Beecher interpreted these results as suggesting that psychological factors, such as an individual's emotional state and secondary gain, affected pain. Secondary gains refer to benefits of being sick or in pain, such as receiving more attention or not having to go to school! In this case secondary gains were most likely experienced by soldiers who were allowed to leave the aversive life-threatening combat zone because of their wounds and probably would eventually be sent home.

There have been other studies demonstrating the importance of our psychological state in the perception of pain. For example, Sternbach (1966) reported that pain increases as the anxiety level of the individual increases (see Figure 11.4). In an earlier study Hill et al. (1952) had shown that anxiety-induced conditions were associated with higher intensities of pain than were low anxiety conditions. Another interesting finding of this study was that morphine was much more effective in decreasing pain when the patient's anxiety level was high; it had little or no effect if that individual's anxiety level was low. Stress also affects pain, with those experiencing more stress also reporting more pain (Sternbach, 1986), and coping responses also appear to affect pain and suffering (Williams and Keefe, 1991).

Cultural and social factors also influence the perception of pain (see Weisenberg, 1977a,b). For example, Tursky and Sternbach (1967) and Sternbach and Tursky (1965) showed significant differences in reactions to electric

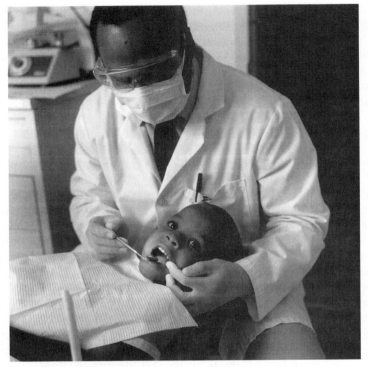

FIGURE 11.4. The importance of psychological state in the sensation of pain is evident in the case of dental pain. People feel more pain or discomfort when they are anxious or fearful but less pain if they are relaxed or distracted. Dentists have learned ways of relaxing or distracting patients, often with positive results.
Source: Elizabeth Garvey/Monkmeyer

shock among ethnic groups: "Yankees" (Protestants of British descent) had a "matter of fact" orientation toward pain and assumed it was a common experience; Irish subjects tended to inhibit their pain expressions and suffering; Italians demonstrated an immediacy to pain experience and emotionally exaggerated their pain, demanding fast relief; Jews also emotionally exaggerated their pain and had great concerns about the meaning and any future implications of the pain.

Some differences in attitudes and responses to pain appear to be learned. In Chapter 10 we discussed the fact that modeling or imitation learning is an important form of learning. For example, investigations of dental fears in children have found that a child's family attitudes and feelings toward dental treatment are important in determining the child's own anxiety about dental treatment (Milgrametal, 1995). In one such study children with anxious mothers showed significantly more emotionally negative behavior during a tooth extraction than did children of mothers with low anxiety (Weisenberg, 1977b). Negative expectations can also affect pain. Chronic pain patients reported more negative self-statements and social thoughts and reported more severe pain than did other patients, suggesting that these negative thoughts intensify or prolong pain (Gil et al., 1990).

In a rather dramatic demonstration of how pain perception and response can be modified through learning, Pavlov (1927) observed what happened when a slight change was made in a classical conditioning procedure (discussed in Chapter 10). Instead of being preceded by a bell [the conditioned stimulus (CS)], the food [the unconditioned stimulus (UCS)] was preceded by an aversive stimulus such as electric shock or a skin prick. Normally, such stimuli presented alone will produce a variety of negative emotional responses. What Pavlov found was that after this conditioning, the dogs failed to demonstrate any emotional response to the aversive stimuli. Instead, the dogs began perceiving these stimuli as signals that food was on the way. They actually elicited salivation and approach behaviors!

Of course, such examples do not imply that all pain is learned. The point is that our pain perceptions and responses often have a significant psychological learning component that directly and significantly contributes to the experiences of pain. Social learning and one's developing sense of self-efficacy also affect these experiences (Bandura et al., 1987). Psychological variables play a direct role in the pain experience. How one reacts to pain sensations is as important an issue as the specific physiological mechanisms involved in transmitting and generating pain experiences. Pain is a complex behavior and not simply a sensory effect.

PAIN BEHAVIOR

Pain, like any other form of complex behavior, must be thought of as having multiple behavioral components. As Fordyce and Steger (1979) indicated, in order to describe pain:

> . . . there must be some form of pain behavior by which diagnostic inference and treatment judgments can be made. A patient will signal the type of pain he or she is experiencing by describing the intensity, frequency, location, and type of pain experienced. In addition to these verbal cues available to the patient's environment as an indication of his or her pain, there is a myriad of nonverbal signs used to communicate pain experiences. These include grimaces, sighs, moans, limps, awkward or strained body positions, the use of a cane or crutch, and many other symbols associated in our society with discomfort or physical problems. (p. 129)

Hilgard (1965) reported that verbal self-report measures of pain tend to produce significantly greater levels of stimulus discrimination and are more closely associated with variation in stimulus presentations than are specific physiological measures. Indeed, there have been a number of self-report measures of pain developed through the years. For example, the McGill pain questionnaire (Melzack, 1975) was developed to assess chronic pain. We discussed this instrument in Chapter 9. As you will recall, it consists of three classes or categories of words that patients use in describing the subjective qualities of their pain experience (see Table 11.1). These descriptive words relate to either sensory, affective, or evaluative aspects of the pain experience (see Figure 11.3).

This allows for a more comprehensive evaluation of the qualitative aspects of pain than a unidimensional rating of pain as mild, moderate, or severe. Williams (1988) has provided a comprehensive review of many other self-report tests and measures of pain and the interested reader is referred there for more details.

Many clinicians, wary of potential reporting biases in self-report measures, developed additional ways of measuring the behaviors associated with pain that could be observed and objectively measured by independent raters. These alternative ways of measuring pain include the use of observation of "pain behaviors" such as "lying down time," sighing, grimacing, rubbing, bracing, and

TABLE 11.1. Items from the McGill pain questionnaire

Some of the words below describe your *present* pain. Circle *only* those words that best describe it. Leave out any category that is not suitable. Use only a single word in each appropriate category—the one that applies the most.

1	2	3	4
Flickering	Jumping	Pricking	Sharp
Quivering	Flashing	Boring	Cutting
Pulsing	Shooting	Drilling	Lacerating
Throbbing		Stabbing	
Beating		Lancinating	
Pounding			

5	6	7	8
Pinching	Tugging	Hot	Tingling
Pressing	Pulling	Burning	Itchy
Gnawing	Wrenching	Scalding	Smarting
Cramping		Searing	Stinging
Crushing			

9	10	11	12
Dull	Tender	Tiring	Sickening
Sore	Taut	Exhausting	Suffocating
Hurting	Rasping		
Aching	Splitting		
Heavy			

13	14	15	16
Fearful	Punishing	Wretched	Annoying
Frightful	Grueling	Blinding	Troublesome
Terrifying	Cruel		Miserable
	Vicious		Intense
	Killing		Unbearable

17	18	19	20
Spreading	Tight	Cool	Nagging
Radiating	Numb	Cold	Nauseating
Penetrating	Drawing	Freezing	Agonizing
Piercing	Squeezing		Dreadful
	Tearing		Torturing

Source: Reprinted from R. Melzack. The McGill pain questionnaire: Major properties and scoring methods. *Pain*, 1975a, *1*, 277–299, with kind permission of Elsevier Science-NL, Sara Burgerhartstraat 25, 1055 KV Amsterdam, The Netherlands.

the like (see Follick et al., 1985; Keefe and Block, 1982). The need for standardized or "objective" indices of pain has led to the development of taxonomies of pain behavior such as the one developed by Follick et al., 1985, shown in Table 11.2.

TABLE 11.2. Operational Definitions for 16 Pain Behaviors

1. *Asymmetry*
   Imbalance of 20 degrees from vertical in posture of body alignment, improper weight bearing during movement, favoring one side.
2. *Slow response time*
   Latency to initiate a response greater than or equal to 5 sec following completion of a command or prior instruction.
3. *Guarded movement*
   Slow, cautious movement relative to baseline; nonmethodical or jerky movement.
4. *Limping*
   Irregular, antalgic gait.
5. *Bracing*
   Pronounced use of extremity on body or object for support; assists movement by leaning on or pushing off chair, wall, body, and so forth; tension or regidity evident in weight-bearing extremity.
6. *Personal contact*
   Rubs body or presses body with palm of hand or with three or more fingers placed flatly on body.
7. *Position shifts*
   Changes in body alignment or in distribution of body weight.
8. *Partial movement*
   Limited range of motivation, does not complete movement. Criteria for specific movements: straight and side leg raises <60 degrees, trunk rotation <75–80 degrees, lateral side bends <45 degrees, sit-up <90 degrees from vertical, toe touch—failure to extend palm below knee.
9. *Absence of movement*
   Does not use body part, does not bend back, back rigid, does not attempt movement.
10. *Eye movement*
    Rolls eyes; repetitive, rapid blinking; eyes closed for greater than 1 sec.
11. *Grimacing*
    Bites lips, grits teeth, pulls back corners of mouth.
12. *Quality of speech*
    Monotone, flat.
13. *Pain statements*
    Statements directly relating to pain, verbalizes pain complaints, states behavior is emitted to avoid pain, discusses pain medications.
14. *Limitation statements*
    Statements relating to disability or impairment, expresses inability, verbalizes hesitation, or questions capacity to perform tasks.
15. *Sounds*
    Any pronounced utterance that is not language—moan, groan, or grunt.
16. *Pain-relief devices*
    TENS, cane, brace on leg or back, crutches, and so forth.

Source: From M. J. Follick, D. K. Ahern, and E. W. Aberger. Development of an audiovisual taxonomy of pain behavior. *Health Psychology*, 1985, 4, 555–568.

Reliance on physiological measures rather than self-report indices does not necessarily yield a more valid or precise measure of an individual's pain than does a verbal report (Fernandez and Turk, 1992). Again, pain is a complex behavior and not purely a sensory event. One needs to consider its multiple components in the assessment and treatment of this behavior. Thus, pain is different from suffering (the former causing the latter), and although caused by real or imagined injury or tissue damage, it is separable from that injury and not simply the sum of all damage to bodily tissue (see Fordyce, 1988).

Organic and Psychogenic Pain

In addition to traditional descriptions of pain in physiological terms, there has been a tendency to view organic pain as a different type of pain from psychogenic pain. The term **psychogenic** was used to imply that the pain was due to psychological causes, or that it was "all in the patient's mind," or that it was not "real" pain because an organic basis for it could not be found. This was an unfortunate belief and its perpetuation as a myth hindered the development of good pain management strategies. Psychogenic pain is not experienced any differently from pain arising from clearly delineated injury or tissue damage. *Psychogenic and organic pain both hurt the same.* Moreover, the diagnosis of organically caused pain does not rule out the important role that psychological variables play for any particular patient. Indeed, in our discussion of the gate control theory of pain we saw how the experience of pain may be produced by psychological factors through the hypothesized central control trigger mechanism.

Psychological factors are important not only to the experience of pain, but also to the response to treatment of pain. For example, Blumetti and Modesti (1976) found that patients suffering from intractable back pain benefited significantly less from surgical intervention techniques if they scored high on the hysteria and hypochondriasis scales of the MMPI. In contrast, patients scoring within normal limits on these two scales showed greater benefits from surgery. Thus, emotional and psychological variables again are shown to play a significant part in pain behavior.

Acute versus Chronic Pain

Before turning to treatment approaches to pain, we must discuss differences between acute and chronic pain. **Acute** pain is often the result of some specific and readily identifiable tissue damage (e.g., a broken leg, surgical lesion). It is short-lived pain, rarely lasting more than 2 to 3 months and usually more transient than that. With this type of pain, a physician usually prescribes a specific treatment that helps to relieve the pain. This is like your dentist prescribing a pain killer for a root canal or a doctor giving morphine to a patient after surgery. As the wound or damage to tissue heals the pain ends. In contrast, while chronic pain usually begins with some specific acute episode, prescribed treatments do not result in any significant reduction of the pain and pain persists for very long periods of time. When traditional medical treatment fails to solve the patient's problem, and chronicity sets in, we call the pain **intractable**, or not responsive to treatment.

Fordyce and Steger (1979) noted that another difference between acute and chronic pain is the type of anxiety experienced by the patient. In acute pain experiences there is usually an increase in anxiety as pain intensity increases, followed by a reduction in this anxiety once treatment begins. As we discussed earlier, a reduction in anxiety generally results in a decrease in pain sensation. Thus, there is a cycle of pain reduction, followed by anxiety reduction, resulting in still more pain reduction. This cycle, however, is very different for chronic pain patients. For these patients the initial anxiety associated with the pain persists and may eventually result in the development of feelings of greater anxiety, despair, and helplessness because of the failure of treatments to alleviate it.

There is evidence that chronic-pain patients develop specific psychological problems related to repeated failure of attempts to alleviate their pain. These problems distinguish them from acute-pain patients. Sternbach et al (1973) compared the MMPI profiles of a group of acute low back pain patients (pain present for less than 6 months) with those of a group of chronic low back pain patients (more than 6 months). The profile patterns are summarized in Figure 11.5. As you can see, there are significant differences between the two groups on the first three clinical scales (hypochondriasis, depression, and hysteria). The combined elevation of these three scales is often referred to as the *neurotic triad* since it is commonly found in neurotic individuals who are experiencing a great deal of anxiety. These results suggested that during the early acute stages of pain, few psychological problems are produced by it. However, as the pain becomes chronic in nature, psychological changes occur. These changes are most likely due to the constant discomfort, despair, and preoccupation with the pain that comes to dominate these patients' lives. As Sternbach (1974) noted in his description of chronic-pain sufferers:

> Pain patients frequently say that they could stand their pain much better if they could only get a good night's sleep. They feel as though their resistance is weakened by their lack of sleep. They never feel rested. They feel worn down, worn out, exhausted. They find themselves getting more and more irritable with their families, they have fewer and fewer friends, and fewer and fewer interests. Gradually as time goes on, the boundaries of their world seem to shrink. They become more and more preoccupied with their pain, less and less interested in the world around them. Their world begins to center around home, doctor's office, and pharmacy (p. 7).

FIGURE 11.5. Comparisons of MMPI profiles of acute and chronic low back pain patients; major differences occurred on the first three clinical subscales: (Hs) hysteria, (D) depression, and (Hy) hypochondriasis. *Source:* Adapted from R. A. Sternbach, S. R. Wolf, R. W. Murphy, and W. H. Akeson. Traits of pain patients: The low-back "loser." *Psychosomatics,* 1973, *14,* 226–229. Copyright © 1973, Academy of Psychosomatic Medicine. Reprinted with permission of the publisher.

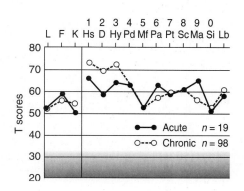

Similar MMPI results have been found in research with patients participating in a comprehensive treatment program for low back pain (discussed later in the chapter). Barnes and colleagues (1992) found significant elevations of a variety of MMPI scales (including scales 1, 2, and 3) before the start of the treatment program in chronic low back pain patients. At a 6-month follow-up period after successful completion of the treatment program there was a significant decrease in these scales to normal levels. These findings suggest that the elevations of scores on psychological tests such as the MMPI that are seen in chronic low back pain patients are most likely due to the trauma and stress associated with their chronic condition and not due to some stable psychological traits. When successfully treated, these elevations disappear.

Chronic pain differs from patient to patient, and one can see particular "types" of chronic pain if one examines a large enough number of cases. For example, Turk and Rudy (1988) categorized referrals to an outpatient pain center into three distinct groups. *Dysfunctional* patients were characterized by severe pain and greater disruption of daily activities. Among *interpersonally distressed* patients, pain appeared to precipitate a crisis or worry and dissatisfaction about how much support was available from family and friends. *Minimizers/adaptive* patients had the least severe pain and the least disruption of daily life. Greater perceived control and overall vigor appeared to contribute to these differences (Turk and Rudy, 1988).

It is obvious that the treatment of the chronic-pain sufferer will often have to deal not only with pain experience, but also with its psychological consequences. Anxiety and depression produced by long-term "wearing down" effects of pain produce a layer of behavioral-psychological problems over the original pain experience itself. A number of approaches currently being used in pain clinics have incorporated behavioral techniques to deal with problems as part of comprehensive treatment. Before discussing comprehensive treatment programs for use with chronic-pain patients, we will briefly review a number of more specific therapeutic methods that have been suggested as effective in relieving pain. (See the box "Pain: A Pervasive Problem.") Although there is evidence for the effectiveness of some of these methods in alleviating acute pain, there is no evidence to support their effectiveness, when used alone, in significantly reducing chronic pain.

SPECIFIC PAIN TREATMENT METHODS

Pain is big business. Treatment of pain has typically been pharmacologic in the past 30 to 40 years, with drugs, such as aspirin, and powerful narcotics, such as morphine. For most minor and/or short-lived pain, analgesics like aspirin or newer ibuprofens are adequate and available in abundance (see Figure 11.6). These drugs inhibit the production of substances needed for pain sensation or interfere with transmission of pain signals to the brain.

Opiates, or narcotics, include opium and a number of drugs made from it (such as morphine or codeine) as well as newer synthetic narcotics. These drugs attach to opiate receptors in the brain and inhibit pain signals or transmission. Unlike aspirin and other anti-inflammatory drugs, narcotics also

Pain: A Pervasive Problem

Pain is one of the most common and perplexing problems we encounter in the United States and in most of the world. Pain related to illnesses, injuries, accidents, tension, and unknown causes is around us all the time. We are bombarded on TV with new and improved pain-killing drugs and our stores are filled with many different remedies for headache pain, muscle soreness, and back pain. The most common kind of pain appears to be headache pain, and it has been suggested that all or nearly all of us experience headaches at least once in a while. Fewer of us have severe headaches, but this figure is large enough to be a problem, with about 10 percent of the population experiencing debilitating headache pain (Salovey et al., 1992). More than one-half of adults in the United

States also suffer from back pain, primarily in the lower back, and this pain can also be disruptive and disabling (Salovey et al., 1992).

Headaches, as we saw in Chapter 7, can be of several types and have different or unknown causes. This is also true of back pain, where damage to muscle, vertebrae, and the disks between the vertebrae of the spine can all account for pain. In addition, damage to these tissues does not appear to be necessary for back pain and there are many cases for which physical causes cannot be identified (Deyo, 1991). Stress, anxiety, fitness, and psychological or emotional disorders can all affect back pain, together or independent of actual tissue damage (Sullivan et al., 1992).

have powerful sedating effects and can enhance mood dramatically. These drugs are addictive and are only used when pain is severe and/or hard to control. They can be effective and reduce routine pain with little risk of side effects. You probably take one or more of the aspirin, acetaminophen, or ibuprofen combinations when you get a headache or experience dental pain. Chronic or excessive use of these drugs can have serious side effects such as gastric distress and ulcers, and they are limited in how well they work against severe pain.

Narcotics are used in cases of unusual pain. You might get a prescription for codeine after having a tooth pulled. Following major surgery, you might be given something even stronger, like morphine. However, these drugs can make it harder for patients to breathe and are very addictive. As a result, their use must be sharply curtailed and controlled. Narcotics are not available without a prescription and are among the most highly monitored drugs available in the United States.

Limitations of these medication approaches and the "last-ditch" nature of surgical intervention to reduce pain have led to the development of behavioral approaches to pain management. In some cases these nonpharmacologic approaches are effective all by themselves, whereas in other cases they are combined with the administration of analgesics to achieve maximum relief. In some stubborn cases the application of these techniques may be the patient's only hope for pain reduction.

Biofeedback

In the last chapter we discussed biofeedback and some of its clinical applications. It has also been used with pain patients. Turk, Meichenbaum, and

FIGURE 11.6. The many brands and kinds of pain-killer drugs highlight the importance of over-the-counter medications and self-treatment of minor ailments. What would happen if we had to see a doctor every time we need an aspirin? Pain reduction and other over-the-counter medications are big business!
Source: Mike Kagan/Monkmeyer

Berman (1979) reviewed the research on the application of biofeedback for the regulation of pain at that time, concluding that biofeedback was no better than other, less expensive, less instrument-oriented treatments such as progressive muscle relaxation training and coping skills training. Moreover, evidence for the effectiveness of biofeedback in reducing pain is marginal at best. The evidence rests mainly on case studies and poorly controlled research. This status has not changed much since the 1979 review (Gatchel and Turk, 1996; Holroyd and Penzien, 1990) although some studies find that biofeedback is useful in reducing pain (Blanchard et al., 1988).

One problem with using biofeedback as the only treatment is that we have no evidence that the etiological variables and pathophysiology of the pain are known and can be voluntarily controlled. Biofeedback training provides subjects with information that will enable them to control voluntarily some aspect of their physiology that may cause pain experience. However, as we have seen, pain is a complex behavior and not merely a pure sensory experience. One cannot expect that dealing solely with a physiological component of the pain will totally eliminate the problem. At best, it may serve as an adjunctive treatment in a comprehensive therapy regimen.

Research is needed to determine for what individuals and for what types of pain biofeedback is a valuable adjunctive method. There is some evidence that people who are more responsive to biofeedback can be identified and that targeting this pain treatment to that subgroup yields good pain control (Flor and Birbaumer, 1993). Biofeedback may prove to be useful primarily in reducing anxiety. Since anxiety and pain perception are closely related, biofeedback may have an impact on the pain process indirectly through reducing anxiety rather than through any pathophysiology per se. Future investigations are needed to delineate such issues more carefully.

Hypnosis

Hypnosis has a long history in clinical medicine. In 1843 James Braid discovered that the nervous system could be artificially induced into a state of "nervous sleep." He eventually named this state "hypnosis" after the Greek god of sleep. It was found that under this special state of sleep, individuals would be very responsive to verbal suggestions given by the hypnotist. Subsequently, during the middle and late nineteenth century a number of prominent physicians including Hippolyte-Marie Bernheim and Jean-Martin Charcot began using hypnotism as a medical treatment. Between 1845 and 1853 James Esdaile, a Scottish surgeon working in India, performed nearly 300 painless major operations, including amputations and cataract removals, with hypnosis as the only anesthetic.

The discovery of ether and other anesthetic drugs led surgeons to prefer physical/pharmacological treatments to psychological treatment such as hypnosis, even though hypnosis has been shown to be equally effective and has fewer side effects and a lower mortality rate for many types of operations (Gatchel and Turk, 1996). However, hypnosis has experienced a revival in clinical medicine, especially in the area of the control of pain, where traditional medical procedures have not been totally effective. There are now many scientific reports that document the effectiveness of hypnosis in alleviating pain (for reviews see Chaves, 1993; Chaves and Barber, 1974). The procedure usually involves the induction of a hypnotic trance state and the suggestion of analgesia (imagining a part of the body to be numb or insensitive to pain).

Relief from pain by hypnosis has been noted in obstetrics, surgery, dentistry, and even cancer treatment (Hilgard and Hilgard, 1975). In addition to reducing or totally eliminating the pain of labor and delivery, hypnosis can also reduce lower back pain and facilitate more rapid recovery. It has the added benefit of eliminating the possible negative effects of anesthesia on the newborn. One obstetrician successfully used hypnosis as the only form of anesthesia in 814 out of 1,000 deliveries, including some cesarean deliveries (Hilgard and Hilgard, 1975). In dentistry Barber (1977) reported the successful use of hypnosis as the sole source of anesthesia in dental procedures on 99 out of 100 patients, many involving extractions. Even with terminal cancer, intense pain can be brought under patients' control so that they no longer have to depend heavily on morphine during the last phases of their lives (Sacerdote, 1966). Research has also indicated that hypnosis is useful in controlling pain in burn patients (Patterson et al., 1992). Syrjala and Abrams (1996) describe other medical situations in which hypnosis and imagery are useful in the treatment of pain. For example, Syrjala, Cummings, and Donaldson (1992) showed that patients who were undergoing bone marrow transplantation could learn and apply hypnosis for pain management with only two sessions of training and some abbreviated "booster" sessions. However, there are few reports of systematic evaluation of the use of hypnosis for pain management in patients with continuous pain. One of the few studies that have been reported was conducted by Spiegel and Bloom (1983). They evaluated the effectiveness of hypnosis in reducing pain among breast cancer patients. Three separate groups were evaluated: a no-treatment group, a support group, and a support group that also received brief hypnosis. After 1 year patients who had been in the hypnosis group reported the lowest pain levels (although these levels were not statistically significantly lower than those in the support group). Across a wide spectrum of illnesses and patient populations, hypnosis appears to be a promising approach to pain management.

Hilgard (1975) concluded that there is more than sufficient evidence demonstrating the usefulness of hypnosis in treating pain conditions. He did not propose that hypnosis should be viewed as an alternative to chemical analgesics and anesthetics, but argued for its use as a supplement in the many cases where anesthetics or analgesia are dangerous or where the patient is excessively anxious. Like meditation or other interventions based on focusing or reorientating one's attention, hypnosis may help to distract us from pain and to achieve a more relaxed state (Kabat-Zinn et al., 1985). It is a method that may prove beneficial on a short-term basis with many patients who are experiencing pain.

Acupuncture

Acupuncture, which originated in ancient China more than 2,000 years ago, was initially based on the theory that the vital organs of the body were connected through tubular systems called *meridians* that radiated underneath the skin. It was believed that life energy or "chi'i" flowed through these meridians. An excess or a deficit of this life energy was believed to produce disease and pain. Insertion of needles into critical points along the meridians could correct imbalances in the life energy and relieve pain and discomfort. Although there has been little experimental support for this "meridian theory," (even the Chinese no longer consider it to be a reasonable explanation for the effectiveness of acupuncture therapy), this therapy is clearly useful in reducing pain (see Figure 11.7).

How does acupuncture actually work? Many believe some psychological mechanisms are involved. Taub (1976) noted that in China the psychological state of the patient is used to determine who will and who will not receive acupuncture as a surgical anesthetic. Pain patients who benefit most from acupuncture are also highly hypnotizable (Katz et al., 1974). However, acupuncture and hypnosis do not operate through identical mechanisms since the observable behaviors of patients undergoing hypnosis and acupuncture differ markedly. The hypnotized patient is unresponsive to the immediate environment, focusing almost all attention on the hypnotist and his or her suggestions to ignore the pain. The acupuncture patient, in contrast, is in contact with the environment and is aware of everything as treatment is being administered. Patients who have received both acupuncture and hypnosis treatments also tell us that the two are very different techniques. Although there appears to be a relationship between hypnotizability and the effectiveness of acupuncture, the reasons for this relationship are not known. Bakal (1979) suggests

FIGURE 11.7. Acupuncture, although largely unexplained, appears to be an effective treatment for some problems for some people.
Source: George S. Zimbel/Monkmeyer.

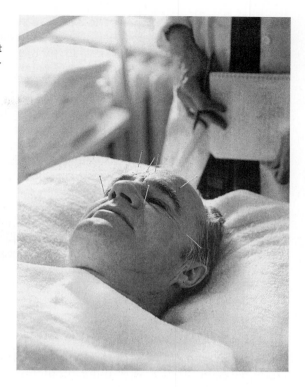

both acupuncture and hypnosis succeed in "closing the gating mechanism" (recall the gate in the spinal cord described in the gate control theory).

The role of endogenous opioid release in acupuncture or hypnosis treatments for pain has also been studied (Mayer et al., 1976). Injections of naloxone reduced the analgesia provided by acupuncture and hypnosis. In this study experimental pain was induced by electrical stimulation of a tooth. One group of subjects were given hypnosis, and the other group acupuncture. Pain estimates indicated that acupuncture increased the pain *thresholds* (the level of electrical stimulation needed to perceive pain) by 27 percent, and hypnosis increased pain thresholds by 85 percent. Following subsequent injections of naloxone, the pain threshold of the acupuncture group fell dramatically, but naloxone had no effect on the pain threshold of the hypnosis group. The investigators, therefore, concluded that acupuncture achieves at least some of its effects by the release of endogenous opiatelike substances from central and periaqueductal gray matter in the brain. Hypnosis most likely achieves its analgesic effects through some higher cortical mechanisms.

In a later study Kiser et al. (1983) evaluated 20 patients with chronic pain of at least 6 months duration who underwent nine sessions of acupuncture. Besides evaluating a host of psychological measures, blood samples were taken immediately before and after the acupuncture treatment regimen, and two opioids were measured: beta-endorphin and met-enkephalin. This treatment resulted in significant improvement of both pain and psychiatric symptoms, and *higher* plasma concentration of met-enkephalin. Plasma beta-endorphin concentrations were unchanged. The extent of symptom relief was highly correlated with the size of increases in plasma met-enkephalin. These results again indicate that acupuncture relieves pain by increasing opioid activity.

Is acupuncture effective in reducing pain? Although additional evidence is needed, it appears that this technique is capable of producing some short-term anesthesia and analgesia, but it is not a proven technique for treating more chronic and persistent complaints of pain (Bakal, 1979). Levine, Gormley, and Fields (1976) evaluated the analgesic effects on patients with chronic pain (pain persisting for more than 6 months) associated with objective evidence of nerve damage and patients with chronic pain without evidence of nerve damage. The majority of chronic-pain patients, although showing some initial relief from pain, eventually reported that the pain returned to pretreatment levels. Moreover, all patients eventually requested the termination of the acupuncture treatment. Other investigators have also reported that pain relief following acupuncture treatment tends to be short-lived (Murphy, 1976). Thus, like hypnosis, acupuncture may be useful for short-term relief of pain. However, it should not be viewed as an alternative to other forms of treatment for chronic pain.

Cognitive-Behavioral Strategies

In recent years there has been a great increase in the use of cognitive strategies for the management of pain (McCaul et al., 1992; Weisenberg, 1977a). Many strategies used to deal with other problems, including relaxation, cognitive reinterpretation, imagery, distraction, and modeling approaches have been used. Although many of these cognitive strategies can significantly modify the perception of experimentally induced pain, only a few studies show direct benefits on clinical pain. Moreover, of those studies of actual clinical pain, most have examined acute rather than chronic pain. A number of these strategies have shown promising results, but we must be cautious about the implications of these studies. Additional investigation is needed to evaluate the effectiveness of these cognitive pain control procedures in dealing with clinical pain, especially of the chronic type (Tollison, Hinnant, and Kriegel, 1991).

Imagine that you have a painful toothache. One way to overcome the pain you feel is to distract yourself, and one very good way to do this is to think about something pleasant and desirable. Relatively early studies of pain found that patients who were trained to engage in positive imagery (e.g., to imagine that they were walking through a lush meadow or swimming in a clear blue lake) reported less discomfort and pain during dental treatment than patients given no special training or who were instructed to visualize a series of two-digit numbers (Horan, Laying, and Pursell, 1976). Similarly, Langer, Janis, and Wolfer (1975) found that patients who were instructed to attend selectively to the positive aspects of their hospitalization (such as relief from work responsibilities and stress) requested less analgesic medication for postsurgery pain than did patients who were merely given presurgery information.

In studies of experimentally induced pain Barber and colleagues (Barber and Cooper, 1972; Chaves and Barber, 1974) also evaluated the cognitive strategy of distracting imagery. They trained subjects to imagine pleasant events, to count aloud, and to attend to other stimuli in the environment (such as counting ceiling tiles) when pain was present. In addition, they were taught to attend selectively to or imagine other sensations such as imagining that the stimulated area was asleep or insensitive, or that it had been injected with novocaine. These cognitive strategies were effective in increasing the pain tolerance of subjects, apparently by diverting attention from the pain and directing it away from the painful sensations. As subjects attend to stimuli that are unrelated to the pain, their tolerance for pain increases.

Other investigators have suggested the use of a "cafeteria style" approach to pain management. In one program, a form of **stress-inoculation training**, the individual is taught a variety of cognitive control strategies of the type discussed earlier, from which he or she may select when confronted with a painful stimulus (Meichenbaum and Turk, 1976). Patients are also assisted in developing a plan to use when the pain becomes more intense, and are instructed to implement the plan at these critical moments. Turk, Meichenbaum, and Genest (1983) have described several major categories of coping strategies (noted in Table 11.3). The use of these strategies shows promise of helping individuals to cope better with their pain (Sanders, 1996). Of course, more research is needed to evaluate the effectiveness of these procedures in dealing with chronic clinical pain.

Comprehensive Operant Treatment Programs

The inpatient strategies generally used in pain clinics can be divided into two basic types: (1) "pure" operant or behavioral treatment programs in which reinforcement procedures for "well behavior" are the major components in treatment and (2) "mixed" behavioral and other treatment programs which treatment involves strategies other than reinforcement such as group discussion with other patients, biofeedback, and family therapy (Fordyce and Steger, 1979). The prototype of the "pure" operant pain treatment program was developed at the University of Washington by Fordyce and his colleagues (1968). This program originally involved a 4- to 8-week inpatient period designed to increase gradually the general activity level and socialization of the patient and to decrease medication use. More recently group administration under other conditions has also been effective (Spence, 1989; Turner and Clancy, 1988). The

---

TABLE 11.3. Major Categories of Coping Strategies

- Imaginative inattention
- Imaginative transformation of pain
- Imaginative transformation of the context of pain
- Attention focused on the physical surroundings of the pain, setting
- Mental distraction (such as counting)
- Somatization or focusing on the body part with a removed, objective view as opposed to an emotional, subjective view of the pain

Source: Adapted from D. C. Turk, D. Meichenbaum, and M. Genest. *Pain and Behavioral Medicine: A Cognitive-Behavioral Perspective.* New York: Guilford Press, 1983.

program is based on the assumption that although pain may initially result from some underlying organic pathology, it is sustained by environmental factors (such as the attention of the patient's family and the rehabilitation staff). These reinforcers can increase pain behaviors such as complaining, grimacing, and requesting pain medication. Viewing pain as an operant behavior, Fordyce assumed that factors such as concern and attention from others, rest, medication, and avoidance of unpleasant responsibilities and duties frequently reinforce pain behavior and hinder a patient's progress in treatment.

Imagine that you have a very painful condition that is severe enough that it has disrupted your life. You cannot attend classes for a while and have been excused from required work until the pain can be controlled. Your friends and family have been very good, paying a lot of attention to you, bringing you gifts, and helping out whenever they can. You can rest, watch television, eat the treats people bring you, and not worry about all the stuff that used to concern you. These secondary gains or benefits of the sick role could make it more difficult to treat and control your pain.

In their treatment program Fordyce and colleagues (1968) systematically controlled environmental events (e.g., attention, rest, medication) and made them contingent on adaptive behaviors rather than on maladaptive ones. A major goal of the program was to increase participation in therapy and physical activity level while decreasing or eliminating pain behaviors. Members of the patient's family are involved in the treatment program and work closely with the rehabilitation staff. They are taught to react to the patient's behavior in ways that will reduce pain and to maximize the patient's compliance with the rehabilitation program. Through this operant approach the patient is taught to reinterpret the sensation of pain and to tolerate it while performing more adaptive behaviors that will gain the attention and approval of others.

An important feature of this program is the reduction in the amount of pain medication used by chronic-pain patients. In addition to minimizing addiction and habituation to analgesic medication, this reduces the patient's general dependence on drugs. Often medication is provided on a "as needed" basis. Unfortunately, the medication is then contingent on the very pain behavior that the rehabilitation staff would like to decrease. To avoid this problem, the delivery of medication may be made contingent on the passage of time rather than on the patient's pain behavior. The intervals between pain medication delivery can then be increased gradually during the treatment program. Another way to reduce the use of medication is to present it to the patient in a liquid that masks the color and taste of the medication (such as cherry syrup). Over a period of approximately 2 months the dosage level of the medication in the "cocktail" is gradually decreased until the patient is given only the masking liquid without an active ingredient. The patient and his or her family are informed of this medication reduction procedure either before or after the medication has been eliminated.

This comprehensive program has produced significant decreases in complaints of pain and in the use of analgesic medication (see Fordyce and Steger, 1979). The following case history illustrates the type of individual for whom this operant procedure has been found to be effective:

Mrs. Y is a 37-year-old white administrator. Since 1948, approximately one year after her marriage, she had virtually constant low back pain, and had been decreasingly able to carry out normal homemaking activities. At the time of admission to the hospital, she complained of a continuous period of activity without an interval of reclining rest as approximately 20 minutes. Her husband reported she was active in the home an average of less than two hours daily. The remainder of her time was spent reclining; either reading, watching television, or sleeping. During Mrs. Y's 18-year history of back pain, she had undergone four major surgical procedures including removal of a herniated disc and a lumbosacral spine fusion. At the time of admission, Mrs. Y was taking four or five habit-forming analgesic tablets per day when she experienced pain. Physical and radiologic examination revealed a stable spine at the fusion site, with no evidence of neurologic deficit (Fordyce et al., 1968, pp. 183–184).

At the end of treatment the patient was able to walk nearly a mile every day. She was also actively participating in occupational therapy 2 hours a day. The narcotic component of the pain medication had been completely eliminated and her pain complaints had been virtually eliminated. Monthly follow-up visits on an outpatient basis indicated that she continued to increase her activity level.

It is not clear whether the long-term use of pain-incompatible behaviors as was evident in these operant procedures will lead to a complete disappearance of pain. Patients may be learning only to avoid attending to and complaining about their pain. Indeed, the available data indicate that patients generally demonstrate only a modest degree of initial relief from their pretreatment pain levels following this behavioral intervention (Bakal, 1979). However, even if such procedures do not totally eliminate pain, they do make a significant difference between unbearable and bearable pain and between an unproductive, sedentary existence and a relatively normal life. More recent applications of this approach suggest that using operant techniques to reduce pain may have greater effects on long-term pain control than do other approaches (Turner and Clanay, 1988).

Functional Restoration: A Sports Medicine Approach to Chronic Low Back Pain

In recent years there has been a newer and even more comprehensive behavioral approach to chronic low back pain termed **functional restoration**. The term refers not only to a treatment methodology for chronic low back pain but also to a wider conceptualization of the entire problem, its diagnosis, and its management. Rather than accepting current limits in history-taking based solely through patients' self-report of pain and of diagnosis through skeletal imaging technology, this method involves more objective information. Structured interviews and quantified self-report measures provide problem-oriented information for patient management. More importantly, objective assessment of physical capacity and effort, with comparison to a normative data base, adds a new dimension to diagnosis. In keeping with a sports medicine approach, this permits the development of treatment programs of varied intensity and duration aimed primarily at restoring physical functional capacity and social performance. Objectives are more ambitious than merely attempting to alter pain complaints and to decrease medications. Improvements in quality of life are greatly enlarged by also focusing on increasing physical capacity and social problems associated with low back pain. Attention to realistic goals such as returning to work and reducing the use of the medical system has already helped to change the focus of traditional treatment programs as well as criteria for evaluation of its effectiveness.

This does not suggest that you should ignore self-reported pain when treating pain in this manner. Rather, self-reports should be interpreted only in the context of overall functioning. Adaptive, positive functioning is sometimes associated with *initial* increases in pain complaints. Indeed, the phrase "no pain, no gain" is appropriately emphasized to people who are undergoing functional restoration. Rather than terminating and delaying further physical training because of these pain complaints, the patient may have to learn to "work through" the pain.

This orientation emphasizes *function.* Fordyce, Roberts, and Sternbach (1985) have argued that it is not enough simply to evaluate and modify an individual's subjective experience of pain. One must comprehensively evaluate *pain behavior* that involves not only what the patient is verbalizing, but also his or her actual functioning. As they emphasize:

> . . . behavioral methods for treating pain problems (chronic pain behaviors) are not intended to "treat pain" in the traditional sense in which this implies directing attention to sources and mechanisms of noxious stimuli generating injury signals which lead to "pain." Behavioral pain methods do not have as their principal objective the modification of nociception, nor the direct modification of the experience of pain, although it very frequently happens that both are influenced by these methods. Rather, *behavioral methods* in pain treatment programs *are intended to treat excess disability and expressions of suffering.* The goal is to render chronic pain patients functional again and as normal in behavior as possible (p. 115).

Indeed, these investigators note that one of the major problems with past treatment and theoretical approaches to chronic pain, including some alleged behavioral ones, was focusing too greatly on merely the subjective experience of pain. A distinction needs to be made between "pain" (the subjective experience) and *pain behavior* or behavioral functioning. This is an extremely important point: The scientific literature tends to support the fact that the most appropriate goal is to modify excessive disability by focusing on *function.* The subjective component of pain (however it is assessed) also is often concurrently changed when functioning is changed. However, it has been found that there usually will be no major change in the subjective expression of "pain" without an improvement in functional activity and disability. This is the hallmark of the functional restoration approach. *One must focus on observable and objectively evaluated functioning along with self-report in order to assess comprehensively chronic-pain behavior.*

The success of this functional restoration approach has been carefully documented in a number of studies (Mayer et al., 1985; Hazard et al., 1989; Mayer et al., 1987). For example, in a 2-year follow-up study of patients administered the functional restoration program (Mayer et al., 1987) significant changes in a number of important realistic outcome measures were found. Nearly 90 percent of the treatment group were actively working, as compared with only about 41 percent of a nontreatment comparison group. Moreover, about twice as many comparison group patients required additional spine surgery and had unsettled worker's compensation litigation relative to the treatment group. The comparison group had approximately five times more patient visits to health professionals and had higher rates of recurrence of reinjury. Finally, there were also significant improvements in self-report measures and physical function measures such as back strength and the range of motion in the treatment group. These results demonstrate the impact that a functional restoration program can have on a range of important outcome measures (Mayer et al., 1987).

There are other forms of multidisciplinary treatments for chronic back pain. In a recent review of the literature Flor, Folydrich, and Turk (1992) concluded that the overall results were quite promising, with significant changes not only in pain and mood but also in behavioral variables such as the return to work and the use of the health care system.

SUMMARY

Pain is an extremely common complaint in medical settings, and traditional medical approaches have frequently proven ineffective. It is one of the most universal forms of stress encountered in medical situations. In fact, it takes into account the vast majority of all physician visits and affects over 50 million Americans. The great deal of research on psychological factors that contribute to pain has stimulated the development of a number of pain management approaches and techniques. In a comprehensive volume reviewing the latest treatment strategies, Gatchel and Turk (1996) summarize the various psychological treatment methods developed for patients suffering from a wide range of pain problems. Treatment approaches based on principles of operant conditioning, cognitive-behavioral interventions, biofeedback, hypnosis, imagery, and group therapy are described. Traditional medical treatments have not worked because pain is a complex phenomenon that involves not only physiological sensations and mechanisms but also significant behavioral/psychological components. A model of pain that integrates both physiological and psychological components has the best chance of allowing a comprehensive understanding of the pain process. The gate control theory of pain proposed by Melzack and Wall (1965) is an early example of such a model. We briefly discussed the physiology of pain, as well as the psychological influences such as anxiety and sociocultural learning factors on pain perception. This has led to an emphasis on the assessment of pain behavior, and not just the physiological components of pain. We must consider pain to be like any other form of complex behavior, consisting of multiple behavioral components.

Several factors affect pain, including ethnic background, stress, anxiety, one's social environment, and the like. Coping and self-efficacy appear to be important too. There are also several types of pain, and it may be distinguished by origin or whether it is acute or chronic. The latter can occur because of treatment failure or intractable pain and seems to be more distressing and disruptive than does acute pain.

A number of specific pain treatment methods were discussed, including biofeedback, hypnosis, acupuncture, and cognitive strategies. Although there is evidence that these techniques are somewhat effective in reducing acute pain, they should be viewed merely as adjunctive treatment methods in a more comprehensive therapy regimen. The initial prototype of the operant pain treatment clinic developed by Fordyce and colleagues (1968) has been effective as well. The functional restoration approach to the treatment of chronic low back pain is an example of a successful comprehensive, multidisciplinary approach to pain and disability management.

RECOMMENDED READINGS

Akil, H., Watson, S. J., Young, E., et al. Endogenous opioids: Biology and function. *Annual Review of Neuroscience*, 1984, 7, 223–255.

Fordyce, W. E., and Steger, J. C. Chronic pain. In O. F. Pomerleau and J. P. Brady (Eds.), *Behavioral medicine: Theory and practice*. Baltimore: Williams & Wilkins, 1979.

Gatchel, R. J., and Turk, D. C. (Eds.), *Psychological approaches to pain management*. New York: Guilford Publications, 1996.

Hilgard, E. R., and Hilgard J. R. *Hypnosis in the relief of pain*. Los Altos, CA: William Kaufmann, 1975.

Holmes, J. A., and Stevenson, C. A. Differential effects of avoidant and attentional coping strategies on adaptation to chronic and recent onset pain. *Health Psychology*, 1990, 9, 577–584.

Holroyd, K. A., and Penzien, D. B. Pharmacological versus non-pharmacological prophylaxis of recurrent migraine headache: A meta-analytic review of clinical trials. *Pain*, 1990, 42, 1–13.

Turk, D. C., Meichenbaum, D. H., and Berman, W. H. Application of biofeedback for the regulation of pain: A critical review. *Psychological Bulletin*, 1979, 86, 1322–1338.

Wall, P. D., and Melzack, R. *Defeating pain*. New York: Plenum Press, 1991.

Weisenberg, M. Pain and pain control. *Psychological Bulletin*, 1977, 84, 1004–1008.

Appetitive and Addictive Behaviors: Obesity, Smoking, and Alcoholism

Being overweight is no fun. Sure, many of us who weigh too much also eat too much (and we sure do like to eat), but obesity is not that simple. It is not healthy; being overweight is a risk factor for almost all major diseases that affect people in adulthood. It is hard to "fix"; losing weight is very difficult and keeping it off is even harder. Also, it is hard to be overweight in a society that values fitness and thinness as much as ours does. In addition, there is evidence that obesity is related to physiological and physical risk factors. Social isolation and sedentary (inactive) lifestyles are related to a depressed mood (see Figure 12.1), and one way that some people keep their weight gains down is by smoking. Cigarette smoking can help us to regulate our appetite and to maintain a desired weight.

Cigarette smoking, which at times is portrayed as the greatest hazard of the twentieth century, is perhaps the most important modifiable risk factor for disease and premature death. Smoking appears to be addictive, and no matter how "cool" it may make us feel, it is a very unhealthy behavior. Recently public opinion has turned against the smoking habit, and no-smoking ordinances in sections of shops, restaurants, and other public places are the norm rather than the exception. Smoking among the general population has decreased since 1960, but it is still much more common than at the beginning of the twentieth century (see Figure 12.2).

Alcohol use is different from smoking in a number of ways. Cigarette smoking is addictive for most of those who engage in it, but most of us who drink alcohol do not become addicted alcoholics. In addition, although smoking does not appear to have any health benefits and carries many health threats, moderate alcohol use may offer some protection from heart disease. However, alcohol use and abuse can be a big problem. Automobile accidents in which alcohol was involved are more serious and costly than when neither party in the accident was under the influence (Rouse, 1995). Up to 25 percent of men ages 21 to 34 and 15 percent of women in their teens drive under the influence of alcohol (see Figure 12.3). And consumption is too high: More than 15

342

CHAPTER 12
*Appetitive and
Addictive Behaviors:
Obesity, Smoking,
and Alcoholism*

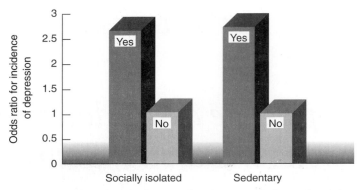

FIGURE 12.1. Incidence of depression by social isolation and physical activity.
Source: From G. A. Kaplan. Biobehavioral risk factors: Reflections on present and future research on biobehavioral risk factors. In S. J. Blumenthal, K. Matthews, and S. M. Weiss (Eds.), *New Research Frontiers in Behavioral Medicine: Proceedings of the National Conference,* 1994, 119–134. NIH Publication No. 94-3772.

percent of men and about 4 percent of women ages 18 to 25 years report heavy use of alcohol (five or more drinks per day on each of 5 of the past 30 days) (Rouse, 1995).

In this chapter we will discuss obesity, smoking, and problem drinking/alcoholism—three common appetitive problem behaviors that have significant

FIGURE 12.2. Cigarette consumption trends over time.
Source: From G. A. Kaplan. Biobehavioral risk factors: Reflections on present and future research on biobehavioral risk factors. In S. J. Blumenthal, K. Matthews, and S. M. Weiss (Eds.), *New Research Frontiers in Behavioral Medicine: Proceedings of the National Conference,* 1994, 119–134. NIH Publication No. 94-3772.

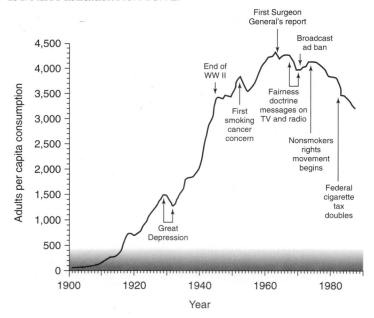

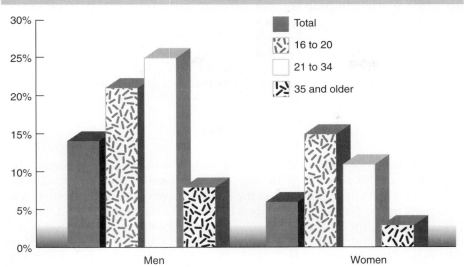

Percent Driving under the Influence of Alcohol or Other Drugs,
by Gender and Age, 1991 to 1993

	Percent of Drivers				Number (millions)			
Cause	Total	16 to 20	21 to 34	35 and older	Total	16 to 20	21 to 34	35 and older
Total	10%	18%	18%	6%	17.9	2.5	9.4	6.0
Men	14%	21%	25%	8%	12.6	1.6	6.4	4.6
Women	6%	15%	11%	3%	5.4	1.0	3.0	1.4

Source notes: Greenblat J and Bertolucci D (1994): *Characteristics of Persons Who Reported Driving under the Influence of
Alcohol or Other Drugs.* Presented at the Joint Statistical Meetings, Toronto. Unpublished data from the 1991, 1992, and 1993
National Household Survey on Drug Abuse (NHSDA) were examined. The NHSDA employs a multistage area probability sample of
the U.S. noninstitutionalized population. Trained interviewers contact the respondents who complete the self-administered
questionnaires on alcohol and other drug use and associated problems in private. Alcoholic beverages include beer, wine, wine
coolers, mixed alcoholic drinks, and distilled spirits. The data shown are estimated annual rates.

FIGURE 12.3. What percent of the population drive under the influence of alcohol or
other drugs? About 10 percent or 18 million people in the United States, age 16 years
and older who drove in the past year, reported that they drove under the influence
(DUI) of alcohol or other drugs. Men of all driving ages are more likely than women to
report DUI. Among men, those age 21 to 34 have the highest rate. Among women,
those age 16 to 20 have the highest rate of DUI.
Source: B. A. Rouse (Ed.). *Substance Abuse and Mental Health Statistics Sourcebook.* DHHS
Publication No. (SMA) 95-3064, Washington, DC: U.S. Government Printing Office, 1995.

health consequences. Behavioral analysis and treatment techniques have been
systematically used to treat these problems. They represent areas in which
health psychology has had a significant and practical impact on public health.
Obesity is considered here because it occupies a central position in the area of
health psychology and behavioral medicine, and was one of the first major
medical concerns to be successfully subjected to systematic behavioral analysis

344

CHAPTER 12
*Appetitive and
Addictive Behaviors:
Obesity, Smoking,
and Alcoholism*

and treatment. This approach was so successful that behavioral approaches are now the primary means of controlling weight and eliminating obesity. Smoking is a major health problem that has received a great deal of attention because it is a behavior that is considered to be the *single most preventable cause of premature death* in the United States and in many other nations (see Chapter 13). Alcoholism is also a major public health problem. There have been some encouraging efforts by behaviorally oriented investigators to understand this problem behavior and to develop possible methods of treatment.

OBESITY

Obesity—or overweight or extreme overweight status—is an important area of study in health psychology because it is a common, chronic condition that directly or indirectly contributes to the development of medical disorders such as hypertension, diabetes, and cancers (Sjostrom, 1993; Stunkard and Wadden, 1993). Diabetes, for example, is associated with obesity when its onset is during adulthood, and nearly 50,000 people died in the United States in 1990 from this chronic disease alone (see Table 12.1). Although there is some controversy as to whether relationships between obesity and health risks are linear (i.e., whether health risks increase in direct proportion to excess weight) (Andrés, 1980), there is a consensus that severe obesity is associated with increased illness and death (Sjostrom, 1993). Recent studies have suggested that thinner men and women live longer, and that relatively modest gains in weight after age 18 can result in a small, but measurable increase in health risks (Manson et al., 1995) (see Figure 12.4). In addition, being overweight is a socially stigmatized condition. Obesity is considered to be unattractive, and extremely overweight people may find themselves shunned, teased, or otherwise not treated very well. Many people want to lose weight, and those who are overweight generally feel bad about themselves (Brownell and Rodin, 1994). Unfortu-

TABLE 12.1. Deaths from Diabetes by Age, 1990[a]

Ages	Number of Deaths			Death Rate per 100,000 Population		
	Total	Male	Female	Total	Male	Female
All ages[b]	47,664	20,266	27,398	19.2	16.7	21.5
45 to 64 years old	9,803	4,983	4,820	21.2	22.5	20.1
65 years old and older	35,523	13,926	21,597	114.3	111.5	116.2

Notes: Diabetes is not a leading cause of death among persons 1 to 44 years old.
[a] Excludes deaths of nonresidents of the United States. Deaths classified according to ninth revision of *International Classification of Diseases.*
[b] Includes those deaths with the age not stated.
Source: 1993 Statistical Abstract of the United States on CD-ROM [machine-readable datafiles]. CD-ABSTR-93. Washington, DC: U.S. Department of Commerce, Economics and Statistics Administration, Bureau of the Census, Data User Services Division, 1993. Primary source: U.S. National Center for Health Statistics. *Vital Statistics of the United States* (annual); and unpublished data.

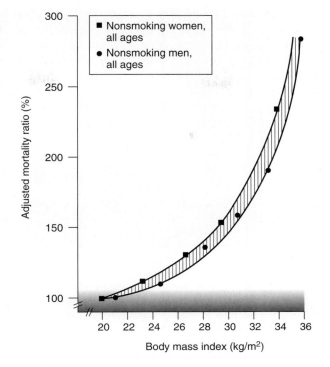

FIGURE 12.4. Mortality ratios by body mass index (kg/m²) for nonsmoking men and women of all ages.
Source: From A. J. Stunkard and T. Wadden. *Obesity: Theory and Therapy* (2nd ed.). New York: Raven Press, 1995.

nately, not everyone can actually control his or her weight, and we may find ourselves gaining weight no matter what we do!

Etiology of Obesity

Obesity is a complex phenomenon with biological, social, and psychological variables involved in its causes and consequences (Stunkard and Wadden, 1993). Despite extensive research and increasing evidence of genetic factors in obesity, there are still large gaps in what we know about the biological and behavioral factors that control food intake. Metabolism, the rate at which energy is produced and used, is also important in obesity. Research on biological causes of obesity has looked at the role of brain centers (such as the hypothalamus), neural mechanisms, and hormones that are involved in eating behavior and hunger regulation (Stunkard and Wadden, 1993). Moreover, there is exciting new work on the molecular biology of obesity suggesting that several genetic mutations that interfere with the body's ability to regulate the number of fat cells one has can cause people to gain weight (Hakas et al., 1995; Ezzell, 1995) (see Figure 12.5). This work proposes that fat tissue secretes a protein called "Ob," which travels through the blood to the hypothalamus in the brain, causing a sequence of physiological responses that suppress the appetite (Ezzell, 1995). In obese individuals, this protein may be lacking or its function may be impaired.

Explanations of why some people become obese have also been based on the notion of **set point**. Set point refers to the idea that the body regulates its

346

CHAPTER *12*
*Appetitive and
Addictive Behaviors:
Obesity, Smoking,
and Alcoholism*

FIGURE 12.5. A mouse with genetic mutations predisposing to obesity (left) is hugely obese compared with a normal mouse (right), which lacks genetic mutations. Researchers believe that a specific gene may encode a brain receptor for the Ob protein, which is secreted by fat cells into the blood to indicate to an individual how much adipose tissue the body has.
Source: Reprinted from C. Ezzel. Fat times for obesity research: Tons of new information, but how does it all fit together? *Journal of NIH Research,* 1995, 7, 39–43. Photograph provided by the Jackson Laboratory.

weight to maintain a certain amount of body fat and energy balance (Keesey, 1993). Each of us has a particular set point, or ideal weight, that is the target for each of us. Unfortunately, for some this set point may be too high! Research has also considered weight regulation based on the number and size of fat cells or adipocytes. It appears that the number of fat cells one has is determined primarily by genetics and/or early nutrition (Faust, 1980; Hirsch and Knittle, 1970). Once an individual matures past childhood, the number of fat cells is determined and impossible to decrease. This suggests that whenever possible, it is important to prevent childhood obesity and the increased number of fat cells that results. If we do not, this individual may have to live with a weight problem for the rest of his or her life.

Important contributions of genetic factors to being overweight are illustrated by an adoption study conducted in Denmark, where records were kept on over 3,500 adoptees and their biological and adoptive parents (Meyer and Stunkard, 1993; Stunkard et al., 1986). By examining relationships between parents and adoptees reared apart or in the same family, this study found a large relationship between the body weight of adoptees and their biological parents, and little relationship between the weight status of offspring and their adopted parents. Obesity was related to genetic factors more strongly than to family environments.

It is very important to recognize that the apparent strength of genetic factors in determining obesity, body weight, and metabolism does not negate or diminish the significant effect that behavior and the environment also have in determining human obesity. Obesity is a product of genetic vulnerability and an unfavorable environment—that is, genetically predisposed individuals are likely to become obese when they are exposed to adverse environmental conditions or develop maladaptive behaviors. The combination of vulnerability and behavior cause them to gain weight.

What appears to be inherited is a tendency to be overweight, but the degree to which people actually become obese is affected by diet and exercise. There is evidence from animal studies that regular activity and a low fat diet can limit genetic tendencies to be obese (Brownell and Wadden, 1992). Social factors, such as cultural norms and attitudes toward thinness, also appear to be important in determining body weight. This was illustrated by results of the midtown Manhattan study, which surveyed a large number of people in New York City and found an inverse relationship between obesity and socioeconomic status, with lower-class individuals more likely to be overweight (Stunkard, 1979) (see Figure 12.6). In addition, study results showed that the longer one's family had been in the United States, the less likely one was to be obese. Obesity becomes less common as individuals become acculturated to American norms, which disapprove of being overweight.

Psychological Aspects of Obesity

Obese people in the United States and in other industrialized nations suffer significant prejudice (Stunkard and Wadden, 1993). This can be seen by the way that obesity and being overweight are portrayed on television, in the movies, and in the print media. Prejudice against overweight people has been

FIGURE 12.6. Decreasing prevalence of obesity with increase in own socioeconomic status (SES) and SES of origin.
Source: From P. B. Goldblatt, M. E. Moore, and A. J. Stunkard. Social factors in obesity. *Journal of the American Medical Association.* 1965, *192,* 1039–1044. Copyright 1965, American Medical Association.

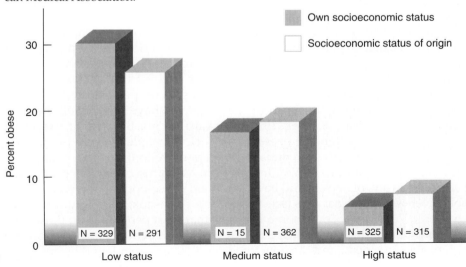

348

CHAPTER 12
Appetitive and
Addictive Behaviors:
Obesity, Smoking,
and Alcoholism

observed in children as young as 6 years old, who in one study described silhouettes of an overweight child as being lazy, stupid, dirty, and ugly (Staffieri, 1967).

Regrettably, even people who are overweight and health care professionals who must provide care appear to share these prejudices against the obese (Wadden and Stunkard, 1993). Despite this, overweight people do not, as a group, suffer more psychological disturbances than do normal weight persons. As might be expected, there are some severely obese patients who seek treatment for their obesity and who experience significant psychological distress that may require treatment (Wadden and Stunkard, 1993). In general, however, most overweight and obese people are well adjusted. In addition, there is little evidence of a discrete personality type associated with obesity and remarkable diversity of personality types among those of us who are overweight. Nevertheless, some overweight people may experience distress related to being obese. Because they are marked by an undesirable condition, their concerns about their weight may reduce quality of life and diminish self-esteem (Wadden and Stunkard, 1993).

Behavioral Aspects of Food Regulation

One way that psychological variables affect obesity is by altering food intake or impairing one's ability to regulate how much one eats. Early research on psychological factors in food regulation was conducted by Schachter and his colleagues (see Schachter and Rodin, 1974). Prompted by the observation that obese individuals did not appear to regulate their eating behavior by internal physiological needs, Schachter (1971) hypothesized that obese people are generally less responsive than other people to internal cues of hunger (such as stomach contractions). Conversely, he believed that obese people *are more* responsive to external environmental food cues such as the smell or sight of food. Obese individuals were seen as more "externally responsive" or "stimulusbound," that is, more strongly affected by stimuli in their immediate environment. For these people external factors like the time of day, reminders about food, television commercials, and other cues, such as the presence or absence of readily available food, are major determinants of eating (Schachter, 1971).

This heightened sensitivity to external factors was not limited to food or eating. Emotionally arousing events, time perception, and reactions to emotional stimuli were also affected (Schachter and Rodin, 1974). Although Schachter and his associates viewed this as a general personality trait or response style commonly found in the obese, others have interpreted these results differently (see Krantz, 1979; Stunkard, 1959). Because of the social stigma associated with being obese in our society, people who are overweight may be highly self-conscious and overly responsive to the social demands in research studies (Krantz, 1978). In addition, a number of studies challenged Schachter's view of obesity and have not found obese-normal differences in responsiveness to external cues (see Nisbett and Temoshok, 1976; Rodin and Slochower, 1976). There is even some evidence that most people—even those who are normal weight are sensitive to external cues such as perceived calorie value, attractiveness, and/or how good food tastes—regulate their intake of food (Pirke and Laessle, 1993). If we did not, those food commercials on TV would not make us so hungry! By the same token, most of us rely on what we think that we are supposed to do in a particular situation. When we "make pigs" of ourselves and when we might want to eat very lightly, we are in part determined by our interpretation of the situation in which we find ourselves.

Dietary Restraint

A series of studies by Herman, Polivy, and their colleagues indicated that the behaviors characterized as "external responsiveness" may be more closely related to dieting or to avoiding food than to obesity per se (Herman and Polivy, 1980; Pirke and Laessle, 1993). For some people, heightened sensitivity to norms regarding eating and body weight results in a pattern of chronic restraint of eating. In such cases we are aware of restraining our eating. Thus, the terms **dietary restraint** or **restrained eating** refer to the tendency to *restrict food intake consciously* in order to prevent weight gain or to promote weight loss. For example, Herman and Mack (1975) hypothesized that the differences in eating behavior between obese and nonobese people were actually due to more frequent dieting among obese people. Based on scores on a questionnaire designed to measure self-monitoring of food intake, they divided normal weight female college students into high and low restraint groups. The study was described to subjects as a taste test, but the experimenters were actually measuring the amount of ice cream that subjects consumed after participants were given either a milkshake "preload" (to fill them up) or after no preload. Unrestrained eaters in the preload condition behaved as expected, eating less during the subsequent ice cream taste test because they had just consumed the milkshake. Restrained eaters, however, behaved in a paradoxical manner, eating *more* after having consumed the milkshake preload. This behavior has been termed **counterregulation** and is explained by the release of restraint or control of food intake in restrained eaters. As a restrained eater, you might have concluded that since you had already exceeded your normal food intake with the milkshake, you might as well eat more (Pirke and Laessle, 1993).

An instrument has been revised and refined and the Revised Restraint Scale (RRS) measures responses to 10 questions asking about dieting and weight fluctuation (Heatherton, Polivy, and Herman, 1991; Herman, 1978). The questionnaire asks, for example, "How often are you dieting?" and "Do you give too much time and thought to food?" Scores range from 1 to 35, with higher values reflecting more dietary restraint (Herman, 1978). Subjects are frequently classified as "restrainers" if their score is equal to or above the median for the sample and "nonrestrainers" if their score is below that value, typically about 15 (Heatherton et al., 1988; Perkins et al., 1995). The degree of restraint in undergraduates has been shown to vary in a number of ways. Females score higher than males, whites score higher than African-Americans, and people who are overweight score higher than those who are normal weight (Klem et al., 1990).

Several other factors have been identified that affect food intake in some way. Among college women, social interaction with male students suppressed eating behavior in average restraint but not in high restraint participants (Copeland, Woods, and Hursey, 1995). Conversely, high restraint women consumed more food following a film that induced negative affect (Schotte, Cools,

350

CHAPTER 12
Appetitive and
Addictive Behaviors:
Obesity, Smoking,
and Alcoholism

and McNally, 1990). The RRS has been used to assess binge eating in disorders like bulimia nervosa (Wilson and Smith, 1989) and in people who are overweight (Marcus, Wing, and Lamparaski, 1985). Using smoking to control weight is more common among smokers who are high in dietary restraint than those who are nonrestrainers (Weekly, Klesges, and Reylea, 1992).

Behavioral Treatment of Obesity

A classic report by Stuart (1967) was a hallmark study responsible for the widespread investigation and subsequent use of behavioral treatment of obesity. We discussed Stuart's program in Chapter 10. Based on the principle of **stimulus control**, Stuart's program consisted of gradually restricting and eliminating stimuli that had come to elicit maladaptive eating behavior. At a 1-year follow-up clients in the program had lost from 26 to 46 pounds, and although weight losses of this magnitude have not been consistently found in studies conducted since Stuart's initial report, the behavioral treatment of obesity has been widespread (Stunkard and Wadden, 1993).

In Chapter 10 we also reviewed an early behavioral treatment study by Mahoney, Moura, and Wade (1973), in which principles of positive reinforcement were used to help individuals gain self-control over eating. Components of treatment that are used in modern behavioral treatment programs for obesity include *self-monitoring*—observing and recording behavior; *problem solving*—training in skills to help manage overeating, weight gain, and nonadherence issues; *nutrition education*—dietary counseling; training to slow the rate of eating; *stimulus control*—limiting exposure to food; *cognitive restructuring*—helping dieters to overcome self-defeating thoughts; and *exercise*—which is considered to be a very important component of long-term weight control (Wadden, 1993). The reader is referred to work by Wadden (1993) and Stunkard and Wadden (1993) for more detailed descriptions of specific behavioral treatment methods.

In most weight loss programs the desired outcome is weight loss and achieving some goal weight. This goal weight is often established with reference to the "ideal" weight standards published by life insurance companies (Metropolitan Life Insurance Company, 1983) or is implemented based on the weight that the client would like to be. Current approaches to treatment of obesity take into account the notion that obesity appears to be a heterogeneous phenomenon, determined by an interaction of many different biological, behavioral, and psychological factors. It is also recognized that different types of treatment approaches may be better suited for patients at levels of obesity. Indeed, in a review of the weight loss literature Brownell and Wadden (1991, 1992) suggest that we abandon the notion that a single treatment approach can be used effectively with all individuals. They propose a three-part process for establishing a treatment plan (see Figure 12.7). First, prior to establishing a plan for weight loss treatment, patients should be classified based on their degree of obesity. Individuals at increasing levels of obesity require a more aggressive and intensive treatment. Next, based on the patient's needs, the least intensive, expensive, and dangerous approaches are used first with all individuals; only nonresponders get the next most intensive step(s), and so on. This conservative approach, of adding additional treatment components as needed,

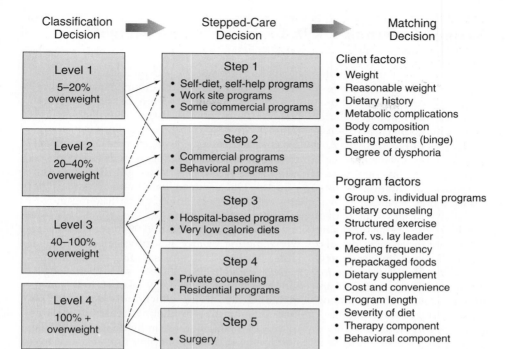

FIGURE 12.7. A conceptual scheme showing a three-stage process in selecting a treatment for an individual. The first stage, the classification decision, divides individuals according to percent overweight into four levels. The level dictates which of the five steps would be reasonable in a second stage, the stepped-care decision. This indicates that the least intensive, costly, and risky approach will be used from among the alternative treatments. The third stage, the matching decision, is used to make the final selection of a program and is based on a combination of client and program variables. The dashed lines with arrows between the classification and stepped-care stages show the lowest level of treatment that may be beneficial, but more intensive treatment is usually necessary for people at the specified weight level.
Source: From K. Brownell & T. Wadden. Reprinted from *Behavior Therapy,* 1991, *22,* 153–177. With permission.

is called *stepped care*. The third element to consider in selecting a weight loss treatment involves a matching decision in which aspects of the individual are used to find the most beneficial program for him or her. For example, some individuals might respond to a group-oriented program and others to individual treatment; some may need supervised exercise, whereas others may be capable of exercising on their own, and so on. (See the box "'The Dieting Maelstrom': Is It Advisable to Lose Weight?")

Interventions for Childhood Obesity

In addition to being a serious problem in adults, the prevalence of obesity in children is rising, with recent estimates suggesting that as many as 25 percent of 11-year-old children and 20 percent of 12 to 18 year olds are obese (Epstein

"The Dieting Maelstrom": Is It Advisable to Lose Weight?

Dieting lies at the heart of a debate that has significant repercussions for the public, health professionals, the media, and a powerful food and diet industry have significant interests. In a recent article Kelly Brownell and Judith Rodin (1994) discuss the pros and cons of this dieting controversy or "maelstrom." On one side of this debate is the cultural ideal that "thin is in" and "fat is not where it's at." The aesthetic ideal of thinness is supported by a vast industry that is valued at over $30 billion per year that supplies diet books, foods, pills, videos, and the like. On the other side are health professionals who recognize the disturbing high prevalence of obesity in our society, are frustrated by the very high relapse rates for diet programs (see below and Chapter 13), and are becoming more and more concerned that dieting itself can have negative effects on health and well-being. For example, recent surveys in the United States indicate that nearly four out of ten women and one-quarter of men report that they are dieting currently. Particularly among women, dieting has become increasingly common, even among normal weight persons—even increasing to epidemic proportions in some groups, such as adolescent girls. In addition, severe dieting is a central feature of a number of eating disorders such as bulimia nervosa, and recent attention has suggested that there may be negative health effects resulting from weight cycling, or repeated bouts of weight loss and regain of weight (Brownell and Wadden, 1992). Indeed, based on evidence of the adverse effects of dieting, an antidieting movement has arisen.

Brownell and Rodin (1994) conclude that while dieting clearly has physical and mental costs, for many individuals dieting has significant benefits as well. They identify several challenges for future health psychology research in this area, including identifying which individuals will be helped or harmed by dieting, reducing the frequency of dieting in those individuals who will be harmed by it, and developing safe and effective means for weight loss and its maintenance in individuals who stand to benefit from it.

et al., 1993). This represents a problem not only because of health risks associated with childhood obesity, but also because obesity in childhood is related to adulthood obesity. Weight loss interventions in childhood have important preventive implications as a result. Research on the treatment of childhood obesity is limited in comparison to the extensive amount of attention it has received with adults. However, a number of successful interventions have been implemented. The majority of treatment programs have focused on treating preadolescent children in the clinical settings, with fewer attempts aimed at younger children and a small number of efforts directed at evaluating school-based or preventive programs (Epstein et al., 1993). Basic components of clinical treatment for obese children include changing the child's diet, providing an exercise program, and implementing parent training.

Since obesity is often a family problem, the success of these programs may depend on the degree to which parents can influence their child's behavior. One common concern for treating young children is the possible negative effects of dieting on growth and height (Epstein et al., 1993). In this regard recent data suggest that in developing children followed for 10 years after being enrolled in a weight loss program, family-based treatments can be maintained throughout development and do not appear to affect eventual growth (Epstein et al., 1993; Epstein et al., 1990). Additional research is needed to enhance both the treatment and the prevention of childhood obesity and the maintenance of weight loss in children enrolled in such programs.

Long-Term Maintenance of Weight Loss

Once an individual has lost weight, what is the best way to help him or her avoid gaining weight back? Although behavioral programs are effective in producing weight loss, the data on helping people to maintain the weight loss are not as impressive (Brownell and Wadden, 1992; Stunkard, 1979; Wadden, 1993). Many individuals are able to lose weight for relatively short periods of time, only to regain the weight. As a result, so-called "yo-yo" dieting is a common phenomenon, which has received attention in terms of its possible adverse health effects (Brownell and Rodin, 1994). As we discuss in Chapter 13, a primary issue with most aspects of health behavior change is the prevention of relapse.

A number of techniques have been used in weight reduction programs to aid in long-term maintenance of weight loss. These include increasing the focus on exercise as a weight loss maintenance strategy; providing coping skills to aid in overcoming high-risk relapse situations and responses to violating diet and/or episodes of binge eating; and emphasizing low fat diets, which may help to overcome some of the adverse metabolic effects of weight loss (Brownell and Wadden, 1992). Programs have also used techniques of social support and multicomponent approaches employing a variety of the techniques described in this section to deal successfully with the problem of maintenance of weight loss (Perri, Sears and Clark, 1993).

CIGARETTE SMOKING AND TOBACCO USE

Nicotine, the principal addictive agent found in tobacco, is a stimulant that increases the general activity level of the central nervous system. This drug is often not included in discussions of drug abuse because it is popular, legal, and widely used. It usually does not distort one's perceptions, decrease mental functioning, or cloud one's memory. However, tobacco addiction is the most common type of drug dependency in this country. Evidence indicates that nicotine can be an extremely addictive substance (Grunberg, Brown, and Klein, 1996). If its use is suddenly discontinued, a period of depression may result. Depression and other symptoms, in part, account for the difficult time that many individuals encounter when attempting to "kick the habit."

Although nicotine produces no apparent psychological damage, the means by which it is ingested creates considerable physiological damage (LaCroix et al., 1991; Orleans et al., 1991). Chronic smoking is a major contributor to a variety of diseases, including lung cancer and cancers of the larynx and esophagus; bronchitis; emphysema; and coronary heart disease (see Figure 12.8). The nastiest effects of smoking appear not to be caused by nicotine but, rather, by tar, smoke, and carbon monoxide that are present in cigarette smoke. The widespread health implications of smoking were sufficient to motivate a series of annual reports by the U.S. Surgeon General on smoking and health. As

354

CHAPTER 12
Appetitive and
Addictive Behaviors:
Obesity, Smoking,
and Alcoholism

Joseph Califano, then Secretary of Health, Education and Welfare, pointed out after he forwarded the 1979 Surgeon General's report to Congress, smoking is "slow motion suicide." Overall, the mortality ratio for male cigarette smokers is 70 percent above that for nonsmokers (USDHHS, 1988).

As a result of evidence documenting the health hazards of tobacco, legislation was passed banning tobacco advertisements from television and radio. Each pack of cigarettes sold in this country is required to include a notice indicating its potentially harmful effects. Regulations about where one can smoke and concerns about the possible health consequences of "second-hand smoke" from other people's cigarettes have turned many against smoking. But despite growing social disapproval of smoking, these widely advertised medical dangers of smoking, and the rising cost of cigarettes, more than 20 percent of American adults still smoke cigarettes. The prevalence of smoking is even higher in other countries. These statistics attest to the potent habit-forming effects of cigarette smoking and the health problems that we face.

Many smokers either cannot quit or, if they do manage to do so, many relapse and return again to the habit (Krantz, Grunberg, and Baum, 1985; Lichtenstein and Glasgow, 1992). In addition, recent data on the prevalence of smoking among 17 to 18 year olds in the United States between 1976 and 1993 indicate that smoking among adolescents is not decreasing, and that tobacco is often the first drug used by young people who go on to use alcohol and illegal drugs (USDHHS, 1994). Because of the frightening list of health dangers associated with cigarettes, health psychologists have sought to determine the reasons why people initiate and maintain the smoking habit.

Initiation of Smoking

Research suggests that social and psychological factors are major causes of smoking initiation. Adolescents often begin to smoke as a response to social pressures to imitate peers, family members, or role models in the media (e.g., actors, athletes) (Warburton et al., 1991). Some young people begin smoking as an expression of adolescent rebellion (Jessor and Jessor, 1977; USDHHS, 1994). Although most of us are aware of the health risks of smoking, misconceptions about these risks and the fact that smoking is addictive can also contribute to the initiation of smoking. Some personality characteristics, such as extroversion, may also be associated with smoking (Eysenck, 1973). It has also been proposed that there are biological factors that affect the quality of an individual's initial experiences with cigarettes. That is, if our early experiences include intense nausea or discomfort, we are not as likely to become a habitual smoker (Silverstein et al., 1982).

Several psychological and sociological theories have been advanced to explain the initiation of the smoking habit. The presence of family or friends who smoke and serve as models, incorrect estimations of peer smoking, the value of the image of independence, lack of social support, being a risk taker, and emotional effects of smoking are related to the initiation of smoking (Camp et al., 1993). The more of these risk factors that you have, the more likely you are to start smoking. Many major theories of psychological development—psychoanalytic, psychosocial, and social learning—have been invoked to explain why people smoke (Grunberg et al., 1996; Krantz et al., 1985). Approaches to

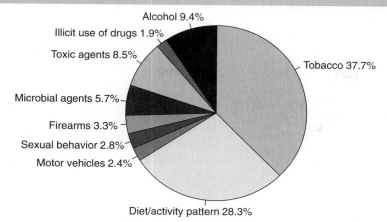

Major Contributions to Preventable Deaths, 1990

- Alcohol 9.4%
- Illicit use of drugs 1.9%
- Toxic agents 8.5%
- Tobacco 37.7%
- Microbial agents 5.7%
- Firearms 3.3%
- Sexual behavior 2.8%
- Motor vehicles 2.4%
- Diet/activity pattern 28.3%

Actual Causes of Death in the United States, 1990

Cause	Preventable Deaths	
	Estimated Number	Percentage of Total
Tobacco	400,000	37.7%
Diet/activity patterns	300,000	28.3
Alcohol	100,000	9.4
Toxic agents	90,000	8.5
Microbial agents	60,000	5.7
Firearms	35,000	3.3
Sexual behavior	30,000	2.8
Motor vehicles	25,000	2.4
Illicit use of drugs	20,000	1.9
Total	1,060,000	100.0

Source notes: McGinnis and Foege (1993): Actual Causes of Death in the United States, *JAMA 270* (18): 2207–2212. A meta-analysis was conducted of government reports, vital statistics, and articles published between 1977 and 1993 to identify and quantify the major nongenetic causes of death. Data from those meeting methodological criteria were synthesized to provide first approximations of the estimated number of deaths in 1990 by the major factors identified. Consult the original source for the various limitations in both approach and available data for this analysis. These include differences in study methodologies, variations in estimated deaths attributed to each cause, paucity of data, and types of assumptions used.

FIGURE 12.8. What percent of preventable deaths can be attributable to alcohol and illicit drug use? Alcohol and illegal drugs together account for 11 percent of preventable deaths. According to the special study of causes of death in 1990, smoking accounts for 39 percent, the greatest proportion of preventable deaths.
Source: B. A. Rouse (Ed.). *Substance Abuse and Mental Health Statistics Sourcebook.* DHHS Publication No. (SMA) 95-3064, Washington, DC: U.S. Government Printing Office, 1995.

356

CHAPTER 12
Appetitive and
Addictive Behaviors:
Obesity, Smoking,
and Alcoholism

the prevention of smoking (see Chapter 13) have applied some of those psychological theories (e.g., social learning theory) discussed in preventing smoking initiation.

Another theory used to explain why people become habitual smokers is the *affect management model*. As proposed by Tomkins (1966, 1968), it focuses on the fact that individuals seek to regulate internal emotional states. Many people smoke in order to create positive emotional states or to reduce negative emotional states. Although initial research yielded results in support of this model, subsequent work raised doubts as to the validity of affect management as an explanation for smoking behavior (Adesso and Glad, 1978; Leventhal and Avis, 1976).

Figure 12.9 presents some positive and negative factors that influence the development of smoking behavior, from the initiation through the maintenance of a habitual behavior. This summary illustrates the array of social, psychological, and biological factors that affect smoking and indicate at what point in the process they operate and whether they generally act to increase (+) or decrease (−) the likelihood of smoking.

Maintenance of Smoking

Many of the same psychological factors that influence the initiation of smoking also maintain this behavior, but additional biological and psychological factors are extremely important. Research leaves little doubt that for heavy smokers smoking is an addictive process, with nicotine being the active drug in this process (USDHHS, 1988). The 1988 U.S. Surgeon General's report went so far as to state that the pharmacological and behavioral processes that determine

FIGURE 12.9. Factors affecting different stages in the development of smoking. *Source:* Adapted with permission from R. Stepney, Smoking behavior: A psychology of the cigarette habit. *British Journal of Diseases of the Chest*, 1980, 74, 325–344.

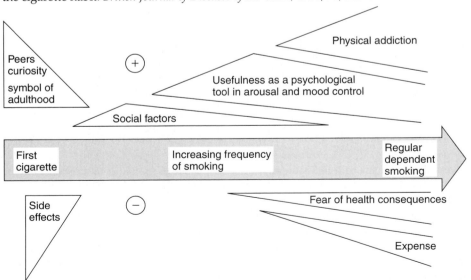

nicotine addiction are comparable in strength with those that determine addiction to drugs such as cocaine and heroin (USDHHS, 1988). An alternative account of maintenance is the *psychological tool model*, suggesting that habitual smokers self-administer tobacco to obtain physiological effects of nicotine that produce psychological rewards such as increased attention or decreased stress (Ashton and Stepney, 1982). Smokers report that having a cigarette helps them focus on their work and makes them more alert. These states are used as tools to better achieve desired goals.

A more commonly held biological model for smoking maintenance is that repeated administration of some component of tobacco (probably nicotine or one of its metabolic products) results in physical dependence (Grunberg et al., 1996; Jarvik, 1979). Support for this viewpoint comes from evidence that rats will self-administer nicotine and that human smokers smoke less when they are given intravenous administration of nicotine or chewing gum that contains nicotine (which is often prescribed to aid smokers in quitting). After physical dependence has been established, a smoker must continue to smoke to avoid unpleasant withdrawal symptoms (irritability, sleep loss, weight gain, etc.; see the next section) (Grunberg et al., 1996; Russell, 1979). They smoke more when given low-nicotine cigarettes (Benowitz et al., 1983). Withdrawal symptoms involving mood, appetite, and insomnia are also evidence of tolerance (Hughes, 1992). However, not all smokers are addicted to nicotine (Shiffman, 1989).

Biological factors alone cannot completely take into account characteristics of the smoking habit. Maintenance of smoking involves the interaction of learning mechanisms with the biochemical and physiological effects of smoking (Hunt and Matarazzo, 1970). Research has shown that the physical effects of smoking may be linked, by conditioning mechanisms, to social and environmental events. For example, heavy smokers may light up a cigarette, even though their previous cigarette is still burning in the ashtray, and smokers may have a stronger urge to smoke in situations where they are used to smoking (such as in a bar or at parties). The "after" cigarette, whether after eating or making love, is an example of the acquired value of smoking.

Another perspective on the complex interplay between biological and psychological processes is the **nicotine-titration model**. This theory is based on the notion that smokers smoke to maintain a certain level of nicotine in the blood and that heavy smokers adjust their smoking rate to keep nicotine at roughly a constant level. Schachter and his colleagues (Schachter, 1978; Schachter et al., 1977) proposed that the acid-base balance (pH) of the urine plays a role in smoking. Specifically, the rate of nicotine excretion depends, in part, on the pH of the urine, which, in turn, can be altered by psychological stress and anxiety. The more acidic or alkaline one's urine is, the faster or slower nicotine leaves the body, and the more or less one wants another cigarette. This means that links among psychological processes, the craving for cigarettes, and increased smoking are mediated by a physiological addiction mechanism involving the pH of the urine.

A series of studies (Schachter et al., 1977) provided support for this hypothesis. First, a sample of heavy smokers consistently smoked more low than high nicotine cigarettes showing that smokers "regulate" nicotine intake (see Figure 12.10). Next it was shown that when urinary pH was manipulated by the administration of alkalizing or acidifying agents, smokers smoked more when

358

CHAPTER 12
Appetitive and
Addictive Behaviors:
Obesity, Smoking,
and Alcoholism

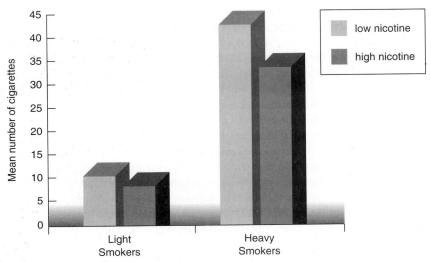

FIGURE 12.10. Effects of nicotine content on smoking. Heavy smokers smoked significantly more low nicotine cigarettes than high nicotine cigarettes.
Source: Adapted from S. Schachter et al. Nicotine regulation in heavy and light smokers. *Journal of Experimental Psychology,* 1977, *106*(1), 5–12.

urine was acidified. A third set of studies examined the urinary pH mechanism as a mediator of psychological determinants of the smoking rate. Urinary pH was found to covary with naturalistic situations (e.g., party going, examinations) that are associated with heavier smoking. The influence of psychological variables (such as stress) on the smoking rate operates because of their effects on the titration mechanism regulating levels of nicotine in the body.

Smoking Cessation

Because of the health risks of cigarette smoking, most research has concentrated on the effects of this behavior rather than on the effects of cessation. Statistics indicate that in the United States as of 1980 nearly 30 percent of men and 16 percent of women in this country were former smokers, compared with a much smaller number in 1965 (USDHHS, 1983). The number of former smokers has increased even more in the past 15 years. These ex-smokers may experience irritability, sleep disturbances, and other psychological and physical problems as they quit (Grunberg et al., 1992). In addition, many ex-smokers gain weight—a situation that discourages some people from trying to quit and that can result in new health hazards for those who quit and gain large amounts of weight (Grunberg et al., 1996; Perkins, 1994). Research suggests that weight gain accompanying withdrawal from nicotine may result from increased preferences for sweet-tasting foods (Grunberg, 1986). In a series of studies smokers who were allowed to smoke ate fewer sweets than did nonsmokers or deprived smokers. The three groups did not differ in consumption of nonsweet foods. A parallel study with animals showed that nicotine administration retarded normal growth and body weight increases in young rats.

Cessation of nicotine was accompanied by marked increases in body weight and concomitant increases in the consumption of sweet foods. Moreover, these effects could not be explained by changes in total food consumption or activity level (Grunberg, 1986).

The ability to tolerate withdrawal is crucial to the maintenance of smoking cessation. Therefore, further investigations of psychological and biological mechanisms responsible for symptoms accompanying withdrawal will suggest techniques for reducing the high relapse rate among those who quit smoking (see Chapter 13). A variety of approaches ranging from hypnosis to traditional group therapy have been used in an attempt to treat chronic smoking behavior and to deal with symptoms of withdrawal. These treatment approaches usually produce an initial period of success followed by relapse. They have produced an estimated long-term abstinence rate (greater than 1 year) of less than 15 percent (Lichtenstein, 1982). Given the addictive nature of nicotine, the introduction and availability of nicotine chewing gum and transdermal patches has helped to mitigate withdrawal symptoms, allowing people to work on behavioral and social habits separately from pharmacologic dependence.

Aversion Strategies

Aversive conditioning techniques have commonly been used to decrease smoking behavior. Aversive stimuli such as electric shock, noise, warm smoky air, and the consequences of rapid smoking are paired with either actual or imagined smoking. The long-term effectiveness of aversive conditioning procedures has been mixed (Lichtenstein, 1982). One illustrative example is the *rapid smoking method*. This method involves the smoking of cigarettes at an extremely rapid rate until additional smoking cannot be tolerated. The rapid smoking treatment sessions are repeated until smokers indicate no additional desire to smoke. "Booster" sessions are subsequently administered if the desire should return. Lichtenstein and Penner (1977) reported an outcome evaluation study that found that 34 to 47 percent of all subjects who entered this type of treatment were still abstinent 2 to 6 years after treatment.

Even though the rapid smoking technique appears to have a good degree of long-term success, it is associated with some problems that limit its use. For example, smokers with cardiovascular or pulmonary diseases (obviously an important target population requiring treatment) may not be able to tolerate such intense rapid smoking without some ill effect. Even for healthy individuals rapid smoking may be dangerous (Hauser, 1974). However, if safeguards are followed (e.g., excluding high-risk subjects and individuals over 55 requiring physician approval for participation, and limiting the duration of exposure to rapid smoking), safety can be maintained (Sachs, Hall, and Hall, 1978).

Stimulus Control

Earlier in this chapter we discussed the concept of stimulus control and how it was employed in the treatment of obesity. This kind of approach has also been used in the treatment of smoking, with the goal being to gradually narrow the stimuli or cues that are associated with smoking (e.g., smoking

360

CHAPTER 12
Appetitive and
Addictive Behaviors:
Obesity, Smoking,
and Alcoholism

only during certain situations or time periods). Results of several studies indicate that stimulus control procedures do not produce results like their use in weight management has (Bernstein and Glasgow, 1979). An interesting finding of these studies is that subjects generally do well in decreasing smoking until they reach 10 to 12 cigarettes a day. However, they then have great difficulty in reducing their consumption rate below this level. Some have suggested that this is because the gradual reduction increases the reinforcement value of each cigarette and makes the remaining cigarettes harder and harder to give up (Flaxman, 1978).

Reinforcement of Nonsmoking

Another operant procedure attempts to eliminate smoking "indirectly" by reinforcing nonsmoking behavior. The most frequently used approach has been some type of monetary reward for nonsmoking during specified periods of time. Although early reviews of the research literature on this technique indicated generally unimpressive results, later research has demonstrated that it may be an effective means of *initiating* changes in smoking behavior (Bernstein and Glasgow, 1979). It appears to be more effective in the short term and more vulnerable to relapse than some other approaches (Stitzer et al., 1986). It may thus be a useful component in a more elaborate and comprehensive treatment package. It also appears to be a strategy that people use on their own when they want to quit smoking. Buying yourself something you want (a CD, some new clothes or jewelry) each week that you are a nonsmoker can be an effective way to quit.

Multimodal Treatment Approaches

As we indicated in Chapter 10, there is a current trend among behavior therapists to use several treatment techniques for a specific disorder in order to deal effectively with all the important controlling or causal variables. Multimodal behavior therapy techniques have been developed to treat smoking. These involve procedures such as the identification of situations that precipitate smoking, the training of new habits that are incompatible with smoking, aversion techniques, group support, and relaxation. Coping skills development also appears to help people quit smoking (Zelman et al., 1992). A number of controlled studies initially produced some very encouraging results and continue to yield promising results (see Lando, 1977; Zelman et al., 1992), but additional evaluative research is needed to document effectiveness more carefully.

Promising new approaches to smoking cessation combine various elements of these kinds of interventions with pharmacological agents. The nicotine patch and nicotine gum are products that contain and impart enough nicotine through the skin or oral tissue to give ex-smokers a "fix" and to minimize physiological craving while quitting. Several studies of cessation programs using these products have been conducted, and most of them suggest that this approach has great potential (Cepeda-Benito, 1993; Tonnesen et al., 1988). However, its value is more limited for long-term as opposed to short-term cessation, and there are instances in which the use of gum or a patch to limit withdrawal symptoms is less effective (Hughes, 1992; Tonnesen et al., 1991). Despite these problems, combined approaches like this probably offer the best hope currently for getting people to successfully quit smoking.

The Problem of Relapse

Some effective techniques to help people quit smoking have been developed. However, in the past investigators have not been as concerned with the important problem of **relapse**. We know that up to 80 percent of smokers who initially succeed at quitting smoking will relapse over a 12-month follow-up period (Hunt and Bespalec, 1974) (see Chapter 13). Because of this, smoking relapse has received increased research attention, and the National Working Conference on Smoking Relapse sponsored by the National Institutes of Health (Shumaker and Grunberg, 1986) took an important first step in addressing this significant health concern.

One major suggestion made by this conference was the use of a "stages of change" conceptualization of relapse prevention developed by Prochaska (1992) (see Chapter 13 for a discussion of the transtheoretical model emphasizing a "stages of change" approach). Simply providing booster sessions to treatment programs is usually not successful in preventing relapse. Rather, it was suggested that relapse-prevention programming be initiated in the early stages of the behavior change process rather than after the individual has remained abstinent for a certain period of time. The major stages include *preparation* and *quitting*, during which efforts are made to change how smokers view their smoking behavior; *early maintenance of change*; *late maintenance of change*; and *recycling* after a temporary relapse has occurred.

Other factors appear to be important in relapse as well. Craving, because of either dependence or strong psychological need, appears to be a major factor in relapse (Killen et al., 1992). The severity of associated feelings, such as anxiety, irritability, and sleeplessness, may also prove to be too much and cause a quitter to relapse (Orleans et al., 1991). The dramatic weight gain and change in eating habits that accompany smoking cessation may cause a relapse (Klesges and Shumaker, 1992) (see Figure 12.11). The strength of previously learned associations (such as smoking while you talk on the phone) may also prove to be obstacles to successful cessation. However, we now know that an isolated relapse is not cause for alarm if it is followed by continued efforts to quit. If we think of a relapse as a "slip" rather than a major defeat and go on as if it never happened, we may be more likely to quit for good.

Smoking Education and Prevention Programs

As we noted earlier in this chapter, many current public health efforts are now using behavioral principles in educating the public to increase good health habits (Lichtenstein and Glasgow, 1992) (see Chapter 13). For many years school and health organizations have been providing education about the dangers of smoking, but only in recent years has attention been directed at modifying the behavioral and social factors involved in the smoking-initiation process. For example, there have been a number of impressive studies demonstrating the use of prevention strategies to discourage children and adolescents

362

CHAPTER 12
Appetitive and
Addictive Behaviors:
Obesity, Smoking,
and Alcoholism

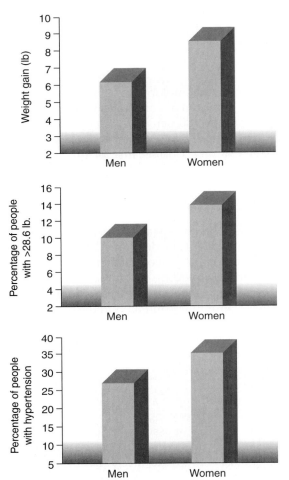

FIGURE 12.11. Weight gain and hypertension following smoking cessation. Women appear to experience more dramatic effects of smoking cessation than do men. *Source:* R. C. Klesges and S. A. Shumaker. Understanding the relations between smoking and body weight and their importance to smoking cessation and relapse. *Health Psychology,* 1992, *11*(suppl.), 1–3.

from initiating smoking (Evans et al., 1981; Flay, 1985) (see Chapter 13). Information, skills training, and appropriate models teaching children that they can decide not to smoke have proven effective (Evans et al., 1984). Work site interventions and education campaigns have also been implemented and are associated with modest gains (Borland et al., 1991; Hymowitz et al., 1991).

In reflecting on research directed at the control of smoking behavior at that time, Hunt and Matarazzo (1982) concluded that although the results of treatments are quite varied, there are encouraging signs that changes are being made in smoking behavior overall. The prevailing "zeitgeist" is one of increasing public intolerance of smoking and increased legislation against smoking. This has been in large part due to the extensive education and prevention programs over the years (Hunt and Matarazzo, 1982). The nonsmoking "ethos" is an important factor in recent statistics indicating a decline in the consumption rate of cigarettes. This nonsmoking ethos and the declining consumption rate, together with the conservative estimate that 25 percent of subjects achieve long-term abstinence after behavioral treatment (a figure that does not include those individuals who voluntarily quit on their own), provide reason for optimism about changing smoking behavior.

ALCOHOL ABUSE AND DEPENDENCE

Approximately one hundred million people in the United States use alcoholic beverages moderately and without harmful effects. Another approximately 5 to 10 million people abuse alcohol and are labeled alcoholics or problem drinkers because of the harm they do to themselves, others, and/or society. Excessive problem drinking on and off the job may cost U.S. industry more than $15 billion a year. Besides these significant economic consequences, alcohol abuse also presents a significant health hazard. It is second only to heroin as an addiction that can cause death. Finally, it has been estimated that two-thirds of the nation's highway fatalities are alcohol-related (see Figure 12.12).

The precise statistics on the incidence of alcohol abuse vary depending on one's definition of alcoholism. There is as yet no one clear, precise, and totally accepted definition of alcoholism. In any consideration of alcohol abuse and dependence one must be aware of the variety of possible drinking patterns and the possible complex of determinants—physiological, psychological, and cultural/situational—of maladaptive drinking behavior (Nathan, 1993). *Episodic heavy drinking* is usually defined as five or more drinks at one time, whereas **alcoholism** is characterized as a disease with genetic, environmental, and behavioral causes (MMWR, 1992; Morse and Flavin, 1992). Alcoholism is usually progressive and can be fatal. Its warning signs include loss of control over drinking, preoccupation with alcohol, and distortions in thought (Morse and Flavin, 1992). Based on existing evidence, most scientists and clinicians agree that genetic transmission is an important factor in the etiology of alcoholism (Dawson et al., 1992; Pickens and Svikis, 1991). Sociocultural factors also play a role in responses to and attitudes toward alcohol (Nathan, 1993).

Behavioral Explanations of Alcoholism

The first influential behavioral explanation of the etiology of alcohol abuse and alcoholism was the *tension-reduction hypothesis*. This hypothesis assumed that alcohol is a tension-reducer and that it is reinforcing for alcoholics because it reduces their tension and anxiety. For example, increased anxiety and increased alcohol intake are associated (McNamee, Mello, and Mendelson, 1968), and anxiety reduction due to alcohol consumption by human subjects has also been demonstrated. More recent research suggests that stress or tension-reducing aspects of alcohol use are one reason that alcohol is used (see Clark and Sayette, 1993).

Although personality factors do not predict alcohol use very well (see Nathan, 1993), research suggests that some individuals may learn to cope with tension-producing life situations by drinking alcohol. However, several studies do not support this aspect of the tension-reduction hypothesis. For example, Nathan and O'Brien (1971) compared a group of male alcoholics and a matched group of nonalcoholics on a variety of behavioral dimensions. After

364

*CHAPTER 12
Appetitive and
Addictive Behaviors:
Obesity, Smoking,
and Alcoholism*

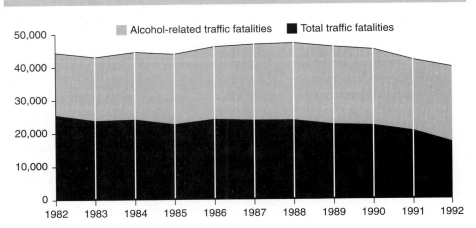

Traffic Fatalities, 1982 to 1992

	Alcohol related	Nonalcohol related	Total	Percent of Alcohol related of Total
1982	25,165	18,780	43,945	57.3%
1983	23,646	18,943	42,589	55.5
1984	23,758	20,499	44,257	53.7
1985	22,716	21,109	43,825	51.8
1986	24,045	22,011	46,056	52.2
1987	23,641	22,749	46,390	51.0
1988	23,626	23,461	47,087	50.2
1989	22,436	23,146	45,582	49.2
1990	22,084	22,515	44,599	49.5
1991	19,887	21,621	41,508	47.9
1992	17,699	21,536	39,235	45.1

Source notes: Data from the National Highway Traffic Safety Administration, Fatal Accident Reporting System, 1993. A variety of indicators are used to determine alcohol-related accidents. These include blood alcohol content (BAC) results and driving while intoxicated (DWI) citations. The Fatal Accident Reporting System (FARS) contains data on a census of fatal traffic crashes within the 50 states, the District of Columbia, and Puerto Rico. To be included in FARS, a crash must involve a motor vehicle travelling on a trafficway customarily open to the public and result in the death of a person (occupant of a vehicle or a non-motorist) within 30 days of the crash. The FARS file contains descriptions, in a standard format of each fatal crash reported. Each crash has more than 100 different coded data elements that characterize the crash, the vehicles, and the people involved. The specific data elements may be modified slightly each year to conform to changing user needs, vehicle characteristics, and highway safety emphasis areas.

FIGURE 12.12. What are the trends in alcohol-related traffic fatalities? Alcohol-related traffic fatalities declined over the past decade. The number of alcohol-related traffic fatalities dropped from 25,165 in 1982 to 17,699 in 1992. The proportion of all traffic fatalities that were alcohol-related also declined. The proportion dropped from 57 percent of all traffic fatalities alcohol-related in 1982 to 45 percent alcohol-related in 1992.
Source: B. A. Rouse (Ed.). *Substance Abuse and Mental Health Statistics Sourcebook.* DHHS Publication No. (SMA) 95-3064, Washington, DC: U.S. Government Printing Office, 1995.

an initial 20- to 24-hour period of drinking during which the anxiety level does decrease, there is a period during which anxiety and depression levels actually *increase*. Thus, despite the physiological tension-reducing properties of alcohol use, there may be an increase in the cognitive or self-report component of anxiety. Personality or predisposing conditions may be related to stress and attentional problems (Alterman and Tartar, 1983; Glenn and Parsons, 1989). Although the tension-reduction model may partly explain why the alcoholic initiates a new episode of drinking, it cannot explain why self-reported anxiety increases following alcohol ingestion. A more comprehensive model is needed to take into account results such as these as well as expectancy effects.

Alcohol and Expectancy Effects

In recent years sophisticated research has assessed the pharmacological effects of alcohol independently of what people expect alcohol will do to them. What had long been considered a pharmacological effect of alcohol was revealed to be the result of a complex interaction of a number of factors. These include our expectations of what the effects of alcohol will be, our past history of alcohol use, the environment in which alcohol use occurs, and the specific actions of alcohol on physiological functioning.

Children of alcoholics have different expectancies about drinking alcohol than do others of the same age and gender. They are usually more likely to believe that the outcomes will be more positive (Martin et al., 1994). Positive expectations, in turn, can motivate people to drink (Brown and Munson, 1987; Cox and Klinger, 1988). Research has also shown that drinking by alcoholic subjects was more strongly related to the *belief* that they were drinking alcohol rather than the pharmacological effects of drinking itself. Marlatt and colleagues (1973) manipulated the type of beverage consumed (alcohol or a tonic water placebo). All subjects were informed that they were participating in a taste-testing experiment on alcohol. One-half the subjects were further told that they would receive alcohol; the other half were told that they were in the "control" condition and would receive only tonic water rather than alcohol. In reality, one-half of the subjects in each of these two groups received alcohol, whereas the other half received tonic water. The actual amount of consumption was determined by whether the subjects thought that they were drinking alcohol and not by the actual alcohol content of the drinks. Thus, expectancy factors appeared to play a significant role in determining beverage consumption by alcoholics.

There have been many other studies of the complex interactions that determine the effect of alcohol. Behaviors and moods such as aggression, anxiety, pain, and sexual arousal may all be important. Wilson and Lawson (1976) found that both men and women reported higher levels of sexual arousal when they believed that they had consumed alcohol (whether or not they had actually done so) than when they believed that they had consumed tonic water. These results suggested that the subjective or psychological effects of alcohol consumption are often independent of physiologically induced effects.

366

CHAPTER 12
*Appetitive and
Addictive Behaviors:
Obesity, Smoking,
and Alcoholism*

Behavioral Treatments of Problem Drinking and Alcoholism

As with other health-impairing habits, a variety of approaches have been tried to reduce problem drinking. Several are similar to those used for obesity or smoking cessation although the relative effectiveness of each may differ. The most critical aspect of treating a drinking problem is getting someone to recognize that he or she has one. Even pointing out that one has several warning signs of alcoholism does not always "work" for some people. Some of us are sure that we can stop drinking anytime, and many people who have major alcohol abuse problems do not believe they do. The importance of making them see their problems cannot be understated. This is a necessary first step on the road to treatment and "cure." Confronting people with alcohol problems, which may be done by friends or family, is one way to make people see these problems. However this is done, the recognition of problems and the willingness to deal with them appear to be critical elements in any treatment plan.

Another issue is dropping out of treatment. We have considered a relapse from smoking cessation and weight management, and it is an important issue in treating alcohol abuse as well. With anything that may be addictive or highly reinforcing, dropping out of treatment or resuming the behavior one gave up is a problem. The desire to "feel good again" can overcome the desire to quit and relapse occurs. Motivation to remain in a cessation program or the strength of one's intention to quit drinking may be the only real protection against relapse in this case. Self-efficacy and a strong sense of perceived control help people to resist relapse and to stay with treatment or abstinence (Rychtarik et al., 1992). Often getting people "clean," or free of alcohol, is the most important single step in the process, and once someone is on the road to recovery, relapses need not spell the end of the treatment. Again, as with smoking and overeating, relapses should be treated as temporary setbacks that can be overcome.

Aversive Therapy

Initial applications of behavioral techniques to treating alcohol abuse are aimed primarily at eliminating the maladaptive drinking behavior. A major method employed was **aversive therapy**. Three different types of aversive stimuli have been used in these approaches: chemical stimuli, including chemical nausea agents such as Antabuse, and drugs that produce muscular paralysis; electric shock; and verbal descriptions of nauseating scenes. Aversion therapy using electrical stimuli typically involves instructing the patient to sip a sample of his or her favorite drink but not to swallow it, at which time an electric shock is administered. The shock can be terminated by spitting out the drink. This technique was used with some success with alcoholics (see Blake, 1967; Miller and Hersen, 1972).

A widely known form of chemical aversion treatment uses Antabuse, a chemical that is taken in pill form by alcoholics each day. Within 2 days of ingestion, it begins to interfere with the metabolic processing of alcohol by the body. Under most conditions Antabuse has no effects on how people feel, but as a patient drinks alcohol, an extremely unpleasant reaction occurs, including nausea and other physiological discomforts. The treatment attempts to make people associate illness with drinking, but one of the problems with this type of treatment is that the patient can discontinue the use of Antabuse after leaving the hospital. Also, like other forms of aversion therapy, it cannot be used for patients with certain physical disorders because of the stressful nature of the chemical treatment.

Wiens and Menustik (1983) reported follow-up data from 685 patients treated with aversion therapy in a hospital. Results indicated that 63 percent of the patients treated maintained continuous abstinence for 1 year. Moreover, approximately one-third the patients reported continuous abstinence for 3 years. Planned after-care contact was a very important component of the treatment program for these patients. More evidence is needed to evaluate the long-term effectiveness of aversion therapy for problem drinking. Although a number of different aversive stimuli have been used, the most effective aversive stimuli have not been identified.

Contingency Contracting/Operant Procedures

Contingency contracting procedures have promise as a method of managing the behavior of alcoholics. The essential ingredient in such programs is reinforcement used to maintain sobriety that is more powerful than the alcohol itself. Bigelow and his associates (see Bigelow et al., 1973) have conducted a number of studies that suggest a potential value of such programs.

One of their first studies assessed the ability of four hospital employees, who were in danger of being fired, to abstain from drinking (Bigelow, Liebson, and Lawrence, 1973). These employees were required, on the basis of a contract, to report on a daily basis to the hospital's alcoholism treatment unit in order to receive Antabuse. It was agreed that failure to report would result in no work and no pay. This contingency contract program produced significant improvements in the job performance and attendance of all four employees. Similar results have been reported in studies of inpatients and outpatients (Griffiths, Bigelow, and Liebson, 1978). A wide variety of other such operant-contingency studies demonstrate that alcoholics can be helped to moderate or terminate their drinking in this manner (Lang and Marlatt, 1982; Nathan and Goldman, 1979). (See the box "From Alcoholic to Social Drinker?")

Alcoholics Anonymous

One of the most widely accepted approaches to the treatment of alcoholism is Alcoholics Anonymous (AA). Many experienced clinicians urge their patients to join and become active in AA, either in conjunction with behavioral treatments or as a sole treatment for alcoholism (Nathan, 1993). Crucial to the understanding of how AA works are the "12 steps," which include the recognition and admission of past sins, the willingness to trust a higher power in pursuit of abstinence, and earnest efforts to stop drinking. Initial interest in AA is quickly followed by complete involvement in a group of caring individuals who provide strong social support and represent an alcohol-free way of life. They are ready to help on the journey along the 12 steps. Although AA has the

From Alcoholic to Social Drinker?

Through the years a controversial question has been whether alcoholics can be treated and retrained to become controlled social drinkers. A common viewpoint, argued by Alcoholics Anonymous (AA), is that alcoholism is an irreversible "disease," and so the alcoholic must totally abstain from drinking. If not, he or she will "lose control" and not be able to stem the "craving" or stop drinking until totally intoxicated. Some recent research questions the notion that total abstinence is needed in the treatment of alcoholism. Techniques have been developed that show great promise for teaching alcoholics to become controlled social drinkers.

Spurred by several studies suggesting that alcoholics could be trained to estimate their blood alcohol level on the basis of subjective feelings of intoxication, a study published in 1975 by the Rand Corporation generated a great deal of controversy because it suggested the possibility of "controlled" social drinking and questioned the dogma of complete abstinence for some alcoholics (Armor, Polick, and Stambul, 1976). Opponents of the controlled drinking approach, primarily AA, argue that public acceptance of this Rand report position may give reformed alcoholics an "excuse" to take a few drinks in an attempt to become controlled drinkers. This might start them on the road back to alcoholism. These opponents generated a great deal of public and political pressure against the Rand report, and attempts were made to force a retraction. This was unfortunate since the report did not advocate "controlled" drinking as a possibility for all alcoholics but suggested that this goal *might* be possible with certain alcoholics. The report emphasized that additional research is needed to determine whether this is a viable approach. Indeed, comprehensive reviews of this "controlled social drinking" literature concluded that because of conceptual and methodological shortcomings of much of the past research in this area, a great deal of additional investigation is needed to determine the viability of this possibility (see Emrick, 1975; Lloyd and Salzberg, 1975; Nathan and Lansky, 1978).

Another important event that "fueled the fire" of this controversy was a study by Penderay, Maltzman, and West (1982). This investigation presented evidence based on a 10-year follow-up of patients originally treated in a study by Sobell and Sobell (1973). This latter study was frequently cited as an example of how controlled drinking behavior could be produced in alcoholics. Penderay and colleagues, after contacting the patients who were administered this form of controlled drinking treatment, significantly cast doubt on the validity of the original findings. They found that some of the treated patients had seriously relapsed, and they also questioned whether some of the original results may have been fabricated. These discrepancies were aired on the television show *60 Minutes* which suggested to the audience that the data were, in fact, seriously flawed. A great deal of negative publicity was thus generated for the controlled drinking approach, and a blue-ribbon panel of independent investigators was formed to review Sobell and Sobell's (1973) experimental results. The investigators concluded that there was no reasonable cause to doubt the scientific or personal integrity of Sobell and Sobell. Subsequently, the Committee on Science and Technology of the U.S. Congress supported this conclusion.

What, then, is the most constructive view to take at the present time on the issue of treatment goals (complete abstinence or controlled drinking)? Recent views of alcoholism and problem drinking have changed the nature of the abstinence/controlled drinking debate. According to Sobell and Sobell (1995), broader models of alcoholism include differentiating alcohol-abusing populations with respect to dependence severity. Epidemiological studies have shown that chronic alcoholics constitute a minority of those with alcohol problems (e.g., Calahan, 1987). Based on this type of evidence, many models of alcohol abuse broadened to include problem drinkers who do not meet the criteria for alcoholism. Problem drinkers have become the focus of research on controlled drinking (Heather, 1990; Sanchez-Craig, Annis, Bornet, and MacDonald, 1984). Indeed, after reviewing 25 years of studies on abstinence versus controlled drinking, Sobell and Sobell (1995) observed that people who were severely dependent on alcohol benefited more from abstinence and that people who were not severely dependent benefited from controlled drinking strategies.

Taking into account both sides of the issue, Nathan and Goldman (1979) suggested the following which still holds true today:

1. Abstinence should be considered the initial goal of treatment for alcoholism.
2. Sober alcoholics should not be led to believe that they can ever drink in a controlled manner. There are currently no unequivocal data to support the validity of this goal.
3. Alcoholics who have repeatedly attempted and failed to stop drinking, who regret having done so, and who are physically able to drink moderately should be considered as possible candidates for controlled-drinking treatment. This view is based on the assumption that controlled social drinking, while less desirable than complete abstinence, is nevertheless more desirable than uncontrolled alcoholism.
4. Additional research comparing the relative long-term effectiveness of abstinence-oriented versus controlled drinking-oriented drinking is greatly needed before any confident decision on treatment goals can be made for anyone.

enormous admiration and respect of clinicians and others in the alcoholism field who believe that it is perhaps the most effective available approach for the alcoholic, it has historically been difficult to evaluate its effectiveness by means of controlled studies (Nathan, 1993).

SUMMARY

This chapter has described how psychological analysis and treatment techniques have been systematically applied to and evaluated with three behavioral problems that have significant health consequences: obesity and weight reduction, smoking, and problem drinking/alcoholism. The area of obesity occupies a central position in the field of health psychology because, historically, it was one of the first major medical concerns to be dealt with by behavioral intervention techniques. We discussed biological and psychosocial factors in the etiology of obesity, including genetics, the concept of set point, and social norms. Next we considered psychological aspects of food regulation as well as the behavioral treatment of obesity. The general conclusion was that behavioral treatment methods are the method of choice to aid people to lose weight. One important question requires further attention, though: Once an individual has lost weight, what is the best method to aid him or her to avoid gaining it back? Although behavioral programs are effective in producing weight loss, the data on helping people to maintain weight loss are not as impressive.

We then discussed the problem of chronic smoking and the social, psychological, and biological factors that contribute to this habit. Initiation of smoking is largely determined by social factors such as peer pressure and social modeling. The nicotine-titration model proposes to explain the maintenance of smoking by suggesting that smokers smoke to keep nicotine at a roughly constant level in the body. Also reviewed in this chapter was research on the consequences of smoking cessation, including weight gain, that impede many people from giving up the smoking habit.

370

*CHAPTER 12
Appetitive and
Addictive Behaviors:
Obesity, Smoking,
and Alcoholism*

We also noted that multimodal treatment techniques show some promise in effectively reducing smoking behavior. Moreover, there are encouraging signs that social pressures are having an effect on smoking behavior. The prevailing "zeitgeist" is one of increasing public intolerance of smoking and increasing legislation against smoking. This nonsmoking ethos is a motivating factor that is important in taking into account recent statistics indicating a decline in the consumption rate of cigarettes.

Lastly, in our discussion of alcoholism we noted that there is no one clear, precise, and totally accepted definition of alcoholism. In any consideration of alcoholism one must be aware of the variety of possible drinking patterns and the possible complexity of determinants—physiological, psychological, and cultural/situational—of maladaptive drinking behavior. We reviewed recent evidence for neurophysiological influences on the craving for alcohol and the interaction of physiological and psychological factors in this process (the neuropsychogenetic model). In addition, we reviewed the various cognitive-behavioral treatment techniques employed for alcoholism, including aversion techniques and contingency contracting-operant methods. Although unidimensional techniques such as aversion therapy show promise for eliminating the maladaptive drinking or consumptive response, one must also simultaneously deal with the situational variables that may be contributing to the maintenance of this drinking behavior. Multimodal behavioral approaches need to be developed to deal with all the important contributing factors.

RECOMMENDED READINGS

Brownell, K., and Wadden, T. Etiology and treatment of obesity: Understanding a serious, prevalent, and refractory disorder. *Journal of Consulting and Clinical Psychology,* 1992, *60*, 505–517.

Grunberg, N. E., Brown, K. J., and Klein, L. C. Tobacco smoking. In A. Baum, C. McManus, S. Newman, et al., (Eds.). *Cambridge handbook of psychology, health, and medicine.* Cambridge: Cambridge University Press, 1997.

Nathan, P. E. Alcoholism: Psychopathology, etiology, and treatment. In P. B. Sutker and H. E. Adams (Eds.), *Comprehensive handbook of psychopathology,* 2nd ed. New York: Plenum Press, 1993.

Stunkard, A. J., and Wadden, T. *Obesity: Theory and therapy,* 2nd ed. New York: Raven Press, 1993.

U.S. Department of Health and Human Services. (USDHHS) *The health consequences of smoking: Nicotine addiction. A report of the surgeon general.* (DHHS Publication No. 82- 50179). Washington, DC: U.S. Government Printing Office, 1988.

CHAPTER 13

Prevention and Health Promotion

Medical treatments are expensive. As we have seen throughout this book, once people are ill, there are a limited number of things that can be done to intervene and these treatments are not always effective. In some cases no treatments are available, and extraordinary medical solutions such as transplants are very costly. To save money and to improve overall health, prevention is an important option. "An ounce of prevention is worth a pound of cure" is an old saying that reflects an early awareness of the fact that it is easier, better, and healthier to prevent disease rather than to treat or cure it. Actually, the dramatic reductions in infectious illnesses and mortality due to diseases like influenza were not because of the discovery of antibiotics alone. Prevention in the form of improved sanitation and diet and the development of vaccines were also critical in this effort. Prevention is still one of the most important issues in medicine today. Having an appropriate diet, exercising, and not smoking may help you to avoid heart disease and the lifelong medication you might have to take. They may also help to eliminate the costs and risks associated with increasingly intense interventions, and to avoid extraordinary medical interventions.

Health psychology has several areas of application showing how prevention can be used to reduce health care costs and disease. Smoking (Chapter 12) and AIDS are critical health problems that have enormous behavioral components. Smoking is a behavior that is clearly easier and more efficient to prevent than treat. AIDS (Chapter 6) currently has no cure, and although new drugs offer hope of controlling the disease, prevention is the most effective way to deal with it. AIDS is spread by behaviors (e.g.,unprotected sex, IV drug use), and if the behaviors that cause this spread can be controlled, the disease can be avoided. By learning more about the risk factors for different diseases and how to counteract them, and how to modify those risks that can be changed, we will be in a better position to prevent the major health threats of our time.

In Chapter 1 we described how, at the turn of the century, the leading causes of morbidity and mortality were infectious diseases such as pneumonia and influenza. Even with the enormous concern and attention recently directed at the AIDS epidemic, infectious diseases are not the primary diseases now. By far the leading causes of death today are chronic diseases such as coronary heart disease and cancers. These diseases are strongly affected by behavioral and environmental factors, and in recent years there has been an enormous increase in attention to behavioral factors in preventive medicine and health promotion. Several major policy reports on health promotion and disease prevention (USDHHS, 1988, 1991), the increase of public and media interest in healthy lifestyles, the growth of health promotion programs in industry, and the focus on promoting healthy behaviors to reduce health care costs are but a few manifestations of this interest in behavioral aspects of prevention. All this attention is certainly fashionable, but is it justified? The overwhelming weight of evidence suggests that it is (USDHHS, 1991)!

BEHAVIORAL IMMUNOGENS AND PATHOGENS

Early reports focusing on the importance of behavioral factors in health estimated that 50 percent of the mortality from the 10 leading causes of death could be attributed to lifestyle (USDHEW, 1979). Those habits that are health-impairing have been called **behavioral pathogens** (Matarazzo, 1984a, b), and beneficial or health-protective behavioral practices have been called **behavioral immunogens** (Matarazzo, 1984b). For example, cigarette smoking is linked with more than 350,000 deaths a year from heart disease, cancers, and chronic lung diseases (Grunberg, 1988). About 200,000 deaths a year can be attributed to excessive consumption of alcohol, and fatal injuries (many alcohol-related or caused by driver error and preventable by use of seat belts) claim more than 100,000 lives each year in the United States (USDHHS, 1990).

A recent analysis of international data (Peto et al., 1992) projected that 3 million deaths worldwide each year can be attributed to smoking. Add to this list recent public concerns about the AIDS epidemic—a disease that has become one of the leading killers of young adults, and which can only be prevented through behavioral change. Other estimates suggest that 7 of the 10 leading causes of death in this country (heart disease, cancer, stroke, automobile accidents, diabetes, cirrhosis of the liver, and arteriosclerosis) could be reduced significantly if vulnerable individuals would change just five behaviors: smoking, alcohol abuse, nutrition, exercise, and adherence to medications to control hypertension (USDHHS, 1990—*Healthy People 2000*).

You have heard all this before: in Chapter 1 when we introduced the field of health psychology and throughout this book as we have addressed specific issues. Behavior is vital to maintaining good health and behavioral factors are important elements in the development and the progression of disease. Prevention is perhaps the "jewel in the crown" of health psychology because it brings to bear the theories and methods of psychology to prevent or modify behaviors that can kill us. Our faith in prevention and our belief that behavior is a critical element in this are, in part, derived from research such as a well-known longitudinal study conducted by Belloc and Breslow (1976). These investigators examined the relationship between personal health practices and subsequent health status and death rates among nearly 7,000 adults. Their survey identified seven specific personal health practices that were highly correlated with physical health. Sleeping 7 to 8 hours per day, eating breakfast almost every day, never smoking cigarettes, rarely eating between meals, being at or near a prescribed weight, having moderate or no use of alcohol, and doing regular physical activity were associated with good health. Those people who followed most or all of these seven simple practices were healthier than those who followed none or few of these practices (Belloc and Breslow, 1976). In a 5½-year follow-up study these initial health practices were compared with subsequent mortality (see Figure 13.1). Summing the number of practices for each individual showed a strong relationship to mortality: The more positive behavioral health practices are, the lower the mortality is at each age group. These findings were subsequently confirmed after nearly 10 years of follow-up (Breslow and Enstrom, 1980).

Looking more closely at the protective *behavioral immunogens*, what is the potential impact of adopting a healthy lifestyle? Other than preventing disease, one obvious answer is a long, healthy, and enjoyable life. To examine the benefits of health-promoting behavior, researchers interested in how to maximize human life expectancy have studied characteristics of people around the world who live long lives, with the idea that perhaps they are doing something right. For example, in areas of the former Soviet Republic of Georgia (now an independent nation), between the Caucasus Mountains and the Black Sea, live the Abkhasians. These people claim to live to very old ages—sometimes as old as 120 to 170 years. In our society the fact that about three individuals are over age 100 per 100,000 people is considered normal (Santrock, 1986). However, a

FIGURE 13.1. Age-specific mortality rates by the number of health practices followed by subgroups of males and females.
Source: Adapted from N. B. Belloc. Relationship of health practices and mortality. *Preventive Medicine,* 1973, 2, 67–81. Copyright 1973, Academic Press.

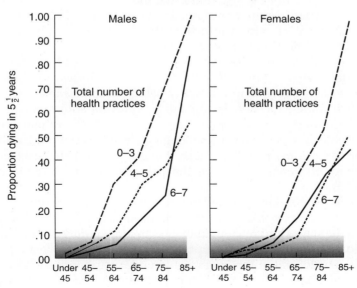

much higher percentage of about 400 centenarians per 100,000 people has been reported among the Abkhasians (Benet, 1974). Moreover, these people stay active, vigorous, and mentally and physically healthy into old age. Most of the elderly there have good hearing and vision, have good posture, and are physically active (Benet, 1974).

We now know that the Abkhasian claims of longevity are exaggerated, partly because no accurate birth records were kept and partly because old people have higher status in their society. It is also believed that the actual upper limits of human life span appear to be about 110 to 120 years (Fries, 1976). Despite exaggerated claims, the Abkhasians do appear to be especially long-lived. This is likely due to their genetic history of longevity, as well as their unique lifestyle (Weg, 1983). The Abkhasians lead predictable lives, and people stay physically and mentally active, maintaining vigorous work roles and habits as long as possible. Their staple diet is low in saturated fat and meat products and high in fruit and vegetables, with no or small amounts of alcoholic beverages and nicotine. Overeating is considered dangerous and obesity is greatly discouraged. In addition, the integration of the elderly into an extended family and into community life as full-functioning members gives them a sense of belonging and a sense of personal control that helps to reduce and avoid stress, and gives the elderly social support and encouragement to maintain their zest for life. These behavioral characteristics are strikingly similar to the behavioral immunogens described by Matarazzo (1984b).

These lifestyle and psychosocial conditions combine to protect these older individuals against the chronic diseases that often accompany old age, and encourage a vigorous, active life that helps them to maintain optimal psychological and physical functions (Fries, 1976; Weg, 1983). Indeed, research has made it possible to estimate one's own predicted life expectancy based on a variety of personal habits, in conjunction with some biological factors such as the longevity of one's parents (see the box "How Long Will You Live?").

The substantial relationships between major chronic diseases and modifiable behavioral factors that are under the individual's control have fostered prevention-oriented research and practice in health psychology. It is possible to classify preventive efforts into three types: **primary prevention**, which refers to the modification of risk factors before disease develops. In many respects this is a highly cost-effective and beneficial strategy, for in the long term the potential costs in lives and dollars of treating disease are likely to outweigh the costs of preventing unhealthy habits. Examples of primary prevention efforts include educational campaigns to prevent adolescents from smoking or to encourage "safe sex" practices to prevent AIDS. Primary prevention is effective, but it is particularly challenging since it is often difficult to motivate otherwise healthy people to make changes in their behavior that may not have immediate benefits, despite the promise of long-term health gains (Miller, 1983).

The terms **secondary prevention** and **tertiary prevention** refer, respectively, to interventions taken to arrest the progress of illness already in early asymptomatic stages and rehabilitation and treatment interventions to stop the progression of disease that is symptomatic. Although less cost-effective and perhaps less beneficial in the long run, secondary and tertiary prevention activities may be easier to accomplish in that appropriate target groups (e.g.,

How Long Will You Live?

This is a rough guide for calculating your personal longevity. The basic life expectancy for males is age 67 and for females it is age 75. Write down your basic life expectancy. If you are in your 50s or 60s, you should add ten years to the basic figure because you have already proven yourself to be quite durable. If you are over age 60 and active, add another two years.

Basic Life Expectancy _____
Decide how each item below applies to you and add or subtract the appropriate number of years from your basic life expectancy.

1. Family history
   Add 5 years if 2 or more of your grand-parents lived to 80 or beyond. _____
   Subtract 4 years if any parent, grandparent, sister, or brother died of heart attack or stroke before 50. Subtract 2 years if anyone died from these diseases before 60. _____
   Subtract 3 years for each case of diabetes, thyroid disorders, breast cancer, cancer of the digestive system, asthma, or chronic bronchitis among parents or grandparents. _____
2. Marital status
   If you are married, add 4 years. _____
   If you are over 25 and not married, subtract 1 year for every unwedded decade. _____
3. Economic status
   Subtract 2 years if your family income is over $40,000 per year. _____
   Subtract 3 years if you have been poor for greater part of life. _____
4. Physique
   Subtract one year for every 10 pounds you are overweight. _____
   For each inch your girth measurement exceeds your chest measurement deduct 2 years. _____
   Add 3 years if you are over 40 and not overweight. _____
5. Exercise
   Regular and moderate (jogging 3 times a week), add 3 years. _____
   Regular and vigorous (long distance running 3 times a week), add 5 years. _____
   Subtract 3 years if your job is sedentary. _____
   Add 3 years if it is active. _____
6. Alcohol
   Add 2 years if you are a light drinker (1 to 3 drinks a day). _____

Subtract 5 to 10 years if you are a heavy drinker (more than 4 drinks per day). _____
Subtract 1 year if you are a teetotaler. _____

7. Smoking
   Two or more packs of cigarettes per day, subtract 8 years. _____
   One to two packs per day, subtract 4 years. _____
   Less than one pack, subtract 2 years. _____
   Subtract 2 years if you regularly smoke a pipe or cigars. _____
8. Disposition
   Add 2 years if you are a reasoned, practical person. _____
   Subtract 2 years if you are aggressive, intense, and competitive. _____
   Add 1 to 5 years if you are basically happy and content with life. _____
   Subtract 1 to 5 years if you are often unhappy, worried, and often feel guilty. _____
9. Education
   Less than high school, subtract 2 years. _____
   Four years of school beyond high school, add 1 year. _____
   Five or more years beyond high school, add 3 years. _____
10. Environment
    If you have lived most of your life in a rural environment, add 4 years. _____
    Subtract 2 years if you have lived most of your life in an urban environment. _____
11. Sleep
    More than 9 hours a day, subtract 5 years. _____
12. Temperature
    Add 2 years if your home's thermostat is set at no more than 68°F. _____
13. Health Care
    Regular medical check ups and regular dental care, add 3 years. _____
    Frequently ill, subtract 2 years. _____

Source: Reprinted, by permission of the publisher, from R. Schulz. *The Psychology of Death, Dying, and Bereavement.* Reading, MA: Addison-Wesley, 1978, pp. 97–98.

those that are ill) can be easily identified and are more motivated to change their behavior.

MODELS OF HEALTH BEHAVIOR AND HEALTH BEHAVIOR CHANGE

As we discussed in Chapter 8, health behaviors can be defined as those actions that people undertake to maintain or enhance their health (Kasl and Cobb, 1966). Health behaviors are affected by social factors, characteristics of the environment, and psychological factors, such as beliefs and attitudes (Leventhal, Prochaska, and Hirschman, 1985). Psychologists and health educators have organized their attempts to understand and modify health behavior in several theories. In the following sections we will discuss some of the most widely studied approaches or models in the health behavior area. These include the *health belief model* (Janz and Becker, 1984), the *theory of reasoned action* (Azjen and Fishbein, 1980), and the *transtheoretical model* (Prochaska, DiClemente, and Norcross, 1992).

The Health Belief Model

The health belief model or HBM (see Janz and Becker, 1984; Rosenstock, 1966) was one of the earliest conceptual approaches developed to explain why people do or do not engage in health behavior. We discussed the model in detail in Chapter 8. It proposed that a person's motivation to engage in health-related behaviors depends on the interaction of several factors: (1) his or her **perceived susceptibility** to a disease (i.e., the person's subjective impression of the risks of getting a serious illness) and the **perceived seriousness** of an illness (i.e., how significantly the disease would affect his or her lifestyle); (2) the individual's belief that engaging in the health behavior will reduce the perceived threat; (3) the person's analysis of whether the *benefits* associated with engaging in that behavior will be greater than the perceived *costs* or *barriers*; and (4) a *cue to action* triggering the appropriate health behavior (Bandura, 1995; Curry and Emmons, 1994; Janz and Becker, 1984).

The HBM has been studied in relation to a wide range of health behaviors, but research on this model has yielded mixed results. For example, Curry and Emmons (1994) reviewed 13 studies in which components of the HBM have been used to answer the questions of why women do or do not engage in breast cancer screening and noted that there is evidence that perceived susceptibility, barriers, and cues to action do influence participation in breast cancer screening behavior. Depending on the study, the relationships among variables predicted by the HBM may be weak. In addition, the HBM has been studied less frequently as a guide to intervention methods for increasing health behaviors.

Theory of Reasoned Action

The theory of reasoned action (TRA) was developed by social psychologists Icek Azjen and Martin Fishbein (see Azjen and Fishbein, 1980) as a general theory to describe the relationships among beliefs, attitudes, intentions, and behavior. According to this theory, people are rational decisionmakers, and behavior that is under voluntary control is determined by beliefs and attitudes. The most immediate influence on behavior is thought to be the *intention* to engage in that behavior. Behavioral intentions are influenced by two categories of beliefs (see Figure 13.2): (1) the person's attitude toward the behavior, which refers to the degree to which a person has a favorable or unfavorable evaluation of the behavior in question; and (2) a social factor called *subjective norm*, which refers to the perceived social pressure to perform or not to perform the behavior. The TRA includes a mathematical formula to specify how different beliefs combine to determine an individual's behavior.

The theory of reasoned action has been applied with some success to the prediction of a variety of health behaviors, including smoking, engaging in exercise, participating in preventive and screening-related health behaviors (e.g., breast self-examination), and delaying seeking medical care (e.g., for breast cancer symptoms). It has also been applied extensively to the prevention of AIDS and HIV infection (see Fishbein, 1996). Although it is possible to derive ideas from the model for ways to increase behavioral intentions (e.g., by affecting social norms), and thereby promote health behaviors, there have been relatively few large-scale interventions that have been based on the TRA (Curry and Emmons, 1994).

The Transtheoretical Model

Prochaska and DiClemente developed the transtheoretical model (TTM) based on their observations of patients in psychotherapy (Prochaska, DiClemente, and Norcross, 1992). The model is now being used in diverse areas of the field of health behavior change. Prochaska and DiClemente noted that patients seemed to go through a similar process of behavior change regardless of the

FIGURE 13.2. Theory of reasoned action.
Source: From I. Ajzen and T. J. Madden. Predictions of goal-directed behavior. Attitudes, intentions, and perceived behavioral control. *Journal of Experimental Social Psychology*, 1986, 22(5), 453–474.

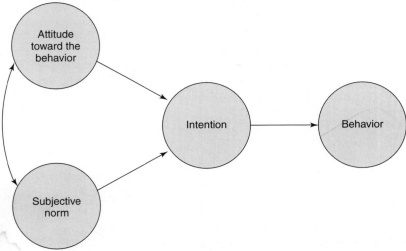

type of psychotherapy that was being applied, and this model is unique in its focus on the process of change and its outcome. TTM describes a set of five stages of readiness to change: (1) *precontemplation*, when there is no intention to change behavior in the foreseeable future; (2) *contemplation*, when the individual starts to think about initiating change but is not actively doing so; (3) *preparation*, taking early steps to change and have unsuccessfully taken action in the past year; (4) *action*, when the individual modifies his or her behavior or the environment in order to overcome his or her problem; and (5) *maintenance*, the stage in which people work to prevent relapse and to consolidate the gains attained during action (Prochaska et al., 1992).

Because relapse is the rule rather than the exception with a variety of health behaviors and addictive behaviors (e.g., smoking cessation, weight loss), Prochaska et al. (1992) observed that people usually do not progress through a linear pattern of change, progressing simply and discretely through each step. Instead, they suggested that a "spiral" pattern of change is usually followed (see Figure 13.3). People can progress from contemplation to preparation to action to maintenance, but most will relapse. During relapse individuals regress to an earlier stage, and although some relapsers will abandon the change process, most will "recycle" back to the contemplation or preparation stages. Each time relapsers recycle, they potentially learn from their mistakes. Thus, the amount of change people make following an intervention is heavily determined by the stage of change at which they were prior to treatment.

In recent years the TTM has been applied to health behaviors, including smoking cessation, engaging in exercise, weight reduction, alcohol treatment, and behaviors related to AIDS prevention and cancer screening (Curry and Emmons, 1994; Prochaska et al., 1992). The TTM has been most extensively studied with respect to smoking cessation. One treatment implication of the TTM re-

FIGURE 13.3. A spiral model of the stages of change—The transtheoretical model.
Source: From J. O. Prochaska, J. C. Norcross, J. L. Fowler, and M. J. Follick. Attendance and outcome in a work site weight control program: Processes and stages of change as process and predictor variables. *Addictive Behaviors*, 1992, 17(1), 35–45. Copyright 1992, with kind permission from Elsevier Science Ltd., The Boulevard, Langford Lane, Kidlington OX5 1GB, UK.

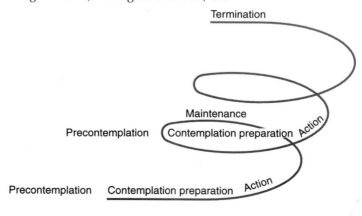

lates to the high relapse and drop-out rates (see below) in treatment and self-help programs for smoking cessation and/or weight reduction. The TTM would predict that treatment programs should not treat all clients as if they were the same but, instead, should tailor the intervention offered to the client's stage of change. As an example, Figure 13.4 shows how the success of a smoking cessation program relates to the stage of change of clients prior to treatment.

BARRIERS TO MODIFYING HEALTH BEHAVIORS

Given the compelling evidence that people's behaviors play such an important role in determining their health, why is it that people still smoke, eat improperly, fail to get adequate exercise, and so on? Unfortunately, unhealthy behaviors are stubborn and resistant to change and are highly subject to relapse. It is possible to identify at least two broad sets of barriers or major obstacles to lifestyle change. The first is the learning theory notion called the **gradient of reinforcement**. This refers to the fact that immediate rewards and punishments are much more powerful than delayed ones (Miller, 1983). Thus, if engaging in a behavior (e.g., eating a particular food) causes immediate relief or

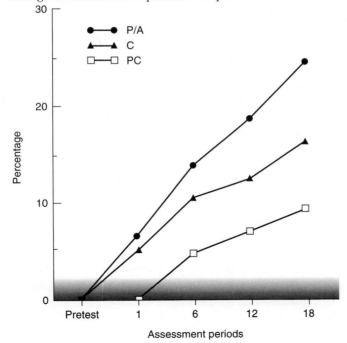

FIGURE 13.4. Percentage of abstinence over 18 months for smokers in precontemplation (PC), contemplation (C), and preparation (P/A) stages before treatment (*N* = 570). *Source:* From J. O. Prochaska. In search of how people change: Applications to addictive behaviors. *American Psychologist,* 1992, *47*(9), 1102–1114. Copyright 1992 by the American Psychological Association. Reprinted with permission.

gratification, or if failing to engage in this behavior provides immediate discomfort, the behavior should be easily acquired and difficult to eliminate. Smokers derive immediate gratification and avoid unpleasant withdrawal symptoms each time they smoke a cigarette, making it difficult to give up. Moreover, the health threats posed by smoking, poor diet, overweight, and lack of exercise seem remote compared with the immediate pleasures of indulging, and the inconvenience and effort involved in adopting more healthful preventive behaviors can also be barriers to behavior change.

A second major set of barriers to lifestyle modification are forces in the social and physical environment. Healthy or unhealthy habits are developed and maintained by social and cultural influences from the family and society (Anderson, 1995). In the last 25 years Americans have made significant progress in changing their attitudes toward exercise and proper nutrition, and have become well informed about the modifiable risk factors for cancers and cardiovascular disorders. However, there are still powerful social pressures that lead teenagers to smoke and economic pressures (such as lack of insurance for helping patients to prevent illness) that lead physicians and other health care providers to put less energy into prevention (Leventhal and Hirschman, 1982; Stachnik et al., 1983). Other economic and physical barriers are found in the higher cost and lower availability of healthier foods and in the lack of time and opportunity for exercise at many work sites (Grunberg, 1988).

Changing Health-Relevant Beliefs and Behaviors

What are some of the strategies used to help people acquire and practice health-promoting behaviors? Research on prevention has used a variety of approaches, ranging from small-scale efforts by using behavior modification to change single risk factors in face-to-face instruction to large-scale public education efforts to change multiple habits by using media communication techniques (see Figure 13.5).

Educational Approaches

A basic premise of health education efforts is that three sets of factors—predisposing factors, enabling factors, and reinforcing factors—influence health behavior and are modifiable by educational interventions. According to Green and Kreuter (1990), **predisposing factors** are those factors that motivate the decisions to take particular health actions. They include the traditional aims of education, such as awareness, understanding, attitudes, and beliefs about health-promoting and health-damaging behavior. **Enabling factors** are the types of skills needed to carry out an action, whether or not the action is motivated. Enabling factors for the prevention or early detection of breast cancer would include whether you know how to do a breast self-examination. **Reinforcing factors** include the rewards that the person obtains for the performance of the health behavior in question (Green and Kreuter, 1990). Examples of reinforcing factors include social and peer approval and stress reduction. Ironically, these very same kinds of reinforcers often lead adolescents to smoke or use drugs. Recent school-based health education campaigns have used the concept of inoculation against peer pressure to counter these influences. In ad-

FIGURE 13.5. Billboards, print media, TV ads, and many other methods have been used to alert and educate people about AIDS. Humor or irony is often used in an attempt to catch people's attention and make the message more memorable.
Source: Barbara Rios/Photo Researchers

ministering these inoculations, students are reinforced for acquiring skills that help them to resist or decline cigarettes or drugs (see Evans, in press; Evans et al., 1981).

Clearly, the most effective health education campaigns combine learning experiences appropriately targeted at all three sets of factors that influence health behavior. As Green (1984) and others have noted, a behavior that is highly reinforced and motivated will not succeed unless enabling factors are also present. Similarly, an enabled and motivated behavior that is socially punished or ridiculed will not endure.

Despite well-formulated health education models and intensive efforts, many health education campaigns have not achieved the goals that they set out to meet. There are several reasons for their lack of success: (1) The campaigns are often not directed or targeted optimally to the appropriate audience. A message about preventing smoking should be targeted at younger audiences, and the social context in which smoking occurs should be addressed as well. (2) The educational campaigns can arouse too much fear that can inhibit behavioral changes. If a message causes people to be very fearful, they may stop listening in order to reduce this fear. (3) Health education efforts may not result in behavior change because peoples' naive theories of illness tell people things that are at odds with the health education message they receive (see Chapter 8).

Effects of Fear Communications

Early laboratory studies examined the role of fear in motivating health attitude and behavior change (Janis, 1967; Leventhal, 1970). One might think that the more fearful a person is about the possible consequences of engaging in a particular behavior, the more likely he or she would be to change the behavior in question. Studies have generally found that higher levels of fear lead to somewhat more attitude change and slightly more behavioral change over a wide range of health issues, including using seat belts, following proper dental hygiene, quitting or reducing cigarette smoking, and taking tetanus inoculations (Leventhal and Hirschman, 1982). These studies also showed that the effects of fear-arousing, threatening messages tended to be short-lived, with behavioral changes dissipating within 1 week of the communication. In addition, when high fear messages fail to persuade, the failure generally reflects the target people's feelings that they were unable to cope with the danger conveyed by the message. Thus, if fear is to lead to a change in behavior in addition to attitude change, instructions as to how to take appropriate action must be added to the threat message (Leventhal, 1980).

In this regard Leventhal (1980) proposed the *parallel process model* of fear and attitude change. In this model the subject copes with the fear communication by two means: fear control and danger control. Danger control refers to the coping behavior directed at reducing the threat—directly manipulating the situation to reduce or eliminate the source of danger. Fear control, on the other hand, refers to coping aimed at making one feel better regardless of the presence of threat. If a health communication is so threatening that individuals become preoccupied with reducing fear, they may do this to the point of ignoring the information about the danger and not coping with it, and not changing their health-related attitudes or behavior. This helps to explain why under certain circumstances high fear messages may fail to persuade.

Commonsense Models of Illness and Their Effects

Leventhal et al. (1980, 1992) have noted that people form their own cognitive models or "representations" of health and illness, models that are used to guide their interpretation of illness and bodily states. These cognitive models may or may not correspond to medical reality as defined by the physician or an outside observer; but as we noted in Chapter 8, it is clear that these representations play an important role in determining health and illness behavior.

Many health-oriented actions that people take focus on illness. When they experience symptoms, and when symptoms are present, people seek a label for illness, take action such as self-care or seek medical care, and expect illness to disappear with treatment. However, in order to interpret bodily states, people need to not only label symptoms but also attach various symptoms to diagnosed disease states (Leventhal, Meyer, and Nerenz, 1980; Pennebaker, 1982). People's representations of health also include notions of the causes of disease, ways to treat them, and ways to prevent illness. Patients generally expect a disease to be a brief one and for a cure to be achieved quickly and definitively. This is true even for patients with chronic diseases, such as cancer. In a study of chemotherapy patients Nerenz (1980) found that when these patients' symptoms disappear, they are distressed by the need for continued treatment. The same is true of prescriptions that you may have received for antibiotics. The instructions you receive usually tell you to take the entire prescription, usually a 10-day course of medication. But your symptoms disappear quickly and it becomes harder and harder to remember to take your medicine.

What are the implications of commonsense illness models for prevention? Preventive behaviors and actions require that people do things that have long-term health benefits. However, these behaviors may or may not affect their experience or explanation of symptoms. Thus, in cases of mismatch between public health or practitioner advice and personal beliefs individuals will be less compliant and less likely to engage in a preventive action. It is important for preventive health messages to be formulated with recognition of the fact that a good deal of preventive behavior is controlled by the person's abstract beliefs about health. By providing enough information about health problems so that patients' misconceptions can be addressed or corrected, also by recognizing and formulating interventions that take into account peoples' representations of illness, we can overcome some or all of these problems.

Cognitive-Behavioral Approaches

As described in Chapter 10, there are a variety of cognitive-behavioral treatment procedures, based in learning theory, that have been applied in medical settings. Several of these techniques have applicability to promoting healthy behavior. Some examples of these applications are presented here.

Applied behavioral analysis is a behavioral change strategy based on the operant conditioning principle that behavior is determined by its antecedents and consequences (Chesney, 1984). This strategy involves identifying a particular target behavior to be modified (e.g., increasing physical exercise levels), observing the current status and antecedents of the behavior, and examining its consequences. After the period of observation the environmental antecedents and consequences are changed to modify the rate of occurrence of the behavior. One example of successful application of applied behavioral analysis is the control of obesity. So widespread is this application that more people have been receiving behavioral treatments for obesity than for all other conditions combined (Stunkard and Wadden, 1993).

The initial stage of behavior modification programs for obesity involves describing the behavior to be changed by keeping a diary record. Each time they eat, patients write down the food, time of day, the people they were with, and the feelings that they were experiencing. Next an analysis of the diary record identifies stimuli or events that may cue the eating (e.g., watching TV, sight of high calorie desserts). These environmental antecedents are then controlled by restricting eating to one place or working with families not to keep high calorie foods on hand (similar to stimulus control procedures discussed in

Chapter 10). In the next stage patients are instructed to modify their eating behavior by reducing their eating speed, by not combining eating with other activities such as reading, television watching, and the like. Finally, the environmental consequences are modified by reinforcing patients for weight loss and for behavioral changes. This may be done by having them give themselves points or other tangible rewards.

In contrast to the applied behavioral analysis approach, the *cognitive-behavioral* perspective is based on the perspective that a large portion of human learning is cognitively mediated. That is, rather than directly responding to their environment, humans react to their thoughts or conceptions of the environment. These approaches recognize the importance of irrational patterns of thinking in causing maladaptive patterns of behavior. In addition, it is considered very desirable to combine and integrate cognitive-based treatment approaches with techniques based purely on performance (Keefe, Dunsmore, and Burnett, 1992). Examples of successful health-promoting cognitive-behavioral interventions are techniques and programs that are implemented in order to train men at risk for AIDS in safer sex and in behavioral assertiveness needed in order to reduce the risk of contracting the HIV virus (Kelly and Murphy, 1992). Other widely used cognitive-behavioral programs include interventions to aid in smoking cessation and maintenance of cessation (Lichtenstein and Glasgow, 1992) and weight reduction (Brownell and Wadden, 1992).

Combinations of social learning, educational, and behavioral modification approaches have also been successfully applied in health promotion efforts. For example, the Stanford Heart Disease Prevention project (Farquhar et al., 1977; Meyer et al., 1980) was a large and well-known prevention effort that used a combination of mass media and face-to-face approaches. Initially, three communities similar in size and socioeconomic status were studied over a 3-year period: One community served as a control, a second was exposed to a mass media campaign, including radio and television announcements, and billboard and printed advertisements about heart disease risk factors (smoking, diet, and exercise). A third community received the same mass media campaign as well as face-to-face behavioral therapy for high-risk people. Results of the study indicated that the media campaign alone produced modest reductions in smoking at a 3-year follow-up. Participants in this group were more informed about cardiovascular risk factors and reported reduced intake of dietary fats and cholesterol. However, the reductions in cardiovascular risk factors were considerably larger when the media campaign was supplemented with face-to-face instruction. The Stanford study suggested that mass media efforts are most successful when incorporated in a more comprehensive program directed at the modification of health habits.

Prevention of Smoking and of Substance Abuse in Adolescents

In spite of a decrease in adult smoking since the release of the 1964 U.S. Surgeon General's Report on Smoking and Health, there has been a discouraging increase in smoking among adolescents—particularly teenage girls. Research has shown that adolescents begin smoking largely in response to social pressures. These social forces include the imitation of peers, family members, and role models (including actors, athletes, and adults in general), and peer pressures in order to be accepted (Flay, 1985). Some youths also begin smoking as an expression of adolescent rebellion or antisocial tendencies (Jessor and Jessor, 1977). Alcohol and drug abuse are also important social and health problems that affect large numbers of adolescents (Hawkins et al., 1992). Pressure from peers and media role models also can foster substance abuse in adolescents (Donaldson and Blanchard, 1995). Psychosocial interventions to reduce alcohol and drug abuse in adolescents and to prevent initial or habitual use have also been studied.

Because of the many psychosocial influences on the initiation of smoking, eclectic, comprehensive preventive interventions in schools have been used to deter smoking in adolescents. These studies have been based with some success on several social psychological theories and use peer modeling, attitude change, and other social learning and social-psychological procedures. One of the earliest and most widely known studies of smoking prevention in adolescents was a 3-year longitudinal study—the Houston project (Evans et al., 1981). This project used an intervention strategy based on Bandura's (1977b) social learning theory. This suggested that by observing others, children acquire expectations and learned behaviors with regard to smoking. For example, by watching their peers and role models smoking and then experiencing positive consequences (e.g., social approval, pleasure from the cigarette), they would be more likely to engage in the same behavior as the model. Based on this assumption, Evans et al. (1981) developed interventions to inoculate students against social influences to smoke.

The Houston project developed persuasive film messages and posters (see Figure 13.6) to teach grade school students about peer and media pressures to smoke, and to educate students about effective coping techniques to avoid trying cigarettes. The types of social pressures that influence adolescents to begin smoking (e.g., peers, smoking parents, and cigarette advertisements) were presented along with a high status, similar-aged model demonstrating ways to resist such pressures (e.g., stalling for time, putting counterpressure on the smoker by telling them the health risks of smoking). These techniques were designed to give students the skills to resist the social pressures to smoke. Other films were also shown to demonstrate the immediate physiological consequences of smoking (e.g., carbon monoxide in the breath). In this study hundreds of students in matched experimental and control groups were compared for cigarette smoking rates at the start of the project and during follow-up periods for 3 years. The results indicated a moderate impact with the experimental groups smoking less frequently and reporting lower intentions to smoke compared with a control group receiving no intervention (Evans et al., 1981).

Since the early 1980s, many programs like this one have been implemented to prevent smoking and/or abuse of other substances (e.g., alcohol or drugs) in adolescents (Donaldson et al., 1995; Flay, 1985). These programs have built and expanded on early studies. More focused attention to social pressures that lead children and adolescents to begin smoking and/or using alcohol or drugs has characterized these programs. For example, older adolescent peer leaders have been used to teach skills for resisting social pressures (i.e., "resistance skill

FIGURE 13.6. Poster used to counteract peer pressure.
Source: Reprinted, by permission, from the Social Psychological
Deterrents of Smoking in Schools Project, Richard I. Evans,
University of Houston, Principal Investigator. Supported by
the National Heart, Lung, and Blood Institute, NIH Grant
17269, 1981.

training") and for teaching students more general social and life skills (Best et
al., 1984; Donaldson et al., 1995; Flay, 1985). These studies have generally reported good success rates, reducing smoking onset rates by 50 percent and reducing the use of alcohol and drugs by a substantial amount. However, attempts to prevent alcohol or substance abuse must be careful that prevention
messages are targeted appropriately to their youthful audience if they are to be
effective (Donaldson et al, 1995). Social learning, attitude change, and resistance skills techniques are now being widely used in the prevention of smoking and drug abuse and are good examples of how health psychology research
is used to address important social and health problems.

Modifying Cardiovascular Risk Factors

As discussed in Chapter 5, potentially modifiable risk factors for cardiovascular disease include cigarette smoking, increased serum cholesterol levels, hypertension, stress and hostility, lack of exercise and sedentary living, and obesity (Ockene and Ockene, 1992). A variety of intervention trials have been conducted to determine whether these behavioral risk factors can be altered and whether this reduces the cardiovascular risk (see Figure 13.7).

The range of prevention strategies used includes interventions involving direct face-to-face interactions between therapists and patients, and public health approaches relying on mass communication (e.g., media advertising) to change attitudes and behavior. As noted earlier in this chapter, behavioral treatments administered through face-to-face treatments have been successful in altering diet (Brownell and Wadden, 1992), smoking (Lichtenstein and Glasgow, 1992), and physical exercise (Dubbert, 1992), but the typical pattern has been short-term success followed by relapse. Well-conducted mass media campaigns directed at large populations can effectively transmit information, alter some attitudes, and produce small shifts in behavior (Meyer et al., 1980). Despite these small changes, these health promotion campaigns are highly cost-effective and practically significant because they reach very large numbers of

FIGURE 13.7. Among the risk factors for heart disease (discussed in Chapter 5) are being male, being overweight, and smoking. Hostility, fat intake, and other risk factors have also been noted. Many of these are modifiable: getting people to quit smoking, to lose weight, to cut fat intake, and to exercise reduces their risk.
Source: Hugh Rogers/ Monkmeyer

people. Face-to-face and public health approaches have been combined in some intervention studies to maximize the effects obtained.

Earlier in this chapter we described the Stanford Heart Disease Prevention Project, which was one of the largest communitywide projects employing a combination of mass media and face-to-face approaches to reduce cardiovascular risk factors (Farquhar et al., 1977; Meyer et al., 1980). Another important risk intervention study is the Lifestyle Heart Study conducted by Ornish and colleagues (1990) described in Chapter 5. This study showed that a comprehensive lifestyle modification program consisting of a very low fat diet, stress management training, smoking cessation, and moderate levels of aerobic exercise could slow and even reverse the progression of coronary heart disease. A large-scale study that yielded less encouraging results was the Multiple Risk Factor Intervention Trial (MRFIT) (MRFIT Group, 1982). This was a large-scale longitudinal study organized to see whether heart disease mortality could be lowered by eliminating three major correctable risk factors—smoking, hypertension, and elevated serum cholesterol. Subjects were over 12,000 men who had elevated risk factors for coronary heart disease—smoking, hypertension, and/or having elevated serum cholesterol—but who had not yet had clinical evidence of heart disease (e.g., heart attack). The participants were randomly assigned to either a special intervention (SI) program, which included treatment for hypertension, intensive counseling for cigarette smoking, and dietary advice for lowering blood pressure levels. These interventions were based in medical clinics and carried out by medical, nursing, or behavioral staff. Patients in the other group (usual care or UC) were referred to their usual sources of medical care (in most cases private practitioners).

At the end of the study the mortality results were not what the study designers had predicted. Instead of lowered coronary mortality in the SI group, there were *no* significant differences between the SI and UC groups. It appeared that the UC "control group," as well as the SI experimental group, changed their behaviors and decreased cardiovascular risk over the course of the study. The designers of the study had originally anticipated no appreciable decline in risk factors in the UC group. This lowering of risk factors by individuals receiving "usual care" parallels the real reduction in cardiovascular mortality that has occurred in the United States over the last 20 years; see Chapter 5. Another reason that there may not have been significant differences between the SI and UC groups is that some of the medical therapies used for hypertension were unexpectedly harmful for a subset of patients (MRFIT Group, 1982).

The unexpected results of the MRFIT study has sparked considerable controversy, and most who believe in the importance of behavioral factors in prevention probably have mixed reactions to these results. Despite their disappointment over the lack of significant group differences, they are encouraged by the fact that Americans are avoiding high fat and high cholesterol foods, are keeping their blood pressure controlled, are stopping smoking, and are increasing their regular physical activity (Grunberg, 1988). Indeed, results of the Lifestyle Heart Study (Ornish et al., 1990) would suggest that the progression of coronary disease might be reversed if more stringent lifestyle modifications than those implemented in MRFIT had been accomplished. However, this requires that people are willing to undergo stricter lifestyle changes than those implemented in MRFIT—changes that may be acceptable only to a select group of high-risk individuals who are very concerned about heart disease.

Modifying Cancer Risk Factors

Cancer is the second leading cause of mortality in the United States today (Curry and Emmons, 1994; Grunberg, 1988; Thomas, 1992) and is a major cause of death throughout the world. Evidence is accumulating that lifestyle factors, including the foods people eat, whether or not they smoke, and the work they do (i.e., occupational exposure to cancer causing agents) can affect the likelihood of getting cancer. For example, an increase in lung cancer rates in the United States in recent years is largely attributed to smoking and tobacco use but are also due to radon in the home and air pollution, as well as rooted in behaviors or modifiable situations. It has been estimated that more than three-quarters of cancer cases are tied to lifestyle factors (National Cancer Institute, 1984; Thomas, 1992). Thus, interventions to prevent smoking and to promote healthy diets are relevant to cancer prevention.

The associations of smoking with a variety of cancers, especially cancer of the lung, are well known and well established. However, alcohol consumption and dietary factors are gaining increasing attention as possible causes of cancer. For example, human epidemiological and animal laboratory studies indicate that alcohol use and consuming certain kinds of foods is associated with cancers of the stomach, breast, ovary, and prostate (Thomas, 1992). Consumption of high fat diets and particular types of food preparation (e.g., smoking, frying) are associated with increased cancer rates, whereas reducing total food intake and consumption of low fat diets, fruits, and vegetables may actually decrease the likelihood of various cancers (Grunberg, 1988).

There is inconsistent evidence of a relationship between fat intake and breast cancer, and stronger links with cancer of the large intestine, prostate, and other organs (Glanz, 1994; Roberts, 1984). Epidemiological studies also indicate that increased intake of dietary fiber from vegetables, fruits, and whole grain cereals decreases the risk of colorectal cancer. Consumption of vegetables such as broccoli, cabbage, brussel sprouts, and dark green and yellow vegetables that are rich in carotene is thought to be associated with the decreased risk of cancer at several sites, and smoking, barbecuing, and charcoal broiling of foods can deposit carcinogenic substances on food surfaces, and therefore may contribute to cancer risk. Knowledge and awareness of the relationships between what we eat and long-term health have spread, partly due to prevention-oriented educational campaigns conducted by public-service-minded grocery chains.

The associations of diet and breast cancer have led to intervention studies to determine if reducing dietary fat intake in women at risk for breast cancer by virtue of having benign breast disease will lower the incidence of their disease (Glanz, 1994). Similar dietary intervention studies to lower the risk of breast cancer are ongoing in the United States and Canada, and the National Cancer Institute has made public education about the dietary aspects of cancer an important prevention objective. In addition, there is considerable evidence that the use of behavioral and psychological methods can improve breast cancer screening, mammography use, and responses to DNA testing for cancer risks (Glanz, 1994; Lerman, 1995; Rimer, 1994).

Work Site Health Promotion

People spend a large proportion of their time at work, and therefore the occupational setting is a convenient place for health promotion interventions. Prevention activities conducted at work are nearby and accessible, and employers stand to benefit from healthier employees. In addition, the work site is an environment where organizational and social structures can be used to design interventions that are effective.

Work site health promotion programs include a range of activities such as hypertension screening and treatment, smoking cessation, weight loss, stress management, and supervised aerobic physical exercise (Weiss, Fielding, and Baum, 1991). Many corporations now offer at least some of these programs, believing that employee morale will be enhanced, productivity will be improved, and health insurance and hospitalization costs will be reduced by increased wellness. Evaluation research on these programs has been of uneven quality, and scientific evidence of the efficacy of these programs remains unclear. However, these programs appear to be feasible, and health psychologists are currently working on developing more effective, convenient, and cost-effective programs (Weiss, Fielding, and Baum, 1991).

One example of a novel work site health promotion intervention has been a program to achieve weight loss. Typically, weight loss interventions have not translated well from clinical to work settings: Attrition is often higher and resultant weight loss is reported to be less for work site programs. Brownell and colleagues (1984) evaluated several weight loss competitions held in business-industrial settings. In one such competition a challenge to lose the most weight was issued by the presidents of three banks to see which bank could achieve the greatest average weight loss. Workers therefore were not only losing weight for the benefit of their own health but were also part of a group competition. Nearly one-third the work force participated in a 12-week program and the results were very encouraging. The drop-out rate in the competition was exceptionally low and the average weight loss was high. Both employees and management reported positive changes in morale and employee-management relations, and the cost-effectiveness of the weight loss was the best ever reported (see Figure 13.8). This study showed that motivation can be enhanced by harnessing the group loyalty and social support that can be engaged at the work site. As a result of the success of this strategy with weight loss, it is currently being applied to other health habits such as smoking.

Work site physical exercise programs have also become popular. One study evaluated the feasibility and effectiveness of an attempt to increase the exercise levels of all employees at four large companies (Blair et al., 1986). Employees at the intervention sites were exposed to a health promotion program that provided a regular exercise program as well as resources and encouragement for smoking cessation, stress management, weight loss, and hypertension control. When compared with workers at other companies, there was a widespread and clinically significant increase in the number of regularly exercising employees

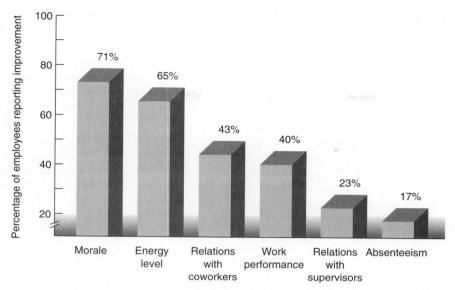

FIGURE 13.8. Percentage of employees reporting improvements in work-related areas due to weight loss. All employees who did not report improvement in an area listed "no change" as a response.
Source: Reprinted by permission of the publisher from K. D. Brownell, et al. Weight loss competitions at the work site: Impact on weight, morale, and cost-effectiveness. *American Journal of Public Health,* 1984, *74,* 1283–1285.

and in employee fitness. The long-term maintenance of exercise habits over a 2-year period was also encouraging. Large numbers of people can be encouraged to adopt healthier lifestyles through effective work site interventions.

PREVENTION OF AIDS

As discussed in Chapter 6, AIDS is a life-threatening disease caused by a virus, HIV, and spread by sexual contact or exposure to substantial amounts of infected blood. Currently there is no vaccine to protect us from AIDS, and because HIV attacks and resides in the T-helper cells of the immune system, victims are made more vulnerable to further infection and other pathogens. Thus, AIDS patients often exhibit other syndromes, particularly "opportunistic" disease such as pneumonia. There is no cure, and effective treatments are currently limited. Once a person is infected with HIV, he or she is likely to develop AIDS; there are no known ways of blocking or reversing this process. The key, then, is to prevent people from ever being infected with HIV, to reduce behaviors that put people at risk for HIV infection. Health psychologists and behavioral scientists have played an important role in this effort.

We have discussed a number of obstacles to the prevention of various diseases, and all of them apply to AIDS as well. Complicating this, however, is both the nature of the disease and its primary modes of transmission. AIDS has been spread primarily through sexual contact and by sharing needles in drug use, and behavior change in these areas has not been very successful in the past. Attempts to curtail teenage pregnancy have not fared particularly well, sexually transmitted disease rates are at all-time highs in some groups, and the dependence involved in drug use makes this behavior very resistant to interventions. Despite this, many risk factors for HIV infection are modifiable and can be addressed by prevention (Coates et al., 1988) (see Figure 13.9). A number of different approaches to preventing the spread of the AIDS virus have been attempted, with some success.

In order to prevent HIV infection, we must modify sexual behavior or drug use. Most approaches to preventing HIV infection seek to modify sexual contact, including the advocacy of abstinence from sex, monogamous sexual relationships, and the use of condoms and the practice of "safer" sex. Limiting the number of different sexual partners can reduce the risk of infection, particularly if one's partners are from low-risk groups. Condoms have been shown to reduce the likelihood of HIV transmission (Conant et al., 1986), and the use of this protection during sex can greatly reduce the risk of infections (Francis and Chin, 1987). It has been difficult to change sexual behavior, however, as the use of condoms is often seen as negative and often resisted by sexual partners. Part of several prevention attempts has been teaching people how to handle resistance to safer sex practices.

The appropriate target groups for the prevention of HIV infection have been debated and described, and, historically, most attention has focused on high-risk groups with relatively high rates of infection. Changes in sexual behavior of gay men, for example, has been a primary focus of research and interventions to prevent the spread of the disease. There have also been concerns about adolescent populations because of their emerging sexuality and past resistance to attempts to change their sexual behaviors (see St. Lawrence, 1993; Weisse et al., 1990). However, these concerns have not yet materialized; the percentage of teens and college students who are HIV positive continues to be low (Gayle et al., 1990) and awareness of AIDS and high-risk behavior is probably at an all-time high. Efforts have also been directed toward changing drug use behavior. If we cannot get people to stop taking drugs, at least we can help them to do it as safely as possible. Programs to provide clean needles or bleach to clean them are among the interventions that take this approach.

A common assumption of many campaigns to reduce risky behaviors is that repetitive media presentation of information about the disease, the ways people get it, and how to minimize risk will lead to a reduction of risk. The findings of a number of studies suggest that education is important but not sufficient by itself to cause behavior change and risk reduction (Leventhal and Cleary, 1980). There is some evidence that publicity and information campaigns have had positive effects on behaviors that increase one's risk of HIV infection. Many people hold very basic misconceptions about AIDS or how one gets the HIV, and how best to protect themselves from infection (St. Lawrence, 1993). However, being well informed about AIDS and HIV infection was not enough to ensure prudent behavior among several different risk groups (DiClemente et al., 1991; Kalichman and Hunter, 1992).

This is not to suggest that education is not necessary. In general, since the identification of high-risk groups and behaviors, our behavior has changed a great deal (Curran, 1985; McKusick et al., 1985; Martin, 1986). Targeted and in-

Modifiable Factors	Nonmodifiable Factors
Poverty	Ethnicity
Alcohol Use	Age
Drug Use	
Knowledge of AIDS	
Self-efficacy	
Perceived costs	
Perceived risks	
Social support	

FIGURE 13.9. Many factors are related to one's risk of becoming infected with the HIV. Most are modifiable and most of these are behavioral factors. Decreasing alcohol use, drug use, and perceived cost while enhancing knowledge, risk perception, and support should decrease the risk of infection.
Source: From T. J. Coates, R. D. Stall, J. A. Catania, and S. Kegeles. Behavioral factors in HIV infection. *AIDS*, 1988, 2(suppl. 1), S239–S246. Copyright 1988, Rapid Science Publishers.

tensive interventions that also respond to individual needs and that emphasize identification and modeling may be effective in further reducing behaviors that increase the risk of HIV infection (Solomon and DeJong, 1986). Changing people's perceptions of their risk as well as their beliefs about being able to control their exposure to HIV appears to be a particularly promising approach (see Goldman and Harlow, 1993; Kline and Strickler, 1993).

Targeting specific high-risk groups is an important aspect of prevention programs. This allows us to tailor the content of the program to fit specifically the needs, lifestyle, and risks of the group being addressed. By selecting target groups, we can address very specific fears, concerns, behaviors, and misconceptions (Kelly et al., 1993). As a result of designing prevention programs for AIDS, several high-risk groups are clear and have been targeted. Homosexuals, sexually active young people, and intravenous drug users are among these groups, but they may be crosscut by sex, culture, ethnic background, and so on. Targeting very small groups may not be economical, but it makes sense that such an approach would be more effective. People who are at risk for AIDS are not all the same—some are young, others are old, some use drugs, some do not, and so on. Knowing whom one is speaking to and what his or her prevalent perceptions are should increase the effectiveness of resulting interventions.

Education campaigns have focused on broad descriptions of the disease, how one can "catch it" and so on. With a disease such as AIDS, information dissemination has been of particular importance, owing to the fear surrounding it. Research has suggested that people overestimate and underestimate their risk of getting AIDS and that people who report being most knowledgeable about the disease often report the least fear of getting it (Harlow et al., 1993; Kline and Strickler, 1993; Cleary et al., 1986). Familiarity appears to be an important aspect of people's ratings of how vulnerable they feel: In San Francisco, where the per capita rate of AIDS is the highest in the United States, only a third of respondents indicated that AIDS was a personal health concern, compared with 57 percent of respondents in New York, 50 percent in Miami, and 47 percent in Los Angeles (see Temoshok, Sweet, and Zich, 1987). This could be explained in many ways, but one likely reason is that in San Francisco, where people have had the most exposure to the disease, to news about it, and to prevention campaigns, there is more information available on which to base risk estimates. More complex estimates of one's risk could be lower than more simplistic guesses about one's risk.

Programs that have paired education with behavioral interventions have had better success in changing high-risk behaviors (see Schneiderman, 1992). Increasing how much information people have about the disease and about high-risk behaviors, *and* providing skills or training in ways to carry out recommended precautions, has modified behavior in several instances. Motivation is important, as are the skills that one needs to insist on safer sex or to avoid compromising situations (Fisher and Fisher, 1992; O'Keeffe et al., 1990). It is important to provide reasons for lowering risk as well as low-cost ways of doing so (see Figure 13.10). Programs that have included these factors in a comprehensive attempt to change attitudes and behaviors have been successful in achieving some prevention goals (Coates, 1990; Kelly and Murphy, 1992).

Knowledge about a disease and our theories about its causes and consequences are also important factors in efforts to prevent illness. This is no different for AIDS, where fear and misconception abound. Since AIDS is a sexually transmitted disease, many of us who do not believe that we are at risk may be in the higher-risk groups. As we noted earlier, sexually active adolescents are likely to come in contact with sexually transmitted diseases. It is estimated that more than one-half the 20 million victims of sexually transmitted diseases reported each year are under 25 years of age (DiClemente, Zorn, and Temoshok, 1987). This means that teenagers, college students, and young adults, by virtue of their greater sexual activity and greater likelihood of having several sexual partners, may be at risk for HIV infection. Skills, assertiveness, and understanding of how risk is conveyed by certain behaviors are not sufficiently well known. College students have been studied, and they have typically expressed

FIGURE 13.10. Factors influencing the adoption of lower-risk behaviors in relation to HIV. *Source:* From M. K. O'Keeffe, S. Nesselhof-Kendal, and A. Baum. Behavior and the prevention of AIDS: Bases of research and intervention. *Personality and Social Psychology Bulletin,* 1990, *16*(1), 177. Copyright © 1990. Adapted by permission of Sage Publications.

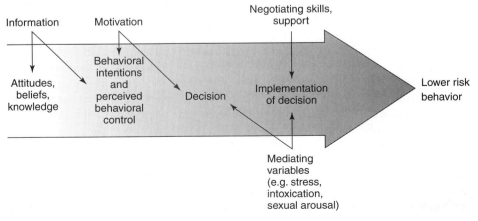

little concern about getting AIDS and did not report changes in their sexual behavior early in the epidemic (Simkins and Eberhage, 1984). In a study of 1,326 students from 10 high schools in San Francisco, DiClemente et al. (1987) found that students knew that AIDS was spread through sexual contact and by sharing needles during drug use. What they did not know was how they could *not* get the disease: Only 41 percent knew that one could not get the disease from kissing someone and 26 percent were not sure that the use of condoms would lower the risk of contracting AIDS. Most of these students were interested in learning more about AIDS.

Drug users may be particularly resistant to behavior change and have been difficult to reach with information or behavior change interventions. Apparently, the media are effective in conveying basic information about AIDS, but it is not likely that this alone will change drug users' behavior sufficiently to reduce the incidence of the disease in this group (Des Jarlais, Friedman, and Strug, 1987). It has been argued that, consistent with the idea of targeting groups, interventions should include very specific information about how the disease is spread and how it can be stopped. Thus, detailed information about how drug users should or should not clean their needles and the like should be included in any attempt to change their behavior (Des Jarlais, Friedman, and Strug, 1987; Stephens et al., 1991).

SUMMARY

The leading causes of death today are chronic diseases that are strongly affected by behavioral factors. Awareness of the importance of personal lifestyle decisions for health and longevity has resulted in renewed interest in behavioral factors in preventive medicine. Health-impairing habits or *behavioral pathogens* have been identified and include such factors as smoking, excessive alcohol consumption, improper diet, and so on. *Behavioral immunogens* or health protective behaviors include the converse or opposite of these practices. Seven specific health practices appear to be highly correlated with better health and lowered mortality: 1) getting a good night's sleep, 2) not smoking, 3) eating breakfast every day, 4) not eating between meals, 5) being at or near prescribed weight, 6) using moderate amounts of or no alcohol, and 7) engaging in regular physical activity. Similar behaviors are characteristic of societies that are known for their longevity.

Several conceptual approaches or models have been developed in order to guide efforts to understand and modify health behavior. These models include the *health belief model*, the *theory of reasoned action*, and the *transtheoretical model*. The first two models attempt to explain health behavior in terms of beliefs, attitudes, and intentions. The transtheoretical model focuses on the process of behavior change and posits that particular stages characterize the process of behavior change.

Some techniques for changing health beliefs and behaviors are educational approaches, including fear communications, and behavioral modification approaches, including applied behavioral analysis and cognitive-behavioral interventions. Despite the fact that health behaviors can be modified by various approaches, it is difficult to maintain these changes over a long period of time and an important problem is that of relapse. Relapse prevention is an important application of cognitive-behavioral treatments to health promotion.

Health promotion programs have been directed at preventing smoking and abuse of alcohol and drugs in adolescents. Many of these programs, which have met with considerable success, have been based on social learning theory and employ techniques of modeling, attitude change, and training in skills to resist social pressures to smoke or take drugs. Programs have also been conducted to modify cardiovascular risk factors. Some of these projects have employed media campaigns supplemented by face-to-face therapy approaches. An example of such a program is the Stanford Heart Disease Prevention project. The Multiple Risk Factor Intervention Trial (MRFIT) was a large study designed to see if mortality could be lowered in men with high coronary risk through intensive face-to-face efforts to modify hypertension, high serum cholesterol, and smoking. The results of the MRFIT were equivocal, with no significant differences between special intervention and control groups. Many people believe this resulted from the fact that the control group also lowered their cardiovascular risk more than anticipated.

Cancer risk may also be lowered by stopping or preventing smoking, and eating a low fat, high fiber diet, and efforts to prevent cancer and to increase compliance to cancer screening through lifestyle interventions have been utilized.

The occupational setting is a convenient place for health promotion interventions. Such activities include work site hypertension screening, antismoking, stress management, physical exercise, and weight control programs. Novel approaches such as weight loss competitions at the work site have been used to increase employee motivation.

AIDS education is another important behavioral health promotion activity. Several approaches to preventing infection from the AIDS virus exist, ranging from the advocacy of sexual abstinence to monogamous sexual relationships to the use of condoms and the practice of "safer" sex. Because of the high AIDS infection risk in intravenous drug users, educational efforts directed at this group are also important.

RECOMMENDED READINGS

Blanchard, E. B. (Ed.). Behavioral medicine: An update for the 1990's. *Journal of Consulting and Clinical Psychology, 60* (4), 491–603, 1992.

Grunberg, N. E. Behavioral factors in preventive medicine and health promotion. In W. Gordon, A. Herd, and A. Baum (Eds.), *Perspectives on behavioral medicine*, vol. 3. New York: Academic Press, 1988.

Prochaska, J. O., DiClemente, C. C., and Norcross, J. C. In search of how people change: Applications to addictive behaviors. *American Psychologist*, 1992, 47, 1102–1114.

Turk, D. C. (Ed.). Mini-series: Advances in behavioral medicine research on breast cancer. *Annals of Behavioral Medicine*, 1994, 16, 298–351.

U. S. Department of Health and Human Services. *Healthy people 2000*: National health promotion and disease prevention objectives (DHHS Publication No. PHS 91–50212). Washington, DC: U.S. Government Printing Office, 1991.

References

Abramson, L. Y., Seligman, M. E. P., and Teasdale, J. Learned helplessness in humans: Critique and reformulation. *Journal of Abnormal Psychology,* 1978, *87,* 49–74.

Achterberg, J., McGraw, P., and Lawlis, G. F. Rheumatoid arthritis: A study of the relaxation and temperature biofeedback training as an adjunctive therapy. *Biofeedback and Self-Regulation,* 1981, *6,* 207–233.

Adams, D. O. Molecular biology of macrophage activation: A pathway whereby psychosocial factors can potentially affect health. *Psychosomatic Medicine,* 1994, *56*(4), 316–327.

Ader, R. Plasma pepsinogen level as a predictor of susceptibility to gastric erosions in the rat. *Psychosomatic Medicine,* 1963, *25,* 221–230.

———. Behavioral influences on immune responses. In S. M. Weiss, J. A. Herd, and B. H. Fox (Eds.), *Perspectives on behavioral medicine.* New York: Academic Press, 1981a.

Ader, R. (Ed.). *Psychoneuroimmunology.* New York: Academic Press, 1981b.

Ader, R., and Cohen, N. Behaviorally conditioned immunosuppression. *Psychosomatic Medicine,* 1975, *37,* 333–340.

Ader, R., and Cohen, N. Conditioned immunopharmacologic responses. In R. Ader (Ed.), *Psychoneuroimmunology.* New York: Academic Press, 1981.

Adesso, V. J., and Glad, W. R. A behavioral test of smoking typology. *Addictive Behaviors,* 1978, *3,* 35–38.

Adler, A. Neuropsychiatric complications in victims of Boston's Cocoanut Grove disaster. *Journal of the American Medical Association,* 1943, *17,* 1098–1101.

Affleck, G. Social comparisons in rheumatoid arthritis: Accuracy and adaptational significance. *Journal of Social and Clinical Psychology,* 1988, *6*(2), 219–234.

Affleck, G., Tennen, H., Pfeiffer, C., and Fifield, J. Appraisals of control and predictability in adapting to a chronic disease. *Journal of Personality and Social Psychology,* 1987, *53*(2), 273–279.

Affleck, G., Tennen, H., Urrows, S., and Higgins, P. Individual differences in the day-to-day experience of chronic pain: A prospective daily study of rheumatoid arthritis patients. *Health Psychology,* 1991, *10*(6), 419–426.

Aiello, J. R., and Thompson, D. Personal space, crowding and spatial behavior in a cultural context. In I. Altman, A. Rappoport, and J. Wohlwill (Eds.), *Human behavior and environment,* vol. 4. New York: Plenum, 1980.

Ajzen, I. Prediction of goal-directed behavior: Attitudes, intentions, and perceived behavioral control. *Journal of Experimental Social Psychology,* 1986, 22(5), 453–474.

Ajzen, I., and Fishbein, M. *Understanding attitudes and predicting social behaviour.* Englewood Cliffs, NJ: Prentice-Hall, 1980.

Azjen, I., and Madden, T. J. Predictions of goal-directed behavior: Attitudes, intentions, and perceived behavioral control. *Journal of Experimental Social Psychology,* 1986, 22(5), 453–474.

Akil, H., Watson, S. J., Young, E., et al. Endogenous opioids: Biology and function. *Annual Review of Neuroscience,* 1984, 7, 223–225.

Aldwin, C., Folkman, S., Shaefer, C., et al. *Ways of coping checklist: A process measure.* Paper presented at the annual American Psychological Association Meeting, Montreal, Canada, 1980.

Alexander, A. B., and Smith, D. D. Clinical applications of EMG biofeedback. In R. J. Gatchel and K. P. Price (Eds.), *Clinical applications of biofeedback: Appraisal and status.* New York: Pergamon, 1979.

Alexander, F. *Psychosomatic medicine: Its principles and applications.* New York: Norton, 1950.

Alloy, L. B., and Clements, C. M. Illusion of control: Invulnerability to negative affect and depressive symptoms after laboratory and natural stressors. *Journal of Abnormal Psychology,* 1992, 101(2), 234–245.

Alloy, L. B., Peterson, C., Abramson, L. Y., and Seligman, M. E. P. Attributional style and the generality of learned helplessness. *Journal of Personality and Social Psychology,* 1984, 46, 681–687.

Alterman, A. I., and Tarter, R. E. The transmission of psychological vulnerability: Implications for alcoholism etiology. *Journal of Nervous and Mental Disease,* 1983, 171, 147–154.

Altmaier, E. M., and Happ, D. A. Coping skills training's immunization effects against learned helplessness. *Journal of Social and Clinical Psychology,* 1985, 3, 181–189.

American Psychiatric Association. *Diagnostic and statistical manual of mental disorders (DSM-IV).* Washington, DC: American Psychiatric Association, 1994.

American Psychiatric Association. *Diagnostic and statistic manual of mental disorders* (revised, 3rd ed.). Washington, DC: American Psychiatric Association, 1987.

Amick, T. L., and Ockene, J. K. The role of social support in the modification of risk factors for cardiovascular disease. In S. A. Shumaker and S. M. Czajkowski (Eds.), *Social support and cardiovascular disease. Plenum series in behavioral psychophysiology and medicine.* University of Massachusetts, Donahue Institute for Governmental Services, Amherst, MA, 1994, pp. 259–278.

Andersen, B. L. A biobehavioral model of cancer stress and disease course. *American Psychologist,* 1994, 49(5), 389–404.

Anderson, C. A., Miller, R. S., Riger, A. L., et al. Behavioral and characterological attributional styles as predictors of depression and loneliness: Review, refinement, and test. *Journal of Personality and Social Psychology,* 1994, 66(3) 549–558.

Anderson, E. A. Preoperative preparation for cardiac surgery facilitates recovery, reduces psychological distress, and reduces the incidence of acute postoperative hypertension. *Journal of Consulting and Clinical Psychology,* 1987, 55, 513–520.

Anderson, N. B. Behavioral and sociocultural perspectives on ethnicity and health: Introduction to the special issue. *Health Psychology,* 1995, 14(7), 589–591.

Anderson, N. B., and Armstead, C. A. Toward understanding the association of socioeconomic status and health: A new challenge for the biopsychosocial approach. *Psychosomatic Medicine,* 1995, 57, 213–225.

Anderson, N. B., McNeilly, M., and Myers, H. Toward understanding race differences in autonomic reactivity: A proposed contextual model. In J. R. Turner, A. Sherwood, and K. C. Light (Eds.), *Individual differences in cardiovascular response to stress.* New York: Plenum, 1992, pp. 125–145.

Andrasik, F., and Blanchard, E. B. The biofeedback treatment of tension headache. In J. P. Hatch, J. G. Fisher, and J. D. Rugh (Eds.), *Biofeedback: Studies in clinical efficacy.* New York: Plenum, 1987, pp. 281–322.

Andrasik, F., Blanchard, E. B., Neff D. F., and Rodichok, L. D. Biofeedback and relaxation training for chronic headache: A controlled comparison of booster treatments and regular contacts for long-term maintenance. *Journal of Consulting and Clinical Psychology,* 1984, *52,* 609–615.

Andrés, R. Effect of obesity on total mortality. *International Journal of Obesity,* 1980, *4,* 381–386.

Angarano, G., Pastore, G., and Monno, L. Rapid spread of HTLV-III infection among drug addicts in Italy. *Lancet,* 1985, *2,* 1302.

Annent, J. *Feedback and human behavior.* Baltimore: Penguin Books, 1969.

Antoni, M. H. Temporal relationship between life events and two illness measures: A cross–lagged panel analysis. *Journal of Human Stress,* 1985, *11,* 21–26.

Antoni, M. H., Baggett, L., Ironson, G., and LaPerriere, A. Cognitive-behavioral stress management intervention buffers distress response and immunologic changes following notification of HIV-1 seropositivity. *Journal of Consulting and Clinical Psychology,* 1991, *59*(6), 906–915.

Antoni, M. H., Schneiderman, N., LaPerriere, A., et al. Mothers with AIDS. In P. Ahmed (Ed.), *Living and dying with AIDS.* New York: Plenum, 1992.

Antony, V. B., Godbey, S. W., Hott, J. W., and Queener, S. F. Alcohol-induced inhibition of alveolar macrophage oxidant release in vivo and in vitro. *Alcoholism, Clinical and Experimental Research,* 1993, *17*(2), 389–393.

Appelbaum, K. A. Cognitive behavioral treatment of a veteran population with moderate to severe rheumatoid arthritis. *Behavior Therapy,* 1988, *19*(4), 489–502.

Arena, J. G., and Blanchard, E. B. Biofeedback and relaxation therapy for chronic pain disorders. In R. J. Gatchel and D. C. Turk (Eds.), *Psychological approaches to pain management: A practitioner's handbook.* New York: Guilford Publications, 1996.

Armitage, J. O. Treatment of non-Hodgkin's lymphoma. *New England Journal of Medicine,* 1993, *328,* 1023–1030.

Armor, D. J., Polich, J. M., and Stambul, H. B. *Alcoholism and treatment.* Santa Monica, CA: Rand Corporation, 1976.

Arnetz, B. B., Edgren, B., Levi, L., and Otto, U. Behavioral and endocrine reactions in boys scoring high on Sennton neurotic scale viewing an exciting and partly violent movie and the importance of social support. *Social Science and Medicine,* 1985, *20*(7), 731–736.

Ashton, H., and Stepney, R. *Smoking: Psychology and pharmacology.* New York: Tavistock, 1982.

Atkinson, J. P., Sullivan, T. J., Kelly, J. P., and Parker, C. W. Stimulation by alcohols of cyclic AMP metabolism in human leukocytes. Possible role of cyclic AMP in the anti-inflammatory effects of ethanol. *Journal of Clinical Investigation,* 1977, *60*(2), 284–294.

Auerbach, S. M., Martelli, M. F., and Mercuri, L. G. Anxiety, information, interpersonal impacts, and adjustment to a stressful health care situation. *Journal of Personality and Social Psychology,* 1983, *44,* 1284–1297.

Ax, A. R. The physiological differentiation between fear and anger in humans. *Psychosomatic Medicine,* 1953, *15,* 433–442.

Ayllon, T., and Azrin, N. H. *The token economy: A motivational system for therapy and rehabilitation.* New York: Appleton-Century-Crofts, 1968.

Babiker, I. Measuring medication compliance using repeated pill counts and riboflavin tracer assay. *International Journal of Methods in Psychiatric Resarch,* 1994, *4*(1), 13–17.

Bachen, E. A., Manuck, S. B., Cohen, S., et al. Sympathetic blockade ameliorates cellular immune alterations induced by acute psychological stress. Presented at the Research Perspectives in Psychoneuroimmunology Fifth Conference, Miami, FL, 1994.

Bachen, E. A., Manuck, S. B., Cohen, S., et al. Adrenergic blockade ameliorates cellular immune responses to mental stress in humans. *Psychosomatic Medicine,* 1995, *57*(4), 366–372.

Bachen, E. A., Manuck, S. B., Marslund, A. L., and Cohen, S. Lymphocyte subset and cellular immune responses to a brief experimental stressor. *Psychosomatic Medicine,* 1992, *54*(6), 673–679.

Baekeland, F., and Lundwall, L. K. Effects of discontinuity of medication on the results of a double-blind study in outpatient alcoholics. *Journal of Studies on Alcohol,* 1975, *36*(9), 1268–1272.

Bagasra, O., Kajdacsy-Balla, A., Lischner, H. W., and Pomerantz, R. J. Alcohol intake increases human immunodeficiency virus type 1 replication in human peripheral blood mononuclear cells. *Journal of Infectious Diseases,* 1993, *167*(4), 789–797.

Baider, L., and Sarell, M. Coping with cancer among Holocaust survivors in Israel: An exploratory study. *Journal of Human Stress,* 1984, *10,* 121–127.

Bakal, D. A. *Psychology and medicine: Psychobiological dimensions of health and illness.* New York: Springer, 1979.

Baker, G. W., and Chapman, D. W. (Eds.). *Man and society in disaster.* New York: Basic Books, 1962.

Ballenger, J. J. Experimental effect of cigarette smoke on human respiratory cilia. *New England Journal of Medicine,* 1960, *263*(17), 832–835.

Ballieux, R. E. The mind and the immune system. *Theoretical Medicine,* 1994, *15*(4), 387–395.

Baltrusch, H. J., Strangel, W., and Titze, I. Stress, cancer, and immunity: New developments in biopsychosocial and psychoneuroimmunologic research. Congress on Brain and Immunity (1991, Naples, Italy). *Acta Neurologica,* 1991, *13*(4), 315–327.

Ban, T. *Recent advances in the biology of schizophrenia.* Springfield, IL: Charles C. Thomas, 1973.

Bandura, A. Modeling approaches to the modification of phobic disorders. In R. Porter (Ed.), *The role of learning in psychotherapy.* London: Churchill, 1968.

———. *Principles of behavior modification.* New York: Holt, Rinehart and Winston, 1969.

———. Psychotherapy based upon modeling principles, In A. E. Bergin and S. L. Garfield (Eds.), *Handbook of psychotherapy and behavior change: An empirical analysis.* New York: Wiley, 1971.

———. Self-efficacy: Toward a unifying theory of behavioral change. *Psychological Review,* 1977a, *84,* 191–215.

———. *Social learning theory.* Englewood Cliffs, NJ: Prentice-Hall, 1977b.

———. The explanatory and predictive scope of self-efficacy theory. Special issue: Self-efficacy theory in contemporary psychology. *Journal of Social and Clinical Psychology,* 1986, *4*(3), 359–373.

Bandura, A. (Ed.). *Self-efficacy in changing societies.* Cambridge, MA: Cambridge University Press, 1995.

Bandura, A., Blanchard, E. B., and Ritter, B. The relative efficacy of desensitization and modeling approaches for inducing behavioral, affective, and attitudinal changes. *Journal of Personality and Social Psychology,* 1969, *13,* 173–199.

Bandura, A., Cioffi, D., Taylor, C. B., and Brouillard, M. E. Perceived self-efficacy in coping with cognitive stressors and opioid activation. *Journal of Personality and Social Psychology,* 1988, *55,* 479–488.

Bandura, A., Grusec, J. E., and Menlove, F. L. Vicarious extinction of avoidance behavior. *Journal of Personality and Social Psychology,* 1967, *5,* 16–23.

Bandura, A., O'Leary, A., Taylor, C. B., et al. Perceived self-efficacy and pain control: Opioid and nonopioid mechanisms. *Journal of Personality and Social Psychology,* 1987, *53,* 563–571.

Bandura, A., Ross, D., and Ross, S. A. Imitation of film-mediated aggressive models. *Journal of Abnormal and Social Psychology,* 1963, *66,* 3–11.

Barber J. Rapid induction analgesia: A clinical report. *American Journal of Clinical Hypnosis,* 1977, *19,* 138–147.

Barber, T. X., and Cooper, B. J. The effects on pain of experimentally induced and spontaneous distraction. *Psychological Reports,* 1972, *31,* 647–651.

Barder, L., Slimmer, L., and LeSage, J. Depression and issues of control among elderly people in health care settings. *Journal of Advanced Nursing,* 1994, *20*(4), 597–604.

Barefoot, J. C., Dahlstrom, W. C., and Williams, R. B. Hostility, CHD incidence, and total mortality: A 25-year follow-up study of 255 physicians. *Psychosomatic Medicine,* 1983, *45,* 59–63.

Barefoot, J. C., Dahlstrom, W. C, and Williams, R. B. Hostility patterns and health implications: Correlations of Cook-Medley hostility scale scores in a national survey. *Health Psychology,* 1991, *10,* 18–24.

Barefoot, J. C., Dodge, K. A., Peterson, B. L., et al. The Cook-Medley hostility scale: Item content and ability to predict survival. *Psychosomatic Medicine,* 1989, *51,* 46–57.

Barefoot, J. C., and Lipkus, I. M. The assessment of anger and hostility. In A. W. Siegman and T. W. Smith (Eds.), *Anger, hostility, and the heart.* Hillsdale, NJ: Lawrence Erlbaum Associates, 1994, pp. 43–66.

Barlow, C. L. A naturalistic study of depression in the elderly. *Dissertation Abstracts, International,* 1988, *49*(4-b), 1378.

Barnes, D., Gatchel, R. J., Mayer, T. G., and Barnett, J. Changes in MMPI profiles of chronic low back pain patients following successful treatment. *Journal of Spinal Disorders,* 1992, *3,* 353–355.

Barnett, R. C. Multiple roles, gender, and psychological distress. In L. Goldberger and S. Breznitz (Eds.), *Handbook of stress: Theoretical and clinical aspects,* 2nd ed. New York: Free Press, 1993, pp. 427–445.

Baron, R. S., Cutrona, C. E., Hicklin, D., and Russell, D. W. Social support and immune function among spouses of cancer patients. *Journal of Personality and Social Psychology,* 1990, *59,* 344–352.

Barry, J., Selwyn, A. P., Nabel, E. G., et al. Frequency of ST segment depression produced by mental stress in stable angina pectoris from coronary artery disease. *American Journal of Cardiology,* 1988, *61,* 989–993.

Barton, A. H. *Communities in disaster.* Garden City, NY: Doubleday, 1969.

Bartrop, R. W., Lazarus, L., Luckhurast, et al. Depressed lymphocyte function after bereavement. *Lancet,* 1977, *1,* 834–836.

Basco, M. R. Compliance with pharmacotherapy in mood disorders. *Psychiatric Annals,* 1995, *25*(5), 269–270, 276, 278–279.

Basco, M. R., and Rush, A. J. Compliance with pharmacotherapy in mood disorders. *Psychiatric Annals,* 1995, *25*(5), 269–270.

Baum, A. Toxins, technology, and natural disasters. In G. R. VandenBos and B. K. Bryant (Eds.), *Cataclysms, crises, and catastrophes: Psychology in action.* Washington, DC: American Psychological Association, 1987, pp. 7–52.

———. Stress, intrusive imagery, and chronic distress. *Health Psychology,* 1990, *9,* 653–675.

———. Behavioral, biological, and environmental interactions in disease processes. In S. J. Blumenthal, K. Matthews, and S. M. Weiss (Eds.), *New research frontiers in be-*

havioral medicine: Proceedings of the National Conference. Washington, DC: U.S. Government Printing Office, 1994, pp. 61–70.

Baum, A., Aiello, J. R., and Calesnick, L. Crowding and personal control: Social density and the development of learned helplessness. *Journal of Personality and Social Psychology*, 1978, *36*, 1000–1011.

Baum, A., Aiello, J. R., and Davis, G. E. Urban stress, withdrawal and health. Paper presented at the annual meeting of the American Psychological Asosciation, New York, 1979.

Baum, A., Cohen, L., and Hall, M. Control and intrusive memories as possible determinants of chronic stress. *Psychosomatic Medicine*, 1993, *55*, 274–286.

Baum, A., Fisher, J. D., and Solomon, S. Type of information, familiarity, and the reduction of crowding stress. *Journal of Personality and Social Psychology*, 1981, *40*(1), 11–23.

Baum, A., and Fleming, I. Implications of psychological research on stress and technological accidents. *American Psychologist*, 1993, *48*(6), 665–672.

Baum, A., Fleming, I., Israel, A., and O'Keeffe, M. K. Symptoms of chronic stress following a natural disaster and discovery of a human-made hazard. *Environment and Behavior*, 1992, *24*, 347–365.

Baum, A., Fleming, R., and Davidson, L. M. Natural disaster and technological catastrophe. *Environment and Behavior*, 1983, *15*, 333–335.

Baum, A., Fleming, R., and Singer, J. R. Coping with victimization by technological disaster. *Journal of Social Issues*, 1983, *39*, 117–138.

Baum, A., and Gatchel, R. J. Cognitive determinants of reactions to uncontrollable events: Development of reactance and learned helplessness. *Journal of Personality and Social Psychology*, 1981, *40*, 1078–1089.

Baum, A., Gatchel, R. J., Aiello, J. R., and Thompson, D. Cognitive mediation of environmental stress. In J. Harvey (Ed.), *Environment, cognition, and social behavior.* Hillsdale, NJ: Erlbaum, 1981.

Baum, A., Gatchel, R. J., Streufert, J., et al. Psychological stress for alternatives of decontamination of TMI-2 reactor building atmosphere. Washington, DC: U.S. Nuclear Regulatory Commision (NUREG/CR-1584), 1980.

Baum, A., and Grunberg, N. E. Gender, stress, and health. *Health Psychology*, 1991, *10*, 80–85.

Baum, A., Grunberg, N. E., and Singer, J. E. The use of psychological and neuroendocrinological measurements in the study of stress. *Health Psychology*, 1982, *1*, 217–236.

Baum, A., and Koman, S. Differential response to anticipated crowding: Psychological effects of social and spatial density. *Journal of Personality and Social Psychology*, 1976, *34*, 526–536.

Baum, A., and Paulus, P. B. Crowding. In D. Stokols and I. Altman (Eds.), *Handbook of environmental psychology*, vol. 1. New York: Wiley-Interscience, 1987, pp. 533–570.

Baum, A., Singer, J. E., and Baum, C. S. Stress and the environment. *Journal of Social Issues*, 1981, *37*, 4–35.

Baum, A., and Valins, S. *Architecture and social behavior: Psychological studies of social density.* Hillsdale, NJ: Erlbaum, 1977.

Bauman, A. E., Craig, A. R., Dunsmore, J., et al. Removing barriers to effective self-management of asthma. *Patient Education and Counseling*, 1989, *14*, 217–226.

Baumann, L. J., and Leventhal, H. "I can tell when my blood pressure is up: Can't I?" *Health Psychology*, 1985, *4*, 203–218.

Beck, A. T. *Depression: Clinical, experimental and theoretical aspects.* New York: Harper & Row, 1967.

———. *Cognitive therapy and emotional disorders.* New York: International Universities Press, 1976.

Beck, A. T., Rush, A. J., Shaw, B. J., and Emery, G. *Cognitive therapy of depression: A treatment manual.* New York: Guilford Press, 1979.

Beck, S. J. *Rorschach's Test I: Basic processes,* 3rd ed. New York: Grune & Stratton, 1961.

Becker, M. H. In hot pursuit of health promotion: Some admonitions. In S. M. Weiss, J. E. Fielding, and A. Baum (Eds.), *Perspectives in behavioral medicine: Health at work.* Hillsdale, NJ: Erlbaum, 1991.

Beckham, J. C., Burker, E. J., Rice, J. R., and Talton, S. L. Patient predictors of caregiver burden, optimism, and pessimism in rheumatoid arthritis. *Behavioral Medicine,* 1995, *20*(4), 171–178.

Bedell, S., and Delbanco, T. L. Choices about cardiopulmonary resuscitation in the hospital—When do physicians talk with patients? *New England Journal of Medicine,* 1984, *310,* 1089–1093.

Beecher, H. K. Relationship of significance of wound to the pain experienced. *Journal of the American Medical Association,* 1956, *161,* 1609–1613.

Belloc, N. B. Relationship of health practices and mortality. *Preventive Medicine,* 1973, *2,* 67–81.

Belloc, N. B., and Breslow, L. Relationship of physical health status and health practices. *Preventive Medicine,* 1976, *1,* 409–421.

Bender, C. M. Cognitive dysfunction associated with cancer and cancer therapy. *Medical Surgical Nursing,* 1995, *4*(5), 398–400.

Benet, S. *Abkhasians: The long-living people of the Caucasus.* New York: Holt, Reinhart and Winston, 1974.

Benowitz, N. L., Hall, S. M., Herning, R. I., et al. Smokers of low-yield cigarettes do not consume less nicotine. *New England Journal of Medicine,* 1983, *309,* 139–142.

Berger, B. G. Running toward psychological well-being: Special considerations for the female client. In M. L. Sachs and G. Buffone (Eds.), *Running as therapy: An integrated approach.* Lincoln: University of Nebraska Press, 1984.

Bergner, M. The sickness impact profile, In N. K. Wenger, M. D. Mattson, and C. D. Furberg (Eds.), *Assessment of quality of life in clinical trials of cardiovascular therapies.* New York: LeJacq Publishing, 1984.

———. Quality of life, health status, and clinical research. *Medical Care,* 1989, *27*(suppl. 3), S148–S156.

Bergner, M. Bobbitt, R., Carter, W., and Gilson, B. The sickness impact profile: Development and final revision of a health status measure. *Medical Care,* 1981, *19*(8), 787–805.

Berkman, L. F., and Syme, S. L. Social networks, host resistance, and mortality: A nine-year follow-up study of Alameda County residents. *American Journal of Epidemiology,* 1979, *109,* 186–204.

Bernstein, D. A., and Glasgow, R. E. Smoking. In O. F. Pomerleau and J. P. Brady (Eds.), *Behavioral medicine: Theory and practice.* Baltimore: Williams & Wilkins, 1979.

Berren, M. R., Biegel, A., and Ghertner, S. A typology for the classification of disasters. *Community Mental Health Journal,* 1980, *16*(2), 103–111.

Best, J. A., Flay, B. R., Towson, S., et al. Smoking prevention and the concept of risk. *Journal of Applied Social Psychology,* 1984, *14,* 257–273.

Bettelheim, B. *The informed heart: Autonomy in a mass age.* Glencoe, IL: Free Press, 1960.

Bieliauskas, L. A. Life stress and aid-seeking. *Journal of Human Stress,* 1980, *6,* 28–36.

Bigelow, G., Libson, I., and Lawrence, C. Prevention of alcohol abuse by reinforcement of incompatible behavior. Paper presented at the annual meeting of the Association for Advancement of Behavior Therapy, December 1973.

Birk, L. (Ed.). *Biofeedback: Behavioral medicine.* New York: Grune & Stratton, 1973.

Bishop. G. D., and Converse, S. A. Illness representations: A prototype approach. *Health Psychology,* 1986, *5*(2), 95–114.

Black, J. L., Dolan, M. P., DeFord, H. A., et al. Sharing of needles among users in intravenous drugs [letter]. *New England Journal of Medicine,* 1986, *314*(7), 446–447.

Blair, S. N., Piserchia, P. V., Curtis, S. W., and Crowder, J. H. A public health intervention model for work-site health promotion: Impact on exercise and physical fitness in a health promotion plan after 24 months. *Journal of the American Medical Association,* 1986, *255*(7), 921–926.

Blake, B. C. The application of behavior therapy to the treatment of alcoholism. *Behavior Research and Therapy,* 1967, *3,* 78–85.

Blalock, S. J., De Vellis, D. M., Afifi, R. A., and Sandler, R. S. Risk perceptions and participation in colorectal cancer screening. *Health Psychology,* 1990, *9,* 792–806.

Blanchard, E. B. (Ed.). Behavioral medicine: An update for the 1990's. *Journal of Consulting and Clinical Psychology, 60*(4), 491–603.

———. Irritable bowel syndrome. In R. J. Gatchel and E. B. Blanchard (Eds.), *Psychophysiological disorders: Research and clinical applications.* Washington, DC: American Psychological Association, 1993.

Blanchard, E. B., and Andrasek, F. Biofeedback treatment of vascular headache. In J. P. Hatch, J. G. Fisher, and J. D. Rugh (Eds.), *Biofeedback: Studies in clinical efficacy.* New York: Plenum, 1987, pp. 1–80.

Blanchard, E. B., Andrasik, F., Neff, D. F., et al. Biofeedback and relaxation training with three kinds of headache: Treatment effects and their prediction. *Journal of Consulting and Clinical Psychology,* 1982, *50,* 562–575.

Blanchard, E. B., Appelbaum, K. A., Guarnieri, P., et al. Two studies of the long-term follow-up of minimal therapist contact treatments of vascular and tension headache. *Journal of Consulting and Clinical Psychology,* 1988, *56,* 427–432.

Bland, S. H., Krogh, V., Winkelstein, W., and Trevisan, M. Social network and blood pressure: A population study. *Psychosomatic Medicine,* 1991, *53,* 598–607.

Blaney, P. H., and Ganellen, R. J. Hardiness and social support. In B. R. Sarason, I. G. Sarason, and G. R. Pierce (Eds.), *Social support: An interactional view.* New York: Wiley, 1990.

Blood, G. W., Simpson, K. C., Dineen, M., and Kauffman, S. M. Spouses of individuals with laryngeal cancer: Caregiver strain and burden. *Journal of Communication Disorders,* 1994, *27*(1), 19–35.

Blum, K. Psychogenetics of drug seeking behavior. In E. E. Muller and A. R. Genezzani (Eds.), *Central and peripheral endorphins: Basic and clinical aspects.* New York: Raven Press, 1984.

Blumenthal, J. A., Burg, M. M., Barefoot, G., et al. Social support, Type A behavior, and coronary artery disease. *Psychosomatic Medicine,* 1987, *49,* 331–340.

Blumenthal, J. A., and McCubbin, J. A. Physical exercise as stress management. In A. Baum and J. E. Singer (Eds.), *Handbook of psychology and health,* vol. 5. Hillsdale, NJ: Erlbaum, 1987.

Blumetti, A. E., and Modesti, L. M. Psychological predictors of success or failure of surgical intervention for intractable back pain. In J. J. Bonica and D. Abbe-Fessard (Eds.), *Advances in pain research and therapy,* vol. 1. New York: Raven Press, 1976.

Bodnar, J., and Kiecolt-Glaser, J. K. Caregiver depression after bereavement: Chronic stress isn't over when it's over. *Psychology Aging,* 1994a, *9,* 372–380.

Bodnar, J., and Kiecolt-Glaser, J. K. Chronic stress and depressive disorders in older adults. *Journal of Abnormal Psychology,* 1994b, *99,* 284–290.

Bonica, J. J. *The management of pain.* Philadelphia: Lea & Febiger, 1953.

Bootzin, R. R. Stimulus control of insomnia. Paper presented at the American Psychological Association, Montreal, Canada, August 1973.

———. *Behavior modification and therapy: An introduction.* Cambridge, MA: Winthrop, 1975.

Borland, R., Owen, N., Hill, D., and Schofield, P. Predicting attempts and sustained cessation of smoking after the introduction of workplace smoking bans. *Health Psychology*, 1991, *10*, 336–342.

Borysenko, M., and Borysenko, J. Stress, behavior, and immunity: Animal models and mediating mechanisms. *General Hospital Psychiatry*, 1982, *4*(1), 413–419.

Bott, E. Teaching of psychology in the medical course. *Bulletin of the Association of American Medical Colleges*, 1928, *3*, 289–304.

Bounds, W., Betzing, K. W., Stewart, R. M., and Holcombe, R. F. Social drinking and the immune response: Impairment of lymphokine-activated killer activity. *American Journal of the Medical Sciences*, 1994, *307*(6), 391–395.

Bovbjerg, D., Ader, R., and Cohen, N. Behaviorally conditioned immunosuppression of a graft versus host response. *Proceedings of the National Academy of Sciences*, 1982, *79*, 583–585.

Boyd, J. R., Covington, T. R., Stanaszek, W. F., and Coussons, R. T. Drug defaulting, II. Analysis of noncompliance patterns. *American Journal of Hospital Pharmacy*, 1974, *31*, 485–491.

Boyle, C. M. Differences between patients' and doctors' interpretation of some common medical terms. *British Medical Journal*, 1970, *2*, 286–289.

Brady, J. V. Ulcers in "executive" monkeys. *Scientific American*, 1958, *199*, 95–100.

Brady, J. V., Porter, R. W., Conrad, D. G., and Mason, J. W. Avoidance behavior and the development of gastroduodenal ulcers. *Journal of Experimental Analysis of Behavior*, 1958, *1*, 69–73.

Braunwald. E. Myocardial ischemia, infarction, and failure: An odyssey. *Cardioscience*, 1994, *5*, 139–144.

Brehm, J. W. *A theory of psychological reactance*. New York: Academic Press, 1966.

Brende, J. O. Electrodermal responses in post-traumatic syndromes. A pilot study of cerebral hemisphere functioning in Vietnam veterans. *Journal of Nervous and Mental Disease*, 1982, *170*(6), 352–361.

Brenner, G. J., Cohen, N., Ader, R., and Moynihan, J. A. Increased pulmonary metastases and natural killer cell activity in mice following handling. *Life Sciences*, 1990, *47*(20), 1813–1819.

Breslau, N., Davis, G. C., Andreski, P., and Peterson, E. Traumatic events and posttraumatic stress disorder in an urban population of young adults. *Archives of General Psychiatry*, 1991, *48*, 216–222.

Breslin, F. C., and Baum, A. S. Alcohol, stress, and immune-related disorders: An interactive model. In R. Vrasti (Ed.), *Alcoholism–New research perspectives*. Still in press.

Breslin, F. C., Hayward, M., and Baum, A. Effect of stress on perceived intoxication and the blood alcohol curve in men and women. *Health Psychology*, 1994, *13*(6), 479–486.

Breslow, L., and Enstrom, J. E. Persistence of health habits and their relationship to mortality. *Preventive Medicine*, 1980, *9*, 469–483.

Brett, J. F., Brief, A. P., Burke, M. J., et al. Negative affectivity and the reporting of stressful life events. *Health Psychology*, 1990, *9*, 57–68.

Broaunwald, E. (Ed.). *Principle of internal medicine*, 12th ed. New York: McGraw-Hill, 1994.

Brown, G. K. A causal analysis of chronic pain and depression. *Journal of Abnormal Psychology*, 1990, *99*(2), 127–137.

Brown, G. K., and Nicassio, P. M. Development of a questionnaire for the assessment of active and passive coping strategies in chronic pain patients. *Pain*, 1987, *31*, 53–63.

Brown, G. K., Wallston, K. A., and Nicassio, P. M. Social support and depression in rheumatoid arthritis: A one-year prospective study. *Journal of Applied Social Psychology*, 1989, *19*, 1164–1181.

Brown, G. W., Bhrolchain, M. N., and Harris, T. Social class and psychiatric disturbance among women in an urban population. *Sociology,* 1975, *9,* 225–254.

Brown, J. D., and Lawton, M. Stress and well-being in adolescence: The moderating role of the physical exercise. *Journal of Human Stress,* 1986, *12,* 125–131.

Brown, J. D., and McGill, K. L. The cost of good fortune: When positive life events produce negative health consequences. *Journal of Personality and Social Psychology,* 1989, *57,* 1103–1110.

Brown, S., and Munson, E. Extroversion, anxiety and the perceived effects of alcohol. *Journal of Studies on Alcohol,* 1987, *48,* 272–276.

Brownell, K. D. Adherence to dietary regimens: 2. Components of effective interventions. *Behavioral Medicine,* 1995, *20*(4), 155–164.

Brownell, K. D., Cohen, R. Y., Stunkard, A. J., et al. Weight loss competitions at the work site: Impact on weight, morale, and cost-effectiveness. *American Journal of Public Health,* 1984, *74,* 1283–1285.

Brownell, K. D., and Rodin, J. The dieting maelstrom: Is it possible and advisable to lose weight? *American Psychologist,* 1994, *49,* 781–791.

Brownell, K. D., and Wadden, T. A. The heterogeneity of obesity: Fitting treatments to individuals. *Behavior Therapy,* 1991, *22,* 153–177.

Brownell, K. D., and Wadden, T. A. Etiology and treatment of obesity: Understanding a serious, prevalent, and refractory disorder. *Journal of Consulting and Clinical Psychology,* 1992, *60,* 505–517.

Bruns, C., and Geist, C. S. Stressful life events and drug use among adolescents. *Journal of Human Stress,* 1984, *10,* 135–139.

Bulman, R. J., and Wortman, C. B. Attribution of blame and coping in the "real world": Severe accident victims react to their lot. *Journal of Personality and Social Psychology,* 1977, *35,* 351–363.

Bundek, N. I., Marks, G., and Richardson, J. L. Role of health locus of control beliefs in cancer screening of elderly Hispanic women. *Health Psychology,* 1993, *12,* 193–199.

Burch, J. Recent bereavement in relation to suicide. *Journal of Psychosomatic Research,* 1972, *16,* 361–366.

Burdette, B. H., and Gale, E. N. The effects of treatment on masticatory muscle activity and mandibular posture in myofascial pain-dysfunction patients. *Journal of Dental Research,* 1988, *67,* 1126–1130.

Burish, T. G., and Jenkins, R. A. Effectiveness of biofeedback and relaxation training in reducing the side effects of cancer chemotherapy. *Health Psychology,* 1992, *11,* 17–23.

Burke, M. Lawmakers: Cost factors override cost concerns. *Hospitals,* 1992, *66*(10), 60.

Burks, N., and Martin, B. Everyday problems and life change events: Ongoing versus acute sources of stress. *Journal of Human Stress,* 1985, *11,* 27–35.

Burt, R. W., DiSario, J. A., and Cannon-Albright, L. Genetics of colon cancer: Impact of inheritance on colon cancer risk. *Annual Review of Medicine,* 1995, *46,* 371–379.

Buske-Kirschbaum, A., Kirschbaum, C., Stierle, H., et al. Conditioned increase of natural killer cell activity (NKCA) in humans. *Psychosomatic Medicine,* 1992, *54*(2), 123–132.

Buske-Kirschbaum, A., Kirschbaum, C., Stierle, H., et al. Conditioned manipulation of natural killer (NK) cells in humans using a discriminative learning protocol. *Biological Psychology,* 1994, *38*(2–3), 143–155.

Buss, A. H., and Plomin, R. *A temperament theory of personality development.* New York: Wiley, 1975.

Buysse, D. J., Reynolds, C. F., Monk, T. H., and Berman, S. R. The Pittsburgh Sleep Quality Index: A new instrument for psychiatric practice and research. *Psychiatry Research,* 1989, *28*(2), 193–213.

Byrne, D. Repression-sensitization as a dimension of personality. In B. Mayer (Ed.), *Progress in experimental personality research,* vol. 1. New York: Academic Press, 1964.

Cacioppo, J. T., Malarkey, W. B., Kiecolt-Glaser, J. K., et al. Heterogeneity in neuroendocrine and immune response to brief psychological stressors as a function of autonomic cardiac activation. *Psychosomatic Medicine,* 1995, *57,* 154–164.

Caggiula, A., Epstein, L. H., and Antelman, S. Acute stress of corticosterone administration reduces responsiveness to nicotine: Implications for a mechanism of conditioned tolerance. *Psychopharmacology,* 1993, *111*(4), 499–507.

Cahalan, D. Studying drinking problems rather than alcoholism. In M. Galanter (Ed.), *Recent developments in alcoholism.* New York: Plenum, 1987, pp. 363–372.

Caizza, A. A., and Ovary, Z. Ethanol intake and the immune system of guinea pigs. *Journal of Studies on Alcohol,* 1976, *37*(7), 959–964.

Calhoun, J. B. Ecological factors in the development of behavior anomalies. In J. Zubin and H. F. Hunt (Eds.), *Comparative psychopathology.* New York: Grune & Stratton, 1967.

———. Space and the strategy of life. *Ekistics,* 1970, *29,* 425–437.

Calhoun, L. G., and Cann, A. Differences in assumptions about a just world: Ethnicity and point of view. *Journal of Social Psychology,* 1995, *134*(6), 765–770.

Califano, J. A. *Healthy people: The Surgeon General's report on health promotion and disease prevention.* Washington, DC: U.S. Government Printing Office, 1979.

Cameron, J. S., Glasgow, E. F., Ogg, C. S., et al. Membranoproliferative glomerulonephritis and persistent hypocomplementemia. *British Medical Journal,* 1970, *4,* 7–14.

Camp, D. E., Klesges, R. C., and Relyea, G. The relationship between body weight concerns and adolescent smoking. *Health Psychology,* 1993, *12,* 24–32.

Campbell, L. A. Preparing children with congenital heart disease for cardiac surgery. Special section: Hospitalization/surgery. *Journal of Pediatric Psychology,* 1995, *20*(3), 313–328.

Campbell, R. J., and Henry J. P. Animal models of hypertension. In D. S. Krantz, A. Baum, and J. E. Singer (Eds.), *Handbook of psychology and health,* vol. 3, *Cardiovascular disorders and behavior.* Hillsdale, NJ: Erlbaum, 1983.

Canning, R. D., Dew, M. A., Armitage, J. M., et al. Psychological distress among caregivers to heart transplant recipients. *Social Science in Medicine,* still in press.

Cannon, W. B. The emergency function of the adrenal medulla in pain and the major emotions. *American Journal of Physiology,* 1914, *33,* 356–372.

———. The James-Lange theory of emotions: A critical examination and an alternative. *American Journal of Psychology,* 1927, *39,* 106–124.

———. Neural organization for emotional expression. In M. L. Reymert (Ed.), *Feelings and emotions: The Wittenberg symposium.* Worcester, MA: Clark University Press, 1928.

———. *Bodily changes in pain, hunger, fear and rage.* Boston: Branford, 1929.

———. Studies on the conditions of activity in the endocrine organs, XXVII. Evidence that the medulliadrenal secretion is not continuous. *American Journal of Physiology,* 1931, *98,* 447–452.

———. Stresses and strains of homeostasis (Mary Scott Newbold lecture). *American Journal of Medical Sciences,* 1935, *189,* 1–14.

Cannon, W. B., and de la Paz, D. Emotional stimulation of adrenal secretion. *American Journal of Physiology,* 1911, *28,* 64–70.

Caplan, R. D., Cobb, S., and French, J. R. P., Jr. Relationships of cessation of smoking with job stress, personality, and social support. *Journal of Applied Psychology,* 1975, *60,* 211–219.

Carey, M. P., and Burish, T. G. Etiology and treatment of the psychological side effects associated with cancer chemotherapy: A critical review and discussion. *Psychological Bulletin,* 1988, *104,* 307–325.

Carlens, E. Smoking and the immune response in the air passages. *Broncho-Pneumologie,* 1976, *26,* 322–323.

Carne, C. A., Weller, I. V., Sutherland, S., et al. Rising prevalence of human T-lymphotropic virus Type III (HTLV-III) infection in homosexual men in London. *Lancet,* 1985, *1,* 1261–1262.

Carney, R. M., Freedland, K. E., Rich, M. W., and Jaffe, A. S. Depression as a risk factor for cardiac events in established coronary heart disease: A review of possible mechanisms. *Annals of Behavioral Medicine,* 1995, *17,* 142–149.

Carney, R. M., Rich, M. W., TeVelde, A., et al. Major depressive disorder in coronary artery disease. *American Journal of Cardiology,* 1987, *60,* 1273–1275.

Carver, C. S., Pozo, C., Harris, S. D., et al. How coping mediates the effects of optimism on distress: A study of women with early stage breast cancer. *Journal of Personality and Social Psychology,* 1993, *65*(2), 375–390.

Carver, C. S., Pozo-Kaderman, C., Harris, S. D., et al. Optimism versus pessimism predicts the quality of women's adjustment to early stage breast cancer. *Cancer,* 1994, *73*(4), 1213–1220.

Carver, C. S., Scheier, M. F., and Pozo, C. Conceptualizing the process of coping with health problems. In H. S. Friedman (Ed.), *Hostility, coping, and health.* Washington, DC: American Psychological Association, 1992, pp. 167–187.

Carver, C. S., Scheier, M. F., and Weintraub, J. K. Assessing coping strategies: A theoretically based approach. *Journal of Personality and Social Psychology,* 1989, *56*(2), 267–283.

Case, R. B., Moss, A. J., Case, N., et al. Living alone after myocardial infarction: Impact on prognosis. *Journal of the American Medical Association,* 1992, *267,* 515–519.

Cassem, N. H., and Hackett, T. P. Psychiatric consultation in a coronary care unit. *Annual Internal Medicine,* 1971, *75,* 9–14.

Cassileth, B. B., Lusk, E. J., Miller, D. S., et al. Psychosocial correlates of survival in advanced malignant disease. *New England Journal of Medicine,* 1985, *312,* 1551–1555.

Cattell, R. B. *The culture-free intelligence test.* Champaign, IL: Institute for Personality and Ability Testing, 1949.

Cautela, J. R. The treatment of alcoholism by covert sensitization. *Psychotherapy: Theory, research, and practice,* 1970, *1,* 83–90.

Cella, D. F., Jacobsen, P. B., Orav, E. J., et al. A brief POMS measure of distress for cancer patients. *Journal of Chronic Diseases,* 1987, *40*(10), 939–942.

Cella, D. F., Mahon, S. M., and Donovan, M. I. Cancer recurrence as a traumatic event. *Behavioral Medicine,* 1990, *16,* 15–22.

Cella, D. F., and Tross, S. Psychological adjustment to survival from Hodgkin's disease. *Journal of Consulting and Clinical Psychology,* 1986, *54,* 616–622.

Cella, D. F., Tross, S., Orav, E. J., et al. Mood states of patients after the diagnosis of cancer. *Journal of Psychosocial Oncology,* 1989, *7*(1–2), 45–54.

Cella, D. F., Tulsky, D. S., Gray, G., et al. The functional assessment of cancer therapy scale: Development and validation of the general measure. *Journal of Clinical Oncology,* 1993, *11*(3), 570–579.

Centers for Disease Control. *Acquired immunodeficiency syndrome (AIDS) weekly surveillance report.* United States, Atlanta, GA, September 1996.

Cepeda-Benito, A. Meta-analytical review of the efficacy of nicotine chewing gum in smoking treatment programs. *Journal of Consulting and Clinical Psychology,* 1993, *61,* 822–830.

Chaitchik, S., and Kreitler, S. Induced versus spontaneous attendance of breast-screening tests by women. *Journal of Cancer Education,* 1991, *6*(1), 43–53.

Chambers, W. N., and Reiser, M. F. Emotional stress in the precipitation of congestive heart failure. *Psychosomatic Medicine,* 1953, *15,* 38–60.

Charlesworth, E. A., and Nathan, R. G. *Stress management: A comprehensive guide to wellness.* Houston, TX: Biobehavioral Press, 1982.

Chaves, J. F. Hypnosis in pain management. In J. W. Rhue, S. J. Lynn, and I. Kirsch (Eds.), *Handbook of clinical hypnosis.* Washington, DC: American Psychological Association, 1993, pp. 511–553.

Chaves, J. F., and Barber, T. X. Cognitive strategies, experimenter modeling, and expectation in the attenuation of pain. *Journal of Abnormal Psychology,* 1974, *83,* 356–363.

Chen, E., and Cobb, S. Family structure in relation to health and disease. *Journal of Chronic Diseases,* 1960, *12,* 544–567.

Chesney, M. A. Behavior modification and health enhancement. In J. D. Matarazzo, S. M. Weiss, J. A. Herd, et al. (Eds.), *Behavioral health: A handbook of health enhancement and disease prevention.* New York: Wiley, 1984.

Chovaz, C. J., McLachland, R. S., Derry, P. A., and Cummings, A. L. Psychosocial function following temporal lobectomy: Influence of seizure control and learned helplessness. *Seizures,* 1994, *3*(3), 171–176.

Christensen, A. J., Smith, T. W., Turner, C. W., et al. Type of hemodialysis and preference for behavioral involvement: Interactive effects on adherence in end-stage renal disease. *Health Psychology,* 1990, *9*(2), 225–236.

Clark, D. B., and Sayette, M. A. Anxiety and the development of alcoholism: Clinical and scientific issues. *American Journal on Addictions,* 1993, *2,* 59–76.

Claser, R. Plasma cortisol levels and reactivation of latent Epstein-Barr virus in response to examination stress. *Psychoneuroendocrinology,* 1994, *19*(8), 765–772.

Cleary, P. D., Rogers, T. F., Singer, E., and Avorn, J. Health education about AIDS among seropositive blood donors. *Health Education Quarterly,* 1986, *13*(4), 317–329.

Clement, V. Emotions, lifestyle defenses and coping in breast cancer patients. *Dissertation Abstracts, International [B],* 1994, *52*(2), 585.

Clover, R. D., Abell, T., Becker, L. A., and Crawford, S. Family functioning and stress as predictors of influenza B infection. *Journal of Family Practice,* 1989, *28*(5), 535–539.

Coates, D., and Wortman, C. B. Depression maintenance and interpersonal control. In A. Baum and J. E. Singer (Eds.), *Advances in environmental psychology,* vol. 2, *Applications of personal control.* Hillsdale, NJ: Erlbaum, 1980, pp. 149–182.

Coates, R. A., Soskoline, C. L., Calzavara, L., et al. The reliability of sexual histories in AIDS-related research: Evaluation of an interview-administered questionnaire. *Canadian Journal of Public Health,* 1987, *77*(5), 343–348.

Coates, T. J. Strategies for modifying sexual behavior for primary and secondary prevention of HIV disease. *Journal of Consulting and Clinical Psychology,* 1990, *58,* 57–69.

Coates, T. J., Stall, R. D., Catania, J. A., and Kegeles, S. Behavioral factors in HIV infection. *AIDS 1988,* 1988, *2*(suppl. 1), S239–S246.

Cobb, S. Social support as a moderator of life stress. *Psychosomatic Medicine,* 1976, *38,* 300–314.

Cobb, S., and Rose, R. M. Hypertension, peptic ulcer, and diabetes in air traffic controllers. *Journal of the American Medical Association,* 1973, *224,* 489–492.

Cohen, A. J., Li, F. P., Berg, S., et al. Heredity renal-cell carcinoma associated with a chromosomal translocation. *New England Journal of Medicine,* 1979, *301,* 592–595.

Cohen, E. A. *Human behavior in the concentration camp.* New York: Norton, 1953.

Cohen, F., and Lazarus, R. S. Active coping processes, coping dispositions, and recovery from surgery. *Psychosomatic Medicine,* 1973, *35,* 375–389.

Cohen, F., and Lazarus, R. S. Coping with the stresses of illness. In G. C. Stone, F. Cohen, and N. E. Ader (Eds.), *Health psychology—A handbook.* San Francisco: Jossey-Bass, 1979.

Cohen, L., Delahanty, D., Schmitz, J. B., et al. The effects of mild stress on natural killer cell activity in healthy men. *Journal of Applied Biobehavioral Research,* 1993, *1*(2), 120–132.

Cohen, R. E., and Tennen, H. Self-punishment in learned helplessness and depression. *Journal of Social and Clinical Psychology,* 1985, *3*, 82–96.

Cohen, S. Environmental load and allocation of attention. In A. Baum, J. E. Singer, and S. Valins (Eds.), *Advances in environmental psychology,* vol. 1. Hillsdale, NJ: Erlbaum, 1978.

———. Aftereffects of stress on human performance and social behavior. A review of research and theory. *Psychological Bulletin,* 1980, *88*, 82–108.

Cohen, S., Doyle, W. J., Skoner, D. P., et al. State and trait negative affect as predictors of objective and subjective symptoms of respiratory viral infections. *Journal of Personality and Social Psychology,* 1995, *68*, 159–169.

Cohen, S., Evans, G. W., Stokols, D., and Krantz, D. S. *Behavior, health, and environmental stress.* New York: Plenum, 1986.

Cohen, S., and Herbert, T. B. Health psychology: Psychological factors and physical disease from the perspective of human psychoneuroimmunology. In J. T. Spence, J. M. Darley, and D. J. Foss (Eds.), *Annual review of psychology,* vol. 47. El Camino, CA: Annual Review, in press.

Cohen, S., and Hoberman, H. M. Positive events and social supports as buffers of life change stress. *Journal of Applied Social Psychology,* 1983, *13*, 99–125.

Cohen, S., Kamarck, T., and Mermelstein, R. A global measure of perceived stress. *Journal of Health and Social Behavior,* 1983, *24*, 385–396.

Cohen, S., Kaplan, J. R., and Manuck, S. B. Social support and coronary heart disease: Underlying psychological and biologic mechanisms. In S. Shumaker and S. Czajkowski (Eds.), *Social support and cardiovascular disease.* New York: Plenum, 1994, pp. 195–221.

Cohen, S., and McKay, G. Social support, stress, and the buffering hypothesis: A theoretical analysis. In A. Baum, J. E. Singer, and S. E. Taylor (Eds.), *Handbook of psychology and health,* vol. 4. Hillsdale, NJ: Erlbaum, 1984.

Cohen, S., and Rodriguez, M. S. Pathways linking affective disturbances and physical disorders. *Health Psychology,* 1995, *14*, 374–380.

Cohen, S., Rothbart, M., and Phillips, S. Locus of control and the generality of learned helplessness in humans. *Journal of Personality and Social Psychology,* 1976, *34*, 1049–1056.

Cohen, S., and Syme, S. L. *Social support and health.* Orlando, FL: Academic Press, 1985.

Cohen, S., Tyrrell, D. A. J., and Smith, A. P. Psychological stress and susceptibility to the common cold. *New England Journal of Medicine,* 1991, *325*, 606–612.

Cohen, S., and Williamson, G. M. Stress and infectious disease in humans. *Psychological Bulletin,* 1991, *190*, 5–24.

Cohen, S., and Wills, T. A. Stress, social support, and the buffering hypothesis: A critical review. *Psychological Buletin,* 1985, *98*, 310–357.

Cohn, J. K. Psychological ramifications of silent myocardial ischemia. *Cardiology Clinics,* 1986, *4*(4), 747–750.

Colerick, E. J. Stamina in later life. *Social Science and Medicine,* 1985, *21*(9), 997–1006.

Colligan, R. C., Offord, K. P., Malinchoc, M., et al. Caveing the MMPI for optimism-pessimism scale: Seligman's attributional model and the assessment of explanatory style. *Journal of Clinical Psychology,* 1994, *50*(1), 71–95.

Collins, A., and Frankenhaeuser, M. Stress responses in male and female engineering students. *Journal of Human Stress,* 1978, *4*, 43–48.

Collins, D. L., Baum, A., and Singer, J. E. Coping with chronic stress at Three Mile Island: Psychological and biochemical evidence. *Health Psychology,* 1983, *2*, 149–166.

Compas, B. E., Worsham, N. L., Epping-Jordan, J. E., and Grant, K. E. When mom or dad has cancer: Markers of psychological distress in cancer patients, spouses, and children. *Health Psychology,* 1994, *14*(6), 507–515.

Conant, M., Hardy, D., Sernatinger, J., et al. Condoms prevent transmission of AIDS-associated retrovirus [letter]. *Journal of the American Medical Association,* 1986, *255*(13), 1706.

Conge, G. A., and Gouche, P. Effet de l'alcool sur la reponse d'immunité á mediation cellulaire de la souris. *Food and chemical toxicology,* 1985, *23*(12), 1099.

Conger, J. J. Reinforcement theory and the dynamics of alcoholism. *Quarterly Journal of Studies on Alcoholism,* 1956, *17,* 296–305.

Contrada, R. J. Type A behavior, personality hardiness, and cardiovascular responses to stress. *Journal of Personality and Social Psychology,* 1989, *57,* 895–903.

Contrada, R. J., Leventhal, E. A., and Anderson, J. A. Psychological preparation for surgery: Marshalling individual and social resources to optimize self-regulation. In S. Maes, H. Leventhal, and M. Johnston (Eds.), *International review of health psychology,* vol. 3. Chichester: Wiley, 1994.

Conyer, R. C. T., Amor, J. S., Medina-Mora, E. M., et al. Prevalence of post-traumatic stress syndrome in survivors of a natural disaster. *Salud Publico de Mexico,* 1987, *29*(5), 406–411.

Cook, N. R., Evans, D. A., Funkenstein, H. H., et al. Correlates of headache in a population-based cohort of elderly. *Archives of Neurology,* 1989, *46,* 1338–1344.

Cook, W. W., and Medley, D. M. Proposed hostility and pharisaic virtue scales for the MMPI. *Journal of Applied Psychology,* 1954, *38,* 414–418.

Cooper, C. L., et al. Incidence and perception of psychosocial stress: The relationship with breast cancer. *Psychological Medicine,* 1989, *19,* 415–422.

Cooper, C. L., and Faragher, E. B. Psychosocial stress and breast cancer: The interrelationship between stress events, coping strategies and personality. *Psychological Medicine,* 1993, *23*(3), 653–662.

Copeland, C. S., Woods, D. J., and Hursey, K. G. Social interaction effects on restrained eating. *International Journal of Eating Disorders,* 1995, *17,* 97–100.

Copeland, P. M., Sachs, N. R., and Herzog, D. B. Longitudinal follow-up of amenorrhea in eating disorders. *Psychosomatic Medicine,* 1995, *57*(2), 121–136.

Corah, N. L., and Boffa, J. Perceived control, self-observation, and response to aversive stimulation. *Journal of Personality and Social Psychology,* 1970, *16,* 1–4.

Cottingham, E. M., Matthews, K. A., Talbott, E., and Kuller, L. H. Environmental events preceding sudden death in women. *Psychosomatic Medicine,* 1980, *42*(6), 567–574.

Coussons-Read, M. E., Dykstra, M. E., Lysle, L. A., and Pavlovian, D. T. Pavlovian conditioning of morphine-induced alterations of immune status: Evidence for opioid receptor involvement. *Journal of Neuroimmunology,* 1994, *55*(2), 135–142.

Cox, D. J., and Gonder-Frederick, L. Major developments in behavioral diabetes research. *Journal of Consulting and Clinical Psychology,* 1992, *60,* 628–638.

Cox, J. P., Evans, J. F., and Jamieson, J. L. Aerobic power and toxic heart rate responses to psychosocial stressors. *Personality and Social Psychology Bulletin,* 1979, *5,* 160–163.

Cox, W. M., and Klinger, E. A motivational model of alcohol use. Special issue: Models of addiction. *Journal of Abnormal Psychology,* 1988, *97,* 168–180.

Coyne, J. C., and Lazarus, R. S. Cognitive style, stress perspective, and coping. In J. L. Kutash and L. B. Schlesinger (Eds.), *Handbook on stress and anxiety.* San Francisco: Jossey-Bass, 1980.

Cramer, L. A., Mattson, R. H., Prevey, M. L., et al. How often is medication taken as prescribed? *Journal of the American Medical Association,* 1989, *261,* 3272–3277.

Crary, B., Hauser, S. L., Borysenko, M., et al. Epinephrine-induced changes in the distribution of lymphocyte subsets in peripheral blood of humans. *Journal of Immunology,* 1983, *131*(1), 1178–1181.

Creer, T. L., and Bender, B. G. Asthma. In R. J. Gatchel and E. B. Blanchard (Eds.), *Psychophysiological disorders: Research and clinical applications.* Washington, DC: American Psychological Association, 1993.

Creer, T. L., and Bender, B. G. Recent trends in asthma research. In A. J. Goreczyn (Ed.), *Handbook of health and rehabilitation psychology.* New York: Plenum, 1994.

Cromwell, R. L., Butterfield, E. C., Brayfield, F. M., and Curry, J. J. *Acute myocardial infarction: Reaction and recovery.* St. Louis: C. V. Mosby, 1977.

Croog, S. H. Problems of barriers in the rehabilitation of heart patients: Social and psychological aspects. *Cardiac Rehabilitation,* 1975, *6,* 27.

———. Recovery and rehabilitation of coronary patients: Psychological aspects. In D. S. Krantz, A. Baum, and J. E. Singer (Eds.), *Handbook of psychology and health,* vol. 3, *Cardiovascular disorders and behavior.* Hillsdale, NJ: Erlbaum, 1983.

Crowne, D. P., and Marlowe, D. A. A new scale of social desirability independent of psychopathology. *Journal of Consulting Psychology,* 1960, *24,* 349–354.

Cruse, J. M., Lewis, R. E., Jr., Bishop, G. R., et al. Decreased immune reactivity and neuroendocrine alterations related to chronic stress in spinal cord injury and stroke patients. *Pathobiology,* 1993, *61*(304), 192–193.

Cumming, C., Handman, M., Lees, A., et al. Psychological profiles of breast cancer patients on adjuvant hormone therapy (meeting abstract). *International Association for Breast Cancer Research,* Biennial Meeting, April 25–28, 1993, Calgary, Alberta, Canada, A90.

Cummings, N. A., Pallak, M. S., Dorken, H., and Henke, C. J. *The impact of psychological services on medical utilization and costs* (HCFA Contract No. 11-C-98344/9). Baltimore: Health Care Financing Administration, 1992.

Cunliffe, W. J., Hull, S. M., and Hughes, B. R. *The benefit of isotretinoin for the severely depressed/dysmorphophobic patient.* Abstract presented at the Second International Congress on Psychiatry and Dermatology, University of Leeds, Leeds, UK, 1989.

Curran, J. W. The epidemiology and prevention of acquired immunodeficiency syndrome. *Annals of Internal Medicine,* 1985, *103,* 657–662.

Curran, J. W., Morgan, W. M., Hardy, A. M., et al. The epidemiology of AIDS: Current status and future prospects. *Science,* 1985, *229,* 1352–1357.

Curry, S. J., and Emmons, K. M. Theoretical models for predicting and improving compliance with breast cancer screening. Mini-Series: Advances in behavioral medicine research on breast cancer. *Annals of Behavioral Medicine,* 1994, *16*(4), 302–316.

Dahl, L. K., Heine, M., and Tassinari, L. Role of genetic factors in susceptibility to experimental hypertension due to chronic excess salt ingestion. *Nature,* 1962, *194,* 480–482.

Dahlstrom, W. G., and Welsh, G. S. *An MMPI handbook.* Minneapolis: University of Minnesota Press, 1960.

Dahlstrom, W. G., Welsh, G. S., and Dahlstrom, L. E. *MMPI handbook,* vol. 1, *Clinical interpretations.* Minneapolis: University of Minnesota Press, 1972.

Dalen, K., Ellersten, B., Espelid, I., and Gronningsaeter, A. G. EMG feedback in the treatment of myofascial pain dysfunction syndrome. *Acta Odontologica Scandinavica,* 1986, *44,* 279–284.

Dalessio, D. J. *Wolff's headache and other head pain.* New York: Oxford University Press, 1972.

Dalkvist, J., Wahlin, T-B. R., Bartsch, E., and Forsbeck, M. Herpes simplex and mood: A prospective study. *Psychosomatic Medicine,* 1995, *57*(2), 127–137.

Daltroy, L. H., and Liang, M. H. Advances in patient education in rheumatic disease. (Review). *Annals of the Rheumatic Diseases,* 1991, *50*(suppl. 3), 415–417.

Davidov, M. E., et al. Bioprolol, a once-a-day beta-blocking agent for patients with mild to moderate hypertension. *Clinical Cardiology,* 1994, *17,* 266.

Davidson, L. M., and Baum, A. Chronic stress and posttraumatic stress disorders. *Journal of Consulting and Clinical Psychology,* 1986, *54*(3), 303–308.

Davidson, L. M., Baum, A., and Collins, D. L. Stress and control-related problems at Three Mile Island. *Journal of Applied Social Psychology,* 1982, *12,* 349–359.

Davis, A. *Social class influences upon learning.* Cambridge, MA: Harvard University Press, 1948.

Davis, M., Eshelman, E. R., and McKay, M. *The relaxation and stress reduction workbook.* Oakland, CA: New Harbinger Publications, 1988.

Davis, M. S. Physiologic, psychological and demographic factors in patient compliance with doctors' orders. *Medical Care,* 1968, *6,* 115–122.

Davis, W. K., Hess, G. E., Van Harrison, R., and Hiss, R. G. Psychosocial adjustment to and control of diabetes mellitus: Differences by disease type and treatment. *Health Psychology,* 1987, *6*(1), 1–14.

Dawes, E. S. Cancer. In P. L. Jackson and J. A. Vessey (Eds.), *Primary care of the child with a chronic condition.* St. Louis: Mosby, 1992, pp. 117–147.

Dawson, D. A., Harford, T. C., and Grant, B. F. Family history as a predictor of alcohol dependence. *Alcoholism: Clinical and Experimental Research,* 1992, *16,* 572–575.

Delahanty, D., Dougall, A. L., Hawken, L., et al. Time course of natural killer cell activity and lymphocyte proliferation in response to two acute stressors in healthy men. *Health Psychology,* 1996, *15*(1), 48–55.

Dembroski, T. M., MacDougall, J. M., Herd, J. A., and Shields, J. L. Perspectives on coronary-prone behavior. In D. S. Krantz, A. Baum, and J. E. Singer (Eds.), *Handbook of psychology and health,* vol. 3, *Cardiovascular disorders and behavior.* Hillsdale, NJ: Erlbaum, 1983.

Dembroski, T. M., MacDougall, J. M, Shields, J. L., et al. Components of the Type A coronary-prone behavior pattern and cardiovascular responses to psychomotor performance challenge. *Journal of Behavioral Medicine,* 1978, *1*(2), 159–176.

Dembroski, T. M., MacDougall, J. M., Williams, R. B., and Gandits, G. A. Components of hostility as predictors of sudden death and myocardial infarction in the multiple risk factors intervention trial. *Psychosomatic Medicine,* 1989, *51,* 514–522.

Derogatis, L. R. *The SCL-90R administration, scoring and procedures Manual I.* Baltimore: Clinical Psychometric Research Unit, Johns Hopkins University, 1977.

Derogatis, L. R., Abeloff, M. D., and Melisaratos, N. Psychological coping mechanisms and survival time in metastatic breast cancer. *Journal of the American Medical Association,* 1979, *242,* 1504–1508.

Derogatis, L. R., Lipman, R. S., and Covi, L. The SCL-90: An outpatient psychiatric rating scale. *Psychopharmacology Bulletin,* 1979, *9,* 13–28.

Derogatis, L. R., Rickels, K., and Rock, A. F. The SCL-90 and the MMPI: A step in the validation of a new self-report scale. *British Journal of Psychiatry,* 1976, *128,* 280–289.

Des Jarlais, D. C., Friedman, S. R., and Strug, D. AIDS and needle sharing within the IV drug use subculture. In D. Feldman and T. Johnson (Eds.), *The social dimensions of AIDS: Methods and theory.* New York: Praeger, 1987.

Deutsch, C. P. Auditory discrimination and learning: Social factors. *Merrill-Plamer Quarterly of Behavior and Development,* 1964, *10,* 277–296.

Devine, E. C., and Cook, T. D. A meta-analysis of effects of psychoeducational interventions on length of postsurgical hospital stay. *Nursing Research,* 1983, *32*(5), 267–274.

Devine, E. C., and Reifschneider, E. A meta-analysis of effects of psychoeducational care in adults with hypertension. *Nursing Research,* 1995, *44*(4), 237–245.

Dew, M. A., Regalski, J. M., Switzer, G. E., and Allen, A. S. Quality of life in organ transplantation: Effects on adult recipients and their families. In P. T. Trzepacz and A. Di

Martini (Eds.), *Transplantation psychiatry: Issues for the 90's.* New York: Cambridge University Press.

Dew, M. A., Simmons, R. G., Roth, L. H., et al. Psychosocial predictors of vulnerability to distress in the year following heart transplantation. *Psychological Medicine,* 1994, *24,* 929–945.

Deyo, R. A. Fads in the treatment of low back pain. *New England Journal of Medicine,* 1991, *325,* 1039–1040.

Dhingra, K., Hittelman, W. N., and Hortobagyi, G. N. Genetic changes in breast cancer—Consequences for therapy? *Gene,* 1995, *159,* 59–63.

Dickinson, J. C., Warshaw, G. A., Gehlbach, S. H., et al. Improving hypertension control: Impact of computer feedback and physical education. *Medical Care,* 1981, *19*(8), 843–854.

DiClemente, R. J., Lanier, M. M., Horan, P. F., and Lodico, M. Comparison of AIDS knowledge, attitudes, and behaviors among incarcerated adolescents and a public school sample in San Francisco. *American Journal of Public Health,* 1991, *81,* 628–630.

DiClemente, R. J., Zorn, R. J., and Temoshok, L. The association of gender, ethnicity, and length of residence in the Bay area to adolescents' knowledge and attitudes about acquired immune deficiency syndrome. Special issue: Acquired immune deficiency syndrome (AIDS). *Journal of Applied Social Psychology,* 1987, *17*(3), 216–230.

Diener, C. I., and Dweck, C. S. An analysis of learned helplessness: Continuous changes in performance, strategy, and achievement cognition following failure. *Journal of Personality and Social Psychology,* 1978, *36,* 451–461.

Diez-Ruiz, A., Tilz, G. P., Gutierrez-Gae, F., et al. Neopterin and soluble tumor necrosis factor receptor Type I in alcohol-induced cirrhosis. *Hepatology,* 1995, *21*(4), 976–978.

Dillard, C. O. *The family viewpoint.* Paper presented at the Cardiac Seminar Program, *Heart Disease, Stress and Industry,* the President's Committee on Employment of the Handicapped, New York, 1982.

DiMatteo, M. R. Enhancing medication adherence through communication and informed collaborative choice. Special issue: Communicating with patients about their medications. *Health Communication,* 1994, *6*(4), 253–265.

DiMatteo, M. R., Hays, R. D., and Prince, L. M. Relationship of physicians' nonverbal communication skill to patient satisfaction, appointment noncompliance, and physician workload. *Health Psychology,* 1986, *5,* 581–594.

DiMatteo, M. R., Sherbourne, C. D., Hays, R. D., et al. Physicians' characteristics influence patients' adherence to medical treatment: Results from the Medical Outcomes Study. *Health Psychology,* 1993, *12*(2), 93–102.

Dimsdale, J. E., Alpert, B. S., and Schneiderman, N. Exercise as a modulator of cardiovascular reactivity. In K. A. Matthews, S. M. Weiss, T. Detre, et al. (Eds.), *Handbook of stress, reactivity, and cardiovascular disease.* New York: Wiley, 1986.

Dirksen, S. R. Search for meaning in long-term cancer survivors. *Journal of Advance Nursing,* 1995, *21*(4), 628–633.

Dishman, R. K. Compliance/adherence in health related exercise. *Health Psychology,* 1982, *1,* 45–59.

Dobson, J. D., and Block, L. Historical philosophical bases of the cognitive-behavior therapies. In K. S. Dobson (Ed.), *Handbook of cognitive-behavior therapies.* New York: Guilford Press, 1988, pp. 3–38.

Dobson, K. S. (Ed.). *Handbook of cognitive-behavioral therapies.* New York: Guilford Press, 1988.

Doehrman, S. R. Psycho-social aspects of recovery from coronary heart disease: A review. *Social Science Medicine,* 1977, *11,* 199–218.

Doherty, W. J., Schrott, H. G., Metcalf, L., and Iasiello-Vailas, L. Effect of spouse support and health beliefs on medication adherence. *Journal of Family Practice,* 1983, *17*(5), 837–841.

Dohrenwend, B. S., and Dohrenwend, B. P. *Stressful life events: Their nature and effects.* New York: Wiley, 1974.

Donaldson, S. I., and Blanchard, A. L. The seven health practices, well-being, and performance at work: Evidence for the value of reaching small and underserved worksites. *Preventive Medicine,* 1995, *24*(3), 270–277.

Donovan, W. L., and Leavitt, L. A. Simulating conditions of learned helplessness: The effects of interventions and attributions. *Child Development,* 1985, *56,* 594–603.

Dougall, A. J. L., Hyman, K. B., Hayward, M. C., et al. Optimism as a mediator of traumatic stress. *Psychosomatic Medicine,* 1996, *58,* 59–97.

Douglas, D., and Anisman, H. Helplessness or expectation incongruence: Effects of aversive consequence on subsequent performance. *Journal of Experimental Psychology: Human Perception and Performance,* 1975, *1,* 411–417.

Drash, A. L. *Clinical care of the diabetic child.* Chicago: Yearbook Publishers, 1987.

Drash, P. W., and Tudor, R. M. Cognitive development therapy: A model for treatment of an overlooked population developmentally delayed preschool children. *Psychotherapy in Private Practice,* 1989, *7*(2), 19–41.

Dressler, W. W. Social support, lifestyle incongruity, and arterial blood pressure in a southern black community. *Psychosomatic Medicine,* 1991, *53,* 608–620.

Dressler, W. W., Grell, G. A., Gallagher, P. N., and Viteri, F. E. Social factors mediating social class differences in blood pressure in a Jamaican community. *Social Science and Medicine,* 1992, *35,* 1233–1244.

Dressler, W. W., Mata, A., Chavez, A., et al. Social support and arterial blood pressure in a central Mexican community. *Psychosomatic Medicine,* 1986, *48,* 338–350.

Drossman, D. A., Sandler, R. S., McKee, D. C., and Lovitz, A. J. Bowel patterns among subjects not seeking health care: Use of a questionnaire to identify a population with bowel dysfunction. *Gastroenterology,* 1982, *83,* 529–534.

Dubbert, P. M. Implementing behavioral treatment for hypertension: Considerations for health psychologists. *Behavior Therapist,* 1992, *15,* 182–185.

Dudgeon, D. The short-form McGill pain questionnaire in chronic cancer pain. *Journal of Pain and Symptom Management,* 1993, *8*(4), 191–195.

Dukro, P. N., Margolis, R. B., and Tait, R. C. Psychological assessment in chronic pain. *Journal of Clinical Psychology,* 1985, *41,* 499–504.

Dunbar, F. *Psychosomatic diagnosis.* New York: Harper & Row, 1943.

Dunbar, H. *Emotions and bodily changes: A survey of literature on psychosomatic relationships: 1910–1933.* New York: Columbia University Press, 1935.

Dunbar, J. Predictors of patient adherence: Patient characteristics. In J. K. Ockene, S. Schumaker, and E. Schron (Eds.), *Handbook of Health Behavior Change.* New York: Springer, 1990.

Dunbar-Jacob, J. Contributions to patient adherence: Is it time to share the blame? *Health Psychology,* 1993, *12*(2), 91–92.

Dutton, D. G., and Aron, A. P. Some evidence for heightened sexual attraction under conditions of high anxiety. *Journal of Personality and Social Psychology,* 1974, *30,* 510–517.

Dweck, C. S. The role of expectations and attributions in the alleviation of learned helplessness. *Journal of Personality and Social Psychology,* 1975, *31,* 674–685.

Dweck, C. S., and Bush, E. S. Sex differences in learned helplessness: 1. Differential debilitation with peer and adult evaluators. *Developmental Psychology,* 1976, *12,* 147–156.

Dweck, C. S., and Gilliard, D. Expectancy statements as determinants of reactions to failure: Sex differences in persistence and expectancy change. *Journal of Personality and Social Psychology,* 1975, *25,* 1077–1084.

Dweck, C. S., and Reppucci, N. D. Learned helplessness and reinforcement responsibility in children. *Journal of Personality and Social Psychology*, 1973, *32*, 109–116.

Dworkin, S. F., Huggins, K. H., LeResche, L., et al. Epidemiology of signs and symptoms in temporomandibular disorders: I. Clinical signs in cases and controls. *Journal of the American Dental Association*, 1990, *120*, 273–281.

Dworkin, S. F., and LeResche, L. (Eds.). Research diagnostic criteria for temporomandibular disorders: Review, criteria, examinations and specifications, critique. *Journal of Craniomandibular Disorders: Facial and Oral Pain*, 1992, *6*, 301–355.

Eales, L. J., Nye, K. E., Parkin, J. M., et al. Association of different allelic forms of group-specific component with susceptibility to and clinical manifestation of human immunodeficiency virus infection. *Lancet*, 1987, *1*, 999–1002.

Edwards, A. L. *Edwards personal preference schedule.* New York: Psychological Corporation, 1959.

Egbert, L. D., Battit, G. E., Welch, C. E., and Bartlett, M. K. Reduction of postoperative pain by encouragement and instruction of patients. *New England Journal of Medicine*, 1964, *270*, 825–827.

Einhorn, H. J., and Hogarth, R. M. Confidence in Judgment: Persistence of the illusion of validity. *Psychological Review*, 1978, *85*, 395–416.

Eliot, R. S., and Buell, J. C. Environmental and behavioral influences in the major cardiovascular disorders. In S. M. Weiss, J. Herd, and B. H. Fox (Eds.), *Perspectives on behavioral medicine.* New York: Academic Press, 1981, pp. 25–39.

Ell, K., Nishimoto, R., Mediansky, L., and Mantell, J. Social relations, social support and survival among patients with cancer. *Journal of Psychosomatic Research*, 1992, *36*(6), 531–541.

Ellis, A. *Reason and emotion in psychotherapy.* New York: Lyle Stuart, 1962.

Emrick, C. D. A review of psychologically oriented treatment of alcoholism. *Journal of Studies on Alcoholism*, 1975, *36*, 88–108.

Engle, G. L. A psychological setting of somatic disease: The giving up-given up complex. *Proceedings of the Royal Society of Medicine*, 1967, *60*, 553–563.

———. A life setting conducive of illness: The giving up-given up complex. *Bulletin of the Menninger Clinic*, 1968, *32*, 355–365.

Enthoven, A., and Kronick, R. A consumer-choice health plan for the 1990s. Universal health insurance: A system designed to promote quality and economy. *New England Journal of Medicine*, 1989, *320*(2), 94–101.

Epstein, L. H. Role of behavior theory in behavioral medicine. *Journal of Consulting and Clinical Psychology*, 1992, *60*, 493–498.

Epstein, L. H., McCurley, J., Wing, R. R., and Valoski, A. Five-year follow-up of family-based behavioral treatments for childhood obesity. *Journal of Consulting and Clinical Psychology*, 1990, *58*, 661–664.

Epstein, L. H., Valoski, A., and McCurley, J. Effect of weight loss by obese children on long-term growth. *American Journal of Diseases of Children*, 1993, *147*(10), 1076–1080.

Eraker, S. A., Kirscht, J. P., and Becker, M. H. Understanding and improving patient compliance. *Annals of Internal Medicine*, 1984, *100*, 258–268.

Erichsen, J. E. *On concussion of the spine: Nervous shock and other injuries of the nervous system in their clinical and medicolegal aspects.* London: Longmans, Green, 1982.

Erlenmeyer-Kimling, J., and Jarvik, L. F. Genetics and intelligence: A review. *Science*, 1963, *14a*, 1477–1479.

Essence, H. J. Personality and the maintenance of the smoking habit. In W. L. Dun (Ed.), *Smoking behavior: Motives and incentives.* New York: Wiley, 1973.

Esterling, B. A. Relaxation and exercise intervention as a means of modulating antibody to Epstein-Barr and human herpes virus Type-6 in an asymptomatic HIV-1 seropositive and seronegative cohort. *Dissertation Abstract International,* 1992, 52(11-B), 6113.

Esterling, B. A., Antoni, M. H., Schneiderman, N., et al. Psychosomatic modulation of antibodies to Epstein-Barr viral capsid antigen and human herpes virus type VI in HIV infected and at risk gay men. *Psychosomatic Medicine,* 1992, 54, 354–371.

Esterling, B. A., Kiecolt-Glaser, J. K., Bodnar, J., and Glaser, R. Chronic stress, social support, and persistent alterations in the natural killer cell response to cytokines in older adults. *Health Psychology,* 1994, 13(4), 291–299.

Esterling, B. A., Kiecolt-Glaser, J. K., and Glaser, R. Psychosocial modulation of cytokin-induced natural killer cell activity in older adults. *Psychosomatic Medicine,* in press.

Evans, G. W. Human spatial behavior: The arousal model. In A. Baum and Y. M. Epstein (Eds.), *Human response to crowding.* Hillsdale, NJ: Erlbaum, 1978.

Evans, G. W., Hygge, S., and Bullinger, M. Chronic noise and psychological stress. *Psychological Science,* in press.

Evans, G. W., and Jacobs, S. V. Air pollution and human behavior. *Journal of Social Issues,* 1981, 37, 95–125.

Evans, R. I. Smoking in children and adolescents: Psychosocial determinants and prevention strategies. In *Smoking and health: A report of the Surgeon General* (DHEW publication No. [PHS] 79-50066). Washington, DC: U.S. Government Printing Office, 1979.

———. University of Houston, Principal Investigator. Supported by the National Heart, Lung and Blood Institute, NIH Grant 17269, 1981.

———. Social influences in etiology and prevention of smoking and other health threatening behaviors in children and adolescents. In A. Baum, T. A. Revenson, and J. E. Singer (Eds.), *Handbook of health psychology.* Hillsdale, NJ: Erlbaum, in press.

Evans, R. I., Rozelle, R. M., Maxwell, S. E., et al. Social modeling films to deter smoking in adolescents: Results of a three year filed investigation. *Journal of Applied Psychology,* 1981, 66, 399–414.

Evans, R. I., Smith, C. K., and Raines, B. E. Deterring cigarette smoking in adolescents: A psychosocial-behavioral analysis of an intervention strategy. In A. Baum, S. E. Taylor, and J. E. Singer (Eds.), *Handbook of psychology and health,* vol. 4, *Social psychological aspects of health.* Hillsdale, NJ: Erlbaum, 1984, pp. 301–318.

Exner, J. A. *The Rorschach: A comprehensive system: Vol. 1, Basic foundations,* 2nd ed. New York: Wiley, 1986.

Eysenck, H. J. Personality and the maintenance of the smoking habit. In W. L. Dunn (Ed.), *Smoking behavior: Motives and incentives.* New York: Wiley, 1973.

———. Cancer, personality and stress: Prediction and prevention. *Advances in Behaviour Research and Therapy,* 1994, 16(3), 167–215.

Ezzell, C. Fat times for obesity research: Tons of new information, but how does it all fit together. *Journal of NIH Research,* 1995, 7, 39–43.

Fahrian, S., Norris, P., Green, A., et al. Biobehavioral treatment of essential hypertension: A group outcome study. *Biofeedback and Self-Regulation,* 1986, 11, 257–264.

Fairbank, J. A., Hansen, D. J., and Fitterling, J. M. Patterns of appraisal and coping across different stressor conditions among former prisoners of war with and without posttraumatic stress disorder. *Journal of Consulting Clinical Psychology,* 1991, 59(2), 274–281.

Fairley, M. *Tropical cyclone Oscar: Psychological reactions of a Fijian population.* Paper presented at the Disaster Research workshop, Mt. Macedon, Victoria, Australia, 1984.

Farquhar, J. W., Wood, P. D., Breitrose, H., et al. Community education for cardiovascular health. *Lancet,* 1977, 1, 1192–1195.

Faulstich, M. E., Williamson, D. A., Duchman, E. G., et al. Psychophysiological analysis of atopic dermatitis. *Journal of Psychosomatic Research,* 1985, *29,* 415–417.

Faust, I. M. Nutrition and the fat cell. *International Journal of Obesity,* 1980, *4,* 314–321.

Faust, J. Same-day surgery preparation: Reduction of pediatric patient arousal and distress through participant modeling. *Journal of Consulting and Clinical Psychology,* 1991, *59*(3), 475–478.

Fawzy, F. I. A structured psychoeducational intervention for cancer patients. Special section: A structured psychoeducational intervention for cancer patients. *General Hospital Psychiatry,* 1994, *16*(3), 149–192.

————. The benefits of a short-term group intervention for cancer patient. *Advances,* 1994, *10*(2), 17–19.

Fawzy, F. I., and Fawzy, N. W. A structured psychoeducational intervention for cancer patients. *General Hospital Psychiatry,* 1994, *16*(3), 149–192.

Fawzy, F. I., Fawzy, N. W., Hyun, C. S., et al. Malignant melanoma: Effects of an early structured psychiatric intervention, coping, and affective state on recurrence and survival 6 years later. *Archives of General Psychiatry,* 1993, *50*(9), 681–689.

Fawzy, F. I., Kemeny, M. E., Fawzy, N. W., et al. A structured psychiatric intervention for cancer patients, II. Changes over time in immunological measures. *Archives of General Psychiatry,* 1990, *47,* 729–735.

Felton, G., Huss, K., Payne, E. A., and Srsic, K. Preoperative nursing intervention with the patient for surgery: Outcomes of three alternative approaches. *International Journal of Nursing Studies,* 1976, *13,* 83–96.

Fernandez, E., and Turk, D. C. Sensory and affective components of pain: Separation and synthesis. *Psychological Bulletin,* 1992, *112,* 205–217.

Festinger, L. A theory of social comparison processes. *Human Relations,* 1954, *7,* 117–140.

Fife, B. L. The conceptualization of meaning in illness. *Social Science and Medicine,* 1994, *38*(2), 309–316.

Fillingham, R. B., and Fine, M. A. The effects of internal versus external information processing on symptom perception in an exercise setting. *Health Psychology,* 1986, *5*(2), 115–123.

Fink, R., Shapiro, S., and Roester, R. Impact of efforts to increase participation in repetitive screening for early breast cancer detection. *American Journal of Public Health,* 1972, *62,* 328–336.

Finkelman, J. M., and Glass, D. C. Reappraisal of the relationship between noise and human performance by means of a subsidiary task measure. *Journal of Applied Psychology,* 1970, *54,* 211–213.

Finklea, J. F., Sandifer, S. H., and Smith, D. D. Cigarette smoking and epidemic influenza. *American Journal of Epidemiology,* 1969, *90*(1), 390–399.

Finney, J. W. Evaluation of two health education strategies for testicular self-examination. *Journal of Applied Behavior Analysis,* 1995, *28*(1), 39–46.

Finney, J. W., Hook, R. J., Friman, P. C., and Rapoff, M. A. The overestimation of adherence to pediatric medical regimens. *Children's Health Care,* 1993, *22*(4), 297–304.

Fisher, C. L., Gill, C., Daniels, J. C., et al. Effects of the space flight environment on man's immune system. *Aerospace Medicine,* 1972, *43,* 856–859.

Fisher, J. D., and Fisher, W. A. Changing AIDS-risk behavior. *Psychological Bulletin,* 1992, *111*(3), 455–474.

Fishman, B., Jacobsberg, L., Frances, A., et al. Effectiveness of psychoeducational interventions after HIV antibody testing. *International Conference on AIDS,* 1990, *6*(3), 252.

Fisk, M. Challenge and defeat: Stability and change in adulthood. In L. Goldberger and S. Breznitz (Eds.), *Handbook of stress: Theoretical and clinical aspects,* 2nd ed. New York: Free Press, 1993, pp. 413–426.

Flanders, W. D., and Rothman, K. J. Interaction of alcohol and tobacco in laryngeal cancer. *American Journal of Epidemiology,* 1982, *115*(3), 371–379.

Flaxman, J. Quitting smoking now or later: Gradual, abrupt, immediate, and delayed quitting. *Behavior Therapy,* 1978, *9,* 260–270.

Flay, B. R. Psychosocial approaches to smoking prevention: A review of findings. *Health Psychology,* 1985, *4,* 449–488.

Fleming, I. C. *The stress reducing functions of specific types of social support for victims of a technological catastrophe.* Unpublished doctoral dissertation, University of Maryland, College Park, 1985.

Fleming, I. C., Baum, A., Davidson, L. M., et al. Chronic stress as a factor in physiologic reactivity to challenge. *Health Psychology,* 1987, *6*(3), 221–237.

Fleming, I. C., Wasson, J. H., Albertsen P. C., et al. A decision analysis of alternative treatment strategies for clinically localized prostate cancer. *Journal of the American Medical Association,* 1993, *269,* 2650–2658.

Fleming, R., Baum, A., Gisriel, M. M., and Gatchel, R. J. Mediating influences of social support on stress at Three Mile Island. *Journal of Human Stress,* 1982, *8*(3), 14–22.

Flor, H., and Birbaumer, N. Comparison of the efficacy of electromyographic biofeedback, cognitive-behavioral therapy, and conservative medical interventions in the treatment of chronic musculoskeletal pain. *Journal of Consulting and Clinical Psychology,* 1993, *61,* 653–658.

Flor, H., Fydrich, T., and Turk, D. C. Efficacy of multidisciplinary pain treatment centers: A meta-analytic review. *Pain,* 1992, *49,* 221–230.

Flor, H., Schugens, M. M., and Birbaumer, N. Discrimination of muscle tension in chronic pain patients and health controls. *Biofeedback and Self-Regulation,* 1992, *17,* 165–177.

Flor, H., and Turk, D. C. Psychophysiology of chronic pain: Do chronic pain patients exhibit symptom-specific psychophysiological responses? *Psychological Bulletin,* 1989, *105,* 215–259.

Folkins, C. H., and Sime, W. E. Physical fitness training and mental health. *American Psychologist,* 1981, *36,* 373–389.

Folkman, S., and Lazarus, R. S. An analysis of coping in a middle-aged community sample. *Journal of Health and Social Behavior,* 1980, *21,* 219–239.

Follick, M., Smith, T., and Ahern, D. The sickness impact profile: A global measure of disability in chronic low back pain. *Pain,* 1985, *21,* 67–76.

Follick, M. J., Ahern, D. K., and Aberger, E. W. Development of audiovisual taxonomy of pain behavior. *Health Psychology,* 1985, *4,* 555–568.

Fontaine, K. R. Effect of dispositional optimism on comparative risk perceptions for developing AIDS. *Psychology Reports,* 1994, *74*(3 Pt. 1), 843–846.

Ford, C. E., and Neale, J. M. Learned helplessness and judgments of control. *Journal of Personality and Social Psychology,* 1985, *49,* 1330–1336.

Fordyce, W. E. Pain and suffering: A reappraisal. *American Psychologist,* 1988, *43,* 276–283.

Fordyce, W. E., Fowler, R. S., Lehmann, J. F., and DeLateur, B. J. Some implications of learning in problems of chronic pain. *Journal of Chronic Diseases,* 1968, *21,* 179–190.

Fordyce, W. E., Roberts, A. H., and Sternbach, R. A. The behavioral management of chronic pain: A response to critics. *Pain,* 1985, *22*(2), 113–125.

Fordyce, W. E., and Steger, J. C. Chronic pain. In O. F. Pomerleau and J. P. Brady (Eds.), *Behavioral medicine: Theory and practice.* Baltimore: Williams & Wilkins, 1979.

Foreyt, J. P., Scott, L. W., Mitchell, R. W., and Gotto, A. M. Plasma lipid changes in the normal poulation following behavioral treatment. *Journal of Consulting Clinical Psychology,* 1979, *47,* 440–452.

Fosco, E., and Geer, J. H. Effects of gaining control over aversive stimuli after differing amounts of no control. *Psychological Reports,* 1979, *29,* 1153–1154.

Fox, B. H. Behavioral issues in prevention of cancer. *Preventive Medicine,* 1976, *5*(1), 106–121.

Fox, P. E., and Oakes, W. F. Learned helplessness: Noncontingent reinforcement in video game performance produces adversement on performance on a lexical decision task. *Bulletin of the Psychosomatic Society,* 1984, *22,* 113–116.

Francis, D. P., and Chin, J. The prevention of acquired immunodeficiency syndrome in the United States. An objective strategy for medicine, public health, business, and the community. *Journal of the American Medical Association,* 1987, *257*(10), 1357–1366.

Francis, V., Korsch, B. M., and Morris, M. J. Gaps in doctor-patient communication. *New England Journal of Medicine,* 1969, *280,* 535–540.

Frank, J. D. *Persuasion and healing.* New York: Schocken Books, 1961.

Frankenhaeuser, M. Behavior and circulating catecholamines. *Brain Research,* 1971, *31,* 241–262.

———. Biochemical events, stress, and adjustment. Reports from the Psychological Laboratories, University of Stockholm (368), 1972.

———. Experimental approaches to the study of catecholamines and emotion. Reports from the Psychological Laboratories, University of Stockholm (392), 1973.

———. The role of peripheral catecholamines in adaption to understimulation and overstimulation. In G. Serban (Ed.), *Psychopathology of human adaptation.* New York: Plenum, 1976.

———. Quality of life: Criteria for behavioral adjustment. *International Journal of Psychology,* 1977, *12,* 99–110.

———. Coping with job stress: A psychobiological approach. Reports from the Department of Psychology, University of Stockholm (532), 1978.

———. Psychoneuroendocrine approaches to the study of emotion as related to stress and coping. In H. E. Howe and R. Dienstbier (Eds.), *Nebraska symposium on motivation 1978.* Lincoln: University of Nebraska Press, 1979.

———. The sympathetic-adrenal and pituitary-adrenal response to challenge: Comparison between the sexes. In T. M. Dembroski, T. H. Schmidt, and G. Blumchen (Eds.), *Biobehavioral bases of coronary heart disease.* Basel: Karger, 1983.

Frankenhaeuser, M., and Gardell, B. Underload and overload in working life: Outline of a multidisciplinary approach. *Journal of Human Stress,* 1976, *2*(3), 35–46.

Frankenhaeuser, M., Jarpe, G., and Mattell, G. Effects of intravenous infusions of adrenaline and noradrenaline on certain psychological and physiological functions. *Acta Physiologica Scandinavia,* 1961, *51,* 175–186.

Frankenhaeuser, M., and Johansson, G. Stress at work: Psychobiological and psychosocial aspects. Paper presented at the 20th International Congress of Applied Psychology, Edinburgh, 1982.

Frankenhaeuser, M., Lundberg, U., Fredrikson, M., and Melin, B. Stress on and off the job as related to sex and occupational status in white-collar workers. *Journal of Organizational Behavior,* 1989, *10*(4), 321–346.

Frankenhaeuser, M., Nordheden, B., Myrsent, A. L., and Post, V. Psycho-physiological reactions to under-stimulation and over-stimulation. *Acta Psychologica Scandinavia,* 1971, *35,* 298–308.

Frankenhaeuser, M., and Rissler, A. Effects of punishment on catecholamine release and efficiency of performance. *Psychopharmacologia,* 1970, *17,* 378–390.

Franklin, G. J., Haug, J., Heyer, N. J., et al. Outcome of lumbar fusion in Washington State worker's compensation. *Spine,* 1994, *19,* 1897–1904.

Franklin, M., Krauthamer, M., Tai, A. R., and Pinchot, A. *The Heart Doctors' Heart Book.* New York: Grosset and Dunlap, 1974.

Frasure-Smith, N., Lesperance, F., and Talajic, M. Depression following myocardial infarction: Impact on 6-month survival. *Journal of the American Medical Association,* 1993, *270,* 1819–1825.

Frasure-Smith, N., and Prince, R. H. The Ischemic Heart Disease Life Stress Monitoring Program: Possible therapeutic mechanisms. *Psychology and Health,* 1987, *1*(3), 273–285.

Frasure-Smith, N., and Prince, R. H. Long-term follow-up of the ischemic health disease life stress monitoring program. *Psychosomatic Medicine,* 1989, *51*(5), 485–513.

Fredrikson, M., Furst, C. J., Lekander, M., et al. Trait anxiety and anticipatory immune reactions in women receiving adjuvant chemotherapy for breast cancer. *Brain, Behavior, and Immunity,* 1993, *7*(1), 79–90.

Freud, S. *Collected papers,* vols. I–V. New York: Basic Books, 1959.

Friedland, G. H. Early treatment for HIV: The time has come. *New England Journal of Medicine,* 1990, *322*(14), 1000–1002.

Friedland, G. H., Harris, C., Butkus-Small, C., et al. Intravenous drug abusers and the acquired immunodeficiency syndrome (AIDS). Demographic, drug use, and needle-sharing patterns. *Archives of Internal Medicine,* 1985, *145*(8), 1413–1417.

Friedman, H. S., and Booth-Kewley, S. The "disease-prone personality": A meta-analytic view of the construct. *American Psychologist,* 1987, *42*(6), 539–555.

Friedman, M., Byers, S. O., Diamanti, J., and Rosenman, R. H. Plasma catecholamine response of coronary-prone subjects (Type A) to a specific challenge. *Metabolism,* 1975, *4,* 205–210.

Friedman, M., and Rosenman, R. H. Association of specific overt behavior pattern with blood and cardiovascular findings. *Journal of the American Medical Association,* 1959, *169,* 1286–1296.

Friedman, M., and Rosenman, R. H. *Type A behavior and your heart.* New York: Knopf, 1974.

Friedman, M., Rosenman, R. H., and Carol, V. Changes in the serum cholesterol and blood clotting time in men subjected to cyclic variation of occupational stress. *Circulation,* 1958, *17,* 852–861.

Friedman, M., Thoresen, C., Gill, J., et al. Alteration of Type A behavior and its effects on cardiac recurrences in post myocardial infarction patients: Summary results of the recurrent coronary prevention project. *American Heart Journal,* 1986, *112,* 653–665.

Friedman, R., and Iwai, J. Genetic predisposition and stress-induced hypertension. *Science,* 1976, *193,* 161–192.

Friedman, R., Sobel, D., Myers, P., et al. Behavioral medicine, clinical health psychology, and cost offset. *Health Psychology,* 1995, *14,* 509–518.

Friedman, S., Hatch, M. L., and Paradis, C. M. Dermatological disorders. In R. J. Gatchel and E. B. Blanchard (Eds.), *Psychophysiological disorders: Research and clinical applications.* Washington, DC: American Psychological Association, 1993.

Friedman, S., Hatch, M. L., Paradis, C. M., et al. Obsessive compulsive disorders in two black ethnic groups: Incidence in an urban dermatology clinic. *Journal of Anxiety Disorders,* 1993, *7*(4), 343–348.

Friedman, S. B., Glasgow, L. A., and Ader, R. Psychosocial factors modifying host resistance to experimental infections. *Annals of the New York Academy of Sciences,* 1969, *164*(Art. 2), 381–392.

Fries, J. F. Aging, natural death, and the compression of morbidity. *New England Journal of Medicine,* 1976, *303,* 130–135.

Froese, A., Hackett, T. P., Cassem, N. H., and Silverberg, E. L. Trajectories of anxiety and depression in denying and nondenying acute myocardial infarction patients during hospitalization. *Journal of Psychosomatic Research,* 1974, *18,* 413–420.

Fromm, E. *The sane society.* New York: Rinehart, 1955.

Funch, D. P., and Gale, E. N. Biofeedback and relaxation therapy for chronic temporo-mandibular joint pain: Predicting successful outcomes. *Journal of Consulting and Clinical Psychology,* 1984, *52,* 928–935.

Funch, D. P., and Marshall, J. The role of stress, social support and age in survival from breast cancer. *Journal of Psychosomatic Research,* 1983, *27,* 77–83.

Gabbay, F. H., Krantz, D. S., Kop, W. J., et al. Triggers of myocardial ischemia during daily life in patients with coronary artery disease: Physical and mental activities, anger, and smoking. *Journal of the American College of Cardiology,* 1996, *27,* 585–592.

Gale, E. M. Epidemiology. In B. G. Sarnat and D. M. Laskin (Eds.), *The temporomandibular joint: A biological basis for clinical practice,* 4th ed. Philadelphia: Saunders, 1992, pp. 237–248.

Gallucci, W. T., Baum, A., Laue, L., et al. Sex differences in sensitivity of the hypothalamic-pituitary-adrenal axis. *Health Psychology,* 1993, *12*(5), 420–425.

Garcia, J., Hankins, W. G., and Rusinak, K. W. Behavioral regulation of the milieu interne in man and rat. *Science,* 1974, *185,* 825–831.

Garmezy, N. Stressors of childhood. In N. Garmezy and M. Rutter (Eds.), *Stress, coping, and development in children.* New York: McGraw-Hill, 1983.

Garrity, T. F. Social involvement and activeness as predictors of morale six months after myocardial infarction. *Social Science and Medicine,* 1973a, *7,* 199–207.

———. Vocational adjustment after first myocardial infarction: Comparative assessment of several variables suggested in the literature. *Social Science and Medicine,* 1973b, *7,* 705–717.

———. Morbidity, mortality, and rehabilitation. In W. D. Gentry and R. B. Williams (Eds.), *Psychological aspects of myocardial infarction and coronary care.* St. Louis: C. V. Mosby, 1975.

Garrity, T. F., McGill, A., Becker, M., et al. Report of the task group of cardiac rehabilitation. In S. M. Weiss (Ed.), *Proceedings of the National Heart and Lung Institute working conference on health behavior* (DHEW Publication No. 76-868). Washington, DC: U.S. Government Printing Office, 1976.

Garrity, T. F., and Marx, M. B. Critical life events and coronary disease. In W. D. Gentry and R. B. Williams (Eds.), *Psychological aspects of myocardial infarction and coronary care,* 2nd ed. St. Louis: C. V. Mosby, 1979.

Garrity, T. F., and Ries, J. B. Health status as a mediating factor in the life change-academic performance relationship. *Journal of Human Stress,* 1985, *11,* 118–124.

Gass, K. A., and Chang, A. S. Appraisals of bereavement, coping, resources, and psychosocial health dysfunction in widows and widowers. *Nursing Research,* 1989, *38*(1), 31–36.

Gatchel, R. J. Biofeedback and the treatment of fear and anxiety. In R. J. Gatchel and K. P. Price (Eds.), *Clinical application of biofeedback: Appraisal and status.* Elmsford, NY: Pergamon, 1979.

———. Effectiveness of two procedures for reducing dental fear: Group-administered desensitization and group education and discussion. *Journal of the American Dental Association,* 1980, *101,* 634–637.

Gatchel, R. J., and Blanchard, E. B. (Eds.), *Psychophysiological disorders: Research and clinical applications.* Washington, DC: American Psychological Association, 1993.

Gatchel, R. J., Deckel, A. W., Wienberg, N., and Smith, J. E. Learned helplessness, depression, and physiological responding. *Psychophysiology,* 1977, *14,* 25–31.

Gatchel, R. J., Deckel, A. W., Weinberg, N., and Smith, J. E. The utility of the Millon Behavioral Health Inventory in the study of chronic headaches. *Headache,* 1985, *25,* 49–54.

Gatchel, R. J., McKinney, M. E., and Koebernick, L. F. Learned helplessness, depression, and physiological responding. *Psychophysiology,* 1977, *14*(1), 25–31.

Gatchel, R. J., Mayer, T. G., Capra, P., et al. Millon Behavioral Health Inventory: Its utility in predicting physical function in low back pain patients. *Archives of Physical Medicine and Rehabilitation, 1986, 67,* 878–882.

Gatchel, R. J., and Price, K. P. (Eds.). *Clinical applications of biofeedback: Appraisal and status.* Elmsford, NY: Pergamon, 1979.

Gatchel, R. J., and Proctor, J. D. Physiological correlates of learned helplessness in man. *Journal of Abnormal Psychology, 1976, 85,* 27–34.

Gatchel, R. J., Schaeffer, M. A., and Baum, A. A psychological field study of stress at Three Mile Island. *Psychophysiology, 1985, 22,* 175–181.

Gatchel, R. J., and Turk, D. C. *Psychological treatment for pain: A practitioner's handbook.* New York: Guilford Publications, 1996.

Gayle, H. D., Keeling, R. P., Garcia-Tunon, M., et al. Prevalence of the human immunodeficiency virus among university students. *New England Journal of Medicine, 1990, 323,* 1538–1541.

Geer, J. H. Biofeedback and the modification of sexual dysfunctions. In R. J. Gatchel and K. P. Price (Eds.), *Clinical applications of biofeedback: Appraisal and status.* Elmsford, NY: Pergamon, 1979.

Geer, J. H., Davison, G. C., and Gatchel, R. J. Reduction of stress in humans through nonveridical perceived control of aversive stimulation. *Journal of Personality and Social Psychology, 1970, 16,* 731–738.

Gentry, W. D., and Kobasa, S. C. O. Social and psychological resources mediating stress-illness relationships in humans. In W. D. Gentry (Ed.), *Handbook of behavioral medicine.* New York: Guilford Press, 1984.

Gentry, W. D., and Matarazzo, J. D. Medical psychology: Three decades of growth and development. In L. A. Bradley and C. K. Prokep (Eds.), *Medical psychology: Contributions to behavioral medicine.* New York: Academic Press, 1981.

Gerin, W., Pieper, C., Levy, R., and Pickering, T. G. Social support in social interaction: A moderator of cardiovascular reactivity. *Psychosomatic Medicine, 1992, 57,* 35–44.

Ghanta, V., Hiramoto, N., Soong, S., and Hiramoto, R. Conditioning the cytotoxic T-lymphocyte secondary response to YC8 tumor (meeting abstract). *Proceedings of the Annual Meeting of the American Association of Cancer Research, 1994, 35,* A265.

Gil, K. M. Coping effectively with invasive medical procedures: A descriptive model. *Clinical Psychology Review, 1984, 4,* 339–362.

Gil, K. M., Keefe, F. J., Sampson, H. A., et al. Direct observation of scratching behavior in children with atopic dermatitis. *Behavior Therapy, 1988, 19,* 213–227.

Gil, K. M., and Sampson, H. A. Psychological and social factors of atopic dermatitis. *Allergy, 1989, 44,* 84–98.

Gil, K. M., Williams, D. A., Keefe, F. J., and Beckham, J. C. The relationship of negative thoughts to pain and psychological distress. *Behavior Therapy, 1990, 21,* 349–362.

Gilberstadt, H. A modal MMPI profile type in neurodermatitis. *Psychosomatic Medicine, 1962, 24,* 471–476.

Gilberstadt, H., and Duker, J. *A handbook for clinical and actuarial MMPI interpretation.* Philadelphia: Saunders, 1965.

Girdler, S. S., Hinderliter, A. L., and Light, K. C. Peripheral adrenergic receptor contributions to cardiovascular reactivity: Influence of race and gender. *Journal of Psychosomatic Research, 1993, 37,* 177–193.

Girdler, S. S., Pedersen, C. A., Stern, R. A., and Light, K. C. Menstrual cycle and premenstrual syndrome: Modifiers of cardiovascular reactivity in women. *Health Psychology, 1993, 12(3),* 180–192.

Glanz, K. Reducing breast cancer risk through changes in diet and alcohol intake: From clinic to community. Mini-Series: Advances in behavioral medicine research on breast cancer. *Annals of Behavioral Medicine, 1994, 16(4),* 334–346.

Glaros, A. G., and Glass, E. G. Temporomandibular disorders. In R. J. Gatchel and E. B. Blanchard (Eds.), *Psychophysiological disorders: Research and clinical applications.* Washington, DC: American Psychological Association, 1993.

Glaser, R., Kiecolt-Glaser, J. K., Bonneau, R., et al. *Psychosomatic Medicine*, 1992, *54*, 22–29.

Glaser, R. J., Kiecolt-Glaser, J., Speicher, C. E., and Holliday, J. E. Stress, loneliness and changes in herpes virus latency. *Journal of Behavioral Medicine*, 1985, *8*, 249–260.

Glaser, R., Rice, J., Speicher, C. E., et al. Stress depresses interferon production concomitant with a decrease in natural killer cell activity. *Behavioral Neuroscience*, 1986, *100*(5), 675–678.

Glaser, R., Thorn, B. E., Tarr, K. L., et al. Effects of stress on methyltransferase synthesis: An important DNA repair enzyme. *Health Psychology*, 1985, *4*(5), 403–412.

Glasgow, M. S., and Engel, B. T. Clinical issues in biofeedback and relaxation therapy for hypertension: Review and recommendations. In J. P. Hatch, J. G. Fisher, and J. D. Rugh (Eds.), *Biofeedback: Studies in clinical efficacy.* New York: Plenum, 1987, pp. 81–122.

Glasgow, R. E. Behavioral research on diabetes at the Oregon Research Institute. *Annals of Behavioral Medicine*, 1995, *17*(1), 32–40.

Glasgow, R. E., and Lichtenstein, E. Long-term effects of behavioral smoking cessation interventions. *Behavior Therapy*, 1987, *18*(4), 297–324.

Glasner, P. D., and Kaslow, R. A. The epidemiology of human immunodeficiency virus infection. *Journal of Consulting and Clinical Psychology*, 1990, *58*(1), 13–21.

Glass, C. R., and Levy, L. H. Perceived psychophysiological control: The effects of power versus powerlessness. *Cognitive Therapy and Research*, 1982, *6*, 91–103.

Glass, D. C., Krakoff, L. R., Contrada, R., et al. Effect of harassment and competition upon cardiovascular and plasma catecholamine responses in Type A and Type B individuals. *Psychophysiology*, 1980, *17*, 453–463.

Glass, D. C., and Singer, J. E. *Urban stress.* New York: Academic Press, 1972.

Glass, D. C., Singer, J. E., and Friedman, L. N. Psychic cost of adaptation to an environmental stressor. *Journal of Personality and Social Psychology*, 1969, *12*, 200–210.

Glass, D. C., Singer, J. E., Leonard, H. S., et al. Perceived control of aversive stimulation and the reduction of stress responses. *Journal of Personality*, 1973, *41*, 577–595.

Glenn, S. W., and Parsons, O. A. Alcohol abuse and familial alcoholism: Psychosocial correlates in men and women. *Journal of Studies on Alcohol*, 1989, *50*, 116–127.

Godding, P. R., McAnulty, R. D., Wittrock, D. A., and Britt, D. M. Predictors of depression among male cancer patients. *Journal of Nervous and Mental Disease*, 1995, *183*(2), 95–98.

Goedert, J. J., Biggar, R. J., Melbye, D. L., et al. Effect of T4 count and cofactors on the incidence of AIDS in homosexual men infected with human immunodeficiency virus. *Journal of the American Medical Association*, 1987, *257*, 331–334.

Goedert, J. J., Biggar, R. J., Weiss, S. H., et al. Three year incidence of AIDS in five cohorts of HTLV-III infected risk group members. *Science*, 1986, *231*, 992–995.

Goffman, E. *Asylums.* Garden City, NY: Doubleday, 1961a.

———. *Encounters: Two studies in the sociology of interaction.* Indianapolis: Bobbs-Merrill, 1961b.

———. *Stigma.* Englewood Cliffs, NJ: Prentice-Hall, 1963.

Goldblatt, P. B., Moore, M. E., and Stunkard, A. J. Social factors in obesity. *Journal of the American Medical Association*, 1965, *192*, 1039–1044.

Goldfried, M. R., and Davison, G. C. *Clinical behavior therapy.* New York: Holt, Rinehart and Winston, 1976.

Goldiamond, I. Self-control procedures in personal behavior problems. *Psychological Reports*, 1965, *17*, 851–868.

Goldman, J. A., and Harlow, L. L. Self-perception variables that mediate AIDS-preventive behavior in college students. *Health Psychology*, 1993, *12*(6), 489–498.

Goldstein, A. P., and Stein, N. *Prescriptive psychotherapies.* Elmsford, NY: Pergamon, 1976.

Gonder-Frederick, L. A., Cox, D. J., Bobbitt, S. A., and Pennebaker, J. W. Mood changes associated with blood glucose fluctuations in insulin-dependent diabetes mellitus. *Health Psychology,* 1989, *8,* 45–59.

Goodall, T. A., and Halford, W. K. Self-management of diabetes mellitus: A critical review. *Health Psychology,* 1991, *10,* 1–8.

Goodkin, K., Antoni, M. H., Helder, L., and Sevin, B. Psychosocial factors in the progression of cervical intraepithelial neoplasia. *Journal of Psychosomatic Research,* 1993, *37*(6), 685.

Goodwin, J. S., Hunt, W. C., Key, C. R., and Samet, J. M. The effect of marital status on stage, treatment and survival of cancer patients. *Journal of the American Medical Association,* 1987, *258,* 3125–3130.

Gordis, L. Methodologic issues in the measurement of patient compliance. In D. L. Sackett and R. B. Haynes (Eds.), *Compliance with therapeutic regimens.* Baltimore: Johns Hopkins University Press, 1976.

Gordis, L., Markowitz, M., and Lillienfield, A. M. Why patients don't follow medical advice: A study of children on long-term antistreptococcal prophylaxis. *Journal of Pediatrics,* 1969, *75,* 957–968.

Gore, S. The influence of social support and related variables in ameliorating the consequences of job loss. Ph.D. dissertation, University of Pennsylvania, 1973.

Gorelick, E. L., and Herberman, R. B. Immunological control of tumor metastases. *Cancer Growth Progression,* 1989, *1,* 134–143.

Gortner, S. R., and Shinn, J. A. Improving recovery following cardiac surgery: A randomized clinical trial. *Journal of Advanced Nursing,* 1988, *13,* 649–661.

Grace, W. J., and Graham, D. T. Relationship of specific attitudes and demotions to certain bodily diseases. *Psychosomatic Medicine,* 1952, *14,* 242–251.

Graham, C., Bond, S. S., Gerkovich, M. M., and Cook, M. R. Use of the McGill Pain Questionnaire in the assessment of cancer pain: Replicability and consistency. *Pain,* 1980, *8,* 377–387.

Graham, D. T. Psychosomatic medicine. In N. S. Greenfield and R. A. Sternbach (Eds.), *Handbook of psychophysiology.* New York: Holt Rinehart and Winston, 1972.

Graham, D. T., Lundry, R. M., Benjamin, L. S., et al. Specific attitudes in initial interviews with patients that have different "psychosomatic" diseases. *Psychosomatic Medicine,* 1962, *24,* 257–266.

Graham, D. T., Stern, J. A., and Winokur, G. Experimental investigation of the specificity hypotheses in psychosomatic disease. *Psychosomatic Medicine,* 1958, *20,* 446–457.

Graham, N. M., Douglas, R. M., and Ryan, P. Stress and acute respiratory infection. *American Journal of Epidemiology,* 1986, *124*(3), 389–401.

Green, B. L. Identifying survivors at risk: Trauma and stressors across events. In J. P. Wilson and B. Raphael (Eds.), *International handbook of traumatic stress syndromes.* New York: Plenum, 1993.

Green, B. L., Lindy, J. D., Grace, M. C., et al. Buffalo Creek survivors in the second decade: Stability and change of stress symptoms over 14 years. Unpublished manuscript, 1989.

Green, B. L., Wilson, J. P., and Lindy, J. D. Conceptualizing post-traumatic stress disorder: A psychosocial framework. In C. Figley (Ed.), *Trauma and its wake,* vol. I. New York: Brunner/Mazel, 1985.

Green, G. M., and Carolin, D. The depressant effect of cigarette smoke on the in vitro antibacterial activity of alveolar macrophages. *New England Journal of Medicine,* 1967, *276,* 421–427.

Green, L. W. Health education models. In J. D. Matarazzo, S. M. Weiss, J. A. Herd, et al. (Eds.), *Behavioral health: A handbook of health enhancement and disease prevention.* New York: Wiley, 1984.

Green, L. W., and Kreuter, M. W. Health promotion as a public health strategy for the 1990s. *Annual Review of Public Health*, 1990, *11*, 319–334.

Green, R. G. Stress and accidents. *Aviation, Space, and Environmental Medicine*, 1985, *56*, 638–641.

Green, V., Stansfield, B. J., and Davidson, C. Cardiac rehabilitation in the United Kingdom. *Physiotherapy*, 1988, *74*, 363–365.

Greenberg, C. I., and Baum, A. Compensatory response to anticipated densities. *Journal of Applied Social Psychology*, 1979, *9*, 1–12.

Greene, R. L. *The MMPI-2MMPI: An interpretive manual*. Boston: Allyn & Bacon, 1991.

Greene, W. A. The psychosocial setting of the development of leukemia and lymphoma. *Annals of the New York Academy of Science*, 1966, *125*, 794–801.

Greene, W. A., Betts, R. F., and Ochitull, H. N. Psychosocial factors and immunity: Preliminary report. Paper presented at the annual meeting of the American Psychosomatic Society, Washington, DC, 1978.

Greene, W. C. The molecular biology of human immunodeficiency virus type 1 infection. *New England Journal of Medicine*, 1991, *324*, 308–317.

Greenwald, H. P., and Nevitt, M. C. Physician attitudes toward communication with cancer patients. *Social Science and Medicine*, 1982, *16*(5), 591–594.

Greer, S. Psychological response to cancer and survival. *Psychological Medicine*, 1991, *21*, 43–49.

Greer, S., and Morris, T. Psychological attributes of women who develop breast cancer: A controlled study. *Journal of Psychosomatic Research*, 1975, *19*, 147–153.

Greer, S. E., and Calhoun, J. F. Learned helplessness and depression in acutely distressed community residents. *Cognitive Therapy and Research*, 1983, *7*, 205–222.

Griffiths, R. R., Bigelow, G. E., and Liebson, I. The relationship of social factors to ethanol self-administration in alcoholics. In P. E. Nathan, G. A. Marlatt, and T. Y. Loberg (Eds.), *Alcoholism: New directions in behavioral research and treatment*. New York: Plenum, 1978.

Grinker, R. R., and Spiegel, J. P. *War neuroses*. Philadelphia: Blakiston, 1945.

Grossarth-Maticek, R., and Eysenck, H. J. Coca-Cola, cancers, and coronaries: Personality and stress as mediating factors. *Psychological Reports*, 1991, *68*(3, Pt. 2), 1083–1087.

Grossman, A., Astley, S. J., Liggitt, H. D., et al. Immune function in offspring of nonhuman primates (Macaca nemestrina) exposed weekly to 1.8 g/kg ethanol during pregnancy: Preliminary observations. *Alcoholism, Clinical and Experimental Research*, 1993, *17*(4), 822–827.

Grossman, C. J., Nienaber, M., Mendenhall, C. L., et al. Sex differences and the effects of alcohol on immune response in male and female rats. *Alcoholism, Clinical and Experimental Research*, 1993, *17*(4), 832–840.

Grove, J. R. Attributional correlates of cessation self-efficacy among smokers. *Addictive Behaviors*, 1993, *18*(3), 311–320.

Grummon, K., Rigby, E. D., Orr, D., et al. Psychosocial variables that affect the psychological adjustment of IVDU patients with AIDS. *Journal of Clinical Psychology, 50*(4), 488–502.

Grunberg, N. E. Behavioral and biological factors in the relationship between tobacco use and body weight. In E. S. Katkin and S. B. Manuck (Eds.), *Advances in behavioral medicine*, vol. 2. Greenwich, CT: JAI Press, 1986.

———. Behavioral factors in preventive medicine and health promotion. In W. Gordon, A. Herd, and A. Baum (Eds.), *Perspectives on behavioral medicine*, vol. 3. New York: Academic Press, 1988.

Grunberg, N. E., and Baum, A. Biological commonalities of stress and substance abuse. In S. Shiffman and T. Wills (Eds.), *Coping and substance abuse*. Orlando, FL: Academic Press, 1985.

Grunberg, N. E., Brown, K. I., and Klein, L. C. Tobacco smoking. In A. Baum, C. Mc-Manus, S. Newman, et al. (Eds.), *Cambridge handbook of psychology, health and medicine.* Cambridge: Cambridge University Press, 1996.

Grunberg, N. E., Greenwood, M. R. C., Collins, F., et al. Task Force 1: Mechanisms relevant to the relations between cigarette smoking and body weight. *Health Psychology,* 1992, *11*(suppl.), 4–9.

Gryfe, C. I., and Gryfe, B. M. Drug therapy of the aged: The problem of compliance and the roles of physicians and pharmacists. *Journal of the American Geriatrics Society,* 1984, *32*(4), 301–307.

Guthrie, E., Creed F., Dawson, D., and Tomenson, B. A controlled trial of psychological treatment for the irritable bowel syndrome. *Gastroenterology,* 1991, *100,* 450–457.

Gutterman, E. M., Erhardt, A. A., Markowitz, J. S., and Link, B. G. Vulnerability to stress among women with in utero Diethylstilbestrol (DES) exposed daughters. *Journal of Human Stress,* 1985, *11,* 103–110.

Guyton, A. C. *Textbook of medical physiology.* Philadelphia: Saunders, 1981.

Hackett, T. P., Rosenbaum, J. F., and Tesar, G. E. Emotion, psychiatric disorders, and the heart. In E. Braunwald (Ed.), *Heart disease: A textbook of cardiovascular medicine,* 3rd ed. Philadelphia: Saunders, 1988.

Hackett, T. P., and Weisman, A. D. Reactions to the imminence of death. In G. H. Grosser, H. Wechsler, and H. Greenblatt (Eds.), *The threat of impending disaster.* Cambridge, MA: MIT Press, 1964.

Haefner, D. P., and Kirscht, J. P. Motivational and behavioral effects of modifying health beliefs. *Public Health Reports,* 1970, *85,* 478–484.

Haggard, E. A. Some conditions determining adjustment during and readjustment following experimentally induced stress. In S. S. Tomkins (Ed.), *Contemporary psychopathology.* Cambridge, MA: Harvard University Press, 1946.

Hagglund, K. J., Roth, D. L., Haley, W. E., and Alarcon, G. S. Discriminate and convergent validity of self-report measures of affect distress in patients with rheumatoid arthritis. *Journal of Rheumatology,* 1989, *16*(11), 1428–1432.

Hakas, J. L., Gajiwala, K. S., Maffei, M., et al. Weight reducing effects of the plasma protein encoded by the obese gene. *Science,* 1995, *269,* 543–546.

Hall, E. T. *The hidden dimension.* New York: Doubleday, 1966.

Hall, M., and Baum, A. Intrusive thoughts as determinants of distress in parents of children with cancer. *Journal of Applied Social Psychology,* 1995, *25*(14), 1215–1230.

Hall, M., Dougall, A. J. L., Buysse, D. J., et al. Sleep quality following traumatic event predicts future health and psychological distress. *Health Psychology,* 1996, still under review.

Halliday, J. L. *Psycho-social medicine: A study of the sick society.* New York: Norton, 1948.

Halstead, W. C. *Brain and intelligence.* Chicago: University of Chicago Press, 1947.

Hammen, C., Ellicott, A., and Gitlin, M. Vulnerability to specific life events and prediction of course of disorder in unipolar depressed patients. Special issue: Clinical depression. *Canadian Journal of Behavioral Science,* 1989, *21*(4), 377–388.

Hanson, D. R., and Gottesman, L. I. The genetics, if any, of infantile autism and childhood schizophrenia. *Journal of Autism and Childhood Schizophrenia,* 1976. *6,* 209–234.

Harburg, E., Erfurt, J. D., Haunstein, L. S., et al. Socioecologic stress, suppressed hostility, skin color and black-white male blood pressure: Detroit. *Psychosomatic Medicine,* 1973, *35,* 276–296.

Harlow, L. L., Rose, J. S., Morokoff, P., and Quina, K. Types of HIV-risk takers: Behavior and attitudes. *International Conference on AIDS,* 1993, *9*(2), 6–11.

Harris, D., Vann, A., and Wrightson, K. Toward a healthy state: Report of the State Commission on Health Education and Illness Prevention. *New York State Journal of Medicine,* 1981, *81*(12), 1798–1801.

Harris, J. R., Lippman, M. E., Veronesi, U., and Willett, W. Breast cancer (1 Pt. 3). *New England Journal of Medicine,* 1992a, *327,* 319–328.

Harris, J. R., Lippman, M. E., Veronesi, U., and Willett, W. Breast cancer (2 Pt. 3). *New England Journal of Medicine,* 1992b, *327,* 473–480.

Harris, P. R. Lifestyle behaviors and time period. In *Health United States 1980.* Washington DC: U.S. Government Printing Office, 1981.

Hartman, C. R., and Burgess, A. W. Information processing of trauma. Special issue: Clinical recognition of sexually abused children. *Child Abuse and Neglect,* 1993, *17,* 47–58.

Harvey, R. F., Hinton, R. A., Gunary, R. N., and Barry, R. E. Individual and group hypnotherapy in treatment of refractory irritable bowel syndrome. *Lancet,* 1989, *1,* 424–425.

Hatch, J. P. Headache. In R. J. Gatchel and E. B. Blanchard (Eds.), *Psychophysiological disorders: Research and clinical applications.* Washington, DC: American Psychological Association, 1993.

Hatch, J. P., Fisher, J. G., and Rugh, J. D. *Biofeedback: Studies in clinical efficacy.* New York: Plenum, 1987.

Hatch, J. P., Gatchel, R. J., and Harrington, R. Biofeedback: Clinical applications in medicine. In R. J. Gatchel, A. Baum, and J. E. Singer (Eds.), *Behavioral medicine and clinical psychology: Overlapping areas.* Hillsdale, NJ: Erlbaum, 1982.

Hatch, M. L., Paradis, C., Friedman, S., et al. Obsessive compulsive disorders in patients with chronic pruritic conditions: Case studies and discussion. *Journal of the American Academy of Dermatology,* 1992, *26,* 549–551.

Hathaway, S. R., and McKinley, J. C. *MMPI manual.* New York: Psychological Corporation, 1943.

Hauser, R. Rapid smoking as a technique of behavior modification: Caution in the selection of subjects. *Journal of Consulting and Clinical Psychology,* 1974, *42,* 625–630.

Hawkins, J. D., Catalano, R. F., and Miller, J. Y. Risk and protective factors for alcohol and drug problems in adolescence and early adulthood: Implications for substance abuse prevention. [Review.] *Psychological Bulletin,* 1992, *112*(1), 64–105.

Hawley, D. J., and Wolfe, F. Anxiety and depression in patients with rheumatoid arthritis: A prospective study of 400 patients. *Journal of Rheumatology,* 1988, *15,* 932–941.

Haynes, R. B. A critical review of the "determinants" of patient compliance with therapeutic regimens. In D. L. Sackett and R. B. Haynes (Eds.), *Compliance with therapeutic regimens.* Baltimore: Johns Hopkins University Press, 1976.

Haynes, R. B., Taylor, D. W., and Sackett, D. L. *Compliance in health care.* Baltimore: Johns Hopkins University Press, 1979.

Haynes, S. G., and Feinleib, M. Women, work, and coronary disease: Prospective findings from the Framingham Heart Study. *American Journal of Public Health,* 1980, *70,* 133–141.

Haynes, S. G., Feinleib, M., and Kannel, W. B. The relationship of psycho-social factors in coronary heart disease in the Framingham Study III: Eight year incidence of coronary heart disease. *American Journal of Epidemiology,* 1980, *111,* 37–58.

Haynes, S. G., Feinleib, M., and Kannel, W. B. Women, work, and coronary heart disease. *American Journal of Public Health,* 1980, *70,* 133–141.

Haythornethwaite, J. A., Pratley, R. E., and Anderson, D. E. Behavioral stress potentiates the blood pressure effects of a high sodium intake. *Psychosomatic Medicine,* 1992, *54*(2), 231–239.

Hazard, R. G., Fenwick, J. W., Kalisch, S. M., et al. Functional restoration with behavioral support: A one year perspective study of patients with chronic low back pain. *Spine,* 1989, *14,* 157–161.

Heater, B. S., Becker, A. M., and Olson, R. K. Nursing interventions and patient outcomes: A meta-analysis of studies. [Review.] *Nursing Research,* 1988, *37*(5), 303–307.

Heather, N. Brief intervention strategies. In R. K. Hester and W. R. Miller (Eds.), *Handbook of alcoholism treatment approaches: Effective alternatives.* New York, Pergamon, 1990, pp. 93–116.

Heatherton, T. F., Herman, C. P., Polivy, J., and King, G. A. The (mis)measurement of restraint: An analysis of conceptual and psychometric issues. *Journal of Abnormal Psychology,* 1988, *97,* 19–28.

Heatherton, T. F., Polivy, J., and Herman, C. P. Restraint, weight loss, and variability of body weight. *Journal of Abnormal Psychology,* 1991, *100,* 78–83.

Heaton, R. K., Grant, I., and Matthews, C. G. *Comprehensive norms for an expanded Halstead-Reitan battery: Demographic corrections, research findings and clinical applications.* Odessa, FL: Psychological Assessment Resources, Inc., 1991.

Hegel, M. T., Ayllon, T., Thiel, G., and Oulton, B. Improving adherence to fluid restriction in male hemodialysis patients: A comparison of cognitive and behavioral approaches. *Health Psychology,* 1992, *11*(5), 324–330.

Heimberg, R. G., Klosko, J. S., Dodge, C. S., and Shadick, R. Anxiety disorders, depression, and attributional style: A further test of the specificity of depressive attributions. *Cognitive Therapy and Research,* 1989, *13*(1), 21–36.

Heirch, I., Kvale, G., Jacobson, B. K., and Bjelke, E. Use of alcohol, tobacco and coffee, and risk of pancreatic cancer. *British Journal of Cancer,* 1983, *48*(5), 637–643.

Hellerstein, H. K., and Friedman, E. H. Sexual activity and the post-coronary patient. *Archives of Internal Medicine,* 1970, *125,* 987–999.

Helmers, K., Posluszny, D., and Krantz, D. S. Associations of hostility and coronary artery disease: A review of studies. In A. Siegman and T. Smith (Eds.), *Anger, hostility and the heart.* Hillsdale, NJ: Erlbaum, 1994.

Henderson, M. M., Kushi, L. H., Thompson, D. J., et al. Feasibility of a randomized trial of a low-fat diet for the prevention of breast cancer: Dietary compliance in the Women's Health Trial Vanguard Study. *Preventive Medicine,* 1990, *19*(2), 115–133.

Henry, J. P., and Cassel, J. C. Psychosocial factors in essential hypertension: Recent epidemiologic and animal experimental data. *American Journal of Epidemiology,* 1969, *90,* 171–200.

Henry, J. P., Ely, D. L., Watson, F. M. C., and Stephens, P. M. Ethological methods as applied to the measurement of emotion. In L. Levi (Ed.), *Emotions: Their parameters and measurement.* New York: Raven Press, 1975.

Henry, J. P., and Stephens, J. C. *Stress, health, and the social environment.* New York: Springer-Verlag, 1977.

Herberman, R. B., and Holden, H. T. Natural cell-mediated immunity. *Advances in Cancer Research,* 1978, *27,* 305–377.

Herbert, T. B., and Cohen, S. Title: Depression and immunity: A meta-analytic review. *Psychology Bulletin,* 1993, *113,* 472–486.

Herbst, A. L., Ulfelder, H., and Poskanzer, D. C. Adenocarcinoma of the vagina: Association of maternal stilbestrol therapy with tumor appearance in young women. *New England Journal of Medicine,* 1971, *284,* 878–881.

Herity, B., Murphy, J., Moriarty, M., et al. Study of squamous-cell carcinoma of the cervix uteri. *Irish Journal of Medical Science,* 1982, *151*(4), 128.

Herman, C. P. Restrained eating. *Psychiatric Clinics of North America,* 1978, *1,* 593–607.

Herman, C. P., and Polivy, J. Restrained eating. In A. J. Stunkard (Ed.), *Obesity.* Philadelphia: Saunders, 1980.

Herman, P., and Mack, D. Restrained and unrestrained eating. *Journal of Personality,* 1975, *43,* 646–660.

Herman, W. H., Teutsch, S. M., and Geiss, L. S. Diabetes mellitis. In R. W. Amler and H. B. Dull (Eds.), *Closing the gap: The burden of unnecessary illness.* New York: Oxford University Press, 1987, pp. 72–82.

Hernstein, R. J. *I.Q. in the meritocracy.* Boston: Atlantic Monthly Press, 1973.

Hernstein, R. J., and Murray, C. *The bell curve: Intelligence and class structure in American life.* New York: Free Press, 1994.

Heston, L. L. Psychiatric disorders in foster home reared children of schizophrenic mothers. *British Journal of Psychiatry,* 1966, *112,* 819–825.

Hewitt, P. L., Flett, G. L., and Mosher, S. W. The perceived stress scale: Factor structure and relation to depression symptoms in a psychiatric sample. *Journal of Psychopathology and Behavioral Assessment,* 1992, *14*(3), 247–257.

Hieb, E., and Wang, R. Compliance: The patient's role in drug therapy. *Wisconsin Journal of Medicine,* 1974, *73,* 152–154.

Higgins, E. M., and du Vivier, A. W. Cataneous disease and alcohol misuse. *British Medical Bulletin,* 1994, *50*(1), 85–98.

Higgins, M. W., and Luepker, R. V. Preface in M. W. Higgins, and R. V. Luepker (Eds.), *Trends in coronary heart disease mortality.* New York: Oxford University Press, 1988, pp. vii–x.

Hilgard, E. R. *Hypnotic susceptibility.* New York: Harcourt, Brace and World, 1965.

———. The alleviation of pain by hypnosis. *Pain,* 1975, *1,* 213–231.

Hilgard, E. R., Atkinson, R. C., and Atkinson, R. L. *Introduction to psychology* (7th ed.). New York: Harcourt Brace Jovanovich, 1979.

Hilgard, E. R., and Hilgard, J. R. *Hypnosis in the relief of pain.* Los Altos, CA: William Kaufmann, 1975.

Hill, H. E., Kornetsky, C. G., Flanary, H. G., and Wilder, A. Effects of anxiety and morphine on the discrimination of intensities of pain. *Journal of Clinical Investigation,* 1952, *31,* 473–480.

Hilton, B. A. The relationship of uncertainty, control, commitment, and threat of recurrence to coping strategies used by women diagnosed with breast cancer. *Journal of Behavioral Medicine,* 1989, *12*(1), 39–54.

Hiroto, D. S. Learned helplessness and locus of control. *Journal of Experimental Psychology,* 1974, *102,* 187–193.

Hiroto, D. S., and Seligman, M. E. P. Generality of learned helplessness in man. *Journal of Personality and Social Psychology,* 1975, *31,* 311–327.

Hirsch, J., and Knittle, J. L. Cellularity of obese and nonobese human adipose tissue. *Federation Proceedings,* 1970, *29,* 1516–1521.

Hirschorn, M. W. AIDS is not seen as a major threat by many heterosexuals on campuses. *Chronicle of Higher Education,* 1987, *33,* 1.

Hoffman, L., Watson, P. B., Wilson, G., and Montgomery, J. Low plasma beta-endorphin in post-traumatic stress disorder. *Australian and New Zealand Journal of Psychiatry,* 1989, *23*(4), 442.

Hokanson, J. E., and Burgess, M. The effects of three types of aggression on vascular processes. *Journal of Abnormal and Social Psychology,* 1962, *64,* 446–447.

Holland, J. C., Rowland, J., Lebovits, A., and Rusalem, R. Reactions to cancer treatment: Assessment of emotional response to adjuvant radiotherapy as a guide to planned interventions. *Psychiatric Clinics of North America,* 1979, *2,* 347–358.

Holland, J. C., and Tross, S. The psychosocial and neuropsychiatric sequelae of the acquired immunodeficiency syndrome and related disorders. *Annals of Internal Medicine,* 1985, *103,* 760–764.

Holmes, D. S. Aerobic fitness and the response in psychological stress. In P. Seraganian (Ed.), *Exercise psychology: The influence of physical exercise on psychological processes.* New York: Wiley, 1993.

Holmes, T. H., and Rahe, R. H. The social readjustment rating scale. *Journal of Psychosomatic Research,* 1967, *11,* 213–218.

Holroyd, K. A., and Penzien, D. B. Pharmacological versus non-pharmacological prophylaxis of recurrent migraine headache: A meta-analytic review of clinical trials. *Pain,* 1990, *42,* 1–13.

Holt, P. G., and Keast, D. Environmentally induced changes in immunological function: Acute and chronic effects of inhalation of tobacco smoke and other atmospheric contaminants in man and experimental animals. *Bacteriological Reviews*, 1977, *41*(1), 205–216.

Horan, J. J., Laying, F. C., and Pursell, C. H. Preliminary study of effects of "in vivo" emotive imagery on dental discomfort. *Perceptual and Motor Skills*, 1976, *42*(1), 105–106.

Horowitz, M., Wilner, N., and Alvarez, W. Impact of event scale: A measure of subjective stress. *Psychosomatic Medicine*, 1979, *41*, 209–218.

Horowitz, S. M., Morgenstern, H., DiPietro, L., et al. Determinants of pediatric injuries. *American Journal of Diseases of Children*, 1988, *142*, 605–611.

Hospers, H. J., Molenar, S., and Kok, G. Focus group interviews with risk-taking gay men: Appraisal of AIDS prevention activities, explanations for sexual risk-taking, and needs support. *Patient Education and Counseling*, 1994, *24*(3), 299–306.

House, J. S., Landis, K. R., and Umberson, D. Social relationships and health. *Science*, 1988, *241*, 540–545.

House, J. S., and Smith, D. Evaluating health effects of demanding work on and off the job. In T. F. Drury (Ed.), *Assessing physical fitness and physical activity in population based surveys.* Hyattsville, MD: National Center for Health Statistics, 1989, pp. 481–508.

Houston, B. K., Chesney, M. A., Black, G. W., et al. Behavioral clusters and coronary heart disease risk. *Psychosomatic Medicine*, 1992, *54*(4), 447–461.

Howard, J. H., Cunningham, D. A., and Rechnitzer, P. A. Effects of personal interaction on triglyceride, uric acid, and coronary risk among managers. *Journal of Human Stress*, 1986, *12*, 53–63.

Healky, M. A., Lam, L. C., Lee, K. L., et al. Job strain and the prevalence and outcome of coronary artery disease. *Circulation*, 1995, *92*(3), 327–333.

Hudgens, R. W. Personal catastrophe and depression. In B. S. Dohrenwend and B. P. Dohrenwend (Eds.), *Stressful life events: Their nature and effects.* New York: Wiley, 1974.

Hughes, H., Brown, B. W., Lawlis, G. F., and Fulton, J. E. Treatment of acne vulgaris by biofeedback relaxation and cognitive imagery. *Journal of Psychosomatic Research*, 1983, *27*, 185–191.

Hughes, J. R. Observer reports of smoking status: A replication. *Journal of Substance Abuse*, 1992, *4*(4), 403–406.

Hunt, W. A., Barnett, L. W., and Ranch, L. G. Relapse rates in addiction programs. *Journal of Clinical Psychology*, 1971, *27*, 455–456.

Hunt, W. A., and Bespalec, D. A. An evaluation of current methods for modifying smoking behavior. *Journal of Clinical Psychology*, 1974, *30*, 431–438.

Hunt, W. A., and Matarazzo, J. D. Habit mechanisms in smoking. In W. A. Hunt (Ed.), *Learning mechanisms in smoking.* Chicago: Aldine, 1970.

Hunt, W. A., and Matarazzo, J. D. Changing smoking behavior: A critique. In R. J. Gatchel, A. Baum, and J. E. Singer (Eds.), *Behavioral medicine and clinical psychology: Overlapping areas.* Hillsdale, NJ: Erlbaum, 1982.

Hymowitz, N. Long-term smoking intervention at the worksite: Effects of quit-smoking groups and an "enriched milieu" on smoking cessation in adult white-collar employees. *Health Psychology*, 1991, *10*(5), 366–369.

Hyson, R. L., Ashcraft, L. J., Drugan, R. C., et al. Extent and control of shock affects naltrexone sensitivity of stress-induced analgesia and reactivity to morphine. *Pharmacology, Biochemistry, and Behavior*, 1982, *17*(5), 1019–1025.

Ironson, G., Taylor, C. B., Boltwood, M., et al. Effects of anger on left ventricular ejection fraction in coronary artery disease. *American Journal of Cardiology*, 1992, *70*(3), 281–285.

Ironson, G., Wynings, C., Schneiderman, N., et al. Post-traumatic stress symptoms, intrusive thoughts, loss and immune function after Hurricane Andrew. *Psychosomatic Medicine*, still in press.

Irwin, M., Patterson, T., Smith, T. L., et al. Reduction of immune function in life stress and depression. *Biological Psychiatry*, 1990, *27*, 22–30.

Jackson, J. K. The problem of alcoholic tuberculosis patients. In P. F. Sparer (Ed.), *Personality stress and tuberculosis.* New York: International Universities Press, 1954.

Jackson, R. L., Maier, S. F., and Coon, D. J. Long-term analgesic effects of inescapable shock and learned helplessness. *Science*, 1979, *206*(4414), 91–93.

Jacob, R. G., and Chesney, M. A. Psychological and behavioral methods to reduce cardiovascular reactivity. In K. A. Matthews, S. M. Weiss, T. Detre, et al. (Eds.), *Handbook of stress, reactivity, and cardiovascular disease.* New York: Wiley, 1986.

Jacobs, M. A., Spilken, A. Z., Norman, M. M., and Anderson, L. S. Life stress and respiratory illness. *Psychosomatic Medicine*, 1970, *32*, 233–242.

Jacobs, S., Kasl, S., Schaefer, C., and Ostfeld, A. Conscious and unconscious coping with loss. *Psychosomatic Medicine*, 1994, *56*(6), 557–563.

Jacobson, E. *Progressive relaxation.* Chicago: University of Chicago Press, 1938.

James, W. *The principles of psychology.* New York: Holt, 1890.

Janes, C. R. Migration, changing gender roles and stress: The Samoan case. *Medical Anthropology*, 1990, *12*(2), 217–248.

Janes, C. R., and Pawson, I. G. Migration and biocultural adaptation: Samoans in California. *Social Science and Medicine*, 1986, *22*(8), 821–834.

Janeway, J., and Travers, C. A. *Immunobiology.* New York: Garland, 1994.

Janis, I. L. *Psychological stress: Psychoanalytic and behavioral studies of surgical patients.* New York: Wiley, 1958.

———. Effects of fear arousal on attitude change: Recent developments in theory and experimental research. In L. Berkowitz (Ed.), *Advances in experimental social psychology*, vol. 3. New York: Academic Press, 1967.

Janis, I. L., and Leventhal, A. Psychological aspects of physical illness and hospital care. In B. Wolman (Ed.), *Handbook of clinical psychology.* New York: McGraw-Hill, 1965.

Janoff-Bulman, R. Characterological versus behavioral self blame: Inquiries into depression and rape. *Journal of Personality and Social Psychology*, 1979, *37*(10), 1798–1809.

———. The aftermath of victimization: Rebuilding shattered assumptions. In C. Figley (Ed.), *Trauma and its wake.* New York: Brunner/Mazel, 1985.

———. Assumptive worlds and the stress of traumatic events: Applications of the schema construct. Special issue: Stress, coping, and social cognition. *Social Cognition*, 1989, *7*(2), 113–136.

———. *Shattered assumptions: Towards a new psychology of trauma.* New York: Free Press, 1992.

Janz, N., and Becker, M. The health belief model: A decade later. *Health Education Quarterly*, 1984, *2*, 1–47.

Jarvik, M. E. Biological influences on cigarette smoking. In *Smoking and health: A report of the Surgeon General* (DHEW Publication No. [PHS] 79-50066). Washington, DC: U.S. Government Printing Office, 1979.

Jay, S. M., Elliot, C. H., Woody, P. D., and Siegel, S. An investigation of cognitive-behavior therapy combined with oral vallium for children undergoing painful medical procedures. *Health Psychology*, 1991, *10*, 317–322.

Jeffery, R. W. Long-term effects of interventions for weight loss using food provision and monetary incentives. *Journal of Consulting and Clinical Psychology*, 1995, *63*(5), 793–796.

Jellinek, M. S., et al. The need for multidisciplinary training in counseling the medically ill: Report of the training committee of the Linda Pollin Foundation. Special supplement issue: A model for counseling the medically ill: The Linda Pollin Foundation approach. *General Hospital Psychiatry*, 1992, *14*(suppl. 6), 3–10.

Jenkins, C. D. Psychosocial and behavioral factors. In N. Kaplan and J. Stamler (Eds.), *Prevention of coronary heart disease*. Philadelphia: Saunders, 1983.

Jenkins, C. D., Rosenman, R. H., and Friedman, M. Development of an objective psychological test for the determination of the coronary-prone behavior pattern in employed men. *Journal of Chronic Diseases*, 1967, *20*, 371–379.

Jenkins, C. D., Rosenman, R. H., and Zyzanski, S. J. Prediction of clinical coronary heart disease by a test for the coronary-prone behavior pattern. *New England Journal of Medicine*, 1974, *290*, 1271–1275.

Jenkins, C. D., Zyzanski, S. J., and Rosenman, R. H. Progress toward validation of a computer-scored test for the Type A coronary-prone behavior pattern. *Psychosomatic Medicine*, 1971, *33*, 193–202.

Jenkins, F. J., and Baum, A. Stress and reactivation of latent herpes simplex virus: A fusion of behavioral medicine and molecular biology. *Annals of Behavioral Medicine*, 1995, *17*(2), 116–123.

Jennings, G., Nelson, L., Nestel, P., et al. The effects of changes in physical activity on major cardiovascular risk factors, hemodynamics, sympathetic function, and glucose utilization in man: A controlled study of four levels of activity. *Circulation*, 1986, *73*, 30–40.

Jensen, A. R. How much can we boost I.Q. and scholastic achievement? *Harvard Educational Review*, 1969, *39*, 1–123.

Jensen, M. P., Karoly, P., and Braver, S. The measurement of clinical pain intensity: A comparison of six methods. *Pain*, 1986, *27*, 117–126.

Jessner, I., Blom, G., and Waldfogel, S. Emotional implications of tonsillectomy and adenoidectomy on children. *Psychoanalytic Study of Children*, 1952, *7*, 126–169.

Jessor, R., and Jessor, S. L. *Problem behavior and psychosocial development: A longitudinal study of youth*. New York: Academic Press, 1977.

Jiang, W., Blumenthal, J. A., Thyrum, E. T., et al. The effects of depression on left ventricular performance in patients with coronary disease. *Psychosomatic Medicine*, 1994 (abstract), *56*, 158.

Joasoo, A., and McKenzie, J. M. Stress and the immune response in rats. *International Archives of Allergy and Applied Immunology*, 1976, *50*, 659–663.

Johansson, G. Case report on female catecholamine excretion in response to examination stress. Reports from the Department of Psychology, University of Stockholm (515), 1977.

Johnson, J. E. Psychological interventions and coping with surgery. In A. Baum, S. E. Taylor, and J. E. Singer (Eds.), *Handbook of psychology and health*, vol. IV. Hillsdale, NJ: Erlbaum, 1984, pp. 167–188.

Johnson, J. E., and Leventhal, H. Effects of accurate expectations and behavioral instructions on reactions during a noxious medical examination. *Journal of Personality and Social Psychology*, 1974, *29*, 710–718.

Johnson, S., Knight, R., Marmer, D. J., and Steele, R. W. Immune deficiency in fetal alcohol syndrome. *Pediatric Research*, 1981, *15*, 908–911.

Johnson, W. D., Stokes, P., and Kaye, D. The effect of intravenous ethanol on the bactericidal activity of human serum. *Yale Journal of Medicine*, 1969, *42*, 71–85.

Johnston, M., and Vogele, C. Benefits of psychological preparation for surgery: A meta-analysis. *Annals of Behavioral Medicine*, 1993, *15*(4), 245–256.

Jones, M. C. Personality correlates and antecedents of drinking patterns in adult males. *Journal of Consulting and Clinical Psychology*, 1968, *32*, 2–12.

———. Personality antecedents and correlates of drinking patterns in women. *Journal of Consulting and Clinical Psychology*, 1971, *36*, 61–69.

Jones, S. L., Nation, J. R., and Massad, P. Immunization against learned helplessness in man. *Journal of Abnormal Psychology,* 1977, *86,* 75–83.

Julius, S., and Esler, M. Autonomic nervous cardiovascular regulation in borderline hypertension. *American Journal of Cardiology,* 1975, *36,* 685–696.

Kabat-Zinn, J., Lipworth, L., and Burney, R. The clinical use of mindfulness meditation for the self-regulation of chronic pain. *Journal of Behavioral Medicine,* 1985, *8*(2), 163–190.

Kaels, L., Glaros, A. G., and McGlynn, F. D. Psychophysiological responses to stress in patients with myofascial pain-dysfunction syndrome. *Journal of Behavioral Medicine,* 1989, *12,* 397–406.

Kahn, R. L., and French, J. R. P., Jr. Status and conflict: Two themes in the study of stress. In J. E. McGrath (Ed.), *Social and psychological factors in stress.* New York: Holt, Rinehart and Winston, 1970.

Kalichman, S. C., and Hunter, T. L. The disclosure of celebrity HIV infection: Its effects on public attitudes. *American Journal of Public Health,* 1992, *82*(10), 1374–1376.

Kallman, F. J. The genetic theory of schizophrenia: An analysis of 691 schizophrenic twin index families. *American Journal of Psychiatry,* 1946, *103,* 309–322.

Kamarck, T. W., Annunziato, B., and Amateau, L. M. Affiliation moderates the effects of social threat on stress-related cardiovascular responses: Boundary conditions for a laboratory model of social support. *Psychosomatic Medicine,* 1995, *57*(2), 183–194.

Kamarck, T. W., Jennings, J., Richard, J., et al. Reliable responses to a cardiovascular reactivity protocol: A replication study in a biracial female sample. *Psychophysiology,* 1993, *30*(6), 627–634.

Kamin, L. J. *The science and politics of I.Q.* Hillsdale, NJ: Erlbaum, 1974.

Kandil, O., and Borysenko, M. Decline of natural killer cell target binding and lytic activity in mice exposed to rotation stress. *Health Psychology,* 1987, *6*(2), 89–99.

Kane, R. A. Psychosocial issues. Psychological and social issues for older people with cancer. (Review.) *Cancer,* 1991, *68*(suppl. 11), 2514–2518.

Kannel, W. B., Castelli, W. P., and Gordon, T. Cholesterol in the prediction of atherosclerotic disease: New perspectives based on the Framingham study. *Annals of Internal Medicine,* 1979, *90,* 85–91.

Kanner, A. D., Coyne, J. C., Schaeffer, C., and Lazarus, R. S. Comparison of two modes of stress measurement: Daily hassles and uplifts versus major life events. *Journal of Behavioral Medicine,* 1981, *4,* 1–39.

Kapel, L., Glaros, A. G., and McGlynn, F. D. Psychophysiological response to stress in patients with myofascial pain-dysfunction syndrome. *Journal of Behavioral Medicine,* 1989, *12,* 397–406.

Kaplan, G. A. Biobehavioral risk factors: Reflections on present and future research on biobehavioral risk factors. In S. J. Blumenthal, K. Matthews, and S. M. Weiss (Eds.), *New research frontiers in behavioral medicine: Proceedings of the National Conference.* NIH Publication No. 94-3772, 1993, pp. 119–134.

Kaplan, J. E., Spira, T. J., Fishbein, D. B., et al. Lymphadenopathy syndrome in homosexual men. Evidence for continuing risk of developing the acquired immunodeficiency syndrome. *Journal of the American Medical Association,* 1987, *257*(3), 335–337.

Kaplan, J. E., Spira, T. J., Fishbein, D. B., and Lyn, H. S. 14-year follow-up of HIV-infected homosexual men with lymphadenopathy syndrome [letter]. *Journal of Acquired Immune Deficiency Syndromes and Human Retrovirology,* 1996, *11*(2), 206–208.

Kaplan, J. R., Adams, M. R., Clarkson, T. B., and Koritnik, D. R. Psychosocial influences on female "protection" among cynomolgus macaques. *Atherosclerosis,* 1984, *53,* 283–295.

Kaplan, J. R., Manuck, S. B., Clarkson, T. B., et al. Social status, environment, and atherosclerosis in cynomolgus monkeys. *Atherosclerosis,* 1982, *2,* 359–368.

Kaplan, N. M. Non-drug treatment of hypertension. *Annals of Internal Medicine,* 1985, *102,* 359–373.

Kaplan, R. M. Value judgment in the Oregon Medicaid experiment. *Medical Care,* 1994, *32,* 975–988.

Kaplan, R. M., and Anderson, J. P. A general health policy model: Update and applications. *Health Services Research,* 1988, *23,* 203–235.

Kaplan, R. M., Anderson, J. P., Patterson, T. L., et al. Validity of the quality of well-being scale of persons with human immunodeficiency virus infection. *Psychosomatic Medicine,* 1995, *57*(2), 138–147.

Kaplan, R. M., Atkins, C. J., and Reinsch, S. Specific efficacy expectations mediate exercise compliance in patients with COPD. *Health Psychology,* 1984, *3,* 223–242.

Kaplan R. M., and Bush J. W. Health related quality of life measurement for evaluation research and policy analysis. *Health Psychology,* 1982, *1,* 61–80.

Karasek, R. A., and Theorell, T. G. *Healthy work.* New York: Basic Books, 1990.

Karasek, R. A., Theorell, T. G., Schwartz, J., et al. Job, psychological factors and coronary heart disease: Swedish prospective findings and U.S. prevalence findings using a new occupational inference method. *Advances in Cardiology,* 1982, *29,* 62–67.

Karasek, R. A., Theorell, T. G., Schwartz, J., Schnall, P., et al. Job characteristics in relation to the prevalence of myocardial infarction in the U.S. Health Examination Survey (HES) and the Health and Nutrition Examination Survey (HANES). *American Journal of Public Health,* 1988, *78,* 910–918.

Kardiner, A., and Spiegel, H. *War stress and neurotic illness.* London: Paul B. Hoeber, 1941.

Kark, J. D., Goldman, S., and Epstein, L. Iraqi missile attacks on Israel. The association of mortality with a life-threatening stressor. *Journal of the American Medical Association,* 1995, *273*(10), 1208–1210.

Kasl, S. V. Issues in patient adherence to health care regimens. *Journal of Human Stress,* 1975, *1,* 5–17.

Kasl, S. V., and Cobb, S. Health behavior, illness behavior, and sick role behavior, Vol. 2. *Archives of Environmental Health,* 1966, *12,* 531–541.

Kasl, S. V., and Cobb, S. Blood pressure changes in men undergoing job loss. A preliminary report. *Psychosomatic Medicine,* 1970, *32,* 19–38.

Kasprowicz, A. L., Manuck, S. B., Malkoff, S. B., and Krantz, D. S. Individual differences in behaviorally evoked cardiovascular response: Temporal stability and hemodynamic patterning. *Psychophysiology,* 1990, *27,* 605–619.

Katkin, E. S., and Goldband, S. The placebo effect in biofeedback. In R. J. Gatchel and K. P. Price (Eds.), *Clinical applications of biofeedback: Appraisal and status.* Elmsford, NY: Pergamon, 1979.

Katon, W., and Sullivan, M. Depression and chronic medical illness. *Journal of Clinical Psychiatry,* 1990, *6,* 3–11.

Katz, I. R. Prevention of depression, recurrence, and complications in late life. Symposium: Disease prevention research at NIH: An agenda for all (1993, Bethesda, MD). *Preventive Medicine: An International Journal Devoted to Practice and Theory,* 1994, *23*(5), 743–750.

Katz, R. L., Kao, C. U., Spiegel, H., and Katz, G. J. Pain, acupuncture, hypnosis. In J. J. Bonica (Ed.), *Advances in neurology,* vol. 4. International symposium on pain. New York: Raven Press, 1974.

Kazdin, A. E. Covert modeling, model similarity, and reduction of avoidance behavior. *Behavior Therapy,* 1974, *5,* 325–340.

Keefe, F. J., and Williams, D. A. New directions in pain assessment and treatment. *Clinical Psychology Review,* 1989, *9*(5), 549–568.

Keefe, F. J., and Block, A. R. Development of an observation method for assessing pain behavior in chronic low back pain. *Behavior Therapy,* 1982, *13,* 363–375.

Keefe, F. J., Brown, G. K., Wallston, K. A., and Caldwell, D. S. Coping with rheumatoid arthritis pain: Catastrophizing as a maladaptive strategy. *Pain,* 1989, *37,* 51–56.

Keefe, F. J., Dunsmore, J., and Burnett, R. Behavioral and cognitive-behavioral approaches to chronic pain: Recent advances and future directions. [Review]. *Journal of Consulting and Clinical Psychology,* 1992, *60*(4), 528–536.

Keefe, F. J., and Williams, D. A. Assessment of pain behaviors. In D. C. Turk and R. Melzack (Eds.), *Handbook of pain assessment.* New York: Guilford Press, 1992, pp. 277–292.

Keesey, R. E. Psychological regulation of body energy: Implications for obesity. In A. J. Stunkard and T. A. Wadden (Eds.), *Obesity: Theory and therapy.* New York: Raven Press, 1993, pp. 77–96.

Keller, S. Physical fitness hastens recovery from psychological stress. *Medical Science Sports Exercise,* 1980, *12,* 118–119.

Kelley, H. H. Attribution theory in social psychology. In D. Levine (Ed.), *Nebraska symposium on motivation,* vol. 15. Lincoln University of Nebraska Press, 1967.

Kelly, J. A., and Murphy, D. A. Psychological interventions with AIDS and HIV: Prevention and treatment. [Review]. *Journal of Consulting and Clinical Psychology,* 1992, *60*(4), 576–585.

Kelly, J. A., Murphy, D. A., Bahr, R., et al. Factors associated with severity of depression and high risk sexual behavior among persons diagnosed with human immunodeficiency virus (HIV) infection. *Health Psychology,* 1993, *12*(3), 215–219.

Keltner, D., Ellsworth, P. C., and Edwards, K. Beyond simple pessimism: Effects of sadness and anger on social perception. *Journal of Personality and Social Psychology,* 1993, *64*(5), 740–752.

Kemp, A., and Berke, G. Effects of heparin and benzyl alcohol on lymphocyte-mediated cytotoxicity in vitro. *Cellular Immunology,* 1973, *7,* 512–515.

Kendall, R. A., and Targan, S. The dual effect of prostaglandin (PGE2) and ethanol on the natural killer cytolytic process: Effector activation and activation and NK-cell-target cell conjugate lytic inhibition. *Journal of Immunology,* 1980, *7,* 2770–2777.

Kennedy, G. H., Hafer, M. A., Cohen, D., et al. Significance of depression and cognitive impairment in patients undergoing programmed stimulation of cardiac arrhythmias. *Psychosomatic Medicine,* 1987, *49,* 410–421.

Kety, S. S., Rosenthal, D., Wender, P. H., and Schulsinger, F. Mental illness in the biological and adoptive families of adopted schizophrenics. *American Journal of Psychiatry,* 1971, *128,* 302–306.

Keys, A. Overweight, obesity, coronary heart disease and mortality. *Nutrition Review,* 1980, *38,* 297–307.

Keys, A., Taylor, H. L., Blackburn, H., Brozek, J., et al. Mortality and coronary heart disease among men studied for 23 years. *Archives of Internal Medicine,* 1971, *128,* 201–214.

Kiecolt-Glaser, J. K., Garner, W. K., Speicher, C., et al. Psychosocial modifiers of immunocompetence in medical students. *Psychosomatic Medicine,* 1984, *46*(1), 7–14.

Kiecolt-Glaser, J. K., and Glaser, R. Psychosocial moderators of immune function. *Annals of Behavioral Medicine,* 1987, *9*(2), 16–20.

Kiecolt-Glaser, J. K., Glaser, R., Gravestein, S., et al. Chronic stress alters the immune response to influenza virus vaccine in older adults. *Proceedings of the National Academy of Science,* 1996, *93*(7), 3043–3047.

Kiecolt-Glaser, J. K., Glaser, R., Shuttleworth, E. C., et al. Chronic stress and immunity in family caregivers of Alzheimer's disease victims. *Psychosomatic Medicine,* 1987, *49*(5), 523–535.

Kiecolt-Glaser, J. K., Glaser, R., Strain, E. C., et al. Modulation of cellular immunity in medical students. *Journal of Behavioral Medicine,* 1986, *9,* 311–320.

Kiecolt-Glaser, J. K., Glaser, R., Williger, D., et al. Psychosocial enhancement of immunocompetence in a geriatric population. *Health Psychology,* 1985, *4*(1), 24–41.

Kiecolt-Glaser, J. K., Malarkey, W., Cacioppo, J. T., and Glaser, R. In R. Glaser and J. K. Kiecolt-Glaser (Eds.), *Handbook of human stress and immunity.* San Diego: Academic Press, 1994, pp. 321–339.

Kiecolt-Glaser, J. K., Marucha, P. T., Malarkey, W. B., et al. Slowing of wound healing by psychological stress. *Lancet,* 1995, *346,* 1194–1196.

Kiecolt-Glaser, J. K., Stephens, R. E., Lipetz, P. D., et al. Distress and DNA repair in human lymphocytes. *Journal of Behavioral Medicine,* 1985, *8*(4), 311–320.

Killen, J. D., Fortmann, S. P., Kraemer, H. C., et al. Who will relapse? Symptoms of nicotine dependence predict long-term relapse after smoking cessation. *Journal of Consulting and Clinical Psychology,* 1992, *60*(5), 797–801.

Killworth, D., and Bernard, H. A. A model of human group dynamics. *Social Science Research,* 1976, *5,* 173–224.

Kinney, R. K., Gatchel, R. J., and Mayer, T. G. The SCL-90R evaluated as an alternative to the MMPI for psychological screening of chronic low-back pain patients. *Spine,* 1991, *16,* 940–942.

Kirsner, J. B. Peptic ulcer: A review of the current literature on various clinical aspects. *Gastroenterology,* 1968, *54,* 610–618.

Kiser, R. S., Khatami, M., Gatchel R. J., et al. Acupuncture relief of chronic pain syndrome correlates with increased plasma net-enkephalin concentrations. *Lancet,* 1983, *2,* 1394–1396.

Kiyak, H. A., Vitaliano, P. P., and Crinean, J. Patients' expectations as predictors of orthognathic surgery outcomes. *Health Psychology,* 1988, *7*(3), 251–268.

Klein, D. C., and Seligman, M. E. P. Reversal of performance deficits and perceptual deficits in learned helplessness and depression. *Journal of Abnormal Psychology,* 1976, *85,* 11–26.

Klein, R. F., Kliner, V. A., Zipes, D. P., et al. Transfer from a coronary care unit. *Archives of Internal Medicine,* 1968, *122,* 104–108.

Klem, C. P. Restrained eating. *Psychiatric Clinics of North America,* 1978, *1,* 593–607.

Klem, M. L., Klesges, R. C., Bene, C. R., and Mellon, M. W. A psychometric study of restraint: The impact of race, gender, weight, and marital status. *Addictive Behaviors,* 1990, *15,* 147–152.

Klesges, R. C., and Shumaker, S. A. Understanding the relations between smoking and body weight and their importance to smoking cessation and relapse. *Health Psychology,* 1992, *11*(suppl.), 1–3.

Kline, A., and Strickler, J. Perceptions of risk for AIDS among women in drug treatment. *Health Psychology,* 1993, *12*(4), 313–323.

Klopfer, B., Ainsworth, M., Klopfer, W. G., and Holt, R. R. *Developments in the Rorschach technique,* vol. 1, *Techniques and theory.* Yonkers-on-Hudson, NY: World Book, 1954.

Kobasa, S. C. Stressful life events, personality and health: An inquiry into hardness. *Journal of Personality and Social Psychology,* 1979, *39,* 1–11.

Kobasa, S. C., Maddi, S. R., and Kahn, S. Hardiness and health: A prospective study. *Journal of Personality and Social Psychology,* 1982, *42,* 168–177.

Kobasa, S. C., Maddi, S. R., Salvatore, R., et al. Effectiveness of hardiness, exercise and social support as resources against illness. *Journal of Psychosomatic Research,* 1985, *29*(5), 525–533.

Koos, E. *The health of Regionville.* New York: Columbia University Press, 1954.

Koriat, A., Melkman, R., Averill, J. R., and Lazarus, R. S. The self-control of emotional reactions to a stressful film. *Journal of Personality,* 1972, *40,* 601–619.

Kormos, R. L., Murali, S., Dew, M. A., et al. Chronic mechanical circulatory support: Rehabilitation, low morbidity and superior survival after heart transplant. *Annals of Thoracic Surgery,* 1994, *57,* 51–58.

Kormos, R. I., Murali, S., Dew, M. A., et al. Development of a quality of life protocol for left ventricular assist device clinical trials. *ASAIO (American Society for Artificial Internal Organs)*, 1995, *41*, 32–41.

Kornblith, A. B., Herr, H. W., Ofman, U. S., et al. Quality of life of patients with prostate cancer and their spouses. The value of a data base in clinical care. *Cancer*, 1994, 73(11), 2791–2802.

Kornblith, A. B., and Holland, J. C. *Handbook of measures for psychological, social and physical function in cancer, Volume 1: Quality of life.* New York: Memorial Sloan-Kettering Cancer Center, 1994.

Korsch, B. M., Fine, R. N., and Negrete, V. F. Noncompliance in children with renal transplants. *Pediatrics*, 1978, *61*, 872–876.

Korsch, B. M., Freeman, B., and Negrete, V. F. Practical implications of doctor-patient interactions. Analysis for pediatric practice. *American Journal of Diseases of Children*, 1971, *121*, 110–114.

Korsch, B. M., Gozzi, E. K., and Francis, V. Gaps in doctor-patient communication, 1. Doctor-patient interaction and patient satisfaction. *Pediatrics*, 1968, *42*, 855–871.

Korsch, B. M., and Negrete, V. F. Doctor-patient communication. *Scientific American*, 1972, *227*, 66–74.

Kotler, T. Avoidant attachment as a risk factor for health. *British Journal of Medical Psychology*, 1994, *67*(3), 237–245.

Krantz, D. S. A naturalistic study of social influences on meal size among moderately obese and nonobese subjects. *Psychosomatic Medicine*, 1979, *41*(1), 19–27.

———. Cognitive processes and recovery from heart attack: A review and theoretical analysis. *Journal of Human Stress*, 1980, *6*(3), 27–38.

Krantz, D. S., Baum, A., and Singer, J. E. (Eds.). *Handbook of psychology and health*, vol. 3, *Cardiovascular disorders and behavior.* Hillsdale, NJ: Erlbaum, 1983.

Krantz, D. S., Baum, A., and Wideman, M. H. Assessment of preferences for self-treatment and information in health care. *Journal of Personality and Social Psychology*, 1980, *39*, 977–990.

Krantz, D. S., Contrada, R. J., LaRiccia, P. J., et al. Effects of beta-adrenergic stimulation and blockade on cardiovascular reactivity, affect and Type A behavior. *Psychosomatic Medicine*, 1987, *49*, 146–158.

Krantz, D. S., and Deckel, A. W. Coping with coronary heart disease and stroke. In T. G. Burish and L. A. Bradley (Eds.), *Coping with chronic disease: Research and applications.* New York: Academic Press, 1983.

Krantz, D. S., and Durel, L. A. Psychobiological substrates of the Type A behavior pattern. *Health Psychology*, 1983, *2*, 393–411.

Krantz, D. S., Glass, D. C., Contrada, R., and Miller, N. E. Behavior and health. *National Science Foundation's second five-year outlook on science and technology.* Washington, DC: U.S. Government Printing Office, 1981.

Krantz, D. S., Glass, D. C., and Snyder, M. L. Helplessness, stress level, and the coronary-prone behavior pattern. *Journal of Experimental Social Psychology*, 1974, *10*, 284–300.

Krantz, D. S., Grunberg, N. E., and Baum, A. Health psychology. *Annual Review of Psychology*, 1985, *36*, 349–383.

Krantz, D. S., Kop, W. J., Santiago, H. T., and Gottdiener, J. S. Mental stress as a trigger of myocardial ischemia and infraction. *Cardiology Clinics of North America*, 1996, *14*, 271–277.

Krantz, D. S., and Manuck, S. B. Acute psychophysiologic reactivity and risk of cardiovascular disease: A review and methodologic critique. *Psychological Bulletin*, 1984, *96*, 435–464.

Krantz, D. S., Sanmarco, M. I., Selvester, R. H., and Matthews, K. A. Psychological correlates of progression of atherosclerosis in men. *Psychosomatic Medicine*, 1979, *41*, 467–475.

Krantz, D. S., and Schulz, R. A model of life crises, control, and health outcomes: Cardiac rehabilitation and relocation of the elderly. In A. Baum and J. E. Singer (Eds.), *Advances in environmental psychology*, vol. 2. Hillsdale, NJ: Erlbaum, 1980.

Krasner, L. Assessment of token economy programs in psychiatric hospitals. In N. H. Miller and R. Porter (Eds.), *Learning theory and psychotherapy*. London: CIBA Foundation, 1968.

Krasnoff, A. Psychological variables and human cancer. A cross-validation study. *Psychosomatic Medicine*, 1959, *21*(4), 291–295.

Kreis, B., Peltier, A., Fournaud, S., et al. Reaction de precipitation entre certains serum humains et des extraits solubles de tabac. *Annales de Medicine Interne* (Paris), 1970, *121*, 437–440.

Krueger, R. B., Levy, E. M., Cathcart, E. S., et al. Lymphocyte subsets in patients with major depression: Preliminary findings. *Advances*, 1984, *1*, 5–9.

Kulik, J. A., and Mahler, H. I. M. Effects of preoperative roommate assignment on preoperative anxiety and recovery from coronary bypass surgery. *Health Psychology*, 1987, *6*, 525–543.

Kulik, J. A., and Mahler, H. I. M. Stress and affiliation research: On taking the laboratory to health field settings. *Annals of Behavioral Medicine*, 1990, *12*(3), 106–111.

Kulik, J. A., Moore, P. J., and Mahler, H. I. M. Stress and affiliation: Hospital roommate effects on preoperative anxiety and social interaction. *Health Psychology*, 1993, *12*, 118–124.

Kulka, R., Schlenger, W., Fairbank, J., et al. Assessment of the prevalence of posttraumatic stress disorder in a community epidemiological study: The national Vietnam veterans readjustment study. Paper presented at the American Psychological Association annual meeting, Atlanta, GA, August 1988.

Kune, G. A., Kune, S., Watson, L. F., and Bahnson, C. B. Personality as a risk factor in large bowel cancer: Data from the Melbourne Colorectal Cancer Study. *Psychological Medicine*, 1991, *21*(1), 29–41.

Lacey, J. I. Somatic response patterning and stress: Some revisions of activation theory. In M. H. Appley and R. Trumbull (Eds.), *Psychological stress*. New York: McGraw-Hill, 1967.

LaCroix, A. Z., and Haynes, S. G. Gender differences in the health effects of workplace roles. In R. C. Barnett, L. Biener, and G. K. Baruch (Eds.), *Gender and stress*. New York: Free Press, 1987.

LaCroix, A. Z., Lang, J., Scherr, P., et al. Smoking and mortality among older men and women in three communities. *New England Journal of Medicine*, 1991, *324*, 1619–1625.

Lalonde, M. The diseases of choice are in our hands. *Dimensions in Health Service*, 1974, *51*, 8, 11.

Lambley, P. The role of psychological processes in the aetiology and treatment of cervical cancer: A biopsychological perspective. *British Journal of Medical Psychology*, 1993, *66*(1), 43–60.

Lando, H. A. Successful treatment of smokers with a broad-spectrum behavioral approach. *Journal of Consulting and Clinical Psychology*, 1977, *41*, 361–366.

Lang, A., and Marlatt, G. A. Problem drinking: A social learning perspective. In R. J. Gatchel, A. Baum, and J. E. Singer (Eds.), *Behavioral medicine and clinical psychology: Overlapping disciplines*. Hillsdale, NJ: Erlbaum, 1982.

Lang, P. J. Autonomic control or learning to play the internal organs. *Psychology Today*, 1970, *4*, 39–44, 82–84.

Lang, P. J., Melamed, B. G., and Hart, J. A. Psychophysiological analysis of fear modification using automated desensitization procedure. *Journal of Abnormal Psychology,* 1970, *76,* 220–234.

Lange, C. The emotions. In K. Dunlap (Ed.), *The emotions.* Baltimore: Williams & Wilkins, 1922.

Lange, W. R., and Dax, E. M. HIV infection and international travel. *American Family Physician,* 1987, *36*(3), 197–204.

Langer, E. J. The illusion of control. *Journal of Personality and Social Psychology,* 1975, *32,* 311–328.

Langer, E. J., Janis, I. L., and Wolfer, J. A. Reduction of psychological stress in surgical patients. *Journal of Experimental Social Psychology,* 1975, *11,* 155–165.

Langer, E. J., and Rodin, J. The effects of choice and enhanced personal responsibility for the aged: A field experiment in an institutional setting. *Journal of Personality and Social Psychology,* 1976, *34,* 191–198.

Langer, E. J., and Roth, J. Heads I win, tails it's chance: The illusion of control as a function of the sequence of outcomes in a purely chance task. *Journal of Personality and Social Psychology,* 1975, *32,* 951–955.

Langer, E. J., and Saegert, S. Crowding and cognitive control. *Journal of Personality and Social Psychology,* 1977, *35,* 175–182.

Lanza, A. F., Cameron, A. E., and Revenson, T. A. Perceptions of helpful and unhelpful support among married individuals with rheumatic diseases. *Psychology and Health,* 1995, *10,* 449–462.

LaPerriere, A., Fletcher, M. A., Antoni, M. H., et al. Aerobic exercise training in an AIDS risk group. *International Journal of Sports Medicine,* 1991, *12,* S53–S57.

Laudenslager, M. L., Ryan, S. M., Drugan, R. C., et al. Coping and immunosuppression: Inescapable but not escapable shock suppresses lymphocyte proliferation. *Science,* 1983, *221,* 568–570.

Laux, D. C., and Klesius, P. H. Suppressive effects of caffeine on immune-response of mouse to sheep erythrocytes. *Proceedings of the Society for Experimental Biology and Medicine,* 1973, *144*(2), 633–638.

Lawler, J. E., Barker, G. F., Hubbard, J. W., and Allen, M. T. The effects of conflict on tonic levels of blood pressure in the genetically borderline hypertensive rat. *Psychophysiology,* 1980, *17,* 363–370.

Lawlis, G. F., Selby, D., Hinnant, D., and McCoy, C. E. Reduction of postoperative pain parameters by presurgical relaxation instructions for spinal pain patients. *Spine,* 1985, *10,* 649–651.

Lazarus, A. A. *Behavior therapy and beyond.* New York: McGraw-Hill, 1971.

Lazarus, R. S. Story telling and the measurement of motivation: The direct versus substitutive controversy. *Journal of Consulting Psychology,* 1966, *30,* 483–487.

———. Cognition and motivation in emotion. Ninety-eighth Annual Convention of the American Psychological Association Distinguished Scientific Contributions Award Address, 1990, Boston, MA. *American Psychologist,* 1991, *46*(4), 352–367.

———. From psychological stress to the emotions: A history of changing outlooks. *Annual Review of Psychology,* 1993, *44,* 1–21.

Lazarus, R. S., and Alfert, E. The short-circuiting of threat by experimentally altering cognitive appraisal. *Journal of Abnormal and Social Psychology,* 1964, *69,* 195–205.

Lazarus, R. S., and Cohen, J. B. Environmental stress. In I. Attman and J. F. Wohlwill (Eds.), *Human behavior and the enviuronment: Current theory and research,* vol. 2. New York: Springer, 1977.

Lazarus, R. S., and Cohen, J. B. Environmental stress. In I. Altman and J. F. Wohlwill (Eds.), *Human behavior and the environment: Current theory and research,* vol. 2. New York: Plenum, 1978, pp. 89–127.

Lazarus, R. S., and Folkman, S. *Stress, appraisal and coping.* New York: Springer, 1984.

Lazarus, R. S., and Launier, R. Stress-related transactions between person and environment. In L. A. Pervin and M. Lewis (Eds.), *Internal and external determinants of behavior.* New York: Plenum, 1978.

Lazarus, R. S., Opton, E. M., Jr., Nomikos, M. S., and Rankin, N. O. The principle of short-circuiting of threat: Further evidence. *Journal of Personality,* 1965, *33,* 622–635.

Leedham, B. Positive expectations predict health after heart transplant. *Health Psychology,* 1995, *14*(1), 74–79.

Lemanek, K. L. Commentary: Childhood asthma. Special issue: Pediatric chronic disease. *Journal of Pediatric Psychology,* 1995, *20*(4), 423–427.

Lemieux, A. M., and Coe, C. L. Abuse related PTSD: Evidence for chronic neuroendocrine activation in women. *Psychosomatic Medicine,* 1995, *57*(2), 105–115.

Leon, G. R. *Case histories of deviant behavior: An interactional perspective* (2nd ed.). Boston: Allyn and Bacon, 1977.

Le Panto, R., Moroney, W., and Zenhausern, R. The contribution of anxiety to the laboratory investigation of pain. *Psychonomic Science,* 1965, *3,* 475.

Lepore, S. J., Evans, G. W., and Palsane, M. N. Social hassles and psychological health in the context of chronic crowding. *Journal of Health and Social Behavior,* 1991, *32,* 357–367.

Lepore, S. J., Evans, G. W., and Schneider, M. L. Role of control and social support in explaining the stress of hassles and crowding. *Environment and Behavior,* 1992, *24,* 795–811.

Lerman, C. Genetic testing for heritable cancer risk: Challenges for behavioral medicine scientists. Paper presented at the meeting of the Academy of Behavioral Medicine Research, Williamsburg, VA, June 1995.

Lerman, C., Trock, B., Rimer, B. K., et al. Psychological side effects of breast cancer screening. *Health Psychology,* 1991, *10,* 259–267.

Lerner, D. J., and Kannel, W. B. Patterns of coronary heart disease mortality in the sexes: A 26-year follow-up of the Framingham population. *American Heart Journal,* 1986, *111,* 383–390.

Le Shan, L. L. Psychological states as factors in the development of malignant disease: A critical review. *Journal of the National Cancer Institute,* 1959, *29,* 1–18.

Lester, N., Smart, L., and Baum, A. Measuring coping flexibility. *Psychology and Health,* 1994, *9,* 409–424.

Leventhal, H. Findings and theory in the study of fear communications. In L. Berkowitz (Ed.), *Advances in experimental social psychology,* vol. 5. New York: Academic Press, 1970.

———. Toward a comprehensive theory of emotion. In L. Berkowitz (Ed.), *Advances in experimental social psychology,* vol. 13. New York: Academic Press, 1980, pp. 139–207.

Leventhal, H., and Avis, N. Pleasure, addiction, and habit: Factors in verbal report on factors in smoking behavior. *Journal of Abnormal Psychology,* 1976, *85,* 478–488.

Leventhal, H., and Cleary, P. D. The smoking problem: A review of the research and theory in behavioral risk modification. *Psychological Bulletin,* 1980, *88,* 370–405.

Leventhal, H., Diefenbach, M., and Leventhal, E. A. Illness cognition: Using common sense to understand treatment adherence and affect cognition interactions. Special issue: Cognitive perspectives in health psychology. *Cognitive Therapy and Research,* 1992, *16*(2), 143–163.

Leventhal, H., and Hirshman, R. S. Social psychology and prevention. In G. E. Sanders and J. Suls (Eds.), *Social psychology of health and illness.* Hillsdale, NJ: Erlbaum, 1982.

Leventhal, H., Meyer, D., and Nerenz, D. The common sense representation of illness danger. In S. Rachman (Ed.), *Medical psychology,* vol. 2. New York: Pergamon, 1980.

Leventhal, H., Nerenz, D., and Leventhal, E. Feeling of threat and private views of illness: Factors in dehumanization in the medical care system. In A. Baum and J. E.

Singer (Eds.), *Advances in environmental psychology,* vol. 4. Hillsdale, NJ: Erlbaum, 1982.

Leventhal, H., Prohaska, T. R., and Hirshman, R. S. Preventive health behavior across the life span. In J. C. Rosen and L. J. Solomon (Eds.), *Prevention in health psychology.* Hanover, NH: University Press of New England, 1985.

Levi, L. The urinary output of adrenalin and noradrenalin during pleasant and unpleasant emotional stress. *Psychosomatic Medicine,* 1965, *27,* 80–85.

———. Psychosocial stress and disease: A conceptual model. In E. K. Gunderson and R. H. Rahe (Eds.), *Life stress and illness.* Springfield, IL: Charles C. Thomas, 1974.

Levi, L., (Ed.). *Society, stress and disease: Male/female roles and relationships,* vol. 3. London: Oxford University Press, 1978.

Levine J. D., Gordon, N. C., and Fields, H. L. The mechanism of placebo analgesia. *Lancet,* 1978, *2,* 654–657.

Levine, J. D., Gormley, J., and Fields, H. L. Observations on the analgesic effects of needle puncture (acupuncture). *Pain,* 1976, *2,* 149–159.

Levy, R. S., Tendler, C., VanDevanter, M., and Cleary, P. D. A group intervention model for individuals testing positive for HIV antibody. *American Journal of Orthopsychiatry,* 1990, *60*(3), 452–459.

Levy, S. M. Death and dying: Behavioral and social factors that contribute to the process. In T. G. Burish and L. A. Bradley (Eds.), *Coping with chronic disease: Research and applications.* New York: Academic Press, 1983.

Levy, S. M., Herberman, R. B., Lippman, M., et al. Immunological and psychological predictors of disease recurrence in patients with early stage breast cancer. *Behavioral Medicine,* 1991, *17*(2), 67–75.

Levy, S. M., Herberman, R. B., Maluish, A. M., et al. Prognostic risk assessment in primary breast cancer by behavioral and immunological parameters. *Health Psychology,* 1985, *4,* 99–113.

Levy, S. M., Herberman, R. B., Whiteside, T., et al. Perceived social support and tumor estrogen/progesterone receptor status as predictors of natural killer cell activity in breast cancer patients. *Psychosomatic Medicine,* 1990, *52,* 73–85.

Lewin, B., Robertson, J. H., Cay E. L., et al. Effects of self-help post-myocardial-infarction rehabilitation on psychological adjustment and use of health services. *Clinical Practice,* 1992, *339,* 1036–1040.

Lewinsohn, P. M. The coping-with depression course. In R. F. Monoz (Ed.), *Depression prevention: Research directions. The series in clinical and community psychology,* 1987, 159–170.

Lewinsohn, P. M., Hoberman, H. M., and Rosenbaum, M. A prospective study of risk factors for unipolar depression. *Journal of Abnormal Psychology,* 1988, *97*(3), 251–264.

Ley, P. Psychological studies of doctor-patient communication. In S. Rachman (Ed.), *Contributions to medical psychology.* New York: Pergamon, 1977.

Ley, P., Bradshaw, P. W., Kincey, J., and Atherton, S. T. Increasing patients' satisfaction with communication. *British Journal of Social and Clinical Psychology,* 1976, *15,* 403–413.

Ley, P., and Spelman, M. S. *Communicating with the patient.* London: Staples Press, 1967.

Lezack, M. D. *Neuropsychological assessment.* New York: Oxford University Press, 1976.

Lichtenstein, E. The smoking problem: A behavioral perspective. *Journal of Consulting and Clinical Psychology,* 1982, *50*(6), 804–819.

Lichtenstein, E., and Glasgow, R. E. Smoking cessation: What have we learned over the past decade? Special issue: Behavioral medicine: An update for the 1990s. *Journal of Consulting and Clinical Psychology,* 1992, *60*(4), 518–527.

Lichtenstein, E., and Penner, M. D. Long-term effects of rapid smoking treatment for dependent cigarette smokers. *Addictive Behaviors,* 1977, *2,* 109–112.

Lichtman, R. R., and Taylor, S. E. Close relationships and the female cancer patient. Women with cancer: Psychological perspectives. In B. L. Andersen (Ed.), *Contributions to psychology and medicine.* New York: Springer-Verlag, 1988, 233–256.

Light, K. C., and Sherwood, A. Race, borderline hypertension, and hemodynamic responses to behavioral stress before and after beta-adrenergic blockade. *Health Psychology,* 1989, *8*(5), 577–595.

Lin, E. H. B., and Peterson, C. Pessimistic explanatory style and response to illness. *Behavior Research and Therapy,* 1990, *28,* 243–248.

Lin, E. H. B., et al. The role of the primary care physician in patients' adherence to antidepressant therapy. *Medical Care,* 1995, *33*(1), 67–74.

Lin, E. H. B., Von Korff, M., Katon, W., and Bush T. The role of the primary care physician in patients' adherence to antidepressant therapy. *Medical Care,* 1995, *33*(1), 67–74.

Lindsley, D. B., and Sassamon, W. H. Autonomic activity and brain potentials associated with "voluntary control of the pilomotors." *Journal of Neurophysiology,* 1938, *1,* 342–349.

Lindzey, G., Loehlin, J., Manosevitz, M., and Thiessen, D. Behavioral genetics. *Annual Review of Psychology,* 1971, *22,* 39–94.

Linet, M. G., Stewart, W. F., Clentano, D. D., et al. An epidemiologic study of headache among adolescents and young adults. *Journal of the American Medical Association,* 1989, *261,* 2211–2216.

Lipkus, I. M., Barefoot, J. C., Feaganes, J., and Williams, R. B. A short MMPI scale to identify people likely to begin smoking. *Journal of Personality Assessment,* 1994, *62*(2), 213–222.

Lipkus, I. M., Barefoot, J. C., Williams, R. B., and Siegler, I. C. Personality measures as predictors of smoking initiation and cessation: The UNC Alumni Heart Study. *Health Psychology,* 1994, *13*(2), 149–155.

Lipowski, Z. J. Psychosomatic medicine in the seventies: An overview. *American Journal of Psychiatry,* 1977, *134,* 233–243.

Lipp, M. R., Looney, J. G., and Spitzer R. L. Classifying psychophysiologic disorders: A new idea. *Psychosomatic Medicine,* 1977, *39,* 285–287.

Lloyd, R. W., and Salzberg, S. C. Controlled social drinking: An alternative to abstinence as a treatment goal for some alcohol abuses. *Psychological Bulletin,* 1975, *82,* 815–842.

Locke, S. E., Hurst, M. W., Williams, R. M., and Heisel, I. S. The influences of psychosocial factors on human cell-mediated immune function. Paper presented at the meeting of the American Psychosomatic Society, Washington, DC, 1978.

Loesser, J. D. Dorsal rhizotomy: Indications and results. In J. J. Bonica (Ed.), *Advances in neurology: International symposium on pain,* vol. 4. New York: Raven Press, 1974.

Long, D. M. Use of peripheral and spinal cord stimulation in the relief of chronic pain. In J. J. Bonica and D. Albe-Fessard (Eds.), *Advances in pain research therapy,* vol. 1. New York: Raven Press, 1976.

Lorig, K., Chastain, R. L., Ung, E., et al. Development and evaluation of a scale to measure perceived self-efficacy in people with arthritis. *Arthritis and Rheumatism,* 1989. *32,* 37–44.

Louria, D. B. Susceptibility to infection during experimental alcohol intoxication. *Transactions of the Association of American Physicians,* 1963, *76,* 102–110.

Lous, I., and Olesen, J. Evaluation of pericranial tenderness and oral function in patients with common migraine, muscle contraction headache and combination headache. *Pain,* 1982, *12,* 385–393.

Luborsky, L., Crits-Christoph, P., Brady, J. P., et al. Antihypertensive effects of behavioral treatments and medications compared. *New England Journal of Medicine,* 1980, *302,* 586.

Luborsky, L., Mintz, J., Brightman, J., and Katcher, A. Herpes simplex virus and moods: A longitudinal study. *Journal of Psychosomatic Research*, 1976, *20*, 543–548.

Ludwick-Rosenthal, R., and Neufeld, W. J. Stress management during noxious medical procedures: An evaluation review of outcome studies. *Psychological Bulletin*, 1988, *104*, 326–342.

Ludwig, E. G., and Collette, J. Dependency, social isolation, and mental health in a disabled population. *Social Psychiatry*, 1970, *5*, 92–95.

Luft, F., Block, R., Weyman, A., Murray, Z., and Weinberger, M. Cardiovascular responses to extremes of salt intake in man. *Clinical Research*, 1978, *26*, 265A.

Lumley, M. A., Abeles, L. A., Melamed, B. G., and Pistone, L. M. Coping outcomes in children undergoing stressful medical procedures: The role of child-environment variables. *Behavioral Assessment*, 1990, *12*(2), 233–238.

Lund, A. K., and Kegeles, S. Increasing adolescents' acceptance of long-term personal health behavior. *Health Psychology*, 1982, *1*, 27–43.

Lundberg, U., and Frankenhaeuser, M. Adjustment to noise stress. Reports from the Department of Psychology, University of Stockholm (484), 1976.

Lundy, J., Raaf, J. H., Deakins, S., et al. The acute and chronic effects of alcohol on the human immune system. *Surgery, Gynecology and Obstetrics*, 1975, *141*(2), 212–218.

Luria, A. R. *The mind of a mnemonist*. Translated by L. Solotaroff. New York: Basic Books, 1958.

Lutgendorf, S. K., Antoni, M. H., Kumar, M., and Schneiderman, N. Changes in cognitive coping strategies predict EBV-antibody titer change following a stressor disclosure induction. *Journal of Psychosomatic Research*, 1994, *38*(1), 63–78.

Lutz, R. W., Silbret, M., and Olshan N. Treatment outcome and compliance with the therapeutic regimens: Long-term follow-up of a multidisciplinary pain program. *Pain*, 1983, *17*(3), 301–308.

Lynch, H. T., Watson, P., Smyrk, T. C., et al. Colon cancer genetics. (Review.) *Cancer*, 1992, *70*(suppl. 5), 1300–1312.

Lynch, P. N., and Zamble, E. A controlled behavioral treatment of irritable bowel syndrome. *Behavior Therapy*, 1989, *20*, 509–523.

MacLeod, A. K., Williams, J. M., and Bekerian, D. A. Worry is reasonable: The role of explanations in pessimism about future personal events. *Journal of Abnormal Psychology*, 1991 *100*(4), 478–486.

McCann, B. S., Bovbjerg, V. E., Brief, D. J., et al. Relationship of self-efficacy to cholesterol lowering and dietary change in hyperlipidemia. *Annals of Behavioral Medicine*, 1995, *17*(3), 221–233.

McCaul, K. D., Monson, N., and Maki, R. H. Does distraction reduce pain-produced distress among college students? *Health Psychology*, 1992, *11*(4), 210–217.

McClelland, D. C., Atkinson, J. W., Clark, R. A., and Lowell, E. L. *The achievement motive*. New York: Appleton, 1953.

McClelland, D. C., David, W. N., Kahn, R., and Wanner, E. *The drinking man*. New York: Free Press, 1972.

McClure, C. M. Cardiac arrest through volition. *California Medicine*, 1959, *90*, 440–446.

McCreary, C. P., Clark, G. T., Merril, R. L., et al. Psychological distress and diagnostic subgroups of temporomandibular disorder patients. *Pain*, 1991, *44*, 19–24.

McFall, M. E., Murburg, M. M., Ko, G. N., and Veith, R. C. Autonomic responses to stress in Vietnam combat veterans with posttraumatic stress disorder. *Biological Psychiatry*, 1990, *27*(10), 1165–1175.

McFall, R. M., and Lillesand, D. V. Behavior rehearsal with modeling and coaching in assertive training. *Journal of Abnormal Psychology*, 1971, *77*, 313–323.

McFall, R. M., and Marston, A. An experimental investigation of behavior rehearsal in assertive training. *Journal of Abnormal Psychology*, 1970, *76*, 295–303.

McFall, R. M., and Twentyman, C. T. Four experiments on the relative contribution of rehearsal, modeling, and coaching to assertive training. *Journal of Abnormal Psychology,* 1973, *81,* 199–218.

McFarland, P. H., and Stanton, A. L. Preparation of children for emergency medical care: A primary prevention approach. *Journal of Pediatric Psychology,* 1991, *16,* 489–504.

McGrath, J. E. *Social and psychological factors in stress.* New York: Holt, Rinehart and Winston, 1970.

McHorney, C. A., Ware, J. E., and Raczek, A. E. The MOS 36-item short-form health survey (SF-36): II. Psychometric and clinical tests of validity in measuring physical and mental health constructs. *Medical Care,* 1993, *31*(3), 247–263.

McHugh, S., and Vallis, T. M. (Eds.). *Illness behavior: A multidisciplinary model.* New York: Plenum, 1986.

McKean, K. J. Using multiple risk factors to assess the behavioral, cognitive, and affective effects of learned helplessness. *Journal of Psychology,* 1994, *128*(2), 177–183.

McKenna, F., and Wright, V. Pain and rheumatoid arthritis. *Annals of Rheumatic Disease,* 1985, *44,* 805.

McKenney, J. M., Slining, J. M., Henderson, H. R., et al. The effect of clinical pharmacy services on patients with essential hypertension. *Circulation,* 1973, *48,* 1104–1111.

McKinnon, W., Weisse, C. S., Reynolds, C. P., et al. Chronic stress, leukocyte sub-populations, and humoral response to latent viruses. *Health Psychology,* 1989, *8,* 389–402.

McKusick, L., Horstman, W., and Coates, T. AIDS and sexual behavior reported by gay men in San Fransisco. *American Journal of Public Health,* 1985, *75,* 493–496.

McLaughlin, M., Cormier, L. S., and Cormier, W. H. Relation between coping strategies and distress, stress, and marital adjustment of multiple-role women. *Journal of Counseling Psychology,* 1988, *35*(2), 187–193.

McMahan, C. E., and Hastrup, J. L. The role of imagination in the disease process: Post-Cartesian history. *Journal of Behavioral Medicine,* 1980, *3,* 205–217.

McNair, D. M., Lorr, M., and Dropelman, L. F. *Profile of mood states.* San Diego: Educational and Testing Service, 1981.

McNamee, H. B., Mello, V. K., and Mendelson, T. H. Experimental analysis of drinking patterns of alcoholics: Concurrent psychiatric observations. *American Journal of Psychiatry,* 1968, *124,* 1063–1071.

Magni, G., Caldieron, C., Rigatti-Luchini, S., and Merskey, M. Chronic musculoskeletal pain and depressive symptoms in the general population: An analysis of the First National Health and Nutrition Examination Survey data. *Pain,* 1990, *43,* 299–307.

Mahler, H. I. M., and Kulik, J. A. Health care involvement preferences and social-emotional recovery of male coronary-artery-bypass patients. *Health Psychology,* 1991, *10,* 399–408.

Mahler, H. I. M., Kulik, J. A., and Hill, M. R. Effects of videotape preparations of recovery of female coronary bypass surgery patients. *Mind/Body Medicine,* 1995, *1*(3), 121–129.

Mahoney, M. J. *Cognition and behavior modification.* Cambridge, MA: Ballinger, 1974.

Mahoney, M. J., and Arnkoff, D. B. Self-management. In O. F. Pomerleau and J. P. Brady (Eds), *Behavioral medicine: Theory and practice.* Baltimore: Williams & Wilkins, 1979.

Mahoney, M. J., Moura, N. G. M., and Wade, T. C. The relative efficacy of self-reward, self-punishment, and self-monitoring techniques for weight loss. *Journal of Consulting and Clinical Psychology,* 1973, *40,* 404–407.

Maier, S. F., Laudenslager, M. L., and Ryan, S. M. Stressor controllability, immune function, and endogenous opiates. In F. R. Brush and H. J. B. Overmier (Eds.), *Affect, conditioning and cognition: Essays on the determinants of behavior.* Hillsdale, NJ: Erlbaum, 1985.

Maier, S. F., Sherman, J. E., Lewis, J. W., et al. Opioid-nonopioid nature of stress-induced analgesia and learned helplessness. *Journal of Experimental Psychology-Animal Behavior Processes*, 1983, *9*(1), 80–90.

Maier, S. F., Watkins, L. R., and Fleshner, M. Psychoneuroimmunology. The interface between behavior, brain, and immunity. *American Psychologist*, 1994, *49*(12), 1004–1017.

Malarkey, W. B., Kiecolt-Glaser, J. K., Pearl, D., and Glaser, R. Hostile behavior during marital conflict alters pituitary and adrenal hormones. *Psychosomatic Medicine*, 1994, *56*, 41–51.

Malloy, P. E., Fairbank, J. A., and Keane, T. M. Validation of a multimethod assessment of post-traumatic stress disorder in Vietnam veterans. *Journal of Consulting and Clinical Psychology*, 1983, *4*, 488–494.

Malmo, R. B., and Shagass, C. Physiologic study of symptom mechanisms in psychiatry patients under stress. *Psychosomatic Medicine*, 1949, *11*, 25–29.

Mann, G. V. Diet-heart: End of an era. *New England Journal of Medicine*, 1977, *297*, 644–650.

Manne, S. L., Bakeman, R., Jacobsen, P. B., and Gorfinkle, K. Adult-child interaction during invasive medical procedures. *Health Psychology*, 1992, *11*(4), 241–249.

Manson, J. E., Willett, W. C., Stampfer, M. J., et al. Body weight and mortality among women. *New England Journal of Medicine*, 1995, *333*(11), 677–685.

Manuck, S. B. Cardiovascular reactivity in cardiovascular disease: "Once more unto the breach." *International Journal of Behavioral Medicine*, 1994, *1*, 4–31.

Manuck, S. B., Cohen, S. C., Rabin, B. S., et al. Individual differences in cellular immune response to stress. *Psychological Science*, 1991, *2*, 111–115.

Manuck, S. B., Kaplan, J. R., and Clarkson, T. B. Behaviorally-induced heart rate reactivity and atherosclerosis in cynomolgous monkeys. *Psychosomatic Medicine*, 1983, *45*, 95–108.

Manuck, S. B., Kaplan, J. R., and Matthews, K. A. Behavioral antecedents of coronary heart disease and atherosclerosis. *Arteriosclerosis*, 1986, *6*(1), 1–14.

Manyande, A., Berg, S., Gettins, D., and Stanford, C. S. Preoperative rehearsal of active coping imagery influences subjective and hormonal responses to abdominal surgery. *Psychosomatic Medicine*, 1995, *57*(2), 177–182.

Manyande, A., Berg, S., Gettins, D., et al. Preoperative rehearsal of active coping imagery influences subjective hormonal responses to abdominal surgery. *Psychosomatic Medicine*, 1995, *57*(2), 177–182.

Marcus, M. D., Wing, R., and Lamparaski, D. M. Binge eating and dietary restraint in obese patients. *Addictive Behaviors*, 1985, *10*, 163–168.

Markoff, R. A., Ryan, P., and Young, T. Endorphins and mood changes in long-distance running. *Medical Science Sports Exercise*, 1982, *14*, 11–15.

Marks, G., Richardson, J. L., Graham, J. W., and Levine, A. Role of health locus of control beliefs and expectations of treatment efficacy in adjustment to cancer. *Journal of Personality and Social Psychology*, 1986, *51*, 443–450.

Marlatt, G. A. Relapse prevention: Theoretical rationale and overview of the model. In G. A. Marlatt and J. R. Gordon (Eds.), *Relapse prevention*. New York: Guilford Press, 1985.

Marlatt, G. A., Demming, B., and Reid, J. B. Loss of control drinking in alcoholics: An experimental analogue. *Journal of Abnormal Psychology*, 1973, *81*, 233–241.

Marlatt, G. A., and Gordon, J. R. (Eds.). *Relapse prevention*. New York; Guilford Press, 1973.

Marmot, M. G. Stress, social and cultural variations in heart disease. *Journal of Psychosomatic Research*, 1983, *27*(5), 377–384.

Marquart, D. I., and Bailey L. L. An evaluation of the culture-free test of intelligence. *Journal of Genetic Psychology*, 1955, *86*, 353–358.

Marsh, J. T., and Rasmussen, A. F., Jr. Effects of exposure to fear-producing stressors on mouse organ weights and leukocyte counts. *Federation Proceedings, Federation of American Societies for Experimental Biology,* 1959, *18,* 583.

Marshall, G. D., and Zimbardo, P. G. Affective consequences of inadequately explained physiological arousal. *Journal of Personality and Social Psychology,* 1979, *37,* 970–988.

Martelli, M. F., Auerbach, S. M., Alexander, J., and Mercuri, L. G. Stress management in the health care setting: Matching interventions with patient coping styles. *Journal of Consulting and Clinical Psychology,* 1987, *55,* 201–207.

Martin, E. D., and Sher, K. J. Family history of alcoholism, alcohol use disorders and the five-factor model of personality. *Journal of Studies on Alcohol,* 1994, *55*(1), 81–90.

Martin, J. L. Demographic factors, sexual behavior patterns, and HIV antibody status among New York City gay men. Paper presented at the annual meeting of the American Psychological Association, Washington, DC, 1986.

Martin, R. A., Kazarian, S. S., and Breiter, H. J. Perceived stress, life events, dysfunctional attitudes, and depression in adolescent psychiatric inpatients. *Journal of Psychopathology and Behavioral Assessment,* 1995, *17*(1), 81–95.

Maslach, C. Negative emotional biasing of unexplained arousal. *Journal of Personality and Social Psychology,* 1979, *37,* 953–969.

Maslow, A. H. *Motivation and personality.* New York: Harper & Row, 1954.

Mason, J. W. A review of the psychoendocrine research on the pituitary-adrenal cortisol system. *Psychosomatic Medicine,* 1968, *30,* 576–607.

———. A historical view of the stress field. *Journal of Human Stress,* 1975, *1,* 22–36.

———. The use of psychoendocrine strategies in post-traumatic stress disorder. Special issue: Traumatic stress: New perspectives in theory, measurement, and research: II. Research findings. *Journal of Applied Social Psychology,* 1990, *20*(21 Pt. 1), 1822–1846.

Mason, J. W., Brady, J. V., and Tolson, W. W. Behavioral adaptations and endocrine activity. In R. Levine (Ed.), *Endocrines and the central nervous system.* Baltimore: Williams & Wilkins, 1966.

Mason, J. W., Giller, E. L., Costen, T. R., et al. Urinary free cortisol levels in posttraumatic stress disorder patients. *Journal of Nervous and Mental Disease,* 1986, *174,* 145–149.

Mason, J. W., Kosten, T. R., Southwick, S. M., and Giller, E. L. The use of psychoendocrine strategies in post-traumatic stress disorder. Special issue: Traumatic stress: New perspectives in theory, measurement, and research: II. Research findings. *Journal of Applied Social Psychology,* 1990, *20*(21 Pt. 1), 1822–1846.

Mason, J. W., Sachar, E. J., Fishman, J. R., et al. Corticosteroid responses to hospital admission. *Archives of General Psychiatry,* 1965, *13,* 1–8.

Masters, J. C., Cerreto, M. C., and Mendlowitz, D. R. The role of the family in coping with chronic illness. In T. G. Burish and L. A. Bradley (Eds.), *Coping with chronic disease: Research and applications.* New York: Academic Press, 1983.

Matarazzo, J. D. Behavioral health and behavioral medicine: Frontiers for a new health psychology. *American Psychologist,* 1980, *35,* 807–817.

———. Behavioral health: *A handbook of health enhancement and disease prevention.* New York: Wiley, 1984a.

———. Behavioral immunogens and pathogens in health and illness. In B. L. Hammonds and C. J. Scheirer (Eds.), *Psychology and health: The master lecture series,* vol. 3. Washington, DC: American Psychological Association, 1984b.

———. Clinical psychological test interpretations by computer: Hardware outpaces software. Special issue: Computer assessment and interpretation: Prospects, promise and pitfalls. *Computers in Human Behavior,* 1985, *1,* 235–253.

Matthews, K. A. Psychological perspectives on the Type A behavior pattern. *Psychological Bulletin,* 1982, *91,* 293–323.

———. Coronary heart disease and Type A behaviors: Update on and alternative to the

Booth-Kewley and Friedman (1987) quantitative review. *Psychological Bulletin,* 1988, *104,* 373–380.

Matthews, K. A., Glass, D. C., Rosenman, R. H., and Bortner, R. W. Competitive drive, pattern A and coronary heart disease: A further analysis of some data from the Western Collaborative Group Study. *Journal of Chronic Diseases,* 1977, *30,* 489–498.

Matthews, K. A., and Haynes, S. G. Type A behavior patterns and coronary disease risk: Update and critical evaluation. *American Journal of Epidemiology,* 1986, *123*(6), 923–960.

Matthews, K. A., Weiss, S. M., Detre, T., et al. *Handbook of stress, reactivity, and cardiovascular disease.* New York: Wiley, 1986.

Mavrias, R., Peck, C., and Coleman, G. The timing of preoperative preparatory information. *Psychology and Health,* 1990, *5,* 39–45.

Maxwell, K. W., Marcus, S., and Renzetti, A. D. Effect of tobacco smoke on phagocytic and cytopeptic activity of guinea pig alveolar macrophages. *American Review of Respiratory Illness,* 1967, *96,* 156.

May, R. M., and Anderson, R. M. Transmission dynamics of HIV infections. *Nature,* 1987, *326*(6109), 137–142.

Mayer, D. J., Price, D. D., Barber, J., and Rafii, A. Acupuncture analgesia: Evidence for activation of a pain inhibitor system as a mechanism of action. In J. J. Bonica and D. Albe-Fessard (Eds.), *Advances in pain research and therapy,* vol. 1. New York: Raven Press, 1976.

Mayer, R. G., Gatchel, R. J., Kishino, N., et al. Objective assessment of spine function following industrial injury: A prospective study with comparison group and one-year follow-up. *Spine,* 1985, *10,* 482–492.

Mayer, T. G., Gatchel, R. J., Mayer, J., et al. A prospective two-year study of functional restoration in industrial low back injury utilizing objective assessment. *Journal of the American Medical Association,* 1987, *258,* 1763–1767.

Mayer, T. G., Mooney, V., and Gatchel, R. J. (Eds.). *Contemporary conservative care of painful spinal disorder.* Philadelphia: Lea & Febiger, 1991.

Mears, F. G., and Gatchel, R. J. *Fundamentals of abnormal psychology.* Chicago: Rand McNally, 1979.

Mechanic, D. Effects of psychological distress on perceptions of physical health and use of medical and psychiatric facilities. *Journal of Human Stress,* 1978, *4*(4), 26–32.

———. The concept of illness behaviour: Culture, situation and personal predisposition. *Psychological Medicine,* 1986, *16*(1), 1–7.

Mechanic, D., and Jackson, D. Stress, illness behavior, and the use of general practitioner services: A study of British women. Manuscript, Department of Sociology, University of Wisconsin, 1968.

Meehl, P. E. *Research results for counselors.* St. Paul, MN: State Department of Education, 1951.

———. Schizotaxia, schizotypy, schizophrenia. *American Psychologist,* 1962, *17,* 827–838.

Mehrabian, A. A questionnaire measure of individual differences in stimulus screening and association differences in arousability. *Environmental Psychology and Nonverbal Behavior,* 1977, *1,* 89–103.

Meichenbaum, D. H. Clinical implications of modifying what clients say to themselves. *University of Waterloo Research Reports in Psychology,* December 1972, 42.

———*Cognitive-behavior modification,* New York: Plenum, 1977.

Meichenbaum, D. H., and Jaremko, M. E. (Eds.). *Stress reduction and prevention.* New York: Plenum, 1983.

Meichenbaum, D. H., and Turk, D. The congitive-behavioral management of anxiety, anger, and pain. In P. O. Davidson (Ed.), *The behavioral management of anxiety, depression and pain.* New York: Brunner/Mazel, 1976.

Meisel, S. R., Kutz, I., Dayan, K. I., et al. Effect of Iraqi missile war on incidence of acute myocardial infarction and sudden death in Israeli civilians. *Lancet*, 1991, *338*(8768), 660–661.

Melamed, B. G., and Siegel, L. Reduction of anxiety in children facing hospitalization and surgery by use of filmed modeling. *Journal of Consulting and Clinical Psychology*, 1975, *43*, 511–521.

Melamed, B. G. Introduction to the special section: The neglected psychological-physical interface. *Health Psychology*, 1995, *14*, 371–373.

Meliska, C. J., Stunkard, M. E., Gilbert, D. G., et al. Immune function in cigarette smokers who quit smoking for 31 days. *Journal of Allergy and Clinical Immunology*, 1995, *95*(4), 901–910.

Mellman, T. A., David, D., Kulick-Bell, R., et al. Sleep disturbance and its relationship to psychiatric morbidity after Hurricane Andrew. *American Journal of Psychiatry*, 1995, *152*(11), 1659–1663.

Melzack, R. *The puzzle of pain.* Harmondsworth, England: Penguin, 1973.

———. The McGill pain questionnaire: Major properties and scoring methods. *Pain*, 1975a, *1*, 227–299.

———. Prolonged relief of pain by brief, intense, transcutaneous somatic stimulation. *Pain*, 1975b, *1*, 357–373.

———. The short form McGill Pain Questionnaire. *Pain*, 1991, *30*, 191–197.

———. Pain: Past, present, and future. *Canadian Journal of Experimental Psychology*, 1993, *47*(4), 615–629.

Melzack, R., Katz, J., and Jeans, M. E. The role of compensation in chronic pain: Analysis using a new method of scoring the McGill pain questionnaire. *Pain*, 1985, *23*, 101–112.

Melzack, R., and Wall, P. D. Pain mechanisms: A new theory. *Science*, 1965, *150*, 971–979.

Mendelson, S. D., and McEwen, B. S. Autoradiographic analyses of the effects of adrenalectomy and corticosterone on 5-HT1A and 5-HT1B receptors in the dorsal hippocampus and cortex of the rat. *Neuroendocrinology*, 1992, *55*(4), 444–450.

Menninger, K. A., and Menninger, W. C. Psychoanalytic observations in cardiac disorders. *American Heart Journal*, 1936, *11*, 10.

Metalsky, G. I., Halberstadt, L. J., and Abramson, L. Y. Vulnerability to depressive mood reactions: Toward a more powerful test of the diathesis-stress and causal mediation components of the reformulated theory of depression. *Journal of Personality and Social Psychology*, 1987, *52*(2), 386–393.

Metropolitan Life Insurance Company. The 1983 Metropolitan height and weight tables. Reproduced in M. A. Boyle and G. Zyla. *Personal Nutrition.* St. Paul, MN: West Publishing, 1993.

Meyer, A. *Psychobiology: A science of man.* Springfield IL: Charles C. Thomas, 1957.

Meyer, A J., Nash, J. D., McAlister, A. L., et al. Skills training in a cardiovascular education campaign. *Journal of Consulting and Clinical Psychology*, 1980, *48*, 129–142.

Meyer, D., Leventhal, H., and Gutmann, M. Common-sense models of illness: The example of hypertension. *Health Psychology*, 1985, *4*, 115–135.

Meyer, J. M., and Stunkard, A. J. Genetics and human obesity. In A. J. Stunkard and T. A. Wadden (Eds.), *Obesity: Theory and therapy.* New York: Raven Press, 1993, pp. 137–149.

Meyer, R. J., and Haggerty, R. J. Streptococcal infections in families: Factors altering individual susceptibility. *Pediatrics*, 1962, *29*, 539–549.

Meyer, T. J. Effects of psychosocial interventions with adult cancer patients: A meta-analysis of randomized experiments. *Health Psychology*, 1995, *14*(2), 101–108.

Meyerhoff, J. L., Oleshansky, M. A., and Mougey, E. H. Psychologic stress increases plasma levels of prolactin, cortisol, and POMC-derived peptides in man. *Psychosomatic Medicine,* 1988, *50,* 295–303.

Mikulincer, M. Attributional processes in the learned helplessness paradigm: Behavioral effects of global attributions. *Journal of Personality and Social Psychology,* 1986, *51,* 1248–1256.

Milgrom, P., Mancl, L., King, B., and Weinstein, P. Origins of childhood dental fear. *Behavior Research and Therapy,* 1995, *33*(3), 313–319.

Miller, B. F., and Keane, C. B. *Encyclopedia and dictionary of medicine, nursing, and allied health,* 4th ed. Philadelphia: Saunders, 1987.

Miller, D. M., and Eisler, R. M. Alcohol and drug abuse. In W. E. Craighead, A. E. Kayden, and M. J. Mahoney (Eds.), *Behavioral modification principles, issues, and application.* Boston: Houghton Mifflin, 1976.

Miller, D. M., and Hersen, M. Quantitative changes in alcohol consumption as a function of electrical aversive conditioning. *Journal of Clinical Psychology,* 1972, *28,* 590–593.

Miller, M. E. Behavioral medicine: Symbiosis between laboratory and clinic. *Annual Review of Psychology,* 1983, *34,* 1–31.

Miller, N. E. Learning of visceral and glandular responses. *Science,* 1969, *163,* 434–445.

Miller, S. M. Monitoring and blunting: Validation of a questionnaire to assess style information seeking under threat. *Journal of Personality and Social Psychology,* 1987, *52*(2), 345–353.

Miller, S. M., and Mangan, C. E. The interacting effects of information and coping style in adapting to gynecologic stress: Should the doctor tell all? *Journal of Personality and Social Psychology,* 1983, *45,* 223–236.

Miller, W. R., and Seligman, M. E. P. Depression and learned helplessness in man. *Journal of Abnormal Psychology,* 1975, *84,* 228–238.

Millon, T. *Modern psychopathology.* Philadelphia: Saunders, 1969.

Mineka, S., and Kelly, K. A. The relationship between anxiety, lack of control, and loss of control. In A. Steptoe and A. Appels (Eds.), *Stress, personal control and health.* New York: Wiley, 1989, pp. 163–192.

Minnick, S. A., Miller, S. L., and Wehner, J. M. The effects of acute stress on ethanol absorption in LS and SS mice. *Alcohol,* 1995, *12*(3), 257–263.

Miranda, J., and Munoz, R. Intervention for minor depression in primary care patients. *Psychosomatic Medicine,* 1994, *56,* 136–147.

Mirsky, I. A. Physiologic, psychologic, and social determinants in the etiology of duodenal ulcer. *American Journal of Digestive Diseases,* 1958, *3,* 285–314.

Mirsky, I. A., Fritterman, P., and Kaplan, S. Blood plasma pepsinogen. II. The activity of the plasma from "normal" subjects, patients with duodenal ulcer and patients with pernicious anemia. *Journal of Laboratory and Clinical Medicine,* 1952, *40,* 188–195.

Mitchell, J. (Ed.). *The ninth mental measurements yearbook.* Lincoln: University of Nebraska Press, 1985.

Mittleman, M. A., Maclure, M., Sherwood, J. B., et al. Triggering of acute myocardial infarction onset by episodes of anger. Determinants of myocardial infarction onset study investigators. *Circulation,* 1995, *92*(7), 1720–1725.

Mittleman, M. A., Maclure, M., Tofler, G. H., et al. Triggering of acute myocardial infarction by heavy physical exertion. Protection against triggering by regular exertion. Determinants of myocardial infarction onset study investigators. *New England Journal of Medicine,* 1993, *329*(23), 1677–1683.

MMWR. Alcohol-related hospitalizations—Indian Health Service and tribal hospitals, United States, May 1992. *Morbidity and Mortality Weekly Report,* 1992, *41*(41), 757–760.

Moffat, F. L., Jr., and Clark, K. C. Optimism versus pessimism predicts the quality of women's adjustment to early stage breast cancer. *Cancer,* 1994, *73*(4), 1213–1220.

Monjan, A. A stress and immunologic competence: Studies in animals. In R. Ader (Ed.), *Psychoneuroimmunology.* New York: Academic Press, 1981.

Monjan, A., and Collector, M. Stress-induced modulation of the immune response. *Science*, 1977, *96*(1), 307–308.

Monjan, A. A., and Mandell, W. Fetal alcohol and immunity: Depression of mitogen-induced lymphocyte blastogenesis. *Neurobehavioral toxicology*, 1980, *2*, 213–215.

Monroe, S. M., and Simons, A. D. Diathesis-stress theories in the context of life stress research: Implications for the depressive disorders. *Psychological Bulletin*, 1991, *110*, 406–425.

Montano, D. E., and Taplin, S. H. A test of an expanded theory of reasoned action to predict mammography participation. *Social Science and Medicine*, 1991, *32*(6), 733–741.

Moore, A. D., and Stambrook, M. Cognitive moderators of outcome following traumatic brain injury: A conceptual model and implications for rehabilitation. (Review). *Brain Injury*, 1995, *9*(2), 109–130.

Morokoff, P. J., Holmes-Johnson, E., and Weisse, C. S. A psychosocial program for HIV-seropositive persons. *Patient Education and Counseling*, 1987, *10*, 287–300.

Morrow, G. R., Asbury, R., Hamman, S., et al. Comparing the effectiveness of behavioral treatment for chemotherapy-induced nausea and vomiting when administered by oncologists, oncology nurses, and clinical psychologists. *Health Psychology*, 1992, *11*, 250–256.

Morrow, K. A., Thoreson, R. W., and Penney, L. L. Predictors of psychological distress among infertility clinic patients. *Journal of Consulting Clinical Psychology*, 1995, *63*(1), 163–167.

Morse, R. M., and Flavin, D. K. The definition of alcoholism. The Joint Committee of the National Council on Alcoholism and Drug Dependence and the American Society of Addiction Medicine to Study the Definition and Criteria for the Diagnosis of Alcoholism. *Journal of the American Medical Association*, 1992, *268*(8), 1012–1014.

Mosnaim, A. D., Wolf, M. E., Maturana, P., et al. In vitro studies of natural killer cell activity in post traumatic stress disorder patients. Response to methionine-enkephalin challenge. *Immunopharmacology*, 1993, *25*(2), 107–116.

Motley, R. J., and Finlay, A. Y. How much disability is caused by acne? *Clinical and Experimental Dermatology*, 1989, *14*, 194–198.

Mott, F. W. *War neuroses and shell shock*. London: Oxford Medical Publications, 1919.

Mount, B. M., Jones, A., and Patterson, A. Death and dying attitudes in a teaching hospital. *Urology*, 1974, *4*(6), 741–748.

Mowrer, O. H., and Viek, P. An experimental analogue of fear from a sense of helplessness. *Journal of Abnormal and Social Psychology*, 1948, *43*, 193–200.

MRFIT Research Group. Multiple risk factor intervention trial: Risk factor changes and mortality results. *Journal of the American Medical Association*, 1982, *248*, 1465–1477.

Mroczek, D. K., Shapiro, A., 3rd., Aldwin, C. M., et al. Construct validation of optimism and pessimism in older men: Findings from the normative aging study. *Health Psychology*, 1993, *12*(5), 406–409.

Mufti, S. I. Alcohol acts to promote incidence of tumors. *Cancer Detection and Prevention*, 1992, *16*(3), 157–162.

Mullen, B., and Suls, J. The effectiveness of attention and rejection as coping styles. *Journal of Psychosomatic Research*, 1982, *26*, 43–49.

Muller, J. E., Abela, G. S., Nestro, R. W., and Tofler, G. H. Triggers, acute risk factors, and vulnerable plaques: The lexicon of a new frontier. Journal of the American College of Cardiology, 1994, *23*, 809–813.

Muller, R., Stark, K., Guggenmoos-Holzmann, I., et al. Imprisonment: A risk factor for HIV infection counteracting education prevention programmes for intravenous drug users. *AIDS*, 1995, *9*(2), 183–190.

Munck, A., and Guyre, P. M. Glucocorticoids and immune function. In R. Ader, D. L. Felten, and N. Cohen (Eds.), *Psychoneuroimmunology* (2nd ed.). San Diego, CA: Academic Press, 1991.

Munsinger, H. The adopted child's IQ: A critical review. *Psychological Bulletin,* 1975, *82,* 623–659.

Murphy, T. M. Subjective and objective follow-up assessment of acupuncture therapy without suggestion in 100 chronic pain patients. In J. J. Bonica and D. Albe-Fessard (Eds.), *Advances in pain research and therapy,* vol. 1. New York: Raven Press, 1976.

Murray, H. A. *Explorations in personality.* New York: Oxford, 1938.

———. *Explorations in personality.* New York: Oxford, 1979.

Myers, A., and Dewar, H. A. Circumstances attending 100 sudden deaths from coronary artery disease with coroner's necropsies. *British Heart Journal,* 1975, *37*(11), 1133–1143.

Naliboff, B., Benton, D., Solomon, G., et al. Immunological changes in young and old adults during brief laboratory stress. *Psychosomatic Medicine,* 1991, *53,* 121–132.

Nappi, G., Bono, G., Sandrini, G., et al. (Eds.). *Headache and depression: Serotonin pathways as a common clue.* New York: Raven Press, 1991.

Nathan, P. E. Alcoholism: Psychopathology, etiology, and treatment. In P. B. Sutker and H. E. Adams (Eds.), *Comprehensive handbook of psychopathology,* 2nd ed. New York: Plenum, 1993.

Nathan, P. E., and Goldman, M. S. Problem drinking and alcoholism. In O. F. Pomerleau and J. P. Brady (Eds.), *Behavioral medicine: Theory and practice.* Baltimore: Williams & Wilkins, 1938.

Nathan P. E., and Lansky, D. Management of the chronic alcoholic: A behavioral viewpoint. In J. P. Brady and H. K. H. Brodie (Eds.), *Controversy in psychiatry.* Philadelphia: Saunders, 1978.

Nathan, P. E., and O'Brien, J. S. An experimental analysis of the behavior of alcoholics and nonalcoholics during prolonged experimental drinking. *Behavior Therapy,* 1971, *2,* 455–476.

National Cancer Institute. Cancer prevention (NIH Publication No. 84-2671). Bethesda, MD: National Institutes of Health, 1984.

National Heart, Lung, and Blood Institute. Report of the task force on research in epidemiology and prevention of cardiovascular diseases, 1994.

National Institute for Health Care Management. Health care problems. Variation across states (Publication No. 94FMS230). NIHCM Lewin. Valhi, Inc., 1994.

Navia, B., Jordan, B., and Price, R. The AIDS dementia complex: I. Clinical features. *Annals of Neurology,* 1986, *19,* 517–524.

Neale, A. V., Tilly, B. C., and Vernon, S. W. Marital status, delay in seeking treatment and survival from breast cancer. *Social Science and Medicine,* 1986, *23*(3), 305–312.

Nemiah, J. C. Psychology and psychosomatic illness. Reflections in theory and research methodology. In J. Freyberger (Ed.), *Topics of psychosomatic research. Proceedings of Ninth European Conference on Psychosomatic Research.* London: Karger, 1973.

———. Denial revisited: Reflections on psychosomatic theory. *Psychotherapy and Psychosomatics,* 1975, *26,* 140–147.

Nerenz, D. R. *Control of emotional distress in cancer, chemotherapy.* Ph.D. dissertation, University of Wisconsin, 1980.

Nerenz, D. R., Leventhal, H., and Love, R. R. Factors contributing to emotional distress during cancer chemotherapy. *Cancer,* 1982, *50,* 1020–1027.

Neuhaus, W., Zok, C., Gohring, U. J., and Scharl, A. A prospective study concerning psychological characteristics of patients with breast cancer. *Archives of Gynecology and Obstetrics,* 1994, *255*(4), 201–209.

Newberry, B. H., Gildow, J., Wogan, J., et al. Inhibition of Huggins tumors by forced re-straint. *Psychosomatic Medicine,* 1976, *38*(3), 155–162.

Newman, H. H., Freeman, F. N., and Holzinger, K. J. *Twins: A study of heredity and environment.* Chicago: University of Chicago Press, 1937.

Nieburgs, H. E., Weiss, J., Navarrete, M., et al. The role of stress in human and environmental oncogenesis. *Cancer Detection and Prevention,* 1979, *2*(2), 307–336.

Nisbett, R. E., and Temoshok, L. Is there an external cognitive style? *Journal of Personality and Social Psychology,* 1976, *33,* 36–47.

Nolen-Hoeksema, S., Girgus, J. S., and Seligman, M. E. P. Learned helplessness in children: A longitudinal study of depression, achievement, and explanatory style. *Journal of Personality and Social Psychology,* 1986, *51,* 435–442.

Nolen-Hoeksema, S., Girgus, J. S., and Seligman, M. E. P. Predictors and consequences of childhood depressive symptoms: A 5-year longitudinal study. *Journal of Abnormal Psychology,* 1992, *101*(3), 405–422.

Nolen-Hoeksema, S., Parker, L. E., and Larson, J. Ruminative coping with depressed mood following loss. *Journal of Personality and Social Psychology,* 1994, *67*(1), 92–104.

Nomikos, M. S., Opton, E. M., Jr., Averill, J. R., and Lazarus, R. S. Surprise versus suspense in the production of stress reaction. *Journal of Personality and Social Psychology,* 1968, *8,* 204–208.

Norman, D. C., Chang, M. P., Wong, C. M., et al. Changes with age in the proliferative response of splenic T cells from rats exposed to ethanol in utero. *Alcoholism, Clinical and Experimental Research,* 1991, *15*(3), 428–432.

North, C. S., Smith, E. M., McCool, R. E., and Lightcap, P. E. Acute post-disaster coping and adjustment. *Journal of Traumatic Stress,* 1989, *2*(3), 353–360.

Norvell, N. K., Hills, H. A., and Murrin, M. R. Understanding stress in female and male law enforcement officers. *Psychology of Women Quarterly,* 1993, *17*(3), 289–301.

Nuckolls, K. B., Cassel, J., and Kaplan, B. H. Psychosocial assets, life crisis, and the prognosis of pregnancy. *American Journal of Epidemiology,* 1972, *95,* 431–441.

Nungester, W. J., and Klesper, R. G. A possible mechanism of lowered resistance of pneumococci infection. *Journal of Infectious Diseases,* 1939, *63,* 94–102.

Oakley, G. The use of an information booklet to reduce the anxiety of hospitalization for elderly patients. Bachelor thesis: University of Leicester, 1988.

Ockene, I. S., and Ockene, J. K. *Prevention of coronary heart disease.* Boston: Little, Brown, 1992.

Ogden, E., and Shock, M. W. Voluntary hypercirculation. *American Journal of the Medical Sciences.* 1939, *198,* 329–342.

O'Keeffe, M. K., Nesselhof-Kendall, S., and Baum, A. Behavior and the prevention of AIDS: Bases of research and intervention. *Personality and Social Psychology Bulletin,* 1990, *16*(1), 166–180.

O'Leary, A., Shoor, S., Lorig, K., and Holman, H. R. A congitive-behavioral treatment for rheumatoid arthritis. *Health Psychology,* 1988, *7,* 527–544.

O'Leary, M. R., Donovan, D., Kreuger, K. J., and Cysenski, B. Depression and perception of reinforcement: Lack of differences in expectancy change among alcoholics. *Journal of Abnormal Psychology,* 1978, *87,* 110–112.

Orleans, C. T., Schoenbach, V. J., Wagner, E. H., and Quade, D. Self-help quit smoking interventions: Effects of self-help materials, social support instructions, and telephone counseling. *Journal of Consulting and Clinical Psychology,* 1991, *59*(3), 439–448.

Ornish, D., Brown, S. E., Scherwitz, L. W., et al. Can lifestyle changes reverse coronary heart disease? *Lancet,* 1990, *336,* 129–133.

Osler, W. *Lectures on angina pectoris and allied states.* New York: Appleton, 1897.

Ostfeld, A., and Eaker, E. (Eds.). Measuring psychosocial variables in epidemiologic studies of cardiovascular disease (NIH Publication No. 85-2270). Bethesda, MD: National Institutes of Health, 1985.

Ouellet, B. L., Romeder, J. M., and Lance, J. M. Premature mortality attributable to smoking and hazardous drinking in Canada. *American Journal of Epidemiology,* 1979, *109*(4), 451–463.

Overmier, J. B., and Seligman, M. E. P. Effects of inescapable shock upon subsequent escape and avoidance responding. *Journal of Comparative and Physiological Psychology,* 1967, *63,* 28–33.

Page, H. *Injuries of the spine and spinal cord without apparent mechanical lesions.* London: J. and A. Churchill, 1885.

Page, L., Danion, A., and Moellering, R. C. Antecedents of cardiovascular disease in six Solomon Island societies. *Circulation,* 1970, *49,* 1132–1140.

Pallak, M. S., Cummings, N. A., Dorken, H., and Henke, C. J. Effect of mental health treatment on medical costs. *Mind/Body Medicine,* 1995, *1,* 7–12.

Palmblad, J., Cantell, K., Stander, H., et al. Stressor exposure and immunological response in man: Interferon producing capacity and phagocytes. *Journal of Psychosomatic Research,* 1976, *20,* 193–199.

Palmblad, J., Pertini, B., and Wasserman, J. Lymphocyte and granulocyte reactions during sleep deprivation. *Psychosomatic Medicine,* 1979, *41,* 273–278.

Panayatopoulos, S., Gotsis, N., Papazoglou, N., et al. Antigenic study of Nicotiana tabacum and research on precipitins against tobacco antigens in the serum of smokers and nonsmokers. *Allergologia et Immunopathologia,* 1974, *2,* 111–114.

Pardine, P., and Napoli, A. Physiological reactivity and recent life-stress experience. *Journal of Consulting and Clinical Psychology,* 1983, *51*(3), 467–469.

Parjis, J., Joosens, J. V., Van der Linden, L., et al. Moderate sodium restrictions and diuretics in the treatment of hypertension. *American Heart Journal,* 1973, *85,* 22–25.

Parker, S. D., Brewer, M. B., and Spencer J. R. Natural disaster, perceived control, and attributions to fate. *Personality and Social Psychology Bulletin,* 1980, *6,* 454–459.

Parkes, C. M. *Bereavement: Studies of grief in adult life.* New York: International Universities Press, 1972.

Parkes, C. M., Benjamin, B., and Fitzgerald, R. G. Broken heart: A statistical study of increased mortality among widowers. *Behavioral Medicine Journal,* 1969, *1,* 740.

Parsons, T. *The social system.* New York: Free Press, 1951.

Patkai, P. Catecholamine excretion in pleasant and unpleasant situations. *Acta Psychologica,* 1971, *35,* 352–363.

Patterson, D. R., Everett, J. J., Burns, G., et al. Hypnosis for the treatment of burn pain. *Journal of Consulting and Clinical Psychology,* 1992, *60,* 713–717.

Patterson, S. M., Zakowski, S. G., Hall, M. H., et al. Psychological stress and platelet activation: Differences in platelet reactivity in healthy men during active and passive stressors. *Health Psychology,* 1994, *13*(1), 34–38.

Pattishall, E. G. The development of behavioral medicine: Historical models. Society of Behavioral Medicine Ninth Annual Scientific Sessions, Boston, MA, 1988. *Annals of Behavioral Medicine,* 1989, *11*(2), 43–48.

Pavlov, I. P. *Conditioned reflexes.* New York: Dover, 1927.

Penderay, M. L., Maltzman, I. M., and West, L. T. Controlled drinking by alcoholics? New findings and a reevaluation of a major affirmative study. *Science,* 1982, *217,* 169–174.

Pennebaker, J. W. Environmental determinants of symptom perception. Paper presented at the meeting of the American Psychological Association, New York, September 1979.

———. *The psychology of physical symptoms.* New York: Springer-Verlag, 1982.

————. *Emotions, disclosure, and health.* Washington, DC: American Psychological Association, 1995.

Pennebaker, J. W., and Brittingham, G. Environmental and sensory cues affecting the perception of physical symptoms. In A. Baum and J. E. Singer (Eds.), *Advances in environmental psychology: Environment and health,* vol 4. Hillsdale, NJ: Erlbaum, 1982.

Pennebaker, J. W., and Newtson, D. The psychological impact of Mt. St. Helens. Manuscript, University of Virginia, 1981.

Peretz, T. Psychological distress in female cancer patients with Holocaust experiences. *General Hospital Psychiatry,* 1994, *16*(6), 413–418.

Perkins, K. A. Issues in the prevention of weight gain after smoking cessation. *Annals of Behavioral Medicine,* 1994, *16,* 46–52.

Perkins, K. A., Epstein, L. H., Fonte, C., and Mitchell, S. L. Gender, dietary restraint, and smoking's influence on hunger and the reinforcing value of food. *Physiology and Behavior,* 1995, *57*(4), 675–680.

Perri, M. G., Sears, S. F., Jr., and Clark, J. E. Strategies for improving maintenance of weight loss. Toward a continuous care model of obesity management. *Diabetes Care,* 1993, *16*(1), 200–209.

Perrin, G. M., and Pierce, I. R. Psychosomatic aspects of cancer—A review. *Psychosomatic Medicine,* 1959, *21*(5), 397–421.

Perrin, L. A. The need to predict and control under conditions of threat. *Journal of Personality,* 1963, *31,* 570–587.

————. *Current controversies and issues in personality.* New York: Wiley, 1978.

Perry, S., Fishman, B., Jacobsberg, L., and Young, J. Effectiveness of psychoeducational interventions in reducing emotional distress after human immunodeficiency virus antibody testing. *Archives of General Psychiatry,* 1991, *48*(2), 143–147.

Persky, V. W., Kempthorne-Rawson, J., and Skelle, R. B. Personality and risk of cancer: Twenty-year follow-up of the Western Electric Study. *Psychosomatic Medicine,* 1987, *49,* 435–449.

Pervin, L. A. The need to predict and control under conditions of threat. *Journal of Personality,* 1963, *31,* 570–587.

Peterson, C., and De Avila, M. E. Optimistic explanatory style and the perception of health problems. *Journal of Clinical Psychology,* 1995, *51*(1), 128–132.

Peterson, C., Rosenbaum, A. C., and Conn, M. K. Depressive mood reactions to breaking up: Testing the learned helplessness model of depression. *Journal of Social and Clinical Psychology,* 1985, *3,* 161–169.

Peterson, L., and Ridley-Johnson, R. Pediatric hospital response to survey on prehospital preparation for children. *Journal of Pediatric Psychology,* 1980, *5*(1), 1–7.

Peterson, L., and Shigetomi, C. One year follow-up of elective surgery, child patients receiving preoperative preparation. *Journal of Pediatric Psychology,* 1982, *7*(1), 43–48.

Peto, R., Lopez, A. D., Boreham, J., et al. Mortality from tobacco in developed countries: Indirect estimation from national vital statistics. *Lancet,* 1992, *339*(8804), 1268–1278.

Pickens, R. W., and Svikis, D. S. Genetic influences in human substance abuse. *Journal of Addictive Diseases,* 1991, *10*(1–2), 205–213.

Pickering, T. G. Personal views on mechanisms of hypertension. In J. Genest, E. Koiw, and O. Kuchel (Eds.), *Hypertension: Physiopathology and treatment.* New York: McGraw-Hill, 1977.

Pilisuk, M., and Parks, S. H. Structural dimensions of social support groups. *Journal of Psychology,* 1980, *106,* 157–177.

Pilkonis, P. A., Imler, S. D., and Rubinsky, P. Dimensions of life stress in psychiatric patients. *Journal of Human Stress,* 1985, *11,* 5–10.

Pillow, D. R., West, S. G., and Reich, J. W. Attributional style in relation to self-esteem and depression: Mediational and interactive models. *Journal of Research in Personality,* 1991, *25*(1), 57–69.

Pilot, M. L., Lenkoski, L. D., Spiro, H. M., and Schaeffer, R. Duodenal ulcer in one of identical twins. *Psychosomatic Medicine,* 1957, *19,* 221–229.

Pinel, T. *Biopsychology.* Boston: Allyn & Bacon, 1993.

Pirke, K. M., and Laessle, R. G. Restrained eating. In A. J. Stunkard and T. A. Wadden (Eds.), *Obesity: Theory and therapy.* New York: Raven Press, 1993, pp. 151–162.

Pistrang, M. The partner relationship in psychological response to breast cancer. *Social Science and Medicine,* 1995, *40*(6), 789–797.

Pittman, N. L., and Pittman, T. S. Effects of amount of helplessness training and internal-external locus of control on mood and performance. *Journal of Personality and Social Psychology,* 1979, *37,* 39–47.

Pliner, P., and Cappell, H. Modification of affective consequences of alcohol: A comparison of social and solitary drinking. *Journal of Abnormal Psychology,* 1974, *83,* 418–425.

Podell, R. N. *Physician's guide to compliance in hypertension.* West Point, PA: Merck and Co., 1975.

Polonsky, W. H. Psychosocial issues in diabetes mellitus. In R. G. Gatchel and E. B. Blanchard (Eds.), *Psychophysiological disorders: Research and clinical applications.* Washington, DC: American Psychological Association, 1993.

Porter, R. W., Brady, J. V., Conrad, D., et al. Some experimental observations on gastrointestinal lesions in behaviorally conditioned monkeys. *Psychosomatic Medicine,* 1958, *20,* 379–394.

Posluszny, D. M., Hyman, K. B., and Baum, A. Group interventions in cancer: Patient adjustment, self-efficacy, and coping skill enhancement in small group settings. In R. S. Tindale, J. Edwards, E. J. Posacas, et al. (Eds.), *Application of theory and research on groups to social issues,* vol. IV, *Social psychological application to social issues.* New York: Plenum, in press.

Pratt, S. A., Finley, T. N., Smith, M. H., and Ladman, A. J. A comparison of alveolar macrophages and pulmonary surgactant obtained from the lungs of human smokers and nonsmokers by endobronchial lavage. *Anatomical Record,* 1969, *163,* 497–507.

Price, K. P. Biofeedback and migraine. In R. J. Gatchel and K. P. Price (Eds.), *Clinical applications of biofeedback: Appraisal and status.* Elmsford, NY: Pergamon, 1979.

Price K. P., and Gatchel, R. J. A perspective on clinical biofeedback. In R. J. Gatchel and K. P. Price (Eds.), *Clinical biofeedback: Appraisal and status.* Elmsford NY: Pergamon, 1979.

Prochaska, J. O. In search of how people change: Applications to addictive behaviors. *American Psychologist,* 1992, *47*(9), 1102–1114.

———. A transtheoretical model of behaviour change: Learning from mistakes with majority populations. In D. M. Becker, D. R. Hill, J. S. Jackson, et al. (Eds.), *Health behavior research in minority populations: Access, design, and implementation.* Washington, DC: National Institutes of Health, 1992, pp. 105–109.

Prochaska, J. O., DiClemente, C. C., and Norcross, J. C. In search of how people change: Applications to addictive behaviors. *American Psychologist,* 1992, *47*(9), 1102–1114.

Prochaska, J. O., Norcross, J. C., Fowler, J. L., and Follick, M. J. Attendance and outcome in a worksite weight control program: Processes and stages of change as process and predictor variables. *Addictive Behaviors,* 1992, *17*(1), 35–45.

Ptacek, J. T., Ptacek, J. J., and Dodge, K. L. Coping with breast cancer from the perspectives of husbands and wives. *Journal of Psychosocial Oncology,* 1994. *12*(3), 47–72.

Purcell, K., Brady, K., Chai, H., et al. The effect on asthma in children of experimental separation from the family. *Psychosomatic Medicine,* 1969, *31,* 144–164.

Putnam, D. E. Enhancing commitment improves adherence to a medical regimen. *Journal of Consulting and Clinical Psychology,* 1994, *62*(1), 191–194.

Quarantelli, E. L., and Dynes, R. R. When disaster strikes. *Psychology Today*, 1972, 5(9), 66–70.

Quirk, F. H., and Jones, P. W. Patients' perception of distress due to symptoms and effects of asthma on daily living and an investigation of possible influential factors. *Clinical Science*, 1990, 79, 17–21.

Rabkin, J. G., and Struening, E. L. Life events, stress, and illness. *Science*, 1976, *191*, 1013–1020.

Radojevik V., Nicassio, P. M., and Weisman, M. H. Behavioral intervention with and without family support for rheumatoid arthritis. *Behavioral Therapy*, 1992, 23, 13–30.

Ragland, D. R., and Brand, R. J. Type A behavior and mortality from coronary heart disease. *New England Journal of Medicine*, 1988, 318, 65–69.

Rahe, R. H. Life changes and near-future illness reports. In L. Levi (Ed.), *Emotions: The parameters and measurements*. New York: Raven Press, 1975.

———. Recent life changes, emotions, and behaviors in coronary heart disease. In A. Baum and J. E. Singer (Eds.), *Handbook of psychology and health*, vol. 5. *Stress*. Hillsdale NJ: Erlbaum, 1987.

Rahe, R. H., Mahan, J. L., and Arthur, R. J. Prediction of near-future health change from subjects' preceding life changes. *Journal of Psychosomatic Research*, 1970, 14, 401–406.

Rahe, R. H., Ryman, D. H., and Ward, H. W. Simplified scale for life change events. *Journal of Human Stress*, 1980, 6, 22–27.

Raphael, B. Psychiatry " 'at the coal-face.' " Annual Congress of the Royal Australian and New Zealand College of Psychiatrists, 1985, Hobart, Australia. *Australian and New Zealand Journal of Psychiatry*, 1986, 20, 316–332.

Raps, C., Peterson, C., Jones, M., and Seligman, M. Patient behavior in hospitals: Helplessness, reactance, or both. *Journal of Personality and Social Psychology*, 1982, 42, 1036–1041.

Reardon, K. K., and Aydin, C. E. Changes in lifestyle initiated by breast cancer patients: Who does and who doesn't? *Health Communication*, 1993, 5(4), 263–282.

Reed, G. M. Perceived control and psychological adjustment in gay men with AIDS. *Journal of Applied Social Psychology*, 1993, 23(10), 791–824.

Rees, L. The importance of psychological allergic and infective factors in childhood asthma. *Schizophrenia Bulletin*, 1964, 8, 1–11.

Regland, B., Cajander, S., Wiman, L. G., and Falkmer, S. Scanning electron microscopy of the bronchial mucosa in some lung diseases using bronchoscopy specimens. *Scandinavian Journal of Respiratory Diseases*, 1976, 57, 171–182.

Reidy, K., and Caplan, B. Causal factors in spinal cord injury: Patients; evolving perceptions and association with depression. *Archives in Physical Medicine Rehabilitation*, 1994, 75(8), 837–842.

Reisen E., Abel, T., Modan, M., et al. Effect of weight loss without salt restriction on the reduction of blood pressure in overweight hypertensive patients. *New England Journal of Medicine*, 1978, *298*, 1–6.

Reitan, R. M. Certain differential effects on left and right cerebral lesions in human adults. *Journal of Comparative and Physiological Psychology*, 1955, 48, 474–477.

———. Psychological deficits resulting from cerebral lesions in man. In J. M. Warren and K. A. Kent (Eds.), *The frontal granular cortex and behavior*. New York: McGraw-Hill, 1964.

Reitan, R., and Wilson, D. *The Halstead-Reitan neuropsychology test battery: Theory and clinical interpretation*. Tuscars Neuropsychology Press, 1985.

Renneker, R. Cancer and psychotherapy. In J. Goldberg (Ed.), *Psychotherapeutic treatment of cancer patients*. New York: Free Press, 1981.

Revenson, T. A. The role of social support and rheumatic disease. *Ballieres Clinical Rheumatology*, 1993, 7(2), 377–396.

Revenson, T. A., Schiaffino, K. M., Majerovitz, S. D., and Gifbofsky, A. Social support as a doube-edged sword: The relation of positive and problematic support to depression among rheumatoid arthritis patients. *Social Science and Medicine*, 1991, *33*, 807–813.

Reynolds, P., and Kaplan, G. A. Social connections and risk for cancer: Prospective evidence from the Alameda County Study. *Behavioral Medicine*, 1990, *16*(3), 101–110.

Richardson, J. L., Danley, K., Mondrus, G. T., and Deapen, D. Adherence to screening examinations for colorectal cancer after diagnosis in a first-degree relative. Special issue: Nonsteroidal anti-inflammatory drug use and cancer workshop. *Preventive Medicine: An International Journal Devoted to Practice and Theory*, 1995, *24*(2), 166–170.

Riley, C. S. Patients' understanding of doctors' instruction. *Medical Care*, 1966, *4*, 34–37.

Riley, J. L., Robinson, M. E., Geisser, M. E., et al. Relationship between MMPI-2 cluster profiles and surgical outcome in low back pain patients. *Journal of Spinal Disorders*, 1995, *8*, 213–219.

Riley, V., Fitzmaurice, M. A., and Spackman, D. H. Animal models in biobehavioral research. Effects of anxiety stress on immunocompetence and neoplasia. In S. M. Weiss, J. A. Herd, and B. H. Fox (Eds.), *Perspectives in behavioral medicine*. New York: Academic Press, 1981.

Rimer, B. K. Mammography use in the U.S.: Trends and the impact of interventions. *Annals of Behavioral Medicine*, 1994, *16*, 317–326.

Rimm, D. C., and Masters, J. C. *Behavior therapy: Techniques and empirical findings*. New York: Academic Press, 1974.

Rinehart, J. J. Sagone, A. L., Baceryak, S. P., et al. Effects of corticosteroid therapy on human monocyte function. *New England Journal of Medicine*, 1975, *292*, 236–241.

Rippetoe, P. A. Effects of components of protection-motivation theory on adaptive and maladaptive coping with a health threat. *Journal of Personality and Social Psychology*, 1987, *52*(3), 596–604.

Rizley, R. Depression and distortion in the attribution of causality. *Journal of Abnormal Psychology*, 1978, *87*, 32–48.

Roberts, C. S., Cox, C. E., Shannon, V. J., and Wells, N. L. A closer look at social support as a moderator of stress in breast cancer. *Health and Social Work*, 1994, *19*(3), 157–164.

Robertson, C., Gatchel, R. J., and Fowler, C. Effectiveness of a videotaped behavioral intervention in reducing anxiety in emergency oral surgery patients. *Behavioral Medicine*, 1991, *17*, 77–85.

Robinson, P. J. Development and evaluation of a presurgical preparation program. *Journal of Pediatric Psychology*, 1991, *16*(2), 193–212.

Robinson, P. J., and Kobayashi K. Adelaide Children's Hospital, Division of Child and Adolescents Mental Health Services, SA, Australia. *Journal of Pediatric Psychology*, 1991, *16*(2), 193–212.

Rodin, J. Health, control, and aging. In M. M. Baltes and P. B. Baltes (Eds.), *The psychology of control and aging*. Hillsdale NJ: Erlbaum, 1986, pp. 139–165.

Rodin, J., and Langer, E. J. Long-term effects of a control-relevant intervention with institutionalized aged. *Journal of Personality and Social Psychology*, 1977, *35*, 897–902.

Rodin, J., Rennert, K., and Solomon, S. K. Intrinsic motivation for control: Fact or fiction. In A. Baum and J. E. Singer (Eds.), *Advances in environmental psychology: Applications of personal control*, vol. 2. Hillsdale, NJ: Erlbaum, 1980.

Rodin, J., and Slochower, J. Externality in the nonobese: The effects of environmental responsiveness on weight. *Journal of Personality and Social Psychology*, 1976, *33*, 338–344.

Rodin, J., Solomon, S., and Metcalf, J. Role of control in mediating perceptions of density. *Journal of Personality and Social Psychology*, 1978, *36*, 988–999.

Rogentine, G. N., Van Kammen, D. P., Fox, B. H., et al. Psychological factors in the prognosis of malignant melanoma: A prospective study. *Psychosomatic Medicine*, 1979, *41*, 647–655.

Rogers, M., and Rippetoe, P. A. Effects of components of protection-motivation theory on adaptive and maladaptive coping with a health threat. *Journal of Personality and Social Psychology*, 1987, *52*(3), 596–604.

Rogers, M., and Reich, P. Psychological intervention with surgical patients: Evaluation outcome. *Advances in psychology and gynecological problems*. London: Tavistock, 1986, pp. 161–188.

Rogers, M. P., Dubey, D., and Reich, P. The influence of the psyche and the brain on immunity and disease susceptibility: A critical review. *Psychosomatic Medicine*, 1979, *41*, 147–164.

Roitt, I., Brostoff, J., and Male, D. *Immunology*. St. Louis: C. V. Mosby, 1985.

Rose, R. M., Jenkins, C. D., and Hurst, M. W. Air traffic controller health change study (FAA Contract No. DOT-FA73WA-3211). Boston: Boston University School of Medicine, 1978.

Rosen, R. C., Brondolo, E., and Kostis, J. B. Non-pharmacological treatment of essential hypertension: Research and clinical applications. In R. J. Gatchel and E. Blanchard (Eds.), *Psychophysiological disorders: Research and clinical application*. Washington, DC: American Psychological Association, 1994.

Rosenbaum, M., and Jaffee, Y. Learned helplessness: The role of individual differences in learned resourcefulness. *British Journal of Social Psychology*, 1983, *22*, 215–225.

Rosenman, R. H. The interview method of assessment of the coronary-prone behavior pattern. In T. M. Dembroski, S. M. Weiss, J. L. Shields, et al. (Eds.), *Coronary-prone behavior*. New York: Springer-Verlag, 1978a.

———. The role of the Type A behavior pattern in ischaemic heart disease: Modification of its effects by beta-blocking agents. *British Journal of Clinical Practice*, 1978b, *32*, 58–65.

Rosenman, R. H., Brand R. J., Jenkins, C. D., et al. Coronary heart disease in the Western Collaborative Group Study: Final follow-up experience of $8 \frac{1}{2}$ years. *Journal of the American Medical Association*, 1975, *233*, 872–877.

Rosenstock, I. M. Why people use health services. *Milbank Memorial Fund Quarterly*, 1966, *44*, 94–127.

———. The health belief model and preventive health behavior. *Health Education Monographs*, 1979, *2*, 354–386.

Rosenthal, D. *Genetic theory and abnormal behavior*. New York: McGraw-Hill, 1970.

Rosenzweig, M. R., Leiman, A. L., and Breedlove, S. M. *Biological psychology*. Sunderland, MA: Sinauter Associates, 1996, p. 232.

Roskies, E., Seraganian, P., Oseasohn, R., et al. The Montreal Type A intervention project: Major findings. *Health Psychology*, 1986, *5*, 45–69.

Ross, R., and Glosmet, J. A. The pathogenesis of arthersclerosis. *New England Journal of Medicine*, 1976, *295*, 369–377, 420–425.

Ross, T. A. *Lectures on war neuroses*. London: Edward Arnold, 1941.

Roter, D. L. Patient question asking in physician-patient interaction. *Health Psychology*, 1984, *3*(5), 395–409.

Roth, S., and Bootzin, R. R. Effects of experimentally induced expectancies of external control: An investigation of learned helplessness. *Journal of Personality and Social Psychology*, 1974, *29*, 253–264.

Roth, S., and Krubal, L. Effects of noncontingent reinforcement on tasks of differing importance: Facilitation of learned helplessness. *Journal of Personality and Social Psychology*, 1975, *32*, 680–691.

Rotter, J. B. Generalized expectancies for internal versus external control of reinforcement. *Psychological Monographs*, 1966, *80*, (Whole No. 609), 1–28.

Rotton, J., Oszewski, D., Charleton, M., and Soler, E. Loud speech, conglomerate noise, and behavioral aftereffects. *Journal of Applied Psychology*, 1878, *63*, 360–365.

Rouse, B. A. (Ed.). *Substance abuse and mental health statistics sourcebook*. (DHHS Publication No. [SMA] 95-3064). Washington, DC: Superintendent of Documents: U.S. Government Printing Office, 1995.

Ruberman, W., Weinblatt, E., Goldberg, J. D., and Chaudhary, B. S. Psychosocial influences on mortality after myocardial infarction. *New England Journal of Medicine,* 1984, *311,* 552–559.

Rubonis, A. V., and Bickman, L. Psychological impairment in the wake of disaster. The disaster-psychopathology relationship. *Psychological Bulletin,* 1991, *109*(3), 384–399.

Rudd, P. The measurement of compliance: Medication taking. In N. A. Krasnegor, L. H. Epstein, S. B. Johnson, and S. J. Yaffe (Eds.), *Developmental aspects of health compliance behavior.* Stanford, CA: Stanford University, 1993, pp. 185–213.

Russel, M. A. H. Tobacco dependence: Is nicotine rewarding or aversive? In *Cigarette smoking is a dependence process* (NIDA Research Monograph No. 23, DHEW Publication No. ADM 79-800). Washington, DC: U.S. Government Printing Office, 1979.

Rybstein-Blinchik, E. Effects of different cognitive strategies on chronic pain experience. *Journal of Behavioral Medicine,* 1979, 2, 93–101.

Rychtarik, R. G., Prue, D. M., Rapp, S. R., and King, A. C. Self-efficacy, aftercare and relapse in a treatment program for alcoholics. *Journal of Studies on Alcohol,* 1992, *53*(5), 435–440.

Sacerdote, P. Hypnosis in cancer patients. *American Journal of Clinical Hypnosis,* 1966, *9,* 100–108.

Sach, D. P. L., Hall, R. G., and Hall, S. M. Effects of rapid smoking. Physiological evaluation of a smoking-cessation therapy. *Annals of Internal Medicine,* 1978, *88,* 639–641.

Sackett, D. L., and Haynes, R. B. *Compliance with therapeutic regimens.* Baltimore: Johns Hopkins University Press, 1976.

Saile, H., Burgmeier, R., and Schmidt, L. R. A meta-analysis of studies on psychological preparation of children facing medical procedures. *Psychology and Health,* 1988, *2,* 107–132.

St. Lawrence, J. S. African-American adolescents' knowledge, health-related attitudes, sexual behavior, and contraceptive decisions: Implications for the prevention of adolescent HIV infection. *Journal of Consulting and Clinical Psychology,* 1993, *61*(1), 104–112.

Sakakibara, T. Effects of brightness or darkness on carcinogenesis. *Nagoya Shirisj Daigaku Igakkai Sasshi,* 1966, *19,* 525–547.

Salloway, J. C., and Dillon, P. B. A comparison of family network and friend network in health care utilization. *Journal of Comparative Family Studies,* 1973, *4,* 131–142.

Salovey, P., Sieber, W. J., Smith, A. F., et al. Reporting chronic pain episodes on health surveys. *Vital and health statistics. (Series, 6, No. 6,* 1-71 [DHHS] Publication No. 92–1081). Washington, DC, U.S. Government Printing Office, 1992.

Salter, A. *Conditioned reflex therapy.* New York: Capricorn Books, 1949.

Samson, J. A., Mirin, S. M., Hauser, S. T., et al. Learned helplessness and urinary MHPG levels in unipolar depression. *American Journal of Psychiatry,* 1992, *149*(6), 806–809.

Sanchez-Craig, M., Annis, H. M., Bornet, A. R., and MacDonald, K. R. Random assignment to abstinence and controlled drinking: Evaluation of a cognitive-behavioral program for problem drinkers. *Journal of Consulting and Clinical Psychology,* 1984, *52,* 390–403.

Sanders, S. H. Operant conditioning with chronic pain: Back to basics. In R. J. Gatchel and D. C. Turk (Eds.), *Psychological approaches to pain management: A practitioner's handbook.* New York: Guilford Publications, 1996.

Santrock, J. W. *Life-span development,* 2nd ed. Dubuque, IA: William C. Brown, 1986.

Sarason, I. G., Johnson, J. H., and Siegel, J. M. Assessing the impact of life changes: Development of the life experiences survey. *Journal of Consulting and Clinical Psychology,* 1978, *46,* 932–946.

Saxena, A. K., Sing, K. P., Srivastava, S. N., et al. Immunomodulation effects of caffeine (1, 3, 7-trimethylxanthine) in rodents. *Indian Journal of Experimental Biology,* 1984, *22,* 298–301.

Scarf, M. Images that heal: A doubtful idea whose time has come. *Psychology Today,* 1980, *14*(4), 32–46.

Schachter, S. *The psychology of affiliation.* Stanford, CA: Stanford University Press, 1959.

———. *Emotion, obesity and crime.* New York: Academic Press, 1971.

———. Pharmacological and psychological determinants of smoking. *Annals of Internal Medicine,* 1978, *88,* 104–114.

Schachter, S., and Rodin, J. *Obese humans and rats.* Hillsdale, NJ: Erlbaum, 1974.

Schachter, S., Silverstein, B., Kozlowski, L. T., et al. Studies of the interaction of psychosocial and pharmacological determinants of smoking. *Journal of Experimental Psychology: General,* 1977, *106,* 3–40.

Schachter, S., and Singer, J. E. Cognitive, social, and physiological determinants of emotional state. *Psychological Review,* 1962, *69,* 379–399.

Schachter, S., and Singer, J. E. Comments on the Maslach and Marshall-Zimbardo experiments. *Journal of Personality and Social Psychology,* 1979, *37,* 989–995.

Schaeffer, M. A., and Baum, A. Adrenal cortisol response to stress at Three Mile Island. *Psychosomatic Medicine,* 1984, *46,* 227–237.

Schedlowski, M., Jacobs, R., Stratmann, G., et al. Changes of natural killer cells during acute psychological stress. *Journal of Clinical Immunology,* 1993, *13,* 119–125.

Scheier, M. F. Optimism, coping, and health: Assessment and implications of generalized outcome expectancies. *Health Psychology,* 1985, *4*(3), 219–247.

Scheier, M. F., and Bridges, M. W. Person variables and health: Personality predispositions and acute psychological states as shared determinants for disease. *Psychosomatic Medicine,* 1995, *57*(3), 255–268.

Scheier, M. F., and Carver, C. S. Optimism, coping, and health: Assessment and implications of generalized outcome expectancies. *Health Psychology,* 1985, *4,* 219–247.

Scheier, M. F., and Carver, C. S. Dispositional optimism and physical well-being: The influence of generalized outcome expectancies on health. Special issue: Personality and physical health. *Journal of Personality,* 1987, *55*(2), 169–210.

Scheier, M. F., and Carver, C. S. Effects of optimism on psychological and physical well-being: Theoretical overview and empirical update. *Cognitive Therapy and Research,* 1992, *16,* 201–228.

Scheier, M. F., Matthews, K. A., Owens, J. F., et al. Dispositional optimism and recovery from coronary artery bypass surgery. *Journal of Personality and Social Psychology,* 1989, *57,* 1024–1040.

Scheier, M. F., Weintraub, J. K., and Carver, C. S. Coping with stress: Divergent strategies of optimists and pessimists. *Journal of Personality and Social Psychology,* 1986, *51,* 1257–1264.

Schiffman, E. L., Fricton, J. R., Haley, D. P., and Shapiro, B. L. The prevalence and treatment needs of subjects with temporomandibular disorders. *Journal of the American Dental Association,* 1990, *120,* 295–303.

Schleifer, S. J., Keller, S. E., Bond, R. N., et al. Major depressive disorder and immunity. *Archives of General Psychiatry,* 1989, *46,* 81–87.

Schleifer, S. J., Keller, S. E., Camerino, M., et al. Suppression of lymphocyte stimulation following bereavement. *Journal of the American Medical Association,* 1983, *250*(3), 374–377.

Schleifer, S. J., Keller, S. E., McKegney, F., and Stein, M. Bereavement and lymphocyte function. Paper presented at the American Psychiatric Association, Montreal, Canada, May 1980.

Schleifer, S. J., Keller, S. E., Meyerson, A. T., et al. Lymphocyte function in major depressive disorder. *Archives of General Psychiatry,* 1984, *41,* 484–486.

Schmale, A. H. Relationship of separation and depression to disease. *Psychosomatic Medicine,* 1958, *20,* 259–277.

———. Giving up as a final common pathway to changes in health. *Advances in Psychosomatic Medicine,* 1972, *8,* 20–40.

Schmoling, P. Human reactions to the Nazi concentration camps: A summing up. *Journal of Human Stress,* 1984, *10,* 108–120.

Schnall, P., Pieper, C., Schwartz, J., et al. The relationship between "job strain," workplace diastolic blood pressure and left ventricular mass index. *Journal of the American Medical Association,* 1990, *263,* 1929–1935.

Schneider, A. M., and Tarshis, B. *Elements of physiological psychology.* New York: McGraw-Hill, 1995, p. 356.

Schneider, A. P., 2d., Nelson, D. J., and Brown, D. D. In-hospital cardiopulmonary resuscitation: A 30-year review. *Journal of the American Board of Family Practice,* 1993, *6*(2), 91–101.

Schneider, P., and Cable, G. Compliance clinic: An opportunity for an expanded role for pharmacists. *American Journal of Hospital Pharmacy,* 1978, *35,* 288–295.

Schneiderman, N. Animal behavior models of coronary heart disease. In D. S. Krantz, A. Baum, and J. E. Singer (Eds.), *Handbook of psychology and health,* vol. 3, *Cardiovascular disorders.* Hillsdale, NJ: Erlbaum, 1983.

Schneiderman, N., Antoni, M. H., Ironson, G., et al. Applied psychological science and HIV-1 spectrum disease. *Applied and Preventive Psychology,* 1992, *1*(2), 67–82.

Schoenen, J., Bottin, D., Hardy, F., and Garard, P. Cephalic and extracephalic pressure pain thresholds in chronic tension-type headache. *Pain,* 1991, *40,* 65–75.

Schofield, W. The role of psychology in the delivery of health service. *American Psychologist,* 1969, *24,* 565–584.

Schotte, D. E., Cools, J., and McNally, R. J. Film-induced negative affect triggers overeating in restrained eaters. *Journal of Abnormal Psychology,* 1990, *99,* 317–320.

Schroeder, D. H., and Costa, P. T., Jr. Influences of life event stress on physical illness: Substantive effects of methodological flaws? *Journal of Personality and Social Psychology,* 1984, *46*(4), 853–863.

Schultz, J. H., and Luthe, W. *Autogenic training: A psychophysiological approach in psychotherapy.* New York: Grune & Stratton, 1959.

Schulz, R. *The psychology of death, dying, and bereavement.* Reading, MA: Addison-Wesley, 1978, pp. 97–98.

Schulz, R., and Aderman, D. Effect of residential change on the temporal distance to death of terminal cancer patients. *Omega: Journal of Death and Dying,* 1973, *4*(2), 157–162.

Schulz, R., and Brenner, G. F. Relocation of the aged: A review and theoretical analysis. *Journal of Gerontology,* 1977, *32,* 323–333.

Schwartz, G. E. Psychophysiological patterning and emotion from a systems perspective. *Social Science Information,* 1982, *21*(6), 781–817.

Schwartz, G. E., and Kline, J. P. Depression, emotional disclosure, and health: Theoretical, empirical, and clinical considerations. In J. Pennebaker (Ed.), *Emotions, disclosure, and health.* Washington, DC: American Psychological Association, 1995.

Schwartz, G. E., and Weiss, S. What is behavioral medicine? *Psychosomatic Medicine,* 1977, *36,* 377–381.

Schwartzberg, S. S., and Janoff-Bulman, R. Grief and the search for meaning: Exploring the assumptive worlds of bereaved college students. *Journal of Social and Clinical Psychology,* 1991, *10*(3), 270–288.

Scientific Registry. Number of U.S. Transplants. Richmond, VA: United Network for Organ Sharing, July 31, 1995.

Sedek, G., Kofta, M., and Tyszka, T. Effects of uncontrollability on subsequent decision making: Testing the cognitive exhaustion hypothesis. *Journal of Personality and Social Psychology,* 1993, *65*(6), 1270–1281.

Seeman, T. E., Berkman, L. F., Blazer, D., and Rowe, J. W. Social ties and support and neuroendocrine function: The MacArthur studies of successful aging. *Annals of Behavioral Medicine,* 1994, *16,* 95–106.

Seligman, M. E. P. *Helplessness: On depression, development and death.* San Francisco: W. H. Freeman, 1975.

———. Learned helplessness and depression in animals and men. In J. T. Spence, R. C. Carson, and J. W. Thibaut (Eds.), *Behavioral approaches to therapy.* Morristown, NJ: General Learning Press, 1976.

Seligman, M. E. P., Abramson, L. Y., Semmel, A., and Von Baeyer, C. Depressive attributional style. *Journal of Abnormal Psychology,* 1979, *88,* 242–247.

Seligman, M. E. P., Maier, S. F., and Geer, J. The alleviation of learned helplessness in the dog. *Journal of Abnormal and Social Psychology,* 1967, *73,* 256–262.

Seligman, M. E. P., and Visintainer, M. A. Tumor rejection and early experience of uncontrollable shock in the rat. In F. R. Brush and J. B. Overmier (Eds.), *Affect conditioning and cognition: Essays on the determinants of behavior.* Hillsdale, NJ: Erlbaum, 1985.

Selwyn, P. A. AIDS—What is now known. Psychological aspects, treatment prospects. *Hospital Practice,* 1986, *21*(6), 125.

Selye, H. The stress of life. New York: McGraw-Hill, 1956.

———. *The stress of life.* (rev. ed.). New York: McGraw-Hill, 1976.

———. *The stress of life.* (rev. ed.). New York: McGraw-Hill, 1984.

Shapiro, A. K. Placebo effects in medicine, psychotherapy, and psychoanalysis. In A. E. Bergin and S. L. Garfield (Eds.), *Handbook of psychotherapy and behavior change: An empirical analysis.* New York: Wiley, 1971.

Shapiro, A. P. The non-pharmacologic treatment of hypertension. In D. S. Krantz, A. Baum, and J. E. Singer (Eds.), *Handbook of psychology and health,* vol. 3, *Cardiovascular disorders and behavior.* Hillsdale, NJ: Erlbaum, 1983.

Shapiro, A. P., Schwartz, G. E., Ferguson, D. C. E., et al. Behavioral methods in the treatment of hypertension: I. Review of their clinical status. *Annals of Internal Medicine,* 1977, *86,* 626–636.

Shattuck-Eidens, D., et al. Assessment and counseling for women with family history of breast cancer: A guide for clinicians. *Journal of the American Medical Association,* 1995, *273,* 577–585.

Sheeran, P., and Abraham, C. Measurement of condom use in 72 studies of HIV-preventive behaviour: A critical review. Special issue: Current perspective: AIDS/HIV education and counseling. *Patient Education and Counseling,* 1994, *24*(3), 199–216.

Sheffer, A. L. Guidelines for the diagnosis and management of asthma. *Pediatric Asthma, Allergy, and Immunology,* 1991, *5,* 57–188.

Shekelle, R. B., Gale, M., Ostfeld, A. M., and Paul, O. Hostility, risk of coronary heart disease and mortality. *Psychosomatic Medicine,* 1983, *45,* 109–114.

Shekelle, R. B., Hulley, S. B., Neaton, J., et al. The MRFIT behavioral pattern study. II: Type A behavior pattern and risk of coronary death in MRFIT. *American Journal of Epidemiology,* 1985, *122,* 559–570.

Shepherd, J. T., and Vanhoutte, P. M. *The human cardiovascular system: Facts and concepts,* New York: Raven Press, 1979, p. 3.

Sher, K. J. Stress response dampening. In H. T. Blane and K. E. Leonard (Eds.), *Psychological theories of drinking and alcoholism.* New York: Guilford Press, 1987, pp. 227–271.

Sherrod, D. R. Crowding, perceived control, and behavioral aftereffects. *Journal of Applied Social Psychology,* 1974, *4,* 171–186.

Sherrod, D. R., and Downs, R. Environmental determinants of altruism: The effects of stimulus overload and perceived control on helping. *Journal of Experimental Social Psychology,* 1974, *10,* 468–479.

Sherrod, D. R., Hage, J. N., Halpern, P. L., and Moore, B. S. Effects of personal causation and perceived control on responses to an aversive environment: The more control, the better. *Journal of Experimental Social Psychology,* 1977, *13,* 14–27.

Sherwood, R. J. Compliance behavior of hemodialysis patients and the role of the family. *Family Systems Medicine,* 1983, *1*(2), 60–72.

Shiffman, S. Tobacco "chippers": Individual differences in tobacco dependence. *Psychopharmacology,* 1989, *97*(4), 539–547.

Shiffman, S., Fischer, L. B., Zettler-Segal, M., and Benowitz, N. L. Nicotine exposure among nondependent smokers. *Archives of General Psychiatry,* 1990, *47*(4), 333–336.

Shiffman, S., Shumaker, S. A., Abrams, D. B., et al. Models of smoking relapse. *Health Psychology,* 1986, *5 suppl.,* 13–27.

Shore, J. H., Tatum, E. L., and Vollmer, W. M. The Mount St. Helens stress response syndrome. In J. H. Shore (Ed.), *Disaster stress studies: New methods and findings.* Washington, DC: American Psychiatric Press, 1987, pp. 7–97.

Shrut, S. Attitudes toward old age and death. In R. Fulton (Ed.), *Death and identity.* New York: Wiley, 1965.

Shumaker, A., and Peguegnat, W. Hospital design, health providers, and the delivery of effective health care. In E. H. Zube and G. T. Moore (Eds.), *Advances in environment, behavior, and design,* vol. 2. Bethesda, MD: National Institutes of Health, Lung, and Blood, 1989, pp. 161–199.

Shumaker, S. A., and Czajkowski, S. M. *Social support and cardiovascular disease.* New York: Plenum, 1994.

Shumaker, S. A., and Grunberg, N. E. Proceedings of the National Working Conference on Smoking Relapse. *Health Psychology,* 1986, *5*(suppl.), 13–27.

Shumaker, S. A., Schrom, E. B., and Ockene, J. (Eds.). *The handbook of health behavior change.* New York: Springer, 1990.

Sieber, W. J., Rodin, J., Larson L., et al. Modulation of human natural killer cell activity by exposure to uncontrollable stress. *Brain, Behavior, and Immunity,* 1992. *6,* 141–156.

Siegel, K., Raveis, V. H., and Karus, D. Psychological well-being of gay men with AIDS: Contribution of positive and negative illness-related network interactions to depressive mood. *Social Science and Medicine,* 1994, *39*(11), 1555–1563.

Siegel, S. Morphine tolerance acquisition as an associate process. *Journal of Experimental Psychology: Animal Behavior Processes,* 1977, *3,* 1–13.

Siegman, A., and Smith, T. W. *Anger, hostility, and the heart.* Hillsdale, NJ: Erlbaum, 1994.

Sifneos, P. E. Clinical observations in some patients suffering from a variety of psychosomatic diseases. *Proceedings of the Seventh European Conference on Psychosomatic Research.* London: Karger, 1967.

Silverman, N. A., Potvin, C., Alexander, J. C., and Chretien, P. B. In vitro lymphocyte reactivity and T-cell levels in chronic cigarette smokers. *Clinical and Experimental Immunology,* 1975, *22,* 285–292.

Silverstein, B., Kelley, E., Swan, J., and Kozlowski, L. Physiological predisposition towards becoming a cigarette smoker: Experimental evidence for sex differences. *Addictive Behavior,* 1982, *7,* 83–86.

Simkins, L., and Eberhage, M. Attitudes towards AIDS, herpes II, and toxic shock syndrome. *Psychological Reports,* 1984, *55,* 779–786.

Sims, J. H., and Baumann, D. D. The tornado threat: Coping styles of the North and South. In J. H. Sims and D. D. Baumann (Eds.), *Human behavior and the environ-*

ment: Interactions between man and his physical world. Chicago: Maaroufa Press, 1974.

Singer, J. E., Lundberg, U., and Frankenhaeuser, M. Stress on the train: A study of urban commuting. In A. Baum, J. E. Singer, and S. Valins (Eds.), *Advances in environmental psychology,* vol. 1. Hillsdale, NJ: Erlbaum, 1978.

Sinyor, D., Schwartz, J. G., Peronnet, F., et al. Aerobic fitness level and reactivity to psychosocial stress. *Psychosomatic Medicine,* 1983, *45,* 205–217.

Sjostrom, L. Impacts of body weight, body composition, and adipose tissue distribution on mobility and mortality. In A. J. Stunkard and T. A. Wadden (Eds.), *Obesity: Theory and therapy.* New York, Raven Press, 1993, pp. 13–42.

Sklar, L. S., and Anisman, H. Stress and coping factors influence tumor growth. *Science,* 1979, *205,* 513–515.

Sklar, L. S., and Anisman, H. Stress and cancer. *Psychological Bulletin,* 1981, *89,* 369–406.

Skodak, M., and Skeels, H. M. A final follow-up study of one hundred adopted children. *Journal of Genetic Psychology,* 1949, *75,* 85–125.

Skre, I., Onstad, S., Togerson, S., and Kringlen, E. High interrater reliability for the structured clinical interview for DSM-III-R Axis I (SCID-1). *Acta Psychiatrica Scandinavica,* 1991, *84,* 167–173.

Sloan, P. Posttraumatic stress in survivors of an airplane crashlanding: A clinical and exploratory research intervention. *Journal of Traumatic Stress,* 1988, *1*(2), 211–229.

Smith, C. D., Carney, J. M., Starke-Reed, P. E., et al. Excess brain protein oxidation and enzyme dysfunction in normal aging and in Alzheimer's disease. *Proceedings of the National Academy of Sciences, USA,* 1991, *88,* 10540–10543.

Smith, E. M., North, C. S., McCool, R. E., et al. Acute post-disaster psychiatric disorders: Identification of those at risk. *American Journal of Psychiatry,* 1989, *147*(2), 202–206.

Smith, S. The unique power of music therapy benefits Alzheimer's patients. *Activities, Adaptation and Aging,* 1990, *14*(4), 59–63.

Smith, T. W. Hostility and health: Current status of a psychosomatic hypothesis. *Health Psychology,* 1992, *11,* 139–150.

Smith, T. W., Turner, C. W., Ford, M. H., et al. Blood pressure reactivity in adult male twins. *Health Psychology,* 1987, *6,* 209–220.

Snow, B. Level of aspiration in coronary prone and noncoronary prone adults. *Personality and Social Psychology Bulletin,* 1978, *4,* 416–419.

Snyder, M. Self-monitoring of expressive behavior. *Journal of Personality and Social Psychology,* 1974, *30*(4), 526–537.

Snyder, M., and Miene, P. K. Stereotyping of the elderly: A functional approach. *British Journal of Social Psychology,* 1994, *33*(Pt. 1), 63–82.

Snyder, S. Opiate receptors and internal opiates. *Scientific American,* 1977, *236,* 44–56.

Sobal, J., and Stunkard, A. J. Socioeconomic status and obesity: A review of the literature. *Psychological Bulletin,* 1989, *105*(2), 260–275.

Sobel, D. S. Mind matters, money matters: The cost-effectiveness of clinical behavioral medicine. In S. J. Blumenthal, K. Matthews, and S. M. Weiss (Eds.), *New research frontiers in behavioral medicine: Proceedings of the National Conference,* 1994, p. 25.

Sobell, M. B., and Sobell, J. C. Controlled drinking after 25 years: How important was the great debate? *Addiction,* 1995, *90,* 1149–1153.

Sobell, M. B., and Sobell, L. C. Individualized behavior therapy for alcoholics. *Behavior Therapy,* 1973, *4,* 49–72.

Soloman, Z., Mikulincer, M., and Arad, R. Monitoring and blunting: Implications for combat-related posttraumatic stress disorder. *Journal of Traumatic Stress,* 1991 *4*(2), 209–221.

Solomon, G. F. Stress and antibody response in rats. *International Archives of Allergy and Applied Immunology,* 1969, *35,* 97.

Solomon, G. F., and Amkraut, A. A. Neuroendocrine aspects of the immune response and their implications for stress effects on tumor immunity. *Cancer Detection and Prevention,* 1979, *2,* 197–224.

Solomon, G. F., Temoshok, L., O'Leary, A., and Zich, J. An intensive psychoimmuno-logic study of long-surviving persons with AIDS. Pilot work, background studies, hypotheses, and methods. *Annals of the New York Academy of Sciences,* 1987, *496,* 647–655.

Solomon, M. S., and DeJong, W. Recent sexually transmitted disease prevention efforts and their implications for AIDS health education. *Health Education Quarterly,* 1986, *13,* 4.

Somes, G. W., Harshfield, G. A., Alpert, B. S., et al. Genetic influences on ambulatory blood pressure patterns: The Medical College of Virginia Twin Study. *American Journal of Hypertension,* 1995, *8,* 474–478.

Southward, E. E. *Shell shock.* Boston: W. M. Leonard, 1919.

Southwick, S. M., Bremnere, D., Krystal, J. H., and Charney, D. S. Psychobiologic re-search in post-traumatic stress disorder. *Psychiatric Clinics of North America,* 1994, *17*(2), 251–264.

Spackman, D. H., and Riley, V. Stress effects of the LDH-virus in alternating the Gard-ner tumor in mice. *Proceedings of the American Association for Cancer Research,* 1975, *16,* 170.

Spagnuolo, P. J., and MacGregor, R. R. Acute ethanol effect on chemotaxis and other components of host defense. *Journal of Laboratory and Clinical Medicine,* 1975, *70,* 295–301.

Spector, N. H., Provinciali, M., di Stegano, G., et al. Immune enhancement by condition-ing of senescent mice. Comparison of old and young mice in learning ability and in ability to increase natural killer cell activity and other host defense reactions in re-sponse to a conditioned stimulus. *Annals of the New York Academy of Sciences,* 1994, *741,* 283–291.

Speisman, J., Lazarus, R. S., Mordkoff, A., and Davidson, L. Experimental reduction of stress based on ego defense theory. *Journal of Abnormal and Social Psychology,* 1964, *68,* 367–380.

Spence, S. H. Congitive-behavior therapy in the management of chronic, occupational pain of the upper limbs. *Behaviour Research and Therapy,* 1989, *27*(4), 435–446.

Spiegel, D., and Bloom, J. R. Group therapy and hypnosis reduce metastatic breast car-cinoma pain. *Psychosomatic Medicine,* 1983, *45,* 333–339.

Spiegel, D., Bloom, J. R., Kraemer, H. C., and Gottheil, E. Effects of psychosocial treat-ment on survival of patients with metastatic breast cancer. *Lancet,* 1989, *2,* 888–891.

Spiegel, D., Bloom, J. R., and Yalom, I. Group support for patients with metastatic can-cer: A randomized prospective outcome study. *Archives of General Psychiatry,* 1981, *38,* 527–533.

Spitzer, R. L., and Endicott, J. DIAGNO II: Further developments in computer program for psychiatric diagnosis. *American Journal of Psychiatry,* 1969, *125,* 12–21.

Spitzer, R. L., Williams, J. B. W., Gibbon, M., and First, M. B. *Structured clinical interview of DSM-III-R.* New York: State Psychiatric Institute, 1988.

Spitzer, S. B., Llabre, M. M., Ironson, G. H., et al. The influence of social situations on ambulatory blood pressure. *Psychosomatic Medicine,* 1992, *54,* 79–86.

Stacey, N. H. Inhibition of antibody-dependent cell-medicated cytotoxicity by ethanol. *Immunology,* 1984, *8,* 155–161.

Stachnik, T., Stoffelmayr, B., and Hoppe, R. B. Prevention, behavior change, and chronic disease. In T. Burish and L. A. Bradley (Eds.), *Coping with chronic disease.* New York: Academic Press, 1983.

Staffieri, J. R. A study of social stereotype of body image in children. *Journal of Personality and Social Psychology,* 1967, *7*(1), 101–104.

Staub, E., Tursky, B., and Schwartz, G. E. Self-control and predictability: The effects on reactions to aversive stimulation. *Journal of Personality and Social Psychology,* 1971, *18,* 157–162.

Stavraky, K. M. Psychological factors in outcome of human cancer. *Journal of Psychosomatic Research,* 1968, *12,* 251.

Stein, M. Stress, depression, and the immune system. Symposium: Interrelations between depression, the immune system, and the endocrine system. *Journal of Clinical Psychiatry,* 1989, *50*(suppl.), 35–40.

Stein, M., Keller, S. E., and Scheifer, S. J. Stress and immunomodulation: The role of depression and neuroendocrine function. *Journal of Immunology,* 1985, *135*(suppl. 2), 827–833.

Stein, M. J., Wallston, K. A., and Nicassio, P. M. Factor structure of the Arthritis Helplessness Index. *Journal of Rheumatology,* 1988, *15,* 427–432.

Steinglass, P., and Gerrity, E. Natural disasters and post-traumatic stress disorder: Short-term vs. long-term recovery in two disaster-affected communities. *Journal of Applied Social Psychology,* 1989, *20,* 1746–1765.

Stephens, R. C., Feucht, T. E., and Roman, S. W. Effects of an intervention program on AIDS-related drug and needle behavior among intravenous drug users. *American Journal of Public Health,* 1991, *81*(5), 568–571.

Stepney, R. Smoking behavior: A psychology of the cigarette habit. *British Journal of Diseases of the Chest,* 1980, *74,* 325–344.

Sterling, B. Science: Bitter resistance. *Fantasy and Science Fiction,* February 1995, 89–101.

Sternbach, R. A. *Principles of psychophysiology.* New York: Academic Press, 1966.

———. *Pain patients: Traits and treatment.* New York: Academic Press, 1974.

———. Pain and "hassles" in the United States: Findings of the Nurpin Pain Report. *Pain,* 1986, *27*(1), 69–80.

Sternbach, R. A., and Tursky, B. Ethnic differences among housewives in psychophysical and skin potential responses to electric shock. *Psychophysiology,* 1965, *I,* 241–246.

Sternbach, R. A., Wolf, S. R., Murphy, R. W., and Akeson, W. H. Traits of pain patients: The low-back "loser." *Psychosomatics,* 1973, *14,* 226–229.

Sternberg, R. J. *In search of the human mind.* Fort Worth, TX: Harcourt Brace and Company, 1995, p. 158.

Stevens, J., Cook, M., and Jordan, C. Reactivation of latent herpes simplex virus after pneumococcal pneumonia in mice. *Infectious Immunology,* 1975, *11,* 635–639.

Stewart, W. F., Lipton, R. B., Celentano, D. D., and Reed, M. L. Prevalence of migraine headache in the United States. Relation to age, income, race, and other sociodemographic factors. *Journal of the American Medical Association,* 1992, *267,* 84–89.

Stitzer, M. L., Rand, C. S., Bigelow, G. E., and Mead, A. M. Contingent payment procedures for smoking reduction and cessation. *Journal of Applied Behavior Analysis,* 1986, *19*(2), 197–202.

Stone, A. A. Event content in a daily survey is differentially associated with concurrent mood. *Journal of Personality and Social Psychology,* 1987, *52*(1), 56–58.

Stone, A. A., Cox, D. S., Valdimarsdottir, H., and Neale, J. M. Secretory IgA as a measure of immunocompetence. *Journal of Human Stress,* 1987, *13,* 136–140.

Stone, A. A., Porter, L. S., and Neale, J. M. Daily events and mood prior to the onset of respiratory illness episodes: A non-replication of the 3–5 day "desirability dip." *British Journal of Medical Psychology,* 1993, *66*(4), 383–393.

Stoney, C. M., Davis, M. C., and Matthews, K. A. Sex differences in physiological responses to stress and coronary heart disease: A causal link? *Psychophysiology,* 1987, *24,* 127–131.

Stoney, C. M., and Engebretson, T. O. Anger and hostility: Potential mediators of the gender difference in coronary heart disease. In A. W. Siegman and T. W. Smith (Eds.), *Anger, hostility, and the heart.* Providence, RI: Brown University, 1994, pp. 215–237.

Stoney, C. M., Matthews, K. A., McDonald, R. H., and Johnson, C. A. Sex differences in lipid, lipoprotein, cardiovascular and neuroendocrine responses to acute stress. *Psychophysiology,* 1988, *25*(6), 645–656.

Storb, R. Preparative regimens for patients with leukemias and severe aplastic anemia (overview): Biological basis, experimental animal studies and clinical trials at the Fred Hutchinson Cancer Research Center. *Bone Marrow Transplantation,* 1994, *14*(suppl. 4), SI-3.

Stotland, E., and Blumenthal A. The reduction of anxiety as a result of the expectation of making a choice. *Canadian Journal of Psychology,* 1964, *18,* 139–145.

Stoudemire, A., and Hales, R. E. Psychological and behavioral factors affecting medical conditions and DSM-IV: An overview. *Psychosomatics,* 1991, *32,* 5–12.

Strain, J. J. Noncompliance: Its origins, manifestations, and management. *The Pharos of Alpha Omega Alpha,* 1978, *41,* 27–32.

Street, N. E., and Mosmann, T. R. Functional diversity of T lymphocytes due to secretion of different cytokine patterns. *FASEB Journal,* 1991, *5*(2), 171–177.

Stryker, J., Coates, T. J., De Carlo, P., et al. Prevention of HIV infection. Looking back, looking ahead. *Journal of the American Medical Association,* 1995, *273*(14), 1143–1148.

Stuart, R. B. Behavioral control of overeating. *Behavior Research and Therapy,* 1967, *5,* 357–365.

Stunkard, A. J. Obesity and the denial of hunger. *Psychosomatic Medicine,* 1959, *21,* 281–289.

———. Behavioral medicine and beyond: The example of obesity. In O. F. Pomerleau and J. P. Brady (Eds.), *Behavioral medicine: Theory and practice.* Baltimore: Williams & Wilkins, 1979.

Stunkard, A. J., Sorensen, T. I. A., Hanis, C., et al. An adoption study of human obesity. *New England Journal of Medicine,* 1986, *314*(4), 193–197.

Stunkard, A. J., and Wadden T. *Obesity: Theory and therapy,* 2nd ed. New York: Raven Press, 1993.

Suinn, R. M. Intervention with Type A behavior. *Journal of Consulting and Clinical Psychology,* 1982, *50,* 933–949.

Sullivan, M. J., Ressor, K., Mikail, S., and Fisher, R. The treatment of depression in chronic low back pain: Review and recommendations. *Pain,* 1992, *50*(1), 5–13.

Sullivan, P. L., and Welsh, G. S. A technique for objective configural analysis of MMPI profiles. *Journal of Consulting Psychology,* 1952, *16,* 383–388.

Suls, J., and Fletcher B. The relative efficacy of avoidant and nonavoidant coping strategies: A meta-analysis. *Health Psychology,* 1985, *4*(3), 249–288.

Surgeon General. *Smoking and health* (DHEW Publication No. [PHS] 79-50066). Washington, DC: U.S. Government Printing Office, 1979.

Surwit, R. S., and Jordan, J. S. Behavioral treatment of Raynaud's syndrome. In J. P. Hatch, J. G. Fisher, and J. D. Rugh (Eds.), *Biofeedback: Studies in clinical efficacy.* New York: Plenum, 1987, pp. 255–280.

Swenson, R. M., and Vogel, W. H. Plasma catecholamine and corticosterone as well as brain catecholamine changes during coping in rats exposed to stressful foot shock. *Pharmacology, Biochemistry and Behavior,* 1983, *18*(5), 689–693.

Symington, T., Currie, A. R., Curran, R. S., and Davidson, J. N. The reaction of the adrenal cortex in conditions of stress. In *Ciba Foundations Colloquia on Endocrinology,* vol. 8. Boston: Little, Brown, 1955.

Syrjala, K. L., and Abrams, J. R. Hypnosis and imagery in the treatment of pain. In R. J. Gatchel and D. C. Turk (Eds.), *Psychological approaches to pain management: A practioner's handbook.* New York: Guilford Publications, 1996.

Syrjala, K. L., Cummings, C., and Donaldson, G. Hypnosis or cognitive-behavioral training for the reduction of pain and nausea during cancer treatment. A controlled clinical trial. *Pain,* 1992, *48,* 137–146.

Tache, J., Selye, H., and Day, S. B. *Cancer, stress, and death.* New York: Plenum, 1979.

Taggart, V. S., Zuckerman, A. E., Sly, R. M., et al. You can control asthma: Evaluaton of an asthma education program for hospitalized inner-city children. *Patient Education and Counseling,* 1991, *17,* 35–47.

Tarlov, A. R., Ware, J. E., and Greenfield, S. The medical outcomes study: An application of methods for monitoring the results of medical care. *Journal of the American Medical Association,* 1989, *262,* 925.

Taub, A. Acupuncture "anesthesia": A critical review. In J. J. Bonica and D. Albe-Fessard (Eds.), *Advances in pain research and therapy,* vol. 1. New York: Raven Press, 1976.

Taub, E. Self-regulation of human tissue temperature. In G. E. Schwartz and J. Beatty (Eds.), *Biofeedback: Therapy and research.* New York: Academic Press, 1977.

Taylor, A. N., Ben-Eliyahu, S., Yirmiya, R., et al. Alcohol and alcoholism. *Alcohol,* 1993, (suppl. 2), 69–74.

Taylor, D. W., Sackett, D. L., Haynes, R. B., et al. Compliance with antihypertensive drug therapy. *Annals of the New York Academy of Science,* 1978, 390–403.

Taylor, S. E. Hospital patient behavior: Reactance, helplessness, or control? *Journal of Social Issues,* 1979, *35,* 156–184.

————. Adjustment to threatening events: A theory of cognitive adaptation. *American Psychologist,* 1983, *38*(11), 1161–1173.

————. Health psychology: The science and the field. *American Psychologist,* 1990, *45,* 40–50.

————. *Health psychology.* New York: McGraw-Hill, 1995.

Taylor S. E., and Brown, J. D. Illusion and well-being: A social psychological perspective in mental health. *American Psychologist,* 1988, *103*(2), 193–210.

Taylor, S. E., Helgeson, V. S., Need, G. M., and Skokan, Z. Q. Self-generated feelings of central and adjustment to physical illness. *Journal of Social Issues,* 1991, *47*(4), 91–109.

Taylor, S. E., Kemeny, M. E., Aspinwall, L. G., et al. Optimism, coping, psychological distress, and high-risk sexual behavior among men at risk for acquired immunodeficiency syndrome (AIDS). *Journal of Personality and Social Psychology,* 1992, *63,* 460–473.

Taylor, S. E., Lichtman, R. R., and Wood, J. V. Attributions, beliefs about control, and adjustments to breast cancer. *Journal of Personal and Social Psychology,* 1984, *45*(3), 489–502.

Taylor, W. R., and Newacheck, P. W. Impact of childhood asthma on health. *Pediatrics,* 1992, *90,* 657–662.

Temoshok, L. Biopsychosocial studies on cutaneous malignant melanoma: Psychosocial factors associated with prognostic indicators, progression, psychophysiology, and tumor-host response. Special issue: Cancer and the mind. *Social Science and Medicine,* 1985, *20*(8), 833–840.

Temoshok, L., Sweet, D. M., and Zich, J. A three city comparison of the public's knowledge and attitudes about AIDS. *Psychology and Health,* 1987, *1,* 43–60.

Tennen, H., and Eller, S. J. Attributional components of learned helplessness and facilitation. *Journal of Personality and Social Psychology,* 1977, *35,* 265–271.

Tessaro, I., Eugenia, E., and Smith, J. Breast cancer screening in older African-American women: Qualitative research findings. *American Journal of Health Promotion,* 1994, *8*(4), 286–293.

Tessler, R., Mechanic, D., and Diamond, M. The effect of psychological disorders on physician utilization: A prospective study. *Journal of Health and Social Behavior,* 1976, *17,* 353–364.

Testa, M. A., Anderson, R. B., Nackley, J. F., et al. Quality of life and antihypertensive therapy in men: A comparison of captopril with enalapril. *New England Journal of Medicine,* 1993, *328,* 907–913.

Theorell, T., Blomkvist, V., Jonsson, J., and Schulman, S. Social support and the development of immune function in human immunodeficiency virus infection. *Psychosomatic Medicine,* 1995, *57*(1), 32–36.

Theorell, T., Knox, S., Svensson, J., and Waller, D. Blood pressure variations during a working day at age 28: Effects of different types of work and blood pressure level at age 18. *Journal of Human Stress,* 1985, *11,* 36–41.

Theorell, T., Leymann, H., Jodko, M., and Konarski, K. "Person under train" incidents: Medical consequences for subway drivers. *Psychosomatic Medicine,* 1992, *54*(4), 480–488.

Thoits, P. A. Social support as coping assistance. *Journal of Consulting and Clinical Psychology,* 1986, *54*(4), 416–423.

Thomas, C. B., and Duszynski, K. R. Closeness to parents and the family constellation in a prospective study of five disease states: Suicide, mental illness, malignant tumor, hypertension, and coronary heart disease. *Johns Hopkins Medical Journal,* 1974, *134,* 251–270.

Thomas, D. B. Cancer. In J. M. Last, and R. B. Wallace (Eds.), *Maxcy-Rosenau-Last public health and preventive medicine.* Norwalk, CT: Appleton and Lange, 1992.

Thomas, W. R., Holt, P. G., and Keast, D. Cellular immunity in mice chronically exposed to fresh cigarette smoke. *Archives of Environmental Health,* 1973, *27*(6), 372–375.

Thompson, S. C., Soboilew-Shubin, A., Galbraith, M. E., and Schwankovsky, L. Maintaining perceptions of control: Finding perceived control in low-control circumstances. *Journal of Personality and Social Psychology,* 1993, *64*(2), 293–304.

Thompson, S. M., Dahlquist, L. M., Koenning, G. M., and Bartholomew, L. K. Brief report: Adherence-facilitating behaviors of a multidisciplinary pediatric rheumatology staff. Special section: Pediatric health care. *Journal of Pediatric Psychology,* 1995, *20*(3), 291–297.

Thompson, W. G., Creed, F., Drossman, D. A., et al. Functional bowel disease and functional abdominal pain. *Gastroenterology International,* 1992, *5,* 75–91.

Thornton, J. W., and Powell, C. D. Immunization to and alleviation of learned helplessness in man. *American Journal of Psychology,* 1974, *87,* 351–367.

Thurlow, H. J. General susceptibility to illness: A selective review. *Canadian Medical Association Journal,* 1967, *97,* 1397–1404.

Thurn, J. R. HIV worldwide. What has happened? What has changed? *Postgraduate Medicine,* 1992, *91*(8), 99–100.

Todarello, O., Casamassima, A., Marinaccio, M., and La Pesa, M. W. Alexithymia, immunity and cervical intraepithelial neoplasia: A pilot study. *Psychotherapy and Psychosomatics,* 1994, *61*(3–4), 199–204.

Tofler, G. H., Stone, P. H., Maclure, M., et al. Analysis of possible triggers of acute myocardial infarction (the MILI study). *American Journal of Cardiology,* 1990, *66*(1), 22–27.

Tollison, C. D., Hinnant, D. W., and Kriegel, M. L. Psychological concepts of pain. In T. G. Mayer, V. Mooney, and R. J. Gatchel (Eds.), *Contemporary conservative care for painful spinal disorders.* Philadelphia: Lea & Febiger, 1991.

Tomkins, S. S. Psychological model for smoking behavior. *American Journal of Public Health,* 1966, *56,* 17–20.

————. A modified model of smoking behavior. In E. Borgatta and R. Evans (Eds.), *Smoking, health and behavior.* Chicago: Aldine, 1968.

Tonnesen, H., Kaiser, A. H., Nielsen, B. B., and Pedersen, A. E. Reversibility of alcohol-induced immune depression. *British Journal of Addiction,* 1992, *87*(7), 1025–1028.

Tonnesen, P., Fryd, V., Hansen, M., and Helsted, J. Effect of nicotine chewing gum in combination with group counseling on the cessation of smoking. *New England Journal of Medicine,* 1988, *318*(1), 15–18.

Tonnesen, P., Norregaard, J., Simonsen, K., and Sawe, U. A double-blind trial of a 16-hour transdermal nicotine patch in smoking cessation. *New England Journal of Medicine,* 1988, *325*(5), 311–315.

Tonnesen, P. N., Norregaard, J., Simonsen, K., and Sawe, U. A double-blind trial of a 16-hour transdermal nicotine patch in smoking cessation [see comments]. *New England Journal of Medicine,* 1991, *325*(5), 311–315.

Trimble, M. R. *Neuropsychiatry.* Chichester, England: Wiley, 1981.

Troop, N. A., Holbrey, A., Trowler, R., and Treasure, J. L. Ways of coping in women with eating disorders. *Journal of Nervous Mental Disorders,* 1994, *182*(10), 535–540.

Tryon, R. C. Genetic differences in maze learning in rats. In *National Society for the Study of Education: The Thirty-Ninth Yearbook.* Bloomington, IL: Public School Publishing, 1940.

Turk, D. C. Biopsychosocial perspective on chronic pain. In R. J. Gatchel and D. C. Turk (Eds.), *Psychological approaches to pain management: A practitioner's handbook.* New York: Guilford Publications, 1996.

Turk, D. C., Meichenbaum, D. H., and Berman, W. H. Application of biofeedback for the regulation of pain: A critical review. *Psychological Bulletin,* 1979, *86,* 1322–1338.

Turk, D. C., Meichenbaum, D., and Genest, M. *Pain and behavioral medicine: A cognitive-behavioral perspective.* New York: Guilford Press, 1983.

Turk, D. C., and Rudy, T. E. Toward an empirically derived taxonomy of chronic pain patients: Integration of psychological assessment data. *Journal of Consulting and Clinical Psychology,* 1988, *56*(2), 233–238.

Turner, J. A., and Clancy, S. Comparison of operant behavioral and cognitive-behavioral group treatment for chronic low back pain. *Journal of Consulting and Clinical Psychology,* 1988, *56*(2), 261–266.

Turner, J. A., and Romano, J. M. Cognitive behavioral therapy. In J. J. Bonica (Ed.), *Management of pain,* 2nd ed. Philadelphia: Lea & Febiger, 1990.

Turner, R. A., Irwin, C. E., Jr., Tschann, J. M., and Millstein, S. G. Autonomy, relatedness, and initiation of health risk behaviors in early adolescents. *Health Psychology,* 1993, *12*(3), 200–208.

Tursky, B., and Sternbach, R. A. Further physiological correlates of ethnic differences in responses to shock. *Psychophysiology,* 1967, *4,* 67–74.

Turuk-Nowakowa T. Model pracy psychologa w klinice onkologicznej. *Polski Tygodnik Lekarski,* 1993, *48*(23–24), 534–535.

Uchino, B. N., Cacioppo, J. T., and Kiecolt-Glaser, J. K. The relationship between social support and physiological processes: A review with emphasis on underlying mechanisms and implications for health. *Psychology Bulletin,* still in press.

Uchino, B. N., Cacioppo, J. T., Malarkey, W., et al. Appraisal support predicts age-related differences in cardiovascular function in women. *Health Psychology,* 1995, *14*(6), 556–562.

U.S. Department of Health and Human Services. *The health consequences of smoking: Cardiovascular disease* (DHEW Publication No. [PHS] 84-50204). Rockville, MD: Public Health Service Publication, 1983.

————. *The health consequences of smoking: Nicotine addiction. A report of the Surgeon General.* (DHHS Publication No. 82-50179). Washington, DC: U.S. Government Printing Office, 1988.

————. *Healthy people 2000: National health promotion and disease preventions objectives.* Washington, DC: U.S. Government Printing Office, 1990.

————. *Healthy people 2000: Health promotion and disease prevention objectives* (DHHS Publication No. PHS 91-50212). Washington, DC: U.S. Government Printing Office, 1991.

————. Vital Health Statistics: Detailed diagnosis and procedures, National Hospital Discharge Survey, 1991. (DHSS Publication No. [PHS] 94-1776). Hyattsville, MD, 1994.

U.S. Department of Health, Education, and Welfare. *Healthy people: Surgeon General's report on health promotion and disease prevention* (DHEW Publication No. 79-55071). Washington, DC: U.S. Government Printing Office, 1979.

Van der Meerren, H. L. M., Van der Shaar, W. W., and Van den Hurk, C. M. The psychological impact of severe acne. *Cutis*, 1985, 7, 84–86.

VanDevanter, N., Shipton-Levy, R., Steilen, M., et al. A model comprehensive counseling and clinical care program for HIV positive persons. *International Conference on AIDS*, 1990, 6(2), 462.

Van Komer, R. W., and Redd, W. H. Personality factors associated with anticipatory nausea/vomiting in patients receiving cancer chemotherapy. *Health Psychology*, 1985, 4, 189–202.

Vanwesenbeeck, I., van Zessen, G., de Graaf, R., and Straver, C. J. Contextual and interactional factors influencing condom use in heterosexual prostitution contacts. *Patient Education and Counseling*, 1994, 24(3), 302–322.

Varni, J. W. *Clinical behavioral pediatrics: An interdisciplinary biobehavioral approach.* New York: Pergamon, 1983.

Visintainer, M. A., and Seligman, M. E. P. Fighting cancer: The hope factor. *American Health*, 1983, 2, 58–61.

Vitaliano, P. P., Maiuro, R. D., Russo, J., and Katon, W. Coping profiles associated with psychiatric, physical health, work, and family problems. *Health Psychology*, 1990, 9(3), 348–376.

Vitaliano, P. P., Russo, J., Carr, J. E., et al. The ways of coping checklist: Revision and psychometric properties. *Multivariate Behavioral Research*, 1985, 20, 3–26.

Wadden, T. A. The treatment of obesity: An overview. In A. J. Stunkard and T. A. Wadden (Eds.), *Obesity: Theory and therapy.* New York: Raven Press, 1993, pp. 197–218.

Waldman, I. D., Weinberg, R. A., and Scarr, S. Racial-group differences in IQ in the Minnesota Transracial Adoption Study: A reply to Levin and Lynn. *Intelligence*, 1994, 19(1), 29–44.

Waldman, R. H., Bond, J. O., Levitt, L. P., et al. An elevation of influenza immunization. Influence of route of administration and vaccine strain. *Bulletin of the World Health Organization*, 1969, 41, 543–548.

Wallasch, T. M. Transcranial Doppler ultrasonic features in episodic tension-type headache. *Cephalalgia*, 1992, 12, 293–296.

Wallston, B. S., Stein, M. J., and Smith, C. A. Form C of the MHLC scales: A condition-specific measure of locus of control. *Journal of Personality Assessment*, 1994, 63(3), 534–553.

Wallston, B. S., and Wallston, K. A. Social psychological models of health behavior: An examination and integration. In A. Baum, J. E. Singer, and S. Taylor (Eds.), *Handbook of psychology and health.* Hillsdale, NJ: Erlbaum, 1984.

Wallston, B. S., Wallston, K. A., Kaplan, G. D., and Maides, S. A. Development and validation of the health locus of control (HLC) scale. *Journal of Consultation and Clinical Psychology*, 1976, 44, 580–585.

Wallston, K. A., and Wallston, B. S. Development of the multidimensional health locus of control (MHLC) scales. *Health Education Monographs,* 1978, *6,* 160–170.

Waltz, B., and Watson, R. R. Role of alcohol abuse in nutritional immunosuppression. *Journal of Nutrition, 122,* (suppl. 3), 733–737.

Waltz, M. A., Price, R. W., and Notkins, A. L. Latent ganglionic infections with herpes simplex virus types 1 and 2: Viral reactivation *in vivo* after neurectomy. *Science,* 1974, *184,* 1185.

Warburton, D. M., Revell, A. D., and Thompson, D. H. Smokers of the future. Special issue: Future directions in tobacco research. *British Journal of Addiction,* 1991, *86*(5), 621–625.

Waxler-Morrison, N., Hislop, T., Gregory, T. G., et al. Effects of social relationships on survival for women with breast cancer: A prospective study. *Social Science and Medicine,* 1991, *33*(2), 177–183.

Wayner, E. A., Flannery, G. R., and Singer, G. The effects of taste aversion conditioning on the primary antibody response to sheep red blood cells and Brucella abortus in the albino rat. *Physiology and Behavior,* 1978, *21,* 995–1000.

Weber, B. L. Genetic testing for breast cancer. *Scientific American: Science and Medicine,* 1996, *3,* 12–21.

Weekly, C. K., Klesges R. C., and Reylea, G. Smoking as a weight control strategy and its relationship to smoking status. *Addictive Behaviors,* 1992, *17,* 259–271.

Weg, R. B. Changing physiology of aging. In D. S. Woodruff and J. E. Birren (Eds.), *Aging: Scientific perspectives and social issues,* 2nd ed. Monterey, CA: Brooks/Cole, 1983.

Wegner, D. M., and Zanakos, S. Chronic thought suppression. Special issue: Psychodynamics and social cognition: Perspective on the representation and processing of emotionally significant information. *Journal of Personality,* 1994, *62*(4), 615–640.

Weick, B. G., Ritter, S., and Ritter, R. C. Plasma catecholamines: Exaggerated elevation is associated with stress susceptibility. *Physiology and Behavior,* 1980, *24,* 869–874.

Weiner, H. *Psychobiology and human disease.* New York: Elsevier, 1977.

Weiner, H., Thaler, M., Reiser, M. F., and Mursky, I. A. Etiology of duodenal ulcer: 1. Relation of specific psychological characteristics to rate of gastric secretion (serum pepsiogen). *Psychosomatic Medicine,* 1957, *19,* 1–10.

Weinstein, N. D. Unrealistic optimism about susceptibility to health problems: Conclusions from a community-wide sample. *Journal of Behavioral Medicine,* 1987, *10*(5), 481–500.

———. Effects of personal experience on self-protective behavior. *Psychological Bulletin,* 1989, *105*(1), 31–50.

Weinstein, R. M. Stigma and mental illness: Theory versus reality. *Journal of Orthomolecular Psychiatry,* 1982, *11*(2), 87–99.

Weisenberg, M. Cultural and racial reactions to pain. In M. Weisenberg (Ed.), *The control of pain.* New York: Psychological Dimensions, 1977a.

———. Pain and pain control. *Psychological Bulletin,* 1977b, *84,* 1004–1008.

Weiss, F., and Miller, F. G. The drive theory of social facilitation. *Psychological Review,* 1971, *78,* 44–57.

Weiss, J. M. Effects of coping response on stress. *Journal of Comparative and Physiological Psychology,* 1968, *65,* 251–260.

———. Effects of coping behavior in different warning signal conditions on stress pathology in rats. *Journal of Comparative and Physiological Psychology,* 1971a, *77,* 1–13.

———. Effects of coping behavior with and without feedback signal on stress pathology in rats. *Journal of Comparative and Physiological Psychology,* 1971b, *77,* 22–30.

Weiss, K. B., Gergen, P. J., and Hodgson, T. A. An economic evaluation of asthma in the United States. *New England Journal of Medicine*, 1992, *326*, 862–866.

Weiss, S., Fielding, J., and Baum, A. (Eds.). *Perspectives in behavioral medicine: Health at work*. Hillsdale, NJ: Erlbaum, 1991.

Weisse, C. S., Nesselhof, S. E. A., Fleck-Kandath, C., and Baum, A. Psychosocial aspects of AIDS prevention among heterosexuals. In J. Edwards, L. Heath, S. Tindale, et al. (Eds.), *Applying social influence processes in preventing social problems*. New York: Plenum, 1990.

Weisse, C. S., Pato, C. N., McAllister, C., et al. Differential effects of controllable and uncontrollable acute stress on lymphocyte proliferation and leukocyte percentages in humans. *Brain, Behavior, and Immunity*, 1990, *4*, 339–351.

Welgan, P., Meshkinpour, H., and Hoehler, F. The effect of stress on colon motor and electrical activity in irritable bowel syndrome. *Psychosomatic Medicine*, 1985, *47*, 139–149.

Wells, J. A. Chronic life situations and life change events. In A. M. Ostfeld and E. D. Eaker (Eds.), *Measuring psychosocial variables in epidemiological studies of cardiovascular disease* (NIH Publication No. 85-2270). Bethesda, MD: National Institutes of Health, 1985.

Werner, E. E. Resilient children. In H. E. Fitzgerald and M. G. Walraven (Eds.), *Annual ed.: Human Development 87/88*. Guilford, CT: Dushkin, 1987.

Whipple, B. Methods of pain control: Review of research and literature. *Image: Journal of Nursing Scholarship*, 1987, *19*(3), 142–146.

Whitcher, S. J., and Fisher, J. D. Multidimensional reaction to therapeutic touch in a hospital setting. *Journal of Personality and Social Psychology*, 1979, *37*, 87–96.

White, R. F. *Clinical syndromes in adult neuropsychology: The practitioner's handbook*. Amsterdam: Elsevier, 1992.

White, R. W. Motivation reconsidered: The concept of competence. *Psychological Review*, 1959, *66*, 297–333.

Whitehead, W. E. Biofeedback treatment of gastrointestinal disorders. *Biofeedback and Self-Regulation*, 1992, *17*, 59–69.

Whitehead, W. E., Winget, C., Fedoravicius, A. S., et al. Learned illness behavior in patients with irritable bowel syndrome and peptic ulcer. *Digestive Diseases and Sciences*, 1982, *27*, 202–208.

Wiebe, D. J., and McCallum, D. M. Health practices and hardiness as mediators in the stress–illness relationship. *Health Psychology*, 1986, *5*(5), 425–438.

Wiedenfeld, S. A., O'Leary, A., Bandura, A., et al. Impact of perceived self-efficacy in coping with stressors on components of the immune system. *Journal of Personality and Social Psychology*, 1990, *59*(5), 1082–1094.

Wiens, A. N., and Menustik, C. E. Treatment outcome and patient characteristics in an aversion therapy program for alcoholism. *American Psychologist*, 1983, *38*, 1089–1096.

Wilbur, J. A., and Barrow, J. G. Reducing elevated blood pressure. *Minnesota Medical*, 1969, *52*, 1303.

Wilcox, V. L., Kasl, S. V., and Berkman, L. F. Social support and physical disability in older people after hospitalization: A prospective study. *Health Psychology*, 1994, *13*(2), 170–179.

Wilkins, W. Desensitization: A reply to Morgan. *Psychological Bulletin*, 1973, *79*, 376–377.

Williams, D. A., and Keefe, F. J. Pain beliefs and the use of cognitive-behavioral coping strategies. *Pain*, 1991, *46*(2), 185–190.

Williams, D. A., Lewis-Fanning, E., Rees, L., et al. Assessment of the relative importance of the allergic, infective and psychological factors in asthma. *Acta Allergologista*, 1958, *12*, 376–385.

Williams, D. A., Robinson, M. E., and Geisser, M. E. Pain beliefs: Assessment and utility. *Pain,* 1994, *59*(1), 71–78.

Williams, J. B., Gibbon, M., First, M. B., et al. The structured clinical interview for DSM-III-R(SCIDF)*II. Archives of General Psychiatry,* 1992, *49,* 630–636.

Williams, P. D., Valderrama, D. M., Gloria, M. D., and Pascogiun, L. G. Effects of preparation for mastectomy/hysterectomy on women's post-operative self-care behaviors. *International Journal of Nursing Studies,* 1988, *25*(3), 191–206.

Williams, P. G., Wiebe, D. J., and Smith, T. W. Coping processes as mediators of the relationship between hardiness and health. *Journal of Behavioral Medicine,* 1992, *15,* 237–255.

Williams, R., Zyzanski, S. J., and Wright, A. L. Life events and daily hassles and uplifts as predictors of hospitalization and outpatient visitation. *Social Science and Medicine,* 1992, *34,* 763–768.

Williams, R. B., Barefoot, J. C., Califf, R. M., et al. Prognostic importance of social and economic resources among medically treated patients with angiographically documented coronary artery disease. *Journal of the American Medical Association,* 1992, *267,* 515–519.

Williams, R. C. Toward a set of reliable and valid measures for chronic pain assessment and outcome research. *Pain,* 1988, *35,* 239–251.

Wills, T. A. Supportive functions of interpersonal relationships. In S. Cohen and S. L. Syme (Eds.), *Social support and health.* Orlando, FL: Academic Press, 1985.

Wilson, D. K., Homes, D. S., Arheart, R., and Alpert, B. S. Cardiovascular reactivity in black and white siblings versus matched controls. *Annals of Behavioral Medicine,* 1995, *17*(3), 207–212.

Wilson, G. T., and Lawson, D. M. Expectancies, alcohol, and sexual arousal in male social drinkers. *Journal of Abnormal Psychology,* 1976, *85,* 587–594.

Wilson, G. T., and Smith, D. Assessment of bulimia nervosa: An evaluation of the eating disorders examination. *International Journal of Eating Disorders,* 1989, *8,* 173–179.

Windle, M., Mondul, T., Whitney, R. B., et al. A discriminant function analysis of various interferon parameters among alcoholics and heavy smokers. *Drug and Alcohol Dependence,* 1993, *31*(2), 139–147.

Winemiller, D. R., Mitchell, E. M., Sutliff, J., and Cline, D. J. Measurement strategies in social support: A descriptive review of the literature. *Journal of Clinical Psychology,* 1993, *49,* 638–648.

Wishnie, H. A., Hackett, T. P., and Cassem, N. H. Psychological hazards of convalescence following myocardial infarction. *Journal of the American Medical Association,* 1971, *215,* 1292–1296.

Wittkower, E. D., and Dudek, S. Z. Psychosomatic medicine: The mind-body-society interaction. In B. Wolman (Ed.), *Handbook of general psychology.* Englewood Cliffs, NJ: Prentice-Hall, 1973.

Wittrock, D. A., Larson, L. S., and Sandgren, A. K. When a child is diagnosed with cancer: II. Parental coping, psychological adjustment, and relationships with medical personnel. *Journal of Psychosocial Oncology,* 1994, *12*(3), 17–32.

Wolf, S. *The stomach.* New York: Oxford, 1965.

Wolf, S., and Wolff, H. G. *Human gastric function: An experimental study of a man and his stomach.* New York: Oxford University Press, 1947.

Wolfe, W. H., Miner, J. C., and Michalek, J. E. Immunological parameters in current and former U.S. Air Force personnel. *Vaccine,* 1993, *1*(5), 545–547.

Wolfer, J., and Visintainer, M. Pediatric surgical patients' stress responses and adjustment as a function of psychologic preparation and stress-point nursing care. *Nursing Research,* 1975, *24,* 244–255.

Wolff, H. G. Life stress and cardiovascular disorders. *Circulation,* 1950, *1,* 187–203.

———. *Stress and disease.* Springfield, IL: Charles C. Thomas, 1953.

Wollershein, J. P. Effectiveness of group therapy based upon learning principles in the treatment of overweight women. *Journal of Abnormal Psychology,* 1970, *76,* 562–574.

Wolpe, J. *Psychotherapy by reciprocal inhibition.* Stanford, CA: Stanford University Press, 1958.

Wong, M., and Kaloupek, D. G. Coping with dental treatment: The potential impact of situational demands. *Journal of Behavioral Medicine,* 1986, *9*(6), 579–597.

Wortman, C. B. Some determinants of perceived control. *Journal of Personality and Social Psychology,* 1975, *31,* 282–294.

Wortman, C. B., and Brehm, J. W. Responses to uncontrollable outcomes. An integration of reactance theory and the learned helplessness model. In L. Berkowitz (Ed.), *Advances in experimental social psychology,* vol. 8. New York: Academic Press, 1975.

Wortman, C. B., and Dintzer, L. Is an attributional analysis of the learned helplessness phenomenon viable? A critique of the Abramson-Seligman-Teasdale reformulation. *Journal of Abnormal Psychology,* 1978, *87,* 75–90.

Wynder, E. L., Kajitani, T., Kuno, J., et al. A comparison of survival rates between American and Japanese patients with breast cancer. *Surgery, Gynecology and Obstetrics,* 1963, *117*(2), 196.

Yeager, J., and Weiner, H. Observations in man. *Advances in Psychosomatic Medicine,* 1970, *6,* 40–55.

Yeates, D. B., Aspin, N., Levinson, H., et al. Mucociliary tracheal transport rates in man. *Journal of Applied Physiology,* 1975, *39*(3), 487–495.

Yehuda, R., Boisoneau, D., Lowy, M. T., and Giller, E. L., Jr. Dose-response changes in plasma cortisol and lymphocyte glucocorticoid receptors following dexamethasone administration in combat veterans with and without posttraumatic stress disorder. *Archives of General Psychiatry,* 1995, *52*(7), 583–593.

Yehuda, R., Giller, E. L., Jr., and Mason, J. W. Psychoneuroendocrine assessment of posttraumatic stress disorder: Current progress and new directions. *Progress in Neuropsychopharmacol Biological Psychiatry,* 1993, *17*(4), 541–550.

Yehuda, R., Kahana, B., Schneidler, J., and Southwick, S. M. Impact of cumulative lifetime trauma and recent stress on current posttraumatic stress disorder symptoms in Holocaust survivors. *American Journal of Psychiatry,* 1995, *152*(12), 1815–1818.

Yehuda, R., Resnick, H., Kahana, B., and Giller, E. L. Long-lasting hormonal alterations to extreme stress in humans: Normative or maladaptive? *Psychosomatic Medicine,* 1993, *55,* 287–297.

Yehuda, R., Southwick, S. M., and Giller, E. L. Exposure to atrocities and severity of chronic posttraumatic stress disorder in Vietnam combat veterans. *American Journal of Psychiatry,* 1993, *149*(3), 333–336.

Yehuda, R., Southwick, S. M., Giller, E. L., et al. Urinary catecholamine excretion and severity of PTSD symptoms in Vietnam combat veterans. *Journal of Nervous Mental Disorders,* 1992, *180,* 321–325.

Yehuda, R., Southwick, S. M., Krystal, J. H., and Bremner, D. Enhanced suppression of cortisol following dexamethasone administration in posttraumatic stress disorder. *American Journal of Psychiatry,* 1993, *150*(1), 83–86.

Yehuda, R., Teicher, M. H., and Giller, E. L. Lack of significant cortisol and growth hormone changes in Israeli civilians during the Gulf War. *American Journal of Psychiatry,* 1995, *152*(4), 652–653.

Young, G. P., Weyden, M. B., Rose, I. S., and Dudley, F. J. Lymphopenic and lymphocyte transformation in alcoholics. *Experientia,* 1979, *35,* 286–289.

Young, L. D. Rheumatoid arthritis. In R. J. Gatchel and E. B. Blanchard (Eds.), *Psychophysiological disorders: Research and clinical applications.* Washington, DC: American Psychological Association, 1993, pp. 269–298.

Young, L. D., and Allin, J. M., Jr. Repression-sensitization differences in recovery from learned helplessness. *Journal of General Psychology,* 1992, *119*(2), 135–139.

Young, L. D., Richter, J. E., Anderson, K. O., and Bradley, L. A. The effects of psychological and environmental stressors on peristaltic esophageal contractions in healthy volunteers. *Psychophysiology,* 1987, *24*(2), 132–141.

Zakowski, S. G., Cohen, L., Hall, M. H., et al. Differential effects of active and passive laboratory stressors on immune function in healthy men. *Internatinal Journal of Behavioral Medicine,* 1994, *1*(2), 163–184.

Zakowski, S. G., McAllister, C., Deal, M., and Baum, A. Stress, reactivity, and immune function. *Health Psychology,* 1992, *11,* 223–232.

Zastowny, T. R., Kirschenbaum, D. S., and Meng, A. L. Coping skills training for children: Effects on distress before, during, and after hospitalization for surgery. *Health Psychology,* 1986, *5*(3), 231–247.

Zautra, A. J., and Manne, S. L. Coping with rheumatoid arthritis: A review of a decade of research. *Annals of Behavioral Medicine,* 1992, *14,* 31–39.

Zelman, D. C., Brandon, T. H., Jorenby, D. E., and Baker, T. B. Measures of affect and nicotine dependence predict differential response to smoking cessation treatments. *Journal of Consulting and Clinical Psychology,* 1992, *60*(6), 943–952.

Zola, I. K. Culture and symptoms: An analysis of patients' presenting complaints. *American Sociological Review,* 1966, *31,* 615–630.

Zubin, J. Role of vulnerability in the etiology of schizophrenic episodes. In L. J. West and D. E. Flinn (Eds.), *Treatment of schizophrenia: Progress and prospects.* New York: Grune & Stratton, 1976.

Zubin, J., and Spring, B. Vulnerability: A new view of schizophrenia. *Journal of Abnormal Psychology,* 1977, *86,* 103–126.

Zuckerman, M. Dimensions of sensation seeking. *Journal of Consulting and Clinical Psychology,* 1971, *36,* 35–52.

Glossary

a-delta fibers Thinly myelinated nerve fibers that conduct nociceptive messages to the spinal cord.

acne Inflammatory diseases of the hair follicles or sebaceous glands.

acquired immune deficiency syndrome (AIDS) A disease caused by the human immunodeficiency virus (HIV) that weakens the immune system and causes people to develop opportunistic infections.

acupuncture The Chinese practice of inserting needles into peripheral nerves to deaden pain, anesthetize, and heal.

acute (ah-kut') A short and relatively severe course.

acute stress Short-lived stress.

adherence The act or quality of doing what one is told or asked to do.

adrenal cortex (ah-dre'nal kor'teks) Outer layers of the adrenal glands that secrete mineral corticoids, androgens, and glucocorticoids.

adrenal medulla (ah-dre'nal mah-dul'ah) The central part of the adrenal gland that secretes epinephrine and some norepinephrine.

adrenaline (ah-dren'ah-len) See *epinephrine.*

adrenocorticotrophic hormone (ACTH) (ad-re" no-kor" teh-ko-trof' ik' hormone) A hormone produced by the pituitary gland that stimulates the adrenal cortex to release glucocorticoids.

aftereffects Effects of a stressor that appear after the stressor is over.

alcoholism A chronic nonclinical term for a disorder characterized by excessive and/or repeated drinking of alcoholic beverages to an extent that interferes with the drinker's health or social or economic well-being.

alexithymia (ah-lex'-ah-thi'-me-ah) The inability to express or describe one's feelings.

alveoli (al-ve' o-li) Small saclike parts of the lung.

anabolic system The constructive process by which living cells or organisms convert simple substances into more complex compounds.

angina pectoris (an-ji'nah pek'to-ris) A chest pain due most often to an insufficient oxygen supply to heart tissue.

antibodies Products of B lymphocytes that are induced by contact with a specific antigen. Antibodies attack antigens in several different ways but can only work against the antigen for which they were produced.

antigen (an' tah-jen) Anything that does not "belong" in the body and that causes an immune response. Discovery of antigens evokes an immune response against them.

anxiety disorders Disorders in which the major symptom is anxiety.

apperception The power of receiving, appreciating, and interpreting sensory impressions.

applied behavioral analysis A field of inquiry based on operant conditioning.

appraisals Interpretations of events or situations in which people find themselves and of their own capabilities.

arrhythmias (ah-rith' me-ah) Irregular or variable heartbeats that are different from normal heartbeats.

arteries Blood vessels that carry blood away from the heart.

artherosclerosis Disease characterized by thickening and loss of elasticity of arterial walls.

assertiveness training Training that helps people to make legitimate demands and to say no.

atopic dermatitis A chronic skin disorder of unknown etiology (although allergic, hereditary, and psychogenic factors appear to be involved).

aura (aw' rah) A subjective sensation or sensory-motor phenomenon that precedes and marks the onset of a recurrent attack, such as an epileptic attack or a migraine headache.

autonomic nervous system (aw" to-nom'ik) The portion of the nervous system concerned with the regulation of the activity of cardiac muscles, smooth muscles, and glands.

aversion therapy The behavior therapy that pairs an unpleasant stimulus with undesirable ones causing the patient to avoid them.

axon The extension of a neuron by which impulses travel away from the cell body.

background stressors Low-magnitude, everyday events that are aversive or disruptive and that produce a chronic elevation in stress.

behavioral genetics The study of individual differences in behavior that are attributable in part to differences in genetic makeup.

behavioral immunogen (ih'myoo-no-jen) A health-protective behavioral practice.

behavioral pathogen (path' o-jen) A health-impairing habit.

beta-endorphins A group of endogenous substances that bind to opiate receptors in various areas of the brain and thereby increase pain threshold.

bias Something that inhibits accurate or impartial judgment.

biofeedback The process of learning to control the autonomic body functions using visual or auditory cues.

blastogenesis (blas"to-jen'e-sis) The rapid replication of cells when stimulated to proliferate.

blood pressure The pressure of blood on the walls of the arteries. The maximum pressure, or *systolic pressure,* that occurs at the end of the output of the left ventricle. The minimum pressure, or *diastolic pressure,* that occurs between beats. High blood pressure is termed *hypertension;* low blood pressure is called *hypotension.*

bone marrow The soft organic material in the cavities of bones.

brain stem The part of the brain connecting the cerebral hemisphere with the spinal cord and made up of the pons, medulla oblongata, and mesencephalon.

bronchiole (brong"ke-ol) One of the finer subdivisions of the bronchia in the lungs.

c-fibers Unmyelinated postganglionic fibers of the autonomic nervous system, found at the dorsal roots and at free nerve endings.

capillaries (kap'i-lar"e) Local extensions of arteries, carrying blood to the smallest units in the body.

cardiovascular reactivity The magnitude and/or pattern of blood pressure or heart rate change when one is stressed or challenged.

cardiovascular system (kar' de-o-vas' kyoo-ler) The system composed of the heart and the blood vessels that is responsible for circulation of blood.

catabolic process (kat" ah-bol'ik) The process by which living cells break down complex substances into simpler compounds.

cataclysmic event (kat-ah-kliz" mik) A major life change or extensive and severely disruptive stressor.

catecholamines (kat" eh-ko" leh-meen') Hormones that mimic and extend the effects of sympathetic nervous system activity. Epinephrine (adrenaline), norepinephrine (noradrenaline), and dopamine are catecholamines. Epinephrine and norepinephrine are secreted by the adrenal medulla and by neurons throughout the nervous system.

cell body The larger protoplasmic mass of a neuron.

central nervous system (CNS) The part of the nervous system consisting of the brain and spinal cord.

cerebellum (ser"eh-bel'um) The brain structure involved in the coordination of movement.

cerebral cortex The layer of gray matter on the surface of the cerebral hemisphere.

chemotaxis (ke"mo-tak'sis) The movement of an organism or an individual cell, such as a leukocyte, in response to a chemical stimulus.

chronic stress Stress that persists over a long period of time.

classical conditioning Learning in which a response is elicited by a neutral stimulus that previously has been presented repeatedly together with the stimulus that originally elicited the response.

cognitive restructuring Making explicit use of cognitive concepts to understand and modify overt behavior.

comorbidity Co-occurrence of two or more disorders, as in the case of heart disease patients who are also depressed.

compliance with medical regimens Willingness or ability to follow recommended treatment.

complication The concurrence of two or more diseases in the same patient.

conditioned reflex A response to a stimulus developed through classical conditioning.

condom (kahn' dum) A cover for the penis, worn during sexual activity to prevent infection or pregnancy.

contact desensitization (de-sen" sih-tih za'shun) A form of systematic desensitization combining modeling and guided participation.

contingency management (kon-tin'jen-se) A behavior modification technique that changes the frequency of a behavior by controlling the reinforcing consequences of that behavior.

control The ability to affect outcomes, to regulate or otherwise influence events or occurrences.

control group Subjects used in an experimental procedure for comparison with the procedure characterized by the absence of the factor(s) being studied.

coping behavior A way of dealing with stress or threats.

coronary heart disease (CHD) (kor' o-neh-re) A disease of the heart and blood vessels (e.g., arteriosclerosis).

counterconditioning Training to elicit a new response to replace an unwanted one.

cytokines Hormone-like substances secreted by lymphocytes and other immune cells.

cytotoxic cell An immune cell that has a specific toxic action on foreign matter.

daily hassles Minor, everyday events that often produce stress.

defensive avoidance The psychological mechanism used to minimize the significance of a threat.

dendrites Area of neuron comprising most of its receptive surface.

depersonalization (de-per′ sun-al-eh-za′-shun) The loss of one's sense of personal identity.

depressive disorders Psychological disorders characterized by persistent sadness and discouragement.

diastole (di-as′to-le) The dilation of the heart ventricles occurring between the first and the second heart sound.

diathesis-stress model of illness (di-ath′eh-sis) A psychophysiological model assuming that individuals are predisposed toward a particular disorder and manifest that disorder when affected by stress.

dietary restraint Concern about and behavioral limitation of food intake.

digestive system The organs in the body involved in converting food into usable substances. It includes the mouth, pharynx, stomach, intestines, and related glands.

dizygotic twins (di″ zi-gaht′ ik) Fraternal twins, developed from separate fertilized ova.

dominant Controlling; in genetics, capable of expression when carried by only one of a pair of homologous chromosomes.

duodenal ulcers (du″o-de′nal) Ulcers in the small intestine.

electrocardiogram (EKG) (e-lek′tro-kar″de-o-gram″) A recording of electrical activity of the heart, used to reveal abnormalities in the heart function or beat.

enabling factors Skills or situations necessary to acquire health-protective behaviors.

endocrine system (en′do-krin) The system of glands that produces and secretes hormones into the circulatory system of the body.

enkephalin Endogenous opioids that occur in nerve endings of brain tissue, spinal cord, and the gastrointestinal tract and bind to opiate receptors.

epinephrine (adrenaline) (ep′eh-nef′rin) A hormonal stimulator of the sympathetic nervous system secreted by the adrenal medulla.

esophagus (e-sof′ah-gus) The passage extending from the pharynx to the stomach.

essential hypertension An unexplained chronic elevation in blood pressure.

eugenics (u-jen′iks) The belief that one can improve hereditary qualities of a race or breed by selectivity breeding for specific genes.

exhaustion A lack of energy with the consequent inability to respond to stimuli.

extinction Gradual disappearance of a conditioned response when it is no longer reinforced.

fraternal twins nonidentical twins, developed from two separate fertilized ova.

gamete (gam′et) A mature, functional reproductive cell.

gastric ulcers (gas′trik) A lesion in the mucosal lining of the stomach.

gastrointestinal (GI) system (gas″tro-in-tes′ teh-nal) The organs of digestion, including the stomach, small intestine, and large intestine.

gate control theory A theory of pain sensation positing a regulatory mechanism in the spinal column.

general adaptation syndrome (GAS) Selye's description of the reaction of the individual to excessive stress consisting of the alarm reaction, the stage of resistance, and the stage of exhaustion.

genotype (jee′no-tipe) The genetic constitution of an organism.

glucocorticoids (gloo″ko-kor′teh-koids) Substances produced by the adrenal cortex that raise the level of blood sugar in the body. The most important glucocorticoids are cortisol and corticosterone.

gradient of reinforcement The learning theory principle suggesting that the strength of a reinforcer is greater when in proximity to a behavior. Behaviors providing short-term gratification (even if health impairing in the long term) are easy to acquire and resistant to change.

health behaviors Behaviors related to health as in health-impairing behaviors or those that improve health.

health psychology A field of psychology studying behavioral factors in the prevention and treatment of illness and the maintenance of health.

helper cells A subtype of T lymphocytes that cooperate with B lymphocytes for the synthesis of an antibody to many antigens; these cells play an integral role in immunoregulation.

hepatic system The liver and related structures.

hippocampus Part of the brain responsible for the transfer of information into long-term memory.

human immunodeficiency virus (HIV) (im″ yoo-no-de-fish′en-se) A virus presumed to be responsible for the disease AIDS.

humoral Pertaining to the humors of the body. *See* also under *theory.*

hybrid (hi′brid) The offspring of two parents that differ in one or more heritable characteristics or are of two different species.

hypertension (hi″ per-ten′shun) A marked and sustained elevation of diastolic and systolic blood pressure.

hypothalamus (hi″ po-thal′ ah-mus) A cortical structure located beneath the thalamus that regulates peripheral autonomic and endocrine activity.

identical twins Two individuals who developed from the same ovum and share an identical chromosome pattern.

idiopathic condition (ihd″e-o-path′ik) A condition with an unknown origin.

illness behaviors Behaviors that characterize people who are ill.

illusion of control The belief that one has more control than is actually available to him or her.

immunocompetence (im″u-no-kom′pe-tens) The ability or capacity to develop an immune response (e.g., antibody production and/or cell-mediated immunity) following exposure to antigen; also called *immunologic competence.*

immunoglobulin (Ig) (im″ yoo-no-glob′ yoo lin) A constituent element of antibodies. B lymphocytes secrete five types of Ig.

immunosurveillence (im″u-no-ser-va′lens) The monitoring function of the immune system in recognizing and reacting against newly developed aberrant cells such as malignant cells.

insulin A protein hormone formed from proinsulin in the beta cells of the pancreatic islets. It promotes the storage of glucose in the liver, skeletal muscle, and adipose tissue.

intractable Not responsive to treatment.

intrusive thoughts Unbidden, uncontrollable, and/or spontaneous thoughts about past or future events or people.

job strain A condition of stress resulting from high job demands and low job control.

learned helplessness A psychological state resulting from repeated exposure to non-contingent behavior and outcome. A person learns that events are not controllable and the feeling can generalize to other situations.

leukocytes (loo'ko-sites) The white cells in the blood; they comprise most cells of the immune system.

limbic system A part of the brain concerned with autonomic functions and emotion.

locus of control Expectations people have for perceived control over behavior. Individuals are classified as having an *internal* locus of control or an *external* locus of control.

lymph (limf) The fluid of the lymph system that drains dead antigen cells from the body, helps to trap antigens near lymph nodes, and carries lymphocytes and macrophages.

lymph nodes (limf) Areas in the body where the system of lymph vessels join. There are lymph nodes throughout the body, each containing lymphocytes and other immune cells.

lymphocytes (lim' feh-sites) A type of white blood cell (leukocyte) that is a major component of the immune system. There are two primary types of lymphocytes: T cells and B cells.

lymphokines (lim-feh-kines) Substances released by lymphocytes, including interferon and interleuken-2, that help to signal and coordinate immune cells.

lyse To kill or split.

macrophages (mak'ro-fajes) Large phagocytic leukocytes that develop from monocytes, perform phagocytic functions, and present antigens to lymphocytes to allow lymphocytes to recognize them.

medulla oblongata Part of the brain that deals with vital bodily functions such as respiration, circulation, and special senses.

metastasis (me-tas'tah-sis) The growth or spread of disease from one organ or part of the body to another not directly connected with it.

migraine headache (mi'grane) A vascular headache, commonly associated with irritability, nausea, and vomiting.

mineralocorticoid (min"er-al-o-kor'ti koid) A corticoid secreted by the adrenal cortex that affects the retention of sodium and potassium.

mitogen (mi' to-jen) A substance that causes immune cells to multiply. Proliferation in the face if a mitogen is used as a measure of the immune system function.

modeling Learning by observing and imitating the behavior of others.

monocyte (mah' no-site) A type of white blood cell (leukocyte) that engulfs and devours foreign particles.

monokines Cytokines produced by monocytes.

monozygotic twins (mon' o-zi-got'ik) Identical twins, developed from the same ovum and sharing identical inheritance.

myocardial infarction (MI) (mi" o-kar' de-al infark' shun) The death of heart tissue as a result of interruption of the blood supply to the area.

myocardial ischemia An interruption of blood supply to the heart.

naloxone (nal-ak'sahn) A chemical used as a narcotic antagonist.

natural killer (NK) cells Leukocytes that kill cells infected by viruses as well as cancerous cells or foreign cells or organisms. They do not require prior sensitization to an antigen in order to attack it.

natural selection The nonrandom reproduction of genotypes resulting from interactions among a variety of phenotypes and the environment.

nervous system The system of the body that causes and coordinates the adjustments and reactions of an organism to internal and environmental conditions.

neurons Any of the conducting cells of the nervous system.

neuropsychological assessment Assessment of brain/cognitive function with objective tests.

neurotransmitter A chemical substance (i.e., norepinephrine, acetylcholine, dopamine) that is released from the axon terminal of a presynaptic neuron.

neutrophils (nu'tro-fils) Short-lived leukocytes that are phagocytic cells that attack bacteria. These cells do not require prior sensitization to bacteria and migrate to areas where they are needed by chemotaxis.

nicotine (nik' eh-teen) A poisonous, colorless, soluble alkaloid obtained from tobacco or produced synthetically.

nicotine-titration model A theory positing that nicotine dependence works to produce and protect a steady level of nicotine in the body.

nociceptor A pain receptor.

noncompliance See *compliance.*

noncontingent When a behavior has no consistent relationship with an outcome.

noradrenaline (nor" ah-dren' ah-lin) See *norepinephrine.*

norepinephrine (noradrenaline) (nor" epeh-nef' rin) A hormone secreted by sympathetic neurons and by the adrenal medulla.

obesity Excessive body weight beyond the limitation of skeletal and physical requirements.

observational learning The learning of patterns of behavior by watching others.

occupational stress Stress experienced in the workplace.

operant conditioning (op' eh-rant) See *instrumental conditioning.*

optimism The expectation that things will work out and that good things will happen.

parasympathetic nervous system (par" ah-sim" pah-thet'ik) The portion of the autonomic nervous system that opposes the sympathetic system and is important for homeostasis of the body.

pathogen Any disease-producing microorganism.

perceived susceptibility How vulnerable people feel to diseases or other misfortunes.

peripheral nervous system (pe-rif' er-al) The portion of the nervous system consisting of the nerves and ganglia outside the brain and spinal cord.

peristalsis (per"i-stal'sis) The movement by which the gastrointestinal tract propels its contents.

pessimism (pes'i-mizm) A disposition to assume the worst.

phagocytes (fag'o-sit) Cells that ingest microorganisms or other cells and foreign particles.

phenotype (fe'no-tipe) The entire physical, biochemical, and physiological makeup of an individual as determined both genetically and environmentally.

phlegm (flem) The mucus secreted in large amounts through the mouth.

phlegmatic (fleg-mat'ik) Characterized by an excess of the supposed humor called phlegm; dull and apathetic.

pituitary gland (pi-tu' eh-ter" e) The "master gland" of the body, which secretes hormones that regulate the proper functioning of the thyroid, gonads, adrenals, and other endocrine organs.

placebo (plah-se' bo) An inactive substance or treatment given to satisfy the patient's desire or need for therapy and used in controlled studies to determine the efficacy of medicinal substances.

plaque (plak) Fatty material that forms in arteries and causes damage by narrowing the passage for blood flow.

plasma (plaz'mah) The fluid portion of the blood in which the particulate components are suspended.

platelets (plat'let) Disk-shaped structures found in the blood, known for their role in blood coagulation.

posttraumatic stress disorder (PTSD) A profound syndrome of distress and withdrawal following exposure to severe stressors.

predisposing factors Factors, such as awareness and comprehension, that motivate an individual to take health action.

primary prevention Changing risk factors before one develops disease.

progressive muscle relaxation A method of achieving relaxation based on repeated contraction and relaxation of muscles.

prospective studies Studies that predict future events and then assess the incidence of these events over time.

psychogenic pain (si" ko-jen' ik) A pain originating in the mind or in mental or emotional conflict.

psychological reactance A psychological response to real or threatened loss of control.

psychophysiological reactivity (si" ko-fiz" e-ah-loj'ik) The changes in an individual's mood and responses, from resting levels during stress or challenge.

psychoneuroimmunology A field of study concerned with brain-behavior immune system relationships.

psychosomatic disorders (si" ko-so-mat'ik) Another term for psychophysiological disorders.

rational-emotive therapy (RET) A form of psychotherapy focusing on the use of cognitive and emotional restructuring to foster adaptive behavior.

reactivity Changes in mood; a physiological measure of arousal caused by a stressor.

receptor A molecule on cell surfaces or within a cell that recognizes and binds with other molecules (e.g., neurotransmitters).

recessive Incapable of expression unless the responsible allele is carried by both members of a pair of homologous chromosomes. A recessive allele or trait.

red blood cells One of the elements of the peripheral blood responsible for the transport of oxygen.

reinforcing factors Rewards or positive responses, such as peer approval, to carrying out a particular health behavior.

relapse Returning to an undesirable behavior that an individual has attempted to extinguish.

renal Pertaining to the kidneys.

reproductive Pertaining to the production of offspring.

respiratory system (re-speh' rah-tor" e) The organs and structures by which air-blood gas exhange take place, including the nose, mouth, trachea, and lungs.

respondent conditioning See *classical conditioning*.

response acquiescence The tendency to agree with test items on a self-report inventory, regardless of content.

restrained eating See *dietary restraint*.

reticular activating system (re-tik'yoo-lar) A system of cells in the brain that controls the overall degree of central nervous system activity, including wakefulness, attentiveness, and sleep.

retrospective studies (reh-tro-spek'tive) Studies that attempt to retrace earlier events in the life of the subject.

safer sex Limiting sexual activity to specific situations and partners using protective methods during sexual activity to prevent the exchange of bodily fluids (e.g., blood and semen).

secondary prevention Practices intended to halt a disease in early asymptomatic stages.

self-efficacy The sense one has that he or she can be successful or can control something.

set point Ideal or normal weight for an individual.

shaping The instrumental conditioning in which all responses resembling the desired one are reinforced initially, with only closer approximations being reinforced progressively until the desired response is obtained.

sick role A role provided by society for an individual suffering from severe physical or mental disorders.

slip An isolated instance of returning to an undesirable health habit that has previously been extinguished.

social desirability A tendency to answer questions about oneself in a socially approved manner.

social support Tangible, psychoemotional, or esteem support provided for a person by social contact or networks.

specific attitudes theory The hypothesis that certain attitudes are associated with certain psychophysiological disorders.

spinal cord The part of the central nervous system that consists of a thick vertical bundle of nerve fibers extending from the brain.

stimulus Any agent, act, or influence that produces functional or trophic reaction.

stimulus control A clinical approach based on the manipulation of environmental stimuli responsible for problems under treatment.

stimulus substitution The classical conditioning phenomenon studied by Pavlov in which an organism has a tendency to respond to a formerly neutral (conditioned) stimulus as if it were an unconditional stimulus.

stress A state or condition characterized by threat, harm, loss, or excessive demand and characterized by psychological and biological changes.

stressors Events that cause stress.

stress-induced analgesia Stress-related increases in pain thresholds.

stress-inoculation A clinical approach intended to provide patients with skills that they can use to cope with stress.

stress management methods Methods and techniques for reducing physiological or psychological aspects of stress.

structured interview (SI) A method for determining Type A and Type B behavior.

successive approximations See *shaping*.

suppressor cells Lymphoid cells that inhibit humoral and cell-mediated immune responses to antigen.

sympathetic nervous system (SNS) The branch of the nervous system responsible for activating or energizing the body to respond.

synaptic knobs Vesicles in the axon where neurotransmitters reside before they are released into the synapse.

systematic desensitization (sis-te-mat′ ik de-sen′ sih-tih-za-shun) A behavior therapy technique whereby the therapist systematically exposes patients to levels of a feared stimulus, reducing the intensity of anxiety that the patient feels and replacing it with a relaxation response.

systole (sis′ to-le) The contraction of the ventricles of the heart.

T-cells Lymphocytes that control other cells as well as kill antigens directly. T-helper cells help B cells to make antibodies and help T-cytotoxic cells, which kill cells infected by viruses and release lymphokines to regulate other cells. T-suppressor cells also regulate other cells by suppressing their function.

tertiary prevention Practices intended to stop the progression of clinically manifest diseases.

thalamus (thal′ah-mus) The main relay center for sensory impulses to the cerebral cortex.

thought-stopping A technique in which patients are to suppress or interrupt troubling thoughts.

thymus (thi'mus) A lymphoid organ.

token economy A behavior modification procedure in which participants are given rewards for constructive behavior. The tokens can be exchanged for desirable items or activities.

twin studies Tests to determine the concordance rate for monozygotic twins as compared with dizygotic twins in the diagnosis of schizophrenia.

Type A behavior A behavior pattern characterized by agressiveness, ambitiousness and restlessness, and living under severe time pressures; associated with coronary heart patients.

Type B behavior The pattern of behavior characterized by the absence of Type A characteristics.

unconditioned reflexes The response always elicited by the unconditioned stimulus in a classical conditioning experiment.

upper motor neuron disorders Dysfunctions occurring in the upper level of the central nervous system (e.g., cerebral palsy, incomplete spinal cord lesions, paresis).

veins Vessels through which blood passes from various organs or parts back to the heart.

white blood cells White or colorless cells found in the blood, part of the immune system, many of them functioning as a defense against infections.

XXX chromosomal type (kro"mah-so'mal) A female with an extra X chromosome. The extra chromosome may cause abnormalities in the genotype.

XYY chromosomal type (kro" mah-so'mal) A male with an extra Y chromosome, considered a "supermale." The extra chromosome has been considered an important contributor to aggressive or criminal behavior.

Index